CISCO CERTIFIED NETWORK PROFESSIONAL

CCNP Cisco Internetwork Troubleshooting Study Guide

(Exam 640-440)

Syngress Media, Inc.

Osborne McGraw-Hill

Berkeley New York St. Louis San Francisco Auckland Bogotá Hamburg London Madrid Mexico City
Milan Montreal New Delhi Panama City Paris São Paulo Singapore Sydney Tokyo Toronto

Osborne McGraw-Hill
2600 Tenth Street
Berkeley, California 94710
U.S.A.

For information on translations or book distributors outside the U.S.A., or to arrange bulk purchase discounts for sales promotions, premiums, or fund-raisers, please contact Osborne/**McGraw-Hill** at the above address.

CCNP Cisco Internetwork Troubleshooting Study Guide (Exam 640-440)

1234567890 DOC DOC 90198765432109

ISBN 007-211912-8

Publisher Brandon A. Nordin	**Series Editor** Mark Buchmann	**Indexer** Jack Lewis
Associate Publisher and Editor-in-Chief Scott Rogers	**Editorial Management** Syngress Media, Inc.	**Computer Designers** Jani Beckwith Gary Corrigan
Acquisitions Editor Gareth Hancock	**Technical Editor** Tony Costa	**Illustrators** Brian Wells Beth Young
Project Editor Jody McKenzie	**Copy Editor** Carol Henry	
Editorial Assistant Tara Davis	**Proofreader** Stefany Otis	**Series Design** Roberta Steele
		Cover Design Regan Honda

From Global Knowledge

At Global Knowledge we strive to support the multiplicity of learning styles required by our students to achieve success as technical professionals. In this testing product, it is our intention to offer the reader a valuable tool for successful completion of the CCNP certification.

As the world's largest IT training company, Global Knowledge is uniquely positioned to offer these books. The expertise gained each year from providing instructor-led training to hundreds of thousands of students worldwide has been captured in book form to enhance your learning experience. We hope that the quality of these books demonstrates our commitment to your lifelong learning success. Whether you choose to learn through the written word, computer-based training, Web delivery, or instructor-led training, Global Knowledge is committed to providing you the very best in each of those categories. For those of you who know Global Knowledge, or those of you who have just found us for the first time, our goal is to be your lifelong competency partner.

Thank you for the opportunity to serve you. We look forward to serving your needs again in the future.

Warmest regards,

Duncan Anderson
President and Chief Operating Officer, Global Knowledge

The Global Knowledge Advantage

Global Knowledge has a global delivery system for its products and services. The company has 28 subsidiaries, and offers its programs through a total of 60+ locations. No other vendor can provide consistent services across a geographic area this large. Global Knowledge is the largest independent information technology education provider, offering programs on a variety of platforms. This enables our multi-platform and multi-national customers to obtain all of their programs from a single vendor. The company has developed the unique CompetusTM Framework software tool and methodology which can quickly reconfigure courseware to the proficiency level of a student on an interactive basis. Combined with self-paced and on-line programs, this technology can reduce the time required for training by prescribing content in only the deficient skills areas. The company has fully automated every aspect of the education process, from registration and follow-up, to "just-in-time" production of courseware. Global Knowledge, through its Enterprise Services Consultancy, can customize programs and products to suit the needs of an individual customer.

Global Knowledge Classroom Education Programs

The backbone of our delivery options is classroom-based education. Our modern, well-equipped facilities staffed with the finest instructors offer programs in a wide variety of information technology topics, many of which lead to professional certifications.

Custom Learning Solutions

This delivery option has been created for companies and governments that value customized learning solutions. For them, our consultancy-based approach of developing targeted education solutions is most effective at helping them meet specific objectives.

Self-Paced and Multimedia Products

This delivery option offers self-paced program titles in interactive CD-ROM, videotape and audio tape programs. In addition, we offer custom development of interactive multimedia courseware to customers and partners. Call us at 1 (888) 427-4228.

Electronic Delivery of Training

Our network-based training service delivers efficient competency-based, interactive training via the World Wide Web and organizational intranets. This leading-edge delivery option provides a custom learning path and "just-in-time" training for maximum convenience to students.

ARG

American Research Group (ARG), a wholly-owned subsidiary of Global Knowledge, one of the largest worldwide training partners of Cisco Systems, offers a wide range of internetworking, LAN/WAN, Bay Networks, FORE Systems, IBM, and UNIX courses. ARG offers hands on network training in both instructor-led classes and self-paced PC-based training.

Global Knowledge Courses Available

Network Fundamentals

- Understanding Computer Networks
- Telecommunications Fundamentals I
- Telecommunications Fundamentals II
- Understanding Networking Fundamentals
- Implementing Computer Telephony Integration
- Introduction to Voice Over IP
- Introduction to Wide Area Networking
- Cabling Voice and Data Networks
- Introduction to LAN/WAN protocols
- Virtual Private Networks
- ATM Essentials

Network Security & Management

- Troubleshooting TCP/IP Networks
- Network Management
- Network Troubleshooting
- IP Address Management
- Network Security Administration
- Web Security
- Implementing UNIX Security
- Managing Cisco Network Security
- Windows NT 4.0 Security

IT Professional Skills

- Project Management for IT Professionals
- Advanced Project Management for IT Professionals
- Survival Skills for the New IT Manager
- Making IT Teams Work

LAN/WAN Internetworking

- Frame Relay Internetworking
- Implementing T1/T3 Services
- Understanding Digital Subscriber Line (xDSL)
- Internetworking with Routers and Switches
- Advanced Routing and Switching
- Multi-Layer Switching and Wire-Speed Routing
- Internetworking with TCP/IP
- ATM Internetworking
- OSPF Design and Configuration
- Border Gateway Protocol (BGP) Configuration

Authorized Vendor Training

Cisco Systems

- Introduction to Cisco Router Configuration
- Advanced Cisco Router Configuration
- Installation and Maintenance of Cisco Routers
- Cisco Internetwork Troubleshooting
- Cisco Internetwork Design
- Cisco Routers and LAN Switches
- Catalyst 5000 Series Configuration
- Cisco LAN Switch Configuration
- Managing Cisco Switched Internetworks
- Configuring, Monitoring, and Troubleshooting Dial-Up Services
- Cisco AS5200 Installation and Configuration
- Cisco Campus ATM Solutions

Bay Networks

- Bay Networks Accelerated Router Configuration
- Bay Networks Advanced IP Routing
- Bay Networks Hub Connectivity
- Bay Networks Accelar 1xxx Installation and Basic Configuration
- Bay Networks Centillion Switching

FORE Systems

- FORE ATM Enterprise Core Products
- FORE ATM Enterprise Edge Products
- FORE ATM Theory
- FORE LAN Certification

Operating Systems & Programming

Microsoft

- Introduction to Windows NT
- Microsoft Networking Essentials
- Windows NT 4.0 Workstation
- Windows NT 4.0 Server
- Advanced Windows NT 4.0 Server
- Windows NT Networking with TCP/IP
- Introduction to Microsoft Web Tools
- Windows NT Troubleshooting
- Windows Registry Configuration

UNIX

- UNIX Level I
- UNIX Level II
- Essentials of UNIX and NT Integration

Programming

- Introduction to JavaScript
- Java Programming
- PERL Programming
- Advanced PERL with CGI for the Web

Web Site Management & Development

- Building a Web Site
- Web Site Management and Performance
- Web Development Fundamentals

High Speed Networking

- Essentials of Wide Area Networking
- Integrating ISDN
- Fiber Optic Network Design
- Fiber Optic Network Installation
- Migrating to High Performance Ethernet

DIGITAL UNIX

- UNIX Utilities and Commands
- DIGITAL UNIX v4.0 System Administration
- DIGITAL UNIX v4.0 (TCP/IP) Network Management
- AdvFS, LSM, and RAID Configuration and Management
- DIGITAL UNIX TruCluster Software Configuration and Management
- UNIX Shell Programming Featuring Kornshell
- DIGITAL UNIX v4.0 Security Management
- DIGITAL UNIX v4.0 Performance Management
- DIGITAL UNIX v4.0 Intervals Overview

DIGITAL OpenVMS

- OpenVMS Skills for Users
- OpenVMS System and Network Node Management I
- OpenVMS System and Network Node Management II
- OpenVMS System and Network Node Management III
- OpenVMS System and Network Node Operations
- OpenVMS for Programmers
- OpenVMS System Troubleshooting for Systems Managers
- Configuring and Managing Complex VMScluster Systems
- Utilizing OpenVMS Features from C
- OpenVMS Performance Management
- Managing DEC TCP/IP Services for OpenVMS
- Programming in C

Hardware Courses

- AlphaServer 1000/1000A Installation, Configuration and Maintenance
- AlphaServer 2100 Server Maintenance
- AlphaServer 4100, Troubleshooting Techniques and Problem Solving

About Syngress Media

Syngress Media creates books and software for Information Technology professionals seeking skill enhancement and career advancement. Its products are designed to comply with vendor and industry standard course curricula, and are optimized for certification exam preparation. You can contact Syngress via the Web at http://www.syngress.com.

Contributors

Ryan Russell (CCNA, CCNP) has been employed in the networking field for more than ten years, including more than five years working with Cisco equipment. He has held IT positions ranging from help-desk support to network design, providing him with a good perspective on the challenges that face a network manager. Recently, Ryan has been contributing to information security projects involving network security and firewalls.

Eric Dean (CCIE#2708) has been employed with Global One since 1994 in the Internetwork Engineering department designing and developing enterprise, Internet, and Dial solutions for the Global One marketplace. Eric holds a master's degree in telecommunications from the University of Maryland, and a bachelor's degree in electrical engineering from George Mason University. He dedicates this book to his extremely patient wife, Lynn Ann, and their soon-to-be-born baby girl.

Vernon Hall graduated with a bachelor of science degree in computer science from James Madison University in 1992 and has been working as a consultant and network engineer for the past six years. He designs, installs, and supports large Novell NetWare networks. His experience includes support for file servers, peripherals, and infrastructure components from manufacturers such as Cisco, Bay Networks, and 3Com. Currently he is Director of MIS for M.C. Dean, Inc., in Chantilly, Virginia.

Ken Peterson (CCIE) is the President of KapNet Technologies, Inc., in Raleigh, North Carolina, a firm specializing in voice/data integration using Cisco routers and Selsius Ethernet phones. Ken has been teaching Cisco voice, Cisco router, and UNIX classes for two years. He holds a bachelor of science degree in electrical engineering from Georgia Tech. Ken's expertise includes Ethernet phones, IP PBXs, voice-over IP/Frame Relay, and Cisco ISDN dial services. Ken is currently developing the Global Knowledge ECRC computer-based training CD-ROMs that complement the Cisco ACRC course.

Natashia Maull is a network engineer in a large telecommunications corporation on the East Coast, specializing in high-speed networking, installation, and troubleshooting. She has experience in Cisco router configuration, ATM technology, the Catalyst 5000 product series, and Cisco internetwork troubleshooting. She is currently implementing an ATM backbone infrastructure using Cisco Products.

Kevin E. Greene works in the telecommunications industry as a Network Security Professional. He holds a master of science degree in information systems and a bachelor of science degree in management information systems from the New Jersey Institute of Technology. In addition, he has attained CheckPoint Firewall-1 certification as a System Engineer and System Administrator.

Shawn H Costigan is a Senior Network Analyst and the Technical Supervisor for BBN's (now GTE Internetworking) Dial Access Group. The network is a 300,000 modem access network and one of the largest EIGRP router networks in the world. He also serves as technical trainer to and mentors the Dialinx Controller Group. Shawn has also served four years of enlisted duty in the USAF, where he was part of the 621st Mobility Squadron that, during contingencies, set up mobile networking communications via WANs to provide encrypted transmissions to various strategic points and back to the United States.

Richard D. Hornbaker (CCIE, CNX, MCSE, Master CNE) is an architect with the Forté Consulting Group, a Phoenix-based firm specializing in strategic network design. With more than 15 years in the industry, Richard holds several certifications including Cisco CCIE, Network General CNX, Microsoft MCSE, and Novell Master CNE. His skills are diverse, ranging from operating systems and software to telephony systems and data networks. Richard has just completed the overhaul of a 12,000-node campus network and is designing a 20,000-site WAN for a major corporate merger. He is a participant in the Internet Engineering Task Force (IETF) and a member of the Institute of Electrical and Electronics Engineers (IEEE). He can be reached at Richard@Hornbaker.com.

From the Classroom Sidebars

Glenn Lepore is a senior network engineer with Niche Networks, LLC, in Herndon, Virginia. He has more than 13 years experience in LAN and WAN design, installation, and troubleshooting. His background includes Frame Relay, X.25, TCP/IP, IPX, and SNA. His experience includes Novell and UNIX administration, Web page design, and Internet Service Provider network operations. He is working toward his CCIE and MCSE certifications.

Technical Review

Tony Costa (CCIE #4140, MCSE, CNE) started his networking career in 1979 installing Gandalf synchronous modems. Since then he has worked extensively in TCP/IP and IBM SNA networks. He installed some of the earliest Banyan Vines LANs in the U.S. Department of Defense, and now occasionally assists in replacing them with Microsoft Windows NT networks. Tony spends his weekends at his home in New Mexico. During the week, he teaches Cisco technology to Cisco's engineers and delivers Cisco IOS router and Cisco Catalyst switch classes to the public through Chesapeake Computer Consultants, Inc.

Acknowledgments

We would like to thank the following people:

- Bridget Robeson at Niche Networks, for all her help.
- Richard Kristof of Global Knowledge for championing the series and providing us access to some great people and information. And to Shelley Everett and Chuck Terrien for all their cooperation.
- Imran Qureshi and Tina Dupart at Cisco for their time and insight.
- To all the incredibly hard-working folks at Osborne/McGraw-Hill: Brandon Nordin, Scott Rogers, Gareth Hancock, and Jody McKenzie for their help in launching a great series and being solid team players.

CONTENTS

5 Novell's Internetwork Packet Exchange (IPX) Protocol **191**

PREFACE

This book's primary objective is to help you prepare for and pass the required CIT exam so you can begin to reap the career benefits of CCNP certification. We believe that the only way to do this is to help you increase your knowledge and build your skills. After completing this book, you should feel confident that you have thoroughly reviewed all of the objectives that Cisco has established for the exam.

In This Book

This book is organized around the topics covered within the Cisco exam administered at Sylvan Testing Centers. Cisco has specific objectives for the CIT exam: we've followed their list carefully, so you can be assured you're not missing anything.

In Every Chapter

We've created a set of chapter components that call your attention to important items, reinforce important points, and provide helpful exam-taking hints. Take a look at what you'll find in every chapter:

- Every chapter begins with the **Certification Objectives**—what you need to know in order to pass the section on the exam dealing with the chapter topic. The Certification Objective headings identify the objectives within the chapter, so you'll always know an objective when you see it!

- **Certification Exercises** are interspersed throughout the chapters. These are step-by-step exercises that mirror vendor-recommended labs. They help you master skills that are likely to be an area of focus on the exam. Don't just read through the exercises; they are hands-on practice that you should be comfortable completing. Learning by doing is an effective way to increase your competency with a product.

■ **Exam Watch** notes call attention to information that is critical knowledge for the CCNP exams. These helpful hints are written by Cisco-certified professionals.

■ **On the Job** notes point out procedures and techniques important for coding actual applications for employers or contract jobs.

■ **From the Classroom** sidebars describe the issues that come up most often in the training classroom setting. These sidebars give you a valuable perspective into certification- and product-related topics. They point out common mistakes and address questions that have arisen from classroom discussions.

■ **Q & A** sections lay out problems and solutions in a quick-read format:

QUESTIONS AND ANSWERS

What are some helpful general troubleshooting tools?	Ping is the most useful general-help tool. It will tell you whether a device is reachable by sending ICMP echo request and waiting for a reply. If no reply comes back, you know there's a problem with that device. A protocol analyzer is also a good troubleshooting tool. A traceroute is also helpful.
How can I connect two dissimilar LANs?	You can achieve this by way of encapsulation. *Translational encapsulation* is a method of transparently bridging LANs that have dissimilar Physical and Data Link architecture (MAC sublayer protocols), such as Token Ring to Ethernet.

■ The **Certification Summary** is a succinct review of the chapter and a re-statement of salient points regarding the exam.

■ The **Two-Minute Drill** at the end of every chapter is a checklist of the main points of the chapter. It can be used for last-minute review.

■ **Tables** are liberally sprinkled throughout the chapters. You'll find that these provide an easy way to look up information and show material you may find worthy of memorization:

Protocol	Familiar Name	Port
Trivial File Transfer Protocol	TFTP	69
Domain Name Service	DNS	53
Time Service	-	37
NetBIOS Name Server	-	137
NetBIOS Datagram Server	-	138
Boot Protocol (Client and Server)	BOOTP	67 and 68
TACACS	TACACS	49

■ The **Self Test** offers questions similar to those found on the certification exams. The answers to these questions, as well as explanations of the answers, can be found in Appendix A. By taking the Self Test after completing each chapter, you'll reinforce what you've learned from that chapter, while becoming familiar with the structure of the exam questions.

Some Pointers

Once you've finished reading this book, set aside some time to do a thorough review. You might want to return to the book several times and make use of all the methods it offers for reviewing the material:

1. *Re-read all the Two-Minute Drills*, or have someone quiz you. You also can use the drills as a way to do a quick cram before the exam.

2. *Review all the Q & A scenarios* for quick problem solving.

3. *Re-take the Self Tests*. Taking the tests right after you've read the chapter is a good idea, because it helps reinforce what you've just learned. However, it's an even better idea to go back later and do all the questions in the book in one sitting. Pretend you're taking the

exam. (For this reason, you should mark your answers on a separate piece of paper when you go through the questions the first time.)

4. *Complete the exercises.* Did you do the exercises when you read through each chapter? If not, do them! These exercises are designed to cover exam topics, and there's no better way to get to know this material than by practicing.

5. *Check out the Web site.* Global Knowledge invites you to become an active member of the Access Global Web site. This site is an online mall and an information repository that you'll find invaluable. You can access many types of products to assist you in your preparation for the exams, and you'll be able to participate in forums, on-line discussions, and threaded discussions. No other book brings you unlimited access to such a resource. You'll find more information about this site in Appendix C.

How to Take a Cisco Certification Examination

by Richard D. Hornbaker (CCIE, CNX, MCSE, MCNE), Forté Consulting Group

This section covers the importance of your CCNP certification and prepares you for taking the actual examination. It gives you a few pointers on methods of preparing for the exam, including how to study register, what to expect, and what to do on exam day.

Catch the Wave!

Congratulations on your pursuit of Cisco certification! In this fast-paced world of networking, few certifications compare to the value of Cisco's program.

The networking industry has virtually exploded in recent years, accelerated by non-stop innovation and the Internet's popularity. Cisco has stayed at the forefront of this tidal wave, maintaining a dominant role in the industry.

Since the networking industry is highly competitive, and evolving technology only increases in its complexity, the rapid growth of the networking industry has created a vacuum of qualified people. There simply aren't enough skilled networking people to meet the demand. Even the most experienced professionals must keep current with the latest technology in order to provide the skills that the industry demands. That's where Cisco certification programs can help networking professionals succeed as they pursue their career.

Cisco started its certification program many years ago, offering only the designation of Cisco Certified Internetwork Expert, or CCIE. Through the CCIE program, Cisco provided a means to meet the growing demand for experts in the field of networking. However, the CCIE tests are brutal, with a failure rate of more than 80 percent. (Fewer than five percent of candidates pass on their first attempt.) As you might imagine, very few people ever attain CCIE status.

In early 1998, Cisco recognized the need for intermediate certifications, and several new programs were created. Four intermediate certifications were added: CCNA (Cisco Certified Network Associate), CCNP (Cisco Certified Network Professional), CCDA (Cisco Certified Design Associate), and CCDP (Cisco Certified Design Professional). Two specialties were also created for the CCIE program: WAN Switching and ISP Dial-up.

CCNP
advice

I would encourage you to take beta tests when they are available. Not only are the beta exams less than the cost of the final exams (some are even free!), but also, if you pass the beta, you will receive credit for passing the exam. If you don't pass the beta, you will have seen every question in the pool of available questions, and can use this information when preparing to take the exam for the second time. Remember to jot down important information immediately after the exam, if you didn't pass. You will have to do this after leaving the exam area, since materials written during the exam are retained by the testing center. This information can be helpful when you need to determine which areas of the exam were most challenging for you as you study for the subsequent test.

Why Vendor Certification?

Over the years, vendors have created their own certification programs because of industry demand. This demand arises when the marketplace needs skilled professionals and an easy way to identify them. Vendors benefit because it promotes people skilled in their product. Professionals benefit because it boosts their career. Employers benefit because it helps them identify qualified people.

In the networking industry, technology changes too often and too quickly to rely on traditional means of certification, such as universities and trade associations. Because of the investment and effort required to keep network certification programs current, vendors are the only organizations suited to keep pace with the changes. In general, such vendor certification programs are excellent, with most of them requiring a solid foundation in the essentials, as well as their particular product line.

Corporate America has come to appreciate these vendor certification programs and the value they provide. Employers recognize that certifications, like university degrees, do not guarantee a level of knowledge, experience or performance; rather, they establish a baseline for comparison. By seeking to hire vendor-certified employees, a company can assure itself that not only has it found a person skilled in networking, but it has also hired a person skilled in the specific products the company uses.

Technical professionals have also begun to realize the value of certification and the impact it can have on their careers. By completing a certification program, professionals gain an endorsement of their skills from a major industry source. This endorsement can boost their current position, and it makes finding the next job even easier. Often, a certification determines whether a first interview is even granted.

Today, a certification may place you ahead of the pack. Tomorrow, it will be a necessity to keep from being left in the dust.

CCNP Advice

Signing up for an exam has become more effortless with the new Web-based test registration system. To sign up for any of CCNP exams, access http://www.2test.com, and register for the Cisco Career Certification path. You will need to get an Internet account and password, if you do not already have one for 2test.com. Just select the option for first time registration, and the Web site will walk you through that process. The registration wizard even provides maps to the testing centers, something that is not available when calling Sylvan Prometric on the telephone.

Cisco's Certification Program

As mentioned previously, Cisco now has six certifications for the Routing and Switching career track, and four certifications for the WAN Switching career track. While Cisco recommends a series of courses for each of these certifications, they are not required. Ultimately, certification is dependent upon a candidate passing a series of exams. With the right experience and study materials, each of these exams can be passed without taking the associated class. Table i-1 shows the various Cisco certifications and tracks.

Figure i-1 shows Cisco's Routing and Switching track, with both the Network Design and Network Support paths. The CCNA is the foundation of the Routing and Switching track, after which candidates can pursue either the Network Design path to CCDA and CCDP, or the Network Support path to CCNP and CCIE.

TABLE i-1   Cisco Certifications

Track	Certification	Acronym
Routing and Switching: Network Support	Cisco Certified Network Associate	CCNA
Routing and Switching: Network Support	Cisco Certified Network Professional	CCNP
Routing and Switching: Network Support	Cisco Certified Internetwork Expert (Routing and Switching)	CCIE-R/S
Routing and Switching: Network Support	Cisco Certified Internetwork Expert (ISP Dial Technology)	CCIE-ISP Dial
Routing and Switching: Network Design	Cisco Certified Design Associate	CCDA
Routing and Switching: Network Design	Cisco Certified Design Professional	CCDP
WAN Switching: Network Support	Cisco Certified Network Associate—WAN switching	CCNA-WAN Switching
WAN Switching: Network Support	Cisco Certified Network Professional—WAN switching	CCNP-WAN Switching
WAN Switching: Network Support	Cisco Certified Internetwork Expert—WAN Switching	CCIE-WAN Switching
WAN Switching: Network Design	Cisco Certified Design Professional—WAN Switching	CCDP-WAN Switching

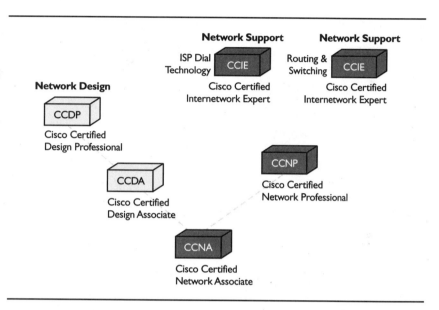

FIGURE i-1

Cisco's Routing and
Switching certification track

Table i-2 shows a matrix of the exams required for each Cisco certification. Note that candidates have the choice of taking either the single Foundation R/S exam, or the set of three ACRC, CLSC, and CMTD exams—all four exams are not required.

TABLE i-2 Examinations Required for Cisco Certifications

Exam Name	Exam #	CCNA	CCDA	CCNP	CCDP	CCIE
CCNA 1.0	640-407	X	X	X	X	
CDS 1.0	9E0-004		X		X	
Foundation Routing and Switching	640-409			X	X	
ACRC	640-403			X	X	
CLSC	640-404			X	X	
CMTD	640-405			X	X	

| TABLE i-2 | Examinations Required for Cisco Certifications (continued) | | | | | |

Exam Name	Exam #	CCNA	CCDA	CCNP	CCDP	CCIE
CIT 3.0	640-406 (or exam 640-440)			X		
CIT 4.0	640-440			X		
CID	640-025				X	
CCIE R/S Qualifying						X
CCIE Lab						X

CCNP Online

In addition to finding the technical objectives that are being tested for each exam, you will find much more useful information on Cisco's Web site at http://www.cisco.com/warp/public/10/wwtraining/ certprog. You will find information on becoming certified, exam-specific information, sample test questions, and the latest news on Cisco certification. This is the most important site you will find on your journey to becoming Cisco certified.

You may hear veterans refer to this CCIE R/S Qualifying Exam as the "Cisco Drake test." This is a carryover from the early days, when Sylvan Prometric's name was Drake Testing Centers and Cisco only had the one exam.

CCNP Advice

When I find myself stumped answering multiple-choice questions, I use my scratch paper to write down the two or three answers I consider the strongest, and then underlining the answer I feel is most likely correct. Here is an example of what my scratch paper looks like when I've gone through the test once:

21. B or C

33. A or C

This is extremely helpful when you mark the question and continue on. You can then return to the question and immediately pick up your thought process where you left off. Use this technique to avoid having to re-read and re-think questions. You will also need to use your scratch paper during complex, text-based scenario questions to create visual images to better understand the question. For example, during the CCNP exam you will need to draw multiple networks and the connections between them. By drawing the layout while you are interpreting the answer, you may find a hint that you would not have found without your own visual aid. This technique is especially helpful if you are a visual learner.

Computer-Based Testing

In a perfect world, you would be assessed for your true knowledge of a subject, not simply how you respond to a series of test questions. But life isn't perfect, and it just isn't practical to evaluate everyone's knowledge on a one-to-one basis. (Cisco actually does have a one-to-one evaluation, but it's reserved for the CCIE Laboratory exam, and the waiting list is quite long.)

For the majority of its certifications, Cisco evaluates candidates using a computer-based testing service operated by Sylvan Prometric. This service is quite popular in the industry, and it is used for a number of vendor certification programs, including Novell's CNE and Microsoft's MCSE. Thanks to Sylvan Prometric's large number of facilities, exams can be administered worldwide, generally in the same town as a prospective candidate.

For the most part, Sylvan Prometric exams work similarly from vendor to vendor. However, there is an important fact to know about Cisco's exams: they use the traditional Sylvan Prometric test format, not the newer adaptive format. This gives the candidate an advantage, since the traditional format allows answers to be reviewed and revised during the test. (The adaptive format does not.)

To discourage simple memorization, Cisco exams present a different set of questions every time the exam is administered. In the development of the exam, hundreds of questions are compiled and refined using beta testers. From this large collection, a random sampling is drawn for each test.

Each Cisco exam has a specific number of questions and test duration. Testing time is typically generous, and the time remaining is always displayed in the corner of the testing screen, along with the number of remaining questions. If time expires during an exam, the test terminates, and incomplete answers are counted as incorrect.

At the end of the exam, your test is immediately graded, and the results are displayed on the screen. Scores for each subject area are also provided, but the system will not indicate which specific questions were missed. A report is automatically printed at the proctor's desk for your files. The test score is electronically transmitted back to Cisco.

CCNP Online

In order to pass these challenging exams, you may want to talk with other test takers to determine what is being tested, and what to expect in terms of difficulty. The most helpful way to communicate with other CCNP hopefuls is the Cisco mailing list. With this mailing list, you will receive e-mail every day from other members discussing everything imaginable concerning Cisco networking equipment and certification. Access http://www.cisco.com/warp/public/84/1.html to learn how to subscribe to this wealth of information.

In the end, this computer-based system of evaluation is reasonably fair. You might feel that one or two questions were poorly worded; this can certainly happen, but you shouldn't worry too much. Ultimately, it's all factored into the required passing score.

CCNP Online

Make it easy on yourself and find some "braindumps." These are notes about the exam from test takers, which indicate the most difficult concepts tested, what to look out for, and sometimes even what not to bother studying. Several of these can be found at http://www.dejanews.com. Simply do a search for CCNP and browse the recent postings. Another good resource is at http://www.groupstudy.com.

Question Types

Cisco exams pose questions in a variety of formats, most of which are discussed here. As candidates progress toward the more advanced certifications, the difficulty of the exams is intensified, both through the subject matter as well as the question formats.

CCNP Advice

Many experienced test takers do not go back and change answers unless they have a good reason to do so. Only change an answer when you feel you may have misread or misinterpreted the question the first time. Nervousness may make you second-guess every answer and talk yourself out of a correct one.

True/False

The classic true/false question format is not used in the Cisco exams, for the obvious reason that a simple guess has a 50 percent chance of being correct. Instead, true/false questions are posed in multiple-choice format, requiring the candidate to identify the true or false statement from a group of selections.

Multiple Choice

Multiple choice is the primary format for questions in Cisco exams. These questions may be posed in a variety of ways.

"SELECT THE CORRECT ANSWER."   This is the classic multiple-choice question, where the candidate selects a single answer from a list of about four choices. In addition to the question's wording, the choices are presented in a Windows "radio button" format, where only one answer can be selected at a time.

"SELECT THE 3 CORRECT ANSWERS."   The multiple-answer version is similar to the single-choice version, but multiple answers must be provided. This is an "all-or-nothing" format; all the correct answers must be selected, or the entire question is incorrect. In this format, the question specifies exactly how many answers must be selected. Choices are presented in a check box format, allowing more than one answer to be selected. In addition, the testing software prevents too many answers from being selected.

"SELECT ALL THAT APPLY."   The open-ended version is the most difficult multiple-choice format, since the candidate does not know how many answers should be selected. As with the multiple-answer version, all the correct answers must be selected to gain credit for the question. If too many answers are selected, no credit is given. This format presents choices in check box format, but the testing software does not advise the candidates whether they've selected the correct number of answers.

Freeform Response

Freeform responses are prevalent in Cisco's advanced exams, particularly where the subject focuses on router configuration and commands. In the freeform format, no choices are provided. Instead, the test prompts for user input and the candidate must type the correct answer. This format is similar to an essay question, except the response must be very specific, allowing the computer to evaluate the answer.

For example, the question

Type the command for viewing routes learned via the EIGRP protocol.

requires the answer

```
show ip route eigrp
```

For safety's sake, you should completely spell out router commands, rather than using abbreviations. In the above example, the abbreviated command SH IP ROU EI works on a real router, but might be counted wrong by the testing software. The freeform response questions are almost always commands used in the Cisco IOS.

Fill in the Blank

Fill-in-the-blank questions are less common in Cisco exams. They may be presented in multiple-choice or freeform response format.

Exhibits

Exhibits accompany many exam questions, usually showing a network diagram or a router configuration. These exhibits are displayed in a separate window, which is opened by clicking the Exhibit button at the bottom of the screen. In some cases, the testing center may provide exhibits in printed format at the start of the exam.

Scenarios

While the normal line of questioning tests a candidate's "book knowledge," scenarios add a level of complexity. Rather than just ask technical questions, they apply the candidate's knowledge to real-world situations.

CCNP
@dvice

You will know you are coming up on a series of scenario questions, because they are preceded with a blue screen, indicating that the following questions will have the same scenario but different solutions. You must remember the scenario will be the same during the series of questions, which means you do not have to spend time reading the scenario again.

Scenarios generally consist of one or two paragraphs and an exhibit that describe a company's needs or network configuration. This description is followed by a series of questions and problems that challenge the candidate's ability to address the situation. Scenario-based questions are commonly found in exams relating to network design, but they appear to some degree in each of the Cisco exams.

CCNP @dvice

I have found it extremely helpful to put a check next to each objective as I find it is satisfied by the proposed solution. If the proposed solution does not satisfy an objective, you do not need to continue with the rest of the objectives. Once you have determined which objectives are fulfilled you can count your check marks and answer the question appropriately. This is a very effective testing technique!

Exam Objectives for CIT

Cisco has a clear set of objectives for the CIT exam, upon which the exam questions are based. The following list gives a good summary, by topic, of the things a candidate must know how to do for this exam:

1. Describe information gathering and communications to get the best use of Cisco's service and support services.

2. Use an efficient problem-solving method when troubleshooting and documenting internetwork problems.

3. Identify and apply generic Cisco-specific troubleshooting tools on Cisco routers and switches.

4. Analyze problem symptoms and resolve resolution strategies in TCP/IP (including the Microsoft 95/NT IP stack), Novell IPX, AppleTalk, Ethernet VLANs, Frame Relay, and ISDN BRI.

5. Perform labs that troubleshoot problems (hardware, software, or configuration bugs), then correct these bugs to restore full network operations.

6. Describe the types of and purposes of tools commonly used for network troubleshooting processes.

7. Describe and use the Cisco information resources (especially those in the CCO CD or World Wide Web site) that can assist with troubleshooting processes.

8. List the preferred methods for escalation of troubleshooting issues to Cisco's service and support programs.

9. Use a problem-solving model to systematically troubleshoot a given problem and list the value of using a systematic process.

10. Apply a process for documenting the steps taken to isolate potential causes and determine potential solutions.

11. Demonstrate knowledge of troubleshooting targets for connection-oriented and connectionless protocols.

12. Demonstrate knowledge of common data link layer characteristics and key troubleshooting targets likely to be found in campus LANs.

13. Demonstrate knowledge of connection sequences and key troubleshooting targets within TCP/IP, Novel IPX, and AppleTalk.

14. Handle troubleshooting tools and minimize their impact on a Cisco router's switching type and data flow.

15. Identify and use the innate Cisco IOS software commands and debug utilities to filter, capture, and display protocol traffic flows.

16. Obtain protocol troubleshooting information by capturing and interpreting data with a third-party protocol analyzer.

17. Use proven problem isolation techniques to list the symptoms of common TCP/IP problems that simulate real-life internetworking malfunctions.

18. Apply diagnostic tools to trouble tickets and solve classroom network TCP/IP problems that simulate real-life internetworking malfunctions.

19. Apply diagnostic tools to solve network problems that include systems running TCP/IP with Windows NT/95 clients and servers.

20. Use proven problem isolation techniques to list the symptoms of common Novell IPX problems on router networks.

21. Apply diagnostic tools to trouble tickets and solve classroom network Novell IPX problems that simulate real-life internetworking malfunctions.

22. Use proven problem isolation techniques to list the symptoms of common AppleTalk problems on router networks.

23. Apply diagnostic tools to trouble tickets and solve classroom network AppleTalk problems that simulate real-life internetworking malfunctions.

24. Use proven problem isolation techniques to list the symptoms of Catalyst 5000 and VLAN problems on switched Ethernet networks.

25. Apply diagnostic tools to trouble tickets and solve classroom network Catalyst 5000 problems that simulate real-life networking malfunctions.

26. Apply diagnostic tools to classroom trouble tickets on switched and routed VLAN configuration problems.

27. Use Cisco IOS router troubleshooting commands with Catalyst 5000 switched troubleshooting commands.

28. Use Cisco IOS commands and problem isolation techniques to identify the symptoms of common WAN and Frame Relay problems.

29. Apply diagnostic tools to trouble tickets and solve classroom network Frame Relay problems that simulate real-life WAN malfunctions.

30. Use Cisco IOS commands and problem isolation techniques to identify the symptoms of common ISDN BRI problems.

31. Apply diagnostic tools to trouble tickets and solve classroom network ISDN BRI problems that simulate real-life WAN malfunctions.

Studying Techniques

First and foremost, give yourself plenty of time to study. Networking is a complex field, and you can't expect to cram what you need to know into a single study session. It is a field best learned over time, by studying a subject and then applying your knowledge. Build yourself a study schedule and stick to it, but be reasonable about the pressure you put on yourself, especially if you're studying in addition to your regular duties at work.

CCNP
advice

One easy technique to use in studying for certification exams is the 15-minutes per day effort. Simply study for a minimum of 15 minutes every day. It is a small, but significant commitment. If you have a day where you just can't focus, then give up at 15 minutes. If you have a day where it flows completely for you, study longer. As long as you have more of the "flow days," your chances of succeeding are extremely high.

Second, practice and experiment. In networking, you need more than knowledge; you need understanding, too. You can't just memorize facts to be effective; you need to understand why events happen, how things work, and (most importantly) how they break.

The best way to gain deep understanding is to take your book knowledge to the lab. Try it out. Make it work. Change it a little. Break it. Fix it. Snoop around "under the hood." If you have access to a network analyzer, like Network Associate's Sniffer, put it to use. You can gain amazing insight to the inner workings of a network by watching devices communicate with each other.

Unless you have a very understanding boss, don't experiment with router commands on a production router. A seemingly innocuous command can have a nasty side effect. If you don't have a lab, your local Cisco office or Cisco users group may be able to help. Many training centers also allow students access to their lab equipment during off-hours.

Another excellent way to study is through case studies. Case studies are articles or interactive discussions that offer real-world examples of how technology is applied to meet a need. These examples can serve to cement your understanding of a technique or technology by seeing it put to use. Interactive discussions offer added value because you can also pose questions of your own. User groups are an excellent source of examples, since the purpose of these groups is to share information and learn from each other's experiences.

And not to be missed is the Cisco Networkers conference. Although renowned for its wild party and crazy antics, this conference offers a wealth of information. Held every year in cities around the world, it includes three days of technical seminars and presentations on a variety of subjects. As you might imagine, it's very popular. You have to register early to get the classes you want.

Then, of course, there is the Cisco Web site. This little gem is loaded with collections of technical documents and white papers. As you progress to more advanced subjects, you will find great value in the large number of examples and reference materials available. But be warned: You need to do a lot of digging to find the really good stuff. Often, your only option is to browse every document returned by the search engine to find exactly the one you need. This effort pays off. Most CCIEs I know have compiled six to ten binders of reference material from Cisco's site alone.

Scheduling Your Exam

The Cisco exams are scheduled by calling Sylvan Prometric directly at (800) 204-3926. For locations outside the United States, your local number can be found on Sylvan's Web site at http://www.prometric.com. Sylvan representatives can schedule your exam, but they don't have information about the certification programs. Questions about certifications should be directed to Cisco's training department.

The aforementioned Sylvan telephone number is specific to Cisco exams, and it goes directly to the Cisco representatives inside Sylvan. These representatives are familiar enough with the exams to find them by name, but it's best if you have the specific exam number handy when you call. After all, you wouldn't want to be scheduled and charged for the wrong exam (for example, the instructor's version, which is significantly harder).

Exams can be scheduled up to a year in advance, although it's really not necessary. Generally, scheduling a week or two ahead is sufficient to reserve the day and time you prefer. When scheduling, operators will search for testing centers in your area. For convenience, they can also tell which testing centers you've used before.

Sylvan accepts a variety of payment methods, with credit cards being the most convenient. When paying by credit card, you can even take tests the same day you call—provided, of course, that the testing center has room. (Quick scheduling can be handy, especially if you want to re-take an exam immediately.) Sylvan will mail you a receipt and confirmation of your testing date, although this generally arrives after the test has been taken. If you need to cancel or reschedule an exam, remember to call at least one day before your exam, or you'll lose your test fee.

When registering for the exam, you will be asked for your ID number. This number is used to track your exam results back to Cisco. It's important that you use the same ID number each time you register, so that Cisco can follow your progress. Address information provided when you first register is also used by Cisco to ship certificates and other related material. In the USA, your Social Security Number is commonly used as your ID number. However, Sylvan can assign you a unique ID number if you prefer not to use your Social Security Number.

Table i-3 shows the available Cisco exams and the number of questions and duration of each. This information is subject to change as Cisco revises the exams, so it's a good idea to verify the details when registering for an exam.

TABLE i-3   Cisco Exam Lengths and Question Counts

Exam Title	Exam Number	Number of Questions	Duration (minutes)	Exam Fee (US$)
Cisco Design Specialist (CDS)	9E0-004	80	180	$100
Cisco Internetwork Design (CID)	640-025	100	120	$100
Advanced Cisco Router Configuration (ACRC)	640-403	72	90	$100
Cisco LAN Switch Configuration (CLSC)	640-404	70	60	$100
Configuring, Monitoring, and Troubleshooting Dialup Services (CMTD)	640-405	64	90	$100
Cisco Internetwork Troubleshooting (CIT)*	640-440	77	105	$100
Cisco Certified Network Associate (CCNA)	640-407	70	90	$100
Foundation Routing & Switching	640-409	132	165	$100
CCIE Routing & Switching Qualification	350-001	100	120	$200
CCIE Certification Laboratory	N/A	N/A	2 days	$1,000

*As of this writing, Cisco is still offering the CIT 3.0 exam, exam 640-406, which has 69 questions and runs 60 minutes. The exam will likely retire once the new exam is established.

In addition to the regular Sylvan Prometric testing sites, Cisco also offers facilities for taking exams free of charge at each Networkers conference in the USA. As you might imagine, this option is quite popular, so reserve your exam time as soon as you arrive at the conference.

Arriving at the Exam

As with any test, you'll be tempted to cram the night before. Resist that temptation. You should know the material by this point, and if you're too groggy in the morning, you won't remember what you studied anyway. Instead, get a good night's sleep.

Arrive early for your exam; it gives you time to relax and review key facts. Take the opportunity to review your notes. If you get burned out on studying, you can usually start your exam a few minutes early. On the other hand, I don't recommend arriving late. Your test could be cancelled, or you may not be left with enough time to complete the exam.

When you arrive at the testing center, you'll need to sign in with the exam administrator. In order to sign in, you need to provide two forms of identification. Acceptable forms include government-issued IDs (for example, passport or driver's license), credit cards, and company ID badge. One form of ID must include a photograph.

Aside from a brain full of facts, you don't need to bring anything else to the exam. In fact, your brain about all you're allowed to take into the exam. All the tests are "closed book," meaning you don't get to bring any reference materials with you. You're also not allowed to take any notes out of the exam room. The test administrator will provide you with paper and a pencil. Some testing centers may provide a small marker board instead.

Calculators are not allowed, so be prepared to do any necessary math (such as hex-binary-decimal conversions or subnet masks) in your head or on paper. Additional paper is available if you need it.

Leave your pager and telephone in the car, or turn them off. They only add stress to the situation, since they are not allowed in the exam room, and can sometimes still be heard if they ring outside of the room. Purses, books, and other materials must be left with the administrator before entering the exam. While in the exam room, it's important that you don't disturb other candidates; talking is not allowed during the exam.

Once in the testing room, the exam administrator logs onto your exam, and you have to verify that your ID number and the exam number are correct. If this is the first time you've taken a Cisco test, you can select a brief tutorial for the exam software. Before the test begins, you will be provided with facts about the exam, including the duration, the number of questions, and the score required for passing. Then the clock starts ticking and the fun begins.

The testing software is Windows-based, but you won't have access to the main desktop or any of the accessories. The exam is presented in full screen, with a single question per screen. Navigation buttons allow you to move forward and backward between questions. In the upper-right corner of the screen, counters show the number of questions and time remaining. Most importantly, there is a 'Mark' checkbox in the upper-left corner of the screen—this will prove to be a critical tool in your testing technique.

Test-Taking Techniques

One of the most frequent excuses I hear for failing a Cisco exam is "poor time management." Without a plan of attack, candidates are overwhelmed by the exam or become sidetracked and run out of time. For the most part, if you are comfortable with the material, the allotted time is more than enough to complete the exam. The trick is to keep the time from slipping away during any one particular problem.

The obvious goal of an exam is to answer the questions effectively, although other aspects of the exam can distract from this goal. After taking a fair number of computer-based exams, I've naturally developed a technique for tackling the problem, which I share with you here. Of course, you still need to learn the material. These steps just help you take the exam more efficiently.

Size Up the Challenge

First, take a quick pass through all the questions in the exam. "Cherry-pick" the easy questions, answering them on the spot. Briefly read each question, noticing the type of question and the subject. As a guideline, try to spend less than 25 percent of your testing time in this pass.

This step lets you assess the scope and complexity of the exam, and it helps you determine how to pace your time. It also gives you an idea of where to find potential answers to some of the questions. Often, the answer to one question is shown in the exhibit of another. Sometimes the wording of one question might lend clues or jog your thoughts for another question.

Imagine that the following questions are posed in this order:

Question 1: "Review the router configurations and network diagram in exhibit XYZ (not shown here). Which devices should be able to ping each other?"

Question 2: "If RIP routing were added to exhibit XYZ, which devices would be able to ping each other?"

The first question seems straightforward. Exhibit XYZ probably includes a diagram and a couple of router configurations. Everything looks normal, so you decide that all devices can ping each other.

Now, consider the hint left by the Question 2. When you answered Question 1, did you notice that the configurations were missing the routing protocol? Oops! Being alert to such clues can help you catch your own mistakes.

If you're not entirely confident with your answer to a question, answer it anyway, but check the Mark box to flag it for later review. In the event that you run out of time, at least you've provided a "first guess" answer, rather than leaving it blank.

Take on the Scenario Questions

Second, go back through the entire test, using the insight you gained from the first go-through. For example, if the entire test looks difficult, you'll know better than to spend more than a minute or so on each question. Break down the pacing into small milestones; for example, "I need to answer 10 questions every 15 minutes."

At this stage, it's probably a good idea to skip past the time-consuming questions, marking them for the next pass. Try to finish this phase before you're 50–60 percent through the testing time.

By now, you probably have a good idea where the scenario questions are found. A single scenario tends to have several questions associated with it, but they aren't necessarily grouped together in the exam. Rather than re-reading the scenario every time you encounter a related question, save some time and answer the questions as a group.

Tackle the Complex Problems

Third, go back through all the questions you marked for review, using the Review Marked button in the question review screen. This step includes taking a second look at all the questions you were unsure of in previous passes, as well as tackling the time-consuming ones you deferred until now. Chisel away at this group of questions until you've answered them all.

If you're more comfortable with a previously marked question, unmark it now. Otherwise, leave it marked. Work your way through the time-consuming questions now, especially those requiring manual calculations. Unmark them when you're satisfied with the answer.

By the end of this step, you've answered every question in the test, despite having reservations about some of your answers. If you run out of time in the next step, at least you won't lose points for lack of an answer. You're in great shape if you still have 10–20 percent of your time remaining.

Review Your Answers

Now you're cruising! You've answered all the questions, and you're ready to do a quality check. Take yet another pass (yes, one more) through the entire test, briefly re-reading each question and your answer. Be cautious about revising answers at this point unless you're sure a change is warranted. If there's a doubt about changing the answer, I always trust my first instinct and leave the original answer intact.

Rarely are "trick" questions asked, so don't read too much into the questions. Again, if the wording of the question confuses you, leave the answer intact. Your first impression was probably right.

Be alert for last-minute clues. You're pretty familiar with nearly every question at this point, and you may find a few clues that you missed before.

The Grand Finale

When you're confident with all your answers, finish the exam by submitting it for grading. After what will seem like the longest 10 seconds in of your life, the testing software will respond with your score. This is usually displayed as a bar graph, showing the minimum passing score, your score, and a PASS/FAIL indicator.

If you're curious, you can review the statistics of your score at this time. Answers to specific questions are not presented; rather, questions are lumped into categories, and results are tallied for each category. This detail is also printed on a report that has been automatically printed at the exam administrator's desk.

As you leave the exam, you'll need to leave your scratch paper behind or return it to the administrator. (Some testing centers track the number of sheets you've been given, so be sure to return them all.) In exchange, you'll receive a copy of the test report.

This report will be embossed with the testing center's seal, and you should keep it in a safe place. Normally, the results are automatically transmitted to Cisco, but occasionally you might need the paper report to prove that you passed the exam. Your personnel file is probably a good place to keep this report; the file tends to follow you everywhere, and it doesn't hurt to have favorable exam results turn up during a performance review.

Re-Testing

If you don't pass the exam, don't be discouraged—networking is complex stuff. Try to have a good attitude about the experience, and get ready to try again. Consider yourself a little more educated. You know the format of the test a little better, and the report shows which areas you need to strengthen.

If you bounce back quickly, you'll probably remember several of the questions you might have missed. This will help you focus your study efforts in the right area. Serious go-getters will re-schedule the exam for a couple days after the previous attempt, while the study material is still fresh in their mind.

Ultimately, remember that Cisco certifications are valuable because they're hard to get. After all, if anyone could get one, what value would it have? In the end, it takes a good attitude and a lot of studying, but you can do it!

1

Troubleshooting Methodology

Today in most enterprise networks many components are connected and attached to existing backbone infrastructures, to support the evolving strategies of a corporation. In this enterprise network it is likely that traffic traversing the network is violating the *80/20 rule*. The 80/20 rule simply implies that 80 percent of traffic on a given network is local (destined for targets in the same workgroup); and not more than 20 percent of traffic requires internetworking. With mergers and acquisitions common in industry today, it is difficult to plan, deploy, and implement resources local to all users. As a result, the routers, switches, servers, and other nodes on the network are typically overutilized, thus bottlenecking the LAN segments and the backbone.

As network administrators managing existing networks, plan and design new ones, they must make strategically sound decisions to accommodate additional users and devices. When new users are added to an existing LAN segment at the corporate office in New Jersey, and they require access to resources at branch locations in Baltimore, Richmond, and Atlanta, options are pretty limited. It makes no sense to deploy the same resources locally for one user. That is, from a design perspective it's probably logical; however, it can become quite expensive. This is becoming a major concern for network administrators—the 80/20 rule has of late become the 20/80 rule.

In today's world of data communications and networking, complex heterogeneous network environments often complicate your efforts in solving network problems. And as the network evolves and grows, so does your challenge to deliver quality network service. Modern businesses rely on sophisticated networks for their livelihood; they can tolerate neither downtime nor degrading network performance. Yet it remains true that the very network on which the business depends is in most instances ignored until real problems occur, and you are faced with a crisis situation. Suddenly you're getting calls from the Data Center VP, the head of Operations, the Finance VP—everyone is looking for estimated uptimes and root-cause analyses.

To handle the occurrence of these problems and other complicated issues, LAN administrators must develop a thorough troubleshooting methodology to help resolve and isolate network problems. You can almost guarantee that there will be problems within your network because of design, installation, and product shortcomings. Troubleshooting is the process of:

- Exposing relevant information
- Eliminating irrelevant information
- Deducing, pinpointing, and isolating the problem area
- Devising a corrective action solution to correct the problem

In this chapter we will explore some of the symptoms and causes for many network problems prevalent in networks today. Often, the length of user downtime and out-of-service delays will depend on the plan of action you implement in your efforts to identify and resolve problematic areas. This chapter also outlines a working model for problem solving, presenting a generic model for you to plan your own course of action. Finally, the chapter gives an overview of the characteristics of various protocols.

CERTIFICATION OBJECTIVE 1.01

Symptoms, Causes, and Actions

On any given day, your network could be throttled to its knees. This is somewhat unlikely to happen all of a sudden. When they're in trouble, networks are just like sick children. Just as children will tell a parent when they're not feeling up to par, likewise your network will definitely alert you when it becomes ill. Usually when children are sick you'll begin to notice symptoms: a loss of appetite, high fever, runny noise, coughing and wheezing, stomach aches, and so on. The symptoms indicate the presence of disorder, and you might see anything from a trace indication foretelling the onset of a problem, to major subjective evidence of a severe physical disturbance. Your network, as well, will show symptoms when it's ill.

One of the major symptoms commonly found in networks throughout organizations today is *congestion*. Initially, your network was probably designed to accommodate a reasonably small to medium-sized workgroup, to allow information sharing. Likewise, many interstate highways and parkways were designed to handle a reasonable size of automobile traffic. However, today we see traffic congestion in networks just as we do on highways. Network administrators and city officials are constantly planning and designing workarounds to help alleviate traffic. How often do you see network administrators implement weekend change-controls to fix an emerging or an existing network problem? How often do you see construction workers drilling and building alternative routes in the wee hours of the night to help accommodate the traffic demands?

Slow Response Time

A significant result of network congestion is slow response time, and this delay is of primary concern to the network administrator.

Historically, LANs have been designed around data rates in the millions of bits per second—far in excess of most communications device capabilities. However, technological innovations and advancements in computing and data communications have changed this paradox somewhat. Many devices in today's network infrastructures have the potential to use the full channel capacity of a typical LAN. When many of these powerful devices share the channel, it's almost guaranteed that congestion will occur somewhere in your network. Congestion is a statistical phenomenon; it occurs as a function of traffic patterns. Network congestion will be revealed to LAN administrators and users in many ways.

Essentially all LANs have a certain capacity for carrying data. When presented with a short-term overload, the LAN distributes that load over time. Under a casual load, the time it takes a host to submit a frame for transmission over the LAN will be short. When the offered load is heavy, the average delay will increase. Simply stated, it takes longer to send the same amount of data under congestion conditions than it does when the load is casual. Usually this is transparent to users. However, when the delay is noticeable, the solution center or call center (help desk) gets flooded with calls from users complaining about slow response times.

Performance Alerts and Notifications

Many variables of LAN operations can be used to measure and evaluate network performance. Depending on configurations, some variables are measured by standard controllers and host software; others require special network-monitoring equipment, such as protocol analyzers or remote monitors (RMONs). To get a close-up look at the performance of your network, you can use various quantifiable and qualitative metrics to help identify potential problems. Following are some key indicators that can be used.

Channel Utilization

The percentage of time in which the channel is busy (or fully utilized) carrying data is known as the *channel utilization.* To determine what constitutes reasonable utilization levels, you should take into consideration the number of stations on a LAN segment, application behavior, frame-length distribution, traffic patterns, time of day, and so on. Pay close attention to utilization levels such as the following; they can be helpful in determining excessive load conditions:

- Utilization exceeds 10–20 percent averaged over an eight-hour work day.

- Utilization exceeds 20–30 percent averaged over the heaviest-load hours of the day.

- Utilization exceeds 50 percent averaged over the heaviest-load 15 minutes of the day.

exam
Watch

For every short-term period, network utilization may be peaking toward 100 percent—without noticeable network delays or performance degradation. This is possible during a large FTP file transfer between two high-performance end-stations. One thing to keep in mind is that each application environment behaves differently, depending on variables such as bandwidth, routing protocols, and so on.

User Complaints

We've all had our share of complaints from end-users. When the phone queues are backed up, it's a strong possibility that a crisis situation is occurring on your network. Therefore, we consider user dissatisfaction as the ultimate manifestation of LAN congestion. You can collect and compile, store and compare statistics, but none of that matters if users are complaining about poor network performance. Often overlooked, user reaction and feedback are critical metrics in the early steps of evaluating and troubleshooting your network.

One thing to keep in mind is that user complaints do not actually mean there is a LAN congestion problem. Often what's reasonable to the user is not necessarily indicative of poor network performance. Users generally have high expectations for technology and are reluctant to recognize that technology has its shortcomings.

Collision Rates

When there is an increased rate of collision on an Ethernet segment, it can be indicative of the offered load. Usually LAN administrators view modest collision rates as normal; nor does a high rate necessarily indicate a severe problem. On an Ethernet segment, collision information can be used to redistribute the offered load over the available time, thus maximizing application throughput and channel utilization. On a functional Ethernet segment, you can have what is considered short-term collision rates as high as 20–25 percent; anything exceeding 30 percent, however, should be studied and administered carefully.

Monitoring and worrying about the number of collisions seen on Ethernet networks is a growing preoccupation of network administrators these days. There have been many debates and misperceptions about what an "acceptable" collision rate is, and how to determine when your network is on the verge of collapsing. Even under the most extreme offered loads, collisions use up a very small percentage of available channel capacity. Generally, you can ignore collision statistics as long as users are satisfied with response times and application efficiency. On the other hand, if users begin complaining, consider investigating collision rates as one source of explanation.

Application Performance Degradation

LAN congestion will ultimately affect application throughput. From the user's perspective, "everything is slow." A daily routine file transfer that normally takes 15 to 20 seconds on average is exceeding one minute.

Normal application transactions are behaving sluggishly. If utilization peaks are reached and network loads become burdensome, there is a good chance that an application will be brought to its knees. This may cause a user request to time out, servers to disconnect, and sessions to hang. Usually under these extreme conditions, applications and processes must be restarted and re-initialized to restore functionality.

Within an enterprise network, there are additional symptoms and problems other than network congestion and slow response. However, these two issues are the focus of our discussion here because they are what network administrators must typically troubleshoot on a daily basis—especially in a large distributed environment with diverse application requirements. With these problems at hand, network administrators are looking at other designs to help alleviate and reduce channel loads. Let's take a look at one of these: the switching approach to networking.

CERTIFICATION OBJECTIVE 1.02

Generic Problem-Solving Model

As a troubleshooter, you must have a process or procedure defined to help you resolve a particular network problem. When a plumber comes to your house to fix a plumbing problem, he or she implements a standard procedure to identify the root cause. Likewise, an automobile mechanic must resort to a method or procedure of identifying problematic area(s) in your vehicle. In a network environment, it is imperative for you to use a systematic approach to troubleshooting. A good start would be to devise a *generic problem-solving model* to aid your efforts to identify, isolate, and resolve the problem.

A problem-solving model starts with a broad domain, and as you drill down each phase, the domain narrows as potential signs and symptoms are eliminated. This model flirts with the unknowns and possibilities of a given problem situation. For instance, let's use a simple mathematics problem as supporting evidence:

Solve for x:
$2x + 8 = 12$

In this problem, you have an unknown (x) with a number of possibilities (not necessarily correct answers). You work to eliminate the obvious wrong answers (process of elimination).

Steps to Solving a Problem

The math problem shown earlier is a simplistic view of problem solving. Although applying a problem-solving model to a network crisis situation is much more difficult, there still is a fundamental approach one must take when presented with a number of unknowns and possibilities.

A generic problem-solving model has at least six phases (shown in Figure 1-1) that need to be successfully satisfied before a problem has been resolved. Each phase represents a process in which a particular action is required. This entire process is not just for troubleshooting internetworking problems but can be used in various problematic domains. From this foundation you can build a problem-solving process to suit your own particular crisis situation. Here are the steps of the problem-solving process:

1. Define and state the problem.

2. Gather facts and analyze the problem.

3. Review and evaluate alternatives and possibilities.

4. Design a plan of action (POA).

5. Implement the solution.

6. Evaluate and observe the solution (further analysis).

7. Repeat the process (if needed).

1. Define and State the Problem

A good rule of thumb is to make a list of resources—people, documentation, Web sites, contact information, and the like—that are relevant to the problem you are trying to solve. Utilize these resources to clarify any unfamiliar terms or concepts, and to help identify the problem domain. At this point in the process you are in search of symptoms—evidence that a problem does exist.

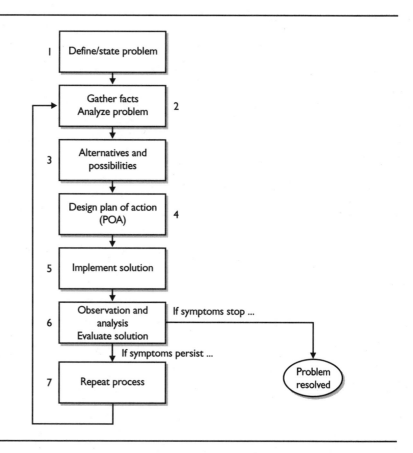

FIGURE I-I

Generic problem-solving
model

When analyzing a network problem, you need to make a clear problem
statement. This will help you to see the big picture and not unduly simplify or
complicate the problem domain.

Try to define the problem in terms of a set of symptoms and potential
causes of those symptoms. For example, say a host or multiple hosts on a
particular LAN segment are not responding to service requests from clients.
One possible cause may be that a host's or router's configuration is
incorrect, resulting in timeouts for service requests.

A good rule of thumb is to ask yourself several questions: Which problem
should I address? If there are several, how do I choose the most critical one?

2. Gather Facts and Analyze the Problem

After you have compiled supporting evidence for the existence of the problem and have defined what that problem is, you can focus on analyzing your findings more thoroughly. You are looking for relevant data that might explain why the problem exists and/or how it occurred. Collect information from sources such as router logs, users' experience, trouble tickets, output from router diagnostics commands, software release notes, protocol analyzer traces, and other troubleshooting commands. This particular phase is aimed at evaluating collected information and data to further isolate possible causes. Ask questions of affected users, network administrators, managers, and other key people.

Using the facts that are gathered, you can begin to eliminate irrelevant issues and narrow the problem domain. For instance, you can completely eliminate hardware as a contributing factor if findings point to other problematic areas, allowing you to focus and pay more attention to pertinent symptoms and specific problem domains.

3. Review and Evaluate Alternatives and Possibilities

First and foremost, your problem solving should begin with an established criteria for evaluating solutions. A good starting point is to set an objective with your team. Based on your definition of the problem and root-cause analysis, the objective should be the specific goal that acceptable solution(s) should attain. If the problem domain is too complex to handle with one objective, the alternative is to evaluate proposed solutions and make a list of Musts and Wants. The Musts are the basic items that require a solution. The Wants are qualities that are desirable in any solution; these should be prioritized from most desirable to least desirable.

4. Design a Plan of Action (POA)

This planning phase is one of the most overlooked steps of the problem-solving model. Designing a plan of action (POA) involves planning and brainstorming. Begin with the most common problem and devise a POA in which only one variable is manipulated.

What are the various alternatives for solving the problem? Once you've established some basis for evaluating the solutions, as described in the preceding Review and Evaluate step, it's important that you brainstorm the solutions. From the list of possible solutions that emerge from this thinking session, select the one that best fits your needs based on your criteria evaluation.

5. Implement the Solution

In this step, ask yourself "How do I make sure the solution is implemented correctly and effectively?" Here you're simply putting the plan into action, performing tasks and testing to ensure that the solution has truly corrected problematic areas.

6. Evaluate and Observe the Solution (Further Analysis)

How did the solution work? What needs to be changed? In this phase you can continue to collect and evaluate information from router logs, users, output from router diagnostics commands, software release notes, protocol analyzer traces, and other troubleshooting commands.

Be on guard for intermittent problems—a symptom that cannot be reproduced by any known procedure. Intermittent problems are very difficult to resolve (troubleshoot). Because you don't know how to reproduce the symptom, it's difficult to know whether the symptom went away because of a test you performed, or because of random chance.

If in fact you can't reproduce the symptom, chances are your only alternative is routine maintenance and guesswork, and you may not be successful in trying to resolve the problem.

7. Repeat the Process

If your network's problem persists, repeat steps 2 through 6. Look again at your facts and try some different solutions.

Pointers for Problem Solving

One thing I'm always mindful to avoid is rushing to a solution too soon. It's best to avoid focusing too much attention on one solution, too early in the troubleshooting process. We've all been guilty of this at some point. Thoroughly go through each phase; don't omit anything. Refrain from acting on the first suggestion of a solution, or before the problem has been adequately defined. Troubleshooting can be like finding a needle in a haystack, so be patient—solutions do not always come on the first go-around.

Many people have a low tolerance for the uncertainty of problem solving; therefore, they dodge problem-solving activities. This impatient approach leads to what I call "patchwork" or "a quick-fix"; this attitude often seeks to eliminate the problem without any thorough evaluation or analysis. Try to remain open-minded, willing to endure the ambiguity and doubt, so that you can perform a thorough analysis by using every step of the problem-solving model.

Recommended Troubleshooting Procedures

In today's world, businesses develop sophisticated enterprise network strategies to gain a competitive advantage in their industry. Because the business relies heavily on its enterprise network, there is no room for ongoing out-of-service delays or poor network performance. Often the small symptoms are ignored, and over time they will flare up into a crisis situation. With every crisis situation you will need a staff of competent individuals who can troubleshoot the problem.

Before you can effectively troubleshoot, you must be able to determine if a problem does exist. In other words, you must have an idea of what your network looks like before it becomes ill. If you never get a clear picture of a functional network, then it will be difficult to determine the true status of your network if a problem does exist. A parent knows how a child behaves before the child becomes sick. By knowing the child's behavior patterns, you can detect a problem if that child's behavior deviates from what is considered the norm. The same applies with your network.

As a network administrator, you should take the pulse of your network through a regularly scheduled sampling of network traffic. These samples will give you an indication of the state of your network, identifying potential areas of concern, potential equipment failures, and performance loss due to the network's having superseded its existing configuration. By taking your network pulse, you can strategically plan maintenance schedules that will help maintain the integrity of your network and fix subtle discrepancies in your network as they emerge.

You can use a *LAN tester* or a *protocol analyzer* to collect network data and store it in the test equipment. Small cable meters and LAN testers can be used to capture and gather readings for a short period of time. Some common devices that can store data for future analysis are Fluke's LANMeter series, Microtest's Compas, and Scope's FrameScope. The large-scale and complex protocol analyzers tend to be PC-equipped. These LAN devices can sample data over a longer period of time, storing megabytes of data. Generally, this information is used to track intermittent network glitches.

An effective troubleshooter should have a hardcopy of network topology, and know and understand host and IP addresses of network devices, routing protocols, circuit identification number (WAN links), slot and port numbers, MAC addresses, and so on. A troubleshooter without a network diagram is like a repairperson without a tool belt.

Consider the following situation: You get a call from the manager of Finance. Users are complaining about network connectivity problems. How do you proceed to troubleshoot the problem? First and foremost you need to have a thorough understanding of the existing network and the protocols directing the flow of network traffic. The following key elements will assist you with your initial troubleshooting. (More tools may be available to you, depending on the problem domain.)

- Topology map
- Access to workstations, PCs, and host configuration information
- IP and MAC addresses and host names (DNS)
- Configuration information for the router on the same LAN segment
- Ping, Traceroute, Telnet, Netstat, and other commands to help determine device status
- LAN test devices and protocol analyzers to monitor and evaluate network traffic

The ping application sends packets of information to a specific address or range of addresses and then notifies the sender when a reply is received, indicating size of packets, packet loss, and the amount of time it took.

After monitoring network traffic, you can use a ping test to actively test your network. These tests will provide you with detailed statistical information (depending on command options used) about network traffic and particular devices.

The Traceroute application provides more descriptive information than Ping. Traceroute returns host and timing information about each "hop" that a data packet takes to get to a specific address. This tool is very helpful when used to determine where packets are being discarded or slowed down.

Another helpful tool for troubleshooting is SNMP (Simple Network Management Protocol), used to monitor routers within a given network.

The basic rule of troubleshooting is to isolate the problem by a process of elimination. A good starting point would be to identify the scope of the problem:

■ Are there any common symptoms?

■ Is the problem only on a single device?

■ Are several, but not all, devices experiencing the same problem?

■ What services are being affected?

Documentation Methods

Managing a network environment is not an easy task, becoming gradually more complicated as the network grows and changes. The more detailed your documentation, the easier it is for you to troubleshoot. Documenting your network is an ongoing process. You should update your documentation whenever a node changes, when an IP address is added or removed, when software or hardware is installed and upgraded, when a network fails, and so on.

Gather and collect statistical information baselining your network, and use that information for documentation. The information can be converted into a spreadsheet or chart for observation and analysis. Accurately documenting your network is critical. Generally, a good rule of thumb is to develop data sheets for your network with the following statistical information:

- Utilization levels (peaks, averages)
- Frame transmission per second (peak, averages)
- Frame size (peak, averages)
- Collision rates (peak, averages)
- Jabbers, runts, and fragment totals
- CRC errors

exam
Ⓦatch

Baselining your network is critical in determining the health of your network, in addition to identifying the problem areas. Baselining also provides network analysis for problem isolation and resolution.

CiscoWorks (discussed in Chapter 8) is an effective management tool for proactive monitoring, providing the functionality for effective baselining. If you can effectively manage your network by deploying network management systems to ensure fault, performance, configuration, security, and accounting management, then half of the battle is won. You are then in a better position to anticipate and identify failures and network problems—before they affect users, servers, and workstations.

For documentation in today's environment, you can build Web sites with online documentation on your corporate intranet. You can develop interactive databases that interface with the front-end of network devices, polling data to populate data records. Posting generic diagrams and system information for internal use only is also a viable method. Since everyone has their own methods for creating documentation, it's in your best interest to install a method for consolidating information. This improves data integrity, and ensures that everyone on your team will have access to the same relevant and accurate documentation. Discrepancies in the documentation can result in ineffective troubleshooting and problem solving, thereby prolonging outage situations.

Cisco's Web site is a good resource for documentation and troubleshooting tips: http://www.cisco.com. There you'll find helpful online documentation of Cisco products, many troubleshooting tips, and assistance with problem resolution.

on the !ob

In the network arena, the elements within the network are constantly changing. Within a year's time the network topology could change at least twice a month. Documentation must be updated to reflect the changes in network design, configurations, hardware locations, contact numbers, process owners, and so on. Ultimately, controlling a full-blown crisis situation could depend on how well you keep accurate and precise documentation. Documentation to a troubleshooter is like a blueprint for an interior decorator, or scouting notes for a coach. In essence, documentation provides the framework for effectively building a clear understanding of a given environment. This will help you conceptualize and interpret the big picture.

CERTIFICATION OBJECTIVE 1.03

Protocol Characteristics Review

You'll need to be familiar with several protocols in order to deliver effective troubleshooting and problem analysis. The flow of traffic across the network is governed by protocols. They work just like traffic regulations and restrictions (speed limits, traffic lights, one-way zones, and so on) that control and regulate the flow of traffic on highways from one destination to another. This section reviews these protocols, discussing their various characteristics.

Connection-Oriented vs. Connectionless

Connection-oriented is comparable to sending a letter that requires a return receipt. It requires adjacent nodes to acknowledge each frame or packet of data received. *Connectionless* service is comparable to sending a letter by standard, regular mail. There is no guarantee that the letter will be delivered on time, thus providing best-effort delivery.

We can use two transport protocols to make the distinction: TCP and UDP. TCP is a connection-oriented, reliable protocol. It provides a control mechanism to ensure that data is sent and received successfully. For instance, if you send certified mail, it requires a signature for delivery, an acknowledgment indicating that the item was delivered and received. TCP provides the reliability by using sequence numbers and acknowledgments. TCP is also responsible for breaking messages into segments, re-assembling them at the destination station, resending anything that wasn't received, and re-assembling messages from the segments. In contrast, UDP is connectionless, responsible only for transmitting the message. UDP provides no software checking for segment delivery, and thus is deemed unreliable.

A connection-oriented protocol has the following characteristics:

- Request for service establishes the circuit (session setup and disconnect, handshakes)
- Provides virtual circuits
- Provides switched virtual circuit
- Provides permanent virtual circuit
- Provides sequential delivery of packets and frames
- Single path through network for all packets and frames

A connectionless protocol has the following characteristics:

- Provides dynamic flow through the network
- Provides alternative paths
- Receiving nodes must be able to manage nonsequential acknowledgments
- There is potential for nonsequential delivery of packets and frames

Figure 1-2 indicates some connection-oriented and connectionless protocols.

Connection-oriented and
connectionless protocols

Connection-oriented Protocols	Connectionless Protocols
SNA	Ethernet
Token Ring	Frame Relay
X.25	IP
FDDI	

Ethernet

Ethernet is the oldest of the LAN technologies commonly used throughout the business industry today. Regardless of its ancient history, Ethernet is still deployed today in traditional LAN infrastructures.

Ethernet's design forces stations to contend against each other for access to media. This contention-based nature of Ethernet prevents stations from exploiting the available 10 Mbps bandwidth. Realistically speaking, each individual station on the shared media only receives a small percentage of the available bandwidth. However, each station is capable of receiving all transmissions from all stations, but only in a half-duplex mode. This means a station cannot send and receive data at the same time.

In the Ethernet architecture, when a station desires to transmit, it checks the network to make sure that no other station on that segment is transmitting. If by chance the network is idle, the station then proceeds with its transmission. The sending station monitors the network to ensure that no other station on the segment is transmitting. There is a strong possibility that two stations on the same network can transmit at the same time, which inevitably produces a collision (Figure 1-3). Once a collision is detected, a special bit pattern called a *jam signal* may be sent by other stations to ensure that all stations recognize the collision and defer any pending transmissions. All stations then stop transmitting for a randomly selected time frame before they are permitted to retransmit.

Collision domain on an
Ethernet LAN segment

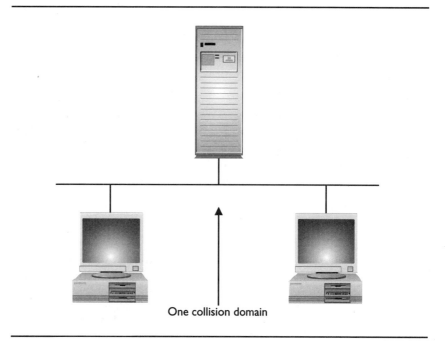

One collision domain

Ethernet uses an access method called Carrier Sense Multiple Access/
Collision Detection (CSMA/CD) to detect the interference caused by
simultaneous transmission by two or more stations. CSMA/CD manages
collisions; however, it also increases transmission time in two ways:

- If two stations transmit simultaneously, the information transmitted
  will collide at some point; therefore, each station must stop its
  transmission and retransmit at a later time.

- Once a stations sends information, an Ethernet LAN will not
  transfer any other information until that information has successfully
  reached its destination.

In essence, although CSMA/CD slows up Ethernet networks, it can
effectively manage transmission on the wire. As a network administrator
you must weigh the pros and cons and determine the most strategically
sound solution for your local networking.

Token Ring

Token Ring, developed by IBM, is a LAN technology in which all stations are connected in a ring or star topology. Token Ring helps reconcile the contention-based access to the transmission medium by granting every station equal access. Token Ring uses a token-passing process to prevent collision between two stations that want to send data at the same time. The token passing allows only the station with the token to have access to the ring for data transmission. When a station wants to transmit, it waits upon the arrival of the token. Essentially, to transmit you need to possess the token. Upon the arrival of the token, the station creates a data frame and transmits it onto the wire. The stations then relay the frame around the ring until the frame reaches its respective destination.

In Token Ring implementation, stations on the ring are connected through a central hub: Media Access Unit (MAU). Often, network administrators will interconnect MAUs to extend the Token Ring LAN connectivity from various floors and parts of the building. Usually, a MAU can connect up to eight Token Ring stations.

The Token Ring operation is quite simple: A station can only transmit when it receives the token frame (though exceptions can be negotiated). A station that receives the token with no data to transmit simply forwards the token to the next station, and this continues until the token reaches a station with data for transmission. The station that seizes the token to transmit data must also alter the T bit of the frame. In Token Ring implementation there is a mechanism in place to permit certain user-designated stations higher priority than other stations on the ring. This allows stations with the highest priority frequent access to the network for data transmission.

To help detect faults on a Token Ring network, an *active monitor* is assigned the role of ring maintenance. The active monitor will discard any frame that traverses the ring continually. This frame can prevent all other stations of the ring from transmitting.

FDDI

Fiber Distributed Data Interface, commonly known as FDDI, is a standard for data transmission on fiber-optic lines within a LAN. FDDI implementation is based primarily on Token Ring implementation. An FDDI network contains two Token Rings: a primary ring, and a secondary ring for failure recovery. FDDI provides extensive reliability by providing up to 100 Mbps capacity. If the secondary ring is not needed for failure recovery, it can carry data, too, increasing capacity to 200 Mbps. The increased capacity makes FDDI the most feasible LAN solution for client/server applications. FDDI can also be deployed for workgroups or at the backbone.

FDDI implementation uses a dual-counter/rotating-ring topology to provide and maintain the necessary fault recovery and data integrity. FDDI consist of the following entities:

■ **Physical Layer Media Dependent (PMD)** defines the physical characteristics of the media interface connectors, cabling, and the services necessary for transmitting signals throughout the network.

■ **Physical Layer Protocol** defines the rules for encoding and framing data for transmission, clocking requirements, and line states.

■ **Media Access Control** mechanism defines the FDDI timed-token protocol, frame and token construction, and transmission on the FDDI ring, in addition to ring initialization and fault isolation functionality.

On an FDDI network you can have stations (nodes with no master ports) and concentrators (nodes with master ports). FDDI standards define two types of stations: dual attached station (DAS) and single attached station (SAS). The DAS connects both the primary and the secondary rings. The SAS connects only one ring; it cannot wrap the ring in case of a fault or link ring failure.

FDDI initializes the ring and transmits data in the following manner:

1. Connections are made between the stations on the ring and their neighbors.

2. Stations negotiate the target token rotation time (TTRT), using the claim-token process.

3. After a node has initialized the ring, the ring begins to operate in a steady state. A steady state simply means that the stations exchange frames using what is called a timed-token protocol (TTP). TTP

defines how the TTRT is set, the length of time for which a station can claim the token, and the method by which a station initializes the ring. The ring will remain in the steady state until a new claim-token process occurs (a new station joins the ring).

4. The stations then pass the token around the FDDI ring.

5. A station on the ring captures the token when it wants to transmit data, and then transmit data to the downstream neighbor.

6. Each station reads and repeats frames as they receive them. If an error is detected, the stations will then set an error indicator.

7. A frame circulates on the ring until it reaches the station that first transmitted it. The station then removes the frame.

8. When the first station has sent all of its frames (or exceed the available transmission time) the token is then released back to the ring.

Transmission Control Protocol/Internet Protocol (TCP/IP)

Early research done by the U.S. Defense Advanced Research Projects Agency (DARPA) in computer interconnectivity gave life to the initial development of the Internet suite of protocols. The TCP/IP suite is governed by a set of standards that specify how computers communicate and the conventions for interconnecting networks and routing traffic. The Department of Defense presented a reference model for this new development, which separates the functions performed by communication protocols into manageable, stackable layers. Each layer controls a certain aspect for data transmission from source to destination. This model is not only designed for protocols to communicate across the network, but can also be used as a platform to develop protocols.

Four layers form this architectural design: the Application layer, Transport layer, Internetwork layer, and the Network Interface layer. The Internetwork layer is commonly used to describe TCP/IP. The TCP/IP stack maps closely to the OSI reference model in the lower layers (see Figure 1-4). The information used in TCP/IP is transferred in a sequence of datagrams.

APPLICATION LAYER This layer of the architectural model provides the functionality for users and programs. It also provides the

FIGURE 1-4

OSI model and TCP/IP
internetworking model

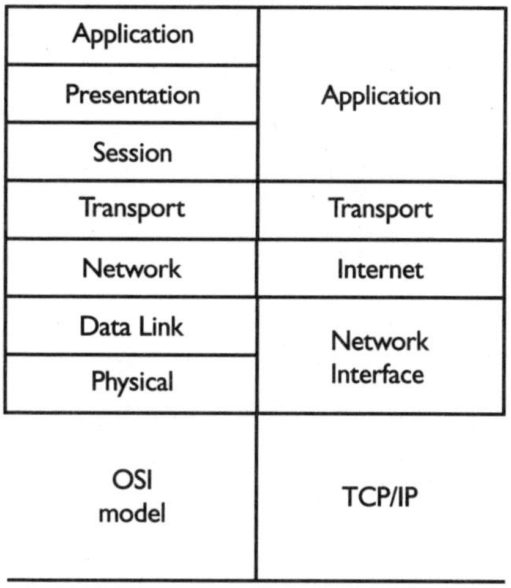

Application	
Presentation	Application
Session	
Transport	Transport
Network	Internet
Data Link	Network Interface
Physical	

OSI model	TCP/IP

services accessed by user applications to communicate over the network. It is the layer in which user-access network processes reside, including all the processes with which users interact directly. One of the most important responsibilities of the Application layer is to manage sessions (connections) between applications.

Application protocols exist for file transfers, Telnet, World Wide Web, e-mail, remote login, and network management elements (SNMP).

TRANSPORT LAYER   The Transport layer provides host-to-host communications. It ensures end-to-end data integrity and provides a reasonably reliable communication service for network elements that want to carry out a two-way communication. This layer also handles flow control, retransmission, and other data management mechanisms. The TCP and UDP protocols reside at the Transport layer.

INTERNETWORK LAYER   These days, the Internetwork layer is called simply Internet Protocol (IP). This layer provides the basic packet-delivery service for all TCP/IP networks. IP is an unreliable, connectionless, best-effort datagram service that does not guarantee packet delivery. If by chance packets are discarded (for whatever reason) the sender and receiver are not notified.

At this layer, a logical systematic scheme for host addresses is used, commonly known as *IP addresses*. These addresses identify devices connected to the network. Furthermore, other autonomous networks in the world use this address implementation to communicate on the information superhighway. The Internetwork and higher layers use these IP addresses for routing functionality. IP addressing consists of a 4-byte or 32-bit addressing scheme with a dotted decimal notation (as in 141.142.153.25). The entire scheme comprises two parts: a network portion and a host portion (see Figure 1-5). The maximum number for each octet is 255; it contains all 1s. Usually the first and last octet are reserved for the network and broadcast addresses, respectively.

Figure 1-6 shows the three conventional Classes (A, B, and C), their address ranges, and local numbers; and gives an example of each addressing scheme. In addition to these addresses, there are special Class D addresses used for multicasting, and a Class E address used for experimenting. The following are the totals of local addresses for each class:

- Class A range ⇔ 1.0.0.0 to 126.0.0.0 ⇔ Number of host addresses: 16,000,000

- Class B range ⇔ 128.0.0.0 to 191.255.0.0 ⇔ Number of host addresses: 64,000

- Class C range ⇔ 192.0.0.0 to 233.255.255.0 ⇔ Number of host addresses: 254

The following paper is a good reference for TCP/IP addressing: *Understanding IP Addressing: Everything You Ever Wanted To Know* by

---

FIGURE 1-5

Internet address format

Network address	Subnet address	Host address

FIGURE 1-6

Conventional address classes

Class	First number	Local numbers	Examples
A	1-126	16,777,216	16.0.0.0-16.100.12.103
B	128-191	65,536	130.15.0.0-130.25.19.102
C	192-223	256	192.149.20.23-192.149.20.255

Chuck Semeria at http://www.3com.com/nsc/501302.html. This paper is recommended reading to get a more in-depth understanding of the addressing scheme and its future implementation in the IP world.

NETWORK INTERFACE LAYER   The Network Interface layer is responsible for getting data across the physical network (Ethernet, Token Ring, etc.). IP datagrams are encapsulated into frames at this layer. Mapping of an IP address to a physical address (MAC) is also performed by this TCP/IP layer. Once information is received from the peer layer (Internetwork), the Network Interface layer is then responsible for routing and adding its necessary routing information to the data (frame headers). The protocols at this layer perform three important functions:

- They define how to use the network to transmit frames across a physical connection.
- They exchange data between the computer and the physical network.
- They deliver data between two end-stations on the same LAN segment, by using the physical addresses of the end-nodes.

Novell IPX

The Novell NetWare Internetwork Packet Exchange (IPX) protocol was derived from the early Xerox Network Systems (XNS) Internet Transport Protocols. The XNS protocol suite is comparable to the TCP/IP protocol suite. Novell IPX utilizes a connectionless datagram protocol. IPX is

NetWare's network layer service, and provides addressing as well as routing capabilities.

■ Internetwork Packet Exchange (IPX) transmits each data unit as an independent entity without establishing a logical connection between the two end-stations. This protocol uses the IEEE 802.3 frame format without the LLC layer.

■ Sequenced Packet Exchange (SPX) protocol is a connection-oriented protocol used for reliable peer-to-peer (client server) communications based on the XNS Sequenced Packet Protocol. SPX is reliable, guaranteeing sequenced packet delivery.

■ NetWare Core Protocol (NCP) is Novell's upper-layer protocol for connection-oriented transmissions. This protocol provides the framework that facilitates interaction between workstations and servers (client/server relationship).

The devices on an IPX network use Service Advertising Protocol (SAP) to advertise NetWare services and addresses. SAP advertisements make service available dynamically. Depending on SAP implementation in an IPX network, SAP broadcasts can be propagated every 60 seconds; however, you can increase this window to effectively manage SAP broadcasts.

In the IPX world, the node number and the network number define the network address, expressed in the *network.node* format. The network number is a 4-byte (32-bit) number that identifies a physical network. Each physical chuck of wire is required to have a single network number, which is the same number that you bind when a file server is configured. In an IPX implementation, Novell servers are inherently routers; therefore, the network number is contained and advertised from the file server.

The node number identifies a node on the network as shown in Figure 1-7 and Figure 1-8. The node number is a 48-bit MAC layer address of the physical interface.

exam
ⓦatch

In the example given in Figure 1-7, a serial interface has a MAC address. Theoretically, this is not realistic, however. In the IPX implementation, serial interfaces use the default Novell address— usually the first address of an active interface.

Addressing scheme used in
an IPX network

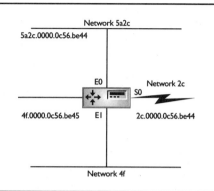

AppleTalk

AppleTalk is considered one of the purest client/server networking systems
that rely on nodes (usually Macintosh workstations) sharing network
resources (servers, printers, files, and so forth). In most cases, the interaction
between devices is transparent to the users, since AppleTalk engages in
network interaction and broadcasting functions, permitting communication
between client and server. Many network professionals in the industry refer
to AppleTalk as a "plug and play" network. An AppleTalk user can plug
right into the network without making major configuration changes. The
network services on the AppleTalk network are easy to locate.

The native routing protocol for AppleTalk is the Routing Table
Maintenance Protocol (RTMP). Routers on the network use this protocol
to exchange and update routing information. RTMP calculates the shortest
path to each destination.

As an AppleTalk network grows, so does the traffic that occurs when
hosts attempt to locate other devices on the network, and when routing

IPX network address, with
interface and network
number and node

Interface	IPX Address	Network Number	Node Number
E0	5a2c.0000.0c56.be44	5a2c	0000.0c56.be44
E1	4f.0000.0c56.be45	4f	0000.0c56.be45
S0	2c.0000.0c56.be44	2c	0000.0c56.be44

information is exchanged by the routers on the network. One way to alleviate this enormous traffic overhead is to use Cisco IOS filters, ultimately improving the scalability of the AppleTalk network.

Devices on the network are deployed in logical groups, commonly known as *zones*. The zone provides a way to localize and manage broadcast traffic and to create "Communities of Interest" (see Figure 1-9). Communities of Interest are equivalent to segmented users in an Ethernet network. Users are logically grouped to share network resources.

A nonextended network allows 127 hosts and 127 servers per network (shown in Figure 1-10). Only a single network number is allowed per wire, and only a single zone is allowed per wire. An extended network allows a total of 253 devices per wire (any combination of hosts and servers). A range of network numbers, called the *cable range,* is allowed per wire.

| FIGURE 1-9 | An example of AppleTalk's Communities of Interest implementation |

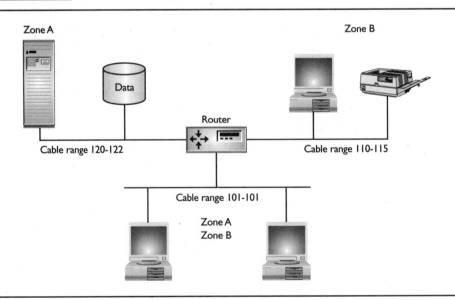

FIGURE 1-10   AppleTalk's implementation of nonextended and extended networks

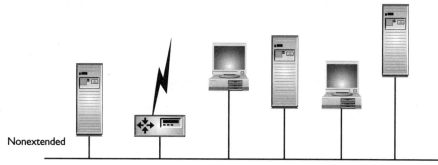

Nonextended

127 hosts, 127 servers per network
Single network number per wire

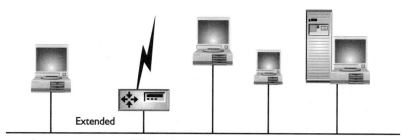

Extended

253 hosts/servers per network
Range of network numbers per wire

CERTIFICATION SUMMARY

The information presented in this chapter presents a realistic framework that can be used to attack most (if not all) network crisis situations. However, if the framework is not utilized properly, quality solutions will not emerge from your troubleshooting efforts. The quality solutions will depend on your commitment and the quality you put into the problem-solving steps.

By getting a complete and accurate symptom description and reproducing the symptoms, you ensure in most instances that you have fixed the symptom, or are at least on your way to resolving the problem.

Avoiding steps could be catastrophic. Stay focused and try to avoid this pitfall. Time is precious and one mistake can often negatively impact the entire troubleshooting process.

When you are at work, you are usually working on a team with other analysts, LAN administrators, and LAN specialists. Usually troubleshooting becomes a team effort; everyone is contributing expertise and helping to get the problem resolved. However, your certification will be a solo effort; therefore, you can't rely on anyone but yourself. It is important for you to develop effective troubleshooting skills on your own. It is even more important for you to understand the problem domain and be able to thoroughly document your findings while analyzing and evaluating symptoms.

Understanding the way in which protocols control the flow of data across the network will provide you with extra ammunition needed for effective troubleshooting. Although each protocol behaves differently, they all are designed to regulate and dictate the flow of traffic from source to destination over some common path.

Finally, remember that troubleshooting is a set of procedures, mental tools, and attitudes that anyone can master. It's up to you to develop the skills that are needed to become an effective troubleshooter. Have an idea of what your network looks like and how it behaves when it's healthy.

 # TWO-MINUTE DRILL

- ❑ One of the major symptoms commonly found in networks throughout organizations today is *congestion*.

- ❑ A significant result of network congestion is slow response time, and this delay is of primary concern to the network administrator.

- ❑ Many variables of LAN operations can be used to measure and evaluate network performance.

- ❑ To determine what constitutes reasonable utilization levels, you should take into consideration the number of stations on a LAN segment, application behavior, frame-length distribution, traffic patterns, time of day, and so on.

- ❑ For every short-term period, network utilization may be peaking toward 100 percent—**without** noticeable network delays or performance degradation. This is possible during a large FTP file transfer between two high-performance end-stations. One thing to keep in mind is that each application environment behaves differently, depending on variables such as bandwidth, routing protocols, and so on.

❑ As a troubleshooter, you must have a process or procedure defined to help you resolve a particular network problem.

❑ The steps of the problem-solving process are:

  ❑ Define and state the problem.

  ❑ Gather facts and analyze the problem.

  ❑ Review and evaluate alternatives and possibilities.

  ❑ Design a plan of action (POA).

  ❑ Implement the solution.

  ❑ Evaluate and observe the solution (further analysis).

  ❑ Repeat the process (if needed).

❑ Troubleshooting can be like finding a needle in a haystack, so be patient—solutions do not always come on the first go-around.

❑ Before you can effectively troubleshoot, you must be able to determine if a problem does exist.

❑ As a network administrator, you should take the pulse of your network through a regularly scheduled sampling of network traffic.

❑ You can use a LAN tester or a protocol analyzer to collect network data and store it in the test equipment.

❑ Some common devices that can store data for future analysis are Fluke's LANMeter series, Microtest's Compas, and Scope's FrameScope.

❑ An effective troubleshooter should have a hardcopy of network topology, and know and understand host and IP addresses of network devices, routing protocols, circuit identification number (WAN links), slot and port numbers, MAC addresses, and so on.

❑ After monitoring network traffic, you can use a ping test to actively test your network. These tests will provide you with detailed statistical information (depending on command options used) about network traffic and particular devices.

❑ The more detailed your documentation, the easier it is for you to troubleshoot.

❑ Documenting your network is an ongoing process.

❑ Baselining your network is critical in determining the health of your network, in addition to identifying the problem areas. Baselining also provides network analysis for problem isolation and resolution.

❑ CiscoWorks (discussed in Chapter 8) is an effective management tool for proactive monitoring, providing the functionality for effective baselining.

❑ You'll need to be familiar with several protocols in order to deliver effective troubleshooting and problem analysis.

❑ TCP is a connection-oriented, reliable protocol. It provides a control mechanism to ensure that data is sent and received successfully.

❑ UDP is connectionless, responsible only for transmitting the message. UDP provides no software checking for segment delivery, and thus is deemed unreliable.

❑ Ethernet is the oldest of the LAN technologies commonly used throughout the business industry today.

❑ Ethernet uses an access method called Carrier Sense Multiple Access/Collision Detection (CSMA/CD) to detect the interference caused by simultaneous transmission by two or more stations.

❑ Token Ring helps reconcile the contention-based access to the transmission medium by granting every station equal access. Token Ring uses a token-passing process to prevent collision between two stations that want to send data at the same time.

❑ Fiber Distributed Data Interface, commonly known as FDDI, is a standard for data transmission on fiber-optic lines within a LAN.

❑ The TCP/IP model is not only designed for protocols to communicate across the network, but can also be used as a platform to develop protocols.

❑ Novell IPX utilizes a connectionless datagram protocol. IPX is NetWare's network layer service, and provides addressing as well as routing capabilities.

❑ AppleTalk is considered one of the purest client/server networking systems that rely on nodes (usually Macintosh workstations) sharing network resources (servers, printers, files, and so forth).

SELF TEST

The following Self Test questions will help you measure your understanding of the material presented in this chapter. Read all the choices carefully, as there may be more than one correct answer. Choose all correct answers for each question.

1. Which of the following agencies did early research in computer interconnectivity?

    A. Department of Defense

    B. Department of Technology

    C. Defense Advanced Research Projects Agency (DARPA)

    D. None of the above

2. The Department of Defense presented what reference model for communication protocols?

    A. Ethernet

    B. Token Ring

    C. TCP

    D. TCP/IP

3. Which of the following are connection-oriented protocols?

    A. Token Ring

    B. Ethernet

    C. FDDI

    D. A and C

    E. A and B

4. Which of the following are connectionless protocols?

    A. Ethernet

    B. IP

    C. ATM

    D. Frame Relay

    E. All of the above

5. Which of the following is the oldest LAN technology?

    A. ATM

    B. NetBIOS

    C. Ethernet

    D. Token Ring

6. What layer or layers of the OSI reference model is/are equivalent to the Network Interface layer?

    A. Data Link

    B. Transport

    C. Physical

    D. A and C

7. The Application layer is responsible for which of the following tasks?

    A. Managing sessions

    B. Providing functionality to users

    C. Providing functionality to programs

    D. All of the above

8. TCP and UDP are both what kind of protocol?

   A. Connection-oriented

   B. Connectionless

   C. Transport

   D. None of the above

9. What kind of protocol is UDP?

   A. Unreliable

   B. Reliable

   C. Fast

   D. IPX

10. An AppleTalk implementation consists of
    _____.

    A. Zones

    B. User segments

    C. Network segments

    D. All of the above

11. Which of the following characterizes congestion on a network?

    A. A statistical phenomenon

    B. A normal state

    C. Overloaded capacity

    D. A and C

12. Which of the following applications sends packet information to the destination and then notifies the sender when a reply is received, indicating size of packets, packet loss, and time taken for a response?

    A. Ping

    B. Telnet

    C. FTP

    D. TFTP

    E. None of the above

13. What is the 80/20 rule?

    A. Eighty percent of traffic should be local, and 20 percent requires internetworking.

    B. Eighty percent of traffic requires internetworking, and 20 percent should be local.

    C. All traffic (100 percent) requires internetworking.

    D. None of the above.

14. What does the term *troubleshooting* mean?

    A. Eliminating irrelevant information

    B. Devising a corrective action plan to fix a problem

    C. Isolating a problematic area

    D. B and C

    E. All of the above except D

15. There are over 16,000,000 local addresses in which of the following address classes?

    A. Class A

    B. Class B

    C. Class C

    D. Class Z

16. Which of the following is a valid Class B address?

    A. 129.232.264

    B. 12.3.34.55

    C. 128.233.23.260

    D. 130.25.19.102

17. Which of the following layers is *not* included in the TCP/IP internetworking model?

    A. Transport layer

    B. Application layer

    C. Data Link layer

    D. Internet layer

18. IP addressing consists of what kind of address scheme?

    A. 8-byte address scheme

    B. 4-byte address scheme

    C. 32-bit address scheme

    D. B and C

    E. A and C

19. Which layer of the TCP/IP internetworking model is responsible for transmitting data across the physical network?

    A. Data Link

    B. Transport

    C. Internet

    D. Network Interface

20. Which of these protocols transmits each data unit as an independent entity without establishing a logical connection between end-stations?

    A. IP

    B. IPX

    C. SPX

    D. A and B

21. Which of the following is a valid IPX network address?

    A. 141.10.10.4

    B. 129.4.4.8

    C. 4f.000.0c56.be45

    D. A and C

22. What is the native routing protocol for AppleTalk?

    A. RIP

    B. IPX

    C. SNA

    D. RTMP

2

LAN
Troubleshooting
Problem Areas

I t's not much fun first thing on a Monday morning getting swamped with calls from employees, clients, and customers complaining about extremely slow network response times. As a network administrator it is your responsibility to isolate the problem and determine the root cause. Often there are no apparent symptoms other than the bottleneck caused by everyone arriving at work and jumping on board to log in to various systems, retrieving e-mail, and surf the Web.

The emergence of corporate intranets presents significant challenges for LAN administrators and network managers. Traditionally, traffic patterns have been governed by the 80/20 rule (80 percent of traffic is destined for a local resource, while 20 percent of traffic requires internetworking). Recently this model has changed to the complete opposite: a 20/80 rule. In today's environment, technology has elevated the level of business in organizations. Network administrators and managers must keep up with new applications and changing traffic patterns, without overextending allocated network budgets.

This chapter discusses some LAN problems that network administrators face in their everyday battle maintaining and troubleshooting. In the first section we'll examine the responsibilities of the first two layers of the OSI model. We will also study various LAN technologies, highlighting the characteristics and problems associated with each. Subsequent sections cover ATM LAN Emulation (LANE), discussing its role in a network infrastructure; and methods for encapsulating protocol data units (PDUs) transmitted to receiving station(s).

CERTIFICATION OBJECTIVE 2.01

Physical Layer Responsibilities

The *Physical layer* is at the bottom of the Open System Interconnection (OSI) reference model (Figure 2-1). This conceptual model illustrates the flow of data from one computer software application to another over some type of network medium. There are seven layers, each having a specific function of data communications between two functional computer systems.

FIGURE 2-1

Seven-layer OSI model

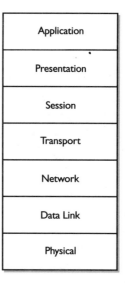

| Application |
| Presentation |
| Session |
| Transport |
| Network |
| Data Link |
| Physical |

The Physical layer provides the necessary mechanical, electrical, functional, and procedural characteristics to initiate, establish, maintain, and deactivate connections for data. This layer is responsible for carrying information from the source system to its destination. One of the main functions of the Physical layer is to carry the signaling to the Data Link layer of the remote system. Repeaters and hubs are Physical layer devices. These devices are not intelligent; in other words, they can only provide electrical signaling on a wire.

CERTIFICATION OBJECTIVE 2.02

Data Link Layer Responsibilities

The second layer up in the OSI model is the Data Link layer, which is responsible for transmitting data across a physical link with a reasonable level of reliability. For instance, if there are multiple stations utilizing one common path for transmission, there must be some type of control mechanism in place for all stations to share that common path. The Data Link layer may provide this control functionality as well as others, such as synchronization, error control, and flow control, to ensure successful data transmission and reception between remote systems.

At the Data Link layer are the specifications for topology and communication between two end-stations. The Data Link layer connects the physical network functionality (cables, signaling, and digital pulses) with the abstract world of software and data streams. At this layer you will see devices such as bridges and switches, both using frame information to control the flow of traffic across the network. In addition, the Data Link layer creates packet headers and checksum trailers, encapsulates datagrams into frames, and does error detection. Hardware addresses are also mapped with IP addresses (commonly known as Address Resolution Protocol (ARP)) at this layer.

After data is received from the Network layer, the Data Link layer puts data into a frame format. All information received from the upper layers of the OSI model must be put into the data field of the frame (between 46 and 1500 bytes). A frame is added with source and destination MAC addresses, along with data field information, and a CRC trailer is created. At this point, the Data Link layer puts the frame on the network for transmission.

As data is being received on a system, the Data Link layer reads the incoming frame. If the MAC address in the destination field is its own, the Data Link layer must process the incoming information. A CRC check is then performed on the frame, comparing the results to information in the frame trailer. If the information matches, the header and trailer are removed in order to forward the data information to its peer layer (the Network layer). On the other hand, if the information is different, a request is sent to the sending station requesting a retransmission.

The Institute of Electrical and Electronics Engineers (IEEE) has subdivided the Data Link layer into two sublayers: Media Access Control (MAC) and Logical Link Control (LLC), as shown in Figure 2-2.

FIGURE 2-2

Data Link sublayers:
LLC and MAC

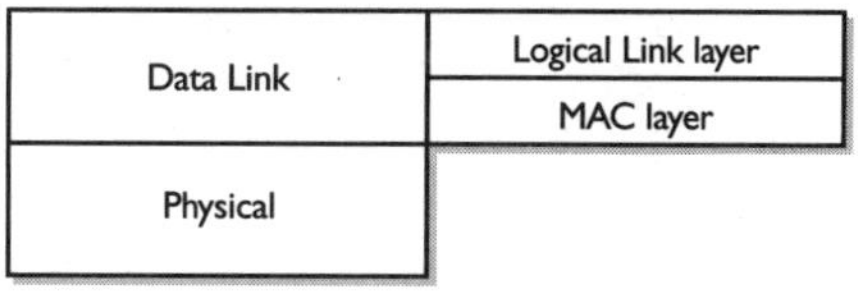

Data Link	Logical Link layer
	MAC layer
Physical	

MAC Layer

The Media Access Control (MAC) sublayer is the interface between user data and the physical placement and retrieval of data on a network. Generally, the MAC has four major functions:

MAC Layer Functions	Tasks
Transmitting data operations	■ Responsible for accepting data from the LLC sublayer and creating a frame by appending a preamble and start-of-frame delimiter; inserts source and destination addresses. ■ Performs calculation on CRC and places information in the FCS field.
Management of transmitting medium's access	■ If the medium is busy, the MAC layer suspends transmission. ■ Presents a serial bit stream to the Physical layer for transmission. ■ Stops all transmission when a collision is detected. ■ Propagates jam signal to stations for collision notification. ■ Manages retransmission when channel becomes idle.
Management of receiving medium's access	■ Verifies byte and length of frame. ■ Receives serial bit stream from the Physical layer. ■ Discards frames that are not an even 8 bits and are less than minimum frame length.

MAC Layer Functions	Tasks
Receiving data operations	■ Performs CRC check. ■ Discards frames not addressed to receiving stations. ■ Passes data to LLC. ■ Removes the preamble, start-of-frame delimiter, source and destination addresses, and FCS. ■ Monitors broadcasts.

Logical Link Layer

IEEE standard 802.2 defines the Logical Link Control field (LLC). It is a Data Link control layer that is used by 802.3 and 802.5 and other networks. LLC was originally designed by IBM as a sublayer in the Token Ring architecture. In essence, this sublayer generates and interprets commands to control the flow of data, including recovery operations for error detection.

The Logical Link layer also provides the connectionless and connection-oriented data transfers. Connectionless data transfers are frequently designated as LLC Type 1, or LLC1. This transfer service does not require data links or link stations to be established. Once a Service Access Point (SAP) has been enabled, the SAP can transmit and receive data from a remote SAP using connectionless service, as well. The connection-oriented portion of data transfers are designated as LLC Type 2, or LLC2. This transfer service requires the establishment of link stations. Once a connection has been established, a mode setting command is required, thus requiring each link station to manage its own link state information.

The LLC protocol is a subset of a High Level Data Link Control (HDLC) protocol, a specification presented by the ISO standards body (International Standard Organization). The protocol enables link stations to operate as peers, in that all stations have equal status on the LAN.

LAN administrators supporting NetBIOS and SNA traffic across LAN segments should be familiar with LLC. Most often you will see LLC2 used when SNA traffic is traversing your network. There is also a possibility that you can see it directly encapsulated into Frame Relay. In these instances the router simply forwards LLC2 frames and often implements LLC link stations. NetBIOS uses LLC to locate resources, and then LLC2 connection-oriented sessions are established.

LLC Type I Operation

With the exception of SNA and the multitude of vendors supporting NetBIOS over NetBEUI, Type 1 is the most prevalent class of LLC. LLC1 is generally used by Novell, TCP/IP, OSI, Banyan, Microsoft NT, IBM, Digital, and most other network protocols. No specific subset exists for the operation of LLC1. The information transfer mode is the only form of operation for LLC1.

The application most commonly used with LLC1 is called Subnetwork Access Protocol (SNAP). Typically, LLC1 operation is through this special subsection of the IEEE 802.2 specification. LAN vendors often implement this protocol. The SNAP application was presented to simplify network protocols' adjustment to the new frame formats introduced by the IEEE 802.2 committee. SNAP is implemented with Novell, Apple, Banyan, TCP/IP, OSI and many other fully stackable protocols that are OSI driven.

The IEEE has defined two fields known as DSAP (Destination Service Address Protocol) and SSAP (Source Service Access Protocol). For the most part, the SAP fields are reserved for protocols which have implemented the IEEE 802.*x* protocols. One of the reserved SAP fields is designated for non-IEEE protocols. To enable SNAP, the SAP values in both the DSAP and SSAP are set to AA (hexadecimal). The control field is set to 03 (hexadecimal). This will help distinguish the various protocols running.

In LLC Type 1 operation, the DSAP and SSAP are both set to AA, and the control field is set to 03 to indicate unnumbered information packets. The SNAP header in an Ethernet packet has four components:

- The Data Link encapsulation headers (destination and source address, and the CRC trailer)
- The 3-byte 802.2 headers (set to AA, AA, and 03)
- The 5-byte protocol discriminator immediately following the 802.2 header
- The data field of the packet

The SNAP allows for Ethernet vendors to quickly switch their drivers and network protocols over the IEEE 802.*x* packet format without rewriting the program code. In addition, vendors who have drivers written for Ethernet systems can port the network operating code quickly over the Token Ring/Data Link frame format. You will find many vendors using the SNAP method to implement their existing code to execute on Token Ring. SNAP is efficient, with a high degree of simplicity, allowing multivendor operation between different vendors.

In networking today, vendors are translating their codes over to the LLC frame format. For example, Novell NetWare previously used a proprietary Ethernet frame. Novell has registered their NetWare operating system with the IEEE and can now use the SAP address of EO in their LLC frames. IEEE 802.*x* frames are now the standard default for NetWare 3.12 and 4.*x* implementations.

The decision to choose a connection-oriented network instead of a connectionless network centers on the functionality desired and needed. Using a connection-oriented system can incur substantial overhead; however it does provide data integrity. On the other hand, connectionless operation consumes less overhead but is susceptible to errors. Thus, it may be practical to provide connection-oriented services for a LAN. The application as well as the upper-layer software usually provide for error control for LANs (at the Transport layer). Today, with LAN network protocols handling connection-oriented services, connectionless methods are more prevalent.

LLC Type 2 Operation

Of the two Link Layer Control services, LLC2 is the more complicated. This service provides the functionality needed for reliable data transfer (quite similar to Layer 4 function). LLC2 also allows for error recovery and flow and congestion controls. The protocol supports specific acknowledgments connection establishment, as well as providing for flow control, making sure that the data arrives in the order it was sent. LLC2 service incurs more overhead than LLC1.

The connection-oriented services are used in LAN services today. The protocols that do not invoke a Transport or Network layer (NetBIOS and

NetBEUI) are the most common. Microsoft NT, Sun Solarnet, IBM Warp Server, and others use this type of connection. Most LAN protocols do not use this mode of LLC. Most LAN protocols have Network, Transport, and Session layers built into the protocol, and use a connectionless mode of LLC.

Ethernet / IEEE 802.3

Ethernet is the oldest LAN technology commonly used throughout the business industry today, and is still deployed in most traditional LAN infrastructures. This technology conforms to the lower layers (Physical and Data Link) of the OSI model. Ethernet remains an effective LAN technology if implemented and deployed strategically.

The nodes on an Ethernet network implement a simple rule: Listen before speaking. In an Ethernet environment, only one node on the segment is allowed to transmit at any given time, due to the CSMA/CD protocol (Carrier Sense Multiple Access/Collision Detection). Although this manages packet collisions, it increases transmission time in two ways: If two nodes transmit at the same time, the information will eventually collide, which will require each node to stop and retransmit at a later time (see Figure 2-3).

CSMA/CD Protocol

CSMA/CD is an access technique used in Ethernet that is categorized as a listen-then-send access method. When a station has data to send, it must first listen to determine whether other stations on the network are talking (communicating). Ethernet primarily uses one channel for transmitting data and does not employ a carrier. As a result, Ethernet encodes data using a Manchester code. In Manchester coding, a timing transition occurs in the middle of each bit, and the line codes maintain an equal amount of positive

FIGURE 2-3

Sending Stations A and D collide

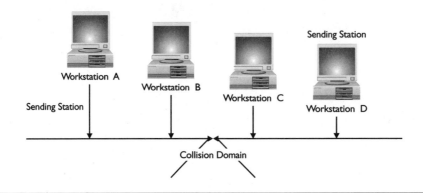

and negative voltage. Many LANs that don't use a clocking mechanism use either Manchester or Differential Manchester encoding. The timing transition has good-timing signaling for clock recovery from data received. In an Ethernet network, Manchester coding provides the functionality of a carrier signal, since Ethernet does not transmit data by a carrier.

If a channel is busy on an Ethernet network, other stations cannot transmit; they must wait until that channel is idle (meaning that there is no data being transmitted on the network) to contend for transmission. In the Ethernet implementation there is a likelihood that two stations can simultaneously transmit (once the channel is idle). Often this produces what is known as a *collision*. When a collision is detected, a signal is propagated to other stations sharing that common wire. A random timer is set on each station to prevent other collisions from occurring.

Network administrators should not be alarmed by increased collision rates. Collisions don't necessarily result in poor Ethernet performance. In many instances, an increasing collision rate indicates that there is more offered load. Ethernet actually uses collisions to distribute shared bandwidth among stations on the network wanting to utilize the channel for transmission. Ethernet uses the collision information to redistribute the instantaneous offered load over the available time, thereby utilizing the channel effectively.

Let's assume that Station A (Figure 2-3) has the channel occupied, and Stations C and D are contending stations waiting for an idle channel in order to transmit. In this case, Station C is closer to Station A than Station D, and C seizes the channel before Station D because the signal reaches C first. Station C is now ready to transmit, although Station D sees the channel as idle. Station C begins its transmission, and then Station D transmits, resulting in a collision. Here the collision is a direct function of the propagation delay of a signal, and the distance between the contending stations.

Many network administrators believe that CSMA/CD is better utilized in an environment where the cable length is much shorter. This access technique is probably best suited for networks on which intermittent transmissions are prevalent. When there is increased traffic volume on an Ethernet segment, the chances for collision increases because that particular segment is being utilized more frequently.

Collision Detection

Under the Manchester coding, a binary 1 is represented by a high-to-low voltage transition. A binary 0 is represented by a low-to-high voltage transition. This representation helps determine if a carrier sense is present on the network. If the network detects a carrier signal, the station proceeds with monitoring the channel. When existing transmission is done, the monitoring station transmits its data while examining the channel for collisions. In an Ethernet network, transceivers and interface cards can detect collisions by examining and monitoring the voltage level of the signal line that Manchester produces.

If a collision is detected during transmission, the station in the process of transmitting will suspend its transmission to initiate a *jam pattern*. The jam pattern consists of 32–42 bits and is initiated long enough to ensure that other stations on the segment have detected the collision. Once a collision is detected, the transmitting station sets random timers, usually referred to as *slot times*. In essence, the slot represents 512 bits or a minimum frame size of 64 bytes. An integer n is used to calculate the wait time for a station. Once time n expires, the station can then finish transmitting (retransmission). If during the retransmission a collision is detected, the integer n is doubled and the station must then wait the duration before retransmitting.

Ethernet's design causes *packet starvation*—packets experience latencies up to 100 times the average, or completely starve out due to 16 collisions. Packet starvation, commonly known as the *packet starvation effect* (PSE), occurs as a result of the CSMA/CD implementation (the unfairness), as described previously in the CSMA/CD algorithm. The PSE makes CSMA/CD LANs unsuitable for real-time traffic except at offered loads much less than 100 percent. Many network administrators believe that Ethernet LANs behave poorly at offered loads much higher than 50 percent. Errors in Ethernet implementation and the inherent unfairness of CSMA/CD has attributed to this belief.

The theory behind PSE is quite simple. In a CSMA/CD implementation, PSE will occur when two stations compete for access under the CSMA/CD algorithm. The probability of one station winning over another for access to the channel is about the same as the ratio of their maximum backoff values. When the network is idle, two stations prepare for transmission. At approximately the same time, the two station attempt to transmit and cause a collision.

When this occurs, they both back off a random amount based on the number of collisions (N) that the packet has been a part of. If N is less than or equal to 10, the backoff is between 0 and 2N1. It is between 0 and 1023 otherwise. The probability that an older packet selects a smaller backoff value than a newer packet with fewer collisions, is less than the ratio of the newer packet's maximum backoff (2N–1 or 1023) divided by the older packet's maximum backoff. Because this value increases exponentially, unless a packet comes ready when no other host is ready to send, it will usually either get access to the bus very quickly or it will experience 16 collisions and starve out. Under high loads, there is usually another packet waiting to send, and so long delays and packet starvation occur to a significant percentage of packets.

Late Collisions

A *late collision* is a collision that is detected only after a station places a complete frame of the network. A late collision is normally caused by an excessive network segment cable length that causes the time for a signal to propagate from one end of a segment to another part of the segment, to be longer than the time required to place a full frame of the network. This small windowing in late collisions may result in two stations attempting to transmit simultaneously without knowledge of each other's transmissions, causing transmissions to collide. This is somewhat similar to two trains traveling on the same rail (due to schedule conflicts) without anyone aware of the error. At some point, the two trains will collide.

A late collision is detected by a transmitter usually after the first slot time of 64 bytes, and where frames are in excess of 65 bytes. One thing to remember is that both normal and late collisions occur in exactly the same manner; the late one just happens later than normal. Defective and faulty equipment such as repeaters, connectors, Ethernet transceivers, and controllers can also be the cause of late collisions.

To help alleviate some of the throughput on an Ethernet segment, many network administrators deploy routers as a means for maximizing throughput. For example, a two-port bridge splits a logical network into two physical segments and only lets a transmission cross if its destination lies on the other side. The bridge forwards packets only when necessary, reducing network congestion by isolating traffic to one of the segments. In contrast, routers link multiple logical networks together. These networks are physically distinct and must be viewed as separate *collision domains* (Figure 2-4). The router performs not only the physical segmentation (each port has a unique network number), but also provides logical segmentation. In Figure 2-5 a router is used to logically segment the network into three distinct segments, thus maximizing the throughput on each network segment.

Ethernet Statistics for Troubleshooting

The following are key statistics and events that are extremely helpful and necessary for proper baselining and troubleshooting of an Ethernet segment.

Frame Sizes for Ethernet Frames

There is a limit to the size of frames an Ethernet segment can transmit.

- **Minimum** ⇒ 64 bytes
- **Maximum** ⇒ 1518 bytes

Frames that are smaller than 64 bytes are called either *runts* or *fragments,* depending on the validity of the frame check sequence. Frames over the maximum frame size are considered *giants* (oversized).

Collision domain on
Ethernet segment

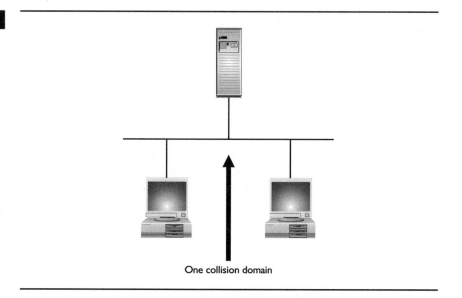

One collision domain

Router segmentation

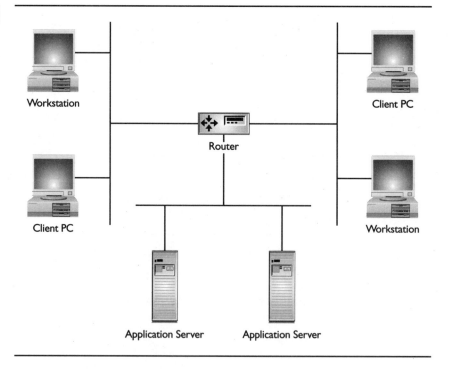

Frame Check Sequence (FCS)

The *frame check sequence* (FCS) provides a mechanism for error detection. Each transmitter computes a CRC with the address fields, the type/length field, and the data field. The CRC is then placed in a 4-byte FCS field.

Keep in mind that faulty network interface cards (NICs) may also result in FCS errors.

Jabbers

Jabbers are long, continuous frames exceeding 1518 bytes that provide a self-interrupt functionality which prevents all stations on the network from transmitting data. Unlike the CSMA/CD access technique used in Ethernet, where stations must listen before sending data, jabbering completely violates CSMA/CD implementation by prohibiting stations from transmitting data. Be aware of the fact that jabbering may be the result of defective NICs, which may need to be replaced immediately. A jabbering condition can result in poor network performance, ultimately causing workstation and file-server disconnects.

Cyclic Redundancy Check (CRC Errors)

In the rule of operation, a CRC check on data fields is initialized before any Ethernet transmissions. The results are appended to the data frame in the FCS field which are 4 bytes in length. A CRC check is also conducted when the destination receives the frame. The CRC check on the data field is then compared to the FCS field. If the results do not match, the frame is discarded and the CRC error count is incremented.

Runts

Runts are short frames that are less than 64 bytes long. They are usually the result of collisions. If a runt frame is well formed, however (that is, it has a valid FCS), then it is usually the result of a faulty NIC or its driver.

SHOW INTERFACE Command Output

When troubleshooting Ethernet problems, you can use the SHOW INTERFACE ETHERNET command to look at errors, collision rates, and so on. Figure 2-6 illustrates the output from this command in Cisco routers. This command can be found in Cisco's IOS Software Command Summary reference manual for Release 11.2 and higher.

Output from Cisco's
SHOW INTERFACE
ETHERNET command

```
Telnet - 151.204.19.194                                              _ □ X
Connect  Edit  Terminal  Help
slspmdssrtra#sho int e1/1/3
Ethernet1/1/3 is up, line protocol is up
  Hardware is cxBus Ethernet, address is 00e0.f72f.e02b (bia 00e0.f72f.e02b)
  Description: test lan
  Internet address is 172.25.199.100/24
  MTU 1500 bytes, BW 10000 Kbit, DLY 1000 usec, rely 255/255, load 1/255
  Encapsulation ARPA, loopback not set, keepalive set (10 sec)
  ARP type: ARPA, ARP Timeout 04:00:00
  Last input 00:00:11, output 00:00:04, output hang never
  Last clearing of "show interface" counters never
  Queueing strategy: fifo
  Output queue 0/40, 0 drops; input queue 0/75, 0 drops
  5 minute input rate 2000 bits/sec, 1 packets/sec
  5 minute output rate 0 bits/sec, 1 packets/sec
     1107486292 packets input, 239642738 bytes, 0 no buffer
     Received 2683329 broadcasts, 0 runts, 0 giants, 0 throttles
     0 input errors, 0 CRC, 0 frame, 0 overrun, 0 ignored, 0 abort
     0 input packets with dribble condition detected
     42954429 packets output, 3700495525 bytes, 0 underruns
     11 output errors, 0 collisions, 2 interface resets
     0 babbles, 0 late collision, 535519 deferred
     11 lost carrier, 0 no carrier
     0 output buffer failures, 0 output buffers swapped out
slspmdssrtra#
slspmdssrtra#
◄│                   [            [            [           [          ►│
```

exam
ⓦatch

*Remember to track and monitor excessive collision rates. Keep in
mind the utilization rate, before collisions present serious problems on
the network.*

CERTIFICATION OBJECTIVE 2.04

Token Ring / IEEE 802.5

Token Ring is a LAN technology that helps reconcile the problems of
contention-based access to a media by granting every station equal access.
To accomplish this, the network passes a 3-byte frame commonly known as
a *token* from station to station. When a station wants to transmit, it waits
upon the arrival of the token. Essentially, to transmit you need to possess
the token (see Figure 2-7). When the token arrives, the station creates a data

Token Ring passing

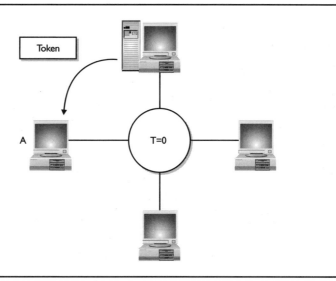

frame and transmits it onto the wire. The stations then relay the frame around the ring until it reaches its respective destination.

One of the major differences between Ethernet and Token Ring is that the Token Ring NICs are intelligent. In other words, Token Ring NICs are able to manage their physical ring, in addition to transmitting and receiving data. NICs are intelligent in the sense that they provide a fault-tolerant solution for Token Ring connected servers. The redundant NIC-enabled drivers switch traffic to a backup NIC if a failure is detected on the active NIC. This keeps your servers connected to the network and reduces downtime.

Understanding MAC Communications

The key to troubleshooting and isolating the inherent problems of Token Ring networks is your ability to understand MAC communications. For that reason, it's important for network administrators and LAN technicians to analyze, observe, and capture the MAC communications by way of a protocol analyzer.

Connecting token stations to a shared medium involves wiring stations to a central hub, commonly known as a *media access unit* (MAU). The MAU may be used to interconnect other MAUs to expand the connectivity. A MAU may also be called a *multistation access unit* (MSAU). Typically, a MSAU connects up to eight Token Ring stations. When interconnecting MSAUs, be sure that they are oriented in the ring. Otherwise, the Token Ring will have a break and it will not operate properly.

In order for new stations to enter the network, a ring-insertion routine must first be conducted. Initially, the station first conducts a media check to check the existing lobe connections (if any exist). After checking the lobe connections, the station then attaches the ring and searches the ring for an active monitor. If no active monitor is on the ring (18-second lapse time) the station then initiates a claim-token process. Then the station transmits a duplicate address test (DAT) frame, which is checked by each active station to see that the new station address is unique. A flag in the frame is set to indicate an error if the station's address duplicates an existing station already on the ring. If no errors are detected, the new station continues with the initialization process.

Token Ring frames always travel in one direction, in a downstream motion. Stations relay frames in a logical ring fashion by repeating the frame, bit for bit. This puts a tremendous amount of dependency on the stations waiting to receive signals from their nearest active upstream neighbor (NAUN). These signals are then repeated to downstream neighbors. A station must always know the MAC address of its NAUN in case it receives incorrect data. A neighbor notification, which occurs every seven seconds, allows stations to discover their MAC address.

Upon receiving data frames, an Address Recognized and Frame Copied bit, usually located in the frame status field, is set at the end of the frame. The frame then traverses the ring until the originator receives it. The originator checks the A and C bits to verify the frame was received. The frame is then stripped, and the token is released by the sender in order for the process to reinitialize. If a station receiving the token has no information to send, the token is forwarded to the next station. One bit of the frame, the T bit, is altered if the station possessing the token has information to receive. Unlike Ethernet, in Token Ring the frames proceed sequentially around the Ring. And because a station must claim the token before transmitting, collisions do not occur in a Token Ring infrastructure.

For efficiency in this LAN architecture, a priority mechanism is used. This priority mechanism permits certain user-designated, high-priority stations to use the network more frequently. There are two fields with Token Ring access fields that control the priority mechanism: the *priority field* and the *reservation field*. Those stations with a priority equal to or higher than the priority of a token can seize that token. Once the token is seized and changed to an information frame, the stations with priority higher than the transmitting station can possess the token for the next pass around the network. The new generated token will include the highest priority of the station seizing the token.

In our discussion we have used the term *frames* in many instances to describe the data portion traversing the network ring. To fully understand exactly how this ring topology operates, you need to understand the frame format. In this format you will have access to the setting information, which determines the ring operation. Following are the fields in the frame format:

- **Starting Delimiter (SD)**   Indicates start of frame
- **Access Control (AC)**   Priority settings
- **Frame Control (FC)**   Indicates frame type
- **Destination Address (DA)**   Specifies the address of destined station
- **Source Address (SA)**   Specifies the address of originating frame
- **Optional Routing Information**   Contains user data (LLC) or control information (MAC frame information)
- **Frame Check Sequence (FCS)**   CRC-32 error check on FC, DA, SA, and information fields
- **Ending Delimiter (ED)**   Indicates end of data or token frame
- **Frame Status (FS)**   Contains A and C bits indicating frame status

To effectively manage the ring, Token Ring stations will frequently assume specific management functionality on the local ring. The *active monitor* is one of the leading management functions for the ring. One station on every ring is assigned to the active monitor role. The active monitor's sole purpose is to ensure integrity. The active monitor has seven main responsibilities:

- Initiate the neighbor notification process
- Monitor the neighbor notification process
- Ensure data frames do not continually traverse the rings
- Detect lost tokens and data frames
- Purge the ring
- Maintain the master clock
- Ensure ring delay

Once a station has been designated as the active monitor, it will continue to perform the tasks until it leaves the ring or experiences extremely high amounts of physical errors. If for some reason the active monitor is unable to assume its responsibility, the remaining stations (otherwise known as the standby stations) will take over the role. The remaining stations will contend for the designated active monitor role, called *token claiming*.

Ring error monitoring is another important and effective management tool. The purpose of the ring-error monitor is to receive soft errors or beacons—MAC frames—that are transmitted from any Token Ring station. A MAC address table is maintained for those stations transmitting errors, as well as active counts and error types. LAN administrators can use protocol analyzers to respond to the ring-error monitor functional address. This will capture beacon and soft-error MAC frames, as well as insert them into a beaconing ring.

A *ring purge* is a normal method of resetting communications on a Token Ring network. This mechanism provides a means for issuing a new token. Ring purges are normal events and are typically encountered during ring insertion and ring de-insertion; however, as with Ethernet collisions, high amounts of ring purges will cause network performance degradation.

When the active monitor enters the ring-purge process, the purge timer starts and the active monitor transmits a ring purge MAC frame. The transmission occurs without waiting for a free token and without releasing a free token upon completion. Continuous idles (0) are sent by the adapters. After the frame has traversed the ring, the active monitor receives the transmission and checks for transmission errors. Such errors could be code violation errors or check sequences (CRC) errors.

Any error detection triggers transmission of ring-purge MAC frames until a frame is received with no transmission errors or until the expiration of the ring-purge timer. This timer's function is to limit the number of retransmission of ring-purge MAC frames during this process. Once the ring-purge MAC frame has traversed the ring error-free, the active monitor sets a one-second timer. After an error-free frame is received, the adapter transmits a free token of a priority equal to the reservation priority in the last ring-purge MAC frame that was stripped by the adapter.

Troubleshooting Token Ring Networks

When troubleshooting Token Ring problems, you can use the SHOW INTERFACE TOKEN RING command to look at errors, collision rates, and so on. Figure 2-8 illustrates the output from the SHOW INTERFACE TOKEN RING command in Cisco routers. This command can be found in Cisco's IOS Software Command Summary reference manual for Release 11.2 and higher.

Being able to understand the ring processes is critical for effectively troubleshooting Token Ring networks. Many LAN administrators overlook such key processes. A good rule of thumb when troubleshooting is to try not to oversimplify the problem-resolution process. The obvious is not always the best indicator; a thorough approach is more realistic for isolating LAN performance problems.

Following are the most common ring processes:

- **Ring Inserting**   A five-phase process that every station must go through to insert into the ring.

- **Token Claiming**   The process by which standby monitors contend and elect a new active monitor.

- **Neighbor Notification**   The process by which a station notifies a downstream neighbor of its MAC address.

FIGURE 2-8

Output from SHOW
INTERFACE TOKEN
RING command

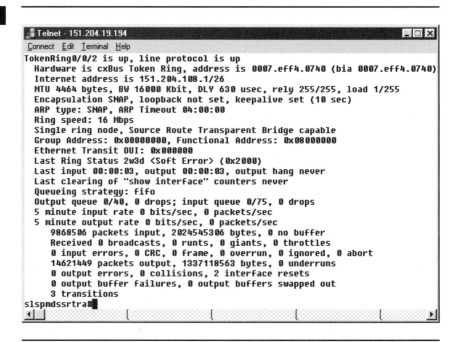

```
Telnet - 151.204.19.194
Connect  Edit  Terminal  Help
TokenRing0/0/2 is up, line protocol is up
  Hardware is cxBus Token Ring, address is 0007.eff4.0740 (bia 0007.eff4.0740)
  Internet address is 151.204.108.1/26
  MTU 4464 bytes, BW 16000 Kbit, DLY 630 usec, rely 255/255, load 1/255
  Encapsulation SNAP, loopback not set, keepalive set (10 sec)
  ARP type: SNAP, ARP Timeout 04:00:00
  Ring speed: 16 Mbps
  Single ring node, Source Route Transparent Bridge capable
  Group Address: 0x00000000, Functional Address: 0x08000000
  Ethernet Transit OUI: 0x000000
  Last Ring Status 2w3d <Soft Error> (0x2000)
  Last input 00:00:03, output 00:00:03, output hang never
  Last clearing of "show interface" counters never
  Queueing strategy: fifo
  Output queue 0/40, 0 drops; input queue 0/75, 0 drops
  5 minute input rate 0 bits/sec, 0 packets/sec
  5 minute output rate 0 bits/sec, 0 packets/sec
     9868506 packets input, 2024545306 bytes, 0 no buffer
     Received 0 broadcasts, 0 runts, 0 giants, 0 throttles
     0 input errors, 0 CRC, 0 frame, 0 overrun, 0 ignored, 0 abort
     14621449 packets output, 1337118563 bytes, 0 underruns
     0 output errors, 0 collisions, 2 interface resets
     0 output buffer failures, 0 output buffers swapped out
     3 transitions
slspmdssrtra#
```

■ **Beaconing**   The process stations utilize in an attempt to remove bad segments.

■ **Ring Purge**   Instructs all NICs to reset. This process is an attempt to recover from a break in the Token Ring. Ring purges are normal reactions to the simple soft errors that occur when stations enter or leave the ring.

■ **Protocol Timers**   There are 14 timers on every Token Ring NIC. Each timer performs its own function.

The following are key statistics and events that are extremely helpful and necessary for proper baselining and troubleshooting of Token Ring networks:

■ **Aborts**   If a station regularly reports that it is aborting transmissions, that station is usually in error. Transmissions are aborted when errors are detected—errors internal to a station, or a token in which the third byte is not an ending delimiter.

- **Beacon** If a beacon alert appears, chances are your ring is inoperable. This situation demands immediate attention. Some protocol analyzers will indicate the beaconing station. Usually the fault occurs between the beaconing station and its upstream neighbor.

- **Beacon Recovery** An event is logged in the system when the ring recovers from a beacon event.

- **Claim Token** The presence of claim frames on the ring means that the ring is going through the monitoring-contention process. You can determine what station initiated monitor contention by analyzing the events that precede the claim tokens.

- **Duplicate MAC Address** This event occurs when a Token Ring station that is trying to enter the ring has the same MAC address as an existing station on the ring.

CERTIFICATION OBJECTIVE 2.05

FDDI

FDDI became a popular LAN networking technology because of its ability to reach 100 Mbps throughput. Today other technologies have closed the gap by providing the demanded throughput. Nevertheless, FDDI still provides network stability and fault tolerance. FDDI supports both a ring and star topology. FDDI's Ring implementation is quite similar to IBM's legacy Token Ring, although FDDI implementation provides more redundancy with a second ring. The second ring is generally used when a failure has occurred on the primary ring.

FDDI transmission is comparable to Token Ring transmission in the sense that a token passes around the ring from station to station. When a station needs to transmit, it must first possess the token. The frame traverses the ring until it is received by its intended destination node. The receiving station copies the frame and continues to forward it along the ring, setting the Frame Copied Indicator (FCI) bit. The transmission is completed when the originating station receives the frame and checks the FCI to make sure it has been properly set. The frame is then removed from the ring, and the next station wishing to transmit can seize the token for transmission, repeating this process.

This communications implementation is much more effective than Ethernet, for the simple reason that larger frames (4096 bytes) are supported. Many network administrators view token passing as less cumbersome than the CSMA/CD access method of communicating. Token passing tends to perform more effectively and efficiently as higher utilization levels are reached.

Attachments to FDDI rings are typically designated as either *dual attached station* (DAS) or *single attached station* (SAS), depending on whether they are attached to both rings or only one ring. Dual attachment stations have the ability to loop back to the secondary ring, if the primary fails. In the FDDI implementation, the DASs are attached to both, whereas SASs have only a single *physical-medium dependent* (PMD) connection to the primary ring by way of a *dual-attached concentrator* (DAC). The DAC provides the necessary connection between multiple networks and the FDDI ring. One way to think of this architectural implementation is to compare it to a highway with access ramps for multiple secondary roads. In the proper implementation, the end-user nodes are rarely connected directly to a FDDI backbone, due to the high costs involved and the fact that end-user nodes seldom need maximum speed at the desktop.

Token possession governs the data flow in the FDDI implementation. However, stations attach new tokens to the ends of their transmissions, and a downstream station is allowed to add its frame to the existing frame. Consequently, at any given time, several information frames can traverse the ring. Unlike Token Ring implementation, all stations monitor the ring for invalid conditions such as lost tokens, persistent data frames, or a break in the ring. Beacon frames are cascaded throughout the FDDI network (identifying failures within the domain) if a node has determined that no tokens have been received from its NAUN during a predetermined time period.

Whenever a station receives its own beacon from an upstream station, it automatically assumes that the ring has been repaired. If beaconing exceeds its timer, DASs on both sides of the failure domain loop the primary ring with the secondary ring in order to maintain full network redundancy.

FROM THE CLASSROOM

Pointers for Effective Troubleshooting and Network Analysis

1. Baseline your network to determine normal operation. When problems occur, it's difficult to determine the state of your network under extreme conditions. LAN administrators must know how their network performs when it's healthy.

2. Approach the problem systematically. Apply problem-solving techniques to the situation and try to eliminate the obvious. It's like working a multiple-choice math problem.

3. Analyze and evaluate symptoms.

4. Isolate the problem area with thorough network analysis.

5. Develop test strategies and apply them to problem areas.

6. Record and document repairs.

And, of course, you should familiarize yourself with Cisco troubleshooting commands, in particular the show commands in Cisco's IOS software.

—*Kevin Greene, Network Engineer*

Baselining your network is critical in determining the problematic areas. Baselining also serves as a very helpful network analysis for problem isolation and resolution.

CERTIFICATION OBJECTIVE 2.06

ATM LAN Emulation (LANE)

Although this topic isn't required for the CIT exam, it is pertinent to the CCIE exam and is beneficial to the reader to have it introduced here.

Many corporations have invested substantial funds in traditional LAN infrastructures. It isn't always feasible for a corporation to reengineer or abandon its current infrastructure, however, a viable solution may be to make subtle changes either at the backbone or on local segments. Whatever the case, a strategic approach is the optimal plan of action. Network administrators must be mindful of the fact that technology is only as good as the plan that drives its design and implementation.

In the traditional and legacy environments, networks were designed with a general assumption that broadcasting to all hosts on a particular LAN was an easy task. Depending on your point of view, you may argue that this is true, given the fact that hosts reside on a shared communications medium. However, Asynchronous Transfer Mode (ATM) approaches networking from a different angle than the traditional legacy LAN. ATM is a widespread technology that carries considerable legacy LAN traffic, or traffic originated by TCP/IP software. But ATM networks are connection-oriented.

ATM was developed around 1983 by AT&T Bell Labs, but it took roughly 10 years before an official forum was created to mature this technology into a working network infrastructure. ATM has the ability to provide high data rates and quality of service within an existing LAN or WAN infrastructure. The ATM Forum's LAN Emulation (LANE) specification defines a mechanism that allows ATM networks to coexist with legacy LANs. Unlike Ethernet and token-based topologies, ATM does not vary its frame size. ATM uses a fixed packet size or cell of 48 bytes for all data communications. This fixed packet size enables a more predictable traffic rate than networks with variable-length packets. ATM can accurately manage, predict, and control bandwidth utilization by regulating the number of packets transmitted.

ATM technology will inevitably play a central role in the evolution of telecommunication and computer data communication. It is widely perceived to be the underlying technology for high-speed networks of the future, such as ISDN. Its advantage over the existing networks is obvious. ATM has high access speed from 1.5 Mbps to 1.2 Gbps. ATM can provide effective throughput for multimedia applications: video, scientific visualization, multimedia conference, distance learning, and so on.

Many network administrators are realizing that there are great difficulties in replacing the existing network totally with ATM. The technological challenge and economical burden make it almost impossible to implement

ATM without the support of established networks. The dilemma for ATM developers is how to integrate existing networks with ATM. Currently, professionals are trying to investigate the technologies of extending the existing network applications to work over ATM.

LAN Emulation (LANE) allows bridging and routing of this traffic over an ATM network. In essence, LANE is a technique used to emulate a shared communication medium similar to Layer 2 LANs, between ATM attached clients (LECs); see Figure 2-9. Today's bridging methods allow these services to support interconnection between ATM networks and the traditional LANs. This implementation supports interoperability between software applications residing on ATM-attached end-nodes and the traditional LAN end-nodes. Different types of emulation can be defined, ranging from emulating the MAC service (such as IEEE 802.*x* LANs) up to emulating the services of OSI Layers 3 and 4.

One of the main purposes of LAN Emulation service is to help provide existing applications with an interface to the ATM network via protocol stacks like APPN, IP, IPX, and AppleTalk—as if they are running over the traditional legacy broadcast networks. These upper protocols use a MAC

FIGURE 2-9

LAN Emulation
Client (LEC)

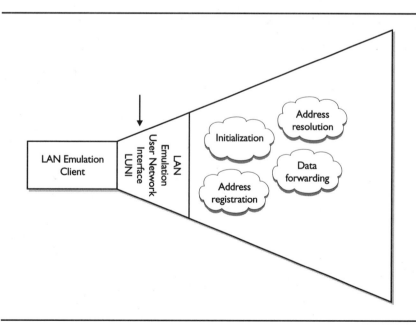

driver for communications; therefore, it is essential for LANE services to use a MAC driver in order to provide access to the ATM network.

In today's current implementation of traditional LANs, stations are able to transmit data without an existing connection. LAN Emulation provides the appearance of a connectionless service to the participating end-nodes so that the state of existing applications remains the same. Hence, LAN Emulation conceals the ATM network from the users. Thus it presents the assumption that the legacy Ethernet and Token Ring are the existing LAN technology. How does this work? Simply by making the ATM network emulate a MAC network, permitting all endpoints to transparently transmit MAC-based packets to each other.

Emulated LANs are somewhat comparable to physical LANs in the sense that both provide communication of data frames among their users. However, users are not able to communicate directly across emulated LAN boundaries, because each emulated LAN is independent of the others. Each emulated LAN comprises a set of LAN Emulation Clients (LECs) and a single LAN Emulation Service (LE Service). The LAN Emulation Services consist of the LAN Emulation Configuration Server (LECS), the LAN Emulation Server (LES), and the Broadcast and Unknown Server (BUS). Each LEC is part of an ATM end-node and represents a set of users, identified by MAC addresses.

Communication among LECs, and between LECs and the LE Service, is performed across ATM Virtual Channel Connections (VCCs). Each LEC must communicate with the LE Service across control and data VCCs. Emulated LANs can in fact operate in numerous environments, such as switched virtual circuits (SVC), Permanent Virtual Circuit (PVC), or both. SVC enables the network to allocate bandwidth on demand from the end-users' service requests. PVCs are virtual channels defined at the users' end-points and along the route that has been predefined for connection.

Following are descriptions of the LAN Emulation components:

- **LAN Emulation Client (LEC)** Provides data forwarding, address resolution, and other control functions. Provides either a MAC-level emulated Ethernet IEEE 802.3 or IEEE 802.5 service interface. A LEC can be a LAN switch, router, Windows 95 client with ATM card and drivers, UNIX host, or file servers.

- **LAN Emulation Server (LES)**   Control-coordination function for emulated LAN. Provides the registering and resolves conflicts with MAC addresses. All queries are sent to the LES to resolve MAC address conflicts. Queries are forwarded directly to clients, or the LES responds directly to queries.

- **Broadcast and Unknown Server (BUS)**   Manages the data sent between LEC and broadcast MAC address; all multicast traffic; and initial unicast frames sent by the LAN Emulation Client before the data-direct target ATM address has been resolved. One BUS is allowed for each Emulated LAN, and each LES can only have one BUS associated with it.

- **LAN Emulation Configuration Server (LECS)**   Comprises the configuration information for all Emulated LANs in the administrative domains. Designates each LEC to an emulated LAN by providing the LEC the LES ATM address.

LEC data frames are sent to the BUS, which in turn serializes the data frames and retransmits them to the attached LECs. In an SVC environment, the BUS is active in the LE Address Resolution Protocol to enable a LEC to locate the BUS. The BUS then becomes the manager of ATM connections and distribution groups. The BUS must always exist in the Emulated LAN, and all LECs must join its distribution group via multicast forward VCC.

In order for clients to map LAN destinations with the ATM address of another client or BUS, an address resolution procedure must manage and resolve any conflicts. Clients use address resolution to set up data-direct VCCs to carry frames. An LE_ARP frame request is forwarded to the LE Service over a control point-to-point VCC for all frame transmissions whose LAN destination is unknown to the client. The LES may then perform one of the following procedures:

- Use a control-distribute VCC or one or more control-direct VCCs to forward the LE_ARP frame to respective client(s). Once a response is received and acknowledged by the client, it is then forwarded over the control VCCs to the originator.

■ Issue an LE_ARP reply for the client that has registered the requested LAN destination with the LES. A LAN destination is sent to the client once a request has been acknowledged.

CERTIFICATION OBJECTIVE 2.07

Encapsulation Methods

Data encapsulation is an extremely important process in peer-to-peer communications—essentially, the process by which layer protocols exchange information among peer layers. In this communications model, there is a sending station and a receiving station that exchange what is known as protocol data units (PDUs). PDUs must either move down or move up the OSI protocol stack, depending on which stations are sending and receiving. The sending station PDUs travel down the protocol stack from the upper-layer protocols. Once the information reaches the receiving station, each lower-level protocol receives the PDUs and passes them up the stack to the protocol's peer layer.

Each layer within the protocol stack depends on its peer service function (as you know, each layer provides some functionality). In order for upper layers to provide services to lower-layer peers, data must be encapsulated as headers and trailers are added to data. In Figure 2-10 there are two stations, A (sending) and B (receiving). As Station A sends data to Station B, the encapsulation process is working behind the scenes at each layer, transparent to users (see Figure 2-11). For instance, as data approaches the Network layer from the upper-layer protocols of Station A, the Network layer encapsulates data received from the Transport layer with its network header. The network header contains source and destination addresses necessary for moving data through the network.

The Data Link layer receives and then will encapsulate the Network layer information into a frame for Data Link services, by appending a frame header and frame trailer. Generally, physical addresses can be found in frames (Ethernet and Token Ring). Finally, the Physical layer will encode the Data Link frame in 1s and 0s (100011111) for transmission on the wire to Station B. Station B will receive the frame and work it to its upper-layer

Peer-to-peer layer
communication

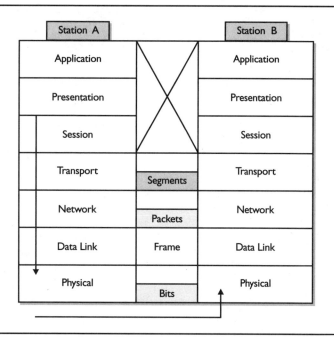

protocols. Before information can be passed along to upper-layer peers,
however, headers and trailers must be stripped off, completing the
decapsulation process.

The encapsulation process
from upper to lower layers
of the protocol stack

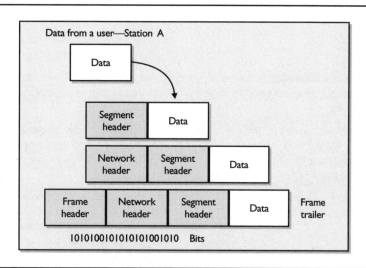

QUESTIONS AND ANSWERS

I'm getting calls from the solution center regarding slow response times.	Rule of thumb: First find out the network segment where users are located, and what resources they are contending for. Check that particular LAN segment (say, slot 2, port 2 of an Ethernet interface E2/2). Look for errors, collision rates, and so on to isolate the problem. Track the problem and convert the data into a statistical analysis for problem isolation and root cause. Check logs and utilization rates for that particular interface. This is a good starting point.
Our Token Ring isn't functioning at all. Where do I start?	Start by using the SHOW INTERFACES TOKEN command to look at a particular token interface. The output will help you determine the status of the interface. If the token interface and line protocol aren't active, try a NO SHUTDOWN command. This will attempt to re-initialize (restart) the interface. Secondly, check cabling to make sure it's physically connected and in good condition. Check configuration, as well, to make sure the interface is configured properly.
I'm getting alarms that indicate duplicate hardware addresses. Why?	This can happen if routers' MAC addresses are administered locally. A good starting point would be to test the duplicate address from a booting device using a network analyzer. If the device gets a response, there is a high probability that another station has the identical MAC address. Correct the problem by changing the MAC address of one of the devices, and re-initialize.
What are some helpful general troubleshooting tools?	Ping is the most useful general-help tool. It will tell you whether a device is reachable by sending ICMP echo request and waiting for a reply. If no reply comes back, you know there's a problem with that device. A protocol analyzer is also a good troubleshooting tool. A Traceroute is also helpful.
What is the difference between nonroutable protocols and routing protocols?	Routed protocols direct user traffic. Routing protocols work between routers to maintain routing tables and paths.
Ten new employees joined my existing workgroup. There is no available space to add additional users to our LAN. What do I do?	You'll probably have to get a hub extender to provide additional ports to accommodate new users. Depending on your current LAN infrastructure, this approach may not be feasible.
How can I connect two dissimilar LANs?	You can achieve this by way of encapsulation. *Translational encapsulation* is a method of transparently bridging LANs that have dissimilar Physical and Data Link architecture (MAC sublayer protocols), such as Token Ring to Ethernet.

CERTIFICATION SUMMARY

The CIT examination details various troubleshooting scenarios. This chapter covers significant issues in problematic areas for troubleshooting LAN problems. It is important to thoroughly investigate network performance; make sure you're tracking errors, application throughput, collision rates, peak utilization periods, and any other statistical analysis information to assist in troubleshooting. A good rule of thumb for LAN troubleshooting is to approach each problem individually with a standardized procedure for effectively isolating and resolving network problems. It's almost impossible for anyone to effectively troubleshoot LAN problems without an intimate knowledge of the existing LAN technologies and infrastructures (Ethernet, Token Ring, and FDDI). A key to the examination is knowing what to look for by understanding symptoms, characteristics, and functionality of the communications protocols stack (Physical, Network, and Data Link layers).

In preparation for the CIT examination, you should focus on understanding the behavioral aspects of Ethernet, Token Ring, and FDDI in terms of providing a medium for connected stations to communicate. Hands-on troubleshooting is crucial; for example, you'll want to capture packets on the network with sniffers and protocol analyzers for in-depth data analysis. You should understand Cisco's debug commands, show commands, and other help commands (traceroute, ping, netstat, etc.) for troubleshooting. Know what each command does; during the exam, these commands could be vital in problem isolation and resolution.

Finally, practice makes perfect. It's almost impossible to know the specifics of the exam, so you'll need to know a substantial amount of everything from A to Z. Also, you must be able to pinpoint a problem and know how to break it down from the general to the specific. For instance, you might need to track a slow-response problem to the point where you can see that a particular channel is being overutilized, resulting in the slow response. Try to get as much game-time experience as possible; it's difficult going into the game without any pre-game warm-ups. Take a few snaps on the side and prepare yourself mentally for the challenge. Stay focused and rely on your knowledge of the mechanics to help you overcome the emerging unknowns. Good luck!

TWO-MINUTE DRILL

❏ The Physical layer provides the necessary mechanical, electrical, functional, and procedural characteristics to initiate, establish, maintain, and deactivate connections for data.

❏ The second layer up in the OSI model is the Data Link layer, which is responsible for transmitting data across a physical link with a reasonable level of reliability.

❏ At the Data Link layer are the specifications for topology and communication between two end-stations.

❏ The Media Access Control (MAC) sublayer is the interface between user data and the physical placement and retrieval of data on a network.

❏ The Logical Link Control field (LLC) is a Data Link control layer that is used by 802.3 and 802.5 and other networks.

❏ Type I is the most prevalent class of LLC. LLCI is generally used by Novell, TCP/IP, OSI, Banyan, Microsoft NT, IBM, Digital, and most other network protocols.

❏ The LLC2 service provides the functionality needed for reliable data transfer (quite similar to Layer 4 function).

❏ Ethernet conforms to the lower layers (Physical and Data Link) of the OSI model.

❏ In an Ethernet environment, only one node on the segment is allowed to transmit at any given time, due to the CSMA/CD protocol (Carrier Sense Multiple Access/Collision Detection).

❏ CSMA/CD (Carrier Sense Multiple Access/Collision Detection) is an access technique used in Ethernet that is categorized as a listen-then-send access method.

❏ In the Ethernet implementation there is a likelihood that two stations can simultaneously transmit (once the channel is idle). This is known as a *collision*.

❏ There is a limit to the size of frames an Ethernet segment can transmit.

❏ The frame check sequence (FCS) provides a mechanism for error detection.

❑ *Jabbers* are long, continuous frames exceeding 1518 bytes that provide a self-interrupt functionality which prevents all stations on the network from transmitting data.

❑ In the rule of operation, a CRC check on data fields is initialized before any Ethernet transmissions.

❑ *Runts* are short frames that are less than 64 bytes long. They are usually the result of collisions.

❑ When troubleshooting Ethernet problems, you can use the SHOW INTERFACE ETHERNET command to look at errors, collision rates, and so on.

❑ Remember to track and monitor excessive collision rates. Keep in mind the utilization rate, before collisions present serious problems on the network.

❑ Token Ring is a LAN technology that helps reconcile the problems of contention-based access to a media by granting every station equal access.

❑ One of the major differences between Ethernet and Token Ring is that the Token Ring NICs are intelligent. Token Ring NICs are able to manage their physical ring, in addition to transmitting and receiving data.

❑ It's important for network administrators and LAN technicians to analyze, observe, and capture the MAC communications by way of a protocol analyzer.

❑ When troubleshooting Token Ring problems, you can use the SHOW INTERFACE TOKEN RING command to look at errors, collision rates, and so on.

❑ FDDI became a popular LAN networking technology because of its ability to reach 100 Mbps throughput.

❑ FDDI transmission is comparable to Token Ring transmission in the sense that a token passes around the ring from station to station.

❑ *Data encapsulation* is an extremely important process in peer-to-peer communications—essentially, the process by which layer protocols exchange information among peer layers.

SELF TEST

The following Self Test questions will help you measure your understanding of the material presented in this chapter. Read all the choices carefully, as there may be more than one correct answer. Choose all correct answers for each question.

1. What layer of the OSI model is responsible for providing signaling and mechanical functionality?

   A. Data Link

   B. Network

   C. Physical

   D. Transport

2. Name the layer of the OSI model that is divided into these two sublayers:

   A. Logical Link Control and Data Link

   B. Logical Link Control and Type 2 services

   C. Logical Link Control and Media Access Control (MAC)

   D. None of the above

3. Which of the following symptoms of trouble are found in Ethernet implementations?

   A. Runts

   B. Ring errors

   C. Beaconing

   D. Collisions

   E. A and D

4. Xerox developed which LAN network technology?

   A. Frame Relay

   B. TCP/IP

   C. Ethernet

   D. Token Ring

   E. None of the above

5. Which of the following is a major difference between Ethernet and Token Ring?

   A. Access method

   B. Different vendors

   C. A and B

   D. None of the above

6. In order to transmit in the Token Ring network, you need to:

   A. Possess token

   B. Have a lot of bandwidth

   C. Priority set

   D. A and C

   E. None of the above

7. What is the number of stations assigned to the active monitor role in Token Ring?

   A. 4

   B. 2

   C. 3

   D. 1

8. The LAN Emulation (LANE) protocol uses which layer?

A. Data Link layer

B. Transport layer

C. Network layer

D. Physical layer

9. LAN Emulation is an ATM Forum standard used to connect:

A. ATM switches to ATM desktop connections

B. Multiprotocol routers to an ATM network

C. WANs to an ATM network

D. Legacy LANs and ATM network

10. In an LLC 802.2 layer, Type 2 is the _____.

A. More complicated

B. Least complicated

C. Most structured

11. Token Ring uses what kind of process to help resolve the contention for the active monitoring role?

A. Ring

B. Token claiming

C. Priority

D. Access

12. Which of the following is a function of the MAC layer?

A. Transmitting data operations

B. Transmitting Media Access Management

C. Receiving Media Access Management

D. Receiving data operation

E. All of the above

13. In an FDDI network, what provides for full redundancy?

A. Single Attached Station (SAS)

B. Dual Attached Station (DAS)

C. Node station

D. End-station

14. How do Token Ring frames traverse the network?

A. In two directions, downstream

B. In one direction, downstream

C. Vertically

D. Horizontally

15. MSAU can connect a maximum of how many Token Ring stations?

A. 16

B. 3

C. 4

D. 8

16. What is the minimum frame size for an Ethernet frame?

A. 56 bytes

B. 128 bytes

C. 64 bytes

17. The active monitor role includes which of the following:

A. Detect lost tokens and data frames

B. Monitor the neighbor notification process

C. Purge ring

D. Ensure ring delay

E. All of the above

18. ARP places hardware addresses in the data portion of which layer?

    A. Physical layer

    B. Data Link layer

    C. Frame layer

    D. None of the above

19. LLC Type 1 Operation is used by all the following except:

    A. IBM

    B. Novell

    C. Microsoft

    D. Digital

    E. Sun

20. What is the maximum frame size for an Ethernet frame?

    A. 250 bytes

    B. 320 bytes

    C. 1518 bytes

    D. 1616 bytes

3

WAN
Troubleshooting
Problem Areas

I n this chapter, we will discuss troubleshooting point-to-point and switched protocols. It's very important to understand the concepts and functionality of each protocol. We will discuss the HDLC and SDLC encapsulation methods, as well as both CHAP and PAP authentications via PPP. We will identify ISDN, Frame Relay, X.25, SMDS, and ATM transmissions and common problems associated with each of them.

CERTIFICATION OBJECTIVE 3.01

Point-to-Point Protocols

In the 1980s, the Internet really started to come to life due to its usage by the U.S. government, universities, and large corporations. These hosts were being supported by the Internet Protocol (IP) and connected via a series of LANs. The most common of these LANs was the Ethernet. Other hosts were connected through WANs, using technologies such as X.25. This eventually evolved into the need to transmit data via the original method used before networking was ever established: the point-to-point or serial connection. To accommodate this need, a standard Internet encapsulation protocol, the Point-to-Point Protocol (PPP), was designed. Not only did PPP standardize Internet encapsulation of IP over point-to-point links, it also addressed other issues such as encapsulation and error detection.

PPP Frame

The PPP frame consists of three primary parts (see Figure 3-1). It contains a header, which is subdivided into an 8-bit address field, an 8-bit control field and a 16-bit protocol field. The body or payload of the packet contains a variable length (up to 1500 bytes) of reserved bandwidth for user data. Finally, there is a trailer that contains a 16-bit frame check sequence (FCS). Following are the roles of these fields:

■ **Address** The datagram's destination.

FIGURE 3-1

A sample PPP frame

Flag I byte	Address I byte	Control I byte	Protocol 2 bytes	Data Up to 1500 bytes	Frame check sequence I or 2 bytes

- **Control**   The binary sequence that calls for transmission type of user data in an unsequenced frame.
- **Protocol**   These two bytes identify the protocol encapsulated.
- **Data**   Contains between zero and 1500 bytes for user information.
- **Frame check sequence**   Provides error detection.

LCP/NCP

PPP operates primarily on the second (Data Link) and third (Network) layers of the OSI model (see Figure 3-2). It defines how bits transmitted and received by the Physical layer are recognized as bytes and frames. PPP also defines procedures for error detection and correction, sequencing, and flow control. It does this by using two protocols, LCP (Link Control Protocol) and NCPs (Network Control Protocols):

- **LCP**   The Link Control Protocol is used to establish, configure, test, and terminate the data-link connection.
- **NCP**   The family of Network Control Protocols is used for establishing and configuring the various Network layer protocols.

Once these connections have been established, packets from each Network layer protocol can be sent over the link. The logical connection remains up for point-to-point communications until the link is closed, either directly via a closure code presented by either of the connecting protocols, or from an unknown cause (for example, a modem disconnection). Flow control is generally dictated by the physical medium or actual hardware you are using; this is sometimes actually the root cause of some unknown closures. Obtaining the lists of closure codes and logging them is an excellent step in

FIGURE 3-2

The seven OSI layers

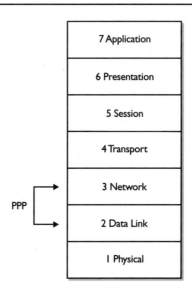

detecting and analyzing your network's trend and for troubleshooting day to day problems.

PPP was also designed to support multiplexing of many higher-level protocols. Although the Internet community is compiled mainly of IP users, it is not limited to them. On top of that, IP networks must often support other protocols as well. These protocols are not discussed in this chapter, but it is important to note that PPP has identified parameters using a family of NCPs for establishing and configuring Network layer protocols such as IP, IPX, and AppleTalk.

Encapsulation

PPP encapsulation is used to decipher multiprotocol datagrams. The family of NCPs will negotiate the protocol being used. It utilizes framing to indicate the beginning and end of the encapsulation. To turn encapsulation on, use the ENCAPSULATION PPP command on the interface. By default, this will enable HDLC for IP on synchronous serial interfaces.

Authentication

To establish a connection using the PPP, there are two standard methods of authentication (if necessary). They are CHAP (Challenge Handshake Authentication Protocol) and PAP (Password Authentication Protocol). These authentication types are utilized in Layer 2 by the LCP.

PAP is the more common of the two and only works to establish an initial link. It is quite vulnerable to attack (or compromise) because it sends its authentication packets throughout the network. Once the link has been established, PAP's role has been completed.

CHAP is used to verify the credibility of a connection using a three-way handshake. After the initial link has been established, it also periodically (and randomly) verifies the validity of the connection by sending a "challenge" message. The connected device will then respond with a calculated hash value that is matched by the challenger. If the values do not match, then the connection is terminated.

To enable these types of authentications, you must add a PPP AUTHENTICATION statement into the interface section of the configuration. Follow this statement with one of the following:

- **chap**   Enables CHAP on the interface.
- **pap**   Enables PAP on the interface.
- **chap pap**   Enables both CHAP and PAP, and performs CHAP before PAP.
- **pap chap**   Enables both CHAP and PAP, and performs PAP before CHAP.

You may also need to set your router's host name and password for call verification. This configuration command syntax is

username *hostname* password *secret*

By default, no PPP authentication type is enabled. Here is a sample configuration:

```
!
interface serial0
```

```
encapsulation ppp
ppp authentication chap
username hostname password secret
```

Link States

When a PPP connection is not functioning properly, it must be declared "down" to prevent the routing of packets from higher-level protocols. A link understood as "up" would be capable of successfully exchanging packets, both to transmit and receive. Another indicator that the PPP connection is not functioning properly is "loopback" detection. It is important to note that PPP is capable of automatically detecting a looped-back link without administrator assistance. Communications equipment often places itself into loopback during troubleshooting to help diagnose problems. It is therefore very important to identify these situations without losing critical information.

If both the serial interface and protocol are down, there are a number of possible problems, including disconnected or faulty physical cabling, provider issues, or hardware failures. If the interface is up and the protocol is down, it may be that keepalives are not incrementing properly, or there may be a misconfiguration, a carrier service problem, timing issues, or hardware failures. These indicators are found using the SHOW INTERFACE command, discussed in the next section.

SHOW INTERFACE and DEBUG Commands

Cisco routers maintain data structures that represent the state of all installed interfaces. To view the interface status, use the SHOW INTERFACE (or SH INT) command. In the following example you will find two examples of this information taken from actual Cisco routers (and slightly masked). This will display the LCP and NCP link states and may identify problems such as input/output errors, CRC errors, and interface resets. Here is an example of this output for a BRI:

```
# show interface BRI0
BRI0: B-Channel is up, line protocol is up
  Hardware is BRI
  MTU 1500 bytes, BW 64 Kbit, DLY 20000 usec, rely 255/255, load 1/255
```

```
Encapsulation PPP, loopback not set, keepalive not set
lcp state = OPEN
ncp state = OPEN ncp ipcp state = OPEN
ncp osicp state = NOT NEGOTIATED ncp ipxcp state = NOT NEGOTIATED
ncp xnscp state = NOT NEGOTIATED ncp vinescp state = NOT NEGOTIATED
ncp deccp state = NOT NEGOTIATED ncp bridgecp state = NOT NEGOTIATED
ncp atalkcp state = NOT NEGOTIATED ncp lex state = NOT NEGOTIATED
Last input 0:00:00, output 0:00:00, output hang never
Last clearing of "show interface" counters never
Output queue 0/40, 0 drops; input queue 0/75, 208 drops
5 minute input rate 0 bits/sec, 1 packets/sec
5 minute output rate 0 bits/sec, 1 packets/sec
   111021403 packets input, 4204243744 bytes, 208 no buffer
   Received 0 broadcasts, 0 runts, 0 giants
   136 input errors, 87 CRC, 14 frame, 17 overrun, 17 ignored, 18 abort
   161882984 packets output, 3434960991 bytes, 0 underruns
   0 output errors, 0 collisions, 35 interface resets, 0 restarts
   0 output buffer failures, 0 output buffers swapped out
   34 carrier transitions
```

Note that the family of NCPs are showing either "open" or "not negotiated." In the event that you were utilizing NCPs rather than IP, they would be negotiated accordingly.

Other important information that can be taken from the show interface command is as follows:

- **BW**   Indicates bandwidth.
- **keepalive**   Shows whether keepalives are sent or not.
- **packets input**   Total number of error-free packets received by the system.
- **no buffer**   Packets that were received but discarded due to buffer allocation problems.
- **input errors**   Total number of "no buffer," runts, giants, CRCs, frame, overrun, ignored, and abort counts.
- **interface resets**   The number of times the interface was completely reset.
- **alarm indications**   Number of CSU alarms.

If no problems are evident in the show interface data, it may be necessary to use Cisco's debug commands.

Note: Be very careful in using the debug commands because they are taxing to the router. Router problems because of CPU utilization have been accidentally caused by leaving this option enabled in the past. When you are finished, be sure to turn off all debugging by typing the **u al** (un-debug all) command. With data scrolling across your monitor, this is the quickest way to ensure that all logging is terminated properly.

With this in mind, here are several debug options to choose from:

- **debug serial interface**   Verifies that HDLC keepalive packets are being passed.

- **debug ppp negotiation**   Shows PPP packets being transferred during startup.

- **debug ppp packet**   Identifies low-level PPP packet dumps. (See Figure 3-3.)

- **debug ppp errors**   Identifies LCP errors during connection and link operation.

- **debug ppp chap/pap**   Shows authentication exchanges.

HDLC

HDLC (High-level Data Link Control) was derived from SDLC (Synchronous Data Link Control). Although commonly referred to as a protocol, HDLC isn't a protocol at all. It's actually a Data Link layer bit-stuffing algorithm that specifies a data encapsulation method for synchronous serial links.

HDLC is the frame-level definition for a number of protocols such as SDLC, BDLC, and X.25, by which frames are identified with special characters called *flags*. HDLC defines a 0 insertion and deletion process (commonly referred to as *bit stuffing*) to ensure that the bit pattern of the delimiter flag does not occur in the fields between flags. Bit stuffing is used to introduce extra 0s in any sequence of more than five 1s. This technique

FIGURE 3-3

Output from debug ppp
packet command

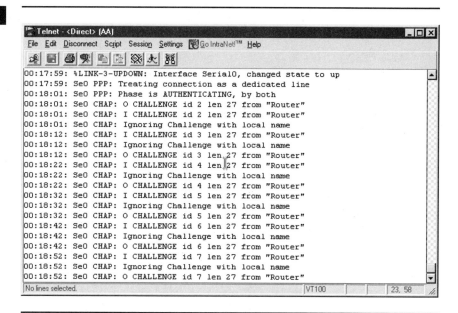

```
Telnet - <Direct> (AA)                                                    _ □ ✕
File  Edit  Disconnect  Script  Session  Settings  🗐 Go IntraNet!™  Help

00:17:59: %LINK-3-UPDOWN: Interface Serial0, changed state to up
00:17:59: Se0 PPP: Treating connection as a dedicated line
00:18:01: Se0 PPP: Phase is AUTHENTICATING, by both
00:18:01: Se0 CHAP: O CHALLENGE id 2 len 27 from "Router"
00:18:01: Se0 CHAP: I CHALLENGE id 2 len 27 from "Router"
00:18:01: Se0 CHAP: Ignoring Challenge with local name
00:18:12: Se0 CHAP: I CHALLENGE id 3 len 27 from "Router"
00:18:12: Se0 CHAP: Ignoring Challenge with local name
00:18:12: Se0 CHAP: O CHALLENGE id 3 len 27 from "Router"
00:18:22: Se0 CHAP: I CHALLENGE id 4 len 27 from "Router"
00:18:22: Se0 CHAP: Ignoring Challenge with local name
00:18:22: Se0 CHAP: O CHALLENGE id 4 len 27 from "Router"
00:18:32: Se0 CHAP: I CHALLENGE id 5 len 27 from "Router"
00:18:32: Se0 CHAP: Ignoring Challenge with local name
00:18:32: Se0 CHAP: O CHALLENGE id 5 len 27 from "Router"
00:18:42: Se0 CHAP: I CHALLENGE id 6 len 27 from "Router"
00:18:42: Se0 CHAP: Ignoring Challenge with local name
00:18:42: Se0 CHAP: O CHALLENGE id 6 len 27 from "Router"
00:18:52: Se0 CHAP: I CHALLENGE id 7 len 27 from "Router"
00:18:52: Se0 CHAP: Ignoring Challenge with local name
00:18:52: Se0 CHAP: O CHALLENGE id 7 len 27 from "Router"

No lines selected.                                      VT100          23, 58
```

ensures that actual data never appears as flag characters. Therefore, the data in HDLC frames appear to be transparent. HDLC operates at the second Data Link layer of the OSI reference model (see Figure 3-2). It utilizes the Physical layer to provide clocking and synchronizing of the transmission and reception of frames.

Data is encapsulated in the (application specific) HDLC frame with embedded information, in an 8- or 16-bit header/trailer. The actual data (Layer 3 frames) is transmitted into the data field, which varies in length depending upon the protocol using the frame. The first two bytes of each frame are defined as the address and control bytes. Each frame also includes two CRC bytes for error checking. The HDLC application decodes the address and control bytes and returns a representation of the contents. The frames are separated by flag sequences that are transmitted between the frames.

Since HDLC is primarily used in a peer-to-peer environment, one station is designated to be the primary and the others become secondary. A session can use one of the following connection modes, which determine how the primary and secondary stations interact:

- **Normal Unbalanced**   Occurs when the secondary station responds only to the primary station.

- **Asynchronous**   When the secondary station initiates the message.

- **Asynchronous Balanced**   Both stations send and/or receive over part of a duplex line.

HDLC is used on both point-to-point and multipoint (multidrop) data links. It also supports full-duplex transparent-mode operation.

SDLC

SDLC is an acronym for Synchronous Data Link Control, and just like HDLC, it is an ISO standard. The SDLC standard was originally invented by IBM to replace the Bisynchronous protocol for WANs, which is known as BDLC. It is structured very similarly to a variation of HDLC called HDLC NRM (Normal Response Mode).

SDLC differs from HDLC in that it is not used for peer-to-peer communications. It is used primarily for multipoint networking. Instead of utilizing the previously mentioned primary and secondary relationships, SDLC is made up of a primary station that controls communications via one or more secondary stations. This primary is usually some type of mainframe or central computer. The secondary nodes act as controllers for all local terminals that transmit the necessary data.

SDLC uses a framing format similar to that of the HDLC frame. An address control field is added, to distinguish conversations between the primary and each of its secondaries, with each secondary having a different address. To streamline transmissions, each secondary reviews all transmissions from the primary but only responds to frames with the secondary's own address. Unlike X.25 or Frame Relay, SDLC is based on dedicated lines with permanent physical connections.

SDLC is capable of full-duplexing but more often than not relies on half-duplexing. This simply means that either the primary or any one of the secondary nodes may be able to transmit simultaneously, but never both. Interference can be created when two or more secondaries transmit at the same time. Often data from both stations is lost as a result. So it becomes important that secondary transmissions are controlled by the primary. In other words, a secondary can only transmit when told to. Further, a limited number of frames may be transmitted before link control is passed back to the primary. SDLC also provides link integrity by using CRC bytes for error detection. Frame acknowledgment is encoded into the control fields. Up to seven frames can be sent from either side before acknowledgment is required.

SDLC typically supports two types of line encoding, either Non-Return to Zero Inverted (NRZi) or non-NRZi. More commonly used, NRZi encoding ensures that one zero is transmitted out of every 5 bit times at a minimum, which aides synchronization.

In fact, one of the most typical problems associated with SDLC is its error recovery. In situations where problems exist, for example when noisy lines create disturbances, the error-recovery mechanism causes many frames to be continually retransmitted and causes latency.

PPP

Several different flavors of PPP are accepted today. The standard, as discussed in the opening section of this chapter, is often referred to as ISPPP (Internet Standard for Point-to-Point Protocol). Here we will briefly discuss Cisco's variation of PPP.

on the **job**

Watch out, don't make the same mistakes that others have made in the past. For instance, I was configuring a network using PPP across several Wellfleet routers and could not get either end to communicate with the other properly. Examining both configurations eventually uncovered that, although I was running PPP on both ends, one was mis-optioned for the default Wellfleet PPP.

Cisco Systems Point-to-Point Protocols

Cisco systems will support asynchronous links using SLIP (Serial Line Internet Protocol), as well as synchronous links using either simple HDLC framing or X.25. It is important to note that SLIP will only support IP traffic. The HDLC framing procedure adds four bytes to the header. The first octet (the address field) is designated as either unicast or multicast. The second octet (the control byte) is left at 0 and simply not checked. Cisco's HDLC is incompatible with other vendors because of the included proprietary type field. You will also encounter problems when directly connecting Cisco equipment over clear-channel or leased connections to non-Cisco boxes.

Cisco uses a keepalive protocol to ensure connectivity of its serial lines, especially those that do not provide an NBMA (nonbroadcast multi-access) service. NBMA provides access to multiple devices which do not broadcast. Therefore, split-horizon is enabled by default on HDLC interfaces. Each end of the link periodically sends two 32-bit sequence numbers to the other side. These numbers are the identifiers of each side. If the numbers are not correct or if no keepalive is sent, the link is considered to be down.

Several other diagnostic tools can be used to help in troubleshooting serial line outages.

■ SHOW CONTROLLERS *interface*/all

This command determines which cable is connected to the interface. Here is an example:

```
# show controllers serial
HD unit 0, idb = 0x7F9C0, driver structure at 0x81480
buffer size 1524  HD unit 0, RS-530 DTE cable
cpb = 0x42, eda = 0x2064, cda = 0x2078
RX ring with 16 entries at 0x422000
00 bd_ptr=0x2000 pak=0x0C866C ds=0x461444 status=80 pak_size=54
TX ring with 4 entries at 0x422800
00 bd_ptr=0x2800 pak=0x000000 ds=0x40C044 status=80 pak_size=44
85 missed datagrams, 43 overruns
0 bad datagram encapsulations, 0 memory errors
0 transmitter underruns
```

■ SHOW BUFFERS

This command displays statistics for the router's buffer pools on the entire router or a specific interface.

- PING

This command sends ICMP requests to the specified IP address. If a response is received, the connection is up. If not, there may be any of several problems occurring, ranging from hardware failures to firewall issues. Here is an example of the output:

```
# ping 204.71.177.35
Sending 5, 100-byte ICMP Echos to 204.71.177.35, timeout is 2 seconds:
!!!!!
Success rate is 100 percent (5/5), round-trip min/avg/max = 76/78/80 ms
```

CERTIFICATION OBJECTIVE 3.02

Switched Protocols

Switched protocols are the set of rules and conventions that govern how devices on a switching network exchange information. These types of protocols include ATM, SMDS, and Frame Relay, among others. In this chapter, we will discuss utilizing and troubleshooting switched-protocol networks.

Frame Relay

The Frame Relay protocol (see Figure 3-4), due to its efficiency, has widely replaced X.25. Frame Relay is a Layer 2 (Data Link) encapsulation method that uses packet switching. This means data is taken and encapsulated

FIGURE 3-4

Frame Relay

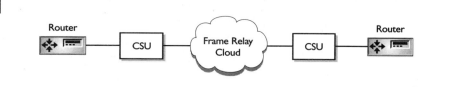

with a formatted Frame Relay header (most often IETF) and sent to its destination, stripped of the encapsulation, and then routed accordingly.

Frame Format

The Frame Relay header is made up of a 10-bit DLCI (data-link connection identifier), a C/R (Command/Response) bit, FECN and BECN (forward/backward explicit congestion notification) bits, and a DE (discard eligible) bit. The data section of this frame immediately follows the header. Finally, a trailer concludes the individual frame. It contains an FCS (frame check sequence) for error detection and frame delineation. Frame Relay standards recommend a maximum frame size of 1600 octets.

The Frame Relay Cloud

The DLCI is actually a locally significant identification to the UNI (User Network Interface) switch in the frame network. Upon entering the Frame Relay network, this DLCI helps the switch identify the path that the frame circuit, known as a PVC (permanent virtual circuit), is provisioned to take. PVCs are responsible for carrying the signal via the configured switches through the Frame Relay network.

This type of network is commonly referred to as a Frame Relay Cloud, because the provider only guarantees the entry and exit points of the connection. Therefore, the actual path the PVC takes is transparent to everybody except the actual provider. A Frame Relay Cloud network contains switches that form dedicated but shared paths for information to pass through (thus the term permanent virtual circuit). Therefore, if a physical path is not being logically used by a specific connection, another PVC may use the path's available bandwidth.

Congestion

Along the PVC, the frame may experience latency due to congestion. This is where the FECNs and BECNs can be useful. These bits explicitly notify a subscriber's device of congestion on the network; they help that device determine whether or not to withhold traffic or reduce its transmission rate until the congestion has cleared. Also, by identifying possible problematic spots in the cloud, some circuits may be reprovisioned to ease connectivity.

Another field that was mentioned but not discussed is the DE (discard eligible) field. If the DE bit is set, then the frame is marked as "discardable" during high-use periods. Although this is not a popular option, providers can encourage customers to use this by assessing lower tariffs.

Error Correction

We will discuss the roles played by CRC error detection in the ISDN section of this chapter. Conceptually similar, the FCS is passed in the trailer of the frame. The destination receives the FCS and computes it. The source then sends the "answer" in the next frame. If the FCS does not match the expected "answer," then the frame is simply discarded and the drop is registered. You may also notice that the interface registers also show runts and giants. These are simply frames that are discarded because they don't fall within the proper size parameters.

Burst Rate and CIR

Transmitting information does not mean that you will be sending out a smooth and steady stream of data. However, you should have some idea of the amount of bandwidth you will be using. The CIR (committed information rate) describes the bandwidth supported during normal operations, but it's possible that you'll go above this amount of bandwidth at any given time. Frame Relay also allows for a committed burst rate, which describes the maximum amount of data a user can put through the network during a specific time interval. Cisco allows you to provide bandwidth statements that solidify your CIR. This is particularly useful if you have dual paths for redundant purposes. In this scenario, you can "traffic shape" by altering the bandwidth statements to primarily utilize a preferred PVC.

Inverse ARP

InARP (Inverse Address Resolution Protocol) is a basic Frame Relay protocol that allows routers on the Frame network to learn the protocol addresses of other routers. Cisco IOS employs InARP to dynamically determine the network information associated with the system's assigned DLCI. If your Cisco router is communicating with a non-Cisco router that does not use InARP, this feature must be eliminated.

LMI

LMI (Local Management Interface) is a basic protocol that is passed through the PVC to verify the validity and state of the link. LMI does not congest traffic on the PVC and is optional. LMI messages perform two functions:

- Verifying a "heartbeat" exchange (the link is running normally)
- Showing PVC status

Several different flavors of LMI are available on Cisco router interfaces. The Cisco default is "gang of four"; others include ANSI Annex A and Annex D. The LMI information must be configured directly into the interface. IOS versions 11.2 and later offer an auto-configuration of LMI. You will see examples of this type of configuration later in this chapter.

The LMI protocol is designed so that the subscriber must initiate information exchange, in order not to tax the network unnecessarily. The exchange consists of a requesting frame comprising a six-octet header and a list of IEs (Information Elements) that carry the status information:

- The first two octets contain the necessary identifiers (similar to the DLCIs).
- The third octet identifies all (LMI) frames as being informational.
- The fourth octet contains a protocol discriminator.
- The fifth octet contains a dummy field that's always set to 0.
- Finally, the sixth octet identifies the message type (either from the subscriber or provider).

And behind the header, LMI recognizes three types of IEs:

- Report type
- Keepalive
- PVC status

Multicasting

Multicasting is an optional feature of Frame Relay that allows users to either send traffic to or receive traffic from multiple users. With this arrangement, the frame network actually duplicates the incoming signal and broadcasts it to the associated MDLCIs (Multicast DLCIs). This is a duplexed operation because traffic flows in both directions.

PVC States

If you experience problems with the link state of your PVC, there are two options you should check: the serial status and the line protocol status. You can do this test using one of three commands:

■ SHOW INTERFACE

This command shows the status of both the physical and line-protocol interface. It also identifies LMI connectivity. An example of this type of output is as follows:

```
Serial0 is up, line protocol is up
  Hardware is XXXXXX
  MTU 1500 bytes, BW 1544 Kbit, DLY 20000 usec, rely 255/255, load 6/255
  Encapsulation FRAME-RELAY IETF, loopback not set, keepalive set (10 sec)
  LMI enq sent  1134915, LMI stat recvd 1133891, LMI upd recvd 0, DTE LMI up
  LMI enq recvd 0, LMI stat sent  0, LMI upd sent  0
  LMI DLCI 0  LMI type is ANSI Annex D  Frame Relay DTE
  Broadcast queue 0/64, broadcasts sent/dropped 0/0, interface broadcasts
5277765
  Last input 0:00:00, output 0:00:00, output hang never
  Last clearing of "show interface" counters never
  Output queue 0/40, 0 drops; input queue 0/75, 0 drops
  5 minute input rate 107000 bits/sec, 32 packets/sec
  5 minute output rate 41000 bits/sec, 47 packets/sec
     46887557 packets input, 1612456289 bytes, 0 no buffer
     Received 0 broadcasts, 0 runts, 0 giants
     2563 input errors, 1690 CRC, 2 frame, 43 overrun, 85 ignored, 61 abort
     57785411 packets output, 2143340051 bytes, 0 underruns
     0 output errors, 0 collisions, 392 interface resets, 0 restarts
     0 output buffer failures, 0 output buffers swapped out
     40 carrier transitions
     DCD=up  DSR=up  DTR=up  RTS=up  CTS=up

Serial0.1 is up, line protocol is up
  Hardware is XXXXXX
```

```
  Internet address is 1.1.1.1 255.255.255.255
  MTU 1500 bytes, BW 1000 Kbit, DLY 20000 usec, rely 255/255, load 6/255
  Encapsulation FRAME-RELAY
Serial0.2 is up, line protocol is up
  Hardware is XXXXXX
  Internet address is 1.1.1.1 255.255.255.255
  MTU 1500 bytes, BW 1544 Kbit, DLY 20000 usec, rely 255/255, load 4/255
  Encapsulation FRAME-RELAY
```

■ SHOW FRAME LMI

This command expands upon the LMI information. Here's an example of this command:

```
LMI Statistics for interface Serial0 (Frame Relay DTE) LMI TYPE = ANSI
  Invalid Unnumbered info 0          Invalid Prot Disc 0
  Invalid dummy Call Ref 0           Invalid Msg Type 0
  Invalid Status Message 0           Invalid Lock Shift 0
  Invalid Information ID 0           Invalid Report IE Len 0
  Invalid Report Request 0          Invalid Keep IE Len 0
  Num Status Enq. Sent 1877971       Num Status msgs Rcvd 1877917
  Num Update Status Rcvd 0           Num Status Timeouts 54
```

■ SHOW FRAME PVC

This command identifies the DLCI and PVC status. It also shows the create and status-change times on the PVC. Here is an example of this command:

```
PVC Statistics for interface Serial0 (Frame Relay DTE)
DLCI = 101, DLCI USAGE = LOCAL, PVC STATUS = ACTIVE, INTERFACE = Serial0.1
  input pkts 60745337       output pkts 83035363      in bytes 2827350014
  out bytes 4097860340      dropped pkts 50           in FECN pkts 0
  in BECN pkts 0            out FECN pkts 0           out BECN pkts 0
  in DE pkts 2266           out DE pkts 0
  pvc create time 31w0d  last time pvc status changed 4w1d
```

If the serial port is physically down, you will want to check the actual physical connections and verify that your provider is not experiencing a problem. However, if the line protocol is showing "down," you need to verify LMI and troubleshoot your configurations. Never be afraid to contact your provider for assistance in the event that you are experiencing a problem.

Ensure that you are troubleshooting the proper problem. The serial port may still be up while the protocol is not functioning properly.

There are a couple of debug commands that you will find particularly useful when troubleshooting Frame Relay problems:

- DEBUG FRAME-RELAY LMI

This displays LMI information.

- DEBUG FRAME-RELAY EVENTS

This shows the exchanges between a router and UNI device in the cloud as shown in Figure 3-5.

- DEBUG FRAME-RELAY PACKET

This command shows the frame packets.

Configuration Example

Following is a sample Frame Relay configuration. This specific router configuration is subinterfaced to use two DLCIs in order to pass traffic

---

FIGURE 3-5

Output from debug frame-relay events command

```
Telnet - <Direct> (AA)
File  Edit  Disconnect  Script  Session  Settings  Go IntraNet!  Help

Router(config-if)#
no shut
Router(config-if)#shut
Router(config-if)#
00:28:26: %LINK-5-CHANGED: Interface Serial0, changed state to administratively
down
00:28:26: %FR-5-DLCICHANGE: Interface Serial0 - DLCI 20 state changed to DELETED
```

through the cloud to redundant points. Note that, as discussed earlier, the bandwidth statements are weighted to pass traffic through a desired path.

```
interface Serial0
 no ip address
 encapsulation frame-relay
 no ip route-cache
 frame-relay lmi-type ansi
!
interface Serial0.1 point-to-point
 ip address 1.1.1.1 255.255.255.255
  bandwidth 1544
 frame-relay interface-dlci 10
!
interface Serial0.2 point-to-point
 ip address 1.1.1.1 255.255.255.255
 bandwidth 1000
 frame-relay interface-dlci 11
```

X.25

X.25 is very similar to Frame Relay because it utilizes packet switching and PVCs. The X.25 standard was approved by the CCITT back in 1976, when other WAN standards were poor at best. X.25 answered several transmission problems by introducing error correction and flow control. Although newer, faster, and more efficient protocols have emerged to replace X.25, it is still being used. So we will discuss it briefly.

Data is transferred via X.25 in the first several layers (Physical, Data Link, and Network) of the OSI model. X.25 relies on the HDLC bit-stuffing algorithm, described in the PPP discussion, to format the information into frames. DTEs (data terminal equipment) and DCEs (data communications equipment) establish connections via PADs (Packet Assemblers/Disassemblers) on logical virtual circuits through either SVCs (switched virtual circuits) or PVCs (permanent virtual circuits), over which the frames are passed.

SVCs and PVCs

Switched virtual circuits are only utilized when the connection is established and are lost when the data is finished being transferred. To establish this connection, the DTE sends a Call Request with the necessary information (source/destination addresses) to establish a connection. If the receiving end sends an acknowledgment back, then transmissions begin and remain up until the necessary information has been passed. This is signaled with a Clear Request packet.

Permanent virtual circuits in X.25 work very similarly to those of Frame Relay. The circuit is a permanent physical connection that is only utilized when data is being transferred.

Addressing

X.25 networks have unique addresses that use the X.121 standard, commonly referred to as NUAs (network user addresses). This addressing scheme dictates that a 14-digit address is assigned; however, only two of these digits are optional (for subaddressing). Using the SHOW INTERFACE command (again), we can see an example of this type of addressing:

```
# show interface serial 1
X25 address 000000010100, state R1, modulo 8, idle 0, timer 0, nvc 1
  Window size: input 2, output 2, Packet size: input 128, output 128
  Timers: T20 180, T21 200, T22 180, T23 180, TH 0
  (configuration on RESTART: modulo 8,
  Window size: input 2 output 2, Packet size: input 128, output 128
  Channels: Incoming-only none, Two-way 5-1024, Outgoing-only none)
  RESTARTs 3/2 CALLs 1000+2/1294+190/0+0/ DIAGs 0/0
```

Error Detection

By using the HDLC error detection, X.25 does have primitive troubleshooting capabilities. However, there are some control messages used to set up, maintain, and tear down communications circuits. Two of these types of messages can indicate a problem: the Disconnect and Reset codes.

- **Disconnect** is used to either reject a connect request or kill an established call.

- **Reset** is used to clear a hung connection or identify synchronization problems.

Finally, whenever the transport service receives a TPDU (Transport Protocol Data Unit) timeout, the message will automatically be resent.

However, if the header contains a protocol error (generally identified in the Transport layer), TPDU will return an ERR cause code and end the connection.

Cisco provides several debugging commands for troubleshooting on X.25:

■ DEBUG X25 EVENTS

This will detect X.25 events and provide cause and diagnostic information as shown in Figure 3-6.

■ DEBUG LAPB

This command displays any Level 2 X.25 information.

SMDS

SMDS (Switched Multimegabit Data Service) was originally released at the beginning of 1992. Throughout this section, you will notice that SMDS is

FIGURE 3-6

Output from debug x25 events command

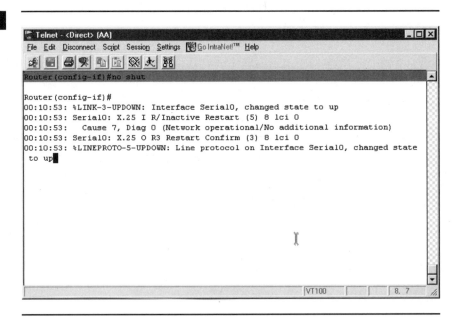

closely related to ATM and Frame Relay technologies. It was engineered to connect LANs to WANS via the local telephone company (telco).

SMDS has a three-tiered architecture:

- A switching infrastructure
- SNIs (Subscriber Network Interfaces) composed of T1 and T3 circuits
- An infrastructure access-control system

Switching Infrastructure

SMDS is connectionless because it does not require that local telcos utilize their switches to establish call paths. Instead, they pass ATM-like 53-byte cells (IEEE 802.6) to a carrier switch (sometimes even through an ATM switch). This switch identifies the destination address and forwards the uniform cells to that destination via the SMDS cloud. The cloud contains a network of switches that permit data to travel over the least-congested paths. The actual SMDS address ensures that the cells arrive in the proper order. This, in turn, allows SMDS to offer a service that provides a faster end-to-end solution, regardless of the bandwidth requirements.

SNI

Another advantage of this type of engineering is that SMDS is scalable. Being connectionless, it's easier for users to expand networks where each site is connected to all other sites. This provides the look and speed of a LAN over a WAN.

Networks can connect to an SMDS cloud via SNIs (Subscriber Network Interfaces), which are generally composed of T1 and T3 circuits. The latest technology, however, allows for bandwidth including 56 Kbps to 64 Kbps. This gives SMDS connectivity to networks in a flexible connectivity range from 56 Kbps to 45 Mbps.

Access-Control System

SMDS uses E.164 addressing, which is very similar to standard telephone numbers. This gives SMDS access-control features such as call screening, verification, and blocking.

Benefits of SMDS

SMDS includes reasonable availability and increased LAN performance. It also provides some data management features, a degree of flexibility, bandwidth on demand, privacy, multiprotocol support, and technology compatibility. SMDS offers a range of accommodating features, including

- End-to-end connectivity
- High-speed, low-delay connectionless data
- Multicasting (group addressing)
- Support of all WAN protocols (for example TCP/IP, Novell, AppleTalk, SNA)
- Scalability
- Security

Compatibility

ATM (discussed next) is compatible with SMDS. They both have similar 53-byte cell-relay packets with 48 bytes for data and a 5-byte address header. In addition, they share compatible headers that simplify transitioning from SMDS to higher ATM speeds.

exam
Ⓦatch

In order to provide Frame Relay users with access to SMDS, a Bellcore standard called the SMDS Interface Protocol Relay Service (a.k.a. SIP Relay) was released. This standard enables SMDS to be encapsulated and transported within Frame Relay, as well.

The Synchronous Optical Network (SONET) is an international standard, fiber-optic transmission that is used for broadband transport. SONET offers a variety of optical line rates (in multiples of 51.84 Mbps) and gives users the ability to send signals at multigigabit rates. SMDS is also compatible to operate at speeds up to 155 Mbps on the SONET's STS-3c interface (OC-3).

Note: The number after the OC is actually the number of STS-1 (Synchronous Transport Signal Level 1) frames, which equals 51.84 Mbps of bandwidth. Therefore, an OC-3 is roughly 155 Mbps of bandwidth.

ATM

ATM stands for Asynchronous Transfer Mode and is often compared to Frame Relay because it is an ISDN (Integrated Services Digital Network) protocol standard. Also, it utilizes both switching and multiplexing technologies. ATM was designed to make Broadband-ISDN (B-ISDN) a reality. B-ISDN was created conceptually as just an extension of ISDN, so it functions as a communications network, providing integrated services. ATM, however, is not guaranteed and utilizes cell switching for much higher speeds and higher volumes over both WANs and LANs. In fact, ATM's primary advantage is that it can use the higher speeds ranging from DS-3 (45 Mbps) through the OC (Optical Carrier) family.

Cell Structure

ATM uses 53-btye cells in order to divide data into smaller and more manageable packets; this allows quicker cell relay across a better range of high-performance communications networks. The ATM cells are composed of 5 bytes for header information, and 48 bytes for actual data (these 48 bytes are typically referred to as the "payload"). The header itself is made up in one of two formats, either UNI (User to Network Interface) or NNI (Network Node Interface).

Both of these contain an 8- to 12-bit VPI (Virtual Path Identifier), a 16-bit VCI (Virtual Circuit Identifier), a 3-bit PT (Payload Type), a 1-bit CLP (Cell Loss Priority), and an 8-bit HEC (Header Error Check). However, the UNI cell contains a GFC (Generic Flow Control) field, which steals 4 bits from the VPI field. See Figure 3-7 for an example. The use of these fixed fields allows for greater speeds because active devices can be configured for set lengths, permitting hardware switching versus the accessing of software routing tables.

Here are descriptions of the fields:

■ **Virtual Path Identifier/Virtual Circuit Identifier**   VPI/VCI fields indicate locally significant virtual path or virtual channel identification numbers, so that the cells belonging to the same connection can be distinguished.

FIGURE 3-7

ATM cell examples

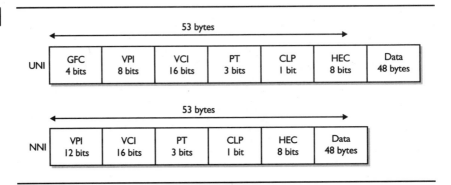

- **Payload Type** This field provides user information (if present) and shows if the cell has suffered traffic congestion.

- **Cell Loss Priority** This field determines whether or not the cell should be dropped by network equipment during periods of congestion.

- **Header Error Check** This field serves a dual purpose. First, it provides CRC error detection. It also provides some cell delineation.

- **Generic Flow Control** This cell header field appears only in UNI systems and bears only local significance. It is intended to provide standardized local functions such as flow control.

Another ATM advantage is that it is the first cell-switched protocol designed specifically to support integrated applications, including voice, video, and data communications. It accommodates transmission speeds from 64 Kbps to gigabit speeds.

The information exchange works via switching across dedicated lines on the network. Circuit paths are allocated to the nodes for data transfer across the network. Channel capacity becomes available and is reserved between the source and destination. Depending on the bandwidth requirements of the application, utilization of the line can vary enormously. At each node, the packet is received, queued in a buffer, and passed on.

There are two basic approaches to the actual transport:

- **Datagram** An example of datagram transport is when each packet can take a separate path through the network and get sorted at the destination. This allows for dynamic congestion handling.

■ **Virtual Circuit**   This type of transport occurs when all the packets are sent through the same path without having the path actually dedicated. The routes are determined between paths through the ATM cloud by the VPI and VCI sections of the cell header before the data is transferred across VCCs (Virtual Channel Connections). An advantage of this method is that the virtual channels allow for sequencing, error detection, and flow control.

Signal Path

A *virtual channel* is a segment of the virtual circuit. A *virtual path* consists of a set of these channels. Each channel and path have locally significant specific identifiers associated with them. The virtual channel and path numbers of a connection may differ from source to destination if the connection is switched at some point within the network. This is because all channels within a single path must have distinct channel identifiers, but may have the same channel identifier as channels in different virtual paths. This makes a VCI uniquely identifiable via both its virtual channel and virtual path number.

Switched virtual circuits establish paths dynamically for the data transfer and then release them once, upon completion. This is especially convenient at the LAN level. It is important to understand that ATM technologies are not only limited to SVCs. ATM switching structures also support PVCs identical to those used in Frame Relay.

QSAAL and ILMI

QSAAL (Q.2100-Signaling ATM Adaptation Layer) is used for UNI signaling across virtual circuits from the router to the ATM switch. It is an ATM Forum-recommended standard that the QSAAL VCI value is 5. ILMI (Integrated Local Management Interface) facilitates administration and configuration of the ATM address and is necessary for the auto-configuration. This is accomplished by informing the switch of its unique ESI (MAC address), which returns the address prefix that is used to construct the entire ATM address. The ATM Forum recommended standard for the ILMI VCI value is 16. These values are necessary in the basic configuration of the router.

Addressing and Encapsulation

ATM uses an NSAP (Network Service Access Point) format address. These addresses are compilations of a unique end-identifier, prefixes that identify individual switches and collections of switches within specific peer groups. The prefix for the ESI (End Station Identifier) will come from the switch via ILMI. The ATM connection is used to transfer information to these addresses. To do this more efficiently, AALs (ATM Adaptation Layers) are used to encapsulate the traffic. AAL is meant to support many classes of services with different transfer requirements. That is why AALs are service dependent.

There are four types of AAL:

- **AAL1** Used for connection-oriented, delay-sensitive services such as DS-1 or DS-3.

- **AAL2** Supports connection-oriented services that do not require a constant bit rate. This is currently an incomplete standard.

- **AAL3/4** Supports both connectionless and connection-oriented protocols that utilize a variable bit-rate such as SMDS. The actual encapsulation type is aal34smds.

- **AAL5** Used for connection-orientated services such as LANE and classic IP over ATM. The actual encapsulation types are aal5snap (Sub-Network Access Protocol), aal5mux (MUX type) and aal5nlpid (Network Layer Protocol Identifier).

Sample Configurations

Although we will not discuss sample configurations in more detail, it's worth noting that there are typically two types of implementation for ATM: IP over ATM, and LANE (LAN Emulation). So as a result, there are various ways to set up an ATM network via your Cisco router. These variables will depend on your networking needs. Following are several router configurations for ATM WAN solutions.

BASIC PVC SAMPLE CONFIGURATION

```
!
interface atm2/0\
   ip address 1.1.1.1 255.255.255.255
   atm pvc 1 0 100 aa15snap
   map-group PVC
!
map-list PVC
   ip 1.1.1.2 atm-vc 1 broadcast
```

BASIC SVC SAMPLE CONFIGURATION

```
!
interface atm2/0\
   Ip address 1.1.1.1 255.255.255.255
   atm pvc 1 0 5 qsaal
   atm pvc 2 0 16 ilmi
   atm esi-address 2222222222.00
   map-group SVC
!
map-list SVC
   ip 1.1.1.1 atm-nsap AA.0000000000.111111111.00 broadcast
```

SHOW Commands

The commands that you will utilize to troubleshoot your ATM network include the following:

■ SHOW ATM INTERFACE ATM

This displays ATM-specific information directly from the ATM interface.

■ SHOW ATM MAP

This displays all of the configured ATM static maps to their remote hosts.

■ SHOW ATM TRAFFIC

This displays the current, global ATM traffic information connected to the router.

■ SHOW ATM VC

This command displays all active permanent and switched virtual circuits, as well as traffic information.

DEBUG Commands

Following are the debug commands you will utilize to troubleshoot your ATM network:

■ DEBUG ATM SIGNAL

Displays all the ATM signaling, including QSAAL and ILMI.

■ DEBUG ATM ILMI

Displays specifically the ILMI signaling.

■ DEBUG SIGNALING

Shows all signaling to the router.

ISDN

Back in 1984, the POTS (Plain Old Telephone Service) could not handle the overwhelming amount of traffic that was necessary to transfer information. So ISDN was brought to life. It allows digital data transfer at a rate of 64 kilobits per second over the analog network infrastructure of today's telephone companies. Today, this need to pass data has only increased, and there are several different ways for it to be accommodated. The ISDN technologies include BRI, MBRI, and PRI.

Before getting started, it is important that you can identify some of the quirks you may encounter with ISDN. First, the ISDN provider will need to give you some necessary information such as the switch type, framing/encoding types, and SPID numbers. The switch information relates to the equipment with which the provider will be connecting you. If you set the wrong option for this parameter, then nothing will come up.

ISDN BRI

The most commonly utilized form of ISDN connectivity is called ISDN BRI (Basic Rate Interface). The reason for its popularity is because it allows quicker Internet connectivity at greater data transfer rates for individual users without tying up a telephone line. It is also reasonably priced for dedicated digital access.

ISDN BRI is often called "2B+D" or "bonded ISDN" because it utilizes two bearer channels with 64 Kbps for data, and one signaling channel with a 16-Kbps bandwidth. See Figure 3-8. The data channels do exactly what they insinuate: pass traffic such as data, voice, video, and so on. The signaling channel communicates with the switch by passing any connection-related traffic.

MBRI

Multiple channels or BRI lines can be multiplexed together (usually in increments of 128 Kbps), depending on your bandwidth needs and the terminal adapter that you possess. This type of technology is known as MBRI (Multiple Basic Rate Interface).

DDR

BRI can be configured to be one type of DDR (dial-on-demand routing) because data is only being transmitted when the connection is established. In other words, the call is placed when data transfer is necessary, and hangs up when the channels are idle. Setting this configuration can be tricky

---

FIGURE 3-8

Basic Rate Interface

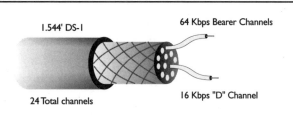

1.544' DS-1

64 Kbps Bearer Channels

24 Total channels

16 Kbps "D" Channel

---

because important roles are placed on idle timeouts and on identifying interesting traffic.

ISDN PRI

ISDN PRI (Primary Rate Interface) is a service provided for companies and others who have a greater need to transfer information. In North America and Japan, this particular type of connection multiplexes 23 Bearer channels for actual data, often called the B channels, and one signaling channel called a D (or data) channel. In Europe, PRIs contain 31 Bearer channels multiplexed with one data channel. The bandwidth of each of these channels, as previously mentioned, is 64 Kbps (kilobits per second).

ISDN PRI differs from BRI as follows:

- No provisions for multipoint connections. This means the connection will be point-to point, directly from the network onto the CPE (Customer Premise Equipment).

- No available DDR.

- Obviously, the available bandwidth will be different.

Layer 2 of ISDN

LAPD (Link Access Procedure on the D channel) is the data-link control protocol used by ISDN. This protocol allows the end devices to communicate via the D channel, which is used primarily for signaling. Signaling is a technique where the provider's equipment (for example, switches such as dms 100s, Seimans, and 5ess) pass their standard set of control signals or messages to the receiving communications equipment. This signaling is used to report incoming connections, call terminations, and any other link-related information. The specific signaling messages are dependent upon the type of ISDN service being utilized.

Layer 3 of ISDN

PRI is capable of supporting the following protocols:

- **ATM** (See Chapter 12) This acronym stands for Asynchronous Transfer Mode and represents the international standard for cell relay.

- **Frame Relay** (See Chapter 12) This is the protocol at the Data Link layer that encapsulates data and transmits it over PVCs (permanent virtual circuits) between logically connected devices.

- **HDLC** (See Chapter 12) This acronym stands for High-level Data Link Control and specifies the Data Link layer data-encapsulation method on synchronous serial links.

- **PPP** (See Chapter 12) This acronym stands for Point-to-Point Protocol, discussed in this chapter.

- **SMDS** (See Chapter 12) This acronym stands for Switched Multimegabit Data Service. It is a high-speed, packet-switched WAN technology and is commonly used in DSL (Digital Subscriber Link). This is the telco's answer to the cable modem.

- **X.25** (See Chapter 12) This is the standard that defines connections for remote terminal access.

PRIs are particularly useful to ISPs (Internet Service Providers) because they can multiplex incoming individual analog connections via the local telco, digitalize the signal, and back-haul the information to their NASs (Network Access Servers). In this scenario, each connection would be assigned to one channel (or DS-0) on the PRI and authenticated as a PPP connection.

T1 WAN Alarms

This brings us to the topic of intrusive and nonintrusive circuit evaluations. There are many ways of testing for possible problems. What can be confusing is identifying exactly what these problems can mean.

There are two types of problems a circuit can experience. Actual WAN alarms are specific signals sent out by the device that sees the problem. They are meant to help troubleshooters identify from which direction the problem is coming. These alarms are:

- **Red Alarm** Identifies that the signal is out of frame or out of synchronization. It generally indicates a break in the line prior to the device that detects or reports the alarm. In other words, the device either does not receive any signal or it is unrecognizable.

- **Yellow Alarm** A signal sent back in the direction from which a red alarm comes. Because this alarm is sent intentionally, it surfaces in one of two signal patterns: Either the second bit in every byte is a 0 (in D4), or it's an alternating pattern of 1s and 0s (in ESF).

- **Blue Alarm** Sometimes referred to as "All Ones." This is also a signal that is sent from a device that detects a red alarm. Because it has not received any passable traffic, the device sends a steady pattern of all 1s to the next device in the circuit path. The receiving device will in turn continue relaying this signal until the red alarm is cleared and traffic is normal.

- **D Channel Failure** Another alarm that falls into the "WAN alarm" category. This alarm indicates that the channel reserved for signaling is failing or unrecognizable. Usually this is a problem that is associated with the source or destination of the signal.

Figure 3-9 illustrates the process by which a signal is generated but does not reach its destination because of a physical media problem. The receiving device is therefore unable to interpret the incoming signal (resulting in a RA, Red alarm) and in turn transmits the appropriate signals to the closest active devices in the span of the signal.

Identifying problems across T1 spans can be done by examining actual errors within the data or problems with synchronization. Here is a list of these types of circuit errors.

- **Bit Errors** This is the basic performance evaluator and can only be tested intrusively by taking the circuit down. By sending predetermined and stressing test patterns through the circuit, these

FIGURE 3-9

Alarms

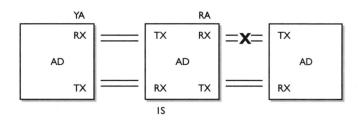

Legend

IS - All Ones	AD - Active Device
RA - Red Alarm	RX - Receive Pair
YA - Yellow Alarm	TX - Transmit Pair
= - Physical Media	X - Signal Disruption

errors are basically logic errors—in other words, 1s that should have been 0s and vice versa.

- **BPVs (Bi-Polar Violations)**   This type of transmission error occurs every time consecutive pulses of the same polarity are transmitted in violation of the bipolar signal format. This type of signal violation can be monitored without taking the circuit down or during pattern testing.

- **Frame Errors**   These errors are measured by the number of times an incorrect value appears in the framing bit position. The circuit can be monitored (not affecting live traffic) to identify these errors, but they are usually difficult to uncover. This is generally because the framing bit is only the 193rd bit in each frame and therefore appears less than one percent of the time.

- **CRC Errors (cyclic redundancy check)**   This method of error detection is both very interesting and very accurate (estimated at over 98 percent). It also is incorporated in any block of live data. The only drawback is that CRC requires the ESF framing format to be utilized. CRC works by building a mathematical equation and transmitting it across the control bits in an ESF frame. The result of the calculation is then transmitted in the next frame. The distant end performs the calculation and compares answers. If the resulting answers do not match, a CRC is incremented.

To identify the errors just listed, you should be able to request that the provider run various tests across your spans. Most providers will require that you have their circuit identification ready. (For example, a World Comm circuit looks something like this: WZ3-123456; and some LECs utilize CLLI codes.) This does not ensure that the technician is actually testing the correct span. So to ensure it's being done properly, monitor the circuit and look for signs that the testers have actually accessed it. If you suspect they might not have, don't be afraid to throw the circuit into alarm by changing either the framing, the encoding, or the switch type, and see if they notice.

The testing patterns most often utilized to test T1 spans are as follows:

- **ALL ONES**   This test sends out an unframed pattern of continuous 1s in an attempt to see if any network devices are dropping bits.

- **QUASI**   This test is often referred to as a STRESS TEST. It's a type of testing that randomly changes the bit pattern (using the pulses – 1s) around in an attempt to create a signal that physically stresses the circuit past the level that normal data transmissions would cause. Often this is an unframed signal. This pattern is meant to test the actual physical media, but it can also show equipment failures.

- **THREE & TWENTY-FOUR**   This is a test pattern that injects three pulses (1s) in every 24 bits (note that this is the minimum 1s density). It is generally used to test active devices in the span. When other testing patterns pass and this one fails, there's often a problem with an active device (a repeater or DAC, for example) along the span.

- **ONE in EIGHT**   This test is a less stressful version of the THREE & TWENTY-FOUR pattern. It basically sends one pulse in every eight, and identifies the same problems.

- **ALL ZEROS**   This test sends out a pattern of all 0s. It is meant to test active network devices in an ESF environment by forcing B8ZS. Any device that does not substitute the zeros pattern with the intentional BPVs would be identified as mis-optioned.

- **FRAMED ONES**   This is a low stress test that inserts 1s into all bits except those reserved for framing. It has a low functionality in the grand scheme and is rarely used to identify less than obvious problems.

CERTIFICATION SUMMARY

Your success at troubleshooting WANs will depend on your understanding of how they work conceptually. In this chapter we discussed both switched and point-to-point protocols and their many attributes.

The PPP standardized Internet encapsulation of IP over point-to-point links, and addressed other previously neglected issues such as encapsulation and error detection. PPP operates on dual layers because it basically comprises two protocols, LCP (Link Control Protocol) and a family of NCPs (Network Control Protocols). PPP supports multiplexing and many higher-level protocols. By utilizing SDLC and HDLC, PPP is able to encapsulate datagrams over point-to-point links. Finally, there are two standard methods of authentication: CHAP (Challenge Handshake Authentication Protocol) and PAP (Password Authentication Protocol).

Switched protocols describe the set of rules and conventions that govern exchange of information among devices on a switching network. In this chapter we discussed, in detail, LAN-to-WAN protocols such as SMDS; higher-speed protocols such as ATM; the older, reliable, pioneering X.25 and its predecessors, including ISDN and Frame Relay.

TWO-MINUTE DRILL

❑ PPP standardized Internet encapsulation of IP over point-to-point links. It also addressed other issues such as encapsulation and error detection.

❑ The PPP frame consists of three primary parts:

  ❑ A header

  ❑ A body or payload of the packet

  ❑ A trailer

❑ PPP operates primarily on the second (Data Link) and third (Network) layers of the OSI model.

❑ The Link Control Protocol (LCP) is used to establish, configure, test, and terminate the data-link connection.

❑ The family of Network Control Protocols (NCP) is used for establishing and configuring the various Network layer protocols.

❑ PPP was also designed to support multiplexing of many higher-level protocols.

❑ PPP encapsulation is used to decipher multiprotocol datagrams.

❑ To establish a connection using the PPP, there are two standard methods of authentication: CHAP (Challenge Handshake Authentication Protocol) and PAP (Password Authentication Protocol).

❑ PAP is the more common of the two and only works to establish an initial link.

❑ CHAP is used to verify the credibility of a connection using a three-way handshake.

❑ It is important to note that PPP is capable of automatically detecting a looped-back link without administrator assistance.

❑ Cisco routers maintain data structures that represent the state of all installed interfaces. To view the interface status, use the SHOW INTERFACE (or SH INT) command.

❑ Be very careful in using the debug commands because they are taxing to the router.

❑ HDLC (High-level Data Link Control) is a Data Link layer bit-stuffing algorithm that specifies a data encapsulation method for synchronous serial links.

❑ SDLC (Synchronous Data Link Control) is used primarily for multipoint networking.

❑ Several different flavors of PPP are accepted today.

❑ *Switched protocols* are the set of rules and conventions that govern how devices on a switching network exchange information.

❑ Frame Relay is a Layer 2 (Data Link) encapsulation method that uses packet switching.

❑ LMI (Local Management Interface) is a basic protocol that is passed through the PVC to verify the validity and state of the link.

❑ Multicasting is an optional feature of Frame Relay that allows users to either send traffic to or receive traffic from multiple users.

❑ Ensure that you are troubleshooting the proper problem. The serial port may still be up while the protocol is not functioning properly.

❑ X.25 is very similar to Frame Relay because it utilizes packet switching and PVCs. X.25 answered several transmission problems by introducing error correction and flow control.

❑ SMDS (Switched Multi-megabit Data Service) has a three-tiered architecture:

  ❑ A switching infrastructure

  ❑ SNIs (Subscriber Network Interfaces) composed of T1 and T3 circuits

  ❑ An infrastructure access-control system

❑ In order to provide Frame Relay users with access to SMDS, a Bellcore standard called the SMDS Interface Protocol Relay Service (a.k.a. SIP Relay) was released. This standard enables SMDS to be encapsulated and transported within Frame Relay, as well.

❑ ATM (Asynchronous Transfer Mode) is often compared to Frame Relay because it is an ISDN (Integrated Services Digital Network) protocol standard. It utilizes both switching and multiplexing technologies.

❑ ISDN allows digital data transfer at a rate of 64 kilobits per second over the analog network infrastructure of today's telephone companies.

❑ LAPD (Link Access Procedure on the D channel) is the data-link control protocol used by ISDN.

❑ PRIs are particularly useful to ISPs (Internet Service Providers) because they can multiplex incoming individual analog connections via the local telco, digitalize the signal, and back-haul the information to their NASs (Network Access Servers).

SELF TEST

The following Self Test questions will help you measure your understanding of the material presented in this chapter. Read all the choices carefully, as there may be more than one correct answer. Choose all correct answers for each question.

1. PPP was designed to do what?

    A. Standardize IP encapsulation

    B. Address error-detection issues

    C. Improve WAN connectivity

    D. All of the above

2. Which of the following fields are included in the PPP frame header?

    A. Control

    B. FCS

    C. Data

3. PPP operates on what layer of the OSI model?

    A. Application

    B. Session

    C. Data Link

    D. Transport

4. The NCP is utilized by PPP on which layer?

    A. Network

    B. Session

    C. Data Link

    D. Transport

5. The most intensive authentication standard for PPP is _____.

    A. TACACS PAP

    B. RADIUS

    C. CHAP

    D. TACACS

6. HDLC is considered a bit-stuffing _____.

    A. Protocol

    B. Algorithm

    C. Encryption

    D. Authentication

7. CRC is primarily used for what?

    A. Error detection

    B. Framing

    C. Encoding

    D. Protocol identification

8. SDLC is primarily used for what?

    A. Peer-to-peer communications

    B. Broadcasting

    C. Multiport networking

9. In Frame Relay headers, FECNs and BECNs (bits) are used for which of the following?

    A. Fragments

    B. Runts

    C. Congestion

    D. Lost frames

10. LMI recognizes only what type of IEs?

    A. Report-type

    B. Keepalive

    C. PVC status

    D. All of the above

11. Which Cisco router command would you use to determine if LMI is up or down?

    A. SH INT

    B. SH FR PVC

    C. SH FR LMI

    D. A and C

12. SVCs identify that sending what signal has completed the signal transmission?

    A. An ACK

    B. A Clear Request

    C. A Termination Request

    D. A NACK

13. SMDS supports which of the following?

    A. OC-3 speed

    B. Encryption

    C. End-to-end connectivity

    D. X.121 addressing

14. How are ATM and SMDS similar?

    A. They use 53-byte uniform cells

    B. They use FCS for error detection

    C. They support VCIs

    D. They support SIP Relay

15. What is the best ATM encapsulation method to use with SMDS?

    A. AAL5snap

    B. AAL34smds

    C. AAL5MUX

    D. QSAAL

16. VCIs are segments of which of the following?

    A. LANs

    B. PVCs

    C. Virtual circuits

17. What type of ISDN standard supports two bearer channels and one signaling channel?

    A. ATM

    B. PRI

    C. X.25

    D. BRI

18. Which of these WAN alarms is caused by a loss of synchronization?

    A. RA

    B. DF

    C. YA

    D. 1s

19. What type of signaling error is a result of pulses registered in consecutive polarity?

    A. BPVs

    B. Framing errors

    C. Bit errors

    D. WAN flaps

20. What T1 test stresses the circuit beyond the point where normal transmissions would be, in an attempt to replicate possible connectivity problems?

    A. 3/24

    B. All 1s

    C. QUASI

    D. All 0s

CISCO CERTIFIED NETWORK PROFESSIONAL

4

The Internet Protocol (IP)

CERTIFICATION OBJECTIVES

Thermost popular network protocol family in existence today is the Transmission Control Protocol/Internet Protocol, commonly abbreviated as TCP/IP. TCP/IP is the fundamental Internet protocol, and its use has increased dramatically in the last several years, due in large part to the popularity of the World Wide Web—although the protocol itself has been around in various forms for over 20 years.

Because of this popularity, many organizations have a connection to the Internet. For simplicity's sake, they may also use TCP/IP as the primary protocol on their internal network (intranet). Most of the network server vendors that for years favored a more proprietary network protocol, such as IPX or AppleTalk, can now operate exclusively over TCP/IP without using any of the other protocols. Network engineers who want to stay current must develop a good understanding of TCP/IP.

In this chapter, we'll cover the details of how TCP/IP works. There are specific sections on the Dynamic Host Configuration Protocol (DHCP) and why it's useful. We'll also cover a selection of application protocols that depend on TCP/IP and are in wide use on the Internet and private networks.

In addition to preparing you for passing the TCP/IP portions of the CIT test, this chapter takes you beyond minimum knowledge of the protocol giving you a look at the way TCP/IP works and why.

CERTIFICATION OBJECTIVE 4.01

Technology Features Recap

If you've been following the standard Cisco certification track, this won't be the first time you've seen information on TCP/IP. Before we get into the troubleshooting specifics, this section examines the details of the underlying protocols. Some of this will be review, but in many cases more detail has been added, along with some examples and anecdotal information.

You'll want to read this recap in its entirety as well as study the troubleshooting section, unless you are already very knowledgeable about

TCP/IP and just don't know the Cisco specifics. Even in the latter case, take a look at the Exam Watch sections to help yourself prepare for the test.

A Note About Terminology

In this chapter we frequently need to refer to a computer or some other device running TCP/IP. In TCP/IP terminology, the word *host* is a fairly generic word for something running TCP/IP. This could be a regular computer, a high-end server, a specialized device, or something else entirely. So, we'll be using *host* to refer to something running TCP/IP.

The one exception will be *routers*. Technically speaking, a TCP/IP router is a host, but it has additional functionality. To be distinct, we'll define *routers* as hosts that perform the routing function.

Another term you'll encounter in this chapter is *TCP/IP stack,* also known as *IP stack* or simply *stack.* This term derives from the layered nature of TCP/IP and other networking software, and the way the layers are "stacked." A TCP/IP stack is simply the TCP/IP software running on the host.

IP, UDP, TCP, ICMP, and Common Ports

TCP/IP traditionally means the entire protocol suite, but the TCP and IP elements hardly comprise a complete list of available protocols. Two other protocols that are essential to most TCP/IP network installations are the User Datagram Protocol (UDP) and the Internet Control Message Protocol (ICMP). UDP is also sometimes dubbed the "Unreliable" Datagram Protocol, for reasons that will become clear later in the chapter. While not technically correct, this nickname describes some of the characteristics of UDP, and serves as a useful way to remember the differences between TCP and UDP.

RFCs

Where did these protocols come from? Specifically, where are their specifications? All of the Internet-related protocols are documented in Request For Comments documents, or RFCs. ("RFC" is a little bit of a misnomer, because the "comment" process is already complete when a document achieves RFC status.) In other words, once a document is assigned an RFC number, it represents the final specification for whatever it is documenting, until it is supplanted by a later RFC.

Throughout this chapter you'll see references to pertinent RFC numbers for the protocol being discussed. It's not necessary to know the approval process for an official RFC in order to understand the protocols, but the process is interesting and worth researching. Networking professionals who want to stay really current on new specifications might consider attending the Internet Engineering Task Force (IETF) meetings and observing the proceedings. See the references section for information, as well as instructions on obtaining copies of RFCs. You'll also find references to other materials that cover the history of TCP/IP and the Internet, and the standards process.

The OSI Layered Model

Without getting into all the specifics of the Open Systems Interconnect (OSI) layered network model, let's briefly cover the hierarchy of various TCP/IP protocols, how they rely on one another, and what that means from a troubleshooting point of view. The OSI model is covered elsewhere in this book; for now, just remember that it's a layered network model. The layers are numbered, and higher layers are more application-specific and closer to the user. For example, e-mail would be considered the highest layer, the Application layer (Layer 7). Other protocols involved in getting that e-mail to the user would likely be considered lower-layer protocols and would have lower numbers.

The IP portion of TCP/IP maps to Layer 3 of the OSI model, the Protocol layer. TCP and UDP are Layer 4 protocols (the Transport layer).

OSI Layers 1 and 2 typically represent elements such as Ethernet, Token Ring, ATM, FDDI, and WAN links. For more information on Layers 1 and 2, see Chapters 2 and 3 of this book. The details of Layers 1 and 2 are ignored here in this chapter except where they are relevant to the overall subject. Typically, this will be when the IP (Layer 3) interacts with the layer immediately below (Layer 2). Higher layers depend on lower layers and, for the most part, won't work if the lower layer isn't functioning. For example, if your Ethernet network is broken, then the TCP/IP protocols trying to use it won't work either.

A TCP/IP network isn't an OSI network. Pure OSI networks do exist in the world, but they are very few and far between. As a consequence, not all protocols in the TCP/IP world map neatly to an OSI layer. Still, the OSI model remains an excellent conceptual teaching tool, and it's fairly common for networking discussions to use OSI concepts. For example, the terms "layer 2 problem" or "layer 4 switch" or "application layer gateway" or "circuit-level proxy" all refer back to the OSI model, and the term "layer 4 switch" doesn't mean much if you don't know what Layer 4 is.

A couple of examples of TCP/IP protocols that don't map neatly to individual OSI layers are the Address Resolution Protocol (ARP) and ICMP. Those two protocols tend to straddle two layers, or act as glue between two layers, depending on how you look at it. More details on ARP and ICMP follow later in the chapter.

Layer 3, IP

We'll start our description of TCP/IP at Layer 3, the Protocol layer; for the TCP/IP protocol suite, Layer 3 is IP. Easily the most distinguishable feature of the IP layer is the IP address. Generally speaking, for devices to communicate over an IP network, each device must have a unique IP address. Under the current version of IP (version 4), this address consists of 4 bytes, or 32 bits. For easier human understanding, the address is usually represented in dotted decimal notation, which looks like this: 192.168.1.1.

IP version 6, now in the works, changes the number of bytes used for IP addresses, as well as a great many other things about IP. IPv6 looks to be still a few years off, and the standard isn't firm yet. It will likely require that most networking professionals be retrained and recertified. Older versions of IP (pre-version 4) also exist. But the Internet reached critical mass under version 4 and that is the current version for the foreseeable future, so this chapter deals exclusively with IPv4.

The later section on Layer 3 contains some basics that probably have been covered in previous study, but we won't be repeating every detail of how IP works. Specifically, you are expected to be familiar with subnetting, subnet masking, IP addressing, and how to convert between binary, decimal, and hexadecimal. If you need a refresher on any of these topics, you can consult *MCSE Microsoft TCP/IP on Windows NT 4.0 Study Guide (Exam 70-59)* (Osborne/McGraw-Hill, 1998) or *CCNA Certified Network Associate Study Guide (Exam 640-407)* (Osborne/McGraw-Hill, 1998).

FROM THE CLASSROOM

IP Version 4 vs. IP Version 6

IP version 4, developed in 1981 (see RFC 791) is currently in use as the standard for IP routing. Since the popularity explosion of the Internet in the past few years, address space is becoming more and more limited. At the rate address space is being allocated, the current available address space will be used up by 2010. The answer to this problem is currently being addressed by the creation of IP version 6 (RFC 1883). IPv6, as it is called, will differ from IPv4 in several areas.

An IPv4 address is 32 bits in length, whereas an IPv6 address will be 128 bits. This will provide a larger amount of available address space, which should last for many years. IPv6 will have, in addition to the standard broadcast address, an "anycast" address that will be used to send packets to a group of devices. The IPv6 header is also different, making some IPv4 fields optional or dropping them altogether. The IPv6 packet has the capability of labeling, allowing packets to be grouped into "flows" so that the sender can identify packets for special handling (such as real-time or nondefault quality of server).

There are three categories of IPv6 addresses: Unicast, Multicast, and Anycast. Unicast is defined as an identifier for a single interface. Multicast is defined as an identifier for a set of interfaces. A packet sent to a Multicast address will be sent to all addresses identified by that address. Anycast is also defined as an identifier of a set of interfaces, except that a packet sent to an Anycast address will be received by the "nearest" device that is identified by that address.

All of the major router vendors have either released software that supports IPv6, or are developing such software to prepare for the day when IPv6 becomes reality.

—*Glenn Lepore, Senior Network Engineer,*
Niche Networks, LLC

Layer 4, TCP and UDP

We'll begin our discussion at OSI Layer 4, the Transport layer. For TCP/IP, this usually means either TCP or UDP. It's fairly uncommon to find other transport protocols at Layer 4 in a TCP/IP network (except for ICMP, which is discussed later). Though IP is an open standard, and other Layer 4 IP protocols do exist and will doubtless be added in the future, their use is negligible compared to TCP and UDP. These two transport protocols provide nearly all the functionality a protocol designer could want for a transport protocol.

We mentioned before that UDP is sometimes nicknamed the "Unreliable" Datagram Protocol. Part of the reason behind this misleading term is that TCP is considered to be a *reliable protocol*. The word *reliable* in this case means that the protocol has specific characteristics that higher-level protocols can take advantage of. It does *not* mean that communications will be 100 percent reliable, and it certainly does not mean that TCP can overcome a network outage.

A Closer Look at TCP

The people working on TCP over the years have had a specific set of characteristics in mind for the protocol. (And keep in mind that there have been different versions, so some of these changes were evolutionary in nature.) TCP's designers wanted a protocol that could solve some of the problems of underlying protocols, specifically those of IP. In a complex, routed IP Internet, a number of things can happen to a packet along its path from point A to point B. A packet may become corrupted, it may be delayed, it may be dropped entirely, it may end up in a loop, and it may arrive out of order compared to other related packets.

TCP addresses all of these issues to some degree. The basic concepts that solve these problems are simple: sequencing and checksumming.

■ *Sequencing* simply means that a number is attached to each packet. Should the packet arrive out of order, or not at all, the other end can tell because it has been keeping track of the sequence numbers.

- *Checksumming* refers to an algorithm called a checksum that is applied to a set of bytes. In the case of TCP, this checksum is applied to a certain portion of the packet, and another number is produced. This number is sent along with the packet so that the receiving end can perform the same calculation and compare the numbers. Any discrepancy indicates that the packet was somehow modified or corrupted in transit and is considered to have not been received. The checksum algorithm used in this case is not complex and does not *guarantee* that the packet wasn't corrupted—only that corruption is highly unlikely. In practice, the checksum is trusted to be 100 percent accurate; the chances are very small that a packet will be corrupt despite passing the checksum test.

When the sequence number and checksum are correct, the host at the far end will then send back a response that says essentially "I got it." If the host at the far end doesn't get a packet at all or if something doesn't match, it does nothing. After a certain amount of time, if the sending host has not received an "I got it" message, it resends the packet.

These behaviors are what earn TCP the title of "reliable." Given a mostly functional IP network, TCP will get the packets to their destination intact and in the right order—eventually. The "eventually" part is an important consideration, which we'll cover shortly; naturally, the details are not as simple.

TCP Communications

Now that we've got the conceptual descriptions out of the way, let's look at the details of how two hosts go about communicating via TCP. In this type of communication one of the hosts is a *client,* and the other is a *server.* It's important to be specific about these words in this particular context, because *client* and *server* (just like *protocol*) mean certain things to certain people, depending on the context. The distinction is easy, though: In the context of a Layer 4 transport protocol under IP, the server is the host that waits, and the client is the host that initiates contact. At a packet level, this means the client is the first one to send a packet.

Up until now, we've been using the word *packet* without specifically defining it. Packet is another one of those words commonly used to describe multiple things, so without context it can be difficult to know exactly what is meant. Packet in this chapter means a collection of bytes that represents the Layer 3 and higher portions of a network communication—specifically, an IP packet without any Layer 2 context, as it might exist in the memory of a host or router. As a byte stream, the packet comprises the bytes that start with the IP header and end with the IP trailer. When a packet is put onto an actual network, Layer 2 headers and possibly trailers are placed around the packet, and it becomes a *frame*. Frames contain packets, and packets contain *connections*.

When two hosts are communicating using the TCP protocol, they are said to have a *TCP connection*. As mentioned, a client initiates contact with a server. For TCP, this represents a very specific process. But before we cover how a TCP connection is set up, we need to discuss TCP port numbers.

TCP Port Numbers

Imagine a server on the Internet, waiting for a TCP connection. It's likely that the client isn't the only host wanting to communicate with the server. It's also likely that the server is capable of offering more than one kind of service. The client and server need some mechanism to determine which host is which, and which service is desired. This is done largely through *port numbers*.

Port numbers are specified in the Layer 4 header inside a packet. For the current version of TCP/IP, port numbers are 16 bits long and unsigned, which gives them a decimal range of 0 through 65535.

A port number represents one of two things, depending on whose port number it is. When a client contacts a server via TCP, the contact is to a particular port on that host, often called the *destination* port. The port on the server usually represents a service, and this is how the client requests a particular service that it thinks the server is offering. If you're an Internet user, you may be familiar with some port numbers already, such as port 80 which represents the default HTTP (Hypertext Transfer Protocol) port, or port 23 which represents the default Telnet server port. (These higher-level protocols are discussed later.) The client also picks a port number for itself, often called a *source* port. The communication is said to be "from" that port number, and that is how the client distinguishes the connection it's using at the moment.

Recall in our example that a server may be offering many services. The client uses the destination port to pick the service it wants. Since the server waits at the same port number for all clients who want the same services, the server needs a way to determine which client is talking. Part of this determination is the IP address. If a server gets 100 requests, all from different IP addresses, then the server knows to send a reply to each of those 100 IP addresses.

But what if the server gets two requests from the same IP address? When the client is a multiuser UNIX host, it's fairly easy to see how this could happen. Two users could be Telnetting or FTPing to the server at the same time (FTP is the File Transfer Protocol). In order to handle this case, TCP's client port number, or source port, comes into play. Now the server has a way to distinguish between different connections coming from the same client. The server keeps track of client IP addresses and port numbers, so it can send the correct response to the correct user on the UNIX host.

It's important to note that port numbers aren't always arbitrarily assigned. There are various classes of port numbers. The classes and their numbers are assigned by the Internet Assigned Numbers Authority (IANA). Following is a section from the IANA's assigned port numbers document, which you can find at

ftp://ftp.isi.edu/in-notes/iana/assignments/port-numbers

as well as other online locations.

```
PORT NUMBERS

The port numbers are divided into three ranges: the Well Known Ports,
the Registered Ports, and the Dynamic and/or Private Ports.

The Well Known Ports are those from 0 through 1023.

The Registered Ports are those from 1024 through 49151

The Dynamic and/or Private Ports are those from 49152 through 65535
```

Of greatest interest to us at present are the well-known ports. These ports are usually the ones that cover the most popular services. Examples include 20 and 21 for FTP (more on why there are two FTP ports later), 23 for Telnet, 25 for Simple Mail Transfer Protocol (SMTP), and 80 for HTTP.

It's entirely possible to run, say, an HTTP server on a port besides 80, and it does happen, but that means the client has to have a way of knowing to use that particular port instead of the well-known one. This can be done by having a link to the special port, or informing the user to use the special port.

Some services (for instance, database servers) don't have assigned ports, so the administrator of the host assigns one and the server runs on that port. The administrator can pick any port number they like. The most common choices fall into the Well Known ports range. Again, the client has to be explicitly told to connect to that port. It's traditional (and a bit of a misnomer) for unregistered servers to run in the Registered ports range. The administrator should consult the referenced IANA document to avoid picking a port that has been assigned to a particular service.

As stated earlier, client hosts need port numbers, too. Typically, the ports handed out for client use fall into the Registered Ports range, but that convention isn't quite as meaningful for clients as it is for servers. Port numbers are assigned by the operating system to avoid conflicts, either with other client programs or with services running on the client host at a particular port. (A host acting as a client can also be running waiting services, making it a server for those services, should some other client decide to connect to it. Remember, in this context the roles of client and server at the Transport layer are determined by who talks first, on a per-connection basis.)

It's fairly uncommon to see ports that fall into the Dynamic/Private ports range in use. I've typically only seen these in use when a firewall or Network Address Translation (NAT) device is used.

The last item about port number ranges has to do with UNIX security. UNIX requires root privileges in order to start a service running in the well-known ports range. Following this convention, UNIX typically chooses ports above that range for client connections. This is so the users on that UNIX host can't run services that masquerade as system services. For example, if the UNIX host weren't running a Telnet service, and users were permitted to run services on port 23, then some unsuspecting user on a client host might come along and Telnet to the server host. When presented with the name and password prompt, the user might type in their name and password, thinking they were going to be logging in to the UNIX host. In fact, they would be supplying their name and password to the malicious user who started the service on port 23.

Other operating systems don't necessarily follow the UNIX conventions and do permit user processes to be run on the low-numbered ports. Specifically, Windows and even Windows NT let any user run a service on any port, although they do follow the convention for client source ports and start at 1024.

The Three-Way Handshake

Now let's examine the process for beginning a TCP connection. A client wants to connect to a server, most often as a result of a command given by a user on the client. The client figures out the IP address of the server and the port number of the desired service, based on information supplied by the user (more details on that process later). Because TCP needs a sequence number and a port number, the client's operating system supplies one of each. The client now has all the information it needs to send the first packet.

Because this is a new connection, the client sends a special type of packet called a SYN packet, SYN being short for *synchronize*. The server responds with a SYN+ACK packet, ACK being short for *acknowledgment*. Finally, the client sends an ACK packet to acknowledge the SYN+ACK packet. This is called the *three-way TCP handshake*. At this point, the client and server are said to have a TCP connection and can exchange data.

Several things happened during this three-packet exchange. Let's take a look at an example, captured using Snoop on a Sparc 5 running Solaris 2.5.1. Snoop is a packet-capture program for Solaris. Again, I've only included the TCP portions here. Normally, Snoop will display the entire frame, including Layer 2 and 3 information.

First, here is the TCP SYN packet. We can tell this because SYN is the only flag bit that is on in the flags section. This is just the TCP portion of the packet, with the Layer 2 and IP headers and trailers stripped off. This type of packet always marks the beginning of a TCP connection.

```
TCP:  ----- TCP Header -----

TCP:

TCP:  Source port = 65445

TCP:  Destination port = 25 (SMTP)

TCP:  Sequence number = 16927230

TCP:  Acknowledgement number = 0

TCP:  Data offset = 28 bytes

TCP:  Flags = 0x02

TCP:          ..0. .... = No urgent pointer

TCP:          ...0 .... = No acknowledgement

TCP:          .... 0... = No push

TCP:          .... .0.. = No reset

TCP:          .... ..1. = Syn

TCP:          .... ...0 = No Fin

TCP:  Window = 8192

TCP:  Checksum = 0x1ef2

TCP:  Urgent pointer = 0

TCP:  Options: (8 bytes)

TCP:    - Maximum segment size = 1460 bytes

TCP:    - No operation

TCP:    - No operation
```

```
TCP:     - Option 4 (unknown - 0 bytes)

TCP:
```

Next is a SYN+ACK packet. The server returns this to the client that sent the SYN packet. By doing so, the server acknowledges that it has received the SYN packet and is listening on the port requested.

```
TCP:  ----- TCP Header -----
TCP:
TCP:  Source port = 25
TCP:  Destination port = 65445
TCP:  Sequence number = 1094177019
TCP:  Acknowledgement number = 16927231
TCP:  Data offset = 24 bytes
TCP:  Flags = 0x12
TCP:       ..0. .... = No urgent pointer
TCP:       ...1 .... = Acknowledgement
TCP:       .... 0... = No push
TCP:       .... .0.. = No reset
TCP:       .... ..1. = Syn
TCP:       .... ...0 = No Fin
TCP:  Window = 8760
TCP:  Checksum = 0x1f7d
TCP:  Urgent pointer = 0
TCP:  Options: (4 bytes)
TCP:     - Maximum segment size = 1460 bytes
TCP:
```

Finally, the client sends an ACK packet. In this case, looking at the flags alone doesn't tell us that this ACK packet is part of a TCP handshake instead of just a regular ACK. At this point, the client and server have verified each other's port numbers and agreed to exchange data using those ports.

```
TCP:  ----- TCP Header -----
TCP:
TCP:  Source port = 65445
TCP:  Destination port = 25 (SMTP)
TCP:  Sequence number = 16927231
TCP:  Acknowledgement number = 1094177020
TCP:  Data offset = 20 bytes
```

```
TCP:  Flags = 0x10
TCP:        ..0. .... = No urgent pointer
TCP:        ...1 .... = Acknowledgement
TCP:        .... 0... = No push
TCP:        .... .0.. = No reset
TCP:        .... ..0. = No Syn
TCP:        .... ...0 = No Fin
TCP:  Window = 8760
TCP:  Checksum = 0x373a
TCP:  Urgent pointer = 0
TCP:  No options
TCP:
```

exam

ⓦatch

Try to get comfortable with examining packet captures. You'll find that a number of questions on the exam will be presented in the form of a frame or packet capture, and you'll be asked to identify individual parts of the capture or identify the purpose of the packet overall. These won't be limited to IP, and the question may involve things that are covered in other sections of this book, such as Token Ring and IP together.

Examine the preceding listing carefully. The key fields here are source port, destination port, sequence number, acknowledgment number, and flags. Flags is a group of bits, and the bits are listed individually immediately below. In this example we're connecting to a mail server, so:

- The *destination port* is 25 (SMTP).

- The *source port* was assigned by the OS. These port number stay fixed during the life of the connection and, along with the IP addresses, represent this connection for both hosts.

- The client gets a *sequence number* from the OS (16927230) and sends it in a SYN packet. We know it's a SYN packet because the only flag set is SYN.

- The server responds from port 25 to port 65445 (reversed from the client's point of view) with its own sequence number (1094177019) and with an *acknowledgment number* of 16927231, which is one more than the sequence number the client originally sent.

- The server also sets both the SYN and ACK *flags,* signifying that it's both synchronizing (sending the sequence number it will be using) and acknowledging the first packet.

- Finally, the client sends an ACK to tell the server it got the reply. Notice that the acknowledgment number has increased by one (the server's sequence number previously).

We now know how TCP goes about establishing a connection. The rest of the connection continues on in this manner, with the sequence and acknowledgment numbers incrementing and the hosts ACKing each other's packets. We have achieved our reliability goals. There's only one problem: we've destroyed performance.

Sliding Window Acknowledgments

Imagine we've got two hosts connected together by a WAN link with approximately 100ms of delay. We need to send some data from one host to another, and because of the maximum frame size that will fit on the WAN link, it's going to take 50 packets to get all of the data across. If we're using TCP as we've described so far, it will take at least 200 milliseconds (ms) to send each packet—100ms for it to get there and 100ms to get back the ACK. Multiply that by 50, and we're up to 10 seconds.

Now imagine some protocol that doesn't require ACKs; it just assumes the packets get there okay and in order. This protocol could simply fire off all the packets in order. If it takes 10ms to cross the wire, then we've got 100ms of initial delay followed by 50 × 10ms, or 0.6 seconds to complete. That's quite a time difference. You're likely thinking, if TCP were really that bad, people wouldn't use it, so there must be some compromise between performance and reliability. Of course, there is: *sliding windows.*

You can't tell when looking at the handshake, but TCP has a performance-enhancing feature called *sliding window acknowledgments.* The three-way handshake waits for the response packet before sending the next one because it has to—each step can't proceed without information from the previous step. The client that sent the SYN packet can't immediately send the ACK packet, because it doesn't yet know the other side's sequence number.

In contrast, the middle part of a TCP conversation is fairly predictable. The numbers go up by the number of bytes sent each time. It stands to reason that we can fire off a number of packets all at once and assume they'll get there. If they don't, the other end won't send the matching ACKs, which we'll know about and can send the packets again. So, back to our example, we send all 50 packets at once for a total of 500ms. Then we collect all the ACKs, which may start coming back as soon as 200ms after we start, taking 500ms. Now we're in the range of 0.7 to 1.0 seconds. Not ideal, but much better than 10 seconds. How about if we could ACK a whole range of packets at once? It's a set of contiguous bytes, so we could send a single, special ACK that says "I got *n* good, ordered bytes in a row." What this amounts to is a simplified form of the TCP sliding window.

The way TCP actually works, however, is not quite as ideal. Imagine that packet number 2 of 50 received at the far end was corrupt or missing. The receiving host would be able to ACK packet number 1, and it might hold a certain number of the next few packets hoping packet 2 would eventually show up. But if the other end is busy sending over 50 packets, the host missing packet 2 will have to eventually give up waiting, throw away the packets it was saving just in case, and all it will be able to ACK is packet 1. Finally, the host sending the 50 packets will get an ACK for only the first packet and realize that it has to start over again, beginning with packet 2. The sending host would have been better off sending a fewer number of packets, letting those get ACKed, and then continuing. Based on those results, the sender might decide to send more or fewer packets before awaiting an ACK. Likewise, the receiving end has to know how many packets are going to be sent at once, so it doesn't wait around for the next packet before it sends an ACK (while the first host is waiting for the ACK before sending any more packets).

SLIDING WINDOW EXAMPLE   TCP starts with a fairly small number of packets at the beginning of a conversation, after the handshake—usually only 1 or 2, depending on the OS. The number of packets sent before an ACK is required is the *window size*. As in our theoretical example, the window size is increased if things are going well, all packets are being ACKed, and the sender isn't having to retransmit. And if the sender is having to resend often, the window size will be decreased.

Why is this concept called a window? Imagine a line of numbers, representing TCP packets:

100 101 102 103 104 105 106 107 108 109 110 111 112 113 114 115 116 117 118 119 120 121

To represent the sliding window, we'll place a box around a portion of the numbers:

100 101 102 │103 104 105│ 106 107 108 109 110 111 112 113 114 115 116 117 118 119 120 121

Our window comprises packets 103, 104, and 105.

Window sizes are actually represented in bytes, but to keep our example simple, we'll pretend the window represents an exact number of packets. In our example, this means we'll send those three packets in a row, without waiting for an ACK in between, and then wait for an ACK for some or all of them. If we receive an ACK for all of them, then we'll slide the window ahead, and repeat the process.

100 101 102 103 104 105 │106 107 108│ 109 110 111 112 113 114 115 116 117 118 119 120 121

Now our window comprises 106, 107, and 108.

The process is repeated. If packets are getting through without our having to do resends, we can increase the window size:

100 101 102 103 104 105 106 107 108 │109 110 111 112│ 113 114 115 116 117 118 119 120 121

Now our window comprises packets 109 through 112, a window size of 4 instead of 3.

It's worth noting that we never slide our window back. If a window has moved beyond a certain number, that means that packet has been ACKed, so we know it got there intact and there is never any reason to send it again.

What happens when communication isn't going well? If packets aren't making it successfully to the other end, then we don't advance the window, at least not as far; and we may shrink it, as well. Suppose we got an ACK back for packets 109 and 110, but not 111 and 112. Then our window becomes this:

100 101 102 103 104 105 106 107 108 109 110 |111 112 113| 114 115 116 117 118 119 120 121

Not only does our window slide forward only 2 packets instead of the full 4, but we've also reduced it back down from 4 packets to 3.

exam
ⓦatch

Another way to think of the sliding window is by considering how many bytes the receiving host has set aside to receive packets. Be prepared to identify window sizes in a packet capture, and to answer questions that call it the "sliding window" or "receive buffer."

We now see how TCP makes up for some of the inefficiencies created by introducing features to help ensure reliable transmission. This discussion, however, does not include some of the details, such as how transmitting hosts know when it's time to retransmit a packet, and how the window size is adjusted and coordinated between the two hosts. If you need further information on the more detailed aspects of TCP, look at RFCs 793, 813, 816, 879, 896, and 1122.

TERMINATING THE CONNECTION   Considering the steps involved in creating a TCP connection, you might also assume that finishing a TCP connection has similar steps as well, and you'd be right. With such an involved connection setup, the connection teardown must also be nontrivial. TCP's graceful close method has a sequence similar to the three-way handshake for setting up a connection.

TCP is a full-duplex communication (both ends can send and receive), and the teardown takes this into account. When one end decides that the conversation should be terminated (as determined by the specific application), that party sends a FIN packet. A FIN packet is a TCP packet with the FIN bit set on in the TCP headers. The other end will ACK the FIN packet. This essentially shuts down only half of the connection, however. The host that sends the FIN bit has indicated that it has no more data to send. At some point after that, the other host will have completed sending its data and will also send a FIN packet. The other host will ACK that FIN packet, and the connection is now marked as closed by both hosts.

There is another way to terminate a TCP connection: with an RST (reset) packet. An RST may be sent when one host needs to terminate the connection abruptly for some reason (for example, the process that owned the connection was terminated). If either host sends an RST packet, the connection is terminated immediately with no further packet exchange.

After a connection has been terminated, the host OS will track which ports and sequence numbers have been used so they are not used again in the near future. This prevents late-arriving packets from previous connections from interfering with any current connections. The tracking is accomplished by use of a timer. Typically, a host will wait a few minutes before it removes a connection from its tables. See the later section on the NETSTAT command for examples of connections being tracked after they are closed.

UDP

After examining the complexities of TCP, you might be wondering if things couldn't be a bit simpler in the world of host communications. We'll now examine the other end of the spectrum: UDP. Compared to TCP, UDP (User Datagram Protocol) imposes almost no structure on conversations between two hosts. The word *User* in User Datagram Protocol means that the user (in this case, the protocol designer) has nearly complete control over UDP's behavior, and all the responsibility for designing their own reliability features.

Like TCP, UDP has port numbers, and they are assigned in the same way by the operating system. Like TCP, UDP uses a checksum. But the similarities pretty much end there. There are no three-way handshakes, no sequence numbers, no system-imposed retransmissions, and no automatic sliding window protocol. This may seem pretty casual to you after reading about all the reasons why TCP uses all these controls, but UDP has some real advantages over TCP: speed, simplicity, and the ability to be connectionless.

Let's go over these in a little more detail. By now, the potential speed advantages are probably obvious. If you've got a very reliable Layer 2 on which to ride—perhaps a well-designed LAN—then TCP's built-in reliability mechanisms may be superfluous and may be imposing unnecessary overhead. Think back to our 50 packet transmission example: UDP can indeed fire off all 50 packets in a row, and it doesn't have to do the handshake. If the message is short, say one packet, the UDP wins hands down. TCP's handshake pretty much guarantees it's going to take several times longer. (We will clarify this with a Domain Name System, DNS, example later on.) Thus, in circumstances where the reliability features are not needed, connectionless protocols offer a performance advantage because they create less network traffic.

exam
ⓦatch

Be aware of the advantages and disadvantages of connection-oriented and connectionless protocols. Also, be aware that UDP isn't the only connectionless protocol. The exam may mix IP connectionless vs. connection-oriented characteristics with the characteristics of other protocols, such as IPX and SPX.

In addition to the speed advantages of UDP, this protocol also offers simplicity. UDP is easier to work with not only for the programmers writing the IP stack for an OS, but also for programmers who want to create programs that communicate by exchanging short messages over an IP network.

The connectionless aspects of UDP are a bit less obvious. Consider that TCP, with its synchronized sequence numbers, window sizes, etc., incurs a lot of overhead. Moreover, that connection is limited to two hosts. In fact, for TCP a connection is defined as communication between two hosts, no more, no less. What if you need to send a message to a group of hosts all at once?

Think back to your previous TCP/IP and LAN study, and remember the concepts of *broadcast* and *multicast*. The advantages of being able to broadcast are obvious. Communicating with 100 hosts via TCP means 100 handshakes, followed by 100 data packets, followed by 100 teardowns—somewhere in the neighborhood of 700 packets. This could all be done with a single UDP packet under the right circumstances. UDP, then, is especially attractive for applications where it's more important for packets to get to their destination quickly than it is to get every single packet; for example, in streaming audio or video.

Let's look at some common applications that use UDP as their transport, and the likely reasons UDP was chosen for them.

SNMP

The role of Simple Network Management Protocol (SNMP) is to manage network devices, such as routers, bridges, printers, and hosts. In essence, SNMP works by sending a short message inside a UDP packet to the device to be managed (usually said to be "running an SNMP agent"), and waits for a reply. SNMP usually works by requesting small bits of information every so often, and there are provisions for collecting the "next item" for lists and other things that don't fit neatly into one packet. This information may be requested frequently, at any desired time interval. It's fairly common to have an automated system that will poll all the network devices on a network at five-minute intervals to make sure they appear to be functioning still.

Because of the frequency of these queries, and the fact that the protocol is intended to manage network equipment, perhaps when the network is under extreme load, implementing SNMP over the TCP transport is impractical. If a host that sends SNMP queries to network devices doesn't get a response right away, it typically resends a number of times before reporting a problem.

on the
job

At a company where it was my job to manage the routers for the network, I once received a call from a user in a remote field office. His network response time was very poor. I tried to Telnet to the router for his office, and my Telnet program would simply hang for a few minutes and then finally report that it was unable to connect. This was a little puzzling because I was able to ping the router, so it appeared to be up. I loaded an SNMP management program and was able to query the router, so I knew for sure it was up. Still, I couldn't Telnet to it. I looked at a number of the available statistics from the SNMP management program and found that the router had run out of memory. It turns out that when you Telnet to a router, it has to allocate memory for buffers and so forth. This router had 0 bytes free, so it was unable to allocate even the small amount needed to establish a TCP connection. Given this information, I was able to determine that the best course of action was to reboot the router, which fixed the problem temporarily, and then schedule a software upgrade after hours. The router's current software version had a memory leak, and if I had simply rebooted the router without investigating the cause of the problem, the same problem would likely have occurred a few more times until I did figure it out. In this case, the lightweight nature of UDP was a huge advantage because the router didn't need to allocate any memory to reply to my query, and I was able to communicate with the router to determine the problem.

Another example of an application that uses UDP for simplicity and resource reasons is DNS (Domain Name System). We'll cover the details of DNS in the DNS and DNS Caching section of this chapter.

NFS

The Network File System (NFS) is one application that uses UDP for performance reasons. NFS is a way for one host to access a directory on another (typically UNIX) host. Originally designed by Sun Microsystems, NFS was later written up as an IETF standard and released as a public protocol. The full details of NFS as discussed in this chapter are located in RFC 1094. (Later RFCs cover newer versions of NFS, but this version suffices for our example.)

Since NFS's purpose is to share files, you would expect it to favor TCP and take advantage of the reliability features. As we mentioned before, however, TCP reliability comes at the price of performance. By using UDP, NFS can pass on to the client much of the work of keeping track of the transfer's progress. NFS is an especially interesting example because it takes some of the features of TCP (specifically, tracking which packets have been received and in what order) and implements them on UDP.

At this point it's useful to point out that a protocol designer could effectively reproduce all the behavior of TCP using UDP, adding in sequencing, acknowledgment, sliding windows, etc. The advantage of UDP is that the protocol designer can pick exactly the features that are needed and implement just those features. The disadvantage, of course, is that the designer must implement the chosen elements in the protocol code rather than being able to take advantage of an existing feature.

It's also worth noting under what circumstances NFS will fail. It's often been stated that NFS was designed with LANs in mind, not WANs. My personal experience is that NFS tends to fail when used across WAN lines that are heavily loaded.

NFS has a much simpler retry mechanism than TCP's. NFS will attempt to retransmit the request at fixed intervals but will give up in a relatively short period of time. Let me give an example. At the company where I work, we have a standing policy with the systems administrators that we don't officially support NFS mounts across our WAN, and we won't guarantee they will work reliably. Between two of our offices that are fairly close geographically, we had a full DS3 45MB link—in other words, a WAN line that had a lot of the performance characteristics of a LAN. The systems administrators had done some independent testing, decided they were satisfied with the performance and reliability of the link, and set up a number of more-or-less permanent NFS mounts across the link.

One day, the DS3 CSU/DSU failed at the far end. Our network had redundant links, but the backup link was only a fractional DS1 Frame Relay link that was good for about 512KB. Of course, the NFS mounts all failed; IP traffic had to be rerouted across a link with a lot more delay and not nearly as much bandwidth. The link didn't fill up entirely, but it would fill at peaks due to the burst nature of NFS. Meanwhile, the other, mostly TCP-based traffic such as HTTP, mail, FTP, and Telnet limped along rather sluggishly but fully functional. (Saying "I told you so" wouldn't help the engineers who couldn't work.)

To be fair, NFS recovers quickly when the adverse conditions are resolved, because it isn't as connection oriented as some other protocols. Also, newer versions of NFS support a TCP option for less reliable links. The protocol previously described is for versions through 2.0. Version 3.0 is already available, and I see a 4.0 in the drafts list at the IETF.

IP Broadcast and Multicast

Finally, let's talk about multicasting and broadcasting and how they work on IP networks. You'll be familiar with the class A, class B, and class C networks from previous IP study, but you may or may not have heard of class D yet.

IP multicast uses *class D network addresses*. Class D networks follow suit with As, Bs, and Cs and fix one more bit in the first octet of the address. (Specifically, binary class As always start 0xxx, class Bs always start 10xx, class Cs always start 110x, and class Ds start 1110.) This gives the class D range a starting address of 224.0.0.0 and, following convention, up through 239.255.255.255, stopping just before 240.0.0.0 (which could be called the start of the class Es). The purpose of classes E and above is currently undefined. All of these standards are documented in RFC 1112.

Like a LAN multicast, an IP multicast is intended to represent a group of hosts. Because of IP's routed nature, if a multicast packet wants to go beyond the local subnet, the router must handle it in some special way. An IP multicast is a way of representing a group of hosts with a single IP address. Since routers normally forward a single copy of a packet based on the destination address, having to forward perhaps multiple copies of a packet to a number of different interfaces represents a departure. The router must keep a separate route table in order to support multicasting, which contains a list of all IP addresses for multicasts in which the router is currently participating, along with a list of all its interfaces that must receive a forwarded copy of those packets.

As you might guess, since this sounds fairly involved, not all routers support IP multicasting. Even most of those that do have it turned off by default, and it must be enabled. For this reason, it usually takes special arrangements to do multicasting between various points on the Internet, and this is one barrier to widespread use of multicasted events. Projects are in place to work around this, such as the MBone (short for Multicast Backbone); see http://www.mbone.com.

The IP multicast information is worth researching, as it will become more popular in the not-too-distant future. Already, you'll find multicasting in use with several applications, such as routing protocols (EIGRP), Microsoft's WINS servers, RealAudio, and others. Be sure to read about the Internet Group Management Protocol or IGMP (RFC 2236), which is how hosts inform routers that they'd like to start receiving a multicast.

IP broadcasts are much simpler conceptually than multicasts. According to the official standard (RFC 919 and RFC 922), the broadcast address is 255.255.255.255 (in binary, all 1s). Standards also exist for local broadcasts such as subnet broadcasts. For a subnet 10.1.1.0 with a mask of 255.255.255.0, the subnet broadcast would be 10.1.1.255. Additional types of broadcasts have been defined, but the all-hosts broadcast and the subnet broadcast are the typical, and support for other types may be spotty by various IP stacks.

To further complicate things, some hosts originally considered 0.0.0.0 to be a broadcast, and 10.1.1.0 would often be described as "this net" and treated like a broadcast, assuming it to mean "all hosts on this net." In practice, this means most hosts will treat either all 0s or all 1s in the appropriate places as broadcasts. Cisco routers will consider either to be a broadcast. This is also the reason that the first and last IP addresses on a subnet are considered "lost" and can't be used for hosts. Routers typically won't forward broadcasts between subnets unless explicitly configured to do so, with a few exceptions (see the description of DHCP forwarding in the IP Helper Addresses section.)

A good example of a broadcast-based protocol is the Routing Information Protocol, or RIP. RFC 1058 covers RIP version 1, and other RFCs cover newer versions. Let's take a look at RIP next.

RIP

The Routing Information Protocol uses a destination of 255.255.255.255 when it broadcasts routing information on a subnet, and a destination port of UDP 520. RIP is a prime example of a protocol that wants to inform everyone at once about some information, and yet it's not critical if some hosts occasionally miss the information.

Without getting too deep into the details of RIP, what it does is send route information to all hosts on a subnet, usually every 30 seconds. Hosts receive this information and keep a copy, using this to make routing decisions for packets if they're headed off the local subnet. Different hosts have different timing for discarding information learned by RIP, but one of the most common behaviors is to hold onto routes learned by RIP for 180 seconds. Therefore, hosts have six chances across a span of three minutes to pick up the broadcast before they give up the cached route. Imagine if the router had to make TCP connections to hundreds of hosts every 30 seconds!

By the way, now that you know what multicasts and broadcasts are, it's useful to know that regular IP packets sent from a single host to a single host are called unicasts.

You've now studied the features of TCP and UDP, and the relative advantages and disadvantages of each. Understanding this information will help you to be a better troubleshooter, and will make tools such as packet analyzers more useful and meaningful to you. This knowledge becomes especially critical when dealing with security devices such as firewalls, and when working with networks under load.

ICMP

The last common protocol we'll cover in this section is ICMP, the Internet Control Message Protocol. ICMP isn't properly a transport protocol like TCP or UDP, and it doesn't fit as neatly into the OSI layers.

We've gone over several examples of problems that can occur in a TCP/IP network. So far we've discussed timeouts, retransmissions, and lack of replies as some mechanisms for indicating problems. ICMP is, however, a better mechanism for informing hosts and routers about status and errors. Strictly speaking, ICMP is a Layer 3 protocol, but you'll see that it has some of the characteristics and functionality of higher-layer protocols, as well. For practical purposes, think of ICMP as a "Layer 3 and up" protocol. There are no formal layers higher than 3, so everything is done in the data portion of the packet except for a small ICMP header. In this section we'll examine the ICMP header's 8-bit Type field, an 8-bit Code field, and a 16-bit checksum. ICMP is officially a required part of TCP/IP and is often built into the operating system or IP stack; therefore, ICMP is almost never seen as a separate daemon or process, except in certain security applications.

ICMP is used by hosts and routers to send error messages and a few other control messages to other routers and hosts. ICMP is an out-of-band information service in the sense that it relies on the same IP networks as other communications, but the messages aren't passed inside Layer 4 connections, even if they are regarding those connections. An example will help clarify.

You'll recall from the discussion of TCP connections that a client sends a SYN packet to a server at a particular port, and waits for a SYN+ACK packet in reply. When everything is going well, that's exactly what the client gets, but what if the server isn't listening on that port? What if the client requests a connection to the Telnet service, and that server isn't offering a Telnet service? One possible result is that your client could keep trying over and over again, giving up after a certain amount of time. That would certainly work, but meanwhile you'll sit there waiting to see if you'll ever connect, and continue sending meaningless packets to the server. This is where ICMP comes in.

An ICMP message type defined as "Destination Unreachable" (which has a subcode defined as "Port Unreachable") is a way for a server to inform a client that it's not listening on the requested port. Destination Unreachable is defined as ICMP type 3, and Port Unreachable is defined as code 3.

Note: A current list of the IANA official types and codes (and corresponding RFCs) can be found at the following URL:

http://www.isi.edu/in-notes/iana/assignments/icmp-parameters

Another common set of ICMP types commonly used to troubleshoot IP networks are type 8 (Echo Request) and type 0 (Echo Reply), collectively known as *ping*. Officially, ping stands for Packet Internet Groper, but that's obviously a bit contrived; it's easier remembered in the context of a ping-pong game. The Echo Request and Echo Reply were intended to be purely diagnostic. The client sends an Echo Request with some arbitrary data (usually *abcdefghi....* repeated as needed to fill in the number of bytes desired to send). The server is expected to echo the same thing back in an Echo Reply. This simple test can yield a couple of useful pieces of information. First, if you get an answer, then the server (or some host at that IP address) is alive and able to respond to ICMP. That usually means the network is at least partially functional, and the server is at least partially up. Second, it's possible to calculate how much time passed between sending the request and getting the reply.

In practical terms, on every operating system I know about, all this functionality is put into a program named ping or possibly some variant. The program ping usually operates in much the same way on any system: The user types **ping host**, and (if everything is working) some number of replies are received, usually with the time listed for the round trip.

```
router>ping www.syngress.com
Translating "www.syngress.com"...domain server (192.168.1.10) [OK]

Type escape sequence to abort.
Sending 5, 100-byte ICMP Echoes to 146.115.28.75, timeout is 2 seconds:
!!!!!
Success rate is 100 percent (5/5), round-trip min/avg/max = 76/78/80 ms
```

The foregoing is an example of a ping done from a Cisco router. Since I did the ping by name, the router did a DNS lookup. I got an answer with address back, which tells me my router can reach my DNS server. If this ping is across the Internet, it probably also means that the other site's DNS servers are working, too. The router sends five Echo Requests, waiting for a reply between each. For Cisco routers, the exclamation point represents an intact reply. The Cisco ping (like many ping programs) gives some round-trip times.

To see what kind of ICMP messages a router is processing, turn on ICMP debugging. To do so, issue the command DEBUG IP ICMP. Don't forget to type the TERMINAL MONITOR command if you are connected to the router remotely via Telnet. You must be in enable mode to debug, or to set your terminal to monitor mode. DEBUG IP ICMP will display a short message for each ICMP packet that your router sends or receives for itself. It will not display anything about ICMP messages being routed through it.

ICMP Redirects

Let's look at one more ICMP example in Figure 4-1 before we move on. Imagine a network consisting of host A on a LAN segment (network A) with two routers. Router B also has network B attached, and router C also has network C attached.

FIGURE 4-1 Host can communicate directly with multiple gateways

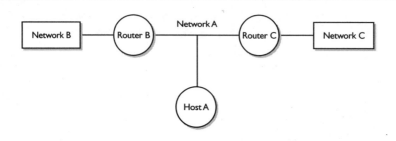

Imagine host A wants to talk to another host not on network A. Host A has two routers through which it can send a packet to reach other networks. How does it decide which router to send to? One possibility is that the host has a complete route table, and it knows which router is the best path to a particular network. This method can either be done manually or via routing protocols. Another possibility is that host A only really knows about one router and has that listed as a default gateway (more on default gateways later). Having only one gateway greatly simplifies things for the host, because it only has to determine whether the other host is on the local (directly attached) network; otherwise, host A needs to send to the (one) router.

Consider this question: If host A sends a packet destined for network C to router B, will it get there? In general, the answer is Yes. As long as routers B and C have current router tables, host A can send to networks B or C via routers B or C, and the packets will eventually get there. But, what happens when host A sends a packet to what is essentially the "wrong" router?

By their nature, routers will forward packets if they are able. That is, if the router has a route listed for the destination of the packet, and the network is functional enough for the router to send packets, it will send them. So, in our example, if host A sends a packet for network C to router B, router B will look in its routing table and send that packet to router C, which then sends it to network C. However, router B now knows that something is slightly amiss, because it just forwarded a packet onto the same network from which it was received. Based on the information router B has about network A, and where it's going to send the packet, router B can determine that host A could be sending directly to router C.

Why does router B care if host A sends packets via router B instead of directly to router C? It's less efficient. In effect, because host A isn't using the best available path, the packet ends up crossing network A twice using extra bandwidth, and adding unnecessary extra delay. Router B will still forward the packet—it's not willing to break network functionality simply because host A is uninformed—but router B will inform host A.

As router B forwards the packet to router C, it will also send an *ICMP type 5 (Redirect) packet* to host A. The Redirect packet tells host A that router B is forwarding the packet, but host A ought to send it to router C, and the Redirect gives host A the IP address for router C. Host A is supposed to take note of this information in its temporary route tables, and use the new router.

The intention of this arrangement is that routers will be better informed about the layout of the network and can inform hosts. Hosts can then start with a relatively simple view of the network, and learn as they go. This should generally mean less administration.

Unfortunately, host support of ICMP Redirects is somewhat spotty. Some hosts ignore them entirely, and some require special configuration to recognize them. Some hosts update their route tables only sporadically, and some update their tables permanently—a problem if the network routing changes. Let me give some specific examples:

- Under Sun's Solaris, you should run gated to get the host to properly receive ICMP Redirects. The gated daemon listens to ICMP Redirects and updates the route table to reflect those changes, as well as a few other functions. Unfortunately, gated may have to be added manually, may only be available with later versions of Solaris, and may cause problems with the route table. I've seen gated corrupt the route table such that manual route adds and deletes wouldn't work until the host was rebooted. In addition, gated doesn't seem to time out route entries, which is a needed function to work properly with Redirects.

■ If your host automatically adds a route as a result of one router informing it of a better route, and if that added route goes away for some reason, the host will not go back and use the original route. The host keeps trying to use the nonfunctional route until it is manually removed. There is no ICMP Redirect for a router to tell a host it *should* be using that route instead of another; there are only Redirects to tell the host it *shouldn't* be using a route. On an operating system that properly times out routes, this isn't too much of an issue. The host will eventually give up the nonfunctional route and go back to the default one.

■ Windows support, too, is spotty. Performance varies among the various Windows versions and depends on which patches and IP stack versions are in place.

In general, newer versions of the operating systems seem to be getting better at handling Redirects. You'll want to check the manuals for your OS and do some testing before you rely on this functionality. Whenever possible, I design my networks so that hosts only have one router to send to. The systems that run on dedicated router equipment (including Cisco routers) generally handle ICMP Redirects properly.

ARP Caching

So far, we've stuck mostly to Layer 3 and above protocols. Most of the work within IP takes place at those levels. At least one protocol that doesn't fall into that category, however, deserves discussion: ARP. ARP, Address Resolution Protocol, is used for mapping IP addresses to Layer 2 addresses. As such, you can think of it as being both Layer 2 and Layer 3, or as a binding between the two.

Recall from previous study in this chapter that for IP packets to be delivered, the addressing at Layer 2 has to be correct. So, for an IP stack to deliver an IP packet to the IP stack on another host, it has to determine the other host's Layer 2 address so that delivery can happen at Layer 2. The mechanism chosen for this determination is automatic mapping of IP addresses to Layer 2 addresses. This is where ARP comes in.

Somewhat like the ping exchanges, ARP exchanges consist of an ARP request and an ARP reply. The ARP request contains the IP address for which the Layer 2 address is desired, and the reply contains both the requested IP address and Layer 2 address. The requestor caches the response to avoid having to ask for it for each message sent to that host. This cached reply has an attached timer, so that it doesn't stick around forever (the reasons for which will become apparent shortly). ARP is strictly a local network protocol. A host never ARPs for an address of another host on a different subnet, but rather ARPs for the address of the router the host will be using to reach that subnet.

We'll use Ethernet for our ARP caching example. Ethernet uses 6-byte, Layer 2 addresses, usually called MAC (Media Access Control) addresses. These MAC addresses are supposed to be globally unique; that is, no two Ethernet cards in the world should have the same MAC address. ARP relies on there being a broadcast mechanism in the Layer 2 network. When one host wants the MAC address that corresponds to an IP address, the host broadcasts an ARP request packet. (This is a Layer 2 broadcast, not an IP broadcast as discussed earlier.) All hosts on the LAN segment process the broadcast. Usually, the IP stack of each host will process the packet, and determine whether its own IP address is the one being requested. If so, the requestor host's IP address is added into the processing host's own ARP cache (I'll explain why in a moment). Each processing host then builds an ARP reply and sends it back to the requesting host.

Why does the host receiving the ARP request cache the requestor's IP address? Because if it didn't, it would have to ARP for the requestor's IP in order to reply, resulting in an *ARP loop*. (Although the replying host could broadcast the reply, that host has enough information to send it directly, and broadcasts are expensive in terms of network resources. Broadcast packets have to go to all hosts and be processed by all hosts.)

Let's look at a capture of an ARP exchange. The following packet is an ARP request, indicated by the opcode number 1:

```
ETHER:    ----- Ether Header -----
ETHER:
ETHER:    Packet 4 arrived at 23:45:41.30
ETHER:    Packet size = 60 bytes
ETHER:    Destination = ff:ff:ff:ff:ff:ff, (broadcast)
ETHER:    Source      = 8:0:20:78:29:f0, Sun
ETHER:    Ethertype = 0806 (ARP)
ETHER:
ARP:      ----- ARP/RARP Frame -----
ARP:
ARP:      Hardware type = 1
ARP:      Protocol type = 0800 (IP)
ARP:      Length of hardware address = 6 bytes
ARP:      Length of protocol address = 4 bytes
ARP:      Opcode 1 (ARP Request)
ARP:      Sender's hardware address = 8:0:20:78:29:f0
ARP:      Sender's protocol address = 10.1.1.33
ARP:      Target hardware address = ?
ARP:      Target protocol address = 10.1.1.34
ARP:
```

This is an ARP reply, indicated by opcode 2:

```
ETHER:    ----- Ether Header -----
ETHER:
ETHER:    Packet 5 arrived at 23:45:41.30
ETHER:    Packet size = 42 bytes
ETHER:    Destination = 8:0:20:78:29:f0, Sun
ETHER:    Source      = 8:0:20:21:37:c3, Sun
ETHER:    Ethertype = 0806 (ARP)
ETHER:
ARP:      ----- ARP/RARP Frame -----
ARP:
ARP:      Hardware type = 1
ARP:      Protocol type = 0800 (IP)
ARP:      Length of hardware address = 6 bytes
ARP:      Length of protocol address = 4 bytes
ARP:      Opcode 2 (ARP Reply)
ARP:      Sender's hardware address = 8:0:20:21:37:c3
ARP:      Sender's protocol address = 10.1.1.34
ARP:      Target hardware address = 8:0:20:78:29:f0
ARP:      Target protocol address = 10.1.1.33
ARP:
```

There are a few interesting things to see in this ARP exchange. As I mentioned, the Layer 2 destination address on the first packet is the broadcast address. You'll also notice that the IP address and MAC addresses are in the Ethernet header as well as in the body of the packet. This is due to the protocol stack mechanism on most operating systems. Usually, lower-layer information is stripped off before it gets passed on to higher-layer handlers. This information is in the body of the ARP packet because ARPs and replies are normally handled by the IP protocol stack on an OS, and by the time the IP stack gets the body of the ARP packet, the Ethernet headers are gone.

You'll also notice that the reply is almost exactly the same as the request, except that the type has been changed from request to reply, the sender and target have been reversed, and the missing MAC address has been filled in. In addition, the reply is sent directly back to the requestor's MAC address rather than broadcast.

We've said that the ARP requestor's information must be cached so that the replying host doesn't have to ARP for the requester in order to reply. Strictly speaking an ARP packet isn't an IP packet. It has a different Ethertype for one thing, and no IP header for another. However, ARP replies are built in much the same way as a regular IP packet, in that there is apparently duplicate information within the body of the ARP packet. For example, the Ethernet MAC address is in the frame header as well as the data portion. When a packet exists in the memory of a host, there is no Layer 2 frame. Likewise, after a packet has been read from the wire, all Layer 2 information is removed and is unavailable, hence the need for the information to be repeated in the IP (or ARP) packet. The IP stack building the ARP reply relies on the ARP cache much as it does when sending a regular IP packet. This gives us a peek into the internals of IP stack management.

ARP Problems

So, ARP seems pretty simple and fairly well defined. What could go wrong?

Recall the caching mechanism. It exists so that a host doesn't have to ARP every time it wants to talk to another host. But if one host is going to send one packet, chances are good that it will want to send more, and probably soon; thus the caching is also the main problem area with ARP. If two hosts have communicated via IP recently, they each have an entry for the other in their ARP caches. They've finished their current communication, but the ARP cache entry is still there, waiting in case they need to communicate again. Often these entries stay for 15 minutes or more.

Perhaps something changes about one of the IP addresses. Maybe a host is removed and a new host is given the old host's IP address. Maybe a network card is swapped out, so that IP address now has a different MAC address. The host that has changed knows it has a new address, and whatever caused the change is also likely to have caused the other host's ARP entry to have been removed, probably because of a reboot. The host that *hasn't* changed, however, still has the ARP entry for the old MAC address. If this host tries to make a connection to the now-incorrect cached MAC address, the packet will be sent to the wrong MAC address and the other host will not get it.

How do we fix this? One choice is to just wait. Eventually the bad ARP entry will time out, and the host will ARP again and get the right information. Unlike ICMP Redirect route updates, ARP entries do time out when they are supposed to. Another solution is to go to the changed host and cause it to contact the confused host. This should cause the changed host to ARP for the confused host; at that point the confused host is supposed to update its ARP table and all should be well. Unfortunately, although most OSs are perfectly willing to cache a new ARP entry for a host that ARPed for them, they aren't always willing to replace an existing one.

The final solution is to manually flush the ARP table on any confused hosts.

ARP Commands

Most hosts have an ARP command. On many UNIX hosts and on Windows hosts, the command to *view* the ARP cache is ARP -A.

```
solaris% arp -a
Net to Media Table
Device   IP Address                 Mask          Flags   Phys Addr
------   -------------------   ---------------   -----   ---------------
le0      solaris2              255.255.255.255           08:00:20:21:37:c3
```

The command to *remove* entries is often ARP -D, but the syntax varies from OS to OS. Consult your documentation.

```
# arp -d solaris2
solaris2 (10.1.1.34) deleted
```

Note the prompt change from solaris% to #. In this case the percent sign changed to a hash or pound sign. Your prompt may vary. On most flavors of UNIX, you have to be root to modify the ARP table manually. The prompt changes to # when I switch to root on my UNIX host.

Checking the ARP table can be a useful troubleshooting step. If a host is having trouble communicating with another IP address, check to see if the ARP has happened successfully. If an ARP entry is missing where there should be one, there may be something broken at Layer 2 or below. If the ARP is there, check to see if it's correct (the right MAC address). If it's there and correct, the problem may well be at Layer 3 or above.

Proxy ARP

Before we leave the subject of ARP, let's touch on another aspect: *proxy ARP.* Proxy ARP is when one host uses its own MAC address to answer an ARP request for another host on a remote net. Normally a router would answer the request in this manner. Proxy ARP is not required functionality for IP, but it can be a useful extra under the right circumstances. On Cisco routers, proxy ARP is on by default.

As you know, hosts determine whether another host is on their same subnet using the subnet mask with which they're programmed. If the other host is within the range indicated by the subnet mask, that host must be on the same subnet, and it can be ARPed for directly. When that host is on a different subnet, the router is ARPed for instead, and the packet is sent to the router's MAC address.

What if the host has the wrong subnet mask? If the mask is too short (that is, it's set to 255.255.0.0 when it should be 255.255.255.0) the host will determine that other hosts that are actually on remote subnets are on the local subnet. The host will try to ARP for the remote host, instead of forwarding packets to the router as it should. Since the ARP wouldn't normally work under those circumstances (hosts can only ARP for other hosts in the same broadcast domain), communications will fail. However, if proxy ARP is turned on at the router, the router will answer for the remote host, and the host with the wrong subnet mask will end up adding the router's MAC address to its ARP table and forwarding the packet to the router. The net effect is comparable to the host's having the correct subnet mask, so the communications works. This can be useful when for some reason it's impractical to reconfigure the host with the correct subnet mask.

To see a Cisco router make and process ARP requests as they happen, issue the DEBUG ARP command. See the earlier "ICMP Redirects" section for information on ICMP debugging and displaying debug results remotely.

DNS and DNS Caching

Until now, we've only discussed the Domain Name System (DNS) in passing. This chapter does not cover the kind of information needed to set up and maintain a DNS server, register it with the InterNIC, and so forth, but we will discuss how it works from a client perspective, and the kinds of things that go wrong.

Briefly, DNS is a system for mapping IP addresses to names, and vice-versa. DNS contains records for other items such as mail servers, but we'll concern ourselves with address mappings here.

For the sake of simplicity and efficiency, DNS uses UDP packets. DNS clients typically need only a short answer to a short question, so UDP is ideal. Let's start by looking at a DNS packet in Figure 4-2.

Figure 4-2 is a partial screen capture of a DNS request packet as displayed by Network Associates' SnifferPro software. I like the DNS decode of the SnifferPro better than what my version of Snoop provides. The DNS request you see here is the simplest type a host can make; it asks its local DNS server to do all the work. The "Recursion desired" flag indicates that the host wants the local DNS server to contact all the other DNS servers along the way and to respond only with a final answer. It's asking for an "A" record, which is a DNS name record. It's asking for www.syngress.com, and it wants it for the Internet family. DNS is

FIGURE 4-2

DNS request packet

```
         IP: No options
         IP:
      UDP: ----- UDP Header -----
         UDP:
         UDP: Source port      = 1035
         UDP: Destination port = 53 (Domain)
         UDP: Length           = 42
         UDP: Checksum         = 081F (correct)
         UDP: [34 byte(s) of data]
         UDP:
      DNS: ----- Internet Domain Name Service header -----
         DNS:
         DNS: ID = 1
         DNS: Flags = 01
         DNS: 0... .... = Command
         DNS: .000 0... = Query
         DNS: .... ..0. = Not truncated
         DNS: .... ...1 = Recursion desired
         DNS: Flags = 0X
         DNS: ...0 .... = Non Verified data NOT acceptable
         DNS: Question count = 1, Answer count = 0
         DNS: Authority count = 0, Additional record count = 0
         DNS:
         DNS: ZONE Section
         DNS:     Name = www.syngress.com
         DNS:     Type = Host address (A,1)
         DNS:     Class = Internet (IN,1)
         DNS:
```

structured to allow for other protocols besides IP, though if it's used with others, it's not widely known.

Figure 4-3 shows the answer to this request packet. As you can see, the answer is 146.115.28.75. Other interesting items to note are

- The time-to-live (43200 seconds), which is how long a DNS caching server should consider this answer to be valid.

- The DNS servers who answer, their IP addresses, and how long that info should be cached, in case there is another query in the syngress.com domain.

What is the importance of that last piece of information (length of cache time)? I deliberately presented a simplified example of a DNS query. The local DNS server that has to do all the work has to take several steps and

FIGURE 4-3

DNS response packet

```
UDP: ----- UDP Header -----
UDP:
UDP: Source port       = 53 (Domain)
UDP: Destination port  = 1035
UDP: Length            = 150
UDP: Checksum          = 818E (correct)
UDP: [142 byte(s) of data]
UDP:
DNS: ----- Internet Domain Name Service header -----
DNS:
DNS: ID = 1
DNS: Flags = 85
DNS: 1... .... = Response
DNS: .... .1.. = Authoritative answer
DNS: .000 0... = Query
DNS: .... '..0. = Not truncated
DNS: Flags = 8X
DNS: ..0. .... = Data NOT verified
DNS: 1... .... = Recursion available
DNS: Response code = OK (0)
DNS: ...0 .... = Unicast packet
DNS: Question count = 1, Answer count = 1
DNS: Authority count = 2, Additional record count = 2
DNS:
DNS: ZONE Section
DNS:      Name = www.syngress.com
DNS:      Type = Host address (A,1)
DNS:      Class = Internet (IN,1)
DNS:
DNS: Answer section:
DNS:      Name = www.syngress.com
DNS:      Type = Host address (A,1)
DNS:      Class = Internet (IN,1)
DNS:      Time-to-live = 43200 (seconds)
DNS:      Length = 4
DNS:      Address = [146.115.28.75]
DNS:
DNS: Authority section 1:
DNS:      Name = syngress.com
DNS:      Type = Authoritative name server (NS,2)
DNS:      Class = Internet (IN,1)
DNS:      Time-to-live = 43200 (seconds)
DNS:      Length = 18
DNS:      Name server domain name = ns1.ma.ultra.net
DNS: Authority section 2:
DNS:      Name = syngress.com
DNS:      Type = Authoritative name server (NS,2)
DNS:      Class = Internet (IN,1)
DNS:      Time-to-live = 43200 (seconds)
DNS:      Length = 6
DNS:      Name server domain name = ns2.ma.ultra.net
DNS:
DNS: Additional record section 1:
DNS:      Name = ns1.ma.ultra.net
DNS:      Type = Host address (A,1)
DNS:      Class = Internet (IN,1)
DNS:      Time-to-live = 43200 (seconds)
DNS:      Length = 4
DNS:      Address = [146.115.8.17]
DNS: Additional record section 2:
DNS:      Name = ns2.ma.ultra.net
DNS:      Type = Host address (A,1)
DNS:      Class = Internet (IN,1)
DNS:      Time-to-live = 43200 (seconds)
DNS:      Length = 4
DNS:      Address = [146.115.8.18]
DNS:
```

talk to several DNS servers along the way to arrive at the final answer given. As is true of most caching, DNS caching assumes that if it was asked once for an answer, it will be asked again, so it hangs on to the answer. The name servers for syngress.com are also stored, in case another host asks for a different host in the syngress.com domain.

Read RFCs 1034 and 1035. They update other RFCs and are, themselves, updated by other RFCs. Nevertheless, they are good starting points for learning about DNS, and they list the other relevant RFCs.

Default Gateway

As discussed in our ICMP Redirect example earlier, most hosts should have a default route set if they expect to be able to communicate with hosts on other networks. When discussing routers, routing, and network paths, we usually call this a default router, but many hosts refer to this as a *default gateway.*

In terms of Layer 3 protocols, "gateway" is usually synonymous with "router," but gateway is another one of those networking terms that means many things to many people, and so its context must be clear. Normally, being "clear" means referring to a default route, but the configuration tools on many types of hosts use the default gateway term. It's important to be familiar with what this term means so that you can give the correct answer to someone over the phone who is trying to fill in the field that says "default gateway." A default gateway is simply the router that a host will use to reach another network when it has no specific information about how to reach that network. The default gateway must be on the same subnet as the host, or the host won't be able to use it.

Most of what can go wrong with default gateways on hosts has to do with misconfiguration. The gateway address may be wrong; it may not be on the same subnet as the host; or the gateway may not be functional in some way. To troubleshoot, you should check to see that the host has a default gateway listed, that it's correct, and that the host is able to ARP for it. If a host can't communicate with hosts on other subnets, but can communicate with hosts on its own subnet, then the problem is likely to be a missing or incorrect default gateway.

Default routes on routers can be a little more complicated. Unlike most hosts, a router doesn't always have a default route. It's quite common for a router connected to multiple subnets to want to learn a default route via a routing protocol, rather than having it statically entered, so that the network can reroute during a failure. Some routers interconnect portions of the Internet, and these routers have to know the path to all portions of the Internet. Given that requirement, it's not appropriate for them to have a default route at all.

When a router or host has a default route, that router/host is deferring to a router that presumably has a more complete routing table. Often this is done for simplicity's sake. For a host that can only reach one router, why should it have anything more than a default route?

Imagine a corporate network that has one Internet connection. All of the corporate routers inform each other of the subnets they control. Therefore, those routers have a complete list of the corporate nets. When one of the routers receives a packet, the packet will be destined for either a corporate net or something else. The router can consult its own complete table to determine if the packet is for the corporate net. If it's not, it must be destined for the Internet because there really isn't any other choice. So, all the corporate routers would have a default route pointing to the router that connects to the Internet. Furthermore, the easiest way to accomplish this is to manually add a default route on the Internet-connected router, and let it advertise that default to all of the other internal routers. This saves configuration time, and allows the other routers to know if that path goes away.

IP Helper Addresses

We discussed broadcasts earlier, stating that they don't usually get forwarded between subnets. There are some protocols, however, for which that arrangement would be an advantage. Specifically, the Dynamic Host Configuration Protocol (DHCP) would benefit from some centralization if the broadcasts could be forwarded. We'll get to the DHCP specifics later in this chapter, but let's touch on it briefly here in connection with *helper addresses*.

The purpose of DHCP is to allow a host to automatically obtain some IP configuration information for the subnet it's currently on. Any network or system administrator who has had to change IP information on many hosts because of a renumbering or a move between nets will appreciate the concept.

DHCP functions by sending a broadcast UDP packet (addressed to 255.255.255.255, with a source address of 0.0.0.0) asking for an address. A DHCP server responds with a similar packet containing an IP address, subnet mask, default gateway, and some other information. At that point, the host has an IP address and can function normally. Since broadcasts don't usually cross subnets, however, what if no DHCP server exists on a particular subnet? One obvious answer is to put one there—but on a network with many subnets, this doesn't scale very easily.

Many routers include a broadcast forwarding mechanism, often for the purpose of forwarding DHCP packets. On a Cisco router, this is called IP HELPER. It's an interface command, meaning it's applied while in config mode and an interface is selected. Here's the syntax:

IP HELPER-ADDRESS *a.b.c.d*

where *a.b.c.d* is the IP address to which you want broadcast packets forwarded, usually a DHCP server.

This command not only causes the broadcasts to be forwarded, it also re-addresses the packet. If the DHCP server were receiving broadcasts from many different subnets, they would look just like broadcasts on the local subnet. Also, the DHCP server wouldn't know where to send the responses, except to broadcast them back, which would again cover only the local subnet. To solve this problem, the broadcast is converted to a unicast when it is forwarded. Thus the destination address becomes the address listed in the IP helper address statement, and the source address becomes the router's primary IP address for the interface that forwarded the broadcast.

This satisfies all the requirements: When it gets the packet, the DHCP server knows which subnet's addresses to hand out, by virtue of the fact that the source address is the router for that subnet, and the DHCP server will be configured to know which addresses it can serve for that subnet. The server also knows to return the reply to the same router address. When it gets the response, the router converts the packet back into a broadcast, and the client gets its IP address.

What if there's more than one DHCP server? You can put in more than one IP helper address. The router will make a copy of the original packet for each of the addresses listed, and modify them as described in the previous two paragraphs. When the router has more than one logical subnet on that interface (that is, it's using secondary addressing), the router will only modify packets to have a source address of the primary address. In order to give out addresses for the other logical subnets, the DHCP server has to know that when it gets a request "from" the primary IP address, it can also hand out addresses in the secondary address space(s). Some DHCP servers don't do this, including the DHCP server that Microsoft ships with Windows NT 4.0.

We'll study DHCP a little more in the section "Obtaining an Address via DHCP."

CERTIFICATION OBJECTIVE 4.02

Common User Tasks

As a network troubleshooter, you'll likely spend a fair percentage of your time answering problem calls from your end-users. Many users don't understand all the steps involved in getting a DHCP address or retrieving a web page, so they often can't describe any symptom more specifically than "it doesn't work." Your job will be to ask the specific questions that give you the information you need to pinpoint and deal with the issue. We can help you with those questions, but you'll also need to develop the diplomatic skills to help you remain polite and helpful when faced with a frustrated and demanding user.

Let's go over some common user tasks, how they work, where they break, and how to fix them.

Obtaining an Address via DHCP

Many of today's operating systems have the ability to automatically obtain an address via DHCP. Examples include Windows 9x, Windows NT,

Solaris 2.6, and many others. There are many excellent reasons to consider using DHCP as a mechanism for assigning addresses, including the ability to move hosts without manually addressing them, and the ability to easily add new hosts. DHCP can help improve the accuracy of your host table as well, since any manual assignment process will invariably incur some errors.

There are also reasons *not* to use DHCP. We won't study those reasons specifically, but many will come up during our discussion, and they should be fairly self-evident.

As we discussed in the section "IP Helper Addresses," the basic purpose of DHCP is to automatically assign IP addresses to hosts. This is accomplished by a request-and-answer protocol between the client and server. Some of the details we've skipped until now include the following:

■ DHCP involves a *leasing mechanism* to ensure that the addresses distributed are eventually reclaimed

■ There is a lease renewal process

■ The initial exchange isn't as simple as we've implied

DHCP Lease Negotiation

Let's examine a packet capture of a DHCP lease negotiation. This is usually done with four packets for a new lease, and each packet represents these four steps: Discover, Offer, Request, and ACK. The following code shows the four steps needed to obtain a new lease. (The packets illustrated here were captured with Snoop.)

Here is a DHCP discover packet, the first packet a DHCP client sends. The discover packet solicits for a DHCP address. Notice that it's broadcast both at the Ethernet and IP levels.

```
ETHER:  ----- Ether Header -----
ETHER:
ETHER:  Packet 1 arrived at 17:46:37.68
ETHER:  Packet size = 342 bytes
ETHER:  Destination = ff:ff:ff:ff:ff:ff, (broadcast)
ETHER:  Source      = 0:0:65:2:68:48, Network General
ETHER:  Ethertype = 0800 (IP)
ETHER:
IP:   ----- IP Header -----
```

```
IP:
IP:     Version = 4
IP:     Header length = 20 bytes
IP:     Type of service = 0x00
IP:           xxx. .... = 0 (precedence)
IP:           ...0 .... = normal delay
IP:           .... 0... = normal throughput
IP:           .... .0.. = normal reliability
IP:     Total length = 328 bytes
IP:     Identification = 58114
IP:     Flags = 0x0
IP:           .0.. .... = may fragment
IP:           ..0. .... = last fragment
IP:     Fragment offset = 0 bytes
IP:     Time to live = 32 seconds/hops
IP:     Protocol = 17 (UDP)
IP:     Header checksum = b6a3
IP:     Source address = 0.0.0.0, OLD-BROADCAST
IP:     Destination address = 255.255.255.255, BROADCAST
IP:     No options
IP:
UDP:    ----- UDP Header -----
UDP:
UDP:    Source port = 68
UDP:    Destination port = 67 (BOOTPS)
UDP:    Length = 308
UDP:    Checksum = CD55
UDP:
DHCP: ----- Dynamic Host Configuration Protocol -----
DHCP:
DHCP: Hardware address type (htype) = 1 (Ethernet (10Mb))
DHCP: Hardware address length (hlen) = 6 octets
DHCP: Relay agent hops = 0
DHCP: Transaction ID = 0x2b852b85
DHCP: Time since boot = 0 seconds
DHCP: Flags = 0x0000
DHCP: Client address (ciaddr) = 0.0.0.0
DHCP: Your client address (yiaddr) = 0.0.0.0
DHCP: Next server address (siaddr) = 0.0.0.0
DHCP: Relay agent address (giaddr) = 0.0.0.0
DHCP: Client hardware address (chaddr) = 00:00:65:02:68:48
DHCP:
DHCP: ----- (Options) field options -----
```

```
DHCP:
DHCP: Message type = DHCPDISCOVER
DHCP: Client Identifier = 0x01000065026848 (unprintable)
DHCP: Requested IP = 10.0.0.3
DHCP: Hostname = dhcpclient
```

Next is a DHCP offer packet. This packet contains enough information for the DHCP client to function. This does not complete the DHCP transaction, though, as previously implied.

```
ETHER: ----- Ether Header -----
ETHER:
ETHER: Packet 2 arrived at 17:46:38.44
ETHER: Packet size = 372 bytes
ETHER: Destination = ff:ff:ff:ff:ff:ff, (broadcast)
ETHER: Source      = 0:c0:4f:b9:c8:b6,
ETHER: Ethertype = 0800 (IP)
ETHER:
IP:    ----- IP Header -----
IP:
IP:    Version = 4
IP:    Header length = 20 bytes
IP:    Type of service = 0x00
IP:          xxx. .... = 0 (precedence)
IP:          ...0 .... = normal delay
IP:          .... 0... = normal throughput
IP:          .... .0.. = normal reliability
IP:    Total length = 358 bytes
IP:    Identification = 57269
IP:    Flags = 0x0
IP:          .0.. .... = may fragment
IP:          ..0. .... = last fragment
IP:    Fragment offset = 0 bytes
IP:    Time to live = 128 seconds/hops
IP:    Protocol = 17 (UDP)
IP:    Header checksum = 7351
IP:    Source address = 10.0.0.170
IP:    Destination address = 255.255.255.255, BROADCAST
IP:    No options
IP:
UDP:   ----- UDP Header -----
UDP:
UDP:   Source port = 67
UDP:   Destination port = 68 (BOOTPC)
```

```
UDP:   Length = 338
UDP:   Checksum = 7ED7
UDP:
DHCP: ----- Dynamic Host Configuration Protocol -----
DHCP:
DHCP: Hardware address type (htype) =  1 (Ethernet (10Mb))
DHCP: Hardware address length (hlen) = 6 octets
DHCP: Relay agent hops = 0
DHCP: Transaction ID = 0x2b852b85
DHCP: Time since boot = 0 seconds
DHCP: Flags = 0x0000
DHCP: Client address (ciaddr) = 0.0.0.0
DHCP: Your client address (yiaddr) = 10.0.0.3
DHCP: Next server address (siaddr) = 10.0.0.170
DHCP: Relay agent address (giaddr) = 0.0.0.0
DHCP: Client hardware address (chaddr) = 00:00:65:02:68:48
DHCP:
DHCP: ----- (Options) field options -----
DHCP:
DHCP: Message type = DHCPOFFER
DHCP: Server Identifier  = 10.0.0.170
DHCP: DHCP Lease time = 300 seconds
DHCP: Lease Renewal (T1) Time = 150 seconds
DHCP: Lease Rebinding (T2) Time = 262 seconds
DHCP: Hostname = dhcpclient
DHCP: Subnet mask = 255.255.255.0
DHCP: Router at = 10.0.0.1
DHCP: DNS server at = 100.0.0.43
DHCP: DNS server at = 10.0.0.53
DHCP: DNS Domain = syngress.com.
DHCP: NetBIOS Name Server = 10.0.0.45
DHCP: NetBIOS Name Server = 10.0.0.11
DHCP: NetBIOS Node Type = Hibrid Node (8)
```

Next we see the client requesting further information, such as DNS servers and WINS servers via DHCP:

```
ETHER:  ----- Ether Header -----
ETHER:
ETHER:  Packet 3 arrived at 17:46:38.44
ETHER:  Packet size = 342 bytes
ETHER:  Destination = ff:ff:ff:ff:ff:ff, (broadcast)
ETHER:  Source      = 0:0:65:2:68:48, Network General
```

```
ETHER:  Ethertype = 0800 (IP)
ETHER:
IP:    ----- IP Header -----
IP:
IP:    Version = 4
IP:    Header length = 20 bytes
IP:    Type of service = 0x00
IP:         xxx. .... = 0 (precedence)
IP:         ...0 .... = normal delay
IP:         .... 0... = normal throughput
IP:         .... .0.. = normal reliability
IP:    Total length = 328 bytes
IP:    Identification = 58626
IP:    Flags = 0x0
IP:         .0.. .... = may fragment
IP:         ..0. .... = last fragment
IP:    Fragment offset = 0 bytes
IP:    Time to live = 32 seconds/hops
IP:    Protocol = 17 (UDP)
IP:    Header checksum = b4a3
IP:    Source address = 0.0.0.0, OLD-BROADCAST
IP:    Destination address = 255.255.255.255, BROADCAST
IP:    No options
IP:
UDP:   ----- UDP Header -----
UDP:
UDP:   Source port = 68
UDP:   Destination port = 67 (BOOTPS)
UDP:   Length = 308
UDP:   Checksum = 5225
UDP:
DHCP:  ----- Dynamic Host Configuration Protocol -----
DHCP:
DHCP: Hardware address type (htype) =  1 (Ethernet (10Mb))
DHCP: Hardware address length (hlen) = 6 octets
DHCP: Relay agent hops = 0
DHCP: Transaction ID = 0x8a858a85
DHCP: Time since boot = 0 seconds
DHCP: Flags = 0x0000
DHCP: Client address (ciaddr) = 0.0.0.0
DHCP: Your client address (yiaddr) = 0.0.0.0
DHCP: Next server address (siaddr) = 0.0.0.0
DHCP: Relay agent address (giaddr) = 0.0.0.0
DHCP: Client hardware address (chaddr) = 00:00:65:02:68:48
```

```
DHCP:
DHCP: ----- (Options) field options -----
DHCP:
DHCP: Message type = DHCPREQUEST
DHCP: Client Identifier = 0x01000065026848 (unprintable)
DHCP: Requested IP = 10.0.0.227
DHCP: Server Identifier  = 10.0.0.170
DHCP: Hostname = dhcpclient
DHCP: Requested Options:
DHCP:  1 (Subnet Mask)
DHCP:  3 (Routers)
DHCP: 15 (DNS Domain Name)
DHCP:  6 (DNS Servers)
DHCP: 44 (NetBIOS RFC 1001/1002 Name Servers)
DHCP: 46 (NetBIOS Node Type)
DHCP: 47 (NetBIOS Scope)
DHCP: Vendor-specific Options (4 total octets):
DHCP: (55) 02 octets0x0000 (unprintable)
```

Finally, we have a DHCP ACK, which answers the queries for further information. It also informs the client how long the lease is good for, and when it should be renewed.

```
ETHER:  ----- Ether Header -----
ETHER:
ETHER:  Packet 4 arrived at 17:46:38.44
ETHER:  Packet size = 372 bytes
ETHER:  Destination = ff:ff:ff:ff:ff:ff, (broadcast)
ETHER:  Source      = 0:c0:4f:b9:c8:b6
ETHER:  Ethertype = 0800 (IP)
ETHER:
IP:   ----- IP Header -----
IP:
IP:   Version = 4
IP:   Header length = 20 bytes
IP:   Type of service = 0x00
IP:         xxx. .... = 0 (precedence)
IP:         ...0 .... = normal delay
IP:         .... 0... = normal throughput
IP:         .... .0.. = normal reliability
IP:   Total length = 358 bytes
IP:   Identification = 58037
IP:   Flags = 0x0
```

```
IP:          .0.. .... = may fragment
IP:          ..0. .... = last fragment
IP:     Fragment offset = 0 bytes
IP:     Time to live = 128 seconds/hops
IP:     Protocol = 17 (UDP)
IP:     Header checksum = 7051
IP:     Source address = 10.0.0.170
IP:     Destination address = 255.255.255.255, BROADCAST
IP:     No options
IP:
UDP: ----- UDP Header -----
UDP:
UDP:    Source port = 67
UDP:    Destination port = 68 (BOOTPC)
UDP:    Length = 338
UDP:    Checksum = E5AE
UDP:
DHCP: ----- Dynamic Host Configuration Protocol -----
DHCP:
DHCP: Hardware address type (htype) =  1 (Ethernet (10Mb))
DHCP: Hardware address length (hlen) = 6 octets
DHCP: Relay agent hops = 0
DHCP: Transaction ID = 0x8a858a85
DHCP: Time since boot = 0 seconds
DHCP: Flags = 0x0000
DHCP: Client address (ciaddr) = 0.0.0.0
DHCP: Your client address (yiaddr) = 10.0.0.227
DHCP: Next server address (siaddr) = 10.0.0.170
DHCP: Relay agent address (giaddr) = 0.0.0.0
DHCP: Client hardware address (chaddr) = 00:00:65:02:68:48
DHCP:
DHCP: ----- (Options) field options -----
DHCP:
DHCP: Message type = DHCPACK
DHCP: Server Identifier  = 10.0.0.170
DHCP: DHCP Lease time = 300 seconds
DHCP: Subnet mask = 255.255.255.0
DHCP: Router at = 10.0.0.1
DHCP: DNS Domain = sybase.com.
DHCP: DNS server at = 10.0.0.43
DHCP: DNS server at = 10.0.0.53
DHCP: NetBIOS Name Server = 10.0.0.45
DHCP: NetBIOS Name Server = 10.0.0.11
```

```
DHCP: NetBIOS Node Type = Hibrid Node (8)
DHCP: Hostname = dhcpclient
DHCP: Lease Rebinding (T2) Time = 262 seconds
DHCP: Lease Renewal (T1) Time = 150 seconds
```

Lease Renewal

The main thing that makes DHCP automatic is that it hands out (that is, leases) IP addresses on a temporary basis only. When the lease for that IP address expires, the client must release it. Clients can request renewals along the way to avoid losing an address they currently have leased. If the client does not request a renewal, the DHCP recovers the address and can give it out to other clients. This way, if a client drops off the network—for example, it is retired or moves to another net—the IP address will get cleaned up automatically.

Web Page Download

As we mentioned at the beginning of the chapter, the Web has been one of the factors driving the growth of the Internet, and hence the growth of TCP/IP. The protocol that is normally used to transfer web pages is the Hypertext Transfer Protocol (HTTP) which runs on TCP port 80 by default.

Let's look at what happens behinds the scenes when you type an address into your web browser.

DNS Resolution

If you type in a name instead of an address, then obviously your host has to perform a *DNS lookup*. We've studied the DNS protocol already, but there is one twist with HTTP servers that we'll examine at the end of this section: It's called *virtual servers*. For now, it's sufficient to say that your browser obtains an IP address and starts a TCP connection.

TCP Session Setup per HTML Object

A typical web page consists of several objects. There is the main HTML code that defines the layout of the page, the appearance of the text, and possibly the look of graphics and other nontext items. What might not be obvious is that each of those objects is transferred (downloaded) separately to the page.

First, the browser transfers the HTML code, because this code tells the browser what other objects to transfer, such as pictures. Then, the browser downloads all of the objects and displays them in the page. In some cases, the page will be drawn only partially on the screen because the browser can't always determine picture size ahead of time and, consequently, how much space it will take up on the screen. After all of the objects have been transferred, the browser declares the page "complete."

HTTP File Transfer

The HTTP protocol itself is relatively simple—at least, in its earliest versions. There are only a few commands, such as GET and POST. HTTP's fundamental purpose in life is to transfer files, and to inform the client what type of file is transferred. HTTP takes advantage of an existing standard to indicate file type: the Multipurpose Internet Mail Extensions (MIME) type. We don't want to delve into all of the details of HTTP here, but let's look at how to make a simple HTTP request, and observe an HTML transfer.

We start with a TELNET command:

```
telnet www.syngress.com 80
```

The 80 at the end of the TELNET command tells it to use port 80 instead of the default 23. This syntax for the command works the same on UNIX and Windows.

At some point, you'll connect, and your Telnet client will just sit there, not displaying anything. Carefully type the following:

```
GET / HTTP/1.0
```

and press ENTER twice. This will not echo on your screen. The results will be the HTML code for that site displayed on your screen, followed immediately by a disconnection. Most HTTP servers will respond to the GET command syntax shown just above.

This technique is useful if you think a browser program might be misbehaving. If you get HTML code back, you know the server is working at least partially. Using TELNET in this manner, to connect to other TCP servers besides Telnet, can be a useful troubleshooting tool.

Multiple Downloads in Parallel

You might wonder, if HTTP transfers one object at a time, isn't that inefficient? It can be. We know that the overhead for TCP can be significant, especially if the amount of information to transfer is small. So, for a web page with many small graphics objects that need to be transferred individually, you pay a fair amount of overhead. It's not as bad as it might be, though. Web browsers are capable of performing transfers *in parallel,* so that after the HTML page is transferred, it can open up a number of simultaneous HTTP connections to grab all the needed objects. This doesn't eliminate the TCP overhead, but it's much faster than if the browser did the transfer serially, waiting for one object to finish before beginning the next.

The next version of HTTP, 1.1, addresses this issue with *persistent connections.* Basically, with a newer browser and newer HTTP server, the various objects can be transferred over one TCP connection. As of the writing of this book, the standards for persistent connections haven't been widely implemented. Check http://www.w3c.org for news on the standard, and watch for upgrades to your favorite browser to support this feature.

Virtual Servers

HTTP has a feature that many other protocols don't: a limited degree of independence from the requirement for different IP addresses to run different versions of the same service. For example, if you wanted to run a number of Telnet servers, each with different prompts, but still keeping them on the standard port 23, you'd probably have to have a different IP address for each server. There just isn't any way (other than having the user pick from a menu) for a server to tell which Telnet version the client is going to want when it connects.

HTTP clients do have a way of telling the server which web page they want, and they do it by default. Starting with version 2.0 of both the Netscape and Microsoft browsers, support has been provided for *virtual servers* (also called virtual hosts or virtual domains). With virtual servers, a number of different web sites can be run on the same IP address (and hence, on the same server). This allows for discrete sites that can still be centralized on fewer servers. Virtual servers are normally transparent to the person doing the browsing, because the browsers send the full URL in each request, which includes the name of the server as typed in by the user. So, if the user types www.domaina.com, the server sees this and serves up web pages for Domain A. When the server sees www.domainb.com, it serves up those pages. Both Domain A and Domain B would resolve to the same IP address.

If you're curious whether a site is hosted on a virtual server, type the IP address into the browser instead of the name. Because the server isn't given a name, it will have to serve up some default page. If you get the same page as you do when using the name, then either that site is the only one on that server, or it's the default page.

Tip: A quick way to get the address for a DNS name is to ping it. Most ping programs report the address for the name being pinged.

FTP Transfer

Next, we'll examine the File Transfer Protocol. FTP is another of those technical acronyms that has become a verb. You'll typically hear people asking you to "FTP a file," and almost never "Use the FTP protocol to transfer a file."

FTP is one of the oldest Internet protocols and has roots in previous networks. It's fairly complex, partly because of limitations on the networks it came from, and partly because of the number of functions it encompasses. FTP handles authentication, simple data translation, security, and various transfer modes.

Authentication and Setup on One Channel, Callback on Another

In the IANA assigned numbers document we referenced in the earlier section on port numbers, FTP has two numbers assigned to it:

```
ftp-data          20/tcp    File Transfer [Default Data]
ftp-data          20/udp    File Transfer [Default Data]
```

```
ftp              21/tcp    File Transfer [Control]
ftp              21/udp    File Transfer [Control]
```

Specifically, port 21 is called the *control port*, and port 20 is called the *data port*. Like many protocols, TCP and UDP ports are assigned together, although standard FTP doesn't use UDP.

The control port is conceptually simple, though the protocol details can be complex. Read RFC 959 for the details on data representation, and so on. Basically, when a client initiates a connection to an FTP server's control port, the server wants the client to be authenticated (i.e., give a username and password). Then the client can issue commands to get a file, send a file, view a directory, and a number of others. All of this takes place over the connection to port 21, similarly to a Telnet connection. In fact, the protocol used to communicate over the control connection is a subset of Telnet.

When a file is to be transferred, the FTP protocol starts to look a little different from the others we've seen so far.

Passive vs. Active FTP

FTP doesn't transfer files over the same connection that it first uses, as HTTP does. FTP requires that a separate connection be set up to transfer the file.

In what's called the "normal," or "active" mode of FTP, the "client" host is required to open a port over which to communicate, and listen for the "server" to connect. The terms client and server are in quotes here because the roles are reversed. The user will still tend to think of the FTP server as being the host that they contact; but in active mode, the file transfer requires the user's host to act as a server. Typically, once a single file has been transferred, the connection closes.

Port 20 (ftp-data) is used as a source port by the FTP server to connect to the user's host. The FTP server has to know which port to connect to on the user's host, so the client FTP program sends its IP address and port number it has allocated to the server before the file request.

In the other FTP mode, passive, the party listening for the file transfer is reversed. The client program issues a PASV command, and the server is expected to respond with its IP address and the port number that will be listening for the data connection.

CERTIFICATION OBJECTIVE 4.03

Common Problems and Fixes

We've explored a number of techniques for troubleshooting problems throughout this chapter. In this section we'll add some additional methods, reiterate (briefly) the ones we've already covered, and look at how to decide which technique to use.

As a network administrator, many times you'll be asked to work on a "network problem." Most networking professionals would probably consider these network problems to be those occurring in Layers 1 through 3. This includes things like dead hubs, broken wires, and down routers. Depending on how your responsibilities are divided, you may or may not be responsible for the higher layers; or your duties may depend on the hosts in question (maybe you're responsible for the servers but not the clients.)

In any case, it doesn't actually matter. As soon as someone has identified the problem as having to do with the network, whether they're correct or not, it's usually up to the network administrator to fix it or to prove that it's *not* a network problem. Both of those solutions usually require your being able to troubleshoot problems beyond the network itself. We won't be explaining everything you need to be a full-time systems administrator, but we'll show you some utility programs that will come in handy to troubleshoot network or network related issues on hosts.

Splitting the Problem in Half

As a troubleshooter, your job is to solve the problem as quickly as possible. Usually the best way to do so is to divide the problem into pieces, pick the most likely pieces to check, check them, and repeat the process until you've (hopefully) narrowed things down to the component at fault.

And don't forget to undo changes that you try out as potential fixes. If it didn't fix it, put it back—or else you may have created another problem.

Ping Test

Probably the shortest test that tells you the most is ping. We've already covered this command, so here's a brief review. Pinging a host by name tests

DNS and Layers 1 and 2 on the path between the two hosts; verifies that packets are passing between the two hosts; and gives a rough measurement of delay and whether packets are being dropped. If the ping works—if the name resolves to the correct IP address, the round-trip times seem reasonable, and no packets were dropped—then you've determined that the difficulty probably isn't a network problem as defined earlier.

One possible exception to this result is that another host has the original host's IP address. Don't forget to consider that the connection may be fine between your host and the one that's supposedly having problems, but it may not be fine from the user's host. You may have to visit the user, or have them perform the test and report the results to you.

If ping reports problems, then you can research those specific problems. If the DNS name doesn't resolve properly or at all, then you know to verify that the host table on the DNS server is correct, and check connectivity between the client and the DNS server. It's fairly common for users to report a particular server as down when it's actually a broken DNS server. If DNS breaks, most of the IP network will be unusable, since so much depends on DNS names being correctly resolved to IP addresses. If the reported symptom is a matter of slow or inconsistent response time, or dropped packets, or no response at all, it may be Layer 1 or 2 that's broken.

If you get no response at all to your ping, and the host being pinged is on another subnet, verify that you can ping the local router.

Oftentimes ping will respond directly with your answer—in the form of "Destination unreachable" messages. If you get a response that router x.x.x.x claims that destination y.y.y.y isn't reachable, you know you've lost a subnet or the router to it. For example:

```
solaris% ping 10.2.2.2
ICMP Host Unreachable from gateway default-router (10.1.1.254)
 for icmp from solaris (10.1.1.1) to 10.2.2.2
```

Packet-Level Debugging

We'll look at one very detailed debugging technique while we're in the neighborhood of Layer 3. *But watch out—this command can cause your router to go down.* So, you'll want to read this section completely before trying any of its procedures.

IOS includes a command, DEBUG IP PACKET, that will display summary information about each packet as it is routed through the router. There are a few circumstances where this type of debugging will be necessary.

Why is this command dangerous? A lot of information can be generated by this command, even on a very lightly loaded router. When working with packet-level debugging, you'll likely be either Telnetted in, or on the actual console of the router. If you're on the router console, probably at 9600 baud, the serial line will be too slow to keep up, and the console will become so backed up that you won't be able to turn off debugging. If you're monitoring via Telnet, the packets for your Telnet connection will be debugged as well. The number of packets being debugged will snowball, and your router will max out trying to keep up with itself.

There's a way around this bottleneck problem: You can apply an access list when using the DEBUG IP PACKET command to limit what kinds of packets you debug. You should be somewhat familiar with Cisco access lists from previous study. Let's refresh your memory. Cisco uses access lists, or things that look like access lists, in many of their IOS features. Access lists and their equivalents are used for operations such as policy-based routing, encryption, and debugging. We'll be focusing on traditional permit- or deny-access lists, much like the ones you would use to permit or block certain kinds of traffic.

For example, let's say you want to allow only a particular IP address to send packets to your router. The IP address is 10.0.0.10. You could create an access list like the following:

```
access-list 110 permit ip host 10.0.0.10 any
access-list 110 deny ip any any
```

You would then apply the access list inbound on the interface for that subnet. This would allow traffic in from address 10.0.0.10, but not from others.

Something to look for when troubleshooting is whether an access list is denying the traffic you want to pass. Access lists are easy to get wrong, so this isn't all that uncommon. Access lists can get you into trouble just as DEBUG IP PACKET can. If you have an access list applied to the interface over which you're Telnetting, you might want to remove the access list from that interface before changing it. After working with access lists extensively for several years, I still manage to lock myself out of a router now and then. When the router is remote and you have no choice but to Telnet in, make sure you have a working configuration saved as the startup-config so that someone at the other end can turn the router off and then back on in case of problems.

DEBUG IP PACKET can also use the same type of access lists to keep you from killing your router when debugging. The syntax is as follows:

```
DEBUG IP PACKET <access list number 1-199>
```

In our example, the command would be

```
debug ip packet 110
```

So, instead of seeing all packets passing through the router, we only see packets from 10.0.0.10. This not only keeps us from killing the router, but also makes it so we don't have to wade through all the other information we might not want.

When might you want to use this command? IP routers work mostly by knowing where to send packets, and they generally aren't concerned with a packet's source. On large private networks, you sometimes see packets from a source address that really doesn't belong on that network. If a network for that source address doesn't exist in the routing tables, then there's no easy way to see where the packet came from originally.

Unfortunately, the only way to track this is to go router-by-router and use the DEBUG IP PACKET command. The command also shows you what interface a packet came into, so you can go back through all the routers until you find the network location that is the source of these packets. For this to work, the packets have to keep passing through periodically, or they won't show up on the debug. So, you'd set up an access list to match the source address(es) in question, and use DEBUG IP PACKET. Once you identify the interface that carried the packet, you repeat the process on any routers that might be directly reachable via that interface.

What can cause this type of situation? I've seen this happen a few times where an outside trainer came on-site to conduct training. Rather than coordinating in advance with the networking personnel, the trainer unwisely just used IP addresses from the outside site.

Troubleshooting Lower Layers

Other sections of this book show you how to troubleshoot Layer 1 and 2 problems, so we won't cover that here. What you do need to bear in mind is the mapping between Layers 2 and 3: ARP. If ARP isn't working properly, then not much else will. The easiest way to check is to examine the ARP table. This was explained in the earlier section, "ARP Caching."

One Layer 2 tool that might help with troubleshooting problems between two Cisco devices is the Cisco Discovery Protocol (CDP). CDP is a proprietary Layer 2 protocol used by Cisco equipment such as routers and switches, to exchange information about themselves. Assuming CDP is turned on (as it is by default), a Cisco device will send CDP packets out through each of its interfaces, and the packets will be received by any other Cisco devices that are on the same network segment as the sending device. The receiving devices keep a table of the information that is contained in the frames. Let's take a look at a portion of the CDP table on a Cisco router:

```
Router1>show cdp neighbors detail
-----------------------
Device ID: router2.domain.com
Entry address(es):
  IP address: 10.0.0.12
  Appletalk address: 9000.127
Platform: cisco 7000,  Capabilities: Router
Interface: Fddi4/0,  Port ID (outgoing port): Fddi3/0
Holdtime : 122 sec

Version :
Cisco Internetwork Operating System Software
IOS (tm) GS Software (GS7-K-M), Version 10.3(12), RELEASE SOFTWARE (fc1)
Copyright (c) 1986-1996 by cisco Systems, Inc.
Compiled Mon 03-Jun-96 12:59 by dschwart
```

There's a lot of useful information in this listing, which can be particularly useful if you can't get two Cisco devices to talk. You can use the SHOW CDP NEIGHBORS DETAIL command on one of the devices, and if you can find the other device in the table, you know things are most likely working correctly up through Layer 2.

Also, notice that Layer 3 addresses and names are available—very useful when troubleshooting a Layer 3 problem, especially if you don't have access to the Cisco device at the other end of a connection. One example of such a situation would be connecting to a new Internet Service Provider (ISP). On a number of occasions, I've worked with an ISP that didn't quite configure things the way they said they would. When they were using a Cisco router, I could look at the CDP table and determine if the link was working through Layer 2, and verify their IP address.

Transport and Above

Once you've been able to eliminate Layers 1 through 3 as the problem, the next thing to focus on is the higher layers, starting with the Transport layer. Suppose you get a complaint that someone can't connect to a server. One of the simplest tests you can do is to ask the user what service they're trying, and then try to connect to that service yourself. You may not even need the client program if the service is TCP.

We already looked at how to check a web server using TELNET. The same works for FTP, SMTP and many others. You just need the port number, and you've got the URL for the IANA document where they're listed. You may not always get a text response, but nearly all Telnet programs will report whether or not they were able to connect. If they connected successfully, then the server was listening on that port, and it completed the three-way handshake.

UDP is a little harder to check, because many UDP servers won't respond at all unless they get a properly formatted request—and besides, there's no standard UDP "telnet" program.

The NETSTAT Command

There's a more direct way to check UDP, though, and that's the NETSTAT command. If you have access to a command prompt on the host in question, many of them include a NETSTAT command. In particular,

```
netstat -a
```

will usually list the open ports. Here's the output of NETSTAT -A on a Windows 98 host. This NETSTAT -AN version of the command simply displays the results without DNS (that is, numeric) names.

```
C:\test>netstat -an

Active Connections

  Proto  Local Address          Foreign Address        State
  TCP    0.0.0.0:1599           0.0.0.0:0              LISTENING
  TCP    0.0.0.0:1600           0.0.0.0:0              LISTENING
  TCP    0.0.0.0:1601           0.0.0.0:0              LISTENING
  TCP    0.0.0.0:1602           0.0.0.0:0              LISTENING
  TCP    0.0.0.0:1603           0.0.0.0:0              LISTENING
  TCP    0.0.0.0:1479           0.0.0.0:0              LISTENING
  TCP    0.0.0.0:1023           0.0.0.0:0              LISTENING
  TCP    0.0.0.0:1023           0.0.0.0:0              LISTENING
  TCP    10.0.0.3:1599          146.115.28.75:80       CLOSE_WAIT
  TCP    10.0.0.3:1600          146.115.28.75:80       CLOSE_WAIT
  TCP    10.0.0.3:1601          146.115.28.75:80       CLOSE_WAIT
  TCP    10.0.0.3:1602          146.115.28.75:80       CLOSE_WAIT
  TCP    10.0.0.3:1603          146.115.28.75:80       CLOSE_WAIT
  TCP    10.0.0.3:137           0.0.0.0:0              LISTENING
  TCP    10.0.0.3:138           0.0.0.0:0              LISTENING
  TCP    10.0.0.3:139           0.0.0.0:0              LISTENING
  TCP    10.0.0.3:1479          10.1.1.11:1352         ESTABLISHED
  UDP    0.0.0.0:1023           *:*
  UDP    10.0.0.3:137           *:*
  UDP    10.0.0.3:138           *:*
```

In the output just shown, the ports marked as LISTENING are the ones to which this host is waiting to connect. A number of the LISTENING ports actually aren't, and we know that because we can see they had been used as source ports to connect to a web server (146.115.28.75:80). That they are marked as LISTENING is probably just a quirk of how NETSTAT reports things on this OS. The ports that are actually listening are TCP 137, 138, and 139, and UDP 137, 138, and 1023.

It's also interesting to note how the OS tracks connections that have been closed, in case it gets a stray packet from an old communication. They're marked CLOSE_WAIT, meaning they're waiting for a timer to expire so they can be taken out of the table. We can also infer that the web page at issue here had four objects in addition to the main HTML page, because there were five connections to it.

NETSTAT is also available on most versions of UNIX.

There are other NETSTAT options worth exploring, as well, including NETSTAT -R, which is often equivalent to the command ROUTE PRINT. Both commands cause the host's route table to be displayed.

The command to display the route table on a Cisco router is SHOW IP ROUTE.

QUESTIONS AND ANSWERS

I want to be able to add or move hosts without having to change their IP addresses.	You can't avoid changing their IP addresses if they move to a different subnet, but you can make the process automatic with DHCP.
One host can't seem to communicate with any other hosts on any subnets.	This is most likely a Layer 1 or 2 problem. If the ARP table is empty, check the cables, check link lights, etc.
I can ping hosts on the same subnet as my host, but not on other subnets.	There are two likely causes: Either bad routing information (missing or wrong default gateway), or the subnet mask is wrong (trying to ARP directly instead of using default gateway).
I have two routers on my subnet. Which do I pick as the default gateway?	It doesn't really matter. If they both have complete routing tables, your packets will always get where they are supposed to go. Consider checking to see if your host can run a routing protocol, or be configured to accept ICMP redirects to improve its routing information.
My host can't get an address via DHCP.	There are many things that might be broken in this scenario. First, check to see if other hosts on that same subnet can get DHCP addresses. If not, check the router forwarding or DHCP server. If other hosts can get the DHCP addresses, check the cables, the NIC, etc. If possible, swap cables with a working host and see if the problem follows the host or the cable.
I can't retrieve a web page from a remote web server.	Ping it. If it doesn't respond, troubleshoot it as a Layer 3 problem, possibly using TRACEROUTE. If the ping works, TELNET to port 80 and issue a GET command. If you get HTML back, check the settings on your browser software.
When I TELNET to a TCP port to test if the server is listening on that port, I get "connection refused."	The server isn't listening on that port, or is configured to refuse connections from your IP address. If you get back a refusal right away instead of having to wait a few minutes for a timeout, it is almost certainly a server problem and not a network problem. The exception would be some sort of firewalling.

CERTIFICATION SUMMARY

TCP/IP is the most widely used protocol family today. It is the set of protocols that make up the Internet, which is the largest collection of networks in existence. The standards that define the TCP/IP suite are created mostly by the IETF and are documented in RFCs.

TCP/IP can be described in terms of the OSI layered model. The IP portion is a Layer 3 protocol, and TCP and UDP are Layer 4 protocols. Other protocols in the TCP/IP suite don't map as neatly into the OSI model. These include ARP, which is a Layer 2 protocol that maps addresses between Layer 2 and Layer 3; and ICMP, a Layer 3 protocol with some Layer 4 characteristics.

In the client-server communications model, the roles of client and server are determined by who initiates the connection. The server is the host that is waiting for a connection, and the client is the host that sends the initial packet.

TCP/IP uses two common transport protocols, TCP and UDP. TCP is considered to be a reliable transport, and handles lost, out-of-order, and mangled packets. UDP is considered an unreliable transport protocol, and the application protocol designer must add any necessary reliability features.

To differentiate among the various services that a server may be offering, the concept of a port is used. A port is a number value in the range 0 through 65535, decimal. Ports are used in both TCP and UDP applications. In addition, clients use port numbers, so that if multiple simultaneous communications occur between the same client and server hosts, the hosts can tell which is which. A TCP communication between two hosts is called a connection.

The IANA is the authority in charge of assigning port (and other) numbers for the Internet. The IANA has declared ports in the 0 through 1023 range as well-known ports, 1024 through 49151 as Registered ports, and 49152 through 65535 as Dynamic or Private ports. On UNIX, only root can start a service that listens on ports in the well-known ports range.

TCP has an initiation phase known as the three-way handshake. The first packet (from the client to the server) is called a SYN packet. The second packet (from the server to the client) is called a SYN+ACK packet. The third packet is a regular ACK, and after that the connection is considered established. This handshake is necessary for hosts to exchange sequence numbers. TCP also ensures that all packets are received, by acknowledging them. Any lost packets won't be acknowledged and will be resent. TCP also has a teardown phase that consists of a FIN packet, followed by an ACK (from the other host) for each host. Alternatively, the connection may be reset with a RST packet.

UDP is preferred for applications that are performance sensitive, need to be simple, or need to do broadcasting or multicasting.

Broadcasting and multicasting under IP are handled by use of special addresses. Addresses for full broadcast would be the all-1s address (255.255.255.255) and the all-0s broadcast (0.0.0.0). IP also includes the concept of directed broadcast or subnet broadcast, in which the host portion of a network address is all 1s or all 0s. For example, for network 10.1.1.0 with a subnet mask of 255.255.255.0, the subnet broadcasts would be 10.1.1.255 and 10.1.1.0. IP also includes provisions for multicasting, a way to send packets to an arbitrary group of hosts. This is accomplished by use of a special set of IP addresses in the range 224.0.0.0 through 239.255.255.255. Routers handle these multicasts through special routing protocols, and hosts join multicast groups by use of the IGMP protocol.

ICMP is used to send control or error messages between routers and hosts. Some of these messages are useful for troubleshooting, including the Echo Request and Echo Reply messages, usually implemented as a ping program. Others are used to save time under error conditions, such as the Destination Unreachable messages. Others, such as the ICMP Redirect, are used to correct bad information.

Hosts typically implement various forms of caching, including ARP caching and DNS caching. This is to prevent having to look up the same information over and over again, especially if it's likely to be needed again immediately. Caching generally only causes problems when something has changed on the network, and the cached information is no longer correct. Most caching mechanisms have timeout facilities to discard stored information; if it's needed again later, it will be requested again. This will eventually purge the bad information being cached. One example of cached information that doesn't always time out properly is the route information learned from ICMP redirects.

DHCP is a protocol used by hosts to automatically obtain an IP address. It employs a leasing and renewal mechanism to reclaim IP addresses that are no longer in use. Since DHCP clients start out with no IP address, they use broadcast addresses to make DHCP requests. If there is no DHCP server on the local subnet, routers can be configured to convert the broadcast into a unicast and forward it to a DHCP server. DHCP clients, if they are still using the IP address they were given, will periodically renew the lease with the DHCP server.

DNS is a UDP-based protocol for resolving mappings between IP addresses and DNS names. Client hosts typically issue DNS requests to servers, which the servers will resolve and then send the answer back to the client. This form of DNS uses UDP because the requests are fairly simple, and the entire query or answer typically fits in one packet. This allows for easy implementation and quick response.

HTTP is the protocol most often used to transfer web pages and related files. HTTP is TCP-based because it needs all of the reliability features of TCP. The HTML for the main web page and each object within the page are transferred via a separate TCP connection in the current version of HTTP (1.0). HTTP is a fairly simple file transfer protocol that sends or receives files and identifies their file type by indicating a MIME type.

The FTP file transfer protocol has been around for many years. It includes provisions for authentication (including anonymous access), security, limited file conversion, and multiple transfer modes. FTP is TCP-based; it uses one connection for passing commands (the control channel), and a separate one for passing data (the data channel). In active mode, FTP expects the "client" host to act as a server and wait for a connection. In passive mode, the server is expected to wait for the data connection. In both cases, the data port is communicated across the control channel by passing the IP address and port number of the host that will act as server for the data connection.

The best strategy for troubleshooting a problem is to divide it up into pieces, perform a test that will steer you toward one of the pieces, check that piece, and repeat as needed. One test that checks many things quickly is the ping test. Other tests include checking whether a port is listening, whether the routing tables are correct, and whether or not the router has a path to the destination.

More information is available at the following web sites:

- **http://www.ietf.org** This is the web site for the Internet Engineering Task Force, the group that defines most of the standard for the Internet. Here, you can find information on IETF Working Groups, join mailing lists, get meeting schedules, see draft standards, and more.

- **http://www.iana.org** The Internet Assigned Numbers Authority is a group dedicated to the business of coordinating functions of the Internet. They are also responsible for assigning various Internet related numbers, such as the Well Known ports.

- **http://www.internic.net** The InterNIC is responsible for a number of root DNS domains, notably .COM, .NET, and .EDU.

- **http://www.cis.ohio-state.edu/hypertext/information/rfc.html** One of the many sites on the Web that contains copies of the RFCs. This archive is particularly nice because they've added some search functions, as well as a couple of specialized groupings of RFCs.

 ## TWO-MINUTE DRILL

- ❑ TCP/IP is the fundamental Internet protocol, and its use has increased dramatically in the last several years.

- ❑ Two other protocols that are essential to most TCP/IP network installations are the User Datagram Protocol (UDP) and the Internet Control Message Protocol (ICMP).

- ❑ *Sequencing* simply means that a number is attached to each packet.

- ❑ *Checksumming* refers to an algorithm called a checksum that is applied to a set of bytes.

- ❑ Try to get comfortable with examining packet captures. You'll find that a number of questions on the exam will be presented in the form of a frame or packet capture, and you'll be asked to identify individual parts of the capture or identify the purpose of the packet overall. These won't be limited to IP, and the question may involve things that are covered in other sections of this book, such as Token Ring and IP together.

❑ TCP has a performance-enhancing feature called *sliding window acknowledgments.*

❑ Another way to think of the sliding window is by considering how many bytes the receiving host has set aside to receive packets. Be prepared to identify window sizes in a packet capture, and to answer questions that call it the "sliding window" or "receive buffer."

❑ Compared to TCP, UDP (User Datagram Protocol) imposes almost no structure on conversations between two hosts.

❑ Like TCP, UDP has port numbers, and they are assigned in the same way by the operating system.

❑ Like TCP, UDP uses a checksum.

❑ UDP has no three-way handshakes, no sequence numbers, no system-imposed retransmissions, and no automatic sliding window protocol.

❑ Be aware of the advantages and disadvantages of connection-oriented and connectionless protocols. Also, be aware that UDP isn't the only connectionless protocol. The exam may mix IP connectionless vs. connection-oriented characteristics with the characteristics of other protocols, such as IPX and SPX.

❑ In addition to the speed advantages of UDP, this protocol also offers simplicity.

❑ The role of Simple Network Management Protocol (SNMP) is to manage network devices, such as routers, bridges, printers, and hosts.

❑ The Network File System (NFS) is one application that uses UDP for performance reasons.

❑ IP multicast uses class D network addresses.

❑ IP broadcasts are much simpler conceptually than multicasts.

❑ RIP is a prime example of a protocol that wants to inform everyone at once about some information, and yet it's not critical if some hosts occasionally miss the information.

❑ ICMP is a better mechanism for informing hosts and routers about status and errors.

❑ ICMP is used by hosts and routers to send error messages and a few other control messages to other routers and hosts.

❑ ARP, Address Resolution Protocol, is used for mapping IP addresses to Layer 2 addresses.

❑ Somewhat like the ping exchanges, ARP exchanges consist of an ARP request and an ARP reply.

❑ DNS is a system for mapping IP addresses to names, and vice-versa.

❑ DNS clients typically need only a short answer to a short question, so UDP is ideal.

❑ Most hosts should have a default route set if they expect to be able to communicate with hosts on other networks; this is referred to as a *default gateway*.

❑ The purpose of DHCP is to allow a host to automatically obtain some IP configuration information for the subnet it's currently on.

❑ As a network troubleshooter, you'll likely spend a fair percentage of your time answering problem calls from your end-users.

❑ There are many excellent reasons to consider using DHCP as a mechanism for assigning addresses, including the ability to move hosts without manually addressing them, and the ability to easily add new hosts.

❑ The protocol that is normally used to transfer web pages is the Hypertext Transfer Protocol (HTTP) which runs on TCP port 80 by default.

❑ FTP handles authentication, simple data translation, security, and various transfer modes.

❑ Usually the best way to troubleshoot is to divide the problem into pieces, pick the most likely pieces to check, check them, and repeat the process until you've (hopefully) narrowed things down to the component at fault.

❑ Don't forget to undo changes that you try out as potential fixes.

❑ Probably the shortest test that tells you the most is ping.

❑ IOS includes a command, DEBUG IP PACKET, that will display summary information about each packet as it is routed through the router. *But watch out—this command can cause your router to go down.*

❑ What you do need to bear in mind is the mapping between Layers 2 and 3: ARP. If ARP isn't working properly, then not much else will.

❑ Once you've been able to eliminate Layers 1 through 3 as the problem, the next thing to focus on is the higher layers, starting with the Transport layer.

SELF TEST

The following Self Test questions will help you measure your understanding of the material presented in this chapter. Read all the choices carefully, as there may be more than one correct answer. Choose all correct answers for each question.

1. Which of the following is a transport protocol?

   A. IP

   B. ICMP

   C. UDP

   D. ARP

2. What is the purpose of ARP?

   A. To map ports to IP addresses

   B. To connect TCP to IP

   C. To broadcast IP addresses

   D. To map Layer 2 addresses to Layer 3 addresses

3. Which of the following programs can be used to connect to many TCP-based services?

   A. Ping

   B. FTP

   C. Telnet

   D. NETSTAT

4. Which range is known as the Well Known ports?

   A. 0 through 1023

   B. 0 through 1024

   C. 1024 through 49151

   D. 49152 through 65535

5. To what IP address does a DHCP client send when requesting a new address?

   A. 0.0.0.0

   B. 10.0.0.1

   C. 127.0.0.1

   D. 255.255.255.255

6. IP multicast is associated with which IP class?

   A. Class A, 1–126

   B. Class B, 128–191

   C. Class C, 192–223

   D. Class D, 224–239

7. When an FTP client opens a port for the FTP server to connect to, this is called:

   A. Active mode

   B. Passive mode

   C. Control channel

   D. Data channel

8. Which is the correct sequence for a TCP three-way handshake?

   A. SYN, ACK, FIN

   B. SYN, SYN+ACK, FIN

   C. SYN, SYN+ACK, ACK

   D. SYN, SYN, ACK

9. IP operates at which OSI layer?

    A. 2

    B. 3

    C. 4

    D. 7

10. If a host can communicate with other hosts on its own subnet, but not with hosts on other subnets, what is a likely cause?

    A. Something is broken at Layer 1 or 2

    B. The router is malfunctioning

    C. The default gateway is not set

    D. DNS isn't working

11. Which commands will display a route table on a host? (Select two.)

    A. NETSTAT -R

    B. ARP -A

    C. TRACEROUTE

    D. ROUTE PRINT

12. Which command displays the route table on a Cisco router?

    A. NETSTAT -R

    B. ROUTE PRINT

    C. SHOW IP ROUTE

    D. SHOW ROUTE

13. Describe the function of the DEBUG IP ICMP command:

    A. To send broadcast ICMP packets from the router to all hosts

    B. To determine if the router is sending and receiving ICMP messages itself

    C. To allow routing of ICMP debugging messages

    D. To cause the router to send diagnostic information via ICMP

14. If a host can communicate with some hosts and not others on its local and on remote subnets, a likely cause is:

    A. Incorrect subnet mask

    B. Misconfigured router

    C. Partial network failure

    D. Bad ARP table

15. Which of the following is a characteristic of a connectionless protocol such as UDP?

    A. Lost packets are retransmitted

    B. There is less network traffic

    C. Port numbers are used to differentiate communications

    D. Packets are delivered in the correct order

16. Which of the following is a routing protocol (used to exchange routes between routers)?

    A. ARP

    B. ICMP

    C. IGMP

    D. RIP

17. Which command is used to display ARP information as the router processes it?

    A. SHOW IP ARP

    B. DEBUG ARP

    C. SHOW ARP

    D. DEBUG IP ARP

18. Which command is probably the best one to use when starting to debug a host-to-host IP networking problem?

    A. PING

    B. ARP

    C. TRACEROUTE

    D. NETSTAT

19. What does the DEBUG IP PACKET command do?

    A. Causes a copy of each packet to be sent to another interface for monitoring by a protocol analyzer

    B. Causes the router to display information about each packet as it is routed

    C. Causes the router to send an ICMP message for each packet received

    D. None of the above

20. What is the command used to configure a Cisco router to forward DHCP broadcasts?

    A. DHCP FORWARD

    B. BOOTP FORWARD

    C. IP FORWARD

    D. IP HELPER

5

Novell's Internetwork Packet Exchange (IPX) Protocol

CERTIFICATION OBJECTIVES

I PX/SPX is the standard communications protocol for Novell networks, just as TCP/IP is the standard protocol for UNIX networks. This chapter covers the fundamental concepts of IPX/SPX, including the various protocols that it uses, common user tasks, routing protocols, and troubleshooting techniques for fixing many associated problems.

CERTIFICATION OBJECTIVE 5.01

IPX Protocol Suite

The Internetwork Packet Exchange (IPX) suite of protocols evolved from the Xerox Network Systems (XNS) Internetwork Datagram Protocol (IDP). IPX was developed by Xerox around the same time it developed Ethernet, with the intention that every network host would be using Ethernet. Novell expanded the IPX protocol suite to handle the requirements of its network operating system, Novell NetWare, enhancing IPX to include numerous services and support for topologies other than Ethernet. Novell NetWare has progressed through several iterations and gained widespread success with the release of NetWare 3.11; even today it is still widely used. From NetWare 2.*xx* to the advent of NetWare 4 and the introduction of NetWare Directory Services, IPX has remained the default communications protocol. With the newly released NetWare 5, Novell has joined the ranks of TCP/IP-based network operating systems, but IPX has such a widespread user base that it will still be around for quite some time.

IPX

Internetwork Packet Exchange (IPX) is a Layer 3 transport protocol used for routing data across a network. This protocol is most commonly used in Novell NetWare networks, and is the default protocol for Novell workstation-to-server and server-to-server communications. The IPX protocol is connectionless, and very similar in nature to the Internet Protocol (IP) side of TCP/IP. Since this protocol is connectionless, there is no guarantee that a packet is delivered, and packets can arrive in any order;

an application using IPX as its transport must have its own method of guaranteeing delivery. Figure 5-1 shows how IPX falls into the OSI model.

IPX is a datagram-based network protocol. When an application sends information to the IPX layer for transmission, the data is encapsulated in an IPX datagram, then sent to the Data Link layer to be handled by the network Interface Card (NIC) driver. The Data Link layer then encapsulates the datagram in an Ethernet packet for broadcast on the network.

Let's step back for a minute and look at IPX from a conceptual view. We will first look at how IPX devices are addressed on an Internetwork. IPX network addresses are 12 bytes (24 hex digits) long and consist of three parts: a network number, a node number (or host address), and a socket number (see Figure 5-2). The usual format for denoting IPX addresses is to separate the fields with a colon. For example, the IPX address of a workstation on network 55 with MAC address 0080C7560D2D would be 0000055:0080C7560D2D. The socket number is dropped when referring to the host itself.

FIGURE 5-1   How IPX fits into the OSI model

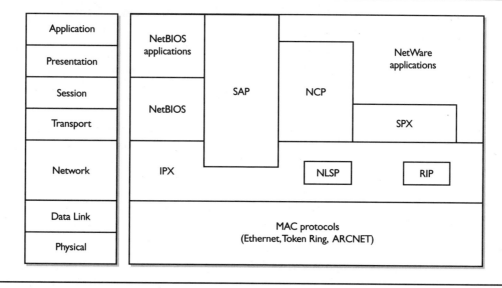

IPX network numbers are 8-digit hex numbers (00000001 to FFFFFFFD) that represent a single cable segment. This number is assigned by an administrator, and it groups together workstations, servers, and devices on a single physical network.

Node numbers are 12-digit hex numbers that uniquely identify a host on the network. This number is usually the Media Access Control (MAC) address of the Ethernet network interface card (NIC) that physically connects the device to the network. This MAC address can be manually assigned in some instances, but is usually derived from the hardware address assigned to the NIC by the manufacturer.

Sockets (ports) are 4-digit hex numbers that identify the source or destination process that generates the packet (such as IPX RIP).

Cisco routers use a slightly different format for enumerating Novell IPX addresses. Cisco designates an IPX network address in the following format:

- Network address, followed by a period
- First four node address hex digits, followed by a period
- Second four network node hex digits, followed by a period
- Last four network node hex digits

The Cisco form of the example in Figure 5-2 would be 00000055.0080.C756.0D2D.

IPX network addresses that identify a network segment are referred to as *IPX external network numbers. Internal network numbers* are used to define a logical network internally within a Novell server. Although you can have multiple servers on the same network sharing a common external network number, each Novell server on an internetwork must have a unique internal network number. This number is used by the server for internal routing of data; it was implemented with NetWare 3.*xx* to handle routing problems

---

FIGURE 5-2

IPX network address format

00000055	0080C7560D2D	0x451
Network Number 8 bytes	Node Number 12 bytes	Socket 4 bytes

associated with having servers connected to multiple networks. Both the internal and external network numbers are assigned to each server during installation by the administrator. Figure 5-3 shows how these numbers are implemented.

Viewing IPX information

The starting point in troubleshooting IPX networks is to ensure that the server and router interfaces are configured correctly. To get the IPX interface configuration on a Cisco router, Telnet to the router and type

```
show ipx interface
```

at the command prompt. This command gives the interface name, the IPX network address, and various settings and statistics.

To view IPX network settings on a Novell server, type

```
config
```

at the system console prompt. This command produces the file server name, the IPX internal network number, and the protocol bindings for the Ethernet interface (including node address, frame type, IPX network number, and so on), as well as the name of the NDS Tree (discussed later), and the Bindery Context.

FIGURE 5-3   Two Novell servers on the same physical network

IPX network number 00000123

Novell Server CORP_1
Network number 00000123
Internal network number 0000012A

Novell Server CORP_2
Network number 00000123
Internal network number 0000012B

Ethernet Frame Types

Frame types are important to the IPX networking model. Ethernet frames are the method in which the data is encapsulated for transmission on the physical media. Each media type (Ethernet, Token Ring, FDDI, and so on) has its own unique framing structures. In an Ethernet environment, IPX supports four frame types:

Ethernet 802.3	Default frame type for Novell 2.*xx*/3.*xx* networks; supports IPX/SPX only. This is the default frame type for NetWare 3.11.
Ethernet II	Supports IPX/SPX, TCP/IP, and AppleTalk Phase I.
Ethernet SNAP	Supports IPX/SPX, TCP/IP, and AppleTalk Phase II.
Ethernet 802.2	Default frame type for Novell 4.*xx* networks, supports IPX/SPX and OSI/GOSIP. This is the default frame type for NetWare 3.12 and above.

Frame types are an important and somewhat unique concept with IPX/SPX networking because they cause problems not typically encountered with other protocols. When you work with Novell networks, frame types are a common issue. The choice of frame type for your network depends upon the network requirements. Ethernet 802.3 is the default for older Novell networks, and as long as IPX/SPX is the only protocol running on your network, 802.3 will work fine. If you need any other protocols running on your network, however, you will have to use different or additional frame types to support those protocols (Ethernet II and Ethernet SNAP are the only two Ethernet frame types that support TCP/IP and AppleTalk).

Let's take an example where you have a Novell server running IPX/SPX and TCP/IP. You can choose to have both protocols using the Ethernet II frame type, or you can use both, having IPX/SPX use Ethernet 802.3 and TCP/IP use Ethernet II. Which choice should you make? There are no hard rules for making this decision, but employing additional frame types means using additional memory on the file server or router. If server memory is not an issue (and these days it often isn't, with memory prices dropping), it boils down to administrator preference.

Novell servers support up to four frame types per network interface, and each frame type is assigned its own unique IPX network address. If you have a Novell server and you load the network interface card (NIC) driver three times, each time you load the driver you must select a different frame type. When you assign an IPX network number to the network card (referred to as *binding*), you must choose a unique network number for each frame type. A single Ethernet NIC can have up to four frame types assigned to it at a time with a unique network address assigned to each frame type. Figure 5-4 shows a Novell server with multiple frame types loaded; each frame type has its own unique network number.

In Figure 5-4, the server has a single network card, and a single internal network number. However, since four frame types have been assigned to this NIC, it has four separate external IPX network numbers associated with it, one for each frame type.

For a workstation and a server to communicate on the same physical network, they must share a common frame type. Figure 5-5 illustrates that a client configured to use one frame type for IPX will not be able to communicate with a server configured to use a different frame type.

On the other hand, when a router connects two networks, a workstation and server can communicate as long as the appropriate frame type has been assigned on each interface of the router. Figure 5-6 illustrates how this works. The client using an 802.3 frame type transmits the packet; the router interface for that network has also been configured to support 802.3 frame type. The router receives the packet, extracts the IPX datagram, then re-encapsulates it in an Ethernet 802.2 frame type and transmits it on the

---

FIGURE 5-4

Novell server with multiple frame types loaded

Frame Type:	Network Number
Ethernet 802.3	00000555
Ethernet 802.2	00000444
Ethernet II	00000333
Ethernet SNAP	00000222

Novell Server
Internal network number 00000001

FIGURE 5-5   A single IPX network with client and server having different frame types

| Novell Client
Ethernet 802.3 only
frame type assigned | NO COMMUNICATION | Novell 4.xx Server
Ethernet 802.2 only
frame type assigned |

network connected to Interface 2. The server, which has been configured with an 802.2 frame type, receives the packet and extracts the datagram.

Consider a scenario with three servers in the following configuration:

CORP1: IPX Network 55 Frame type 802.3
CORP2: IPX Network 44 Frame type 802.2
CORP3: IPX Network 55 Frame type 802.3

How many router interfaces would be required to connect the three servers? Answer: Two. CORP1 and CORP3 have the same network number and frame type—they are on the same network. Network 55 requires one router interface using an 802.3 frame type, and network 44 requires one interface using an 802.2 frame type.

FIGURE 5-6   Different client and server frame types with a connecting router (two IPX networks)

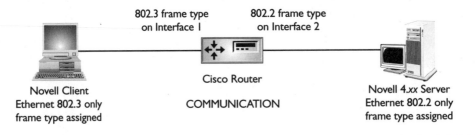

802.3 frame type
on Interface 1

802.2 frame type
on Interface 2

Cisco Router

| Novell Client
Ethernet 802.3 only
frame type assigned | COMMUNICATION | Novell 4.xx Server
Ethernet 802.2 only
frame type assigned |

On Cisco routers, the following Ethernet encapsulation type codes are used when assigning frame types to an interface:

novell-ether	Ethernet 802.3
arpa	Ethernet II
sap	Ethernet 802.2
snap	Ethernet SNAP

Figure 5-6 brings up an important question: if you have a large internetwork consisting of many separate networks connected by routers, how will devices know how to reach the remote networks? The answer is that IPX has its own routing protocols. These routing protocols provide a method for routers and servers on the network to inform their remote neighbors how to reach them. IPX implements two routing protocols, IPX RIP and NLSP. Both of these protocols will be discussed in more detail in this chapter.

SPX

Sequenced Packet Exchange (SPX) is a Layer 4 transport protocol used for providing reliable connections in a Novell environment. Connection-oriented SPX is similar in nature to the Transmission Control Protocol (TCP) Layer 4 protocol of the TCP/IP stack.

SPX uses IPX as the transport protocol but offers a method for sequencing packets and guaranteeing delivery. This protocol gives applications a method for reliable delivery without having to provide one of their own. Using SPX is similar to sending letters through the postal system with a receipt requested. SPX receives data from the applications, fragments it, and passes it to the IPX layer for transmissions as datagrams. IPX in turn passes the datagrams to the Data Link layer for encapsulation into frames and transmission. On the receiving side, the frame is received by the Data Link layer, which in turn extracts the datagram and passes it to the IPX layer. The IPX layer then passes the information to the SPX layer, which reassembles the packets as they arrive and arranges for retransmission in the event any packets are lost.

Think of SPX as a set of executive assistants to two company Vice Presidents (the "applications"). A VP at one location gives Assistant 1 a stack of documents to deliver. Assistant 1 records all the documents received, sorts them, and sends them to the mail room for delivery. The mail room personnel, which correspond to the IPX layer, in turn put documents into numerous envelopes and pass them to the mail delivery system (the Data Link layer). Figure 5-7 illustrates this metaphor for the three layers (SPX, IPX, and Data Link).

When the mail truck arrives at Location 2, the mail carrier removes the letters from the delivery bag and hands the envelopes to the mail room at that location. The mail room then takes the envelopes, removes the documents, and passes them to the executive Assistant 2. The assistant takes the documents, sorts them, and realizes from the numbering that one of the documents is missing. The assistant then runs down to the mail room and gives the staff a receipt noting that all documents but one were received. The mail room puts the receipt in an envelope and gives it to the next delivery truck that comes in. The mail carrier then delivers the mail message back to Location 1. The receipt makes it back up the chain to Assistant 1, who reprints the missing document and sends it back to the mail room for delivery.

FIGURE 5-7

The SPX mail delivery example

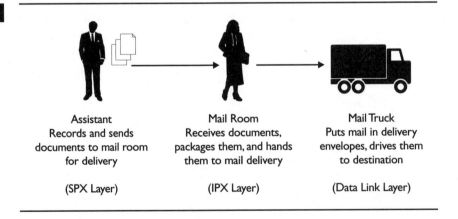

Assistant	Mail Room	Mail Truck
Records and sends documents to mail room for delivery	Receives documents, packages them, and hands them to mail delivery	Puts mail in delivery envelopes, drives them to destination
(SPX Layer)	(IPX Layer)	(Data Link Layer)

The preceding example is very simplified, but it illustrates the model of the guaranteed delivery system. If the VPs relied only upon the mail room to deliver the mail, they would have no way of knowing if the documents were received in their entirety, or received at all for that matter. Applications requiring guaranteed delivery can rely on this Novell built-in delivery system for reliable communications.

Two common scenarios in which the SPX transport is used are

- Print server-to-file server communications (a print server is a device pulling print jobs from a print queue, discussed later in this chapter)

- Modem pooling (workstation-to-modem pooling device)

There are currently two versions of SPX: SPX and SPX II.

SPX and SPX II

SPX II was released in 1992 to address some of the weaknesses of SPX. SPX supports only one outstanding packet at a time; a second packet cannot be transmitted until acknowledgment of the first is received (a positive acknowledgment must be sent to the sender by the receiver). SPX II, on the other hand, allows for multiple packets to be transmitted before a positive acknowledgment is received. If the receiver gets a series of packets and realizes that one of the sequence is missing, a negative acknowledgment (NACK) is sent to the sender. This is known as *windowing* and allows for more efficient delivery of packets by eliminating the one-to-one acknowledgment for transmitted packets.

SPX II also provides for larger packets. Standard SPX supports only a 576-byte packet, but SPX II is limited only by the maximum packet size allowed by the network type being used (such as Ethernet or Token Ring packet size). SPX II was written to be backwards compatible with SPX, and a device using SPX II will revert to standard SPX in order to communicate with a device running the older version of SPX.

Comparing IPX, SPX, and SPX II

The following figures show the difference in the reliable delivery mechanisms of IPX, SPX, and SPX II. IPX (Figure 5-8) is connectionless;

FIGURE 5-8

IPX delivery alone
(no ACK)

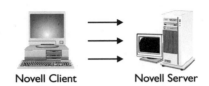

Novell Client   Novell Server

Packets sent, no acknowledgment returned

the packets are simply sent, and upper-layer protocols are expected to provide guaranteed delivery if they require it. SPX (Figure 5-9) still uses IPX to transport the packets, but it fragments a packet, in addition, and returns it to IPX for transmission. Then SPX waits for an acknowledgment before sending the next packet. SPX II (Figure 5-10) also uses IPX, but sends a series of packets and then waits for an acknowledgment from the receiver at the end of the transmission.

NCP

NetWare Core Protocols (NCP) are a set of server routines used for performing application requests. This is essentially the "language" that clients and servers speak among themselves for sending requests for action and then generating a response to those requests. The client generates an NCP request (for printing or file access, for example). The server performs some action and then answers with an NCP reply. NCP is used for virtually all operations between clients and servers, including

FIGURE 5-9

SPX delivery (one packet,
one ACK)

Packet

ACK

Novell Client   Novell Server

Packet sent, acknowledgment returned

FIGURE 5-10

SPX II delivery (multiple
packets, one ACK)

Packets

ACK

Novell Client   Novell Server

Multiple packets sent, single acknowledgment returned

establishing a connection, reading and writing files, setting file attributes, printing, and so forth.

Let's take a quick look at how NCP works. In Figure 5-11, a Novell client PC makes a request of the server. The request generates an NCP packet which is sent to the server; this *NCP request* is one of numerous Novell-defined function calls. For each action that can be requested by a client, there is an established *NCP function request code.* For each reaction that can be generated by a server, there is an established *NCP function reply code* that is sent to the workstation. When the server receives an NCP request, the server performs some corresponding action and generates an NCP reply to alert the client of the results of its request.

A very common example of NCP is a workstation booting up and attempting to connect to a file server. The workstation sends an NCP Create Service Request to the file server, and it answers with an NCP Create Service Reply.

Within the NCP packet itself, a function code must be included to identify the type of request being made, along with any parameters being

FIGURE 5-11

NCP client request
followed by an NCP
server reply

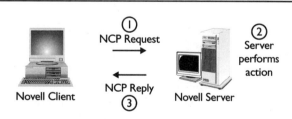

① NCP Request

② Server performs action

NCP Reply ③

Novell Client   Novell Server

passed to that NCP function. Novell has published a directory with the list of functions and their associated codes.

NCP Doesn't Use SPX

NCP uses IPX, not SPX, as its transport. Remember that IPX has no mechanism for guaranteed delivery—so does that mean NCP is an unreliable method for communicating? The answer is no. To ensure reliable delivery, NCP implements its own method of guaranteed delivery. The NCP delivery method is similar to SPX in that there is a one-to-one acknowledgment required for every packet sent. When an NCP read request is generated, a single packet is transmitted, and then an acknowledgment must be received before the next packet is sent.

LIP

Large Internet Packet (LIP) was developed to address a problem of packet size constraints between client workstations and servers. In early releases of the client software, when a client negotiated packet size between itself and the server, the client would set it to the maximum size allowable between the two. However, if a router were detected between the two (the *hop count* was one or greater), the client would automatically drop its packet size to a maximum of 576 bytes for communications to that server. LIP is a remedy for this limitation; the client software allows for the maximum negotiated size, regardless of whether there are routers between the workstation and the server. Larger packets translate into faster communications. Figure 5-12 shows a scenario where LIP greatly improves performance.

Packet Burst

Packet burst is designed to allow multiple packets to be transmitted between Novell clients and servers in response to a single read or write request. Packet burst uses NCP connections to transfer data. NCP alone typically requires an acknowledgment for each packet sent, and packet burst technology allows NCP connections to greatly improve throughput by

FIGURE 5-12	Packet size negotiation between client and server with and without LIP

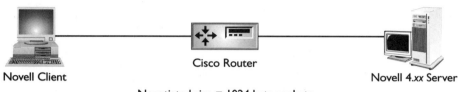

Novell Client   Cisco Router   Novell 4.*xx* Server

Negotiated size = 1024 byte packets
Before LIP: The maximum packet size is 576 bytes
Using LIP: The maximum packet size is 1024 bytes

reducing the number of acknowledgments. Figure 5-13 shows NCP communications *without* packet burst.

There is overhead in this method because it requires continuous two-way communications between the client and server for transmissions. Figure 5-14 shows how communications occur *with* packet burst technology.

Packet burst is a *dynamic window* method of transmitting, which means the number of packets that can be transmitted in the burst window is not statically set. The size of the windows is calculated as (Maximum Reads × Packet Size) for read bursts, and (Maximum Writes × Packet Size) for write bursts. The setting for packet size is negotiated between the client and server upon startup, and the maximum number of reads and writes is an option configured on the client. Older implementations of packet burst have a limitation of 16-burst read packets and 10-burst write packets, but there is no such limit on the newer implementations.

FIGURE 5-13	

NCP communications without packet burst

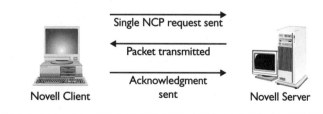

Single NCP request sent →

← Packet transmitted

Acknowledgment sent →

Novell Client   Novell Server

FIGURE 5-14

FIGURE 5-14

NCP communications with
packet burst

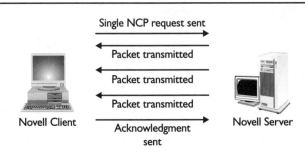

Single NCP request sent

Packet transmitted

Packet transmitted

Packet transmitted

Novell Client   Acknowledgment   Novell Server
                          sent

The packets do not have to be received in order, because the packet burst
component of the client software will sort and assemble them. When the
server has sent all the packets, it then sends an end of transmission flag, and
the client in turn generates an acknowledgment. If any packets were lost,
the client includes them in this acknowledgment, and the server retransmits
them. This continues until all packets are delivered.

IPX NetBIOS

NetBIOS is a Session layer interface specification developed by IBM and
Microsoft. This interface provides for a naming schema on the network that
gives each node a unique network name. NetBIOS is used to provide
connection-oriented sessions over lower-layer protocols such as NetBEUI,
TCP/IP, and IPX. Figure 5-15 shows three NT workstations running
NetBIOS over IPX.

With NetBIOS, each station periodically broadcasts its name on the
network. When a group of NetBIOS-based computers are brought together
on a network, an election occurs. One station is elected a *master browser*,
which means it has the responsibility of listening to all the NetBIOS
broadcasts on the network and storing their information. As you might
imagine, this protocol generates heavy broadcast traffic, and in large
networks the broadcasting can become a problem. We will discuss shortly
how this broadcasting load can be controlled.

FIGURE 5-15

An IPX network
using NetBIOS

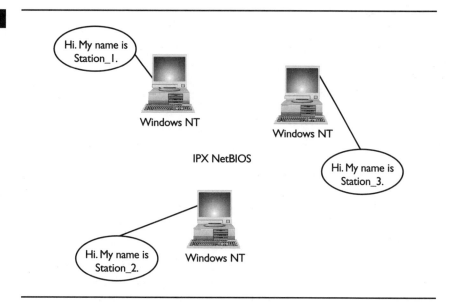

Mixing IPX NetBIOS Encapsulations

NetBIOS is not specific to IPX; it can also be implemented using TCP/IP
and NetBEUI as the transport protocol. How do you think a workstation
and a server would communicate if the workstation were configured to use
TCP/IP and the server is running IPX/SPX? How would the
communication be affected by putting a router between the two?

The answer to the first question is that they would not communicate at
all, because NetBIOS implementations are protocol specific. In essence, the
workstation and server are thinking the same but not speaking the same
language. A client using NetBIOS over TCP/IP will not be able to
communicate with a server configured to use NetBIOS over IPX, as shown
in Figure 5-16.

The answer to the second question is that a router will have no impact at
all on the communications in this scenario. This is not a frame-type issue,
where a router will pull the datagram from the frame on one interface and
re-encapsulate it on another. The router performs no conversions at the

FIGURE 5-16   NetBIOS using two different transport protocols

NT Workstation
running NetBIOS
over TCP/IP

NO COMMUNICATION

NT Server
running NetBIOS
over IPX

protocol level, so there would be no communication between the
workstation and server even if a router connected them.

Cisco routers and Novell NetWare servers support forwarding of IPX
NetBIOS packets. In early implementations of IPX on Novell servers,
NetBIOS packets were supported, but there was no mechanism for
controlling the flow of the packets, and heavy broadcasting by IPX
NetBIOS nodes was a problem. When the IPX upgrade was released for
NetWare servers, new packet type 20 was created for IPX NetBIOS packets.

When viewing IPX NetBIOS packet traces, IPX headers have 0x14 (hex
for 20) in the packet type field, and the destination socket will be 0x455.
The type 20 assignment for packets allows administrators to selectively filter
IPX packets by type; routers can be configured to drop or selectively
forward IPX NetBIOS packets. NetBIOS propagation is limited to 8 hops
across Novell routers.

Novell Control of NetBIOS Forwarding

NetBIOS forwarding is handled on Novell servers in one of three ways,
based upon a server console setting. The following command controls
NetBIOS forwarding on a Novell server:

SET IPX NETBIOS REPLICATION OPTION = [0|1|2|3]

From the Novell server console prompt, you can control the flow of
NetBIOS packets through the Novell routing engine. The settings have the
following impact on NetBIOS routing:

0	Drops all NetBIOS packets (effectively disables NetBIOS routing)
I	Receives NetBIOS packets and propagates them through all interfaces
2	Packets are forwarded using two general rules: (1) A server will not propagate a NetBIOS packet through the same interface on which the server receives (a.k.a. *split-horizon*); and (2) If a server receives a packet through different interfaces from the same source, the server drops all packets after the first (a.k.a. *reverse path forwarding*)
3	Same as method 2, but does not propagate across WAN links

Cisco Control of IPX NetBIOS Broadcasting

By using the ipx type-20-propagation setting on an interface, you can enable IPX NetBIOS forwarding. Since NetBIOS can generate a considerable amount of broadcast traffic, Cisco provides a method for controlling IPX-broadcast packet flow. IPX NetBIOS propagation can be controlled by the use of the ipx helper-address and the ipx helper-list interface commands.

The ipx helper-list sets a list of attributes that packets must meet before they are forwarded through a particular interface. The syntax of the command is

IPX HELPER-LIST *access-list-number*

where *access-list-number* is the hexadecimal value for an access list.

The other mechanism is the ipx helper-address, which uses the syntax

IPX HELPER-ADDRESS *net.host*

where *net.host* is the IPX network address of the host. When the router receives broadcasts that match the access list defined by the helper list, it forwards them to the host specified by the helper address. To specify that IPX NetBIOS packets should be flooded (sent out all interfaces), you can specify the helper address for an interface to be –1.FFFF.FFFF.FFFF

RIP

IPX Routing Information Protocol (RIP) was an early but prevalent routing protocol for IPX networks. This protocol allows routers in an IPX network to automatically exchange routing information about a network. RIP is a *distance-vector protocol,* which means it is based upon the Bellman-Ford algorithm. This algorithm, in a nutshell, uses the number of hops in a route to find the shortest route. IPX RIP uses a slightly different metric, *ticks,* but the mechanics of the protocol are essentially the same. Each router on the network broadcasts its entire routing table, but only to its directly connected neighbors. The neighbors then process the information and pass it on to their neighbors, and so on.

IPX RIP maintains two metrics for remote networks and uses these settings to make routing decisions.

- The first setting is a *tick,* which is the amount of time it takes a packet to reach another network segment. A tick is 1/18 second, and routes that take the fewest ticks are used to forward packets.

- In the event that two routes take the same amount of ticks, the second setting, *hops,* is the tie breaker; the route with the least hops is used. Hops are the number of routers that a packet must cross to reach the destination network. Fifteen is the maximum number of hops in an IPX network using RIP; a hop count of 16 denotes the route is unreachable.

Figure 5-17 shows a network using IPX RIP as the routing protocol.

If RIP broadcasts its entire routing table to its neighbors, why in the example are only two networks being broadcast out on network 999 by both CORP1 and CORP2? It might seem that the servers should broadcast, from all interfaces, all four networks that the servers know about. But doing so can cause problems.

In the Figure 5-17 example, if CORP2 receives information about network 123 (on the interface connected to network 999) from CORP1, and if CORP2 then broadcasts that information back through the same interface to CORP1, you will have a problem. CORP1 will then receive the information and think it can reach network 123 through server CORP2, except with a higher tick and hop count. CORP1 would now have two entries for network 123 in its RIP table, one showing it as a local interface and a second entry with a route through CORP2. Should the CORP1

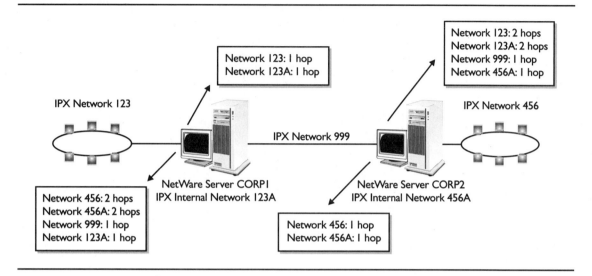

FIGURE 5-17 A Novell network using RIP

Network 123: 2 hops
Network 123A: 2 hops
Network 999: 1 hop
Network 456A: 1 hop

Network 123: 1 hop
Network 123A: 1 hop

IPX Network 123

IPX Network 456

IPX Network 999

NetWare Server CORP1
IPX Internal Network 123A

NetWare Server CORP2
IPX Internal Network 456A

Network 456: 2 hops
Network 456A: 2 hops
Network 999: 1 hop
Network 123A: 1 hop

Network 456: 1 hop
Network 456A: 1 hop

interface connecting it to network 123 go down, CORP1 would then try to route packets to CORP2, which has no connection to 123. To avoid such routing loops, IPX RIP uses a *split-horizon* routing method. Routers that use split horizon do not broadcast routes they receive on one interface back through that same interface.

IPX RIP packets use IPX port 0x0453, and are generated for the following reasons:

- **Router initializing** When a router running IPX RIP initializes, it broadcasts its presence via RIP.

- **Initial table building** When a router running IPX RIP initially builds its routing table, it broadcasts a request for RIP information.

- **Periodically** IPX RIP routers broadcast their presence every 60 seconds.

- **Router being downed** When an IPX RIP router is brought down properly, it broadcasts that all routes through it are unreachable (all routes broadcast with a hop count of 16).

- **Configuration changes** When a router detects a change in its routing tables, it broadcasts those changes so all routers will be updated.

RIP devices broadcast updates every 60 seconds, and a single IPX RIP packet can contain as many as 50 network entries. As you might imagine, if you have a very large and complex network, RIP broadcasts will generate a considerable amount of traffic. RIP is also used by workstations for route discovery to servers. This will be discussed later in this chapter.

When using IPX RIP, if servers or routers are brought down properly, they send a broadcast out to alert the other network devices to the fact that they will be unreachable. They do this by broadcasting their routes with a hop count of 16, which informs other routers that they are unreachable.

It is very helpful to be able to see the routing tables on Novell servers and Cisco routers. This can help identify the source of a problem because you can see where a packet is going. On Cisco routers, to view the IPX routing table, use the

```
show ipx route
```

command at the system prompt.

For Novell servers, to display the networks in the IPX routing table, type

```
display networks
```

at the server console prompt. This will give you all available network numbers and themetrics to reach them in hops and ticks.

SAP

In a Novell environment, we have seen how RIP can provide routing information for remote networks. However, given that there are a multitude of services available in Novell environments, how can servers and workstations find resources on the network? Unless a Novell server can announce to the world (or at least the network) that it is a file server, having a route to it is worthless.

To this end, Novell offers Service Advertising Protocol (SAP). SAP allows servers to not only announce their presence on the network, but also to announce *what kind* of services they are offering. Servers store SAP tables much as they do routing tables. When a server receives a SAP broadcast, it processes the broadcast and stores the information in a local database. Figure 5-18 shows a server receiving SAP broadcasts from various network servers and storing them in its SAP table.

FIGURE 5-18   Servers receive and store SAP information

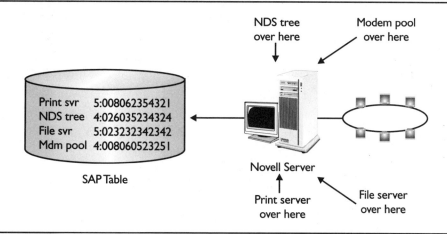

When a client workstation needs to connect to a service, it can request a list of services from the server it is connected to, because servers all store information about all available services on the network. This prevents the client from having to either store all the SAP information itself, or broadcast out on the network every time it needs to connect to a service. Figure 5-19 shows a workstation making a SAP request and the server responding with a reply giving the information.

FIGURE 5-19   Clients can request SAP information from a file server

In several aspects of its behavior, SAP is similar to RIP. Servers maintain internal tables of SAP broadcasts; SAP broadcasts are generated every 60 seconds; SAP uses a split-horizon broadcast scheme; and SAP broadcasts are generated when a server detects a change in its tables. However, SAP is not a routing protocol and does not store information about how to reach remote networks. It is simply a list of available resources and their network addresses. To locate these resources on the network, you must use a routing protocol such as RIP.

SAP packets use IPX as the transport and have a source and destination socket of 0x0452 in the IPX header. Services are broadcast every 60 seconds, and if a service is not broadcast for three minutes, it is dropped from the SAP tables.

FROM THE CLASSROOM

Stop That SAP!

An important concept in the IPX protocol is a Service Advertising Protocol (SAP). SAPs are used by network nodes (servers) to find out what services are available on the network. The three types of SAP packets are Periodic SAP Information packets, SAP Service Requests, and SAP Service Response. If left unchecked, SAP packets can cause congestion on both WAN and LAN links. The best way to keep SAPs from hogging the network is to implement SAP-suppressing filters.

Users at a remote office need access to data on certain NetWare servers at the central office. Because these users do not need to print files or have access to all the available servers, then filters can be implemented to suppress SAP packets that advertise printer services, and to suppress the advertisement of the servers not needed by the remote users across the WAN link to the remote office.

Get Nearest Server (GNS) is a query used by a new client on the network to establish connection with a server. If users located in a certain area have a server that is available, but a server in another area replies first to a request by the client, filters can be implemented to determine which servers can respond to GNS requests from clients.

Through the use of filters on Cisco routers you can "stop that SAP" and prevent unwanted traffic from congesting your network.

—Glenn Lepore, Senior Network Engineer,
Niche Networks, LLC

SAP Broadcast Categories

SAP broadcasts fall into three basic categories: the periodic update broadcasts, SAP service queries, and SAP service responses.

PERIODIC BROADCASTS   These packets are generated by every server on the network to announce the type of service they are offering. SAP broadcast packets can contain SAP information for up to seven servers. When a server makes a periodic broadcast on the network, it sends the packet out with a network address of its locally connected interface, and a node address of FF-FF-FF-FF-FF-FF-FF (all nodes). By doing this, all hosts on the network receive and process the packet. A SAP broadcast contains the following information about network services:

Server Name	The actual name of the resource
Server Type	A Novell-defined value for the type of service being offered. Novell publishes a list of all publicly defined server types (example: 0x0004 is a Novell file server)
Network Address	IPX network number
Node Address	IPX node number (usually MAC address as discussed in the IPX section)
Socket	Port with which the server originating the service will receive service requests

SAP SERVICE QUERIES   To discover what services are available on a network without sitting and waiting for broadcasts, a node can enter a *SAP service query*. Servers that offer a service or services matching the request will answer with a *SAP service reply*. A very common SAP service query in Novell networks is the Get Nearest Server request, which a workstation issues when it is attempting to connect to a file server. A SAP service query contains the following information:

Packet Type	Defines whether the packet is a General Service query (not currently implemented) or a Get Nearest Server query
Server Type	Contains one of the Novell defined server types

For example, if a workstation were trying to connect to a file server, it would issue a request with packet type of 0x0003 (Get Nearest Server) and a server type of 0x0004 (Novell file server).

SERVICE RESPONSE   When a server receives a SAP request, it sends a SAP response. The service response packet contains the following information:

Response Type	Type of response (either General Response or a Nearest Server Response)
Server Type	Type of server (the value here is the same as the Server Type for the service query broadcast)
Server Name	Server name
Network Address	IPX network number of the server
Node Address	Node number of the server
Socket	Socket number (port) of the server that will receive the service requests
Intermediate Networks	Number of routers between the client and server

To see a list of the devices available on the network, both Cisco and Novell provide mechanisms for viewing the SAP table entries. On Cisco routers, to view the list of servers in the SAP table, type **show ipx servers** at the router console. On Novell servers, to view the list of servers in the SAP table, type **display servers** at the server console.

SAP Route Must Be Present

When a server or a router receives a SAP broadcast, it verifies the SAP against its routing table. If there is no route to the device being advertised by the SAP, the SAP is discarded. If a server is set up with only a default route, there can be a potential problem because all SAPs will be dropped.

Novell servers have a switch that allows an administrator to override this feature. At the server console prompt, type

set required network for services = off

This allows SAP entries to be stored even if no route for them is found in the routing table.

Cisco extends the functionality of RIP and SAP by the implementation of IPX Enhanced Interior Gateway Routing Protocol (IGRP), which provides numerous enhancements over standard RIP. Enhanced IGRP works in conjunction with IPX RIP and exchanges routing information between the two protocols when they are both run on the same network.

NLSP

IPX RIP is an effective routing protocol for small- to medium-sized networks, but it is inefficient in large internetworks. RIP servers and routers broadcast their routing tables every 60 seconds, which can lead to heavy traffic if there are a large number of servers and routers making up the internetwork. Also, IPX RIP routers only know about routers directly adjacent to them. Routing decisions are made based upon the number of ticks, which doesn't account for congested routes, bandwidth cost factors, and so on.

To remedy these problems, Novell developed NetWare Link Services Protocol (NLSP). NLSP offers numerous enhancements over RIP; Table 5-1 shows a comparison of the two routing protocols.

NLSP is a *link-state protocol*. The link-state routing algorithm is based upon the Dijkstra algorithm. It is more complex and robust than the Bellman-Ford algorithm used by distance-vector protocols (for instance, RIP). NLSP allows routing decisions to be made based on more than just ticks or hop counts; congestion, routing costs, and other factors can all be taken into account.

Consider an example where RIP would be a very poor choice; Figure 5-20 shows a network that has both an ATM link and a Frame Relay connecting two remote networks. If the ATM link carried a very high price for usage, you might want to use the Frame Relay link, especially if the ATM link were heavily utilized and the Frame Relay link were dedicated to your network. Using RIP, the logical choice would be to use the ATM link, because RIP understands only ticks and hops but not the costs associated with bandwidth.

| TABLE 5-1 | Comparison of IPX RIP and NLSP |

Feature	IPX RIP	NLSP
Update method	Every 60 seconds, or when changes are detected	Only when changes are detected
Maximum hops	15	127
Manageability	Requires proprietary solution	SNMP (Defined MIB)
Service advertisement	SAP	Combines routing protocol with service advertisement (no additional service needed)
Routing information	RIP tables store the next hop only for remote networks	Entire network stored in NLSP table
WAN overhead	Higher, because RIP still sends RIP and SAP broadcasts	Lower; broadcasts are reduced and SAP is eliminated
Parallel paths	Not supported	Supported
Broadcast method	General broadcast to all nodes	Multicast support (limits nodes that handle packet)
Link cost calculation	Calculated first by ticks (1/18 second), then by hops if ticks are equal	Uses a metric calculated on throughput; user can manually assign a metric to override

| FIGURE 5-20 | A network on which NLSP is advantageous |

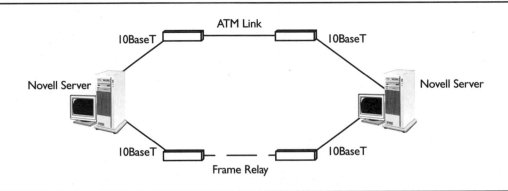

If you were using NLSP, you could assign a metric to each of the links, and this metric would be used in the calculation of the cost from one network to another. The metric could account for any number of factors: the cost of the ATM link, or perhaps the fact that the Frame Relay link isn't shared by your entire corporation. Whatever the rationale, you can assign metrics to the links with NLSP to give the router preference in selecting the paths.

Another enhancement of NLSP is that it reduces the amount of traffic generated by the routing protocols, by not using constant periodic broadcasts of the entire routing table by each device. Instead, NLSP routers build link-state databases, and only send updates when they detect a topology change. They use multicasting and directed transmission instead of general broadcasts.

Routers build *adjacencies* among one another, and exchange "Hello" packets to test the link state. An adjacency implies that two routers know about each other as neighbors and will periodically test for connectivity. An NLSP router takes information from its neighbors and uses that to construct a Link-State Packet (LSP), a packet that describes its immediate neighbor.

When a topology change is detected, NLSP uses two mechanisms to reliably update the NLSP routing tables.

- The first is *flooding;* when a router detects a change, it constructs a new LSP and sends it to all of its neighbors. For WANs, this transmission is a directed packet, and in LANs it is a multicast.

- The second is *receipt-confirmation*, which behaves differently in LANs as opposed to WANs. In WANs, when an adjacent router receives an LSP, it sends an acknowledgment back to the sender. In LANs, there is no direct acknowledgment, but the Designated Router multicasts a Complete Sequence Number Packet (CSNP) that contains all LSP identifiers and sequence numbers for that router's area. All NLSP routers receiving this packet can use it to verify their NLSP tables' accuracy.

Establishing Adjacencies

Figure 5-21 shows an example of how routers establish an adjacency over a WAN. Before the NLSP adjacency is established, the data link connection

FIGURE 5-21   The steps in bringing up an NLSP link

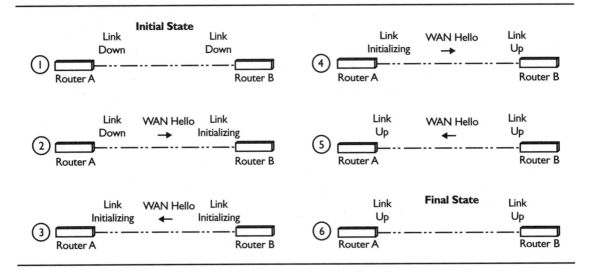

must first be established. Once the physical link is established, the routers use the IPX WAN version 2 protocol to establish the characteristics of the link. Once this is done, the routers can begin exchanging WAN Hello packets.

In step 1, the routers have their link status set to down. Router A starts by sending a Hello packet over the WAN (step 2) with the status field set to down (WAN Hello packets have a status field that is used to specify whether the link is down, initializing, or up). When Router B receives the packet, it changes its link state to initializing.

Its link state now set to initializing, Router B then sends a Hello packet back to Router A (step 3) with the status field set to initializing. When Router A receives the packet, it sets its state to initializing.

Both routers now have their link status set to initializing. Router A then sends another Hello packet back to Router B (step 4) with the status field set to initializing. When Router B receives the second Hello packet, it sets its link state to up.

With its link state set to up, Router B now sends yet another Hello packet to Router A (step 5) with the status field set to up. When Router A receives this packet, it sets its link status to up. In the final step of this sequence (step 6), both interfaces are set to up, and communications can pass across the router. Once the link is up, the routers will begin exchanging LSPs that describe the link states and start forwarding IPX data packets. The routers will periodically exchange Hello packets to maintain the adjacency.

In the NetWare Link Services Protocol Specification, a LAN is defined as a broadcast-based network (broadcasting is available at the Data Link layer). A WAN is defined as a connection-oriented or point-to-point network. As such, NLSP handles LAN adjacencies somewhat differently from WAN adjacencies. Rather than sending a directed Hello packet to establish an adjacency, routers send multicast LAN Hello packets when a LAN circuit is enabled. These multicast packets are used to establish adjacencies and select the Designated Level 1 router, which is the router that will make routing decisions and originate LSPs on behalf of the LAN. Hello packets are periodically broadcast on the LAN, and this information is used to update the link-state database.

NLSP Areas

A major enhancement of NLSP is support for hierarchical grouping of networks, using areas, domains, and global internetworks. In Figure 5-22, two distinct "areas" each have two separate networks running as a logical single network. Routers that connect networks in an area are called Level 1 routers.

An *area* is a collection of networks logically grouped to form a single network (see Figure 5-22). Areas are defined by a common address, which consists of an IPX network address and a network mask. The mask determines how much of the network address is used to define the area. Take the example where you have three separate networks, numbered 55555123, 55555124, and 55555125. If you have a mask of FFFFF000, only the first five digits of the individual network addresses are used to define the area, and the area network address would be 55555000. In other words, the effective part of the address that defines the area would be 55555 (first five digits), and these two networks would be considered to be one area.

A *routing domain* is a group of routing areas that belong to a single organization. The routing domain consists of multiple areas joined together to form an interconnected network. If you take the areas in Figure 5-22 and

Two distinct NLSP areas, comprising six Level I routers

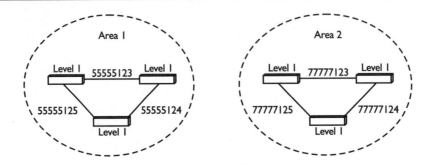

connect them using one of the routers from each area, you end up with a domain that looks like the one in Figure 5-23.

The two routers that connect the areas are now considered Level 2 routers; they each communicate with another area on behalf of their local

An NLSP domain is made up of NLSP areas

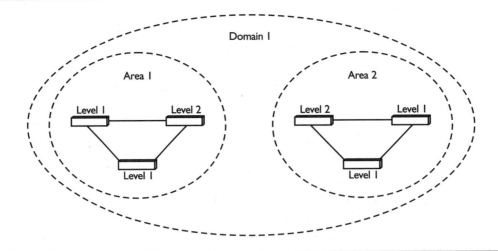

area. They are still considered a Level 1 router within their domain, but they are Level 2 routers to another area. A Level 3 router is a router that connects two domains together; a Level 3 router would also be considered a Level 2 router within its own domain.

Viewing NLSP Configuration

On Cisco routers, several commands can be used to display NLSP information. To view individual interface information, type

```
show ipx interface
```

To view the NLSP link state database, type

```
show ipx nlsp database
```

To view NLSP adjacencies, type

```
show ipx nlsp neighbors
```

To view general routing information and the IPX routing table, type

```
show ipx route
```

Since NLSP combines RIP and SAP functionality, the SAP table on a Cisco router will also display routes when NSLP is enabled. To view the SAP table and routes, type

```
show ipx servers
```

exam
⑩atch

NLSP is the default routing protocol for newer versions of NetWare, but it can be changed to RIP/SAP through the INETCFG server utility. RIP/SAP is automatically enabled on Cisco routers when IPX is configured, but NLSP is not. To enable NLSP, the administrator must first assign an IPX internal address to the router, enable NLSP, then assign an area address and mask. Once this is done, the administrator can enable NLSP on individual router interfaces.

Common Packet Types and Port Numbers

Now that we have discussed IPX and the related protocols that use it, let's take a look at the IPX header and some fields that are used by all of the protocols. Figure 5-24 illustrates the IPX header.

The IPX header immediately follows the Ethernet frame header and occurs in all packets using IPX as the transport protocol. It is always 30 bytes in length, and the first two bytes (the checksum) always contain the value FFFF. Some of the fields, such as source and destination network address, are obvious; these are the IPX network addresses of the sending and receiving host. Source and destination node numbers are the host addresses of the sending and receiving hosts.

Two of the fields—Packet Type and Socket—are not so obvious; let's take a look at these in the context of CIT.

■ **Packet Type**   Packet Type is used to specify what type of service the packet is using for delivery. Valid values for this field are as follows:

0	IPX
4	IPX
5	SPX
17	NCP

FIGURE 5-24   IPX header format

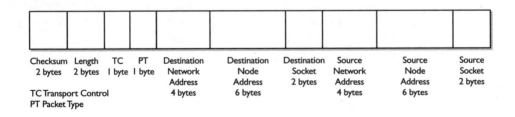

Checksum	Length	TC	PT	Destination Network Address	Destination Node Address	Destination Socket	Source Network Address	Source Node Address	Source Socket
2 bytes	2 bytes	1 byte	1 byte	4 bytes	6 bytes	2 bytes	4 bytes	6 bytes	2 bytes

TC Transport Control
PT Packet Type

■ **Socket (a.k.a. Port)** The source and destination sockets refer to the ports on the sending and receiving hosts that handle the packet. A few of the valid values are as follows:

0x451	NetWare Core Protocol (NCP)
0x452	Service Advertising Protocol (SAP)
0x453	Routing Information Protocol (RIP)
0x455	NetBIOS Packet

SAP Server Types

SAP types are not part of the IPX header itself; the SAP header follows the IPX header. As we mentioned in the SAP section, there are three types of SAP packets, and each has its own structure.

The field in this category that warrants further discussion is the Server Type field. Novell periodically releases an updated list of all publicly defined server types. (This does not include any SAP server types that organizations may implement privately.) This list is available for download from Novell's FTP site and is named DSAP??.EXE, where ?? is the most recent version of the file. Here's a list of a few of the common SAP server types:

0x0004	Novell file server
0x0005	Job server
0x0006	Gateway
0x0007	Print server
0x000A	Job queue
0x0021	SNA gateway
0x0047	Advertising print server
0x009A	Name pipes server
0x009E	Portable NetWare (UNIX)
0x0107	NetWare 386
0x026B	Time synchronization
0x0278	NetWare Directory server

Common User Tasks

Now that we have an overview of IPX/SPX networking, let's take a look at how a typical Novell network works. Theory is great, but there is nothing like seeing how things actually work; let's take a look at some illustrations of how Novell NetWare implements IPX/SPX.

Novell file servers store object and routing databases in one of two ways. In NetWare 3.*xx*, the information is stored in a set of flat database files collectively referred to as the *Bindery*. When users boot up and log into a Novell 3.*xx* network, they are authenticated on a single server using an account in that server's Bindery. In the example in Figure 5-25, there are three Bindery-based servers on a network. Having access to all three requires being authenticated three separate times, once on the Bindery of each server. A major drawback to this scenario is account maintenance; an administrator has to create an account on three separate servers in order to give a user access to all three.

NetWare 4.*xx* servers use NetWare Directory Services (NDS), which is a distributed database that conforms to the X.500 standard for hierarchical directory services. A *tree* is the top level of the NDS database. With NDS, user logins are no longer server-centric; multiple servers can now belong to a single tree, and once a user is authenticated on the tree they have access to any server that is a member of the tree (limited only by the rights the administrator applies). Multiple servers maintain copies of the NDS database, and this database is synchronized between them. With this configuration, an administrator only needs to add an account to a tree once and can assign rights to the user for any resources in the tree. Figure 5-26 shows a logical view of how the NDS tree works.

The first part of setting up a Novell network is bringing up the server. Novell servers start by booting up in DOS, then running an executable file named SERVER.EXE. This executable reads two files as it starts up, STARTUP.NCF and AUTOEXEC.NCF, which are both ASCII text files. STARTUP.NCF is generally used to tell the server program which disk

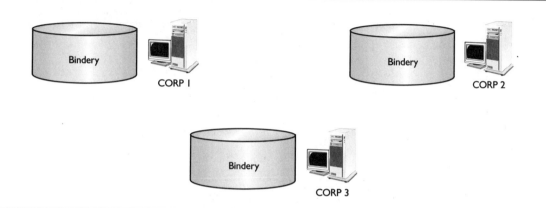

FIGURE 5-25   Three Bindery-based servers

drivers to load in order to support the hardware. SERVER.EXE also makes certain environment settings that are static once the server is up and running. AUTOEXEC.NCF contains the server name, the list of network card drivers to load, the network address assignments, and settings for environment variables that can be dynamically changed.

Once the server is up and running with all drivers loaded and configured, a workstation can be configured to connect to the servers. On workstations

FIGURE 5-26

Servers using
NDS database

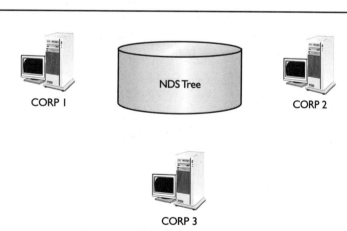

running DOS, four executables are loaded to provide access to the file server; these must be loaded in the following order:

1. **LSL.COM**   The Link Support layer. Handles communications between the MLID and the protocol stacks.

2. **MLID.COM**   A card-specific driver that handles I/O with the network interface card (NIC).

3. **IPXODI.COM**   The IPX protocol stack.

4. One of the following:
   NETX.EXE   The NetWare Shell for Bindery-based networks. Handles NCP I/O and provides the user interface to the Novell server (NetWare 3.*xx* networks).

   OR

   VLM.EXE   The NetWare DOS Requester for NDS-based networks. Serves the same purpose as the NetWare Shell (NetWare 4.*xx* networks).

This driver set makes up the Novell Open Data-link Interface (ODI), which is a standard for supporting multiple protocols on a single network interface. Once the MLID is executed, any vendor wishing to implement its protocol can do so by writing a protocol stack executable that conforms to the ODI specifications. IPXODI.COM is the Novell IPX protocol stack, but any other protocol such as TCP/IP could be loaded just as easily.

These executables use an ASCII text file called NET.CFG for settings such as the NIC IRQ and port, the Ethernet frame type to use, the name of the Preferred Server or Preferred Tree to log into. This functionality has been adapted to the Windows 95 and Windows NT 32-bit protocol stacks and now works without loading DOS terminate-and-stay-resident (TSR) programs, but the fundamentals are the same.

Workstation Bootup (Bindery Mode)

Let's first take a look at the sequence for a Bindery connection. (In this example, a server other than the workstation's Preferred Server responds to its request first). The sequence of events happens in the following order.

Get Nearest Server

When a workstation boots up, there are several steps that must be completed before the user has access to the file server's resources. The first step is to find an initial server to connect to.

The user loads the four drivers (previously listed). These drivers are loaded from a DOS prompt at the workstation (the files are usually in a subdirectory of drive C:). When the NetWare shell (NETX.EXE) loads, it sends out a SAP request for Get Nearest Server (0x004). All NetWare servers that receive the packet respond with a SAP Nearest Server Reply.

The workstation accepts and uses the first SAP response it receives (the fastest server wins). The SAP packet contains the name and IPX internal address of the first file server that responded. The workstation generates a RIP broadcast to find the route to this file server. The file server responds with a RIP reply giving the route to the server.

Lookup Preferred Server

The workstation connects to this file server by issuing an NCP Create Service Connection request. After this connection is established, the workstation issues an NCP request to the server for the IPX internal network address of its Preferred Bindery Server. The server performs a lookup in its SAP table and performs an NCP reply to the workstation with the network address of the workstation's Preferred Server. (If the workstation had no Preferred Server option set, it would remain attached to this first server.)

Find Route to Preferred Server

The workstation generates an NCP Destroy Connection request. Once this connection is gone, the workstation generates a RIP broadcast to find the route to its Preferred Bindery Server (using the information provided by the initial file server). The workstation receives a RIP reply from its Preferred Bindery Server, containing the route to connect to the server.

Connect to Preferred Server

Once the workstation has the route, it then generates an NCP Create Service Connection request to the Preferred Bindery Server. The server responds with an NCP Create Service Connection reply.

Negotiate Settings and Login

Once the workstation has attached to its Preferred Server, it can then negotiate the communications settings for the connection. After these are made, the user can log in and start using the server's resources.

The workstation and server then issue NCP requests and replies back and forth to negotiate LIP and Packet Burst settings.

Finally, the NetWare shell generates an NCP request to the server to get the file server's date and time, which the shell uses to synchronize the PC clock.

The user can then set the active drive to the file server's virtual drive and execute the LOGIN.EXE program. The user's account will be authenticated on the server's Bindery, and the login script will be executed (setting drive mappings, environment settings, and so forth).

exam
Watch

If you wish to configure a server to not automatically answer all NCP Get Nearest Server requests, type the following command at the server console prompt: set reply to get nearest server = off. This command can be added to AUTOEXEC.NCF if you want to make this setting automatically upon server startup.

Workstation Bootup (NDS Mode)

Now let's take a look a how this works when establishing a connection to an NDS tree. When the workstation boots up, it loads the following four drivers, in this order: LSL.COM, MLID.COM, IPXODI.COM, and VLM.EXE. When VLM (the NetWare DOS Requester) loads, it performs the following steps, in the order shown, to connect to the Preferred Directory Server.

Get Nearest Directory Server

The connection procedure is essentially the same for NDS logins as it is for Binder mode. The workstation must first find a server to attach to, but rather than a Bindery Server, the workstation now looks for a Directory Server.

The four NetWare ODI drivers are loaded. In this case, rather than the NETX NetWare shell, the NDS DOS Requester (VLM.EXE) is loaded. The files for the Requester are stored in C:\NWCLIENT by default. When VLM loads, the Requester generates a SAP request for Get Nearest Directory server (0x278). Every server that is running as an NDS Directory Server responds with a SAP Nearest Directory Server reply.

The workstation accepts and uses the first SAP response it receives (the fastest Directory Server wins). The SAP packet contains the name and IPX Internal address of the first Directory Server that responded. The workstation generates a RIP broadcast to find the route to this server. The Directory Server responds with a RIP reply giving the route to it.

Look Up Preferred Directory Tree

The workstation connects to this Directory Server by issuing an NCP Create Service Connection request, and the server responds with an NCP Create Service Connection. The workstation issues an NCP request for IPX internal address of a server in the workstation's Preferred Tree. The server responds with an NCP reply giving the network address of a Directory Server in the workstation's Preferred Tree.

Find Route to Preferred Tree

Once the workstation has attached to an initial Directory Server and found the address of its Preferred Tree, it can then drop the initial connection. After that connection is dropped, the workstation searches for the path to its Preferred Tree.

The workstation generates an NCP Destroy Connection request. Once this connection is gone, the workstation generates a RIP broadcast to find the route to the Directory Server in its Preferred Directory Tree. The workstation receives a RIP reply from the server, giving it the route to connect to the tree.

Connect to Preferred Server

Once the workstation has the route, it then generates an NCP Create Service Connection request to the Directory Server in its tree. The server responds with an NCP Create Service Connection reply.

Negotiate Setting and Login

Once the workstation has attached to a server in its Preferred Tree, it can then negotiate the communications settings for the connection. After these are made, the user can log in to the tree and start using any resources for which it has access.

The workstation and server then issue NCP requests and replies back and forth to negotiate LIP and Packet Burst settings. Once the LIP and Packet Burst negotiations are completed, the NetWare Requester generates an NCP request to the server to get the file server's date and time, which it uses to synchronize the PC clock.

The user can then set the active drive to the file server's virtual drive and execute the LOGIN.EXE program. The user's account will be authenticated on the server's NDS database, and the login script will be executed (setting drive mappings, environment settings, and so on).

How SLIST Really Works

SLIST is Novell's utility for listing available servers on a NetWare 3.*xx* Bindery-based server. For NetWare 4.*xx* NDS-based servers, the command NLIST SERVERS /A/B gives the same results.

When a user executes SLIST or NLIST, the workstation itself does not produce the list of available servers. Rather, the workstation sends an NCP request to the server, and the server answers with the server entries in its SAP tables. Servers store their SAP tables in their Bindery (3.*xx* servers) or NDS database (4.*xx* servers).

How Printing Really Works

Printer sharing is a key component of any network operating system, and Novell NetWare has wide market share for Bindery and NDS support. Printing is essentially the same in Novell 3.*xx* (Bindery) and Novell 4.*xx* (NDS), so we will discuss the simpler scenario of the two: Bindery printing.

For printing to work on a Bindery-based server, two database objects must be created: a *print queue* and a *print server.* A print queue is a location where printing information is stored as users generate print jobs, and a print server pulls these jobs from the queue and sends them to the printer. A print queue is nothing more than a special directory on the file server; print jobs are created as files and put in the directory for handling by a print server.

When a user generates a print job, the NetWare Shell software receives the job, packages it into a file, and puts it in the print queue. This operation is performed using NCP commands between the workstation and server. Once the job is in the queue, the print server can then pull the print job and send it to the printer.

Print servers are devices that connect to the file server using SPX. These show up as active connections (users) on the NetWare MONITOR screen. Print servers constantly check the directory for new print jobs, and when a new one is found, the server pulls it from the queue and sends it to the printer. Figure 5-27 shows this relationship; there is no direct connection between the workstation and printer.

Print servers advertise themselves using SAP, and will show up in the SAP tables of Novell servers and Cisco routers. However, workstations do not communicate directly with the print servers and therefore do not need to broadcast a SAP query to find the network address of the Print Server. They simply print to the queue on the server.

CERTIFICATION OBJECTIVE 5.03

Router Proxy GNS by Default

When workstations boot up, they generate an NCP Get Nearest Server request to attach to a server. What happens if there are no Novell servers on the workstation's local segment? Cisco's answer to this is *Get Nearest Server*

FIGURE 5-27 A workstation prints to a server queue; the print server pulls it from the queue

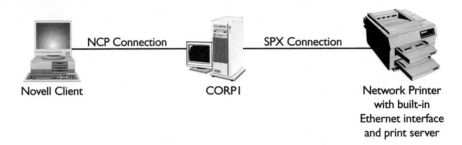

NCP Connection   SPX Connection

Novell Client   CORP1   Network Printer
                                                  with built-in
                                                  Ethernet interface
                                                  and print server

(GNS) proxying, which means that the router will send a GNS reply on behalf of the servers it has stored in its SAP table. In Figure 5-28, a workstation has no servers on its local network, but there are two Novell servers on a remote network.

When the workstation issues a SAP Get Nearest Server request, the Cisco router will answer with a GNS reply for one of the servers in its SAP table. The Cisco IOS determines which server it should use for this reply based

FIGURE 5-28   Cisco router proxying for servers on remote network

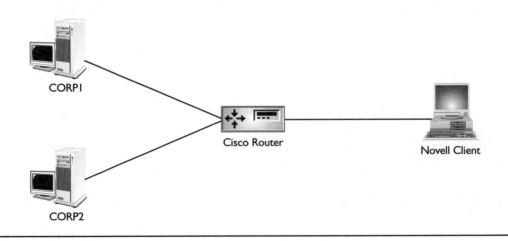

CORP1

CORP2

Cisco Router   Novell Client

upon the version of IOS being used. The important concept here, though, is that the router will answer on behalf of the servers. This Cisco router feature is turned on by default when IPX routing is enabled on an interface.

Common Problems and Fixes

Now that we have covered the concepts of IPX networking, we can explore some of the procedures to troubleshoot typical problems encountered when using this protocol. Common problems include workstations that are unable to connect to servers, difficulty connecting to servers through routers, intermittent connectivity, and faulty NetBIOS forwarding. As with any protocol, an IPX network administrator may encounter many different IPX issues, but here we will cover many of the problems most often seen.

Local Connectivity Problems

Most problems in Novell networks are client connectivity issues; for instance, a workstation cannot log in to a server, or you cannot see servers or resources on remote networks. Following are a few troubleshooting tips.

Check to Ensure the Frame Types Match

If the client is on the same network as the server, ensure that they share the same frame type. Perform the following steps to ensure frame type consistency:

1. Check the NET.CFG file on the workstation and look for the following two lines:

   ```
   Link Driver driver name
   Frame frame type
   ```

2. When you load the MLID, check to see what frame type is loading. If more than one frame type is configured, load IPXODI.COM and

see what frame type(s) the protocol binds to. If there is no frame type line in NET.CFG, the software will load with the defaults (802.3 for the older MLIDs and 802.2 for newer ones).

3. Check the file server to ensure it has the correct frame type loaded for the NIC and that the correct IPX address is bound to that frame type. At the file server console prompt, type

```
config
```

If there are multiple interfaces, ensure that the one connected to the same network as the workstation has the intended frame type bound. If not, either edit the AUTOEXEC.NCF on the server to correct the problem, or use the INETCFG module on newer NetWare servers.

Check the Workstation Connectivity

Perform the following steps to see if the connection problems are workstation based.

1. See if the workstation is able to connect to any server. When you're successfully attached to a server, the workstation will return a success message when you load NETX.EXE or VLM.EXE, and give the name of the server.

2. If you're attached to a server but not the one you want, check the workstation's Preferred Server to ensure the number of licenses has not been exceeded. When a server hits its maximum number of users, it will no longer accept connections.

3. Check NET.CFG to ensure that a section for Preferred Server has been added.

4. If the workstation cannot attach to any server, check the cabling, the card, and the port and IRQ settings in the NET.CFG to ensure the card is loading properly. It's a good idea to put a protocol analyzer on the network and look at any broadcasts originating from the workstation's MAC address. You will be able to see the Get Nearest Server requests and any replies if the workstation is communicating on the network.

Check to Ensure the Server Has Connectivity

If you suspect that the problems may be server based, perform the following steps:

1. At the server console, type

   ```
   display servers
   ```

   and see if the server can detect the other servers on the network. If so, type

   ```
   reset router
   ```

   to clear the SAP tables. Wait approximately 60 seconds, and type

   ```
   display servers
   ```

   again. This will ensure you are not seeing old SAP entries. If the server is communicating with the network, you will see the list of servers within a minute

2. Check the server console for router configuration errors. If a server or router is improperly addressed, all servers on the network will start broadcasting visible and audible error messages from the console.

Connectivity Problems Through a Cisco Router

When IPX networks are connected by a router, other problems may arise. The administrator has to configure the connecting interfaces correctly on any router, of course, but be aware of the following Cisco-specific problems that may occur.

Check to Be Sure the Router Is Configured Properly

If the workstation and server are on different networks, you need to ensure that the frame types on the router interfaces match the frame types on both the workstation and server networks.

1. On the Cisco router, type

   ```
   show ipx interface
   ```

   and ensure the frame types and network numbers are correct.

2. Type

   ```
   show interfaces
   ```

   Check to see that interface and line protocols are up, and see if there are input or output errors on the interfaces connecting the networks. If there are, issue a

   ```
   clear interface counter
   ```

   command to reset the counters.

3. Again, type

   ```
   show interfaces
   ```

   to see if the error counters still increase. This may indicate a media error.

4. Check the remote NetWare server's configuration by typing

   ```
   config
   ```

   at the prompt. Verify the that frame types and network numbers are correct.

The next step is to ensure that the servers and routers are seeing the SAP broadcasts for the device you are trying to connect to. To verify this, perform the following tests:

5. Check the remote server's connectivity by using the DISPLAY SERVERS and RESET ROUTER commands described in the troubleshooting connectivity section. If the remote server has no entries in its SAP table, it has probably lost its connection to the network.

6. To check the SAP tables of the Cisco router, Telnet to the connecting Cisco router and type

   ```
   show ipx servers
   ```

This will show the SAP table on the router. If the remote Novell server shows up in the SAP tables of the router or a local Novell server, but it's not reachable, type

```
reset router
```

from the Novell server console prompt. The SAP table entry for the remote server may no longer be valid, and this command causes the server to rebuild its RIP and SAP tables. If the server no longer shows up after 60 seconds, the server itself may be down or a network link may be down.

7. The next step is to ensure that the router isn't performing any unwanted filtering. At the Cisco router prompt, type

```
show ipx interface
```

Make sure that no RIP or SAP filters have been applied. If filters are present, these can stop the flow of broadcasts to various networks and will cause devices not to show up.

8. In large networks, make sure the hop count is high enough on the routers. The default is 15, which may not be high enough for large networks. Type

```
show ipx route
```

to see what the maximum *hop count* is set to. If the setting is not high enough, raise it by issuing the following command:

```
ipx maximum-hop  hopcount
```

Check for Packet-Related Problems

Make sure that LIP packets are not being negotiated larger than what the router can support. The IPX ping on a Cisco router is useful here, because you can select the datagram size you want to ping with. At the router prompt, type

```
ping
```

When prompted for the protocol, type

```
ipx
```

Enter the address of the server you want to test, in the Cisco format:

```
NNNNNNN.HHHH.HHHH.HHHH
```

and then select the datagram size. Start at 576 and work up; if the ping starts failing as the datagram gets larger, you probably have a problem with LIP support.

Check for IPX Internal Network Number Conflicts

A somewhat more difficult problem to troubleshoot is when an administrator assigns duplicate IPX internal addresses. The symptoms of this happening are users' losing connections and SPX devices' (such as print servers) mysteriously losing connections when all hardware seems to be functioning correctly. There are two methods for checking this situation.

- The first method is to examine the routers' RIP and SAP tables by typing in the SHOW IPX SERVERS and SHOW IPX ROUTE commands. Check to ensure that routes you know to be on one interface are not showing up on another; if you do see this, it's likely that a server connected to the second interface has been assigned a duplicate IPX internal network number.

- The second method is to attach a protocol analyzer to the local network where devices are being dropped. Look at all packets going to and from a device attempting to connect to the server. If you see a workstation or printer trying to attach to a server other than the one for which they were configured, there is a good chance that the server has been assigned the same IPX internal network number as the desired server. The benefit of using the protocol analyzer is that you will get the name of the server causing the problem.

Intermittent Connectivity Problems

If your network is experiencing problems with intermittent connectivity when connected through Cisco routers, here are a few troubleshooting tips.

Check the Cisco Router Settings for RIP and SAP

After you have checked for filters and none have been applied, there are some additional Cisco specific areas to look at.

- If a server is slow when processing SAP updates, it may be due to the fact that Cisco routers can forward broadcasts faster than the router can process them. You can increase the default value of 55ms for the SAP output delay by using the command

  ```
  ipx output-sap-delay value
  ```

  while in configuration mode for a particular interface (where *value* is the number of milliseconds you want for the delay).

- RIP and SAP timer mismatches can also cause problems. The default for RIP and SAP updates on Novell servers is 60. Check the servers to ensure these settings have not been changed.

- Check the routers by issuing the command

  ```
  show running-config
  ```

  to ensure settings are correct. For LANs, it is recommended that you do *not* use a SAP interval, because this setting cannot be changed on servers. Check to see if there is an entry for IPX SAP-INTERVAL. If there is, issue the

  ```
  no ipx sap-interval
  ```

  command. For RIP, type

  ```
  show ipx interfaces
  ```

and see what the update interval is. Make sure it matches the value set on all servers; all routers and servers should have the same value.

■ Over slower WAN links, SAP broadcasts might be getting dropped. If you issue a SHOW IPX SERVERS command at the router and see more entries than there are in the DISPLAY SERVERS output at the Novell console, SAP broadcasts may be getting dropped. There are three Cisco recommendations for this:

■ Use SAP filters to restrict SAP broadcasts as much as possible.

■ Increase the HOLD-QUEUE *length out* setting to increase the output hold-queue length.

■ Increase the bandwidth available across the WAN link.

IPX NetBIOS Problems

Most IPX NetBIOS problems are related to either the forwarding (or lack thereof) of IPX type 20 packets, or NetBIOS filtering. If you have applications that connect to NetBIOS applications over a router and you experience problems, use the following troubleshooting tips:

■ Check the Novell settings. If you are using a Novell server as a router, check to make sure that IPX NetBIOS forwarding is enabled. Type set ipx netbios replication option and see what the value is set to. Refer to the earlier section on IPX NetBIOS for an explanation of the replication options and how they affect NetBIOS.

■ Cisco has extensive support for IPX NetBIOS, including filter lists and forwarding rules that allow an administrator to control NetBIOS traffic flow. When using a Cisco router to forward NetBIOS traffic, check the following settings:

1. At the Cisco router command prompt, issue a

```
show running-config
```

command. Check to see if the ipx type-20-propagation setting is present for every interface that requires the passing of IPX NetBIOS packets. If not, issue the

```
ipx type-20-propagation
```

command for every interface that has this requirement.

2. You should also check the IPX helper-address configuration setting on the router interface of the client to ensure that broadcasts are being forwarded to the appropriate address for the application. If this setting does not exist, issue the

```
ipx helper-address
```

command with the address of the server the client is trying to reach. This setting ensures that the client broadcasts get forwarded to the appropriate location. See the IPX NetBIOS section for information on IPX helper addresses and helper lists.

3. If you have checked all of the settings mentioned here and are still experiencing problems, check the NetBIOS filters and access lists to make sure that the packets aren't being dropped.

CERTIFICATION SUMMARY

The IPX suite of protocols has extensive support due to the widespread success of Novell NetWare as a network operating system. This protocol has gained substantial industry support, and Cisco has made no exception. IPX is the core component of Novell networking, and this chapter presents several key concepts of this protocol.

It is important to understand the roles of IPX as a transport protocol, SPX as a delivery mechanism, and NCP as a communications protocol and a delivery mechanism. Equally important are the roles of RIP and NLSP as routing protocols, and SAP as an advertisement protocol for services on the network. Although not a component of Novell networking, the forwarding of IPX NetBIOS is supported by both Novell and Cisco. This widely used protocol is also a key concept when working with the IPX/SPX protocol.

We have looked at the basics of the various protocols that make up the IPX/SPX suite, and how they are implemented on Novell and Cisco platforms. Understanding these basics is essential to handling problems that arise in IPX-based networks.

✓ TWO-MINUTE DRILL

❑ IPX/SPX is the standard communications protocol for Novell networks, just as TCP/IP is the standard protocol for UNIX networks.

❑ Novell expanded the IPX protocol suite to handle the requirements of its network operating system, Novell NetWare, enhancing IPX to include numerous services and support for topologies other than Ethernet.

❑ Internetwork Packet Exchange (IPX) is a Layer 3 transport protocol used for routing data across a network.

❑ IPX is a datagram-based network protocol.

❑ IPX network addresses that identify a network segment are referred to as *IPX external network numbers*. Internal network numbers are used to define a logical network internally within a Novell server.

❑ Sequenced Packet Exchange (SPX) is a Layer 4 transport protocol used for providing reliable connections in a Novell environment.

❑ SPX uses IPX as the transport protocol but offers a method for sequencing packets and guaranteeing delivery.

❑ NetWare Core Protocols (NCP) are a set of server routines used for performing application requests.

❑ NCP uses IPX, not SPX, as its transport.

❑ Large Internet Packet (LIP) was developed to address a problem of packet size constraints between client workstations and servers.

❑ *Packet burst* is designed to allow multiple packets to be transmitted between Novell clients and servers in response to a single read or write request.

❑ NetBIOS is a Session layer interface specification developed by IBM and Microsoft. This interface provides for a naming schema on the network that gives each node a unique network name.

❑ The RIP protocol allows routers in an IPX network to automatically exchange routing information about a network.

❑ Novell offers Service Advertising Protocol (SAP). SAP allows servers to not only announce their presence on the network, but also to announce *what kind* of services they are offering.

❑ Cisco extends the functionality of RIP and SAP by the implementation of IPX Enhanced Interior Gateway Routing Protocol (IGRP), which provides numerous enhancements over standard RIP. Enhanced IGRP works in conjunction with IPX RIP and exchanges routing information between the two protocols when they are both run on the same network.

❑ NLSP offers numerous enhancements over RIP. NLSP is a *link-state protocol.*

❑ The IPX header immediately follows the Ethernet frame header and occurs in all packets using IPX as the transport protocol.

❑ NetWare 4.*xx* servers use NetWare Directory Services (NDS), which is a distributed database that conforms to the X.500 standard for hierarchical directory services.

❑ With NDS, user logins are no longer server-centric; multiple servers can now belong to a single tree, and once a user is authenticated on the tree they have access to any server that is a member of the tree (limited only by the rights the administrator applies).

❑ If you wish to configure a server to *not* automatically answer all NCP Get Nearest Server requests, type the following command at the server console prompt: **set reply to get nearest server = off**. This command can be added to AUTOEXEC.NCF if you want to make this setting automatically upon server startup.

❑ SLIST is Novell's utility for listing available servers on a NetWare 3.*xx* Bindery-based server.

❑ Printing is essentially the same in Novell 3.*xx* (Bindery) and Novell 4.*xx* (NDS).

❑ When workstations boot up, they generate an NCP Get Nearest Server request to attach to a server. What happens if there are no Novell servers on the workstation's local segment? Cisco's answer to this is *Get Nearest Server (GNS) proxying,* which means that the router will send a GNS reply on behalf of the servers it has stored in its SAP table.

❑ Common problems include workstations that are unable to connect to servers, difficulty connecting to servers through routers, intermittent connectivity, and faulty NetBIOS forwarding.

❑ Most problems in Novell networks are client connectivity issues.

❑ When IPX networks are connected by a router, other problems may arise.

❑ Your network may experience problems with intermittent connectivity when connected through Cisco routers.

❑ Most IPX NetBIOS problems are related to either the forwarding (or lack thereof) of IPX type 20 packets, or NetBIOS filtering.

SELF TEST

The following Self Test questions will help you measure your understanding of the material presented in this chapter. Read all the choices carefully, as there may be more than one correct answer. Choose all correct answers for each question.

1. What layer of the OSI model does IPX correspond to?

    A. Data Link

    B. Network

    C. Transport

    D. Session

2. What two Ethernet frame types support TCP/IP?

    A. Ethernet 802.3

    B. Ethernet 802.2

    C. Ethernet SNAP

    D. Ethernet II

3. Which one of the following three protocols uses a one-to-one acknowledgment for transmitted packets?

    A. IPX

    B. SPX

    C. SPX II

4. NetWare Core Protocols (NCP) uses SPX for guaranteed delivery.

    A. True

    B. False

5. Packet Burst provides greater performance through what enhancement?

    A. Packet sizes are increased when connecting over a router.

    B. The burst mechanism greatly reduces network traffic.

    C. Multiple packets are transmitted in response to a single read or write request.

6. What is the Cisco feature that allows an administrator to control the flow of IPX NetBIOS packets to a particular host?

    A. IPX helper addresses/IPX helper lists

    B. IPX NetBIOS flow control

    C. ipx netbios type-20-propagation

    D. NetBIOS directional caching

7. How often are RIP broadcasts sent by default by Novell servers?

    A. Every 10 seconds

    B. Every 30 seconds

    C. Every 60 seconds

    D. Every 5 minutes

8. What is the command on Cisco routers to view the SAP entries?

    A. SHOW IPX SAP-TABLE

    B. DISPLAY SERVERS

    C. SHOW IPX SERVERS

    D. DISPLAY NETWORKS

9. What is the maximum number of hops that NLSP supports?

   A. 15

   B. 127

   C. 45

   D. 30

10. What is the SAP type for a Novell File Server?

    A. 0x0005

    B. 0x0007

    C. 0x0107

    D. 0x0004

11. When a workstation boots up and loads the drivers for a Bindery connection, what is it most likely trying to connect to?

    A. An NDS tree

    B. A Novell 4.*xx* server

    C. A Novell 3.*xx* server

    D. A Windows NT server

12. When a workstation issues an SLIST command, it generates a SAP Get Nearest Server command and waits for responses from all network servers to build the list it displays.

    A. True

    B. False

13. A workstation printing on a Novell network does not directly send print jobs to the printer, but rather generates print jobs in a queue on the file server itself.

    A. True

    B. False

14. How will a Cisco router handle workstations' Get Nearest Server requests by default if there are no servers on the same interface as the workstation?

    A. The router will drop the request.

    B. The router will forward the request onto all interfaces.

    C. The router will proxy-answer for servers using servers listed in its SAP table.

    D. The router will forward the request to the interface containing the first server in its SAP table.

15. By default, what will servers do if they receive a SAP packet and there is no route for it in their routing table?

    A. The server will send a RIP broadcast to find the route.

    B. The server will drop the SAP packet.

    C. The server will store the SAP information in its SAP tables.

    D. The server will store the SAP until a route is discovered.

6

Apple's AppleTalk Protocol

CERTIFICATION OBJECTIVES

Fans of Apple computers may be familiar with what is sometimes referred to as "The Macintosh Way." Entire books have been written on exactly what The Macintosh Way is, so we won't even try to come close to a complete definition and will limit our discussion here to AppleTalk—Apple Computer Inc.'s networking environment—and its related protocols. For our purposes in this chapter, The Macintosh Way means "making things easy and seamless for the Macintosh user."

Apple has succeeded admirably in its goal of making things easy and seamless for the Macintosh user. However, the company's goal didn't necessarily include making things easy for the AppleTalk network manager.

Most of the time, the Mac is very easy to use, is intuitive, and runs trouble-free, just as Apple says it will. When a failure occurs, however, solving the problem can be maddeningly complex. AppleTalk networking closely parallels how the Macintosh operating system works. Most of the time, things work well, but when problems occur, they can be difficult to solve.

This is not intended to imply that there is something inherently wrong with AppleTalk. On the contrary—Apple was years ahead of other network systems with some of the features available in AppleTalk and related protocols, just as the company led the industry with the Mac OS. Sometimes, though, all of the things that are supposed to work together automatically, don't. When that happens, you as an AppleTalk network manager, have to know what's happening behind the scenes. You also have to know all the little details that the users are not supposed to have to worry about.

This chapter is about the details of AppleTalk, and how to use your understanding of those details to troubleshoot AppleTalk networks. We'll cover how the AppleTalk protocol works, and how to troubleshoot it from desktop computers as well as Cisco routers. Typically, the only reason you'll have an AppleTalk network is because you have Apple Macintoshes. Therefore, most of the desktop computer examples will be with a Mac.

The Evolution of AppleTalk

Let's examine the history of AppleTalk. A form of the AppleTalk protocol was first introduced with the Apple LaserWriter—Apple's first laser printer and the first laser printer with PostScript. This printer was one of the major factors in Apple's dominance of the desktop publishing market, and has much to do with the Mac being as popular as it is. Unfortunately, in the mid-1980s, all these technical innovations came at a fairly steep price, several thousand dollars. Apple realized that these printers would have to be sharable in order to help justify the expense of their purchase.

Actually, early versions of AppleTalk existed *before* the LaserWriter, but the printer's marketing is what really drove the need for Mac networking. Apple built AppleTalk into the ROMs of the LaserWriter and—with an OS update for the Macs and some cables and connectors supplied by Apple—you had a small, serviceable network that allowed sharing of the expensive printer.

LocalTalk

This LaserWriter-generated networking technology, originally called AppleBus, became known as LocalTalk. LocalTalk was a relatively slow (230 Kbps) serial networking technology. Nonetheless, it had one massive advantage: It was already built into nearly every Mac and laser printer that Apple sold, even some of the dot-matrix printers. LocalTalk got even less expensive when third parties such as Farallon (now Netopia) sold versions of the connectors that would function over standard telephone wire.

In contrast to Ethernet and Token Ring networks, on which the work is shared partly by the NIC and partly by the host, LocalTalk devices were strictly dumb. They contained no networking logic to speak of, just some electronics for signal conversion and noise prevention. This meant that the software on the Macs (and printers) were responsible for everything from OSI Layer 2 on up. It also meant that there were no built-in networking addresses to take advantage of. Apple could have required users or administrators to program an address into each device, but that would have been contrary to Apple's goal of seamlessness. Besides, it would have been somewhat difficult on the printers, since there was no keypad of any sort to do so.

What Apple decided to do was, in simple terms, to have AppleTalk devices just pick an address at random. If you've ever had to track down a duplicate-address problem on some other type of network, this approach might sound a little dangerous. Apple took this factor into account, giving AppleTalk a mechanism to ensure that a duplicate address is not picked. When the AppleTalk device picks an address, it does an AppleTalk Address Resolution Protocol (AARP) broadcast, discussed later in this chapter, to see if that address is in use. If it is, another one is picked. As long as most of the addresses aren't already in use, this works fine.

As we'll see later in the chapter, some of these mechanisms designed to make things automatic on small, local networks occasionally don't work in larger networks.

CERTIFICATION OBJECTIVE 6.01

Common Mac User Tasks

Mac users, like any others, expect to be able to boot up their computers and have everything work properly. For the networking component, that means users expect to be able to go to the Chooser, see all the zones they expect to see, and within those zones have access to all the resources that they expect to use. Typically, from the user's point of view, failure during any of these connections and tasks constitutes a "network problem"—and you have to fix it.

Let's review what you, as a network manager, have to do to create an AppleTalk network using Cisco routers. We'll assume that your Layer 2 network is in place, your router interfaces are not in the shut state, and you're ready to add AppleTalk at Layer 3.

The first thing to do is turn on AppleTalk routing. To do so, you enter configuration mode and type this command:

```
appletalk routing
```

By default, using this form of the command turns on Routing Table Maintenance Protocol (RTMP) routing.

Alternatively, you can use Cisco's proprietary Enhanced Interior Gateway Routing Protocol (EIGRP) by issuing this command instead:

```
appletalk routing eigrp network-number
```

Replace the words "network-number" with an integer value from 1 to 65535. This number has to be unique across your entire AppleTalk network. Consider using the starting number of one of your cable ranges on that router as your EIGRP network number. This keeps it unique because your cable ranges must be unique as well.

The relative merits of EIGRP vs. RTMP are discussed briefly in the "Zone Lists" section of this chapter. That section also covers interface configuration commands.

Bootup and Address Assignment

Like nearly all networking protocols, AppleTalk uses a numbering scheme to differentiate nodes. Unlike other protocols that are hard-addressed (IP, DECNet), or automatically assigned according to the MAC address (IPX), AppleTalk uses a dynamic addressing scheme.

AppleTalk Phase I

Let's return for a moment to our LocalTalk/AppleTalk history lesson. Back when LocalTalk was all there was, the version of AppleTalk that would have been in use is now known as *AppleTalk Phase I*. The current version of AppleTalk is *AppleTalk Phase II*. The biggest change is that Phase II supports multiple networks. In Phase I, only a single network of 254 addresses was permitted. In Phase II, 65,535 networks (give or take; see next section) of 254 addresses each are permitted. Multiple network numbers (also called *cable ranges*) can be assigned to a single broadcast domain (except on LocalTalk networks, which are limited to one network number).

Phase I AppleTalk is, for all intents and purposes, obsolete. AppleTalk Phase II was released in 1989, and Apple has been slowly removing Phase I support since that time. Recent AppleTalk devices and Mac OSs may not include the option to use Phase I at all.

on the **! Ob**

If Phase I devices do exist, support is usually provided with a LocalTalk-to-EtherTalk (AppleTalk over Ethernet) router or a converter of some sort. One option is to use an EtherWave adapter from Netopia (under the Farallon brand name). These can be a little expensive, but their cost may be preferable to maintaining LocalTalk-to-EtherTalk routers, depending on how many LocalTalk devices you have to support. You'll find information about the EtherWave adapters on the Web at http://www.farallon.com/ products/ether/adapters/ewmprad.html.

By the way, our history lesson is now over. The rest of this chapter focuses on AppleTalk Phase II, unless otherwise noted, and we'll be ignoring LocalTalk. Cisco does not produce any LocalTalk equipment, and Cisco routers have long been Phase II-compatible.

AppleTalk Phase II

If you're familiar with TCP/IP, you may have noticed a parallel between AppleTalk addresses and IP addresses. AppleTalk uses an addressing scheme with a 16-bit network number followed by an 8-bit node number. Addresses are usually represented in decimal, like this: 1000.10. In IP terms, this is equivalent to a 24-bit address space, with a fixed subnet mask of 255.255.0. The network number range is 0 through 65535, and the node number range is 0 through 255. Of course, there are some reserved addresses in those ranges, which we'll get to later. These addresses operate at OSI Layer 3, much as IP addresses do.

AARP

The parallels between TCP/IP and AppleTalk don't end there. As mentioned briefly earlier, Apple has a protocol called the AppleTalk Address Resolution Protocol, AARP. AARP is much like IP ARP, and is used to map Layer 3

AppleTalk addresses to Layer 2 addresses. Figure 6-1 illustrates a screen from the SnifferPro packet capturing software from Network Associates. On this screen you can see an AARP request. If you compare this to the IP ARP packet format in Chapter 4 of this book, you'll see they are very similar.

exam
Ⓦatch

Try to get used to identifying the various parts of AppleTalk packets. You may be asked to identify the protocol of a packet, its purpose, and so forth.

In Apple terminology, these AARP mappings are maintained in the *Address Mapping Table (AMT)*. The AMT is also commonly called an *ARP*

FIGURE 6-1

An AARP request packet

```
⊟ DLC:  ----- DLC Header -----
   DLC:
   DLC:  Frame 10 arrived at  11:43:31.7840; frame size is 60 (003C hex) bytes.
   DLC:  Destination = Multicast 090007FFFFFF, Atalk_Broadcast
   DLC:  Source      = Station 00107B281E00
   DLC:  802.3 length = 36
   DLC:
⊟ LLC:  ----- LLC Header -----
   LLC:
   LLC:  DSAP Address = AA, DSAP IG Bit = 00 (Individual Address)
   LLC:  SSAP Address = AA, SSAP CR Bit = 00 (Command)
   LLC:  Unnumbered frame: UI
   LLC:
⊟ SNAP: ----- SNAP Header -----
   SNAP:
   SNAP: Type = 80F3 (AARP)
   SNAP:
⊟ AARP: ----- AARP -----
   AARP:
   AARP:   Hardware type             = 1 (Ethernet)
   AARP:   Protocol type             = 809B (AppleTalk)
   AARP:   Hardware address length   = 6 bytes
   AARP:   Protocol address length   = 4 bytes
   AARP:   Command                   = 1 (Request)
   AARP:   Hardware address - Source = 00107B281E00
   AARP:   Protocol address - Source = 9010.119
   AARP:   Reserved ; Value at offset = 000000000000
   AARP:   Protocol address - Desired = 9010.100
   AARP:
   AARP: [Normal end of "AARP".]
   AARP:
   DLC:  Frame padding= 10 bytes
```

table or, for purposes of Cisco commands, the *Apple ARP table*. Here's an example output from a Cisco router for the SHOW APPLE ARP command:

```
Router>show apple arp
Address        Age (min)   Type       Hardware Addr      Encap   Interface
2249.129            6    Dynamic    0800.097e.ce90.0000   SNAP    Ethernet0/0
2249.131            4    Dynamic    0800.0977.721d.0000   SNAP    Ethernet0/0
2249.155            -    Hardware   0000.0c39.cc04.0000   SNAP    Ethernet0/0
2204.180            -    Hardware   0000.0c39.cc09.0000   SNAP    Ethernet0/5
2225.13           169    Dynamic    00c0.4900.5634.0000   SNAP    Ethernet1/0
2225.30           169    Dynamic    00c0.4900.ba19.0000   SNAP    Ethernet1/0
2225.32           173    Dynamic    00c0.4900.563f.0000   SNAP    Ethernet1/0
2225.168            -    Hardware   0000.0c39.cc0c.0000   SNAP    Ethernet1/0
281.43              -    Hardware   0000.0c39.cc0d.0000   SNAP    Ethernet1/1
280.30             12    Dynamic    0800.2012.e4f3.0000   SNAP    Ethernet1/2
280.36             37    Dynamic    0800.0796.740e.0000   SNAP    Ethernet1/2
280.41            177    Dynamic    0000.c51a.1544.0000   SNAP    Ethernet1/2
280.59             55    Dynamic    0800.0726.37ae.0000   SNAP    Ethernet1/2
280.87            160    Dynamic    0800.076f.f6c4.0000   SNAP    Ethernet1/2
280.108           132    Dynamic    0800.079c.51f8.0000   SNAP    Ethernet1/2
280.116            37    Dynamic    0000.9423.05f0.0000   SNAP    Ethernet1/2
280.128           110    Dynamic    0800.09c1.a109.0000   SNAP    Ethernet1/2
280.129           109    Dynamic    0800.097d.b57c.0000   SNAP    Ethernet1/2
280.130           109    Dynamic    0800.0997.a171.0000   SNAP    Ethernet1/2
280.131           108    Dynamic    0800.092d.1396.0000   SNAP    Ethernet1/2
280.132            74    Dynamic    0800.0999.563d.0000   SNAP    Ethernet1/2
280.134           109    Dynamic    0800.092d.53ea.0000   SNAP    Ethernet1/2
```

DDP

Now that you've seen what AppleTalk addressing looks like, let's examine the format of AppleTalk's Layer 3 packets. AppleTalk's Layer 3 protocol is called the Datagram Delivery Protocol, or DDP. Like IP, DDP is an unreliable, connectionless protocol. Also, as in IP, the sequencing, retransmissions, and other features to ensure reliability are the responsibility of higher-layer protocols. Let's look at the fields in the DDP portion of a packet, shown in Figure 6-2.

- **Hop Count**   This is the number of router hops a DDP packet has made while traveling to its destination. Hop count is analogous to the IP TTL counter, but hop count is fixed at a maximum of 15. If the count reaches 15 and the router that currently "has" the packet can't deliver it to a directly attached node, the packet must be discarded.

```
DDP: ----- DDP header -----
  DDP:
  DDP:  Hop count            = 0
  DDP:  Length               = 599
  DDP:  Checksum             = 38CF (Correct)
  DDP:  Destination Network Number = 0
  DDP:  Destination Node     = 255
  DDP:  Destination Socket   = 1 (RTMP)
  DDP:  Source Network Number = 9010
  DDP:  Source Node          = 119
  DDP:  Source Socket        = 1 (RTMP)
  DDP:  DDP protocol type = 1 (RTMP data)
  DDP:
```

The packet shown in Figure 6-2 was a broadcast from an AppleTalk router to a directly attached net, so it has passed through no routers and the hop count is 0. Apple has set aside 6 bits for this field.

■ **Length**   This is the number of bytes of DDP information—that is, the DDP header and data portions. Apple has defined the maximum length to be 599 bytes (13 for the header, and up to 586 for data). This packet is part of a series of several, and the AppleTalk router has filled this first packet to the maximum, in order to keep the number of packets to a minimum. Apple has set the length of this field to 10 bits. This field, plus the 6 bits from the hop count, make up the first two bytes of the DDP header.

■ **Checksum**   This is a 16-bit checksum for the DDP packet, covering all DDP bytes following the Checksum field. This feature is intended to provide a simple check for packet corruption. If the checksum doesn't match the data, the packet must be discarded. According to the protocol specification, the checksum is optional. A checksum of 0 implies the checksum was not calculated, and receiving nodes should not perform a checksum calculation.

■ **Destination Network Number**   This is the network number for which the packet is destined. AppleTalk routers make forwarding decisions based on the destination network, just as IP routers do. This number is also used by nodes to determine if a packet is destined for them. The Destination Network Number field is equivalent to a network or subnetwork number in IP. In our example, the number is 0, which means the packet is destined for "this net." This number can also be thought of as a broadcast number.

- **Source Network Number** This is the network number of the transmitting node. In our example, the AppleTalk router is using an address of 9010.

- **Destination Node** This is the node (station) on the destination network that will receive this packet. This field is equivalent to the host portion of an address in IP. Host number 255 is the broadcast address. Node 0 is used to represent any router for the indicated network number. Node 254 is reserved and should not be used.

- **Source Node** This is the sending node (station) on the source network. The router in our example has a node address of 119. Cisco routers will follow the dynamic addressing process, or the node number can be forced by typing it in.

- **Source Socket** AppleTalk, like IP, uses socket numbers to differentiate among multiple processes running on various nodes. (On IP, sockets are more commonly called ports, but the concept is the same.) Unlike IP, AppleTalk socket numbers are defined at Layer 3, and not Layer 4. Apple uses 8 bits to hold a socket number, so the possible range of values is 0 through 255. Numbers 0 and 255 are reserved.

- Socket numbers 1 through 127 are the Statically Assigned Sockets (SASs). Apple has reserved use of sockets 1 through 63. Sockets 64 through 127 are available for development use and should *only* be used by developers for experimental purposes, *not* in production software.

- Sockets 128 through 254 are the Dynamically Assigned Sockets (DASs) and should be used for user-installed services. The DASs are assigned by the OS via a system call.

In our example, the socket number is 1, which is reserved for RTMP. We'll discuss RTMP more in the RTMP section.

- **Destination Socket** This field contains the socket number of the receiving node (or nodes). Since this packet is an RTMP packet, the destination socket is also 1.

- **DDP Type** This field indicates the transport type. AppleTalk tends to use more transport types than does IP, and AppleTalk's are more application-specific. The transport type in our example is RTMP.

Note that the order of the fields in the foregoing discussion is slightly different from the order shown in Figure 6-2. The discussion order is correct. The SnifferPro software displays the fields in what the SnifferPro developers apparently consider a more readable order.

It's fairly evident that the designers of AppleTalk were familiar with TCP/IP, and made use of similar formats where appropriate.

Address Acquisition

Before we move on from Layer 3, let's take a closer look at how AppleTalk devices acquire a *dynamic address*. When we discussed address acquisition previously, it was in the simplified context of a Phase I/LocalTalk network. That environment does not take into account the network number, since Phase I has only node numbers and no network numbers.

In a Phase II network, the process of choosing the node ID is the same. Specifically, it's usually the job of the AARP software to pick a nonconflicting node ID. It does so by picking an ID at random, and sending an AARP request for that address to see if there are any responses.

In addition to the node ID, the AppleTalk device also has to pick a network number. Apple decided to accomplish this by reserving a particular range of network numbers for this purpose. The range is FF00 through FFFE in hex, or 65280 through 65534 in decimal. This range is the Startup range. When a Mac boots up onto an AppleTalk network for the first time ever, it acquires a node ID in one of the networks listed in this Startup range. The primary purpose of this address is for communication with an AppleTalk router to determine the correct network number(s) to use. This communication is done via the *Zone Information Protocol (ZIP)*.

A new AppleTalk device will send a particular type of ZIP packet, a GetNetInfo request, using the startup address it has chosen. If there are any AppleTalk routers on that network, they will see the request and will reply with a ZIP packet that contains a GetNetInfo reply message. This message contains, among other fields, a starting network number, an ending network number, and the zone name (more about zone names in the upcoming "Zone Lists" section). This is enough information for the node to choose an address in the proper network number range using the same process it used to choose an address in the Startup range.

If there is no router present, the AppleTalk device will keep its startup address and use that to communicate. This facilitates small ad-hoc networks without a router, useful for simple file sharing and printing.

Macs retain their previous address and zone name on the local hard drive, and attempt to use that information next time they boot. Other AppleTalk devices may or may not have nonvolatile storage for the same purpose, but they can always utilize the dynamic process. Storing the previous information is merely a time-saver.

exam
ⓦatch

The Mac stores the previous network address and zone on its hard drive, but it keeps other kinds of information in a special, small section of memory called Parameter RAM (PRAM). PRAM stores special settings about the Mac, mostly hardware information (about the hard drive, video card, and so on). If you're familiar with PC hardware, think of PRAM as similar to the CMOS. PRAM also stores information about the network card. On occasion, PRAM becomes corrupt or miss-set and needs to be cleared. You may need to perform the following procedure if the Mac doesn't seem to be recognizing its network card properly.

To clear the PRAM on a Mac, you restart it; and while it's restarting (before the "happy Mac" picture appears), press and hold down COMMAND-OPTION-P-R. Yes, indeed, that's four keys, all pressed at the same time, while restarting the Mac. When the PRAM has been cleared, the boot process may be different while the Mac rediscovers its hardware.

The process of an AppleTalk device's obtaining an address is one of the common failure points on the network. The details of this process are important and will be discussed in detail in the "Common AppleTalk Problems and Fixes" section.

Zone Lists

Let's take a detailed look at those AppleTalk zones we've mentioned a couple of times in passing so far. The *zone list* is one of the defining characteristics of AppleTalk. A *zone* is simply a name for a logical grouping of AppleTalk devices. Zones are for the benefit of people, and are commonly named according to function, location, department…, and so on—for example, "Houston, San Francisco, Boston…" or perhaps "Legal, HR, Engineering…". The names chosen aren't important, as long as they make sense to the people they represent.

Mac users normally access the zone list by accessing the Chooser from the Apple menu in the upper-left corner of their screen, as shown in Figure 6-3.

Where does the Mac get the zone list? From an AppleTalk router. Just as routers keep address tables, AppleTalk routers also maintain a list of zone names and their associated cable ranges. Apple's term for this list is the Zone Information Table (ZIT). To view the table on a Cisco router, use the SHOW APPLE ZONE command. Here is an example of the output:

```
Router>show apple zone
Name                             Network(s)
Chicago                          2236-2236 2243-2243 210-210
Atlanta                          52 252-252
Madrid                           268-268 68 1013
New York                         18 218-218
Maarssen                         45 245-245
El Segundo                       207-207
Atrium                           270-270 275-275 2208-2208
Tokyo                            295-295 94 95 97 2209-2209 2269-2269
                                 2258-2258
Btrium                           243-243
Frankfurt                        257-257 57 157
Boulder                          1002-1002 1001-1001 1007-1007
Nagoya                           27 297-297
North American Twilight Zone     8017-8017 8006-8006 8005-8005 4011-4011
                                 8035-8035 8000-8000 8032-8032 8002-8002
```

As you can see, several of the zones have multiple associated cable ranges. This allows AppleTalk devices in those areas to be logically grouped together, even if they are on different networks. Also notice that upper- and lowercase are maintained in zone names, and spaces are permitted. This means it's very important that you take care not to add extra spaces or type the names slightly wrong in some way. If you do, you'll end up with two similarly named zones in the Chooser. And if it's because of an extra space at the end of a zone name, you may not be able to tell why the "duplication" is occurring.

At this point, you may be wondering what exactly is the relationship between a zone name and a cable range. As is demonstrated in the output just shown, a zone can consist of more than one cable range. The cable ranges do not have to be contiguous, or related in any way, except that you want them to be in the same zone.

FIGURE 6-3

Zone list in the Chooser
on a Mac

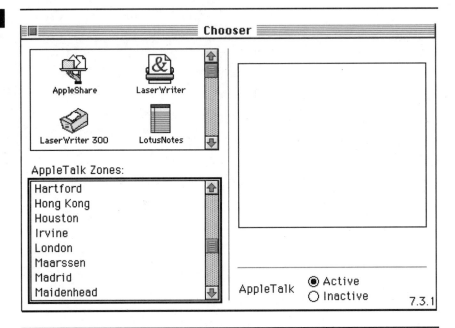

You can also have more than one zone per cable range, which is useful when you want to make more than one logical grouping on one network segment. This creates an interesting situation for AppleTalk devices, as they now have a choice as to what zone they are "in." We'll discuss that issue further in the later section "Chooser Lists."

Router Interface Configuration Commands

In this section we'll review the commands used to configure a Cisco router interface for AppleTalk.

To configure a cable range on a particular router interface, first enter configuration mode, and select the desired interface (for example, with the INTERFACE ETHERNET 0 command). Then use the AppleTalk cable-range command. For example:

```
Router(config-if)#appletalk cable-range 50000-50000
```

One cable range is permitted per interface. In this example, the range given was 50000 through 50000; in other words, "use AppleTalk network number 50000." The allowable range for this cable-range command is 0 through 65279.

Network 0 is special; it's used to place a router into "discovery" mode and will cause the router to obtain its network and node addresses from another router. Discovery mode does not work across serial lines. An AppleTalk router that is *not* in discovery mode is called a *seed router.* Recall that we mentioned earlier that more than one network number is permitted per network segment; a cable range is a contiguous range of AppleTalk network numbers.

If there are two seed routers on the same network segment, you MUST make sure their cable range and zone lists match.

The next step is *to assign one or more zone names to the interface,* with these commands:

```
Router(config-if)#appletalk zone name 1
Router(config-if)#appletalk zone name 2
```

Keep in mind that a zone name cannot be applied if the interface is in discovery mode.

To remove a zone name from an interface, use the "no" version of the command. For example, to get rid of the second name assigned by the second command just shown, use

```
no AppleTalk zone name 2
```

To remove all zone names at once, use

```
no AppleTalk zone
```

by itself.

The final interface command to look at before we move on is for *selecting a routing protocol.* The two common routing protocols are RTMP and EIGRP, as discussed in the next three sections. Here's the command:

```
appletalk protocol {aurp | eigrp | rtmp}
```

Be default, RTMP is enabled. The routing protocols can be added and removed independently. To remove a protocol, use the "no" version of the command (as instructed for the zone name command).

You may be wondering about the AURP in the protocol command's options. AURP stands for AppleTalk Update Routing Protocol; it's used only when AppleTalk is tunneled and can only be applied to tunnel interfaces. If you need to work with tunneled AppleTalk networks, review the Cisco configuration guide for AppleTalk, available at

http://www.cisco.com/univercd/cc/td/doc/product/software/ios120/12cg cr/np2_c/2capple.htm.

Obtaining Zone Lists

Now that we've reviewed the router interface commands, let's return to the question of how an AppleTalk client workstation gets a list of zones. The list of zones is obtained from client's local router.

RTMP In order for the local router to get a list of zones, it first needs to get a list of network numbers via RTMP, the Routing Table Maintenance Protocol. We mentioned RTMP briefly earlier, examining a packet header for an RTMP packet in the "DDP" section.

RTMP is a distance-vector routing protocol, which means it uses a distance number to determine if one route is better than another. In the case of RTMP, the metric is simply the router hop count. RTMP starts at 0 for directly attached networks, and goes up to 15. Networks that are 16 or more hops away are considered unreachable. (RTMP is very similar to RIP, if you're familiar with that IP routing protocol.)

By default, every 10 seconds an RTMP router sends a complete list of network numbers to each of its AppleTalk interfaces. This list is used by routers to build and maintain a list of cable ranges. As AppleTalk routers receive updates for new network numbers, they attempt to retrieve the list of zones for those networks.

ZIP Retrieving the list of zones is done via ZIP (Zone Information Protocol), also briefly mentioned earlier. ZIP is used here in much the same way that it's used during startup, to get a list of zone names for a particular network number. Specifically, the router sends a ZIP request containing multiple network numbers. This may be done using multiple ZIP requests if the list of network numbers will not fit in one packet. A local AppleTalk router sends a ZIP reply containing a list of network numbers, and the zone or zones for each. This response may take multiple ZIP replies if the list will not fit in one packet.

EIGRP   An alternative to RTMP in the Cisco environment is EIGRP. Briefly, EIGRP for AppleTalk offers all the advantages over RTMP that EIGRP for IP offers over RIP. The biggest advantage is that EIGRP only sends updates when necessary, saving possibly a lot of bandwidth. The disadvantage is that EIGRP is proprietary to Cisco and can't be used with non-Cisco equipment (for example, LocalTalk routers). You can use RTMP where you have to, but use EIGRP over your backbone.

Non-Routing Node Obtaining Zone List

Non-routing nodes (for example, client workstations) have things a bit easier than the local router. They don't require a complete network-to-zone mapping. In fact, the way the Mac OS was designed, all they really need is a list of zone names. Client workstations send another type of ZIP request, called a GetZoneList request, to a local router. The workstation's first request asks for a list of zones starting at index 1. Index 1 is simply the first zone in the router's list. The router responds with a list of zones. If there are more zones available than can fit in a single packet, the router sets a flag in the packet that indicates more zones are available. In this case, the workstation makes an additional request, starting at an index number that is one greater than the number of zones it has received so far. The router responds starting at the zone number requested. This exchange is repeated until the router sets the flag that there are no more zones, and the workstation has a complete list.

The workstation repeats this process each time the Chooser is launched. If the Chooser is left open, it will refresh itself every few minutes.

You've learned how routers maintain zone lists, and how workstations get them from routers. Let's take a look at how the zones are used once the workstation has a list.

Chooser Lists

Now that we've seen what zones are and where they come from, what resources are we grouping? The resources we want to group into various zones are services offered by AppleTalk devices. Typically, the two most visible services that Mac users want access to are file servers and printers. The file-sharing protocol used with AppleTalk is the AppleTalk Filing Protocol (AFP). Printing is done via the Printer Access Protocol (PAP).

In order to focus on what's needed to troubleshoot AppleTalk in a Cisco environment, we won't be covering AFP and PAP in detail. We will, however, study how the Chooser works, and the protocols that are used to get to the point where AFP and PAP would come in.

Earlier you observed the Chooser's display of the list of zones on a Mac. Let's take a look at how resources are located once a zone has been selected. Figure 6-4 is another screen capture of the Chooser, showing zones for an AppleShare server.

There are a number of things to note here. First, in the upper-left area of the Chooser are the service types that this Mac can use. In our example, we've got AppleShare and LaserWriter, which are the two most common choices. You can see that we also have a LaserWriter 300 driver loaded. Lotus Notes is also loaded, and it looks like there are more, since the scroll bar is active. In our example, AppleShare has been selected.

In the lower-left area is the zone list you saw in Figure 6-3. Minneapolis is selected. Now you can see more clearly what the zones are for. When AppleShare and Minneapolis are selected, we get a list of AppleShare servers in Minneapolis. In our example, there appears to be a Receptionist Mac that is offering file services.

If you click on LaserWriter instead, you'll see a list of any LaserWriters in Minneapolis. Select Madrid, and you'll see a list of LaserWriters in Madrid.

This makes for a fairly powerful abstraction. Most people who use the Mac find this arrangement for finding network resources fairly intuitive. If you're familiar with Microsoft Windows networking, you'll notice this is somewhat similar to the Windows Internet Name Service (WINS) function (although it works differently behind the scenes, as you'll see).

Name Binding Protocol

There's one very important AppleTalk protocol that we haven't discussed yet: the Name Binding Protocol (NBP). NBP does a couple of different things, depending on how it's used, but its main function is to map a named service to its network number, its node ID, and its socket number. Let's look at an example to clarify how this works.

In Figure 6-4, the user selected AppleShare and Minneapolis. The result was a list of a single server, Receptionist Mac. How did the workstation obtain that name? The short answer is that the workstation broadcasts a request for it. The long answer is that it had some help from the AppleTalk routers.

Recall that Macs don't keep a complete network-to-zone map, so they have to rely on the routers for that. The Mac will build an NBP packet that contains that Mac's own network number, node ID, and the socket with which it wishes to communicate NBP information. The packet also contains two strings, one for the zone desired ("Minneapolis" in our example) and

FIGURE 6-4

AppleShare server in the Chooser on a Mac

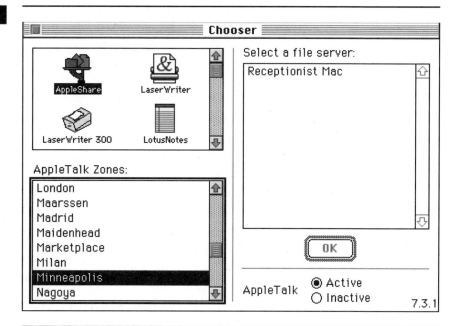

one for the type of service ("AFPServer" for AppleShare). This information makes up an NBP *broadcast request* packet. The Mac forwards this packet to a local router, requesting that the router broadcast the packet. The local router converts this packet into a *forward* request, consults its zone-to-network table, and forwards a copy of the packet to all the networks in that zone.

When the packet reaches a router that is directly attached to one of the networks in that zone, the router converts the forward request into a *lookup request* packet. This packet is largely the same as the original broadcast request packet, but its destination is now a local broadcast. These local broadcast packets reach all the AppleTalk devices on each of the networks in the zone. Each of the AppleTalk devices offering that requested service then sends a *lookup reply* directly to the original node that made the request. The Mac that made the request needs the help of the routers to get the request broadcast to the appropriate networks, but the requesting Mac handles all the replies itself.

Since DDP is not a guaranteed-delivery protocol, the requesting Mac usually sends the same request several times in a short period of time. It ignores duplicate replies.

The service-request process is the same for other services as it is for AFPServer. The requesting workstation simply requests the appropriate service name, which is typically hard-coded into both the server process and client driver. Independent developers can create whatever sort of service they like; they just have to develop the client and server processes and choose a name. File servers, printers, modems, fax gateways, SNA gateways, Lotus Notes, and other services can be made available through the Chooser.

By convention, when an AppleTalk device offers multiple services, they all must appear in the same zone. If an AppleTalk device is on a network segment with more than one zone, the administrator of the device chooses the zone in which the device appears. On a Mac, this is done via the Network Control Panel. Simply launch the Network Control Panel, double-click on the appropriate protocol (for example, EtherTalk), and select the zone in which the device should appear. If only one zone is available, the Control Panel will say so. On a network segment with multiple zones, one of the zones is the default, and that default is where the device will appear unless it's changed. On a Cisco router, the default is the first one programmed in.

Now that we know how AppleTalk works, let's see how it breaks.

Common AppleTalk Problems and Fixes

For a protocol with so many dynamic aspects, AppleTalk works surprisingly well. Still, there are a few issues that the AppleTalk network manager should be aware of. Some of these will be problems that users should be able to solve themselves. Some problems will result from abnormal network conditions. And some problems probably aren't supposed to happen, but do anyway.

Before we get into specifics, there are a few general steps you can take to make your AppleTalk life easier. The biggest favor you can do for yourself is to keep good documentation. In a medium-to-large AppleTalk network, issues such as "How many zones are we supposed to have?" or "What network numbers are available?" can become very big problems. AppleTalk's dynamic nature can be both a curse and a blessing. It's fairly easy to let an AppleTalk network grow itself, but when problems arise, if you don't have good records, it will be difficult to know which zone and network numbers are supposed to be present.

For collecting records, you may want to use something as elaborate as one of the commercial utilities for scanning large AppleTalk networks and generating reports. Or you may get by with something as simple as saving a copy of the output from a command on your router. If you currently manage an AppleTalk network but you don't have records, consider trying some of the troubleshooting commands as you read through this section, and record the results in a text file. The time you save may be your own. If nothing else, by saving your router configurations to an FTP server when you make changes, you can search through those.

Routing Problems

Routing problems are generally pretty straightforward. The root issues of concern are incorrect routes and missing routes. The solution is to correct the bad or missing information. Let's take a look at a few ways to find and fix these problems.

Most of the examples in this section are done on the routers, because routing problems rarely are evident when you're looking at the workstations. Later sections may lead you back to this one.

Missing Routes

The problem of a missing route is the one that most often needs solving. Usually, the problem is simply a down link or router, which is often simple to deal with. In other cases, the router is up and reachable, and it's not clear why the route is missing.

For the latter situation, EIGRP is often at fault (assuming EIGRP is being used to route AppleTalk). For whatever reason (an IOS bug, for instance), EIGRP will occasionally fail to update a neighboring router. This poses a problem because EIGRP does not get automatically updated whether it's needed or not, as do RIP and RTMP. If EIGRP doesn't think you need a route update, you don't get one.

The trick is to somehow force EIGRP to send an update. Some possible ways to do this are to shut/no shut the interface and do a CLEAR APPLETALK ROUTE or CLEAR APPLETALK EIGRP NEIGHBORS. In some extreme cases, you may have to temporarily remove and then reapply EIGRP (not recommended if you can avoid it, because the router can lock up for several minutes); you may even have to reboot the router. Obviously, you'll have to judge for yourself what will be the consequences of using a particular solution to try and fix a particular problem. If the missing network isn't critical, you may want to reboot your router during off-hours.

In other cases, you may discover that it's the receiving router rather than the sending router that has the problem. You may have to repeat the troubleshooting process with the receiving router. It may become apparent, after you've gone as far as rebooting the sending router, that the receiving router is the one having trouble.

The good news about missing routes is that newer versions of IOS don't seem to have as much trouble with EIGRP. Consider running one of the newer IOS versions that has been declared General Deployment, if you aren't already.

With RTMP, the problems tend to be routes coming and going. Because of the way RTMP sends route updates, extremely busy networks will sometimes prevent route updates from reaching their destination, or the receiver may be too busy to process them. The result will be the routes' timing out of the route table. This usually causes a reduction in traffic, as the routers drop packets for which they have no destination. When the traffic slows, the route updates make it through, and the process repeats. Often, this will appear to the end-users as zones disappearing and reappearing in the Chooser.

The only real solution for missing routes is to try and redesign the network in some way to eliminate or segment the excess traffic.

Incorrect Routes

The problem of incorrect routes is usually less common than that of missing routes—but it's rather more difficult to troubleshoot. An incorrect route is one that points to nothing, loops, or points to something you didn't want it to.

Under a protocol such as IP, the network manager would normally do a TRACEROUTE command to see the loops, or to get a final destination. Mac network managers who are in the habit of using a question mark at the IOS command line as a quick online help technique may have noticed this tantalizing command:

```
Router#traceroute appletalk ?
  WORD  Trace route to destination address or hostname
  <cr>
```

Sadly, it is not to be:

```
Router#traceroute apple 50000.1
%Not yet implemented.
```

There is no documentation for this feature in any of the Cisco IOS references. This includes the documentation for IOS version 12, which is the latest version available as of this writing. Hopefully, Cisco will implement it someday.

Unfortunately, this leaves you stuck doing a TRACEROUTE manually. You'll have to log onto each router and do a SHOW APPLETALK ROUTE to look at the interface by which it's connected. Most of the time you'll be managing routers via TCP/IP, so you'll have to figure out the IP address on the next AppleTalk router so you can connect to it. If the router is connected via an interface that has only one router on it, you're probably in good shape. Otherwise, you'll have to look at the AppleTalk address, consult the Apple ARP table, get the MAC address, consult the IP ARP table, and look up the IP address.

exam
ⓦatch

There may be one shortcut available to you while doing a manual TRACEROUTE, if the next router is a Cisco router. As mentioned in previous chapters, Cisco has written a proprietary protocol called the Cisco Discovery Protocol (CDP). CDP's purpose in life is to help various pieces of Cisco equipment find one another, for network management purposes. We can take advantage of this as well, since one item of information passed via CDP is the AppleTalk address. Here is the command to use, followed by its output list of neighboring Cisco devices:

```
Router>show cdp neighbor detail
Device ID: Router2
Entry address(es):
  IP address: 10.0.0.12
  Appletalk address: 9000.127
Platform: cisco 7000,  Capabilities: Router
Interface: Fddi4/0,  Port ID (outgoing port): Fddi3/0
Holdtime : 129 sec

Version :
Cisco Internetwork Operating System Software
IOS (tm) GS Software (GS7-K-M), Version 10.3(12), RELEASE
SOFTWARE (fc1)
Copyright (c) 1986-1996 by cisco Systems, Inc.
Compiled Mon 03-Jun-96 12:59 by dschwart
```

As you can see, CDP provides a handy map of IP address to AppleTalk address. Be prepared to answer questions about CDP on the exams.

So what causes these incorrect routes? A common cause is running two routing protocols between two routers; for example, both RTMP and EIGRP. It's possible to advertise a route over one protocol, and pick it right back up via the other, creating a route loop. Another possible reason is "unofficial" routers that have been added to your network, which can include Macs, Windows NT servers, and UNIX hosts with the right software.

Something Missing on the Network

"Something missing" might be a printer, a file server, a zone, or all of the zones. These gaps are usually observed from the workstations. There's a wide range of causes for "missing pieces" problems, so let's go over some of them.

Service Missing from a Zone

This is a fairly common problem. The call you'll get is usually something to the effect of "I can't see my printer in the XYZ zone" or "When I double-click my alias, it says the server cannot be found." Some of these are network problems; some of them are not.

In some cases, the problem is simple; for example, the printer has been turned off, is offline, has been unplugged, or is out of paper. This is easy to fix, provided you can find the printer to begin with. Even if you have no record of the printer's location, the user can usually show you which printer isn't connected. Only occasionally might you get a request for help with a printer that doesn't appear in the Chooser and whose location the user doesn't know. In this case, the question may actually be whether the printer exists at all.

What about a file server? This may be nothing more than someone's desktop workstation, and the server may be off, or file sharing may have been turned off. Occasionally, on dedicated AppleShare servers, the AppleShare program may crash. The same thing may occur on Novell servers with the AppleShare Value Added Process (VAP) or NetWare Loadable Module (NLM).

As you can see, you'll want to start your troubleshooting by making sure the service still exists. This can usually be verified from another workstation, or by visiting the server offering the service. Another thing to look out for is whether the service has changed zones. Recall that on a network segment with multiple zone names, an AppleTalk device will initially come up on the default zone. It may happen that an AppleTalk device will spontaneously return to the default zone after it has been moved to a different one.

Finally, there is one possible network problem: Recall that when a user clicks on a zone, a broadcast request is made, and the workstation awaits replies. If the broadcast can't get there, or the replies can't get back, the service will not appear in the Chooser. This is normally either a routing or congestion issue and should be corrected using the suggestions in the preceding "Routing Problems" section. If it's truly a routing problem, it's likely that the entire zone will be empty, or a portion of it if the zone covers multiple cable ranges.

Missing Zone

The problem of a missing zone is fairly easy to diagnose, if not to fix. If the user is missing one or more zones, either the full zone list didn't come through when it was requested, due to a congested or failing local network, or the router may not have the zone that's missing. The latter case is the most likely.

Connect to the router, do a SHOW APPLETALK ZONE command, and look for the zone. If it's not there, troubleshoot it as you would a routing problem. This is where your records come in handy, because you'll need to know the cable ranges associated with that zone.

All Zones Missing

When all zones are missing, it means either the local router or the workstation is not working properly. You'll probably know which one is at fault based on feedback from other users in the area. If it's a single workstation that's having trouble, the most likely cause is a Layer 2 connectivity problem. If the workstation has another protocol loaded (for example, TCP/IP) you may be able to use that to troubleshoot the problem.

If you're satisfied that you have good Layer 2 connectivity, then the problem is likely that the workstation couldn't get out of the Startup network range for some reason. This can sometimes be fixed with a reboot. If the workstation is running a fairly old version of the OS and network drivers, an upgrade can be required.

You might also check to see if you're low on addresses in that cable range. In that situation, it will be difficult for the workstation to find an open address at random; it may time out before it finds a good one. To prevent this from happening, consider allocating about twice as much address space as you intend to use.

AppleTalk Interface Goes Down

This is a fairly specific problem. Normal status for an AppleTalk interface on a Cisco router is "address valid," as shown in this output from the show appletalk interface command:

```
Cat-RSM#show appletalk interface vlan 99
Vlan99 is up, line protocol is up
  AppleTalk cable range is 9010-9010
  AppleTalk address is 9010.119, Valid
  AppleTalk zone is "Zone 1"
  AppleTalk address gleaning is disabled
  AppleTalk route cache is enabled
```

Here's the output for an AppleTalk interface that's having trouble:

```
Vlan220 is up, line protocol is up
  AppleTalk node down, Port configuration error
  AppleTalk cable range is 251-251
  AppleTalk address is 251.229, Invalid
  AppleTalk primary zone is "Zone 2"
  AppleTalk additional zones: "test"
  AppleTalk discarded 1 packet due to input errors
  AppleTalk address gleaning is disabled
  AppleTalk route cache is disabled, port initializing
```

Typically, the only time a Cisco router will show its AppleTalk interface in the state illustrated here is if something has told the router that its configuration is wrong—and about the only thing that will do that is another seed router. In the example shown here, I added the "test" zone, and there was another seed router on that network. As soon as the zone list didn't match, the Cisco interface went down. As mentioned in the Router Interface Configuration Commands section earlier in this chapter, make sure that all seed routers on the same network segment have the same configuration.

QUESTIONS AND ANSWERS

I want to be able to use my old LocalTalk devices with my EtherTalk devices.	You have two choices: Buy a converter for each of the LocalTalk devices, or get some LocalTalk-to-EtherTalk routers.
I need to be able to use more than 253 devices on the same network number. How do I arrange this?	You can't. You can, however, achieve the same effect by creating a cable range that consists of multiple, contiguous network numbers. This is, for all intents and purposes, just like having a larger network with a single network number.
I want to document my AppleTalk network so I'm prepared when trouble arises.	Good. Pick a time when your network is operating properly, log in to a router, and copy the output from the SHOW APPLETALK ZONE and SHOW APPLETALK ROUTE commands. Save a backup copy of all of your router configuration files. Create a file to track usage of your network numbers, so you can allocate new ones without conflict. Create a list of network numbers and what router they are on, so you can track them down if they fall out of the routing table.
Should I use RTMP or EIGRP for my AppleTalk routing?	It depends on your environment. If you have a small network with mostly LAN connections, RTMP will probably be simpler. If you have a large network with lots of WAN links, EIGRP is probably better.
One of my users doesn't have any zones in their Chooser. Why?	Go through your normal Layer 1 and 2 troubleshooting sequence (link light, etc.). If there are other protocols on the Mac, try those as well. Do you have enough addresses in your cable range? Is the right protocol selected (for instance, EtherTalk and not LocalTalk)? Have you tried rebooting? Do the drivers need updating?
My user's printer isn't showing up in the zone where it's supposed to be. Why?	Is the printer turned on and otherwise ready to print? Is the printer in the right zone? If it's a printer that prints a "test page" on startup, power it off and back on, and look at the test page to see if it printed which zone it's in. Can anyone else print to the printer? Is all of the networking cabling in place?
I don't have enough addresses for all of my AppleTalk devices. How do I deal with this?	Expand or replace the cable range on that network segment. Try to allocate about twice as much address space as is needed for all the devices. Remember to change the cable range on all seed routers if more than one exists on that network segment.

CERTIFICATION SUMMARY

AppleTalk originally gained popularity as a way to share expensive printers among multiple Macintosh computers, and because it came built into each of those printers and Macintoshes. AppleTalk was designed after TCP/IP was created, and AppleTalk's designers used some of the IP designs.

AppleTalk addressing uses 24 bits: 16 for a network number, and 8 for a node ID. This type of AppleTalk is called AppleTalk Phase II. AppleTalk Phase I was originally used on LocalTalk networks and was limited to 253 devices.

When an AppleTalk device first boots, it must choose an address. This is done by first randomly picking a node ID and network number from the Startup network number range. The device verifies that the address it has picked is not already in use by requesting its own address via an AARP request. If the device receives no reply, it knows it can use the address it has chosen. Once it has picked a startup address, the device can use that to communicate with a local AppleTalk router to determine if there is a cable range assigned to the network segment that the router is on. If so, the device picks another node ID within that range and sends an AARP request for that address, as well.

The protocol AppleTalk uses at Layer 3 is called DDP. DDP is a connectionless, unreliable protocol. Reliability features must be implemented at higher layers.

Mac users typically access network resources through the Chooser. In the Chooser, the user sees a list of service types, and a list of zones from which to choose the services. When the Chooser is first launched, it requests a list of zone names from a local router, via the ZIP protocol. The Mac may need to make more than one request, because all of the zones may not fit in one packet.

Once a list of zones is obtained, the user may select one and ask for a particular service. A list of services of a particular type in a particular zone is obtained by sending a broadcast request to a local router. The local router converts this to a forward request, and forwards it to a directly attached router that can reach a network in the requested zone. Once the forward request has reached the routers that have the appropriate networks attached, the routers convert their copy of the forward request into a lookup request. The lookup request is broadcast to the local network, and all AppleTalk devices that are running the requested service respond directly to the original requesting node. The original request may be sent several times to ensure delivery, since an unreliable protocol is being used.

Troubleshooting AppleTalk problems without accurate network documentation can be difficult, because otherwise there may be little indication of what exactly is wrong. Because AppleTalk is dynamic in nature, much of the information needed to troubleshoot a problem may not be available when the problem is occurring, unless it has been recorded elsewhere.

The closest thing to an official specification for AppleTalk is Apple's book "Inside AppleTalk." They have made it available on the Web (minus a few of the figures) at:

http://www.apple.com/macos/opentransport/docs/Inside_AppleTalk.pdf

Some related specifications can be found at:

http://www.apple.com/macos/opentransport/reference.html#Specs

Cisco provides an excellent Configuring AppleTalk guide at:

http://www.cisco.com/univercd/cc/td/doc/product/software/ios113ed/ 113ed_cr/np2_c/2capple.htm

It contains configuration guides, troubleshooting tips, and information on how to architect an AppleTalk network.

 ## TWO-MINUTE DRILL

- ❑ As a network manager, you'll have to create an AppleTalk network using Cisco routers. Assuming that your Layer 2 network is in place, your router interfaces are not in the shut state, and you're ready to add AppleTalk at Layer 3, the first thing to do is turn on AppleTalk routing.

- ❑ By default, using this form of the command, `appletalk routing`, turns on Routing Table Maintenance Protocol (RTMP) routing.

❑ Alternatively, you can use Cisco's proprietary Enhanced Interior Gateway Routing Protocol (EIGRP) by issuing this command instead: `appletalk routing eigrp network-number`.

❑ AppleTalk uses a numbering scheme to differentiate nodes. AppleTalk uses a dynamic addressing scheme.

❑ Apple has a protocol called the AppleTalk Address Resolution Protocol, AARP.

❑ Try to get used to identifying the various parts of AppleTalk packets. You may be asked to identify the protocol of a packet, its purpose, and so forth.

❑ AppleTalk's Layer 3 protocol is called the Datagram Delivery Protocol, or DDP.

❑ In addition to the node ID, the AppleTalk device also has to pick a network number.

❑ When a Mac boots up onto an AppleTalk network for the first time ever, it acquires a node ID in one of the networks listed in this Startup range. The primary purpose of this address is for communication with an AppleTalk router to determine the correct network number(s) to use. This communication is done via the Zone Information Protocol (ZIP).

❑ If there is no router present, the AppleTalk device will keep its startup address and use that to communicate.

❑ Mac users normally access the zone list by accessing the Chooser from the Apple menu.

❑ AppleTalk routers also maintain a list of zone names and their associated cable ranges called the *Zone Information Table (ZIT)*.

❑ A zone can consist of more than one cable range. The cable ranges do not have to be contiguous, or related in any way, except that you want them to be in the same zone.

❑ To configure a cable range on a particular router interface, first enter configuration mode, and select the desired interface.

❑ To remove a zone name from an interface, use the "no" version of the command.

❏ AURP stands for AppleTalk Update Routing Protocol; it's used only when AppleTalk is tunneled and can only be applied to tunnel interfaces.

❏ The list of zones is obtained from client's local router.

❏ The file-sharing protocol used with AppleTalk is the AppleTalk Filing Protocol (AFP). Printing is done via the Printer Access Protocol (PAP).

❏ Name Binding Protocol (NBP) does a couple of different things, depending on how it's used, but its main function is to map a named service to its network number, its node ID, and its socket number.

❏ The biggest favor you can do for yourself is to keep good documentation.

❏ Routing problems are generally pretty straightforward. The root issues of concern are incorrect routes and missing routes. The solution is to correct the bad or missing information.

❏ There may be one shortcut available to you while doing a manual TRACEROUTE, if the next router is a Cisco router. As mentioned in previous chapters, Cisco has written a proprietary protocol called the Cisco Discovery Protocol (CDP).

SELF TEST

The following Self Test questions will help you measure your understanding of the material presented in this chapter. Read all the choices carefully, as there may be more than one correct answer. Choose all correct answers for each question.

1. Which of the following is a transport protocol?

   A. ID

   B. DDP

   C. RTMP

   D. AFP

2. What is the purpose of AARP?

   A. To map sockets to AppleTalk addresses

   B. To get a list of zones

   C. To transport packets

   D. To map Layer 2 addresses to Layer 3 addresses

3. What is the purpose of NBP?

   A. To map a named service to its network number, node ID, and socket number

   B. To retrieve the default zone for the local network segment

   C. To access files on AppleShare servers

   D. For printing

4. Which protocol is used for file transfers in AppleTalk?

   A. FTP

   B. AFP

   C. PAP

   D. DDP

5. What is the range, in hex, designated as the Startup network range?

   A. FFF0-FFFF

   B. FF00-FFFF

   C. 65280-65534

   D. FF00-FFFE

6. What is AppleTalk's Layer 3 protocol?

   A. ZIP

   B. RTMP

   C. AARP

   D. DDP

7. What is the maximum number of bytes in the DDP portion of an AppleTalk packet?

   A. 65,535

   B. 599

   C. 1000

   D. 1500

8. How does a node determine if its randomly picked address is already in use?

   A. By sending an AARP request

   B. By using ZIP to ask the router

   C. By listening to RTMP broadcasts

   D. By sending NBP requests

9. When will a Cisco router declare its own AppleTalk address invalid and refuse to function?

   A. When it's set to 128

   B. When another seed router tells the Cisco router that it's using an invalid configuration

   C. When it's in dynamic mode

   D. When it's in the Startup range

10. What's the most likely cause of one missing zone on a workstation?

    A. ZIP is running on the wrong socket

    B. The NBP broadcast didn't get a response

    C. The local router doesn't have that zone in its ZIT

    D. A name conflict

11. Which command is used to display AppleTalk routes on a Cisco router?

    A. SHOW APPLETALK ZONE

    B. SHOW APPLETALK ROUTE

    C. SHOW APPLETALK ARP

    D. TRACEROUTE APPLETALK ROUTE

12. How do you display the ZIT on a Cisco router?

    A. SHOW APPLETALK ZONE

    B. SHOW APPLETALK ROUTE

    C. SHOW APPLETALK ARP

    D. SHOW APPLETALK NBP

13. In which zone will an AppleTalk device appear on a network segment that has more than one zone?

    A. The first alphabetically in the Chooser

    B. The default

    C. The longest

    D. The shortest

14. By default, RTMP sends updates how often?

    A. Every 10 seconds

    B. Every 20 seconds

    C. Every 30 seconds

    D. Every 60 seconds

15. A zone is:

    A. A network number

    B. A cable range

    C. A device driver

    D. A group of AppleTalk devices

16. What is the broadcast host ID?

    A. 0

    B. 253

    C. 254

    D. 255

17. What is the maximum number of hops in an AppleTalk network routed with RTMP?

    A. 8

    B. 15

    C. 16

    D. 255

18. What type of packet does a workstation use to get a list of zone names?

    A. GetZoneList

    B. NBP

    C. ZIP

    D. GetNetInfo

19. What's the most likely cause of two zones with the same name in the Chooser?

    A. Duplicate ZIP packets

    B. Corrupted router memory

    C. One hasn't timed out yet

    D. An extra space

20. What's the best way to prepare for problems on an AppleTalk network?

    A. Use EIGRP

    B. Use Phase II

    C. Document the network

    D. Use a Sniffer

7

Common Routing Protocols

When troubleshooting network conditions due to routing protocol anomalies, it is important to have a fundamental knowledge of how the routing protocol functions, the available tools for diagnosis, and an experience base in problem identification and resolution.

This chapter presents an in-depth discussion of the following routing protocols: RIP, IGRP, IPX, AppleTalk, EIGRP, OSPF, and BGP. A number of troubleshooting techniques are also presented. It is important for the reader to experiment and become familiar with the various elements within the router tables, processes, and debug information.

CERTIFICATION OBJECTIVE 7.01

Periodic Broadcast-Based Protocols

Routing protocols are generally subdivided into two categories: periodic broadcast protocols, and event-driven protocols.

Periodic broadcast protocols send route updates at regular, timed intervals. Should a certain number of updates be missed over an extended interval, the routers in the network will assume the route to be inaccessible and will eventually remove the route altogether. This method of routing requires constant updating of the routes, whether there has been a routing table change or not.

Periodic broadcast protocols are considered to be of "legacy" variety. Although periodic broadcast protocols are more antiquated, there still exists a considerable installed base of these protocols, including RIP and IGRP (Cisco's Interior Gateway Routing Protocol). Because these protocols can be a little temperamental and sometimes have obscure effects on routing within large networks, they provide substantial input to the Cisco Certified Internetwork Expert troubleshooting section.

Periodic broadcast protocols such as RIP were used widely within the early ARPANET. As networks grew to scale, elements such as longer convergence times, multiple routing loops, and hierarchical models required more robust and scalable network routing protocols.

Event-driven protocols provide for this more scalable network architecture, in that routing updates are only generated in the event of a network topology change. For instance, when a subnet is disconnected from a router, causing a change in the routing table, an event-driven protocol will broadcast the route's removal. When the subnet re-attaches, then the route will be advertised again.

Often periodic broadcast protocols and event-driven protocols are confused with *distance vector* and *link-state protocols*. However, the correct association of these terms is that distance vector protocols may be either periodic broadcast or event-driven. For example, BGP is a distance vector, event-driven protocol; OSPF is a link-state, event-driven protocol; and IGRP is a distance vector, periodic broadcast protocol.

Distance vector protocols only maintain a database of the destination routes and the metric required to reach the network. Link-state protocols, on the other hand, maintain an entire network topology database and locally determine the best path to each destination network.

Routing Information Protocol (RIP)

As previously mentioned, RIP is one of the "legacy" periodic broadcast, distance-vector routing protocols. It is defined in RFC 1058. RIP functions by broadcasting its full routing table to all other routers in the network. All routers receive the advertised routes and regularly update their forwarding tables. Before sending out route broadcasts, RIP edits its routing table based upon split-horizon, metric limitations, and on variable mask conflicts.

In the event that certain routes are no longer advertised, then it is assumed that those routes are no longer active. Due to the complexity of large periodic broadcast networks using RIP, there can exist various convergence and synchronization issues regarding RIP broadcasts.

RIP maintains a routing table with the following criteria:

Network Destination	Represents the network or subnet for which this packet is destined.
Next Hop	Represents the IP address of the next router on the path to the destination network.

Hop Distance	Represents the number of router hops required to reach the actual destination network. RIP is currently restricted to networks less than 16 hops.
Timers	Represent the update and expiration times associated with the routes.
Flags	Represent the network state of a route.

Following are various timers associated with RIP:

- **Update Timers**   Frequency at which the entire routing table is broadcast. RIP defaults to 30 seconds for the update timer.

- **Invalid Timers**   Interval after which a route is determined to be no longer valid and will no longer be advertised. RIP defaults to 90 seconds for the invalid timer.

- **Flush Timers**   Interval after which a route is removed from the RIP table. RIP defaults to 270 seconds for the flush timer.

RIP generally requires route updates every 30 seconds via broadcasts in order to keep the routes fresh. After the 90-second invalid timer period, the routes are no longer accessible and are no longer advertised. After the 270-second flush timer period, the route originating from the neighbor router is removed. In large-scaled meshed networks with up to 16 routers in a path, waiting four minutes for routing tables to reconverge can be intolerable. A worst case maximum size network can even take up to eight minutes before routing stabilizes.

In order to accommodate various routing loops that may occur within certain network topologies, RIP has implemented a number of features to reduce looping effects:

- **Holddown**   Instructs the router to wait a period of time before reinstating a route that may have been invalid. This prevents downstream routers, which may not yet be aware of invalid routes, from making them valid again.

- **Split-horizon**   Prevents a router from advertising a route back to its source. Split-horizons prevent two-node routing loops, which can cause a "count to infinity" hop count problem.

- **Poison reverse**   Prevents larger, multihop routing loops by using holddowns for routes that have increasing metrics.

Classful Routing

RIP suffers from limitations on its IP addressing abilities. IP RIP is a *classful* routing protocol. In the earlier classful Internet routing networks, IP addresses were categorized based upon their IP addressing range:

- **Class A**   0.0.0.0 – 126.255.255.255
- **Class B**   128.0.0.0 – 191.255.255.255
- **Class C**   192.0.0.0 – 223.255.255.255

In a classful subnetting environment, if one chooses to subdivide a particular class of address space (say the Class A range 10.0.0.0, for instance) into further subnets (such as 255.255.255.0), then the entire address space for the address class would be subnetted with that particular netmask, 255.255.255.0. This means all LANs, as well as point-to-point serial interfaces, are required to use an entire /24 for each subnet. Allowing only one subnetting of the classful IP address space for both LANs and point-to-point networks can be both limiting as well as wasteful within today's networking environments.

The term *classful* refers to a major network number of class A, B, or C. Classful protocols share the characteristic that they do not transmit mask information along with destination network information. Instead, the receiving router infers a mask from that configured on the receiving interface, when the route is a subnet of the same major network number. Since the receiving router must guess at a mask, the sending router edits its routing updates. Updates about destination networks belonging to the same major network number are sent only if they match the mask configured on the receiver's interface.

e x a m
ⓦa t c h

When redistributing routing protocols with classless VLSM networks into RIP, be sure that subnetted static routes with a null next hop are redistributed, as well.

This scheme breaks down when a router must send an advertisement into an interface configured in a different major network number. Here the classful routing protocol creates a summary advertisement representing the entire major network number. When a router receives an advertisement of a network number not belonging to the same major network number as that configured on the receiving interface, that router examines the bits in the host portion of the route. If the bits are all zero, the advertisement is assumed to be a classful summary. If there are nonzero bits in the host portion, the advertisement is considered a host route.

More recent protocols allow for variable-length subnet masking (VLSM), which allows for a nonclassful IP addressing scheme. If a LAN has a subnet address 10.1.1.0/24, for instance, and a frame relay point-to-point subinterface is assigned 10.1.2.0/30, RIP will not propagate the subnet mask information associated with the route. All subnets within the class must have only one netmask, which is associated with a connected interface on the router. Therefore, when using RIP, be sure when subnetting to consistently use the same subnet mask within a network class.

Routing protocols such as RIPv2, OSPF, BGP, and others propagate netmask information along with routing updates. Routing protocols that allow for VLSM updates allow for "classless" routing where subnetting can be of different lengths.

It is a good idea to use one IP address subnet for all point-to-point links assigning a /30 to the subnet, and use another IP subnet for LANs possibly using a /24.

e x a m
ⓦa t c h

Whenever redistributing routes, always include "subnets."

Troubleshooting RIP

When troubleshooting RIP, it is always best to start by looking in the routing table for "RIP." First determine if the routing entry exists, by using the SHOW IP ROUTE RIP command. Then determine its hop count and the next hop. The two values in brackets, shown as [120/1], represent the route's administrative distance and metric, respectively.

If the route exists within the RIP table, you may want to verify that it is in the forwarding table, discussed next. If the route does not exist, then you may need to enable a debug mode and verify that you are receiving the routing updates for the desired networks. (Debug mode is discussed later in the section.)

Consider this router's IP forwarding table:

```
Lab_Con#show ip route rip
     10.0.0.0/24 is subnetted, 4 subnets
R       10.3.1.0 [120/1] via 10.2.1.3, 00:00:16, Ethernet0
R       10.5.1.0 [120/1] via 10.2.1.2, 00:00:23, Ethernet0
R       10.4.1.0 [120/1] via 10.2.1.3, 00:00:16, Ethernet0
```

Although RIP may be advertising a specific route, due to RIP's high administrative distance, another lower administrative distance routing protocol such as EIGRP may also be advertising the same route and be populating the Forwarding Information Base.

In the following example, EIGRP has a lower routing administrative distance than RIP and therefore has preference over RIP in the FIB table as shown by the SHOW IP ROUTE command:

```
RouterA#sh ip route
Codes: C - connected, S - static, I - IGRP, R - RIP, M - mobile, B - BGP
       D - EIGRP, EX - EIGRP external, O - OSPF, IA - OSPF inter area
       E1 - OSPF external type 1, E2 - OSPF external type 2, E - EGP
       i - IS-IS, L1 - IS-IS level-1, L2 - IS-IS level-2, * - candidate default
       U - per-user static route

Gateway of last resort is not set

10.0.0.0/24 is subnetted, 4 subnets
D       10.3.1.0 [90/409600] via 10.2.1.3, 00:04:17, Ethernet0/0
C       10.2.1.0 is directly connected, Ethernet0/0
C       10.6.1.0 is directly connected, Serial5/0/4
C       10.5.1.0 is directly connected, Loopback0
```

Some strange routing occurrences may exist where routes vanish and reappear due to competing routing protocols. Asynchronous updates in lower administrative-distance routing protocols will supersede routes originated by higher administrative-distance protocols. This phenomena can occur with RIP and IGRP originating the same routes. It is therefore important to verify the entry time associated with each route in the FIB.

Table 7-1 depicts all the administrative distances associated with each routing protocol.

exam

ⓦatch

Running RIP with an instance of another periodic broadcast routing protocol, such as IGRP, can result in routing issues. This is due to the asynchronous updates' and administrative distance's competing for inserting routes into the forwarding table.

Resorting to Debug Mode

If all else fails and you can't figure out what is going on in the network, it's time to get into debug mode and start monitoring all RIP packets and updates traversing the network. Verify that the RIP routes are being

TABLE 7-1		
Routing Protocol Administrative Distances	**Route Source**	**Default Distance**
	Connected interface	0
	Static route	1
	Enhanced IGRP summary route	5
	External BGP	20
	Internal enhanced IGRP	90
	IGRP	100
	OSPF	110
	IS-IS	115
	RIP	120
	EGP	140
	External enhanced IGRP	170
	Internal BGP	200
	Unknown	255

advertised correctly and being originated from the appropriate routers, as follows:

```
RouterA#terminal monitor
RouterA#debug ip rip events
RIP event debugging is on

RouterA#
RIP: sending general request on Ethernet0/0 to 255.255.255.255
RIP: sending general request on Serial5/0/4 to 255.255.255.255
RIP: sending general request on Loopback0 to 255.255.255.255
RIP: received v1 update from 10.2.1.1 on Ethernet0/0
RIP: Update contains 1 routes
RIP: sending v1 update to 255.255.255.255 via Ethernet0/0 (10.2.1.2)
RIP: Update contains 2 routes
RIP: Update queued
RIP: Update sent via Ethernet0/0
RIP: sending v1 update to 255.255.255.255 via Serial5/0/4 (10.6.1.1)
RIP: Update contains 2 routes
RIP: Update queued
RIP: Update sent via Serial5/0/4
RIP: sending v1 update to 255.255.255.255 via Loopback0 (10.5.1.1)
RIP: Update contains 2 routes
RIP: Update queued
RIP: Update sent via Loopback0
```

Cisco's Interior Gateway Routing Protocol (IGRP)

Cisco's *Interior Gateway Routing Protocol (IGRP)* is also a periodic broadcast protocol, with stronger decision-making criteria based upon real-time network events and congestion states.

IGRP allows for more-dynamic routing decisions based upon real-time network states, including

- Load
- Reliability
- Bandwidth
- Delay
- MTU

In addition, IGRP has the ability to balance traffic even within unequal multipath networks. For instance, if two neighboring routers have a T1 and a 512K circuit between them, IGRP can balance the traffic by proportionally routing traffic to destinations on each circuit.

IGRP contains three types of routes: interior, system, and exterior. *Interior routes* are part of a router's directly connected interface. *System routes* are routes within the IGRP's autonomous system. *Exterior routes* are learned outside of IGRP's autonomous system.

An autonomous system is a routing domain that contains all routers within an IGRP network, as shown in Figure 7-1. Any external routes to the autonomous system must be learned via an EGP/BGP, redistribution from another routing protocol, or a default route.

The following timers are associated with IGRP:

- **Update Timer**   Frequency of broadcasts of the entire routing table. IGRP defaults to 90 seconds.

- **Invalid Timer**   Interval after which a route is determined to be no longer valid. IGRP defaults to 90 seconds.

- **Holddown Timer**   Interval to wait before revalidating a route. IGRP defaults to 270 seconds.

- **Flush Timer**   Interval after which a route is removed from RIP table. IGRP defaults to 630 seconds.

FIGURE 7-1

IGRP autonomous system

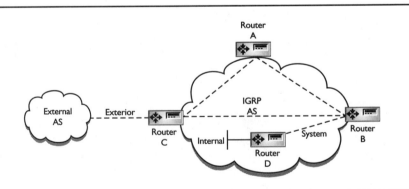

Like RIP, IGRP is a periodic broadcast-based routing protocol. IGRP, however, updates routes at 90-second intervals, designates a route as inaccessible after 270 seconds, and removes the route entirely after 630 seconds. IGRP also uses flash updates for sending immediate route-update messages; as well as poison reverse updates to reduce the possibility of routing loops. If enabled on every router in the network, the poison reverse update will "hold down" the route while the update is being distributed throughout the network.

IGRP is also a classful IP routing protocol. It follows the same IP subnetting rules as RIP.

exam
ⓦatch

When redistributing routing protocols with classless VLSM networks into IGRP, be sure that there are classful static routes with a null next hop redistributed as well.

Troubleshooting IGRP

When troubleshooting an IGRP network, always start with the IGRP routing table. The two values in the brackets, shown as [100/1600], represent the route's administrative distance and metric, respectively. Make sure that the route exists within the IGRP routing table. If it exists, verify that it's in the FIB, by using the SHOW IP ROUTE IGRP command as shown here. Also, ensure the route's entry time shows that it is stable.

```
Lab_Con#show ip route igrp
     10.0.0.0/24 is subnetted, 4 subnets
I       10.3.1.0 [100/1600] via 10.2.1.3, 00:00:38, Ethernet0
I       10.5.1.0 [100/1600] via 10.2.1.2, 00:00:48, Ethernet0
I       10.4.1.0 [100/1200] via 10.2.1.3, 00:00:38, Ethernet0
```

In the event that the IGRP routes are not showing up in the IGRP table, then you should begin debugging IGRP. Look to see that routes containing the routing updates are being received. If they are not being received, then the neighbor router which should be advertising the routes most likely has a filter, access list, or is down. Use the DEBUG IP IGRP command to enable IGRP debugging.

```
RouterA#terminal monitor
RouterA#debug ip igrp events
IGRP event debugging is on

IGRP: sending update to 255.255.255.255 via Loopback0 (10.5.1.1)
IGRP: Update contains 3 interior, 1 system, and 0 exterior routes.
IGRP: Total routes in update: 4
IGRP: sending update to 255.255.255.255 via Ethernet0/0 (10.2.1.2)
IGRP: Update contains 2 interior, 1 system, and 0 exterior routes.
IGRP: Total routes in update: 3
IGRP: sending update to 255.255.255.255 via Serial5/0/4 (10.6.1.1)
IGRP: Update contains 3 interior, 1 system, and 0 exterior routes.
IGRP: Total routes in update: 4
```

IPX RIP and Service Advertising Protocol (SAP)

Although IP has made significant progress within the last few years as the common communications protocol, there is still a significant installed base of IPX (Internetwork Packet Exchange) equipment and networks. Service Advertising Protocol (SAP) is an enterprise network services protocol used to advertise information regarding file servers, print servers, job servers, and so on. IPX can be routed via IPX RIP, IPX EIGRP, or NLSP.

Cisco IPX routing is a packet-based routing protocol; SAP is a services-advertising protocol. *Networking* and *services* can be regarded as somewhat different entities within IPX. IPX networks are represented by an 8-digit hexadecimal number uniquely identifying the cable segment.

Unless you plan to use NLSP (NetWare Link Services Protocol), most IPX networks are nonhierarchical and require either the explicit advertising of every IPX network, or the use of default routes for IPX routing.

Cisco allows for filtering both IPX networks and services based upon the following:

- Standard source and destination network numbers 800–899

- Extended IPX protocol type

- SAP and GNS

- NetBIOS

Filters can be applied to both interfaces and routing updates.

Troubleshooting IPX RIP

When troubleshooting an IPX network, always start with the IPX routing table. Identify each network and make sure that the routing table is complete. Use the SHOW IPX ROUTE command to look at the IPX forwarding table. Make sure that each IPX network and next hop interface are accurate:

```
RouterA#show ipx route
Codes: C - Connected primary network,    c - Connected secondary network
       S - Static, F - Floating static, L - Local (internal), W - IPXWAN
       R - RIP, E - EIGRP, N - NLSP, X - External, A - Aggregate
       s - seconds, u - uses

5 Total IPX routes. Up to 1 parallel paths and 16 hops allowed.

No default route known.

L       CCCC is the internal network
C       AAAA (NOVELL-ETHER),   Et0/0
R       BBBB [02/01] via       AAAA.0060.8394.e940,    8s, Et0/0
R       DDDD [02/01] via       AAAA.0060.5cf4.1554,   54s, Et0/0
R       EEEE [02/01] via       AAAA.0060.8394.e940,    8s, Et0/0
```

To verify that an attached host is available, use the PING IPX command to verify response:

```
RouterB#ping ipx AAAA.0060.8388.bb00

Type escape sequence to abort.
Sending 5, 100-byte IPX cisco Echoes to AAAA.0060.8388.bb00, timeout is 2 seconds:
!!!!!
Success rate is 100 percent (5/5), round-trip min/avg/max = 1/3/4 ms
```

To verify that a Novell server is being advertised throughout the network, use the SHOW IPX SERVER command:

```
RouterB#show ipx server
Codes: S - Static, P - Periodic, E - EIGRP, N - NLSP, H - Holddown, + = detail
1 Total IPX Servers

Table ordering is based on routing and server info

    Type Name                      Net     Address   Port    Route Hops Itf
S      4 FileServer          AAAA.0060.8388.cc00:0023    conn   2  Et10/0
```

It is usually a good idea to debug various routers and verify correct IPX operation. Look for network updates at regular intervals. If certain networks are not being advertised, then a neighbor router may be route filtering, may have access lists, or may be down. Consider the following output:

```
RouterA#debug ipx routing events
IPX routing events debugging is on

IPXRIP: positing full update to AAAA.ffff.ffff.ffff via Ethernet0/0 (broadcast)
IPXRIP: sending update to AAAA.ffff.ffff.ffff via Ethernet0/0
```

Also, view incremental SAP updates for regular activity, as follows:

```
RouterA#debug ipx sap
IPX service events debugging is on

IPXSAP: positing update to AAAA.ffff.ffff.ffff via Ethernet0/0 (broadcast) (full)
```

AppleTalk Routing Table Maintenance Protocol (RTMP)

AppleTalk *Router Table Maintenance Protocol (RTMP)* is another distance vector, periodic broadcast RIP-based protocol. Cisco's support of AppleTalk includes the following:

- Phase 1 and Phase 2 AppleTalk (though they are incompatible)
- Extended and nonextended networks
- AppleTalk Address Resolution Protocol (AARP)
- AppleTalk Port Group
- Datagram Delivery Protocol
- Name Binding Protocol
- Zone Information Protocol
- AppleTalk Echo Protocol
- AppleTalk Transaction Protocol

AppleTalk Phase 1 allows for 254 devices, with 127 end-nodes and 127 servers, and only one zone. AppleTalk Phase 2 allows for 253 node devices per network, with multiple zones per network.

AppleTalk uses a 16-bit decimal, cable network-number addressing scheme concatenated with a node address. It employs a media-dependent address-selection protocol to dynamically assign node addresses. An extended network cable-range can be represented as a single network number or a start/end contiguous network-numbering sequence. A typical cable-range assignment may be represented in the form *4-8*. An AppleTalk node would be represented as *4.53*.

Each AppleTalk network can be a member of one or more zones, but a node is part of only one zone. A *zone* contains a logical group of networks. A single AppleTalk enterprise network can contain up to 255 zones. The various zones localize the nodes (printers, hosts, servers) within a large-scale enterprise network.

Large AppleTalk networks may contain an inordinate number of zones and networks requiring filtering of certain information. Cisco allows for filtering AppleTalk information based upon the following:

- Zones
- Network numbers
- Get Zone List Requests/Replies
- Routing table updates
- Zone Information Protocol (ZIP) replies
- Name Binding Protocol (NBP)

Cisco allows for access lists to apply interface filters on AppleTalk Datagram packets based upon packets' source network, cable range, or zone.

Routing table update filters can also be used to limit advertised AppleTalk zones and networks.

With GZL reply/request filters, Cisco routers can also limit the zone information permitted in the Macintosh Chooser. All routers on the attached network must have the same Get Zone List filters, or the Chooser will receive conflicting information and zones will appear and disappear.

ZIP filters are applied to routing table updates so that zones are not advertised to unauthorized routers.

AppleTalk can also limit the various node devices bound to strings via the Name Binding Protocol.

Troubleshooting AppleTalk Networks

In troubleshooting AppleTalk networks, always start with the routing table. Make sure that the router has all the correct information for forwarding AppleTalk packets. Try using a big whiteboard with lots of color markers—this is often invaluable when trying to localize problems and identify the nature of a problem. By drawing the local network and verifying where packets are being routed, you can more easily verify correct routing.

Here is output from the SHOW APPLETALK ROUTE command:

```
RouterB#show AppleTalk route
Codes: R - RTMP derived, E - EIGRP derived, C - connected, A - AURP
       S - static  P - proxy
1 route in internet

The first zone listed for each entry is its default (primary) zone.

C Net 1-10 directly connected, Ethernet10/0, zone A
```

If the router does not have a complete set of routes or is missing particular zones, then you will probably want to proceed into verifying routing neighbors, filters, and access lists as discussed later in this section. If the router *does* have full routes, then verify that the local LAN segments also have connectivity and that all nodes are reachable, by using the SHOW APPLETALK ARP command:

```
RouterB#show AppleTalk arp
Address       Age (min)  Type      Hardware Addr       Encap   Interface
2.223              12    Dynamic   0060.5cf4.1554.0000  SNAP   Ethernet10/0
2.241               -    Hardware  0060.8394.e940.0000  SNAP   Ethernet10/0
9.210              12    Dynamic   0060.8388.bb00.0000  SNAP   Ethernet10/0
```

If a particular node is not present within the ARP table, try pinging the AppleTalk node and then re-verify its ARP entry:

```
RouterA#ping AppleTalk 2.223

Type escape sequence to abort.
Sending 5, 100-byte AppleTalk Echoes to 2.223, timeout is 2 seconds:
!!!!!
Success rate is 100 percent (5/5), round-trip min/avg/max = 4/5/8 ms
```

If the AppleTalk node is unreachable, then there is probably a cabling problem, an interface problem (CLEAR APPLETALK INTERFACE), or a node problem (reboot).

If you cannot identify any local problems on the router, then you will have to begin looking upstream at the network. Verify that all AppleTalk RTMP neighbors are established and have been available for a considerable period of time. Make sure that the neighbors are not resetting themselves or having intermittent connectivity problems:

```
RouterB#show AppleTalk neighbors
AppleTalk neighbors:
  2.223          Ethernet10/0, uptime 00:13:57, 1 sec
                 Neighbor is reachable as a RTMP peer
  9.210          Ethernet10/0, uptime 00:15:37, 6 secs
                 Neighbor is reachable as a RTMP peer
```

Sometimes an end-user may not see particular zones within the enterprise network. In order to verify that all zones are available, use the SHOW APPLETALK ZONE command to view what zones are known by the router:

```
RouterB#show AppleTalk zone
Name                                    Network(s)
A                                       1-10
Total of 1 zone
```

If a particular zone is not shown on the router, it is probably being filtered by an upstream router. You should verify any access lists being applied on the interface connecting the two routers.

If the router is aware of the zone but a particular cable segment is unable to access that particular zone, it may be that an access list applied to that cable segment's interface is blocking that particular zone's advertisement. To verify the access list applied to the interface, use the SHOW APPLETALK ACCESS-LISTS command:

```
RouterB#show AppleTalk access-lists
AppleTalk access list 600:
  permit cable-range 1-10
  deny other-access
AppleTalk access list 601:
  permit zone A
  deny additional-zones
  deny other-access
```

Putting Debug to Work

Finally, if you cannot determine the nature of the problem or if you want to verify protocol behavior, look at the individual debug information and make sure that updates are occurring at regular intervals.

For instance, DEBUG is also helpful to ensure that ZIP broadcast storms are not congesting the network. A *ZIP broadcast storm* occurs when a route advertisement without a corresponding zone triggers the network with a flood of ZIP requests. You can detect a ZIP storm by looking for many incrementing ZIP requests in succession while enabling DEBUG APPLETALK-EVENTS. IOS 9.01 and above allow for ZIP storms to be prevented.

In order to verify routing operations such as update intervals, use the DEBUG APPLETALK RTMP command:

```
RouterA#debug AppleTalk rtmp
AppleTalk RTMP routing debugging is on

AT: src=Ethernet0/0:9.210, dst=1-10, size=10, 0 rtes, RTMP pkt sent
AT: Route ager starting on Main AT RoutingTable (1 active node)
AT: Route ager finished on Main AT RoutingTable (1 active node)
```

CERTIFICATION OBJECTIVE 7.02

Event-Driven Protocols

With the emergence of large-scaled networks within both the enterprise and the Internet, there exists the requirement to provide for robust, less "chatty" routing protocols. Three such powerful protocols are OSPF (Open Shortest Path First), EIGRP (Enhanced IGRP), and BGP (Border Gateway Protocol).

OSPF is purely an IP-based routing protocol intended for hierarchical large-scale networks. EIGRP is a multiservice routing protocol supporting IPX, AppleTalk, and IP. BGP is used for interconnecting networks and defining strict routing policies.

All three of these routing protocols provide only state-change information rather than regularly sending the entire network tables and trying to periodically synchronize the network. Depending on the routing environment, each one of these protocols is appropriate for certain network architectures.

Open Shortest Path First (OSPF)

OSPF is an IETF standards-based, event-driven link-state protocol based upon RFC 1583. OSPF is intended for enterprise hierarchical networks with a centralized backbone supporting various subordinate networks. An OSPF network architecture (see Figure 7-2) would contain a backbone area 0 with other attached network areas. All areas must attach to at least one portion of the backbone area 0, and must be contiguous.

Each network interface on a router must be associated with an area. A router that has multiple interfaces in various areas, including the backbone, is called an Area Border router. The Area Border router will maintain a separate link-state network topology for each attached area.

OSPF's main features include the following:

- Supporting cost metric
- Allows multipath/equal path
- Type-of-service routing
- Variable-length subnet mask
- Route summarization
- Stub areas

FIGURE 7-2

OSPF hierarchical topology

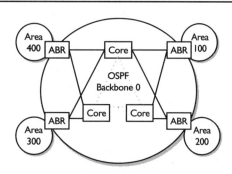

OSPF makes all routing decisions based upon static cost-metric assignments on each interface link. All links and their states are maintained in a link-state database. OSPF uses a Dijkstra link-state algorithm to compute the shortest path to any destination based upon the additive assigned metrics. Each network connection has a binary associated link state as either up or down. In the event of a link-state change, OSPF will flood a link-state advertisement to all adjacent neighbor routers, who will then recompute the shortest path to all known destinations; then routing will reconverge.

Each multi-access segment and NBMA network "elect" a Designated Router and Backup Designated Router for minimizing the exchange of database information on a particular shared network segment.

exam
ⓦatch

Understand how to use OSPF in point-to-point, point-to-multipoint, and broadcast media.

When network conditions change (as in a link failure), the neighbor routers will send link-state advertisements to their neighbors, who then in turn propagate the network change throughout the network.

OSPF supports five packet types:

- Hello
- Database description
- Link State Request
- Link State Update
- Link State Acknowledge

In addition, there are four types of Link State Updates:

- Router Link Advertisements
- Network Link Advertisements
- Summary Link Advertisements
- AS External Advertisements

Cisco's OSPF has a number of attractive features, such as creating virtual links through a transit area to extend a backbone area. Another helpful element of OSPF is the ability to create route summaries within the network, to better aggregate routing.

e x a m
ⓦatch

Be sure to design an OSPF network and assign IP addresses so that they summarize. In addition, beware of summarizing routes and then redistributing them into classful routing protocols.

Troubleshooting OSPF

OSPF has a number of design-related issues that can cause networkwide problems. For instance, a large OSPF network with unstable links can generate a considerable amount of LSA flooding. It is important when designing a hierarchical OSPF network to try and contain most of these LSAs within the areas. Route summarization also helps contain LSAs within each area. You can see evidence of an OSPF network that is too large and has too many unstable links by looking at the CPU usage of the routers. Recomputation of a large SPF database can consume substantial CPU resources—especially if the network is well meshed.

A general rule of thumb is for an area to contain less than 100 routers, and a network less than 700. Although successful larger OSPF networks do exist, and some smaller ones have design problems, other protocols (such as Border Gateway Protocol) are designed for larger, multiconnected networks.

When troubleshooting OSPF networks, start with the OSPF routing process itself, using SHOW IP OSPF. Verify redistribution of selected routes and make sure that the SPF algorithm is not continually recomputing. The "SPF algorithm executed" line shows the network stability. Successive executions of the SHOW IP OSPF command will show how often the network routing is reconverging.

```
Router#sh ip ospf 100
 Routing Process "ospf 100" with ID 1.1.1.1
 Supports only single TOS(TOS0) routes
 It is an autonomous system boundary router
 External Link update interval is 00:30:00 and the update due in 00:26:16
 Redistributing External Routes from,
    connected, includes subnets in redistribution
    static, includes subnets in redistribution
 SPF schedule delay 5 secs, Hold time between two SPFs 10 secs
 Number of areas in this router is 1. 1 normal 0 stub
```

```
Area BACKBONE(0)
    Number of interfaces in this area is 3
    Area has no authentication
    SPF algorithm executed 12 times
    Area ranges are
    Link State Update Interval is 00:30:00 and due in 00:26:14
    Link State Age Interval is 00:20:00 and due in 00:16:14
```

exam
ⓦatch

When redistributing OSPF routes, be sure to include external 1, external 2, and subnets.

After verifing the OSPF process, make sure that the selected routes in the forwarding table are based upon OSPF, by using the SHOW IP ROUTE command. Verify that each route learned also has the appropriate routing code, whether it's O, IA, E1, or E2. Consider the following output:

```
RouterA#show ip route
Codes: C - connected, S - static, I - IGRP, R - RIP, M - mobile, B - BGP
       D - EIGRP, EX - EIGRP external, O - OSPF, IA - OSPF inter area
       E1 - OSPF external type 1, E2 - OSPF external type 2, E - EGP
       i - IS-IS, L1 - IS-IS level-1, L2 - IS-IS level-2, * - candidate default
       U - per-user static route

Gateway of last resort is not set

10.0.0.0/8 is variably subnetted, 5 subnets, 2 masks
O E2    10.3.1.0/24 [110/20] via 10.2.1.3, 00:00:02, Ethernet0/0
C       10.2.1.0/24 is directly connected, Ethernet0/0
O       10.1.1.1/32 [110/11] via 10.2.1.1, 00:00:02, Ethernet0/0
C       10.5.1.0/24 is directly connected, Loopback0
O       10.4.1.0/24 [110/20] via 10.2.1.3, 00:00:02, Ethernet0/0
```

In the event that certain routes are not being advertised, a very common mistake is in the masking of the wildcard bits in the NETWORK statement. Also, make sure that the correct area is assigned to the networks:

```
router ospf 100
 redistribute connected subnets
 redistribute bgp 100 subnets
 passive-interface ATM0/0/0.431
 network 10.10.208.0 0.0.0.255 area 0.0.0.0
```

If you are using virtual links to extend the network backbone area 0, make sure that the virtual links do not attempt to transit an area stub and that the configuration is correct.

exam
ⓦatch

Understand how and where to use virtual links for extending a backbone area.

After verifying correct configuration and local routing, look toward your upstream routers and verify that you have established adjacent neighbor relationships. If an OSPF neighbor is not being established, it may be that the link between the routers is down, or an access list could be misconfigured.

```
Router>show ip ospf neighbor

Neighbor ID     Pri   State         Dead Time   Address        Interface
10.10.208.1     1     FULL/  -      00:00:38    10.10.216.146  ATM0/0/0.633
10.10.216.16    1     FULL/  -      00:00:30    10.10.216.150  ATM0/0/0.634
```

It may also be necessary to view the entire OSPF database and verify that all links are showing up. A lower "age" of the link indicates whether it is an unstable connection. Unstable connections in large OSPF networks tend to cause network "brown-outs" for periods of time while the network reconverges.

```
Router>show ip ospf database

     OSPF Router with ID (10.10.216.1) (Process ID 10281)<R>


             Router Link States (Area 0.0.0.0)

Link ID         ADV Router      Age    Seq#        Checksum Link count
10.10.208.1     10.10.208.1     493    0x800043C6  0x2B25   36
10.10.208.2     10.10.208.2     1054   0x800048D0  0x2EEE   12
10.10.208.7     10.10.208.7     1229   0x800004D5  0xD911   6
10.10.208.14    10.10.208.14    61     0x80000CEE  0x79BC   6
```

Cisco's Enhanced IGRP (EIGRP)

EIGRP is a comprehensive, event-driven Cisco enterprise routing protocol. It effectively routes IP, IPX, and AppleTalk all within a single routing-protocol architecture. EIGRP is a renovated version of IGRP with the following added features:

- Variable-length subnet masking (VLSM)
- More-robust routing
- Faster convergence times
- Partial event-driven updates
- Multiple network layer support
- Full compatibility with IGRP

The stronger routing protocol delivered by EIGRP is the result of the following features:

- Distributed Update Algorithm (DUAL)
- Reliable Transport Protocol
- Neighbor discovery
- Protocol-dependent modules

At the heart of EIGRP is the DUAL finite state machine, which uses a concept called *feasible successors* to select a loop-free balanced routing topology. The topology table maintains a set of minimum-cost downstream routers as feasible successors for each network destination. DUAL uses feasible successors in selecting a least-cost path through the network that is guaranteed not to be part of a routing loop. During a network topology change, DUAL will check for feasible successors (or query its neighbors if none are found) and then reconverge routing.

EIGRP uses both unicast and multicast messages to more efficiently communicate with its neighbors within the EIGRP network. In addition, routing updates are encapsulated within a reliable transport protocol to guarantee delivery, while common Hellos for keepalive purposes are unacknowledged.

EIGRP's strength comes from the breadth of network protocol communication with its neighbors, exchanging routing and real-time network state information only when network events change. EIGRP provides for such a robust routing architecture using various packet types; neighbor tables; topology tables; routing states; and routing tags:

- In attaining real-time network state information, EIGRP uses a variety of packet protocol types, including Hello/Acknowledgment, update (unicast and multicast), queries, replies, and requests.

- In providing valuable neighbor information, EIGRP neighbor tables include the neighbor's address, neighbor's connected interface, and Reliable Transport Protocol information.

- In providing valuable network topology information, EIGRP topology tables include the destination, the neighbor, and the metric.

- EIGRP maintains one of two routing states per network: Active (Recomputing) and Passive (Stable). And one of two routing tags are maintained per network: Internal and External.

Troubleshooting EIGRP

In troubleshooting EIGRP, start by looking locally on the router where the problem exists. Verify all the interfaces on which EIGRP is currently enabled, by using the SHOW IP EIGRP INTERFACE command.

```
RouterA#show ip eigrp interface
IP-EIGRP interfaces for process 100
```

Interface	Peers	Xmit Queue Un/Reliable	Mean SRTT	Pacing Time Un/Reliable	Multicast Flow Timer	Pending Routes
Et0/0	2	0/0	4	0/10	50	0
Se3/0	0	0/0	0	0/10	0	0
Se5/0/4	0	0/0	0	0/10	0	0
Lo0	0	0/0	0	0/10	0	0

Look at the number of EIGRP "Peers" to verify the correct number of neighbors. Sometimes low-bandwidth congested links can cause routing update problems, as well—which EIGRP attempts to assist by pacing the routing updates.

If certain routes are not being received by a router, but all local configuration and connectivity elements seem to be operating at the IP level, then begin looking upstream at the neighboring routers. Start by verifying that all neighbors are established, with the SHOW IP EIGRP NEIGHBOR command:

```
RouterA#show ip eigrp neighbor
IP-EIGRP neighbors for process 100
H   Address                  Interface   Hold Uptime   SRTT   RTO  Q   Seq
                                         (sec)         (ms)        Cnt Num
1   10.2.1.3                 Et0/0         11 00:00:54    1    200  0   2
0   10.2.1.1                 Et0/0         13 00:02:17    8    200  0   4
```

Look at each neighbor and make sure it is established on the appropriate WAN and LAN links. The "Uptime" shows how long the neighbor session has been established and may indicate whether a neighbor is unstable.

Also, make sure that all routes are part of the topology table and that the feasible successors are accurate, by using the SHOW IP EIGRP TOPOLOGY command:

```
RouterA#show ip eigrp topology
IP-EIGRP Topology Table for process 100

Codes: P - Passive, A - Active, U - Update, Q - Query, R - Reply,
       r - Reply status

P 10.3.1.0/24, 1 successors, FD is 409600
        via 10.2.1.3 (409600/128256), Ethernet0/0
P 10.2.1.0/24, 1 successors, FD is 281600
        via Connected, Ethernet0/0
P 10.6.1.0/24, 1 successors, FD is 2169856
        via Connected, Serial5/0/4
P 10.5.1.0/24, 1 successors, FD is 128256
        via Connected, Loopback0
```

If all neighbors are established and the feasible-successor topology table is accurate, verify that the routes in the forwarding table are being advertised via EIGRP. Sometimes other routing protocols may exist, with lower administrative distances whose routes get selected in the forwarding information base. Use the SHOW IP ROUTE command to verify the routes in the FIB and the protocols who made the entry.

```
Lab_Con>sh ip route
Codes: C - connected, S - static, I - IGRP, R - RIP, M - mobile, B - BGP
       D - EIGRP, EX - EIGRP external, O - OSPF, IA - OSPF inter area
       E1 - OSPF external type 1, E2 - OSPF external type 2, E - EGP
       i - IS-IS, L1 - IS-IS level-1, L2 - IS-IS level-2, * - candidate default
       U - per-user static route

Gateway of last resort is not set

     10.0.0.0/24 is subnetted, 4 subnets
D       10.3.1.0 [90/409600] via 10.2.1.3, 04:59:37, Ethernet0
C       10.2.1.0 is directly connected, Ethernet0
D       10.6.1.0 [90/2195456] via 10.2.1.2, 04:59:37, Ethernet0
D       10.5.1.0 [90/409600] via 10.2.1.2, 04:59:37, Ethernet0
```

In troubleshooting IPX EIGRP, verify that the routes in the forwarding table are being advertised via EIGRP and not via IPX RIP or NLSP, as shown here:

```
RouterB#show ipx route
Codes: C - Connected primary network,    c - Connected secondary network
       S - Static, F - Floating static, L - Local (internal), W - IPXWAN
       R - RIP, E - EIGRP, N - NLSP, X - External, A - Aggregate
       s - seconds, u - uses

4 Total IPX routes. Up to 1 parallel paths and 16 hops allowed.

No default route known.

L       BBBB is the internal network
C       AAAA (NOVELL-ETHER),  Et10/0
E       CCCC [45867776/1] via     AAAA.0060.8388.bb00, age 00:01:52,
                     1u, Et10/0
E       DDDD [45867776/1] via     AAAA.0060.5cf4.1554, age 00:01:52,
                     1u, Et10/0
```

For IPX EIGRP, also verify the IPX EIGRP topology for feasible successors:

```
RouterB#show ipx eigrp topology
IPX EIGRP Topology Table for process 100

Codes: P - Passive, A - Active, U - Update, Q - Query, R - Reply,
       r - Reply status
```

```
P DDDD, 1 successors, FD is 45867776
         via AAAA.0060.5cf4.1554 (45867776/45842176), Ethernet10/0
P CCCC, 1 successors, FD is 45867776
         via AAAA.0060.8388.bb00 (45867776/45842176), Ethernet10/0
P BBBB, 1 successors, FD is 45842176
         via Redistributed (45842176/0)
P AAAA, 1 successors, FD is 281600
         via Connected, Ethernet10/0
```

For IPX EIGRP, verify that all EIGRP neighbors are established:

```
RouterB#show ipx eigrp neighbor

IPX EIGRP Neighbors for process 100
H    Address                  Interface    Hold Uptime    SRTT   RTO  Q  Seq
                                           (sec)          (ms)      Cnt Num
1    AAAA.0060.8388.bb00      Et10/0        12 00:01:19    83    498  0  10
0    AAAA.0060.5cf4.1554      Et10/0        14 00:01:19   161    966  0  10
```

For AppleTalk EIGRP, verify that all EIGRP neighbors are established:

```
RouterA#show AppleTalk neighbor
AppleTalk neighbors:
  2.223          Ethernet0/0, uptime 00:05:36, 1 sec
       Neighbor has restarted 2 times in 1d03h.
          Neighbor is reachable as a RTMP & EIGRP peer
  2.241          Ethernet0/0, uptime 00:03:23, 2 secs
       Neighbor has restarted 1 time in 1d03h.
          Neighbor is reachable as a RTMP & EIGRP peer

RouterA>show AppleTalk eigrp neighbor
AT/EIGRP Neighbors for process 1, router id 100
H    Address                  Interface    Hold Uptime    SRTT   RTO   Q  Seq
                                           (sec)          (ms)      Cnt Num
1    2.223                    Et0/0         10 06:59:06     0   3000   0  1
0    2.241                    Et0/0         13 06:59:07     0   3000   0  3
```

Using Debugging

You should become comfortable with debugging EIGRP routing for IP, IPX, and AppleTalk EIGRP networks. Because EIGRP is a robust protocol, it can also be fairly complex. Start with the DEBUG IP EIGRP command and watch the routing updates or network errors:

```
RouterA#debug ip eigrp
IP-EIGRP Route Events debugging is on

IP-EIGRP: 10.6.1.0/24, - do advertise out Ethernet0/0
IP-EIGRP: Int 10.6.1.0/24 metric 2169856 - 1657856 512000
IP-EIGRP: 10.5.1.0/24, - do advertise out Ethernet0/0
IP-EIGRP: Int 10.5.1.0/24 metric 128256 - 256 128000
IP-EIGRP: 10.2.1.0/24, - do advertise out Ethernet0/0
IP-EIGRP: Int 10.3.1.0/24 metric 409600 - 256000 153600
IP-EIGRP: Ext 204.59.159.0/24 metric 1336064 - 1280000 56064
IP-EIGRP: Processing incoming UPDATE packet
```

In debugging AppleTalk EIGRP, make sure that all peers are sending and receiving Hellos and updates:

```
RouterA#debug AppleTalk eigrp-all
RouterA#
atigrp2_router: peer is 2.223
atigrp2_router: received HELLO from 2.223
atigrp2_router: peer is 2.241
atigrp2_router: received HELLO from 2.241
AT: atigrp2_write: about to send packet
Ethernet0/0: output AT packet: enctype UNKNOWN, size 65
07FFFFFF0060FFFFFFFFFFFF00608394E94000461|0041B0D000000009FFD25858580205ECED
00000000000000000000000000000010001000C010001000000000F0204000C0001000A00
```

IPX EIGRP debug allows for you to watch all routing updates from each neighbor and verify that all reachability information is being received:

```
RouterA#debug ipx eigrp events
IPX EIGRP events debugging is on

IPXEIGRP: External CCCC metric 45842176 hop 1 delay 1
IPXEIGRP: External BBBB metric 269312000 hop 2 delay 2
IPXEIGRP: External DDDD metric 269312000 hop 2 delay 2
IPXEIGRP: Received update from AAAA.0060.8394.e940 for net BBBB
IPXEIGRP: Received update from AAAA.0060.8394.e940 for net BBBB
IPXEIGRP: External BBBB metric 4294967295 hop 1 delay 1
IPXEIGRP: DDDD via AAAA.0060.5cf4.1554 metric 45867776
IPXEIGRP: Received update from AAAA.0060.5cf4.1554 for net DDDD
IPXEIGRP: better [0/0/45867776] route for DDDD from AAAA.0060.5cf4.1554,
        flushing old [2/1/0] route/paths
        external hop count in table 1, in update 1
IPXEIGRP: Received update from AAAA.0060.5cf4.1554 for net DDDD
IPXEIGRP: Received update from AAAA.0060.5cf4.1554 for net DDDD
```

Border Gateway Protocol (BGP)

The Border Gateway Protocol (BGP) is the routing protocol of the Internet. Logically, there are two portions to BGP: External BGP (EBGP) and Internal BGP (IBGP).

EBGP exchanges routing information with external networks or autonomous systems. IBGP exchanges routing information with all other routers within the autonomous system. In addition to EBGP and IBGP, there is also an Interior Gateway Protocol (IGP)—including OSPF, IS-IS, and EIGRP—which routes among all the IBGP gateways.

BGP also allows for *route reflectors* and *BGP confederations* to reduce IBGP routing meshing. Without route reflectors or BGP confederations, the entire IBGP network has to be meshed. Route reflectors and BGP confederations allow for localization of IBGP meshes.

The topology illustrated in Figure 7-3 shows the relations between EBGP, IBGP, and IGP.

FIGURE 7-3

BGP internetwork

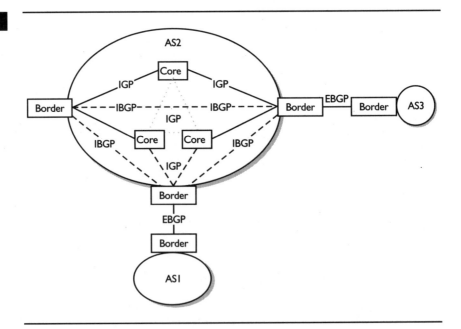

BGP gathers and advertises routes from network external boundaries. Due to the enormous wealth of routes within the Internet, it makes sense that BGP is an event-driven protocol.

BGP does not make per-hop routing decisions but rather functions under an entire network cloud called an Autonomous System (AS). When two ASs connect and exchange routes, it is called *peering*. BGP allows for specific peering policies to be defined at the borders, so that routes may be filtered, deterred, or preferred based upon AS numbers, community tags, metrics, and other criteria.

BGP makes its routing decisions based upon the following priorities, in this order:

1. Must be able to reach the next hop IP Address of the advertised BGP route.

2. Select the route with the largest BGP Administrative Weight value. (Administrative Weight is localized on the router.)

3. Select the route with the highest Local Preference value. (Local Preference is advertised throughout the entire AS.)

4. Select the route originated locally on the router.

5. Select the route with the shortest AS path.

6. Select the route with lowest origin code (IGP < EGP < INCOMPLETE).

7. Select the route advertised with the lowest Multi-Exit Discriminator (MED). (MED is advertised throughout the AS via EBGP.)

8. Select the route advertised via an external path instead of an internal path.

9. Select the route advertised with the lowest IGP metric.

10. Select the route advertised with the lowest IP address.

The Interior Gateway Protocol runs inside the Autonomous System. The IGP provides for intra-AS routing and does not carry external routing information. Common IGPs within an Internet routing environment are OSPF and Integrated IS-IS.

As shown in the BGP internetwork topology in Figure 7-3, AS1 is transiting AS2 to reach AS3. Because AS1's routes are not originated within AS2's IGP but are learned externally via EBGP from AS1, AS2 must disable synchronization with the IGP in order to advertise the routes to AS3. IGP synchronization is disabled with the NO SYNCHRONIZATION configuration command.

exam
ⓦ**atch**   *Synchronization should almost always be disabled.*

In setting up routing exchange information, BGP peers must be manually configured and individually identified. This peering establishment must be performed for all EBGP as well as IBGP peers. In the event that an IBGP peer is not included in the configuration, then that router will not learn any EBGP routes from any other BGP routers.

exam
ⓦ**atch**   *When generating an EBGP route using the NETWORK command, make sure that the route is already in the IGP routing table.*

Cisco provides for a peer-group feature in which a bundle of peers can be identified by a string. When configuring IBGP peering, it is usually helpful to bundle all IBGP peers into a peer group.

Cisco also provides for extensive BGP routing-policy definitions using regular expressions, access lists, community tags, and route maps.

BGP RFC 1163 specifies four different types of BGP message types: Open, Update, Notification, and Keepalive.

Troubleshooting BGP

When troubleshooting BGP, especially with a full Internet routing table, it is best to start with a summary snapshot of BGP. Ensure that all neighbors are established and that all BGP table versions are synchronized for each neighbor. In addition, it's important to see how long the BGP session with each neighbor has been up and established. Use the SHOW IP BGP SUMMARY command to give an overview of the BGP state:

```
RouterA>show ip bgp summary
BGP table version is 159505, main routing table version 159505
1299 network entries (2502/3897 paths) using 274900 bytes of memory
504 BGP path attribute entries using 69380 bytes of memory
142 BGP route-map cache entries using 2272 bytes of memory
0 BGP filter-list cache entries using 0 bytes of memory

Neighbor         V    AS MsgRcvd MsgSent  TblVer  InQ OutQ Up/Down  State/PfxRcd
10.2.1.1         4    1   81106   45150   159505   0    0 4w3d         1059
10.3.1.1         4    2 5128660  173273   159505   0    0 2w2d          146
10.4.1.1         4    1   86799   45155   159505   0    0 2w3d         1296
```

Verify that the number of routing entries is about what is expected, and that no routes are being filtered out.

All of the BGP table versions ("TblVer") should be the same on the router. The "Up/Down" state, which gives you an idea of how long the BGP session has been active, suggests stability.

If a particular session appears to be in a hung state or continues initializing, then it sometimes helps to clear the BGP session with the CLEAR IP BGP command and see if it comes active:

```
RouterA#clear ip bgp 10.2.1.1
```

If there is a particular route you are searching for, use the SHOW IP BGP *x.x.x.x* command to specify the route. (Viewing an entire Internet routing table can take considerable time.) Here's an example:

```
RouterA#sh ip bgp 192.31.7.130
BGP routing table entry for 192.31.7.0/24, version 34967033
Paths: (2 available, best #1, advertised over EBGP)
  65001 65002
    10.2.1.1 (metric 4) from 10.2.1.1 (10.2.1.1)
      Origin IGP, localpref 90, valid, internal, best
      Community: 1:1
      Originator : 10.2.1.1, Cluster list: 10.2.1.1
```

In the SHOW IP BGP *x.x.x.x* output, verify that the proper AS path is shown for the particular route. Also look at the "Originator" to verify that the appropriate BGP router or routers are originating and advertising the route via IBGP.

If routing communities are being used with BGP routes, it may be important to check the route maps associated with the community tags. Route maps can get rather complex, especially with Internet routing. Use the SHOW ROUTE-MAP command to view route maps associated with community routing tags, as shown here:

```
Router>show route-map peer-out
route-map peer-out, permit, sequence 10
  Match clauses:
    community (community-list filter): 53
  Set clauses:
    as-path prepend 1000
  Policy routing matches: 0 packets, 0 bytes
route-map peer-out, permit, sequence 20
  Match clauses:
    community (community-list filter): 20
  Set clauses:
  Policy routing matches: 0 packets, 0 bytes
```

Route maps allow for modifying BGP routing metrics, local preferences, communities, AS PATH prepending, and for influencing other BGP parameters in order to manage BGP routing policies. Although route maps can be very powerful, they can also be confusing and should be structured accordingly.

A typical BGP configuration shown by the SHOW RUNNING-CONFIG command might look like:

```
neighbor test peer-group
neighbor test remote-as 65000
neighbor test version 4
neighbor test distribute-list 110 in
neighbor test distribute-list 111 out
neighbor test route-map peer-in in
neighbor test route-map peer-out out
neighbor test filter-list 50 in
neighbor test filter-list 51 out
```

By default, all BGP advertises all routes to all neighbors. In the event that you want to filter routing advertisements (and you probably do), either in or out, based upon a certain IP address block, you should create access lists specifying the particular IP address range you wish to deny or permit.

```
access-list 110 deny    ip 127.0.0.0 0.255.255.255 255.0.0.0 0.255.255.255
access-list 110 deny    ip 10.0.0.0 0.255.255.255 255.0.0.0 0.255.255.255
access-list 110 deny    ip 192.168.0.0 0.0.255.255 255.255.0.0 0.0.255.255
```

An access list may be applied to a BGP peering session via a route-map or a distribute-list in the BGP peering statement as shown in the following configuration display.

```
neighbor test distribute-list 110 in
neighbor test distribute-list 111 out
```

or

```
route-map peer-in permit 110
match ip address 110
```

If there are particular ASs you wish to filter, then you can create an AS-Path access list.

```
ip as-path access-list 50 deny _65002_
```

You can apply an AS-Path list either via a filter-list or within a route-map.

```
neighbor test filter-list 50 in
neighbor test filter-list 51 out
```

or

```
route-map peer-in permit 10
match as-path 50
```

To view a particular peer-group peering session use the SHOW IP BGP PEER-GROUP command

```
RouterA#sh ip bgp peer-group test

BGP neighbor is test, peer-group leader,  remote AS 65001
Index 2, Offset 0, Mask 0x4
 BGP version 4
 Minimum time between advertisement runs is 5 seconds
 Incoming update network filter list is 110
 Outgoing update network filter list is 111
 Route map for incoming advertisements is peer-in
 Route map for outgoing advertisements is peer-out
```

In viewing the SHOW IP BGP PEER-GROUP output, verify that the appropriate AS number, filter-lists, and route-maps are being applied.

Sometimes a stub IBGP neighbor is used within an AS for remote sites which are not multi-homed or for some larger hierarchical type ASs trying to reduce the size of an IBGP mesh. The route reflector is an IBGP configuration which allows for a peer not to be part of the full IBGP mesh. To verify whether a neighbor is a route reflector use the SHOW IP BGP NEIGHBOR command and the third line should identify whether it is a route reflector or not.

```
RouterA#show ip bgp neighbor 10.2.2.1
BGP neighbor is 10.2.2.1, remote AS 65000, internal link
Index 34, Offset 4, Mask 0x4
 Route-Reflector Client
```

Finally, BGP can often be very processor-intensive; it should be checked periodically to see if it's sustaining high-CPU utilization. If you are maintaining a number of BGP peering sessions on a single router, clearing BGP can cause CPU spikes when processing an inordinate amount of information. Here's an example of the SHOW PROC CPU command:

```
RouterA#show proc cpu
CPU utilization for five seconds: 96%/90%; one minute: 92%; five minutes: 85%
```

CERTIFICATION SUMMARY

Although newer networks are generally not built with periodic broadcast protocols, there still exists a substantial base of legacy networks supporting these routing protocols. These protocols are often used in multivendor routing environments, because periodic broadcast protocols are somewhat simpler and more interoperable. For this reason, it's important to be able to troubleshoot and debug various routing protocols at the lowest level.

RIP is found at the core of many protocols such as IPX and RTMP. Only in exclusive Cisco environments does one have the advantage of bundling IP, IPX, and AppleTalk into a robust event-driven enterprise routing protocol such as EIGRP.

Event-driven protocols are much more scalable and more applicable within larger networks. OSPF and EIGRP each have their own advantages and disadvantages, and each is intended for specific types of network architectures. BGP, as the routing protocol of the Internet, can be very complex, with extremely cryptic and nonintuitive routing policies.

Regardless of the routing environment, protocols, or architecture, it is important to have a solid base of troubleshooting skills and tools for understanding and diagnosing the nature of certain anomalies. Cisco provides a wide range of commands, views, and features to assist in determining where a problem may exist so that a solution may be found.

 # TWO-MINUTE DRILL

- ❑ Routing protocols are generally subdivided into two categories: periodic broadcast protocols, and event-driven protocols.

- ❑ Periodic broadcast protocols send route updates at regular, timed intervals.

- ❑ *Event-driven protocols* provide for a more scalable network architecture, in that routing updates are only generated in the event of a network topology change.

- ❑ RIP functions by broadcasting its full routing table to all other routers in the network. All routers receive the advertised routes and regularly update their forwarding tables.

- ❑ RIP generally requires route updates every 30 seconds via broadcasts in order to keep the routes fresh.

- ❑ In order to accommodate various routing loops that may occur within certain network topologies, RIP has implemented a number of features to reduce looping effects:
  - ❑ Holddown
  - ❑ Split-horizon
  - ❑ Poison reverse

- ❑ When redistributing routing protocols with classless VLSM networks into RIP, be sure that subnetted static routes with a null next hop are redistributed, as well.

❏ Whenever redistributing routes, always include "subnets."

❏ When troubleshooting RIP, it is always best to start by looking in the routing table for "RIP."

❏ Running RIP with an instance of another periodic broadcast routing protocol, such as IGRP, can result in routing issues. This is due to the asynchronous updates' and administrative distance's competing for inserting routes into the forwarding table.

❏ Cisco's Interior Gateway Routing Protocol (IGRP) is also a periodic broadcast protocol, with stronger decision-making criteria based upon real-time network events and congestion states.

❏ The following timers are associated with IGRP:

  ❏ Update Timer

  ❏ Invalid Timer

  ❏ Holddown Timer

  ❏ Flush Timer

❏ When redistributing routing protocols with classless VLSM networks into IGRP, be sure that there are classful static routes with a null next hop redistributed as well.

❏ When troubleshooting an IGRP network, always start with the IGRP routing table.

❏ Although IP has made significant progress within the last few years as the common communications protocol, there is still a significant installed base of IPX (Internetwork Packet Exchange) equipment and networks.

❏ Service Advertising Protocol (SAP) is an enterprise network services protocol used to advertise information regarding file servers, print servers, job servers, and so on.

❏ When troubleshooting an IPX network, always start with the IPX routing table.

❏ AppleTalk Routing Table Maintenance Protocol (RTMP) is another distance-vector, periodic broadcast RIP-based protocol.

❏ In troubleshooting AppleTalk networks, always start with the routing table.

❏ Three powerful event-driven protocols are OSPF (Open Shortest Path First), EIGRP (Enhanced IGRP), and BGP (Border Gateway Protocol).

❏ OSPF is purely an IP-based routing protocol intended for hierarchical large-scale networks.

❏ EIGRP is a multiservice routing protocol supporting IPX, AppleTalk, and IP.

❏ BGP is used for interconnecting networks and defining strict routing policies.

❏ Understand how to use OSPF in point-to-point, point-to-multipoint, and broadcast media.

❏ OSPF has a number of design-related issues that can cause networkwide problems.

❏ When redistributing OSPF routes, be sure to include external 1, external 2, *and* subnets.

❏ Understand how and where to use virtual links for extending a backbone area.

❏ In troubleshooting EIGRP, start by looking locally on the router where the problem exists.

❏ Synchronization should almost always be disabled.

❏ When generating an EBGP route using the NETWORK command, make sure that the route is already in the IGP routing table.

❏ When troubleshooting BGP, especially with a full Internet routing table, it is best to start with a summary snapshot of BGP.

SELF TEST

The following Self Test questions will help you measure your understanding of the material presented in this chapter. Read all the choices carefully, as there may be more than one correct answer. Choose all correct answers for each question.

1. Split-horizon is a feature intended to prevent which of the following?

    A. TTL Expiration

    B. Large Routing Loops

    C. Count-to-Infinity

    D. Two-node routing loops

2. Which of the following metrics is *not* a basis for IGRP routing decisions?

    A. Reliability

    B. Bandwidth

    C. Cost

    D. Delay

3. Which of the following IGRP timers is *not* used for routing updates?

    A. Update timers

    B. Flooding timers

    C. Holddown timers

    D. Flush timers

4. EIGRP has advantages over IGRP based upon all the following criteria *except*

    A. Faster convergence

    B. Variable-length subnet masking

    C. Packet-loss metric

    D. Multiprotocol support

5. Which EIGRP packet is *not* used within the EIGRP protocol suite?

    A. Hello

    B. Update

    C. Reply

    D. Close

6. An IPX Packet Address is a concatenation of

    A. 16-bit XNS address with a 32-bit network-assigned address

    B. 32-bit network-assigned address and a 48-bit MAC address

    C. 32-bit 802.2 address and a 32-bit MAC address

    D. 48-bit NetBIOS address and a 32-bit MAC address

7. AppleTalk RTMP routing is a

    A. Distance vector, periodic broadcast routing protocol

    B. Link-state, event-driven routing protocol

    C. Distance vector, event-driven protocol

    D. Link-state periodic broadcast protocol

8. OSPF is a routing protocol with all the following characteristics except

    A. It allows for hierarchical networks

    B. It's a link-state protocol

    C. It's a periodic broadcast protocol

    D. It's based on the Dijkstra algorithm

9. Which of the following packet types is *not* included in OSPF?

    A. Hello

    B. Link State Reachability

    C. Link State Request

    D. Link State Update

10. OSPF supports Type-of-Service-based routing.

    A. True

    B. False

11. BGP makes routing decisions based upon all the following criteria except

    A. AS path length

    B. Metric

    C. Hop count

    D. IP address

12. BGP is a periodic broadcast protocol.

    A. True

    B. False

13. IPX can be routed via all the following routing protocols except

    A. IPX RIP

    B. RTMP

    C. IPX EIGRP

    D. NLSP

14. IPX access lists can be applied to all of the following except

    A. GNS requests

    B. Service Advertising Protocol (SAP)

    C. IPX addresses

    D. NetBEUI addresses

15. BGP is completely independent of the IGP.

    A. True

    B. False

16. AppleTalk addresses are dynamically assigned.

    A. True

    B. False

17. Which of the following is *not* a limitation of RIP?

    A. Subnetting

    B. Maximum 15-router hop count

    C. Classful routing

    D. Not scalable

18. Nodes on extended AppleTalk networks can belong to multiple zones.

    A. True

    B. False

19. OSPF has a higher administrative distance than IGRP.

    A. True

    B. False

20. IGRP is a

    A. Distance vector, periodic broadcast routing protocol

    B. Link-state, event-driven routing protocol

    C. Distance vector, event-driven protocol

    D. Link-state periodic broadcast protocol

CCNP
CISCO CERTIFIED NETWORK PROFESSIONAL

8

Troubleshooting Tools

M any of the earlier chapters gave techniques for troubleshooting specific technologies such as IP, AppleTalk, LANs and WANs, and emphasizing techniques for handling failure situations. In this chapter, we'll introduce some tools and products that can be used with a wide range of technologies, during normal operations as well as during failures.

We'll describe some of the tools available on Cisco routers. In most cases, these will be general-purpose tools. That is, we won't be rehashing the tools presented in previous chapters, but rather will look at tools that cover the router as a whole, or that are applicable to multiple technologies.

We'll take an introductory look at CiscoWorks, one of Cisco's commercial tools for managing Cisco products. If you're managing more than a few pieces of Cisco equipment, or you need to do substantial detailed analysis of even one piece, it's likely you'll find CiscoWorks to be helpful. CiscoWorks is one of the topics covered on the tests.

Finally, we'll examine a number of third-party tools. You probably already have most of these tools because they came with the operating systems you are using. Some can be obtained for free on the Internet. We'll also look at a few free Cisco tools that you can download (though technically those aren't third-party items).

Many of the tools covered in this chapter make use of the Simple Network Management Protocol (SNMP). SNMP usually runs on top of the IP protocol, though it can be used over others (for example, AppleTalk). In fact, if you haven't noticed already, the vast majority of the tools available to manage Cisco equipment make use of TCP/IP. Because of this, a good understanding of TCP/IP is essential to taking good advantage of the items presented in this chapter. If you haven't already done so, you may wish to read Chapter 4 concerning TCP/IP.

Also, it's very important that you understand how to use the operating system that you've chosen for managing your network. This chapter presents examples for both UNIX and Windows (CiscoWorks runs on Windows NT and a variety of UNIX versions). If you're using something else, you'll find that many of the techniques outlined here are applicable to other OSs, too, as long as you can obtain equivalent software for your OS.

Using Router Diagnostic Tools

Cisco's Internetwork Operating System (IOS) is exactly what its name implies: an operating system. IOS is obviously specialized and optimized for networking, but it's an OS nonetheless. IOS includes a user interface, a file system, an IP stack, a number of network server processes, and network client software. The network client software includes ping, Traceroute, and Telnet utilities.

Why use a router as your network troubleshooting tool? Because it's there. And by this we don't mean "because it exists," but rather "because it's where the problem is." When you're called upon to look at a network issue, often you'll be looking at a location somewhere other than where you are. This location may be on the other side of the world from you, if it's across a WAN connection. Even if it's in the same city, it might be the middle of the night and you don't want to drive into work if you absolutely don't have to. Regardless of the circumstances, at some point you're likely to find yourself working on a network issue remotely.

This presumes, of course, that the problem isn't easily diagnosed from your desktop computer or using some specialized network-management or diagnostic tool. If at least one endpoint of the communication you need to examine is at your own physical location, you may be able to use your regular tools to troubleshoot. But, if you're in the U.S. and the problem is somewhere between Europe and Asia, then it's not likely that you'll be able to solve the problem without involving a remote device.

When you're working remotely, what can be determined from a router? As you've read in the preceding chapters, there are a number of diagnostic tools to troubleshoot specific protocols and specific interfaces. We won't repeat that information here. Instead, let's look at some general-purpose things we can do from a router.

Telnet

As mentioned earlier, Cisco IOS client programs include ping, Traceroute, and Telnet. In Chapter 4, you learned how to use these programs to diagnose a TCP/IP network. These programs can be used from a Cisco router as well.

We'll start with Telnet. Telnet can be used to verify connectivity to most TCP services. The Cisco Telnet utility goes a little farther and makes this task a little easier by allowing us to specify some services by name:

```
Router#telnet host ?
  /debug              Enable telnet debugging mode
  /line               Enable telnet line mode
  /noecho             Disable local echo
  /route:             Enable telnet source route mode
  /source-interface   Specify source interface
  /stream             Enable stream processing
  <0-65535>           Port number
  bgp                 Border Gateway Protocol (179)
  chargen             Character generator (19)
  cmd                 Remote commands (rcmd, 514)
  daytime             Daytime (13)
  discard             Discard (9)
  domain              Domain Name Service (53)
  echo                Echo (7)
  exec                Exec (rsh, 512)
  finger              Finger (79)
  ftp                 File Transfer Protocol (21)
  ftp-data            FTP data connections (used infrequently, 20)
  gopher              Gopher (70)
  hostname            NIC hostname server (101)
  ident               Ident Protocol (113)
  irc                 Internet Relay Chat (194)
  klogin              Kerberos login (543)
  kshell              Kerberos shell (544)
  login               Login (rlogin, 513)
  lpd                 Printer service (515)
  nntp                Network News Transport Protocol (119)
  pop2                Post Office Protocol v2 (109)
  pop3                Post Office Protocol v3 (110)
  smtp                Simple Mail Transport Protocol (25)
  sunrpc              Sun Remote Procedure Call (111)
  syslog              Syslog (514)
```

```
tacacs              TAC Access Control System (49)
talk                Talk (517)
telnet              Telnet (23)
time                Time (37)
uucp                Unix-to-Unix Copy Program (540)
whois               Nicname (43)
www                 World Wide Web (HTTP, 80)
<cr>
```

You will need to know what commands to type to elicit the correct response, but if you connect, at least you know the port is listening. This also serves as a quick way to look up a port number if the service you're after is one of those listed.

Note that the telnet command has some advanced options, including source routing and specifying which interface is used. These options are not always available on a typical workstation ping program.

Ping

The ping program is pretty self-explanatory. Still, there are several items worth noting. One is that the Cisco ping will sometimes report a little more information than a Windows or UNIX ping. For example, if you're trying to ping a host behind a firewall that prohibits ping, the firewall will sometimes send back ICMP type 3, code 10 "Communication with destination host is administratively prohibited." Many ping programs will simply report that the host was not responding. The Cisco ping, however, reports a character that indicates it got back an administratively prohibited code. Check your IOS documentation for details.

There are a number of advanced options offered with the Cisco ping program that typically aren't available with a Windows or UNIX ping. Let's take a look at the options available with the IP ping:

```
Router#ping
Protocol [ip]:
Target IP address: 10.0.0.1
Repeat count [5]:
Datagram size [100]:
Timeout in seconds [2]:
Extended commands [n]: y
```

```
Source address or interface:
Type of service [0]:
Set DF bit in IP header? [no]:
Validate reply data? [no]:
Data pattern [0xABCD]:
Loose, Strict, Record, Timestamp, Verbose[none]:
Sweep range of sizes [n]:
```

These options are available only in enable mode. Usually, you simply ping a destination address. Here, you have the option to specify how many packets are sent, what size they are, and what timeout should be used.

Following the timeout option is a choice for "Extended commands." These options are not universally available in all ping implementations on other operating systems.

- The first is *source address or interface*. This allows you to specify the source address for the ping.

- The next is *type of service*. The default is 0, which is echo request.

- Next is the *set DF bit* option. DF stands for "don't fragment," which is an IP option.

- Next is *Validate reply data?*, which forces the router to check that the data echoed back matches what was sent. Windows ping always validates data in this manner.

- *Data pattern* specifies the string of bytes to be repeated to fill the datagram size.

- Next is a set of options relating to IP source routing.

- Finally, IOS allows you to use a range of sizes instead of a single size for the packets.

Many of these options touch on advanced, rarely used IP options. If you're curious about them, consult an advanced TCP/IP book.

Ping is not limited to IP. The IOS implements a ping client for a number of protocols:

```
Router>ping ?
  WORD      Ping destination address or hostname
  apollo    Apollo echo
```

```
appletalk   Appletalk echo
clns        CLNS echo
decnet      DECnet echo
ip          IP echo
ipx         Novell/IPX echo
vines       Vines echo
xns         XNS echo
```

The word "ping" is usually considered specific to TCP/IP, but the concept is very generic: Send data and have it echoed back. Most protocols provide some sort of provision for these functions, and Cisco has implemented them into the IOS ping software.

Traceroute

The Traceroute command is especially useful for remote diagnosis of TCP/IP network problems. IP routing is one of the things that can be working fine in one part of a network and broken in another. You may be able to Traceroute to a particular IP address with no difficulty from your workstation, but when you do it from the router that's serving the user having trouble, the problem may present itself.

The Traceroute program's operation is interesting because, unlike other services offered on the Internet, Traceroute was not originally intended to be there. Traceroute actually works by taking advantage of a side effect. Recall from Chapter 4 the concept of a Time To Live factor, or TTL. The idea of the TTL is this: In case of a route loop, you avoid having a packet loop forever and quickly filling up links by allowing packets to live only so long on the network. To accomplish this, an initial TTL is picked (a maximum of 255, chosen by the sending host) when the packet is sent. Each router that passes the packet subtracts one from the TTL. That way, if a loop occurs, the packet will loop for a maximum of approximately 254 hops and then be discarded. Routers don't normally silently discard packets, though. They are obliged to send an ICMP message indicating why the packet was discarded. (The reason is type 11, code 0, "Time To Live exceeded in Transit.")

So the Traceroute program simply sends a packet with a TTL of 1. The first hop is the IP address that responds with ICMP type 11, code 0. The program then sends a packet with a TTL of 2, and the second hop is the IP address that responds, and so on.

exam
ⓦatch

Most UNIX operating systems and the Cisco IOS use UDP packets as the packets that are intended to expire along the way. The destination port number is usually somewhere in the 33,000 range. These port numbers don't mean anything in particular because they're intended to expire. The tracert program that comes with Microsoft Windows does something a little different, however: It uses ICMP packets instead of UDP. Specifically, it sends ICMP echo requests, essentially ping packets. The protocol used isn't really important, since it's the side effect that's desired. In practice, though, it may make a difference when a firewall is being used; one type of Traceroute will work across the firewall, while the other won't. If you have a Windows desktop computer, it may be useful to be able to execute UDP-style Traceroutes from your router. On the Cisco exam, be prepared to recognize which type of Traceroute is sent by a particular operating system, and how Traceroute works in general.

For another explanation of how Traceroute works, and a proposed alternative, see RFC 1393 at

http://www.cis.ohio-state.edu/htbin/rfc/rfc1393.html

Accounting

Another tool that Cisco makes available on its routers is the *accounting* feature. Accounting works by keeping some simple statistics about Layer 3 communications, and is applied on a per-interface basis. Cisco supports a number of protocols with accounting capability, including IP, IPX, and DECNet.

When accounting is applied to an interface, the router will keep track of the number of bytes and packets sent between each pair of network addresses. To help clarify, following is an example done on a High Speed

Serial Interface (HSSI). We see source and destination IP addresses, number of packets and number of bytes:

```
Router#configure terminal
Enter configuration commands, one per line.  End with CNTL/Z.
Router(config)#int hssi 1/0/0
Router(config-if)#ip accounting
Router(config-if)#^Z
Router#sho ip accounting
   Source          Destination              Packets              Bytes
   192.168.149.4   198.29.75.75                   1                 65
   192.168.151.34  168.95.0.8                    24              19424
   192.168.149.18  202.96.215.178                 5                213
   192.168.149.18  204.160.241.83                 1                 40
   192.168.149.18  203.138.157.21                 7                280
   192.168.151.34  195.54.9.6                     3               1656
   192.168.149.18  203.245.15.250                 9                365
   192.168.149.18  195.129.14.134                 4                176
   192.168.149.18  205.252.144.99                 7                877
   192.168.149.4   195.40.1.62                   54               6700
   192.168.149.250 200.9.225.10                  16               1490
   192.168.151.73  202.99.104.68                  1                180
   192.168.149.102 207.103.0.2                    2                116
   192.168.151.66  202.98.97.69                   7               9800
   192.168.151.43  203.14.32.6                   58              81888
   192.168.151.73  202.99.96.68                   2                360
   192.168.151.36  202.32.13.5                   34              34801
   192.168.151.34  152.149.247.30                 5               3070
   192.168.149.102 193.131.248.24                 1                 67
   192.168.149.18  194.163.252.76                37               1496
   192.168.151.68  202.101.101.78                26              28950
   192.168.149.102 204.123.2.18                   1                 64
```

The amount of memory set aside for accounting data can be adjusted, but in general it's fairly limited. This limits the usefulness of the accounting data for things like billing, especially on busy links with a wide range of IP addresses crossing them. Still, having this feature available does have some particular uses; for instance, you can spot-check to see what percentage of the bandwidth is being used by a particular address at a particular moment in time.

on the **Job**

A couple of years ago, one of my coworkers received a call from a user in a remote sales office in Asia. The user was complaining that his document wouldn't print. At the time, the link was a relatively small one (56 Kbps), and the print server was in the U.S. In order to print, the user was dependent on the WAN link. We examined the WAN link and found it to be rather full. Assuming this was the cause of the print problems, we turned on the accounting router option to find out what was using the bandwidth. We discovered that a particular IP address in the remote office was using nearly all the bandwidth communicating with an IP address on the Internet. The IP address in the remote office turned out to be the desktop computer of the user who had originally called, and the IP address on the Internet turned out to be what an H.R. department would call "an inappropriate Web site." We called the user back, explained what we thought was causing the problem, and suggested a solution. The user had no further complaints.

Router Web Interface

Newer versions of the Cisco IOS include a *web server* that can be used to issue configuration and monitoring commands. This feature was introduced in 11.0(6) and was made an "official" feature in 11.2 and later. You can set up AAA or TACACS logins to allow various levels of access to network users. For instructions on how to enable the web server and configure permissions and security, see

http://www.cisco.com/univercd/cc/td/doc/product/software/ios112/httpsec.htm

The *web interface* doesn't add anything new. It's basically an HTML interface to the command-line IOS. For example, entering the URL

http://router/exec/-/show/ip/route/CR

will display a list of IP routes, just as if you'd typed SHOW IP ROUTE at the command line.

Even if you are very familiar with the IOS command line, the web interface may have some value to you. Using a web browser to access the router makes certain things easier, such as searching through a long list or saving the output. These actions can be done with a standard Telnet client, as well, but usually not without some trouble. For example, to search through a long output using a Telnet client, you'd probably have to log the output to a file and search the file in a separate window.

The web interface may be less daunting for coworkers who aren't familiar with the IOS. Users can make bookmarks, or you can set up a static web page posted with links to particular URLs on the router to allow easy access to certain features. You could provide less-experienced staff with a list of URLs to check for common problems.

Router Logging

What if your router produced an interesting error message and you weren't watching? You can avoid this by configuring all your routers to log console messages locally, at a minimum. If your routers are used in any kind of a security application, it's best to also configure them to send copies of the messages to a remote syslog server.

To configure your router to log locally, use the

LOGGING BUFFERED [size]

global command. The optional [*size*] parameter is the number of bytes you want to set aside for logging. If you omit that parameter, the router uses the default number of bytes, which varies depending on the type of router.

To configure your router to log to a syslog host, use the global command

LOGGING host

The *host* parameter is the IP address or name of a server running a syslog service. The syslog service is a de facto remote logging standard from the UNIX world. Syslog server software is available for UNIX, Windows NT, and other platforms.

The following document includes a section on how to configure logging:

http://www.cisco.com/univercd/cc/td/doc/product/software/
ios113ed/113ed_cr/fun_c/fcprt4/fctroubl.htm

CERTIFICATION OBJECTIVE 8.02

Introduction to CiscoWorks

So far, most of this chapter (and most of this book) has been about managing and troubleshooting at a fairly detailed level. Most of what we've discussed so far has concerned working with one or two devices at a time. In this section, we'll examine some tools that let you look at your network as a whole, and manage devices as a group rather than individually.

Cisco's product to perform this function is CiscoWorks. CiscoWorks, like a number of other network management packages, gives you a graphical view of your network, including graphical representation of problems. You can "drill down" on the picture to get more specific information, including data on individual devices. You can use CiscoWorks to collect statistical information about your network. Other components of CiscoWorks help you manage your equipment configuration, upgrade software, and check version information for your equipment.

Most network management packages, including CiscoWorks, use SNMP to perform the actual management and reporting functions. So before we examine the tasks you'll do with CiscoWorks, let's make sure we understand the functions of SNMP.

The Role of SNMP

SNMP was covered very briefly in Chapter 4 of this book, but only at a protocol level. We didn't actually cover what SNMP is used for. We'll do that now. This fairly simple protocol is used to build highly complex management systems. Conceptually, SNMP works by getting or setting a value of a particular object on a remote device, using a password. By getting a value, the protocol can determine the state of the remote object. By setting a value, it can change the state. The host doing the querying is usually called the *SNMP manager,* and the host being queried is usually said to be running an *SNMP agent.*

Let's make things a little less abstract. Most SNMP agents will answer a query for a contact name. A *contact name* is simply a string of characters that represents the person responsible for the device being queried. The contact name is usually a person's name, a department name, or perhaps an e-mail address. The idea is that if someone queries the device, they will know whom to contact for questions about it.

Figure 8-1 shows a request packet. This packet was captured using the Sniffer Pro software from Network Associates. Only the UDP and SNMP portions of the packet are illustrated.

There are a few things notable in this request packet. First, the UDP port is 161. The version is 0, which means version 1. The "Community" is public.

The Community string functions as a password of sorts. Let's take a look at it. There's the command, get next request. There's a Request ID to differentiate among multiple requests. There's a facility for error handling, and finally there's the Object ID (OID). The OID is the string of numbers (or equivalent text descriptions) in curly brackets, separated by dots, that

FIGURE 8-1

An SNMP request packet

```
UDP: ----- UDP Header -----
UDP:
UDP: Source port      = 1054
UDP: Destination port = 161 (SNMP)
UDP: Length           = 48
UDP: Checksum         = 71D8 (correct)
UDP: [40 byte(s) of data]
UDP:
SNMP: ----- Simple Network Management Protocol (Version 1) -----
SNMP:
SNMP: Version      = 0
SNMP: Community    = public
SNMP: Command      = Get next request
SNMP: Request ID   = 20139
SNMP: Error status = 0 (No error)
SNMP: Error index  = 0
SNMP:
SNMP: Object = {1.3.6.1.2.1.1.4} (sysContact)
SNMP: Value  = NULL
SNMP:
```

represents a particular SNMP value that is being referenced. The OID is the important piece of the string. It identifies what piece of information we're interested in.

Figure 8-2 shows the response packet. Notice that the response is nearly identical to the request, except the Value field now has a value. This is our answer. As you can see, the answer is "Ryan Russell."

Most of an SNMP manager's job consists of handling and interpreting this type of communication. The manager requests bits of information over and over again to establish trends, chart utilization, keep error counts, and so on. Of course, the information requested is usually something more useful than just the contact name.

On Cisco routers, information is made available via the SNMP agent; it concerns the interfaces installed, whether they are active, what protocols are running, statistical information about traffic being passed, how busy the CPU is, the amount of memory available, and a wide variety of other data.

This type of information is collected every so many seconds. The elapsed interval before collecting the information again is called the *polling* interval. The polling interval can be set to any amount of time, depending on how much traffic you want to generate and how often you need the information. One common default polling interval is every five minutes; shorter intervals are appropriate if the information is needed more often. For example, if you're trying to generate a graph of bandwidth utilization in one-minute increments, you'd probably have to poll at least once per minute. Naturally, the more often you poll, the more network management traffic is generated. The network manager setting up the SNMP management software has to balance the desired frequency of information updates against the extra load the updates place on the network managing them.

On Cisco routers, SNMP must be explicitly enabled, by configuring the router to respond to a particular community string or list of strings. The console port must also be used for at least some initial configuration.

FIGURE 8-2

An SNMP response

```
⊟ 🕮 UDP: ----- UDP Header -----
   📄 UDP:
   📄 UDP: Source port      = 161 (SNMP)
   📄 UDP: Destination port = 1054
   📄 UDP: Length           = 61
   📄 UDP: Checksum         = C382 (correct)
   📄 UDP: [53 byte(s) of data]
   📄 UDP:
⊟ 🖳 SNMP: ----- Simple Network Management Protocol (Version 1) -----
   📄 SNMP:
   📄 SNMP: Version      = 0
   📄 SNMP: Community    = public
   📄 SNMP: Command      = Get response
   📄 SNMP: Request ID   = 20139
   📄 SNMP: Error status = 0 (No error)
   📄 SNMP: Error index  = 0
   📄 SNMP:
   📄 SNMP: Object = {1.3.6.1.2.1.1.4.0} (sysContact.0)
   📄 SNMP: Value  = Ryan Russell
   📄 SNMP:
```

SNMP Traps

There is one more piece of SNMP that hasn't been discussed yet: *SNMP traps*. In all of our examples so far, the SNMP management station contacts the network device. This contact is done at some designated polling interval, or whenever a setting needs to be changed on the device. In some cases, this frequency may not be good enough. For example, a lot can happen on a network during a polling interval of five minutes.

SNMP traps are another mechanism that can be used to trigger events on the SNMP management station. SNMP traps work by delegating some of the event-monitoring responsibility to the network device. Usually, the network management station will set an SNMP trap on a network device, to monitor some threshold or event. When that threshold or event occurs, the network device sends a packet indicating that to the management station. At that point the management station can make further requests of the device, and perform whatever alterations need to be done.

On Cisco routers, SNMP trap capabilities must be enabled when configuring the router. Refer to the IOS documentation for your IOS version for details.

Managing with CiscoWorks

CiscoWorks is Cisco's SNMP management product. More accurately, it's Cisco's *collection* of SNMP management products. This section of the chapter will provide you with a short introduction to CiscoWorks 2000, the latest version of CiscoWorks. This product is fairly complex, and it would take a book or two to cover it comprehensively. Instead, we'll give you an idea of what CiscoWorks can do, and provide you with some of the information on which you're likely to be tested.

Previous versions of CiscoWorks required a third-party resource manager. For SNMP software, a *resource manager* is the portion of the software that is responsible for discovering SNMP devices and for doing the basic polling function. One example is Hewlett-Packard's OpenView. On top of the resource manager is usually some sort of graphical map of the network, employing various shapes and colors to indicate equipment types, link types, and the state of the network. Some SNMP management software also includes *element managers,* which are usually device-specific software used for specialized management functions. For example, an element manager might be managing the modem settings of a modem pool device. Element managers are typically launched by making a selection from the graphical map.

CiscoWorks 2000 includes its own resource manager, so no additional software purchase is necessary. If you desire, CiscoWorks 2000 can also run on top of a number of other resource managers. The main view into CiscoWorks is CiscoWorks for Switched Internetworks, or CWSI (pronounced "swizzy"). (CWSI is the graphical map we mentioned in the preceding paragraph.) Figure 8-3 shows what CWSI looks like.

The main part of the window, in the center, contains the logical network layout. The diagram in Figure 8-4 is of a network of Cisco devices, including routers and switches. Also depicted are a number of interconnecting technologies, including Ethernet, 100MB Ethernet, FDDI, and serial links. Along the right side of the window is a list of device types and link types. In a somewhat complex diagram like this one, it's useful to

FIGURE 8-3

CWSI main screen

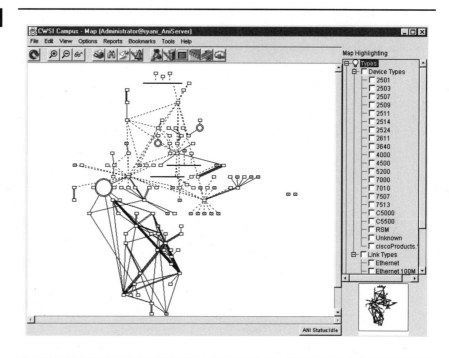

be able to highlight a subset of it. Figure 8-4 reflects the same diagram showing the 100MB Ethernet links.

Multiple items can be checked in the list of devices and links, in order to highlight more than one type at a time. Across the top of the window, under the menus, are the toolbar buttons:

- The circular arrow on the left is used to rediscover the network.

- The next group of three buttons are used for zooming in and out.

- The next four buttons operate a few miscellaneous functions, including printing the map, doing a find, and sending e-mail.

- The last six buttons at the right end of the toolbar are used to launch other applications such as Telnet and Traffic Director.

FIGURE 8-4

CWSI showing 100MB
Ethernet links

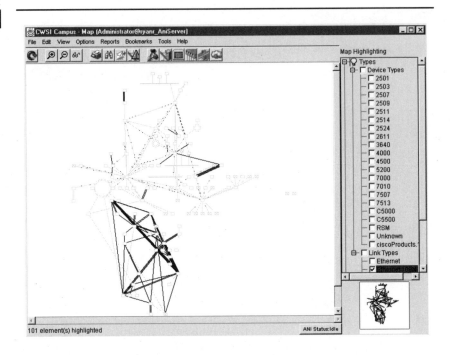

Autodiscovering the Network

The logical view you see in Figure 8-4 was *automatically discovered*. Like
many SNMP management packages, CiscoWorks includes a facility to
autodiscover your network, by querying Cisco devices for Cisco Discovery
Protocol (CDP) information. CDP was mentioned briefly in previous
chapters as a proprietary Cisco protocol used to discover neighboring Cisco
devices, and used by network management software. CiscoWorks is a prime
example of network management software that takes advantage of CDP.

In order to autodiscover your network, when you first set up CiscoWorks
you give it an SNMP community name to use, and a *seed device*. The
SNMP community name is the "password" CiscoWorks will attempt to use
when trying to communicate with discovered devices via SNMP. The seed
device is any Cisco device on which the SNMP community will work, and
which has other neighboring Cisco devices. CiscoWorks will query the first
device for its CDP list, then query the devices on that list, and so on. This
process continues on until all the devices have been contacted.

In some cases, the SNMP community will not work on the discovered devices. In Figure 8-3, a number of devices have Xs through their icons. These are devices that CiscoWorks knows are (or were) there, but with which it can't communicate. This failure may be due to an incorrect SNMP community, an access list established on the router or switch, or some sort of firewalling.

Once you've discovered a portion of your network, you can investigate the devices that couldn't be managed, and start determining what can be done to remedy the situation. After the problem has been corrected, you can rediscover the individual devices or the entire network.

The CiscoWorks Applications

CiscoWorks includes a number of other applications in addition to CWSI.

- **TrafficDirector** is used for statistics gathering via SNMP and RMON.

- **ATMDirector** is used for various ATM switch management and discovery functions.

- **VLANDirector** is a GUI for managing VLANs on Catalyst switches.

- **UserTracker** displays end-station information retrieved from switches and routers.

- **Resource Manager** is used for managing configuration and inventory information.

- **CiscoView** displays and manages individual devices.

exam
ⓦatch

Be prepared to answer somewhat imprecise questions about CiscoWorks. For example, you may be asked which CiscoWorks application is used to manage VLANs across multiple switches (the answer is VLANDirector). In previous CIT exams, the questions haven't been much more specific than that. It's possible that Cisco wants its certified professionals to be aware of CiscoWorks, without requiring much more than that. Be familiar with the various CiscoWorks application names and their basic functions.

CiscoWorks doesn't let you do anything that you couldn't otherwise do by hand via the command-line interfaces—that is, if you've got enough time to spend doing it manually. The point of CiscoWorks (or any network management application) is to save you time and trouble. You will have to weigh the expense of CiscoWorks against the benefits you will realize. Take into account the size of your network when making this decision, since CiscoWorks doesn't add a lot of value to very small networks. Don't forget to consider the amount of time it will take to install, learn, and configure the CiscoWorks software. Sadly, busy network managers often have a problem allowing time to implement the tools that will save them time in the long run.

CERTIFICATION OBJECTIVE 8.03

Using Third-Party Tools

Most veteran network managers have collected an arsenal of tools to assist in their duties. These utilities range anywhere from simple programs that come with most operating systems, to dedicated, expensive test equipment. In this section, we'll take a look at a number of third-party network-management tools, to give you an idea of what's available and what might work for you.

CMU SNMP Library

We've already studied SNMP managers, earlier in this chapter. The commercial SNMP managers referenced there provide a fairly comprehensive management function, including all of the graphics functions. They're also fairly expensive. An alternative to these pricey graphical SNMP managers is a free, command-line SNMP manager.

One of these command-line SNMP managers is the CMU SNMP Library, available at http://www.net.cmu.edu/projects/snmp/. The software comes in source code form, so you'll need some experience in compiling programs to put the Library to work. The software has been written to compile on a number of UNIX environments, as well as Windows.

When it's compiled and installed, CMU SNMP offers a number of command-line programs. These include snmpget, snmpgetnext, snmpset, and snmpwalk. Some of these programs correspond directly to SNMP commands (get, get next, set).

Of particular interest is the snmpwalk program. It's used to dump a table of the SNMP values a device offers. This table is especially useful if you're trying to figure out the OID of a particular value, or if you're just trying to investigate a particular SNMP device. Here's a sample:

```
solaris% snmpwalk 10.0.0.1 public
Name: interfaces.ifTable.ifEntry.ifOutOctets.24 -> Counter: 3265397796
^Cpeanuts% ./snmpwalk 130.214.99.1 public | more
Name: system.1.0 -> OCTET STRING- (ascii):     Cisco Internetwork Operating
System Software ..I
OS (tm) C5RSM Software (C5RSM-DSV-M), Version 11
.2(12a.P1)P1, MAINTENANCE INTERIM SOFTWARE..Copyright (c)
1986-1998 by cisco Systems, Inc...Compiled
Tue 24-Mar-98 23:21 by dschwart
Name: system.2.0 -> OBJECT IDENTIFIER:  .iso.org.dod.internet.private.
enterprises.cisco.ciscoProducts.168
Name: system.3.0 -> Timeticks: (901373979) 104 days, 7:48:59
Name: system.4.0 -> OCTET STRING- (ascii):     Ryan Russell
Name: system.5.0 -> OCTET STRING- (ascii):     Cat55-RSM
Name: system.6.0 -> OCTET STRING-    (hex):
Name: system.7.0 -> INTEGER: 6
Name: interfaces.ifNumber.0 -> INTEGER: 24
Name: interfaces.ifTable.ifEntry.ifIndex.1 -> INTEGER: 1
Name: interfaces.ifTable.ifEntry.ifIndex.2 -> INTEGER: 2
Name: interfaces.ifTable.ifEntry.ifIndex.3 -> INTEGER: 3
Name: interfaces.ifTable.ifEntry.ifIndex.4 -> INTEGER: 4
Name: interfaces.ifTable.ifEntry.ifIndex.5 -> INTEGER: 5
  .
  .
  .
```

So what's the advantage—other than lower cost—of a command-line package like CMU SNMP, as opposed to a graphical commercial package? There are several benefits.

■ You can use the command-line version to script the collecting and receiving of SNMP information. This type of scripting may or may not be available with a given commercial package.

■ Because of the scripting and batch-mode capabilities of a command-line package, it can be used to generate reports and web pages and such.

■ You can distribute this kind of software at will. Some commercial packages, on the other hand, charge for each management station.

■ Finally, customization is infinitely more possible, especially if you're a programmer, because the source code is available.

exam
ⓦatch
Cisco routers provide a way for you to load a configuration file into them, via SNMP and TFTP. This configuration file need not be a complete file, so this also represents a way to execute arbitrary commands. This is very useful if you've lost the Telnet password or enable password, but you have an SNMP password for the router that is allowed to write. Here's an example of this technique:

```
# snmpset router private .1.3.6.1.4.1.9.2.1.53.10.1.99.34 string router-confg
Received GET RESPONSE from 10.1.250.12
requestid 0x5d5b errstat 0x0 errindex 0x0
Name: .iso.org.dod.internet.private.enterprises.cisco.local.1.53.10.1.99.34
-> OCTET STRING- (ascii):         router-confg
#
# cat router-confg
line vty 0 4
password test

# telnet router
Trying 10.1.250.12...
Connected to router.
Escape character is '^]'.


User Access Verification

Password:
Router>
```

You'll substitute your router name or IP address for the word router in the snmpset command, and use the IP address of your TFTP server at the end of the OID (where the example has "10.1.99.34").

The example shown here sets the VTY password to "test." Be prepared to identify this as a password recovery technique on an exam.

This example was prepared using the CMU snmpset program. For further examples (using HP OpenView) see: http://www.cisco.com/ warp/public/490/11.html. Again, for this to work, SNMP must already be configured and you must have an SNMP write password. And watch out—this means anyone who has the SNMP write passwords to your router can have full control of it.

Packet Analyzers

Another important tool for the network manager is the *packet analyzer* or *packet capture program.* These are also commonly called "sniffers," although Sniffer is also the name of a product from Network Associates (previously Network General). The generic term *sniffer* is frequently used to mean a packet analyzer, much as "kleenex" is used for tissue and "to xerox" means making photocopies.

Throughout this book are numerous examples of output from packet analyzers. You've seen output from commercial packet analyzers such as Sniffer Pro from Network Associates, as well as from free (or, at least, included) packages such as snoop. One free product used on a number of UNIX platforms is tcpdump, available at ftp://ftp.ee.lbl.gov/ (look through the list for tcpdump). If you have Solaris, you probably already have snoop.

The various packet analyzers have their own strengths and weaknesses. For example, the AG Group (http://www.aggroup.com/) produces a commercial package called Etherpeek. It originally ran only on Macintoshes, so it has very good AppleTalk decodes, as you might imagine. The UNIX packages are often highly suitable for TCP/IP monitoring, but not always for other protocols. Sniffer Pro is a favorite all-around packet analyzer, but it's expensive.

exam
Ⓦatch

Cisco routers can act as very rudimentary packet analyzers. Chapter 4 presents an example of using a router to examine packet addresses as they are routed. Cisco provides a more comprehensive example with respect to source-route bridging interfaces using the debug list command. You can study it at http://www.cisco.com/warp/public/ 697/7.html. Be prepared to answer questions about this feature.

Packet analyzers are tremendously helpful, but only if you know how to use them. Don't expect to use a packet analyzer for the first time and have everything be crystal clear to you. Like any tool, you will need to spend some time getting familiar with its operation. For packet analyzers, this usually means you should be able to narrow down the output to include only what you need to see, and then be able to understand that output. The two tasks are somewhat similar. In order to specify what packets you want to see, you need to know something about the protocol you're trying to monitor—which is the first step to understanding the packets themselves. This means knowing what MAC addresses to look for, what Layer 3 protocol addresses to look for, and what socket or port numbers to look for.

The best way to learn how to use your packet analyzer is to put it to work monitoring a protocol that is running properly. Like most tools, it's best not to try and learn them while you're working on a problem. If you've been following the Cisco certification track, this likely isn't a problem, since many examples of packet analyzer output are presented throughout. And don't forget that there will be several questions in the tests based on packet analyzer output.

Hardware Tools

In addition to the software tools you've seen so far in this chapter, there are a number of hardware tools that can be very useful as well. Chief among these is the *cable tester*. There are few things more frustrating than spending hours troubleshooting a problem at the protocol level, only to find out later that it was due to a bad or marginal cable. Cable testers offer a wide range of functionality along with a wide range of prices.

You'll use cable testers to check proper operation of your wiring, whether it be in the walls or in a loose patch cable. Most cable installers will test the wiring they put in, during the installation, for proper operation. Some will even provide reports on the quality of the work. Still, cable can go bad due to thermal expansion and contraction, or just plain stress on the wires.

The simplest and least-expensive cable testers are called *continuity testers,* which simply verify that voltage is passed across the wires. The better ones will test pairs individually to make sure that some of the wires haven't been crossed with another pair. Most of these testers operate as a pair of devices, one at each end of a wire, with LEDs on them. Some combination of LED colors will indicate proper operation. Continuity testers are available in wiring stores and communications catalogs.

The more-expensive wire testers are capable of performing a *time-domain reflectometer (TDR) test*. Basically, a TDR test is used to measure the length of a cable, or the distance to a break. This is accomplished by sending a signal down a wire and measuring how long it takes for an echo of the signal to bounce back. This type of feature was slightly more useful when coax cable was more popular, but TDR tests can still be handy when cable runs are behind walls or under floors. They're also very useful for certifying your cable plant. Better cable installers will do this for you and present a report, but it never hurts to spot-check the work. Part of certifying your cable plant involves making sure that none of your cable runs exceed the maximum allowed distance for the media.

For example, for 10bT or 100bT wiring, the maximum allowed length (according to the spec) is 100 meters, or about 328 feet. With a TDR-capable tester, you can pick a few cable runs that you think are farthest from your wiring closet, and test for length. If you're under the limit, you're probably okay. But if you're beyond it, you know to keep an eye out for trouble. 10bT is a lot more forgiving than 100bT. Don't forget to allow length for patch cables at each end.

Other testers are capable of performing *signal-quality testing*. You may have heard the terms "NEXT" and "attenuation" in relation to network cabling. NEXT stands for *near-end crosstalk*. This refers to the tendency for signals to "jump" pairs near the ends of wires where the pairs have been separated and untwisted. *Attenuation* is the tendency for signals to get weaker over distance. The physics behind the phenomenon isn't all that important; what matters is whether your wire is "in spec" or "out of spec." Most of the high-end testers are fairly easy to use. They usually require a calibration for your cable type; after that you usually just have to press a single button. They perform continuity, length, NEXT, and attenuation tests (and possibly others) and report pass or fail. When the cable fails, the tester usually displays what failed.

Some cable testers are also capable of performing a rudimentary protocol analyzer function. Testers exist for fiber in addition to the copper testers mentioned, although obviously some of the tests don't apply.

Companies that produce these types of testers include the following:

QUESTIONS AND ANSWERS

What tool will help me build a visual map of my network?	One of the easiest ways to do this is with an SNMP management package that has an autodiscovery feature, such as CiscoWorks.
I want to build a set of web pages to report various things about my network. How do I do this?	There are a few ways to do this. If you have a network-management package already, see what kind of Web reporting capabilities it has. You can also obtain a scriptable SNMP package such as CMU SNMP and write your own scripts; or use something like the MRTG package designed for just that purpose. You may also be able to make use of the web server feature in newer IOS versions.
How can I tell if a cable is working?	You can either try it to see if it works, and watch the error counters; or you can use a specialized testing device. A tester will perform a better test faster, but may be expensive to purchase. Don't forget that cables which work fine at 10MB may not work well at all at 100MB, even if they're supposed to. If the cables will be used for 100MB operation, test them at 100MB.
I have a remote user complaining about not being able to communicate with a particular host, but I can reach it just fine. What's happening?	Symptoms experienced by remote users will reflect the state of their subnet, their equipment, and so on—not yours. You may need to do your troubleshooting from a device closer to the remote user, such as a router, switch, or UNIX host on their subnet. In some cases, you may have to talk the user through the steps of the tests you'd perform yourself if you were there, and having them read the results to you.
How do I tell if a host is using all the bandwidth on a particular network, and which one is doing it?	Many packet analyzer programs include a "top talker" feature that can be used to determine exactly this information. Also, if the traffic is crossing a router, you can turn on the accounting router feature as another method to get similar information.
How do I tell which switch port a particular host is connected to?	You can script your own tool to pull a list of port-to-MAC-address maps for each switch. Or, if you have CiscoWorks, UserManager will do that for you.

- Fluke (http://www.fluke.com/scripts/nettools/products/templates/products.asp)

- Microtest (http://www.microtest.com)

- Datacom Technologies (do a Web search for lancat)

Other Places to Find Troubleshooting Tools

Don't forget to watch the other chapters of this book for tools and techniques. For example, Chapter 4 includes information on how to use a number of TCP/IP troubleshooting tools you probably already have. In addition:

- Yahoo maintains a short list of network tools at

   http://dir.yahoo.com/Computers_and_Internet/
   Communications_and_Networking/Protocols/TCP_IP/Tools/

- Netcat is a useful utility for IP testing and scripting. Look for it at

   http://www.l0pht.com/~weld/netcat/index.html

- Multi Router Traffic Grapher (MRTG) is a very useful package for producing graphs of network utilization. Go to

   http://ee-staff.ethz.ch/~oetiker/webtools/mrtg/mrtg.html

Please keep in mind that some of these tools come in source code format and may need compiling. Some basic programming experience may be required. Also, web pages on the Internet occasionally move or get a new owner, so if one of the URLs listed doesn't work at some point in the future, use your favorite search engine to track the site down.

CERTIFICATION SUMMARY

In addition to the protocol- and media-specific tools presented throughout this book, there are a number of tools and techniques that you can use to manage your entire network. Some of these tools are built into Cisco equipment, some of them are commercial network-management packages or hardware devices, and some of them are free tools you can download.

Cisco routers, as well (and to some degree, switches) can be used as network troubleshooting tools. One of the chief advantages to using network equipment for troubleshooting, rather than special devices or software, is that network equipment is already installed at the location where the problem is occurring. This can save time and travel when the problem is happening in a remote location.

The types of troubleshooting that can be done with Cisco routers include Traceroutes, ping tests, Telnet tests, accounting, and simple packet debugging.

Many network-management tools are based on SNMP, which is used to query network devices for small, specific pieces of information. This data can be combined or collected repeatedly over time to give a picture of the network and the kind of load it's carrying. SNMP can be used to set the state of network devices, as well, including changing configuration or password information.

SNMP traps can be set on network devices so that network management stations can be notified immediately when some event takes place. The management station sets SNMP traps, and waits for a signal from the network device to indicate the event has occurred.

Cisco's SNMP network-management product is CiscoWorks—a collection of programs that automate various tasks related to Cisco networking equipment. Some of these programs are for specific tasks, such as managing VLANs on Catalyst switches, or ATM networks on Lightstream switches. Some of them are general-purpose utilities, such as CWSI, CiscoView, and Resource Manager. These CiscoWorks applications help automate some of the tasks that a network manager must perform, such as monitoring for down links and managing equipment configuration.

There are also a variety of third-party tools available to help you manage your network. These tools range from free software tools, to expensive dedicated hardware. Some of the free programs include SNMP management packages such as the CMU SNMP Library, and packet-analyzer software such as tcpdump. Many of these software packages come in source code form, and may require modest programming experience to compile and install.

An example of a hardware tool is a cable tester. Some cable testers are capable of very complex testing, including continuity, swapped wires, NEXT, attenuation, and cable length tests, and even rudimentary packet analysis.

TWO-MINUTE DRILL

❑ Cisco IOS client programs include ping, Traceroute, and Telnet.

❑ Telnet can be used to verify connectivity to most TCP services. The Cisco Telnet utility goes a little farther and makes this task a little easier by allowing us to specify some services by name.

❑ The telnet command has some advanced options, including source routing and specifying which interface is used.

❑ Cisco ping will sometimes report a little more information than a Windows or UNIX ping.

❑ The traceroute command is especially useful for remote diagnosis of TCP/IP network problems.

❑ Accounting works by keeping some simple statistics about Layer 3 communications, and is applied on a per-interface basis.

❑ Newer versions of the Cisco IOS include a web server that can be used to issue configuration and monitoring commands.

❑ To configure your router to log locally, use the LOGGING BUFFERED [size] global command.

❑ To configure your router to log to a syslog host, use the global command LOGGING host.

❑ CiscoWorks, like a number of other network management packages, gives you a graphical view of your network, including graphical representation of problems.

❑ Most SNMP agents will answer a query for a contact name.

❑ A contact name is simply a string of characters that represents the person responsible for the device being queried.

❑ On Cisco routers, information is made available via the SNMP agent; it concerns the interfaces installed, whether they are active, what protocols are running, statistical information about traffic being passed, how busy the CPU is, the amount of memory available, and a wide variety of other data.

❑ On Cisco routers, SNMP must be explicitly enabled, by configuring the router to respond to a particular community string or list of strings.

❑ SNMP traps are another mechanism that can be used to trigger events on the SNMP management station.

❑ For SNMP software, a *resource manager* is the portion of the software that is responsible for discovering SNMP devices and for doing the basic polling function.

❑ CiscoWorks includes a facility to autodiscover your network, by querying Cisco devices for Cisco Discovery Protocol (CDP) information.

❑ TrafficDirector is used for statistics gathering via SNMP and RMON.

❑ ATMDirector is used for various ATM switch management and discovery functions.

❑ VLANDirector is a GUI for managing VLANs on Catalyst switches.

❑ UserTracker displays end-station information retrieved from switches and routers.

❑ Resource Manager is used for managing configuration and inventory information.

❑ CiscoView displays and manages individual devices.

❑ You'll use cable testers to check proper operation of your wiring, whether it be in the walls or in a loose patch cable.

❑ The simplest and least-expensive cable testers are called *continuity testers,* which simply verify that voltage is passed across the wires.

❑ A *time-domain reflectometer test* is used to measure the length of a cable, or the distance to a break.

❑ *Attenuation* is the tendency for signals to get weaker over distance.

SELF TEST

The following Self Test questions will help you measure your understanding of the material presented in this chapter. Read all the choices carefully, as there may be more than one correct answer. Choose all correct answers for each question.

1. SNMP can be used for which of the following tasks?

   A. Configuring network equipment

   B. Resetting router passwords

   C. Collecting statistical information

   D. All of the above

2. The Telnet client built into IOS can be used to test connectivity to which of the following protocols?

   A. SNMP

   B. PING

   C. SMTP

   D. SNMP-TRAP

3. Which of the following is *not* a function of CiscoWorks?

   A. Configuring a router for the first time.

   B. Discovering the logical network layout.

   C. Tracking a MAC address to a particular switch port.

   D. Keeping statistics about your network.

4. Which of these programs from the CMU SNMP package is used to dump the SNMP table from a network device?

   A. snmpget

   B. snmpgetnext

   C. snmpwalk

   D. snmpset

5. Traceroute is possible because IP hosts are required to send what?

   A. ICMP echo replies

   B. ICMP TTL-exceeded messages

   C. SNMP traps

   D. Traceroute response packets

6. With respect to wiring, what does "NEXT" mean?

   A. The next patch panel

   B. The next bridge hop

   C. The next router hop

   D. Near-end crosstalk

7. What's the best way to learn how to use a protocol analyzer?

   A. Read the documentation

   B. Monitor a working network

   C. Monitor a failing network

   D. Monitor for "top talkers"

8. Which router feature is used to track traffic between Layer 3 addresses?

   A. Accounting

   B. SNMP

   C. Debugging

   D. HTTP server

9. Which of the following CiscoWorks applications is used to maintain VLAN information in Catalyst switches?

   A. CWSI

   B. ATMDirector

   C. UserManager

   D. VLANDirector

10. Which protocol is used by Cisco devices to discover neighboring Cisco devices?

    A. SNMP

    B. CWSI

    C. CDP

    D. UDP

11. What type of test is used to determine cable length, or distance to cable breaks?

    A. PING

    B. TDR

    C. NEXT

    D. Attenuation

12. What is the name for the list of numbers used to refer to a particular SNMP value?

    A. ICMP

    B. CWSI

    C. OID

    D. CDP

13. If you want to configure your router to log messages outside itself, you will need what kind of server?

    A. Windows NT

    B. UNIX

    C. CWSI

    D. Syslog

14. One of the more important tasks performed when using a packet analyzer is

    A. Keeping copies of the packets

    B. Narrowing down what's being monitored

    C. Sending SNMP requests

    D. Printing packets

15. In what version of IOS was the HTTP server officially introduced?

    A. 11.0(6)

    B. 11.1

    C. 11.2

    D. 12.0

16. What kind of IOS command is used to turn a router into a very rudimentary sniffer?

    A. Set sniffer

    B. Span port

    C. Debug

    D. PING

17. What command is used to configure a router to log to a remote host?

    A. logging *host*
    B. logging buffered
    C. logging syslog
    D. logging *remote*

18. What is used by network devices to notify a management station of some event occurring or threshold being reached?

    A. ICMP
    B. CDP
    C. SNMP
    D. SNMP trap

19. Microsoft Windows uses what protocol in its tracert implementation?

    A. CDP
    B. TCP
    C. UDP
    D. ICMP

20. What is one important difference between most commercial SNMP packages and most free ones?

    A. The ability to do SNMP traps
    B. A GUI
    C. Working over IP
    D. Working with Cisco equipment

9

Cisco's Diagnostic Tools

W hen you're troubleshooting network anomalies and misconfigurations, it is important to have a feature-rich set of tools for determining areas of fault or performance degradation. These diagnostic tools can be used to examine conditions on the interface, in memory, the CPU, and on the network and routing environment. Cisco IOS provides a variety of commands to view router hardware and routing characteristics.

In general, when troubleshooting network problems you should typically begin at the bottom (Physical) layer of the seven-layer OSI model and work up to the Application layer. It's always good to start off by removing any physical problems, whether it be with the cabling, connections, CPU, or a memory overload. After confirming physical connectivity, then work up through Layer 2, the Data Link layer, making sure that all point-to-point and multipoint connections and neighbors are established. Then determine if routing inconsistencies exist at Layer 3.

Cisco IOS has embedded numerous commands to show network events at various layers. This chapter presents the Cisco IOS troubleshooting commands and highlights their specific areas of relevance. It is important to be proficient with these commands, and to be able to identify problem areas with efficiency. Whether the networking problems are intentionally induced within the CCIE lab exam, accidentally occurring within an enterprise network, or causing customer service disruption via a network service provider, efficient troubleshooting is critical.

CERTIFICATION OBJECTIVE 9.01

Interface-Specific Commands

When troubleshooting a network problem, most always you'll start at the interface of origin. Whether it's a network LAN or a customer circuit, start closest to the source and then work out into the network. Cisco IOS has provided an extensive number of interface troubleshooting commands that give you a considerable amount of signaling, error checking, and protocol mapping information.

It's important to first determine if the problem is with a shared LAN segment such as Ethernet or Token Ring, or if the problem exists on a serialized circuit such as Frame Relay, SONET, or ATM. Start within an overview, by looking at the various interfaces and the configured protocols and addresses on each one. Cisco IOS provides interface views for IP, IPX, and AppleTalk over multiple media.

Cisco supports most all interface types and gives detailed statistics on each. The SHOW INTERFACE command is used to monitor both LAN and WAN interface status and statistics. Cisco shows information on the physical interfaces themselves, and a number of other switching, queuing, and accounting statistics can be gathered, as well. Here is output from the SHOW INTERFACE command:

```
RouterA#show interface ?
  ATM               ATM interface
  Ethernet          IEEE 802.3
  Hssi              High Speed Serial Interface
  Loopback          Loopback interface
  Null              Null interface
  POS               Packet over Sonet
  Serial            Serial
  Tunnel            Tunnel interface
  accounting        Show interface accounting
  crb               Show interface routing/bridging info
  fair-queue        Show interface Weighted Fair Queueing (WFQ) info
  mac-accounting    Show interface MAC accounting info
  precedence        Show interface precedence accounting info
  random-detect     Show interface Weighted Random Early Detection (WRED) info
  rate-limit        Show interface rate-limit info
  |                 Output modifiers
  <cr>
```

When viewing the event or statistical counters associated with an interface, execute the SHOW INTERFACE command several times to determine the rate at which counters are increasing. This helps you determine whether packets are being received, packet loss is problematic, collisions are occurring, and errors are incrementing. As you begin troubleshooting the interface, it is also much easier to watch the counters after they are cleared with the CLEAR COUNTERS command.

```
RouterA#clear counters
Clear "show interface" counters on all interfaces [confirm]y
```

Problems are most often detected by an end-user on a LAN segment, so it is often best to start troubleshooting closest to the source of the problem and then look into the network. On the LAN side with regard to Ethernet, you should first start by looking at the Ethernet interface itself:

```
RouterA#show interface ethernet0/0
Ethernet0/0 is up, line protocol is up
  Hardware is cxBus Ethernet, address is 0000.0c66.a300 (bia 0000.0c66.a300)
  Description: Server connection to WWW
  Internet address is 10.1.1.1/28
  MTU 1500 bytes, BW 10000 Kbit, DLY 1000 usec, rely 255/255, load 1/255
  Encapsulation ARPA, loopback not set, keepalive set (10 sec)
  ARP type: ARPA, ARP Timeout 04:00:00
  Last input 00:00:00, output 00:00:00, output hang never
  Last clearing of "show interface" counters never
  Queueing strategy: fifo
  Output queue 0/40, 1299 drops; input queue 0/75, 1688 drops
  5 minute input rate 946000 bits/sec, 59 packets/sec
  5 minute output rate 11000 bits/sec, 23 packets/sec
    679412490 packets input, 2176130895 bytes, 0 no buffer
    Received 5920676 broadcasts, 11 runts, 0 giants
    54 input errors, 0 CRC, 41 frame, 2 overrun, 0 ignored, 0 abort
    0 input packets with dribble condition detected
    338822171 packets output, 3036730793 bytes, 0 underruns
    4578 output errors, 83658269 collisions, 1 interface resets
    0 babbles, 0 late collision, 0 deferred
    0 lost carrier, 0 no carrier
    0 output buffer failures, 0 output buffers swapped out
```

As you can see, the SHOW INTERFACE command is one of the most revealing diagnostic commands. Let's take a look at a few key fields for identifying status on the LAN interface.

■ Of first importance is line two that the interface shows "up/up." Generally, if the Ethernet cable is connected to a hub correctly, the interface will show "up/up." If the cable is broken or there's a problem with a hub or Ethernet switch, the interface will show "down/down."

- On line 3, take note of the *MAC address* and the *IP address* assigned to the interface. The MAC address is always 24 bits or 6 hex digits in length, and is useful in determining if duplicate IP addresses have been assigned on a LAN segment. The SHOW ARP command can be used for detecting duplicate IP addresses.

- On line 5, verify that the assigned IP address is consistent with the appropriate *netmask.*

- Line 6 shows much of the performance link state information used by IGRP/EIGRP.

- On line 7, verify if *keepalives* are set.

- On line 8, look to see if an extended period of time has passed since a packet was input or output on the router. The *last input/output* fields give an indication of when packets were sent or received on the interface.

- When viewing the *byte, packet,* and *error counters,* on line 10, take note of the time since counters were last cleared.

- On line 12, take a look at the *queue depth,* and see if packets have been dropped on either the input or output queue.

- On lines 13 and 14, look at the *load on the interface.* Generally, a LAN Ethernet interface will handle a combined duplex load of 30 percent of the line bandwidth. This maximum load varies with the LAN topology.

- On lines 17 and 20, watch for an increasing number of *errors, ignores,* or *aborts.* As an interface reaches its maximum throughput, certain ignores and aborts may become apparent.

- For an Ethernet, on line 21, it is always important to monitor *collisions.* A high collision rate can slow down throughput and increase delay considerably.

exam
ⓌatchWatch out for *"no keepalives"* during troubleshooting.

exam
Ⓦatch Verify netmasks during troubleshooting.

IP Interfaces

Since most routers have at least IP configured on them, a good starting point is to view all the interfaces and the IP protocols configured on each. Following is output from the SHOW IP INTERFACE BRIEF command:

```
RouterA#show ip interface brief
Interface          IP-Address      OK? Method Status                 Protocol
Ethernet0/0        10.2.1.2        YES NVRAM  up                     up
Ethernet0/1        10.4.1.2        YES manual up                     up
Hssi1/0            unassigned      YES unset  administratively down  down
ATM2/0             unassigned      YES unset  up                     up
ATM2/0.32          unassigned      YES unset  up                     up
ATM2/0.33          10.20.20.1      YES NVRAM  up                     up
ATM2/0.100         unassigned      YES unset  up                     up
Serial3/0          10.60.60.1      YES NVRAM  down                   down
Serial3/1          unassigned      YES unset  down                   down
Serial3/2          unassigned      YES unset  administratively down  down
Serial3/3          unassigned      YES unset  down                   down
Serial5/0/0        unassigned      YES unset  administratively down  down
Serial5/0/1        unassigned      YES unset  administratively down  down
Serial5/0/2        unassigned      YES unset  administratively down  down
Serial5/0/3        unassigned      YES unset  administratively down  down
Serial5/0/4        10.6.1.1        YES manual up                     up
Serial5/0/5        unassigned      YES unset  administratively down  down
Serial5/0/6        unassigned      YES unset  administratively down  down
Serial5/0/7        unassigned      YES unset  administratively down  down
ATM10/0/0          unassigned      YES unset  up                     up
POS12/0/0          10.8.1.1        YES manual up                     up
Loopback0          10.5.1.1        YES NVRAM  up                     up
```

The SHOW IP INTERFACE BRIEF snapshot shows all the interfaces, their IP addresses, and their operational status. This command gives you a quick overview of all interfaces configured on the router. When using the SHOW IP INTERFACE BRIEF command, you can use the output information to verify the following:

- Correct IP address
- Administrative and physical status on each interface is up
- Protocol signaling on the interface shows up

For a particular interface, it is often important to view all the default IP settings that are enabled or disabled. For instance, here is the output from the SHOW CONFIGURATION on Ethernet0/0:

```
interface Ethernet0/0
 description interface to FTP server
 ip address 10.2.1.2 255.255.255.0
 no ip route-cache optimum
 appletalk cable-range 1-10 9.210
 appletalk zone A
 appletalk protocol eigrp
 ipx network AAAA
```

A more detailed configuration, however, is shown by viewing all the default information that is enabled or disabled on the interface. Dependent on the IOS version, certain configuration settings may be enabled or disabled by default. For example:

```
RouterA#show ip interface ethernet0/0
Ethernet0/0 is up, line protocol is up
  Internet address is 10.2.1.2/24
  Broadcast address is 255.255.255.255
  Address determined by non-volatile memory
  MTU is 1500 bytes
  Helper address is not set
  Directed broadcast forwarding is enabled
  Multicast reserved groups joined: 224.0.0.10
  Outgoing access list is not set
  Inbound  access list is not set
  Proxy ARP is enabled
  Security level is default
  Split horizon is enabled
  ICMP redirects are always sent
  ICMP unreachables are always sent
  ICMP mask replies are never sent
  IP fast switching is enabled
  IP fast switching on the same interface is disabled
  IP Optimum switching is disabled
  IP Flow switching is disabled
  IP LES Fast switching turbo vector
  IP Null turbo vector
  IP multicast fast switching is enabled
  IP multicast distributed fast switching is disabled
```

```
Router Discovery is disabled
IP output packet accounting is disabled
IP access violation accounting is disabled
TCP/IP header compression is disabled
Probe proxy name replies are disabled
Gateway Discovery is disabled
Policy routing is disabled
Web Cache Redirect is disabled
BGP Policy Mapping is disabled
```

The SHOW IP INTERFACE command produces an inordinate amount of default and configured settings. You should generally follow a structured approach by starting at the Physical layer, verifying Layer 2 framing, and then look at the network Layer 3.

At Layers 1 and 2, verify that the physical interface and line protocol are both up. At Layer 3, verify the following:

- Correct IP address
- Applied access lists are correct
- Appropriate switching mode is set
- No undesirable default settings

IPX Interfaces

In troubleshooting of IPX networks, it's important to get an overview of the interfaces enabled with IPX. To view the IPX interface configuration, use the SHOW IPX INTERFACE command:

```
RouterA#show ipx interface brief
Interface          IPX Network Encapsulation Status               IPX State
Ethernet0/0        AAAA        NOVELL-ETHER  up                   [up]
Ethernet0/1        unassigned  not config'd  up                   n/a
Hssi1/0            unassigned  not config'd  administratively down n/a
ATM2/0             unassigned  not config'd  up                   n/a
ATM2/0.32          unassigned  not config'd  up                   n/a
ATM2/0.33          unassigned  not config'd  up                   n/a
ATM2/0.100         unassigned  not config'd  up                   n/a
Serial3/0          unassigned  not config'd  down                 n/a
Serial3/1          BBBB        HDLC          down                 [up]
```

The SHOW IPX INTERFACE BRIEF command provides valuable information for verifying the following:

- Assigned network address

- Proper encapsulation: SAP, HDLC, ARPA, Novell-Ether, SNAP

- Interface status is up

- IPX state is up

Also view the IPX interface settings:

```
RouterA#show ipx interface ethernet0/0
Ethernet0/0 is up, line protocol is up
  IPX address is AAAA.0060.8388.bb00, NOVELL-ETHER [up] line-up, RIPPQ: 0, SAPPQ: 0
  Delay of this IPX network, in ticks is 1 throughput 0 link delay 0
  IPXWAN processing not enabled on this interface.
  IPX SAP update interval is 1 minute(s)
  IPX type 20 propagation packet forwarding is disabled
  Incoming access list is not set
  Outgoing access list is not set
  IPX helper access list is not set
  SAP GNS processing enabled, delay 0 ms, output filter list is not set
  SAP Input filter list is not set
  SAP Output filter list is not set
  SAP Router filter list is not set
  Input filter list is not set
  Output filter list is not set
  Router filter list is not set
  Netbios Input host access list is not set
  Netbios Input bytes access list is not set
  Netbios Output host access list is not set
  Netbios Output bytes access list is not set
  Updates each 60 seconds, aging multiples RIP: 3 SAP: 3
  SAP interpacket delay is 55 ms, maximum size is 480 bytes
  RIP interpacket delay is 55 ms, maximum size is 432 bytes
  IPX accounting is disabled
  IPX fast switching is configured (enabled)
  RIP packets received 4548, RIP packets sent 4548
  SAP packets received 0, SAP packets sent 1
```

The SHOW IPX INTERFACE command presents all default IPX settings. At Layers 1 and 2, verify that the physical interface and line protocol are both up. At Layer 3, verify the following:

- The interface address is the concatenation of the network address and MAC address.

- Network delay in ticks is not excessive.

■ SAP update interval.

■ Filters or access lists.

■ RIP and SAP routing information is configured with correct filtering and routing update intervals.

AppleTalk Interfaces

As it does for IP and IPX, Cisco IOS provides for an AppleTalk overview with the SHOW APPLETALK INTERFACE BRIEF summary:

```
RouterA#show appletalk interface brief
Interface       Address      Config        Status/Line Protocol  Atalk Protocol
Ethernet0/0     9.210        Extended      up                    up
Ethernet0/1     unassigned   not config'd  up                    n/a
Hssi1/0         unassigned   not config'd  administratively down n/a
ATM2/0          unassigned   not config'd  up                    n/a
AT8/0/0.36      50.189       Extended      up                    up
```

For AppleTalk, verify the following:

■ Address is within cable range of segment

■ Configuration is extended or nonextended

■ Status on Line and Protocol are both up

In addition, view the AppleTalk interface settings:

```
RouterA#show appletalk interface ethernet0/0
Ethernet0/0 is up, line protocol is up
  AppleTalk cable range is 1-10
  AppleTalk address is 9.210, Valid
  AppleTalk zone is ""A"
  Routing protocols enabled: RTMP & EIGRP
  AppleTalk port configuration verified by 2.223
  AppleTalk address gleaning is disabled
  AppleTalk route cache is enabled
```

At Layers 1 and 2, verify that the physical interface and line protocol are both up. At Layer 3, verify the following:

■ Correct cable range assignment (Phase I or Phase II)

■ AppleTalk address is within cable range

- Zone assignment is correct
- RTMP, EIGRP, or other AppleTalk routing protocols are intentionally enabled

WAN Interfaces

Cisco supports a wide variety of WAN interfaces, each with its own characteristics. When troubleshooting ATM, Frame Relay, HDLC, and other protocol interfaces, use the SHOW commands to determine if errors, packet drops, or other problems are causing performance degradation.

Serial Interfaces

After determining that the LAN side of the network is configured properly and functioning, then look at the WAN connectivity on the router. A number of areas of concern—such as up/up status, IP address, last input/output, and clearing of counters—are similar for both Ethernet and serial interfaces, but for serialized circuits it's important to monitor other fields as well. When viewing serial interfaces, look at the various signaling and performance criteria, shown here:

```
RouterA#show interface serial5/7
Serial5/7 is up, line protocol is up
  Hardware is cxBus Serial
  Description: RouterA Serial
  Internet address is 10.6.1.1/24
  MTU 1500 bytes, BW 1920 Kbit, DLY 20000 usec, rely 255/255, load 36/255
  Encapsulation HDLC, loopback not set, keepalive set (10 sec)
  Last input 00:00:00, output 00:00:00, output hang never
  Last clearing of "show interface" counters 3w3d
  Queueing strategy: fifo
  Output queue 0/40, 896826 drops; input queue 0/75, 3205 drops
  5 minute input rate 282000 bits/sec, 157 packets/sec
  5 minute output rate 277000 bits/sec, 61 packets/sec
     442254793 packets input, 455690937 bytes, 49 no buffer
     Received 0 broadcasts, 0 runts, 0 giants
     16732 input errors, 12547 CRC, 3 frame, 0 overrun, 2837 ignored, 4182 abort
     205404329 packets output, 2223592864 bytes, 0 underruns
     0 output errors, 0 collisions, 144 interface resets
     0 output buffers copied, 0 interrupts, 0 failures
     2 carrier transitions
     RTS up, CTS up, DTR up, DCD up, DSR up
```

The SHOW INTERFACE SERIAL command allows for determining the usage of the WAN resources and network status. Pay attention to the following:

- An excessive number of drops indicates an oversubscribed circuit and can be an important factor in degraded performance. If you compare the number of drops on line 10 with the number of packets input and output on lines 13 and 16, then you can gain an idea of your drop percentage.

- Input and Output rates show the load on the circuits. (Note: You can reduce the default five-minute interval by using the command LOAD INTERVAL.)

- Continue to monitor all errors and other fields over a period of time, and ensure that no problems exist with either circuit quality or router performance.

- Make sure that all serial signals, such as RTS, CTS, DTR, DCD, and DSR, are up. Any of these signals being down can cause serious serial port problems.

ATM Interfaces

Following is the output from a SHOW INTERFACE command for an ATM interface:

```
RouterA#show interface atm10/0/0
ATM10/0/0 is up, line protocol is up
  Hardware is cyBus ENHANCED ATM PA
  MTU 4470 bytes, sub MTU 4470, BW 33920 Kbit, DLY 200 usec, rely 255/255, load
1/255
  Encapsulation ATM, loopback not set, keepalive set (10 sec)
  Encapsulation(s): AAL5 AAL3/4
  4096 maximum active VCs, 2 current VCCs
  VC idle disconnect time: 300 seconds
  Last input never, output 00:00:00, output hang never
  Last clearing of "show interface" counters 03:55:08
  Queueing strategy: fifo
  Output queue 0/40, 0 drops; input queue 0/75, 338 drops
  30 second input rate 4064000 bits/sec, 337 packets/sec
```

```
30 second output rate 0 bits/sec, 1 packets/sec
   3496889 packets input, 979428910 bytes, 0 no buffer
   Received 0 broadcasts, 0 runts, 0 giants
   0 input errors, 0 CRC, 0 frame, 0 overrun, 0 ignored, 0 abort
   9243 packets output, 641692 bytes, 0 underruns
   0 output errors, 0 collisions, 0 interface resets
   0 output buffers copied, 0 interrupts, 0 failures
```

In monitoring an ATM interface, highlight and observe the following specific areas:

- Queuing drops are always a concern and will often lead to poor service quality.

- ATM input errors can occur due to AAL5 trailer CRC errors, via dropped cells in the ATM network. This problem is known as *packet shredding*. The VC parameters should be adjusted to better shape the ATM VC contract.

When troubleshooting ATM networks, another useful view is from the SHOW ATM INTERFACE command:

```
RouterA#show atm interface atm10/0/0
ATM interface ATM10/0/0:
AAL enabled:  AAL5  AAL3/4, Maximum VCs: 4096, Current VCCs: 2
Max. Datagram Size:4528, MIDs/VC: 1024
PLIM Type:E3 - 34Mbps, Framing is G.832/G.804, TX clocking: LINE
Scrambling: ON
3475271 input, 9195 output, 4 IN fast, 4 OUT fast
Config. is ACTIVE
```

Use the SHOW ATM INTERFACE command to obtain specific information for the following consideration:

- Verifying framing encapsulation, whether PLCP or direct mapping
- Verifying whether the clock source is being obtained internally or from the line
- Verifying E3/DS3 scrambling
- Viewing the packet loss

To view all the ATM Virtual Circuits configured on the router, use the SHOW ATM VC command:

```
RouterA#show atm vc
                                  AAL /           Peak  Avg.  Burst
     Interface      VCD  VPI  VCI Type  Encapsulation  Kbps  Kbps  Cells Status
     ATM2/0.32       32    0   32  PVC   AAL5-SNAP      2000  2000    96 ACTIVE
     ATM2/0.33       33    0   33  PVC   AAL5-SNAP      2000  2000    96 ACTIVE
     ATM10/0/0.36    30    0   36  PVC   AAL5-SNAP       800   400    10 ACTIVE
     ATM10/0/0.37    31    0   37  PVC   AAL5-SNAP       800   400    10 ACTIVE
```

When configuring multiple VCCs on a Cisco router, it is important to get a snapshot view of all VCCs in order to verify the following:

- VCD is used for local VCC identification on the router
- VPI/VCI
- AAL5 encapsulation method as AAL5snap, AAL5nlpid, or AAL5mux
- Peak, Sustained, and Burst rates
- Interface is currently active

To look at an individual Virtual Circuit, display the information relevant to its VCD, as shown here:

```
RouterA#show atm vc 31
ATM10/0/0.37: VCD: 31, VPI: 0, VCI: 37, etype:0x0, AAL5 - LLC/SNAP, Flags: 0x30
PeakRate: 800, Average Rate: 400, Burst Cells: 10, VCmode: 0x0
OAM DISABLED, InARP DISABLED
InPkts: 1776004, OutPkts: 3936, InBytes: 2671969328, OutBytes: 259230
InPRoc: 4395, OutPRoc: 23, Broadcasts: 3797
InFast: 0, OutFast: 0, InAS: 1771609, OutAS: 116
InPktDrops: 0, OutPktDrops: 0
CrcErrors: 0, SarTimeOuts: 0, OverSizedSDUs: 0
OAM F5 cells sent: 0, OAM cells received: 0
Status: ACTIVE
```

When using the SHOW ATM VC command to verify statistics and status for a particular VCC, use the output for the following checks:

- Verifying that the packet counters are increasing
- Looking at the packet drops

- Looking at the CRC errors

- Verifying whether OAM cells (if enabled) are being sent and received

Frame Relay Interfaces

When troubleshooting a Frame Relay connection, start by looking at the interface itself with the SHOW INTERFACE command.

```
RouterA#show interface serial4/0
Serial4/0 is up, line protocol is up
  Hardware is cxBus Serial
  Description: Frame Relay Connection
  MTU 1500 bytes, BW 1544 Kbit, DLY 20000 usec, rely 255/255, load 95/255
  Encapsulation FRAME-RELAY, loopback not set, keepalive set (10 sec)
  LMI enq sent  512885, LMI stat recvd 512885, LMI upd recvd 0, DTE LMI up
  LMI enq recvd 0, LMI stat sent  0, LMI upd sent  0
  LMI DLCI 0  LMI type is ANSI Annex D  frame relay DTE
  Broadcast queue 0/64, broadcasts sent/dropped 0/0, interface broadcasts 276571
  Last input 00:00:01, output 00:00:01, output hang never
  Last clearing of "show interface" counters 8w3d
  Input queue: 0/75/0 (size/max/drops); Total output drops: 228
  Queueing strategy: weighted fair
  Output queue: 0/64/228 (size/threshold/drops)
     Conversations  0/96 (active/max active)
     Reserved Conversations 0/0 (allocated/max allocated)
  5 minute input rate 230000 bits/sec, 24 packets/sec
  5 minute output rate 315000 bits/sec, 28 packets/sec
     9830213 packets input, 3255079600 bytes, 1 no buffer
     Received 0 broadcasts, 0 runts, 0 giants
     0 input errors, 0 CRC, 0 frame, 0 overrun, 0 ignored, 0 abort
     16573628 packets output, 2182943705 bytes, 0 underruns
     0 output errors, 0 collisions, 0 interface resets
```

The Frame Relay results of the SHOW INTERFACE command should be used to verify the following:

- LMI Type is Cisco, ANSI, or Q933a

- LMI is established via LMI packets sent and received, and DTE LMI up

- Packets counters are increasing

exam
ⓌatcH   *Be aware of the LMI type used for Frame Relay.*

If you're using serial subinterfaces, verify that each PVC is operational, as follows:

```
RouterA#show interface serial4/0.16
Serial4/0.16 is up, line protocol is up
  Hardware is cxBus Serial
  Description: Frame Relay (DLCI 16)
  Internet address is 10.10.10.1/30
  MTU 1500 bytes, BW 1544 Kbit, DLY 20000 usec, rely 255/255, load 10/255
  Encapsulation FRAME-RELAY
```

When viewing individual Frame Relay PVCs, use the SHOW INTERFACE SERIAL command to verify the following:

- Subinterface is up/up
- Load exists

exam
ⓦatch *Be familiar with both subinterfaces and protocol mapping on a common interface.*

exam
ⓦatch *If using Frame Relay subinterfaces, then split-horizon is on by default. On non-subinterfaces, it is disabled by default.*

It may also be necessary to view all the individual PVCs, as shown here:

```
RouterA#show frame-relay pvc
 PVC Statistics for interface Serial4/0 (Frame Relay DTE)
 DLCI = 16, DLCI USAGE = LOCAL, PVC STATUS = ACTIVE, INTERFACE = Serial4/0.16

   input pkts 117584       output pkts 86792        in bytes 35629074
   out bytes 27842302      dropped pkts 2           in FECN pkts 190
   in BECN pkts 0          out FECN pkts 0          out BECN pkts 0
   in DE pkts 0            out DE pkts 0
   pvc create time 28w6d, last time pvc status changed 09:57:48

 DLCI = 17, DLCI USAGE = LOCAL, PVC STATUS = ACTIVE, INTERFACE = Serial4/0.17

   input pkts 86215        output pkts 103387       in bytes 27414236
   out bytes 29261689      dropped pkts 5           in FECN pkts 0
   in BECN pkts 0          out FECN pkts 0          out BECN pkts 0
   in DE pkts 0            out DE pkts 0
   pvc create time 28w6d, last time pvc status changed 20:50:41
```

The SHOW FRAME-RELAY PVC shows statistics and status on a per-VC basis and should be used for the following checks:

- Verify DLCI
- Verify Active status
- View incrementing counters
- View PVC status change for instability

CERTIFICATION OBJECTIVE 9.02

Memory and Process Commands

When you're receiving slow response from a router, or routing processes are taking a long time to converge, this can be a sign of insufficient CPU space or memory. Cisco IOS provides a few commands to view the state of the router's CPU and memory.

There are various types of memory: internal flash, PCMCIA flash, read-only memory (boot ROM), nonvolatile memory, and volatile memory.

- Internal flash memory can be used to store IOS software images or backup configurations.
- PCMCIA flash allows additional memory for alternative IOS images or configurations.
- ROM chips have subsets of IOS burnt into the chips and are nonconfigurable. Certain IOS revisions require upgrading ROM sets.
- Nonvolatile memory is where start-up configurations are usually saved.
- Volatile memory is dynamically used by routing and other processes.

When adding memory to a router, it is important to verify that the memory is being recognized by the router and that it has been installed correctly. Additional memory SIMMs usually must be inserted in particular slots in a particular order, as specified in the hardware guide for the router.

To verify that the processor type and whether the memory is recognized, use the command SHOW VERSION:

```
RouterA#show version
Cisco Internetwork Operating System Software
IOS (tm) GS Software (RSP-JV-M), Version 11.1(20)CC, EARLY DEPLOYMENT RELEASE
SOFTWARE (fc1)
V111_20_CC_THROTTLE_BRANCH Synced to mainline version: 11.1(20)CA
Copyright (c) 1986-1998 by cisco Systems, Inc.
Compiled Fri 17-Jul-98 21:38 by richardd
Image text-base: 0x60010910, data-base: 0x60ABC000

ROM: System Bootstrap, Version 11.1(2) [nitin 2], RELEASE SOFTWARE (fc1)
ROM: GS Software (RSP-BOOT-M), Version 11.1(472), RELEASE SOFTWARE (fc1)

RouterA uptime is 2 weeks, 4 days, 6 hours, 9 minutes
System restarted by reload at 18:49:48 UTC Fri Sep 18 1998
System image file is "slot0:rsp-jv-mz.111-20.CC", booted via slot0

cisco RSP2 (R4700) processor with 131072K/2072K bytes of memory.
R4700 processor, Implementation 33, Revision 1.0
.

.
123K bytes of non-volatile configuration memory.

16384K bytes of Flash PCMCIA card at slot 0 (Sector size 128K).
20480K bytes of Flash PCMCIA card at slot 1 (Sector size 128K).
8192K bytes of Flash internal SIMM (Sector size 256K).
No slave installed in slot 7.
Configuration register is 0x2102
```

The SHOW VERSION and SHOW HARDWARE commands provide a high-level overview of the router's hardware for verifying the following:

- Boot ROM version

- Installed memory

- Processor type

- NVRAM size

- PCMCIA flash

- Internal flash

Cisco IOS shows each individual process running and the amount of CPU each process has been consuming. Most importantly, the five-second, one-minute, and five-minute CPU averages show how well the router is performing from a CPU perspective. If the CPU is suspiciously high, look at the individual statistics for each Processor ID (PID) and see which one might be the CPU offender.

```
RouterA>show processes cpu
CPU utilization for five seconds: 38%/32%; one minute: 41%; five minutes: 42%
 PID  Runtime(ms)  Invoked  uSecs   5Sec    1Min    5Min TTY Process
   1            0        1       0  0.00%   0.00%   0.00%   0 SSCOP Input
   2     15878664   153691  103317  0.00%   0.46%   0.57%   0 Check heaps
   3        61628    13640    4518  0.00%   0.00%   0.00%   0 Pool Manager
```

SHOW PROCESSOR CPU is one of the commands often executed at every login to the router, in order to:

- View five-second, one-minute, and five-minute CPU utilization

- View individual PIDs for excessive CPU usage

If a router is running BGP and receiving a full Internet routing table, then the router will require at least 64MB of memory. Memory is also used as a buffer for holding packets to be processed. It is also important to make sure that a memory leak is not occurring, in which memory is not being freed up for reuse. Memory leaks are often common bugs in newer IOSs with more recent features.

```
RouterA#show processes memory
Total: 119135744, Used: 43307316, Free: 75828428
 PID TTY  Allocated       Freed    Holding    Getbufs    Retbufs Process
   0   0      54416         304    3417704          0          0 *Init*
   0   0  104446496   100954236      87700     369816       6808 *Dead*
  32   0  996116024    46580624    7731636     176620   63633216 IP Input
  68   0  215246040  3687622384   28582656          0          0 BGP Router
  69   0 3913241184  3732387224    1215444   54673308    3961988 BGP I/O
```

In order to verify the memory usage, use SHOW PROCESSES MEMORY to view the following:

- Total, used, and free memory
- Each PID, looking for memory leaks not freeing up memory, or dead processes retaining memory

A similar summary command lets you view all memory allocations:

```
RouterA#show memory summary
            Head    Total(b)   Used(b)    Free(b)   Lowest(b) Largest(b)
Processor 60E62200  119135744  43235988   75899756  66192808  64004400
     Fast 60E42200    131072    130648       424       424       380
```

To view flash contents, issue the SHOW FLASH command. Generally, flash memory contains IOS and configuration images. In addition, some of the more recent IOS versions may not fit entirely on the flash memory; they may require ROM sets to be upgraded, or possibly more memory. Be aware of available flash when upgrading IOS.

```
RouterA>show flash
-#- ED --type-- --crc--- -seek-- nlen -length- -----date/time------ name
1   .. FFFFFFFF 62D63903 6E6A4C  18   7104972  Sep 19 1998 13:47:11
igs-j-l.111-20.bin
2   .. FFFFFFFF C763888E C5C7C0  22   5725428  Sep 21 1998 07:29:25
rsp-pv-mz.112-4.P.bin
```

exam
ⓦatch

Be aware of what IOS version is loaded on the router.

CERTIFICATION OBJECTIVE 9.03

Buffer and Message-Logging Commands

A router allocates buffers in memory for holding a packet while waiting for the routing table lookup and other processing to finish. Buffers of various sizes are allocated within memory to accommodate the various packets.

Usually after a table lookup is performed, the route is cached on the interface and does not require further table lookups; this means subsequent packets within the flow do not require system buffer space.

The default buffer sizes are as follows:

- Small (104-byte buffers)
- Middle (600-byte buffers)
- Big (1524-byte buffers)
- VeryBig (4520-byte buffers)
- Large (5024-byte buffers)
- Huge (18,024-byte buffers)

In the event no existing "free" buffers are available for a packet, then a "miss" is registered and a creation request is made. Many buffer creations can be CPU-intensive. When buffers cannot be created, then the packet is dropped as a failure. If packets are regularly being dropped due to insufficient buffers, find out which buffer has the highest failure rate. Cisco allows for adjusting of the default buffer sizes to accommodate various packet profiles. The SHOW BUFFERS command displays the various allocation and statistics for the buffer pools.

```
RouterA>show buffers
Buffer elements:
     897 in free list (500 max allowed)
     305531633 hits, 0 misses, 400 created

Public buffer pools:
Small buffers, 104 bytes (total 249, permanent 120):
     196 in free list (20 min, 250 max allowed)
     110770217 hits, 71815 misses, 37161 trims, 37290 created
     38466 failures (0 no memory)
Middle buffers, 600 bytes (total 202, permanent 90):
     193 in free list (10 min, 200 max allowed)
     58597300 hits, 87379 misses, 229930 trims, 230042 created
     2340 failures (0 no memory)
Big buffers, 1524 bytes (total 90, permanent 90):
     89 in free list (5 min, 300 max allowed)
     42329380 hits, 3087 misses, 1289 trims, 1289 created
```

```
                         2201 failures (0 no memory)
            VeryBig buffers, 4520 bytes (total 10, permanent 10):
                 9 in free list (0 min, 300 max allowed)
                 6113678 hits, 1442 misses, 215 trims, 215 created
                 1400 failures (0 no memory)
            Large buffers, 5024 bytes (total 10, permanent 10):
                 10 in free list (0 min, 30 max allowed)
                 699 hits, 701 misses, 98 trims, 98 created
                 701 failures (0 no memory)
            Huge buffers, 18024 bytes (total 0, permanent 0):
                 0 in free list (0 min, 13 max allowed)
                 81 hits, 642 misses, 97 trims, 97 created
                 642 failures (0 no memory)
             Header pools:
```

The SHOW BUFFERS command indicates the typical packet and traffic patterns that are consuming router resources. Use this command to determine the following:

- The highest number of hits characterize the size of most packets

- The number of failures reflect the number of dropped packets

- The number of creations can be CPU-intensive

Cisco allows for extensive logging of commands and network events, maintaining a local log on the router as well as allowing logging to a syslog daemon on a remote server. The log files are always a good place to look for hardware- and other network-event information. Following is output from the SHOW LOG command:

```
RouterA#show log
Syslog logging: enabled (0 messages dropped, 501 flushes, 0 overruns)
    Console logging: level debugging, 17588 messages logged
    Monitor logging: level debugging, 84 messages logged
    Trap logging: level informational, 16291 message lines logged
        Logging to 10.1.1.222, 16291 message lines logged
        Logging to 10.2.1.66, 16291 message lines logged
        Logging to 10.3.1.194, 16291 message lines logged
    Buffer logging: level debugging, 17087 messages logged
Oct  7 16:34:07 UTC: %LINEPROTO-5-UPDOWN: Line protocol on Interface Serial8/2,
changed state to down
Oct  7 16:34:37 UTC: %LINEPROTO-5-UPDOWN: Line protocol on Interface Serial8/2,
changed state to up
```

Using Ping, Extended Ping, and Traceroute to Confirm Network Connectivity

For troubleshooting end-to-end connectivity, some of the most common and most powerful tools are the ping, extended ping, and Traceroute commands. Cisco has built in extensive network troubleshooting tools for supporting IP, IPX, AppleTalk, and other networking protocols.

One of a troubleshooter's greatest friends is the PING command. The following output shows the extensive PING network applications:

```
RouterA#ping ?
  WORD       Ping destination address or hostname
  apollo     Apollo echo
  appletalk  Appletalk echo
  clns       CLNS echo
  decnet     DECnet echo
  ip         IP echo
  ipx        Novell/IPX echo
  vines      Vines echo
  xns        XNS echo
  <cr>
```

An IP ping is an ICMP *echo request* packet that is sent to a remote station. When a remote station receives this ICMP request, the station will simply *echo reply* with the identical packet. By default, a Cisco router will send five consecutive 64-byte pings to a remote end-station. The router will then record the minimum, maximum, and average response times of the *echo replies* and the number of *echo replies* successfully returned as seen in the following PING output.

```
mae-e>ping www.cisco.com

Type escape sequence to abort.
Sending 5, 100-byte ICMP Echoes to 192.31.7.130, timeout is 2 seconds:
!!!!!
Success rate is 100 percent (5/5), round-trip min/avg/max = 76/76/76 ms
```

Ping is a simple tool to determine if access to the remote node is possible. In the event that the ICMP requests do not receive a reply, there could be network problems due to poor routing, network congestion, network failure, access lists or filtering, or a busy remote host. If the ping fails, then further examination must occur.

```
RouterB#ping ipx AAAA.0060.8388.bb00

Type escape sequence to abort.
Sending 5, 100-byte IPX cisco Echoes to AAAA.0060.8388.bb00, timeout is 2
seconds:
!!!!!
Success rate is 100 percent (5/5), round-trip min/avg/max = 1/3/4 ms

RouterA#ping appletalk 2.223

Type escape sequence to abort.
Sending 5, 100-byte AppleTalk Echoes to 2.223, timeout is 2 seconds:
!!!!!
Success rate is 100 percent (5/5), round-trip min/avg/max = 4/5/8 ms
```

exam
ⓦatch **Be sure to ping all interfaces and verify that they all respond.**

The source IP address in an ICMP echo request packet is always assigned to the router's transmitting interface. The interface that will transmit the echo request is chosen in the IP routing process. In order to test that other interfaces and their subnets are being advertised into the network, Cisco's extended ping allows for the source IP address to be modified to something other than the outgoing address.

```
RouterA#ping
Protocol [ip]:
Target IP address: 10.1.1.1
Repeat count [5]:
Datagram size [100]:
Timeout in seconds [2]:
Extended commands [n]: y
Source address or interface: 10.2.2.2
Type of service [0]:
Set DF bit in IP header? [no]:
```

```
Validate reply data? [no]:
Data pattern [0xABCD]:
Loose, Strict, Record, Timestamp, Verbose[none]:
Sweep range of sizes [n]:
Type escape sequence to abort.
Sending 5, 100-byte ICMP Echoes to 10.1.1.1, timeout is 2 seconds:
```

The extended ping also allows for modifying the repeat count, packet size, and type of service. In addition, by setting the timeout to 0 and the repeat count high, the extended ping can become a simple packet generator. When modifying the source IP address, Cisco requires the source IP address to be a valid interface on the router, or the return packet would not get routed back.

To further determine where certain network problems may be occurring, Cisco IOS provides a Traceroute utility that shows each individual network hop along the path to a destination. The Traceroute tool uses UDP packets with invalid ports, and increments their TTL by one so that each hop replies with an ICMP "Timeout Exceeded" message. The source IP address of the ICMP reply message is then used and displayed as a network map of the route to a particular destination.

```
mae-e>traceroute www.cisco.com

Type escape sequence to abort.
Tracing the route to cio-sys.cisco.com (192.31.7.130)

 1 f1-0-0.maeeast.bbnplanet.net (192.41.177.2) 0 msec 4 msec 4 msec
 2 p2-2.vienna1-nbr2.bbnplanet.net (4.0.1.93) [AS 1] 4 msec 4 msec 4 msec
 3 p1-0.vienna1-nbr3.bbnplanet.net (4.0.5.46) [AS 1] 4 msec 4 msec 4 msec
 4 p3-1.paloalto-nbr2.bbnplanet.net (4.0.3.178) [AS 1] 80 msec 80 msec 84 msec
 5 p0-0-0.paloalto-cr18.bbnplanet.net (4.0.3.86) [AS 1] 84 msec 80 msec 84 msec
 6 h1-0.cisco.bbnplanet.net (131.119.26.10) [AS 1] 84 msec 80 msec 80 msec
 7 sty.cisco.com (192.31.7.39) [AS 109] 80 msec 80 msec 80 msec
 8 cio-sys.cisco.com (192.31.7.130) [AS 109] 80 msec *  80 msec)
```

When using the Traceroute command, unusual paths may sometimes show up. Traceroute sometimes produces erroneous routing results, and should therefore be considered a helpful utility but not necessarily definitive. In addition, Traceroute only shows the path from a source to a particular destination. The return path from that destination may follow an entirely different path. When two different paths exist between two particular subnets, this is known as *asymmetrical* routing.

```
RouterA#traceroute ?
  WORD       Trace route to destination address or hostname
  appletalk  AppleTalk Trace
  clns       ISO CLNS Trace
  ip         IP Trace
  oldvines   Vines Trace (Cisco)
  vines      Vines Trace (Banyan)
  <cr>
```

CERTIFICATION SUMMARY

Cisco provides a feature-rich command set for troubleshooting both LAN and WAN interfaces, CPU and memory, and network routing. Fluency with these commands, and the ability to quickly scan through the displayed results, are extremely important skills when you're troubleshooting real network events.

Interface signaling, packet loss, and errors are all indications of a misconfigured or overutilized network. It is important to detect these problems quickly. The CCIE exam gives only a limited amount of time to identify and resolve various problems.

Although the exam does not specifically test for CPU or memory problems, these issues come up every day. When you're adding new features, expanding routing, or increasing utilization, these enhancements all begin to consume more of the routers' resources and must be continually monitored for performance.

Ping and Traceroute are a troubleshooter's friend. These two tools are often used in determining packet loss, delay, routing, and other general problems. Along with some of the other tools mentioned in this chapter, these commands provide adequate information for diagnosing many common problems and issues occurring with your interface, CPU, memory, and routing.

✓ TWO-MINUTE DRILL

- ❑ In general, when troubleshooting network problems you should typically begin at the bottom (Physical) layer of the seven-layer OSI model and work up to the Application layer.

- ❑ When troubleshooting a network problem, most always you'll start at the interface of origin.

- ❑ When viewing the event or statistical counters associated with an interface, execute the SHOW INTERFACE command several times to determine the rate at which counters are increasing.

- ❑ Since most routers have at least IP configured on them, a good starting point is to view all the interfaces and the IP protocols configured on each.

- ❑ The SHOW IP INTERFACE BRIEF snapshot shows all the interfaces, their IP addresses, and their operational status.

- ❑ In troubleshooting of IPX networks, it's important to get an overview of the interfaces enabled with IPX by using the SHOW IPX INTERFACE command.

- ❑ When troubleshooting ATM, Frame Relay, HDLC, and other protocol interfaces, use the SHOW commands to determine if errors, packet drops, or other problems are causing performance degradation.

- ❑ ATM input errors can occur due to AAL5 trailer CRC errors, via dropped cells in the ATM network. This problem is known as packet shredding.

- ❑ When troubleshooting a Frame Relay connection, start by looking at the interface itself with the SHOW INTERFACE command.

- ❑ If using Frame Relay subinterfaces, then split-horizon is on by default. On non-subinterfaces, it is disabled by default.

- ❑ A router allocates buffers in memory for holding a packet while waiting for the routing table lookup and other processing to finish.

❑ The default buffer sizes are as follows: Small (104-byte buffers), Middle (600-byte buffers), Big (1524-byte buffers), VeryBig (4520-byte buffers), Large (5024-byte buffers), and Huge (18,024-byte buffers).

❑ For troubleshooting end-to-end connectivity, some of the most common and most powerful tools are the ping, extended ping, and Traceroute commands.

❑ When two different paths exist between two particular subnets, this is known as asymmetrical routing.

SELF TEST

The following Self Test questions will help you measure your understanding of the material presented in this chapter. Read all the choices carefully, as there may be more than one correct answer. Choose all correct answers for each question.

1. All the following IP IOS interface switching modes are supported, except:

   A. Flow

   B. Optimum

   C. Virtual

   D. Fast

2. A 10 Mbps Ethernet usually saturates at about:

   A. 1 Mbps

   B. 3 Mbps

   C. 6 Mbps

   D. 10 Mbps

3. When using subinterfaces, split-horizon is disabled by default.

   A. True

   B. False

4. Cisco IOS supports all the following Novell IPX encapsulation methods except:

   A. MAC

   B. ARPA

   C. Novell-Ether

   D. SNAP

5. The following indicators may represent interface or network problems, except:

   A. CRC

   B. Drops

   C. Load

   D. Aborts

6. Which of the following signaling states should *not* be up on an active circuit?

   A. CTS

   B. DCR

   C. DCD

   D. DTR

7. Which of the following Frame Relay LMI types is *not* supported?

   A. IETF

   B. ANSI

   C. Q933a

   D. Cisco

8. ATM AAL5 "packet shredding" is indicated by:

   A. Packet drops

   B. Ignores

   C. CRC errors

   D. Overruns

9. Cisco ATM supports all the following AAL5 adaptations except:

   A. AAL5mux

   B. AAL5snap

    C. AAL5nlpid

    D. AAL5head

10. Packet loss is usually attributed to an oversubscribed connection.

    A. True

    B. False

11. Which of the following is *not* a buffer size attributed to various packet sizes?

    A. Little

    B. Medium

    C. VeryBig

    D. Huge

12. The default buffer size for Big is 1518 bytes.

    A. True

    B. False

13. All of the following types of memory are within Cisco hardware, except:

    A. NVRAM

    B. Flash

    C. Swap

    D. ROM

14. All routing tables are stored in:

    A. Flash

    B. NVRAM

    C. VRAM

    D. ROM

15. The startup configuration for booting the router is stored in the boot ROM.

    A. True

    B. False

16. Most newer releases of IOS make better use of memory.

    A. True

    B. False

17. Cisco logging supports all the following except:

    A. Console

    B. Print spooler

    C. Syslog daemon

    D. Local log

18. Ping is really an ICMP redirect.

    A. True

    B. False

19. Traceroute sends pings to each hop.

    A. True

    B. False

20. Extended pings allow for all the following features except:

    A. Modifying packet size

    B. Specifying the route

    C. Replacing the source IP address with that of another router

    D. Modifying the payload content

10

Advanced Diagnostic Tools

CERTIFICATION OBJECTIVES

D oing advanced diagnostics on Cisco hardware and IOS requires an intimate knowledge of each individual platform, whether it be a Cisco 766, 2600, 4700, 5300, CAT5500, Lightstream, 7513, or 12008. Each networking platform has its own hardware architecture and diagnostic methods. In order to identify and resolve the most complex problems, Cisco provides a variety of commands for viewing hardware, network, and protocol events at the lowest level.

Often, the advanced diagnostics are used to gather valuable information when working with Cisco TAC or advanced-support mailing lists. These tools are also used to do the important regular monitoring of the network and hardware, to ensure proper operation. When viewing debug, core dump, or hardware-level information, you can gain considerable insight into the fundamental operations of network protocol or hardware functionality.

CERTIFICATION OBJECTIVE 10.01

Debug Mode

One of the more powerful tools in Cisco's command set is the DEBUG command for viewing ongoing protocol processes and state information. Debug is typically used to gather live protocol information, or for deep investigation of certain anomalies. Cisco allows for debugging most of the networking features. The following DEBUG ? command shows all the services in which debug can be used:

```
RouterA#debug ?
  aaa                 AAA Authentication, Authorization and Accounting
  access-expression   Boolean access expression
  adjacency           adjacency
  all                 Enable all debugging
  apollo              Apollo information
  apple               Appletalk information
  aps                 Automatic Protection Switching
  arp                 IP ARP and HP Probe transactions
  async               Async interface information
  atm                 ATM Signalling
```

```
atm                    ATM interface information
broadcast              MAC broadcast packets
cBus                   ciscoBus events
callback               Callback activity
cdp                    CDP information
channel                Channel interface information
chat                   Chat scripts activity
clns                   CLNS information
cls                    CLS Information
compress               COMPRESS traffic
confmodem              Modem configuration database
custom-queue           Custom output queueing
decnet                 DECnet information
dhcp                   DHCP client activity
dialer                 Dial on Demand
dlsw                   Data Link Switching (DLSw) events
dnsix                  Dnsix information
domain                 Domain Name System
dspu                   DSPU Information
dxi                    atm-dxi information
eigrp                  EIGRP Protocol information
entry                  Incoming queue entries
ethernet-interface     Ethernet network interface events
fastethernet           Fast Ethernet interface information
filesys                File system information
frame-relay            Frame Relay
fras                   FRAS Debug
ip                     IP information
ipc                    Interprocess communications debugging
ipx                    Novell/IPX information
isis                   IS-IS Information
kerberos               KERBEROS authentication and authorization
lane                   LAN Emulation
lapb                   LAPB protocol transactions
lat                    LAT Information
lex                    LAN Extender protocol
list                   Set interface or/and access list for the next debug command
llc2                   LLC2 type II Information
lnm                    Lan Network Manager information
lnx                    generic qllc/llc2 conversion activity
local-ack              Local ACKnowledgement information
modem                  Modem control/process activation
mop                    DECnet MOP server events
nbf                    NetBIOS information
netbios-name-cache     NetBIOS name cache tracing
nhrp                   NHRP protocol
ntp                    NTP information
packet                 Log unknown packets
pad                    X25 PAD protocol
```

```
ppp             PPP (Point to Point Protocol) information
priority        Priority output queueing
probe           HP Probe Proxy Requests
qllc            qllc debug information
radius          RADIUS protocol
rif             RIF cache transactions
sdlc            SDLC information
sdllc           SDLLC media translation
serial          Serial interface information
smf             Software MAC filter
smrp            SMRP information
sna             SNA Information
snapshot        Snapshot activity
snmp            SNMP information
source          Source bridging information
spanning        Spanning-tree information
sscop           SSCOP
standby         Hot standby protocol
stun            STUN information
tacacs          TACACS authentication and authorization
tarp            TARP information
tbridge         Transparent Bridging
telnet          Incoming telnet connections
tftp            TFTP packets
token           Token Ring information
translate       Protocol translation events
tunnel          Generic Tunnel Interface
v120            V120 information
vg-anylan       VG-AnyLAN interface information
vines           VINES information
vlan            vLAN information
x25             X.25 information
xns             XNS information
xremote         XREMOTE
```

As you can see, the debug facility provides options to troubleshoot every service your router provides. Whether you're trying to debug AAA authentication on a dial platform or verifying correct X.25 mappings, debug is a common tool used to verify network operations. For instance, debug is commonly used in troubleshooting routing protocols, to verify correct routing updates and established neighbors. Depending upon the complexity of your networking environment, you will probably use debug commands sparingly.

Debug Mode Cautions

When using the debug command, be aware of the extra CPU and network overhead it imposes on the router and bandwidth. In an active network, for instance, it is generally a good idea to avoid using DEBUG ALL. In fact, Cisco IOS displays a stern warning before enabling DEBUG ALL.

```
RouterA#debug all
This may severely impact network performance. Continue? [confirm]n
```

Unless you're physically sitting next to the router, so that you have the opportunity to power-cycle the router as well as have a terminal plugged directly into the console port, do not use DEBUG ALL. If you are running high-speed links or multiple protocols, you can expect that a DEBUG ALL will lock up your router.

If you're remotely Telnetting to the router via a VTY interface and you want the debug information to stream to your Telnet session, be sure to enable terminal monitor:

```
RouterA#terminal monitor
```

You should also be aware of the effects of enabling debugging for other information-intensive features, such as DEBUG PACKET, DEBUG ETHERNET-INTERFACE, DEBUG FASTETHERNET, DEBUG SERIAL, and DEBUG IP PACKET. When enabling debugging on interfaces, be sure to view the load on the interface, especially when debugging at the packet level. An interface under heavy utilization with debug enabled may lock up the router.

In the event that the screen starts to overflow with information, issue the command NO DEBUG ALL to disable the displaying of all debugging information:

```
RouterA#no debug all
All possible debugging has been turned off
```

Although it may take a while for the remote session to completely clear its buffer of all information, be patient and eventually the display of debug information will stop. It may be helpful to issue the NO DEBUG ALL command again in case it was mistyped.

Enable debugging on the most specific areas of interests and then view how much debug information is being generated. As long as the level of information is not overwhelming, then you can start enabling more general levels of debugging. Don't start with a general debug command like DEBUG PACKET.

Debugging at the Protocol Level

Cisco provides for an extensive number of feature options for debugging IP protocols. You can debug IP routing protocols such as EIGRP, RIP, BGP, or perform basic IP-application debugging, obtaining ICMP, IP, TCP, or UDP protocol information. Most often debugging is used for examining routing protocols and the state information exchanged between routers.

For information about debugging of specific routing protocols, see Chapter 7.

The following IP services can be debugged with the DEBUG IP command:

```
RouterA#debug ip ?
  bgp        BGP information
  cache      IP cache operations
  cef        IP CEF operations
  cgmp       CGMP protocol activity
  drp        Director response protocol
  dvmrp      DVMRP protocol activity
  egp        EGP information
  eigrp      IP-EIGRP information
  error      IP error debugging
  ftp        FTP dialogue
  http       HTTP connections
  icmp       ICMP transactions
  igmp       IGMP protocol activity
  igrp       IGRP information
  mbgp       MBGP information
  mcache     IP multicast cache operations
  mds        IP Distributed Multicast information
  mobile     Mobility protocols
  mpacket    IP multicast packet debugging
  mrouting   IP multicast routing table activity
  ospf       OSPF information
  packet     General IP debugging and IPSO security transactions
  peer       IP peer address activity
  pim        PIM protocol activity
  policy     Policy routing
  rip        RIP protocol transactions
  routing    Routing table events
  sd         Session Directory (SD)
  security   IP security options
  tcp        TCP information
  udp        UDP based transactions
  wccp       WCCP information
```

IP debugging can be used on an IP-application basis. For instance, you can monitor all ICMP packets being processed by the router with the DEBUG IP ICMP command:

```
RouterA#debug ip icmp
ICMP packet debugging is on
RouterA#ping 10.4.1.5

Type escape sequence to abort.
Sending 5, 100-byte ICMP Echoes to 10.4.1.5, timeout is 2 seconds:
!!!!!
Success rate is 100 percent (5/5), round-trip min/avg/max = 1/2/4 ms
RouterA#
ICMP: echo reply rcvd, src 10.4.1.5, dst 10.4.1.2
ICMP: echo reply rcvd, src 10.4.1.5, dst 10.4.1.2
ICMP: echo reply rcvd, src 10.4.1.5, dst 10.4.1.2
ICMP: echo reply rcvd, src 10.4.1.5, dst 10.4.1.2
ICMP: echo reply rcvd, src 10.4.1.5, dst 10.4.1.2
```

An extremely powerful feature of debugging is being able to use the router like a sniffer—you can debug certain packet-based information in a focused mode. Again, it is important to emphasize that you should not debug too much information and overwhelm the router. For this reason, you should restrict the IP information flow via an access list.

The following example shows how to monitor all Web traffic passing through a router:

```
RouterA(config)#access-list 180 permit tcp any any eq www
RouterA #term mon

RouterA#sh access-list 180
Extended IP access list 180
    permit tcp any any eq www (3 matches)

RouterA #debug ip packet ?
  <1-199>  Access list
  detail   Print more debugging detail
  <cr>

RouterA #debug ip packet 180 detail
IP packet debugging is on (detailed) for access list 180
RouterA #
IP: s=192.168.1.1 (Serial1/1/3), d=165.83.213.4 (ATM4/0.36), g=10.1.1.1, len 64, forward
    TCP src=4147, dst=80, seq=2813805505, ack=0, win=8192 SYN
IP: s=192.168.2.3 (Serial1/1/0), d=206.253.217.16 (ATM4/0.36), g=10.1.1.1, len 52, forward
    TCP src=1078, dst=80, seq=1964586, ack=0, win=8192 SYN
IP: s=192.168.1.4 (Serial1/1/3), d=207.46.148.254 (ATM4/0.36), g=10.1.1.1, len 44, forward
    TCP src=4313, dst=80, seq=1078366422, ack=1114922769, win=8576 ACK FIN
```

In order to verify the level of debugging currently enabled on the Cisco router, use the SHOW DEBUG command:

```
RouterA# show debug
Generic IP:
  ICMP packet debugging is on
  IP packet debugging is on (detailed) for access list 180
```

IPX debugging is equally as powerful for monitoring Novell traffic and routing protocol updates. The output of the following DEBUG IPX ? command's categories is self-explanatory.

```
RouterA#debug ipx ?
  compression     IPX compression
  eigrp           IPX EIGRP packets
  ipxwan          Novell IPXWAN events
  nasi            NASI server functionality
  nlsp            IPX NLSP activity
  packet          IPX activity
  redistribution  IPX route redistribution
  routing         IPX RIP routing information
  sap             IPX Service Advertisement information
  spoof           IPX and SPX Spoofing activity
  spx             Sequenced Packet Exchange Protocol
```

When requiring in-depth analysis of an IPX network, this debug information is very powerful. Further analysis would probably require an intelligent sniffer capable of providing detailed analysis of the IPX network.

AppleTalk debugging can be used for determining AppleTalk anomalies, as well. The AppleTalk debugging categories are also somewhat self-explanatory, and you can determine for yourself the best ways of setting up and reviewing the resulting output. Following is output from the DEBUG APPLE ? command:

```
RouterA#debug apple ?
  arp                  Appletalk address resolution protocol
  aurp-connection      AURP connection
  aurp-packet          AURP packets
  aurp-update          AURP routing updates
  domain               AppleTalk Domain function
  eigrp-all            All AT/EIGRP functions
  eigrp-external       AT/EIGRP external functions
  eigrp-hello          AT/EIGRP hello functions
  eigrp-packet         AT/EIGRP packet debugging
  eigrp-query          AT/EIGRP query functions
  eigrp-redistribution AT/EIGRP route redistribution
  eigrp-request        AT/EIGRP external functions
  eigrp-target         Appletalk/EIGRP for targeting address
  eigrp-update         AT/EIGRP update functions
  errors               Information about errors
```

```
events            Appletalk special events
fs                Appletalk fast-switching
iptalk            IPTalk encapsulation and functionality
macip             MacIP functions
nbp               Name Binding Protocol (NBP) functions
packet            Per-packet debugging
redistribution    Route Redistribution
remap             AppleTalk Remap function
responder         AppleTalk responder debugging
routing           (RTMP&EIGRP) functions
rtmp              (RTMP) functions
zip               Zone Information Protocol functions
```

Interface Debugging

When you have to resolve WAN problems, Cisco provides a number of options designed for low-level debugging of Frame Relay, ATM, ISDN, and other WAN technologies. When building a VPN via a data service provider, it is important to view WAN interconnectivity at the Physical and Framing layers. Interface-specific commands for WANs and LANs are discussed in Chapter 9 and will be helpful when you're doing interface debugging.

Frame Relay Debugging

With the DEBUG FRAME-RELAY command, Cisco provides for extensive monitoring of Frame Relay connections within multiprotocol environments.

```
RouterA#debug frame-relay ?
  dlsw      Frame Relay dlsw
  events    Important Frame Relay packet events
  ip        Frame Relay Internet Protocol
  llc2      Frame Relay llc2
  lmi       LMI packet exchanges with service provider
  packet    Frame Relay packets
  rsrb      Frame Relay rsrb
  verbose   Frame Relay
```

It is often important to look at the LMI (Local Management Interface) debug information in the event of a Frame Relay PVC failure. The following DEBUG output example shows an LMI-type misconfiguration and correction. For this example, the correct configuration is with ANSI LMI-type.

```
RouterA(config)#interface Serial4/0:0
 RouterA(config)#encapsulation frame-relay
 RouterA(config)#bandwidth 64000
 RouterA(config)#frame-relay lmi-type ansi
```

Start by turning on Frame Relay LMI debugging:

```
RouterA#debug frame-relay lmi
Frame Relay LMI debugging is on
Displaying all Frame Relay LMI data
```

When the Frame Relay interface is configured properly, the LMI information should show DTE as up on messages being sent out, as shown here:

```
Serial4/0:0(out): StEnq, myseq 65, yourseen 64, DTE up
datagramstart = 0xA6D6BC, datagramsize = 14
FR encap = 0x00010308
00 75 95 01 01 01 03 02 41 40
```

Messages coming in should also be identifiable:

```
Serial4/0:0(in): Status, myseq 2
RT IE 1, length 1, type 1
KA IE 3, length 2, yourseq 2 , myseq 2
```

The interface also shows all signaling as up/up, as shown next. Make sure that the LMI messages are being sent and received.

```
Serial4/0:0 is up, line protocol is up
  Hardware is cxBus E1
  MTU 1500 bytes, BW 64000 Kbit, DLY 20000 usec, rely 255/255, load 1/255
  Encapsulation FRAME-RELAY, loopback not set, keepalive set (10 sec)
  LMI enq sent  13, LMI stat recvd 8, LMI upd recvd 0, DTE LMI up
  LMI enq recvd 0, LMI stat sent  0, LMI upd sent  0
  LMI DLCI 0  LMI type is ANSI Annex D  frame relay DTE
```

When we misconfigure the interface by enabling Cisco LMI-type, the router is no longer able to communicate with the switch and takes the subinterface down:

```
RouterA(config)#int s4/0:0
RouterA(config-if)#frame-relay lmi-type cisco
RouterA#show interface serial4/0:0
Serial4/0:0 is up, line protocol is down
  Hardware is cxBus E1
  MTU 1500 bytes, BW 64000 Kbit, DLY 20000 usec, rely 255/255, load 1/255
  Encapsulation FRAME-RELAY, loopback not set, keepalive set (10 sec)
  LMI enq sent  3, LMI stat recvd 0, LMI upd recvd 0, DTE LMI down
  LMI enq recvd 0, LMI stat sent  0, LMI upd sent  0
  LMI DLCI 1023  LMI type is CISCO  frame relay DTE
```

The debug information reflects that LMI cannot be established between the router and the frame relay switch. LMI messages are still sent out to the switch, and LMI messages are received by the router, but in the wrong protocol format—and thus the two can no longer communicate. Incoming messages, labeled "(in)," are being received in the wrong format for the particular interface or subinterface. The interface will inactivate and then delete PVCs whose LMI is no longer functioning.

```
Jan  2 19:56:42 UTC: %FR-5-DLCICHANGE: Interface Serial4/0:0 - DLCI 30 state changed to
INACTIVE
Jan  2 19:56:42 UTC: %LINEPROTO-5-UPDOWN: Line protocol on Interface Serial4/0:0.1, changed
state to down
Jan  2 19:56:42 UTC: %FR-5-DLCICHANGE: Interface Serial4/0:0 - DLCI 31 state changed to
INACTIVE
Jan  2 19:56:42 UTC: %FR-5-DLCICHANGE: Interface Serial4/0:0 - DLCI 51 state changed to
INACTIVE
Jan  2 19:56:42 UTC: %FR-5-DLCICHANGE: Interface Serial4/0:0 - DLCI 30 state changed to
DELETED
Jan  2 19:56:42 UTC: %LINEPROTO-5-UPDOWN: Line protocol on Interface Serial4/0:0, changed
state to down
```

Finally, after the correct LMI-type is restored to the configuration, the incoming messages are understood and the interface becomes active again:

```
Serial4/0:0(in): Status, myseq 4
RT IE 1, length 1, type 0
KA IE 3, length 2, yourseq 4 , myseq 4
PVC IE 0x7 , length 0x3 , dlci 30, status 0x2
PVC IE 0x7 , length 0x3 , dlci 31, status 0x2
Jan  2 19:57:46 UTC: %FR-5-DLCICHANGE: Interface Serial4/0:0 - DLCI 31 state changed to ACTIVE
PVC IE 0x7 , length 0x3 , dlci 50, status 0x0.
```

ATM Debugging

ATM can be a complicated transmission service, especially when supporting data, voice, and video applications are all on the same service. Often you will require an in-depth look at the ATM operations at its lowest levels. The DEBUG ATM command provides robust ATM debugging information.

```
RouterA#debug atm ?
  arp        Show ATM ARP events
  errors     ATM errors
  events     ATM Events
  ilmi       Show ILMI events
```

```
oam            Dump OAM Cells
packet         ATM packets
sig-all        ATM Signalling all
sig-error      ATM Signalling errors
sig-events     ATM Signalling events
sig-ie         ATM Signalling information elements
sig-packets    ATM Signalling packets
smap-all       ATM Signalling Static Map all
smap-error     ATM Signalling Static Map errors
smap-events    ATM Signalling Static Map events
```

If you have set up ATM service from an ATM Service Provider and are using OAM cells to manage the VC status, you can use the DEBUG ATM OAM command to verify if the OAM cells are being delivered end-to-end. Check to see that the CTags are hexadecimally incrementing. If you are not receiving ATM OAM cells, then the PVC may be down and you should contact your Service Provider.

```
RouterA#
9w4d: ATM OAM LOOP(ATM6/0/0)  I: VCD#637 LoopInd:1 CTag:521A
9w4d: ATM OAM LOOP(ATM6/0/0.637) O: VCD#637 CTag:0
9w4d: ATM OAM LOOP(ATM6/0/0)  I: VCD#637 LoopInd:1 CTag:521B
9w4d: ATM OAM LOOP(ATM6/0/0.637) O: VCD#637 CTag:0
9w4d: ATM OAM LOOP(ATM6/0/0)  I: VCD#637 LoopInd:1 CTag:521C
9w4d: ATM OAM LOOP(ATM6/0/0.637) O: VCD#637 CTag:0
```

ISDN Debugging

If using a dial-up server or dial-on-demand routing (DDR), you will more than likely one day require the help of the DEBUG ISDN command for troubleshooting your ISDN connection.

```
as5300#debug isdn ?
  events   ISDN events
  q921     ISDN Q921 packets
  q931     ISDN Q931 packets\
```

Be sure to understand ISDN DDR in terms of both configuration and troubleshooting.

The following output shows a typical DEBUG ISDN EVENTS session on a Cisco 5300 dial platform:

```
as5300#debug isdn events
ISDN events debugging is on
```

This is a debug output example of an ISDN call setup:

```
as5300#
..Jan  2 17:22:44 EST: ISDN Se0:23: Incoming call id = 0xD4
.Jan  2 17:22:44 EST: ISDN Se0:23: received CALL_INCOMING
.Jan  2 17:22:44 EST: ISDN Se0:23: Event:  Received a Sync call from <unknown> on B9 at 64
Kb/s
.Jan  2 17:22:44 EST: %LINK-3-UPDOWN: Interface Serial0:8, changed state to up
.Jan  2 17:22:44 EST: ISDN Se0:23: received CALL_PROGRESSing
.Jan  2 17:22:44 EST: %LINK-3-UPDOWN: Interface Virtual-Access1, changed state to up
.Jan  2 17:22:45 EST: %LINEPROTO-5-UPDOWN: Line protocol on Interface Serial0:8, changed state
to up
.Jan  2 17:22:45 EST: %LINEPROTO-5-UPDOWN: Line protocol on Interface Virtual-Access1, changed
state to up
.Jan  2 17:22:50 EST: %ISDN-6-CONNECT: Interface Serial0:8 is now connected to  edean
```

In the preceding example, notice the following order:

- The ISDN call is first recognized

- The interface comes up

- The virtual template establishes a PPP session

- The login is verified

- The connection is established

An ISDN call teardown would look like this:

```
Jan  2 17:23:53 EST: %LINK-3-UPDOWN: Interface Virtual-Access1, changed state to down
.Jan  2 17:23:53 EST: %LINEPROTO-5-UPDOWN: Line protocol on Interface Serial0:8, changed
state to down
.Jan  2 17:23:53 EST: %LINEPROTO-5-UPDOWN: Line protocol on Interface Virtual-Access1,
changed state to down
.Jan  2 17:23:53 EST: ISDN Se0:23: entering process_rxstate, CALL_DISC
.Jan  2 17:23:53 EST: %ISDN-6-DISCONNECT: Interface Serial0:8  disconnected from  edean,
call lasted 69 econds
.Jan  2 17:23:53 EST: %LINK-3-UPDOWN: Interface Serial0:8, changed state to down
.Jan  2 17:23:53 EST: leaving CCPRI_ReleaseCall, Allocated CCBs = 1
.Jan  2 17:23:53 EST: ISDN Se0:23: entering process_rxstate, CALL_CLEARED
```

Notice the following order of events:

- The virtual interface link actually times out

- The PPP/LCP line protocol goes down

- The call is disconnected

- The interface is downed

- The call is cleared and available for the next session

Typical misconfigurations of ISDN include errors in switch type and SPIDs. For instance, a mismatch of the ISDN switch type can be detected on an AS5300 when incoming calls keep failing and releasing. The ISDN switch may try to terminate the call on the next channel/port, over and over again, as shown in the following output:

```
as5300#
Jan  2 17:31:46 EST: ISDN Se0:23: Incoming call id = 0x7
Jan  2 17:31:46 EST: ISDN Se0:23: received CALL_INCOMING
Jan  2 17:31:46 EST: ISDN Se0:23: Event:  Received a Voice call from <unknown> on B1 at 64
Kb/s
Jan  2 17:31:46 EST: leaving CCPRI_ReleaseCall, Allocated CCBs = 0
Jan  2 17:31:46 EST: ISDN Se0:23: entering process_rxstate, CALL_DISC
Jan  2 17:31:46 EST: ISDN Se0:23: entering process_rxstate, CALL_CLEARED
Jan  2 17:31:53 EST: ISDN Se0:23: Incoming call id = 0x8
Jan  2 17:31:53 EST: ISDN Se0:23: received CALL_INCOMING
Jan  2 17:31:53 EST: ISDN Se0:23: Event:  Received a Sync call from <unknown> on B2 at 64
Kb/s
Jan  2 17:31:53 EST: %LINK-3-UPDOWN: Interface Serial0:1, changed state to up
Jan  2 17:31:53 EST: leaving CCPRI_ReleaseCall, Allocated CCBs = 0
Jan  2 17:31:53 EST: ISDN Se0:23: entering process_rxstate, CALL_DISC
Jan  2 17:31:53 EST: %LINK-3-UPDOWN: Interface Serial0:1, changed state to down
Jan  2 17:31:53 EST: ISDN Se0:23: entering process_rxstate, CALL_CLEARED
Jan  2 17:31:54 EST: ISDN Se0:23: Incoming call id = 0x9
Jan  2 17:31:54 EST: ISDN Se0:23: received CALL_INCOMING
Jan  2 17:31:54 EST: ISDN Se0:23: Event:  Received a Sync call from <unknown> on B3 at 56
Kb/s
Jan  2 17:31:54 EST: %LINK-3-UPDOWN: Interface Serial0:2, changed state to up
Jan  2 17:31:55 EST: leaving CCPRI_ReleaseCall, Allocated CCBs = 0
Jan  2 17:31:55 EST: ISDN Se0:23: entering process_rxstate, CALL_DISC
Jan  2 17:31:55 EST: %LINK-3-UPDOWN: Interface Serial0:2, changed state to down
Jan  2 17:31:55 EST: ISDN Se0:23: entering process_rxstate, CALL_CLEARED
as5300#
```

When trying to detect ISDN errors, you should look at the Q.921 Layer 2 LAPD protocol initialization, and verify the operations. The following output of DEBUG ISDN Q921 shows a correct incoming call and establishment operation:

```
as5300#debug isdn q921
ISDN Q921 packets debugging is on
as5300#
Jan  2 17:37:39 EST: ISDN Se0:23: RX <-  INFOc sapi = 0  tei = 0  ns = 23  nr =23  i =
0x08020170050402889018103A983867008C136383934343935
Jan  2 17:37:39 EST: ISDN Se0:23: TX -> RRr sapi = 0  tei = 0  nr = 24
Jan  2 17:37:39 EST: %LINK-3-UPDOWN: Interface Serial0:5, changed state to up
Jan  2 17:37:39 EST: ISDN Se0:23: TX -> INFOc sapi = 0  tei = 0  ns = 23  nr = 24  i =
0x08028170021803A98386
```

```
Jan  2 17:37:39 EST: ISDN Se0:23: RX <-  RRr sapi = 0  tei = 0  nr = 24
Jan  2 17:37:39 EST: ISDN Se0:23: TX ->  INFOc sapi = 0  tei = 0  ns = 24  nr = 24  i =
0x08028170071803A98386
Jan  2 17:37:39 EST: ISDN Se0:23: RX <-  RRr sapi = 0  tei = 0  nr = 25
Jan  2 17:37:39 EST: ISDN Se0:23: RX <-  INFOc sapi = 0  tei = 0  ns = 24  nr = 25  i =
0x080201700F
Jan  2 17:37:39 EST: ISDN Se0:23: TX ->  RRr sapi = 0  tei = 0  nr = 25
Jan  2 17:37:39 EST: %LINK-3-UPDOWN: Interface Virtual-Access1, changed state to up
Jan  2 17:37:40 EST: %LINEPROTO-5-UPDOWN: Line protocol on Interface Serial0:5,changed
state to up
Jan  2 17:37:40 EST: %LINEPROTO-5-UPDOWN: Line protocol on Interface Virtual-Access1,
changed state to up
Jan  2 17:37:45 EST: %ISDN-6-CONNECT: Interface Serial0:5 is now connected to  edean
```

If you want to study the details of each of the ISDN fields, visit

http://www.cisco.com/univercd/cc/td/doc/product/software/ios112/
dbook/dipx.htm#xtocid68738

Leaving the DEBUG ISDN Q921 running should produce ongoing messages like the following:

```
Jan  2 17:53:16 EST: ISDN Se0:23: TX ->  RRp sapi = 0  tei = 0 nr = 27
Jan  2 17:53:16 EST: ISDN Se0:23: RX <-  RRf sapi = 0  tei = 0  nr = 26
Jan  2 17:53:46 EST: ISDN Se0:23: TX ->  RRp sapi = 0  tei = 0 nr = 27
Jan  2 17:53:46 EST: ISDN Se0:23: RX <-  RRf sapi = 0  tei = 0  nr = 26
Jan  2 17:54:16 EST: ISDN Se0:23: TX ->  RRp sapi = 0  tei = 0 nr = 27
Jan  2 17:54:16 EST: ISDN Se0:23: RX <-  RRf sapi = 0  tei = 0  nr = 26
```

These messages are just ongoing polling and response messages that are sent back and forth between the ISDN switch and router. They are somewhat like keepalives.

In the event that a misconfiguration exists on the router, involving selection of the wrong ISDN switch type, Q921 LAPD protocol will not establish itself between the router and the switch. Following is an example of an ongoing TEI negotiation failure due to a misconfigured switch type. In this example, each interface is failing during the TEI negotiation, and the ISDN switch is continually attempting to failover onto the next available ISDN channel. Failover occurs when an allocation request on a port fails and then attempts to allocate the next available port.

```
as5300#
Jan  2 17:33:45 EST: ISDN Se0:23: TX ->  RRp sapi = 0  tei = 0 nr = 41
Jan  2 17:33:45 EST: ISDN Se0:23: RX <-  RRf sapi = 0  tei = 0  nr = 41
Jan  2 17:33:55 EST: ISDN Se0:23: RX <-  INFOc sapi = 0  tei = 0  ns = 41  nr = 41  i =
```

```
0x0802016E05040288901803A983847008C136383934343935
Jan  2 17:33:55 EST: ISDN Se0:23: TX -> RRr sapi = 0  tei = 0  nr = 42
Jan  2 17:33:55 EST: %LINK-3-UPDOWN: Interface Serial0:3, changed state to up
Jan  2 17:33:55 EST: ISDN Se0:23: TX -> INFOc sapi = 0  tei = 0  ns = 41  nr = 42  i =
0x0802816E021803A98304
Jan  2 17:33:55 EST: ISDN Se0:23: TX -> INFOc sapi = 0  tei = 0  ns = 42  nr = 42  i =
0x0802816E071803A98304
Jan  2 17:33:55 EST: ISDN Se0:23: RX <- RRr sapi = 0  tei = 0  nr = 42
Jan  2 17:33:55 EST: ISDN Se0:23: RX <- RRr sapi = 0  tei = 0  nr = 43
Jan  2 17:33:55 EST: ISDN Se0:23: RX <- INFOc sapi = 0  tei = 0  ns = 42  nr = 43  i =
0x0802016E5A080282E4
Jan  2 17:33:55 EST: ISDN Se0:23: TX -> RRr sapi = 0  tei = 0  nr = 43
Jan  2 17:33:55 EST: %LINK-3-UPDOWN: Interface Serial0:3, changed state to down
Jan  2 17:33:56 EST: ISDN Se0:23: RX <- INFOc sapi = 0  tei = 0  ns = 43  nr = 43  i =
0x0802016F0504048890218F1803A983857008C136383934343935
Jan  2 17:33:56 EST: ISDN Se0:23: TX -> RRr sapi = 0  tei = 0  nr = 44
Jan  2 17:33:56 EST: %LINK-3-UPDOWN: Interface Serial0:4, changed state to up
Jan  2 17:33:56 EST: ISDN Se0:23: TX -> INFOc sapi = 0  tei = 0  ns = 43  nr = 44  i =
0x0802816F021803A98305
Jan  2 17:33:56 EST: ISDN Se0:23: TX -> INFOc sapi = 0  tei = 0  ns = 44  nr = 44  i =
0x0802816F071803A98305
Jan  2 17:33:56 EST: ISDN Se0:23: RX <- RRr sapi = 0  tei = 0  nr = 44
Jan  2 17:33:56 EST: ISDN Se0:23: RX <- RRr sapi = 0  tei = 0  nr = 45
Jan  2 17:33:56 EST: ISDN Se0:23: RX <- INFOc sapi = 0  tei = 0  ns = 44  nr = 45  i =
0x0802016F5A080282E4
Jan  2 17:33:56 EST: ISDN Se0:23: TX -> RRr sapi = 0  tei = 0  nr = 45
Jan  2 17:33:56 EST: %LINK-3-UPDOWN: Interface Serial0:4, changed state to down
```

CERTIFICATION OBJECTIVE 10.02

Fault-Tracking Commands

Often you will want to look at some historical information on the router, or to proactively send alarms and traps to a server. This usually requires a separate network management platform to allow for message logging, SNMP traps, SNMP polling, and NTP timing. Cisco provides a variety of network management tools to accomplish fault tracking and problem resolution.

Logging

You may want messages or events to be logged locally on the router as well as be archived on a central server. The LOGGING command enables the logging of messages to a variety of sources, as shown in the following output:

```
RouterA(config)#logging ?
  WORD              IP address of the logging host
  buffered          Copy logging messages to an internal buffer
  console           Set console logging level
  facility          Facility parameter for syslog messages
  monitor           Set terminal line (monitor) logging level
  on                Enable logging to all supported destinations
  source-interface  Specify interface for source address in logging transactions
  trap              Set syslog server logging level
```

The LOGGING BUFFERED command helps you maintain local logging on the router for events and messages:

```
RouterA(config)#logging buffered
```

You can then use the SHOW LOGGING command to view the contents of the router's local logging buffer:

```
RouterA#show logging
Syslog logging: enabled (0 messages dropped, 21 flushes, 0 overruns)
    Console logging: level warnings, 8641 messages logged
    Monitor logging: level informational, 19 messages logged
    Trap logging: level informational, 9667 message lines logged
        Logging to 204.59.144.222, 9667 message lines logged
        Logging to 204.59.153.66, 9667 message lines logged
        Logging to 204.59.153.194, 9667 message lines logged
    Buffer logging: level debugging, 92022 messages logged

Log Buffer (4096 bytes):
/0/0): received report type 2
2w3d: atmdx_process_love_letter(ATM5/0/0): 6 VCs core statistics
2w3d: ATM OAM(ATM5/0/0.234): Timer: VCD#234 Status:1 CTag:504306 Tries:365050
2w3d: ATM(ATM5/0/0.234): VCD#234 failed to echo OAM. 365051 tries
2w3d: ATM OAM LOOP(ATM5/0/0.234) O: VCD#234 CTag:7B1F3
2w3d: ATM OAM(ATM5/0/0.234): Timer: VCD#234 Status:1 CTag:504307 Tries:365051
2w3d: ATM(ATM5/0/0.234): VCD#234 failed to echo OAM. 365052 tries
2w3d: ATM OAM LOOP(ATM5/0/0.234) O: VCD#234 CTag:7B1F4
```

When you're setting up a central syslog server to maintain all logging messages, Cisco lets you customize the facility type-logging method with the LOGGING FACILTY command:

```
RouterA(config)#logging facility ?
  auth    Authorization system
  cron    Cron/at facility
  daemon  System daemons
  kern    Kernel
  local0  Local use
  local1  Local use
  local2  Local use
  local3  Local use
  local4  Local use
  local5  Local use
  local6  Local use
  local7  Local use
  lpr     Line printer system
  mail    Mail system
  news    USENET news
  sys10   System use
  sys11   System use
  sys12   System use
  sys13   System use
  sys14   System use
  sys9    System use
  syslog  Syslog itself
  user    User process
  uucp    Unix-to-Unix copy system
```

Typically, you would send the logging information to a syslog server identified by the IP address following the command:

```
RouterA(config)#logging facility syslog
RouterA(config)#logging 10.1.1.222
RouterA(config)#logging 10.1.1.67
```

On the UNIX server identified by the IP address, you would configure the /etc/syslog.conf file so that incoming syslog messages are logged to a known file. Following is an example of a /etc/syslog.conf file:

```
Logger% more /etc/syslog.conf
#ident  "@(#)syslog.conf    1.3    93/12/09 SMI"  /* SunOS 5.0 */
#
# Copyright (c) 1991-1993, by Sun Microsystems, Inc.
#
# syslog configuration file.
#
# This file is processed by m4 so be careful to quote ('') names
# that match m4 reserved words.  Also, within ifdef's, arguments
```

```
# containing commas must be quoted.
#
# Note: Have to exclude user from most lines so that user.alert
#       and user.emerg are not included, because old sendmails
#       will generate them for debugging information.  If you
#       have no 4.2BSD based systems doing network logging, you
#       can remove all the special cases for "user" logging.
#
*.err;kern.notice;auth.notice;user.none              /dev/console
*.err;kern.debug;daemon.notice;auth.info;mail.crit;user.none;local7.info
/var/adm/messages <- Cisco logging
*.alert;kern.err;daemon.err;user.none                operator
*.alert;user.none                                    root
```

With the MORE command, you can view the log file identified in /etc/syslog.conf:

```
Logger% more /var/adm/messages
Jan  2 04:27:36 RouterA-serial8-2.lab.net 2552: Jan  2 09:27:34 UTC: %LINK-3-UPDOWN:
Interface Serial8/4, changed state to down
Jan  2 04:27:37 RouterB-hssi4-0.lab.net 8888: Jan  2 09:27:36 UTC: %CI-3-PSFAIL: Power
supply 2 failure
Jan  2 04:27:37 RouterB-hssi4-0.lab.net 8889: Jan  2 09:27:36 UTC: %CI-3-BLOWER: ps2 fan
failure
Jan  2 04:27:38 RouterA-serial8-2.lab.net 2553: Jan  2 09:27:37 UTC: %LINK-3-UPDOWN:
Interface Serial8/4, changed state to up.
```

Timestamps

If the router is configured with the SERVICE TIMESTAMP command, you will see each event message in the log timestamped. Use the SERVICE TIMESTAMP command to make sure that all logged or debugging information has the appropriate timestamp.

You can use the TIMESTAMP command independently for debug or logging messages:

```
RouterA(config)#service time ?
  debug  Timestamp debug messages
  log    Timestamp log messages
  <cr>
```

When the messages arrive, you can use either the time local to the router, or the up time of the router:

```
RouterA(config)#service time log ?
  datetime  Timestamp with date and time
  uptime    Timestamp with system uptime
  <cr>
```

You can also specify various formats for the timestamp:

```
RouterA(config)#service timestamps log date show-timezone?
  localtime       Use local time zone for timestamps
  msec            Include milliseconds in timestamp
  show-timezone   Add time zone information to timestamp
```

Network Time Protocol

Use of Network Time Protocol (NTP), RFC 1305, is suggested in order to keep the network timing synchronized. NTP will ensure that every device in the network has the same time, so that all timestamps and logging of information are synchronized. NTP is usually reliable within microseconds.

To enable NTP on a router, for synchronization with an NTP server, use the NTP SERVER command:

```
ntp clock-period 17180256
RouterA(config)#ntp server 10.1.1.222
```

Note: The "ntp clock-period" output displayed in the configuration should not be adjusted. The NTP clock-period is automatically stored in the NVRAM and is generated by the NTP process. NTP clock-period is a measure of the drift error in the clock, in units of ticks, and the router will adjust the clock by this amount. Remember—do not attempt to modify this value.

To verify correct NTP operational status, use the SHOW NTP STATUS command:

```
RouterA#show ntp status
Clock is synchronized, stratum 3, reference is 10.1.1.222
nominal freq is 250.0000 Hz, actual freq is 249.9943 Hz, precision is 2**24
reference time is BA394062.DF27DFC3 (01:03:30.871 UTC Sun Jan 3 1999)
clock offset is -1.08 msec, root delay is 114.79 msec
root dispersion is 21.70 msec, peer dispersion is 13.37 msec
```

Take note of the time and the frequency drift to verify correct operation. Descriptions of each NTP status field can be found at the following URL:

http://www.cisco.com/univercd/cc/td/doc/product/software/ios112/ 112cg_cr/1rbook/1rsysmgt.htm#xtocid1962130

In order to view the NTP devices and their reference clocks in the NTP network, use the SHOW NTP ASSOCIATIONS command:

```
RouterA#show ntp associations

      address         ref clock     st  when  poll reach  delay  offset   disp
+ 10.2.1.6          10.1.1.222      3   690  1024  376  153.6   -9.20   21.8
+~10.1.1.222        128.8.10.6      2    78  1024  377    5.2   -3.43   18.7
- 192.168.6.58      10.1.1.222      3   160  1024  376  194.3  -18.66   16.5
  192.168.6.122     10.1.1.222      3   957  1024  137  170.7  120.35  263.7
* 10.1.1.222        193.62.83.9     2   202  1024  377  101.9    1.26    5.5
 * master (synced), # master (unsynced), + selected, - candidate, ~ configured
```

In this output you'll need to view the various clock sources and amount of delay and offset applied to each. At the following URL you'll find a detailed reference of each field:

http://www.cisco.com/univercd/cc/td/doc/product/software/ios112/112cg_cr/1rbook/1rsysmgt.htm#13931

Also, refer to the RFC 1305 for details of NTP itself.

SNMP

Whole books have been written about SNMP (Simple Network Management Protocol). Our discussion here, however, focuses just on Cisco's provision of SNMPv1 and SNMPv2 access for reactively and proactively managing the network.

You'll use the SNMP-SERVER command to set all SNMP properties. An increasing number of SNMP attributes and permissions are configurable on a Cisco device, as shown here:

```
RouterA(config)#snmp-server ?
  access-policy      Define an SNMPv2 access policy (acl)
  chassis-id         String to uniquely identify this chassis
  community          Enable SNMP; set community string and access privs
  contact            Text for mib object sysContact
  context            Define an SNMPv2 context
  enable             Enable SNMP Traps or Informs
  host               Specify hosts to receive SNMP TRAPs
  location           Text for mib object sysLocation
  packetsize         Largest SNMP packet size
```

```
party               Define an SNMPv2 party
queue-length        Message queue length for each TRAP host
system-shutdown     Enable use of the SNMP reload command
tftp-server-list    Limit TFTP servers used via SNMP
trap-authentication Send TRAP messages on receipt of incorrect community string
trap-source         Assign an interface for the source address of all traps
trap-timeout        Set timeout for TRAP message retransmissions
view                Define an SNMPv2 MIB view
```

Of importance are the setting of the SNMP community string, along with read/write permissions and a suggested access list to restrict those who are allowed to poll your router. The following configuration example shows the snmp community option settings.

```
RouterA(config)#snmp-server community ?
  WORD   SNMP community string

RouterA(config)#snmp-server community test ?
  <1-99>  Std IP accesslist allowing access with this community string
  ro      Read-only access with this community string
  rw      Read-write access with this community string
  view    Restrict this community to a named MIB view
  <cr>
```

The following example shows the configuration of the SNMP community string with Read Only access by servers within the access list 2:

```
RouterA(config)#snmp-server community test RO 2
RouterA#show access-list 2
Standard IP access list 2
    permit 10.1.1.68
    permit 10.2.1.6.
```

You will also want to specify the server that is to receive the various traps, and possibly also specify the types of traps you wish to receive. The following configuration example shows the snmp trap server options.

```
RouterA(config)#snmp-server host 10.1.1.68 test ?
  bgp               Allow BGP state change traps
  channel-failures  Allow channel link failure event traps
  config            Allow SNMP config traps
  dspu              Allow dspu event traps
  envmon            Allow environmental monitor traps
  frame-relay       Allow SNMP frame-relay traps
  isdn              Allow SNMP ISDN traps
  llc2              Allow llc2 event traps (currently CIP CSNA only)
  rsrb              Allow rsrb event traps
```

```
sdlc           Allow sdlc event traps
sdllc          Allow sdllc event traps
snmp           Allow SNMP-type traps
stun           Allow stun event traps
tty            Allow TCP connection traps
x25            Allow x25 event traps
<cr>
```

The following configuration shows two different SNMP trap collectors, each with its community string, and one with a customized BGP SNMP trap collector:

```
RouterA(config)#snmp-server host 10.1.1.68 test snmp
RouterA(config)#snmp-server host 10.2.1.66 test snmp bgp
```

CERTIFICATION OBJECTIVE 10.03

Interconnectivity Commands

When you're troubleshooting extensive network problems, it's not unusual to have to traverse the network and access a number of routers in order to determine where a fault may exist. You will have to be comfortable bouncing from router to router—both in-band and out-of-band (that is, via modem or comm-server). When a router is not accessible directly through a remote session such as Telnet, it will be important to be able to access the router via other methods.

exam
ⓦatch

Become intimately familiar with using a Cisco 2511 or 2611 as a multiconsole access device, and with switching between multiple reverse-Telnet sessions.

Cisco supports regular Telnet between routers, provided a password has been defined on the VTY interfaces. You can define local VTY passwords, local username/password combinations, or use a distributed TACACS, TACACS+, or Radius server. These are all-powerful distributed platforms for centralizing Authentication, Authorization, and Accounting (although remote AAA is not included as a subject on the exam).

Be prepared to recover a lost password.

When navigating around a network, Telnet is commonly used to access routers. TELNET is the default command within Cisco IOS. This means you can merely type in the IP address or DNS name of a remote host and gain direct access via Telnet.

```
RouterA#10.1.1.1
```

A Cisco 2511/2611 is popularly used as a communications terminal server in order to gain remote-console access to multiple routers or other devices, as an out-of-band access method.

- When using the 2511, be sure that the line settings are correct on each of the async lines. Most console ports are set by default to 9600,8,N,1.

- When using a 2511 to access multiple routers, you will have to perform a *reverse Telnet* in order to gain access to the async lines. Reverse Telnet is nothing more than Telnetting to the 2511's own IP address, and then to the async line port.

The following listing shows a typical reverse Telnet session with a Cisco 2511:

```
Router-cs#10.1.1.40 2001

Trying 10.1.1.40, 2001 ... Open


User Access Verification

Username: test

Password: _

RouterB>
```

To disconnect from the current async session, press the following keys all at once: CTRL-SHIFT-6. This key sequence brings you back to the 2511 prompt:

```
Router-cs#
```

To return to the last reverse Telnet session, press ENTER. To view the current active sessions on the communication server, use the SHOW SESSION command:

```
Router-cs#show session

Conn Host              Address            Byte  Idle Conn Name

*  1 10.1.1.40         10.1.1.40          0     0 10.1.1.40



Router-cs#10.1.1.40 2003
Trying 10.1.1.40, 2003 ... Open


Router-cs#show session

Conn Host              Address            Byte  Idle Conn Name

   1 10.1.1.40         10.1.1.40          0     1 10.1.1.40

   2 10.1.1.40         10.1.1.40          0     0

*  3 10.1.1.40         10.1.1.40          0     0
```

Sometimes, a console port may be hung or inaccessible. In the event that you cannot access a console port, you may have to clear the line interface several times with the CLEAR LINE command:

```
Router-cs# 10.1.1.40 2004

Trying 10.1.1.40, 2004 ... Open


Router-cs#clear line 4

[confirm]y [OK]

Router-cs#clear line 4

[confirm]
```

```
[OK]

Router-cs#10.1.1.40 2004

Trying 10.1.1.40, 2004 ... Open


User Access Verification

Username: test
```

To close a session, use the DISCONNECT ? command and specify the particular session ID:

```
RouterA#disconnect ?
  <1-20>   The number of an active network connection
  WORD     The name of an active network connection
  <cr>

Router-cs#disconnect 3

Closing connection to 10.1.1.40 [confirm]y
```

e x a m
ⓦ a t c h   *Command level expertise with the Cisco 2511 in moving from session to session can save considerable time when concurrently configuring and monitoring many routers.*

CERTIFICATION OBJECTIVE 10.04

How to Perform a Core Dump

A *core dump* is a dump of the memory registers to a file. Core dumps are rarely performed except when working closely with Cisco's Technical Assistance Center (TAC). Usually, the core dump is then analyzed by senior-level TAC for highly erroneous protocol information. A network operator is not usually expected to read a core dump. As a matter of fact, a core file is usually not viewable. Nevertheless, Cisco provides a tool for decoding a core dump, called Stack Decoder. The following URL links to Cisco's Stack Decoder:

http://www.cisco.com/stack/stackdecoder.shtml

The EXCEPTION CORE command is used to identify the name of the file into which to write the core dump:

```
RouterA(config)#exception ?
  core-file          Set name of core dump file
  dump               Set name of host to dump to
  memory             Memory leak debugging
  protocol           Set protocol for sending core file
  region-size        Size of region for exception-time memory pool
  spurious-interrupt Crash after a given number of spurious interrupts

RouterA(config)#exception core ?
  WORD  Name of the core file

RouterA(config)#exception core RouterA ?
  <cr>
```

A core dump can be performed using RCP, FTP, or TFTP; however, TFTP is limited to a 16MB core file.

■ To perform a core dump using TFTP, first create a file on the TFTP server for writing the core dump. Then, on a UNIX TFTP server platform execute the following:

```
cd /tftpboot

touch RouterA

chmod 777 RouterA
```

■ To use FTP for writing the core file, enter the following FTP configuration for the usernames and passwords, and identify FTP as the file transfer mechanism:

```
RouterA(config)#ip ftp username test
RouterA(config)#ip ftp password testpw
RouterA(config)#exception protocol ftp
Then, prepare the router for writing the core dump
```

```
RouterA(config)#exception core RouterA
RouterA(config)#exception dump ?
  Hostname or A.B.C.D  Hostname or address of dump host

RouterA(config)#exception dump 10.1.1.1 ?
  <cr>

RouterA(config)#exception dump 10.1.1.1
```

When you're ready to write the core file, execute the WRITE CORE command. For routers with substantial memory and large routing tables, a core dump can take considerable time and produce a large core file. The following WRITE CORE output is truncated:

```
RouterA#write core
Remote host? 10.1.1.1
Name of core file to write [RouterA]?
Write file RouterA on host 10.1.1.1? [confirm]
Writing RouterA

!!!!!!!!!!!!!!!!!!!!!!!!!!!!!!!!!!!!!!!!!!!!!!!!!!!!!!!!!!!!!!!!
!!!!!!!!!!!!!!!!!!!!!!!!!!!!!!!!!!!!!!!!!!!!!!!!!!!!!!!!!!!!!!!!!!!!!!
!!!!!!!!!!!!!!!!!!!!!!!!!!!!!!!!!!!!!!!!!!!!!!!!!!!!!!!!!!!!!!!!!!!!!!
!!!!!!!!!!!!!!!!!!!!!!!!!!!!!!!!!!!!!!!!!!!!!!!!!!!!!!!!!!!!!!!!!!!!!!
!!!!!!!!!!!!!!!!!!!!!!!!!!!!!!!!!!!!!!!!!!!!!!!!!!!!!!!!!!!!!!!!!!!!!!
!!!!!!!!!!!!!!!!!!!!!!!!!!!!!!!!!!!!!!!!!!!!!!!!!!!!!!!!!!!!!!!!!!!!!!
!!!!!!!!!!!!!!!!!!!!!!!!!!!!!!!!!!!!!!!!!!!!!!!!!!!!!!!!!!!!!!!!!!!!!!
!!!!!!!!!!!!!!!!!!!!!!!!!!!!!!!!!!!!!!!!!!!!!!!!!!!!!!!!!!!!!!!!!!!!!!
!!!!!!!!!!!!!!!!!!!!!!!!!!!!!!!!!!!!!!!!!!!!!!!!!!!!
```

CERTIFICATION OBJECTIVE 10.05

Hardware Diagnostics

Most newer IOS versions have bundled microcode within the software. Some older IOS versions require a separate microcode upload. In addition, some nonrouter IOS software requires separate microcode software.

To view the running microcode, use the SHOW MICROCODE command. Often you will have to check the hardware release notes to verify what microcode or IOS is required to support a particular hardware device. The SHOW MICROCODE command displays the existing microcode:

```
Router#show microcode ?
  |  Output modifier

Router#show microcode

Card    Microcode    Target Hardware    Description
Type    Version      Version
----    ---------    ---------------    -----------
EIP     20.3              1.x           EIP version 20.3
FIP     20.4              2.x           FIP version 20.4
TRIP    20.2              1.x           TRIP version 20.2
AIP     20.16             1.x           AIP version 20.16
FSIP    20.9              1.x           FSIP version 20.9
HIP     20.2              1.x           HIP version 20.2
MIP     22.3              1.x           MIP version 22.3
FEIP    20.6              2.x           FEIP version 20.6
VIP2    21.40             2.x           VIP2 version 21.40
RSP2    20.0              1.x           RSP2 version 20.0
POSI    20.1              2.x           (null) version 20.1

Microcode flash default images

Card    Microcode
Type    Version      device:filename
----    ---------    --------------------
CIP     22-30        slot0:cip22-30        - Not present
```

Sometimes a newer card or software feature will require new microcode to be loaded on the Cisco device. You should follow the device-specific instructions for copying microcode onto the hardware.

Show Version

The SHOW VERSION command is one of the most frequently used commands when you're looking at a Cisco device. After logging into the router, one of the first commands you type in will usually be SHOW

VERSION. This command gives a good overview of hardware and software on the router, as shown here:

```
Router#show version ?
  |  Output modifiers
  <cr>

Router#show version

Cisco Internetwork Operating System Software

IOS (tm) 3000 Software (IGS-J-L), Version 11.1(7), RELEASE SOFTWARE (fc2)

Copyright (c) 1986-1996 by cisco Systems, Inc.

Compiled Wed 23-Oct-96 20:03 by tej

Image text-base: 0x03038304, data-base: 0x00001000


ROM: System Bootstrap, Version 11.0(10c), SOFTWARE

ROM: 3000 Bootstrap Software (IGS-BOOT-R), Version 11.0(10c), RELEASE SOFTWARE (fc1)


Router uptime is 1 minute

System restarted by reload

System image file is "flash:igs-j-l.111-7.bin", booted via flash


cisco 2511 (68030) processor (revision L) with 2048K/2048K bytes of memory.

Processor board ID 06094429, with hardware revision 00000000

Bridging software.

SuperLAT software copyright 1990 by Meridian Technology Corp).

X.25 software, Version 2.0, NET2, BFE and GOSIP compliant.

TN3270 Emulation software (copyright 1994 by TGV Inc).

1 Ethernet/IEEE 802.3 interface.
```

```
2 Serial network interfaces.

16 terminal lines.

32K bytes of non-volatile configuration memory.

8192K bytes of processor board System flash (Read ONLY)


Configuration register is 0x2102
```

The *configuration register* denotes how the router will boot. If the low-order hexadecimal digit is 0, then the router will boot into ROM monitor mode. For instance, a configuration register set to 0x141 will ignore NVRAM and boot from ROM. In addition, on some routers the ROM IOS subset does not support routing.

exam
ⓦatch

Be prepared to change configuration register settings to recover passwords or a hung router.

Test

Cisco IOS also provides a testing feature for examining various hardware and protocol criteria. The TEST commands will perform some hardware validation tests on various interfaces, protocols, and devices. *Note:* Most of these TEST commands are used by Cisco's factory personnel and are generally not to be used in the field.

```
RouterA#test ?
  appletalk    APPLETALK diagnostic code
  interfaces   Network interfaces
  ipc          Interprocess communications test commands
  memory       Non-volatile and/or multibus memory
  vines        VINES diagnostic code
```

For instance, you can test the router's memory, as shown next. However, be sure to rewrite the configuration to NVRAM after using this command, because the test overwrites the memory.

```
RouterA#test memory
Test NVRAM card [y/n] ? y
Passed
```

You can test all interfaces, as well. The interface test is used primarily for factory testing of the physical hardware, and not for operational testing. On certain routers that support MCI and ciscoBus Ethernet, as well as all serial interfaces, you can send a loopback ICMP request ping to the interface and take note of any errors. Errors would indicate a hardware or environmental physical-plant problem, such as lack of ventilation or electromagnetic interference. Here is output from the TEST INTERFACES command:

```
RouterA#test interfaces
Test Ethernet0/0 [y/n] ? y
!!!!!!!!!!!!!!!!!!!!!!!!!!!!!!!!!!!!!!!!!!!!!!!!!!!!!!!!!!!!!!!!!!!!!!!!!!!!!!
!!!!!!!!!!!!!!!!!!!!! Passed
Test Ethernet0/1 [y/n] ?
!!!!!!!!!!!!!!!!!!!!!!!!!!!!!!!!!!!!!!!!!!!!!!!!
```

Show Env

Cisco also provides a means to gather valuable environmental status and measurements, using the SHOW ENV command. This is especially handy for routers in remote locations with unpredictable HVAC.

```
RouterA#show env ?
  all    All environmental monitor parameters
  last   Last environmental monitor parameters
  table  Temperature and voltage ranges
  |      Output modifiers
  <cr>

RouterA#show env
All measured values are normal
```

The SHOW ENV LAST command displays the environmental settings of the router when it was last shut down. You will want to make sure that the shutdown was not due to power or temperature irregularities.

```
RouterA>show env last
  RSP(2) Inlet      previously measured at 25C/77F
  RSP(2) Hotpoint   previously measured at 28C/82F
  RSP(2) Exhaust    previously measured at 31C/87F
  RSP(3) Inlet      previously measured at 23C/73F
  RSP(3) Hotpoint   previously measured at 29C/84F
  RSP(3) Exhaust    previously measured at 33C/91F
  +12 Voltage       previously measured at 12.03
  +5 Voltage        previously measured at 5.11
  -12 Voltage       previously measured at -11.98
  +24 Voltage       previously measured at 24.06
```

The SHOW ENV ALL command provides a comprehensive view of the router's voltage and temperature operating environment. This command also produces some helpful information for when you're working with TAC, such as the serial numbers, part numbers, board revision numbers, firmware versions, and even RMA numbers of certain devices and interfaces. When upgrading IOS software, be sure to check the release notes and verify that the Hardware level is supported.

```
RouterA#show env all
Arbiter type 1, backplane type 7513 (id 2)
Power supply #1 is 1200W AC (id 1), power supply #2 is removed (id 7)
Active fault conditions: none
Fan transfer point: 100%
Active trip points: Restart_Inhibit
15 of 15 soft shutdowns remaining before hard shutdown


                    1
             0123456789012
Dbus slots: XXXX XX X X X

   card      inlet      hotpoint      exhaust
RSP(6)     26C/78F     35C/95F      31C/87F

Shutdown temperature source is 'hotpoint' on RSP(6), requested RSP(6)

+12V measured at 12.03
 +5V measured at 5.15
-12V measured at -11.93
+24V measured at 24.15
+2.5 reference is 2.48

PS1 +5V Current    measured at 60.39 A (capacity 200 A)
PS1 +12V Current   measured at 0.27 A (capacity 35 A)
PS1 -12V Current   measured at 0.09 A (capacity 3 A)
PS1 output is 315 W

RouterA#


          Physical slot 0, ~physical slot 0xF, logical slot 0, CBus 0
          Microcode Status 0xC
          Master Enable, LED, WCS Loaded
          Board is analyzed
          Pending I/O Status: Debug I/O
          EEPROM format version 1
          FEIP controller, HW rev 2.2, board revision D0
          Serial number: 04391979  Part number: 73-1374-04
          Test history: 0x00        RMA number: 00-00-00
```

```
        Flags: cisco 7000 board; 7500 compatible

        EEPROM contents (hex):
           0x20: 01 13 02 02 00 43 04 2B 49 05 5E 04 00 00 00 00
           0x30: 68 00 00 00 00 00 00 00 00 00 00 00 00 00 00 00

        Slot database information:
        Flags: 0x4      Insertion time: 0x2EFBD408 (27w4d ago)

        PA 0 Information:
                Fast-Ethernet PA, 1 port, 100BaseTX-nISL
                EEPROM format version 1
                HW rev 1.0, Board revision A0
                Serial number: 03097304  Part number: 73-1376-03

        PA 1 Information:
                Fast-Ethernet PA, 1 port, 100BaseTX-nISL
                EEPROM format version 1
                HW rev 1.0, Board revision A0
                Serial number: 03585214  Part number: 73-1376-03
Slot 1:
        Physical slot 1, ~physical slot 0xE, logical slot 1, CBus 0
        Microcode Status 0x0
        Master Enable, LED, WCS Loaded
        Board is analyzed
        EEPROM format version 1
        FSIP controller, HW rev 1.1, board revision A0
        Serial number: 01667283  Part number: 73-1126-05
        Test history: 0x00         RMA number: 00-00-00
        Flags: cisco 7000 board; 7500 compatible

        EEPROM contents (hex):
           0x20: 01 07 01 01 00 19 70 D3 49 04 66 05 00 00 00 00
           0x30: F1 00 FF 00 00 00 00 00 00 00 00 00 00 00 00

        Slot database information:
        Flags: 0x4      Insertion time: 0xD88 (28w6d ago)
```

Show Tech

When you're working with Cisco TAC, they will often request that you e-mail to them a SHOW TECH output when opening a case. It's a good idea to look through the subcommands of SHOW TECH and understand why they are vital to TAC. Many of the SHOW TECH subcommands have been covered in earlier chapters. In this discussion, for brevity's sake, the longer subcommand listings have been truncated and comments are interleaved within the output listing.

First in the SHOW TECH subcommands is SHOW VERSION, which lists the running IOS version along with the supported ROM version:

```
RouterA>show tech

----------------- show version -----------------

Cisco Internetwork Operating System Software
IOS (tm) 4500 Software (C4500-AJS-M), Version 11.2(9), RELEASE SOFTWARE (fc1)
Copyright (c) 1986-1997 by cisco Systems, Inc.
Compiled Tue 23-Sep-97 00:38 by ckralik
Image text-base: 0x600088A0, data-base: 0x60924000

ROM: System Bootstrap, Version 5.2(7b) [mkamson 7b], RELEASE SOFTWARE (fc1)
BOOTFLASH: 4500 Bootstrap Software (C4500-BOOT-M), Version 10.3(7), RELEASE SOFTWARE (fc1)
```

In the event that the router boots from the ROM IOS image, older ROM versions will often not support newer software features within the NVRAM configuration. You may lose a number of valuable services or possibly have a router stranded out in the network as inaccessible. (Always be sure to have a modem or some out-of-band access to remote routers.) In addition, Cisco 2500 series routers do not support routing at all when booted in ROM mode.

The output of the SHOW TECH command continues:

```
lab4000 uptime is 2 weeks, 6 days, 3 hours, 52 minutes
System restarted by power-on
System image file is "flash:c4500-ajs-mz.112-9.bin", booted via flash

cisco 4500 (R4K) processor (revision D) with 32768K/16384K bytes of memory.
Processor board ID 04023213
R4700 processor, Implementation 33, Revision 1.0
G.703/E1 software, Version 1.0.
Bridging software.
SuperLAT software copyright 1990 by Meridian Technology Corp).
X.25 software, Version 2.0, NET2, BFE and GOSIP compliant.
TN3270 Emulation software.
2 Ethernet/IEEE 802.3 interface(s)
2 Serial network interface(s)
128K bytes of non-volatile configuration memory.
8192K bytes of processor board System flash (Read/Write)
4096K bytes of processor board Boot flash (Read/Write)

Configuration register is 0x2102
.
```

With SHOW RUNNING-CONFIG, you can produce the entire running configuration so that TAC can check for conflicting or erroneous configurations:

```
------------------ show running-config ------------------
```

SHOW CONTROLLERS identifies the capabilities of each interface card, as well as any hardware failures:

```
------------------ show controllers ------------------

LANCE unit 0, NIM slot 2, NIM type code 9, NIM version 3
Media Type is AUI
idb 0x60D03A24, ds 0x60D05548, eim_regs = 0x3C200000
IB at 0x400581CC: mode=0x0000, mcfilter 0000/0000/8100/0000
station address 0060.471e.c71a  default station address 0060.471e.c71a
buffer size 1524
RX ring with 32 entries at 0x40058210
Rxhead = 0x40058210 (0), Rxp = 0x60D05560 (0)
00 pak=0x60D0CFC0 ds=0xA8072E0E status=0x80 max_size=1524 pak_size=0
01 pak=0x60D0CDE0 ds=0xA8072756 status=0x80 max_size=1524 pak_size=0
02 pak=0x60D0CC00 ds=0xA807209E status=0x80 max_size=1524 pak_size=0
03 pak=0x60D0CA20 ds=0xA80719E6 status=0x80 max_size=1524 pak_size=0
.
.
.
```

The SHOW STACKS subcommand helps TAC view the state of the router when it last was rebooted or crashed.

```
------------------ show stacks ------------------


Minimum process stacks:
 Free/Size    Name
10496/12000   Init
 9912/12000   Virtual Exec
 5196/6000    Router Init
10104/12000   Exec

Interrupt level stacks:
Level    Called Unused/Size  Name
   2   88464466   5520/6000  Network interfaces
   3          0   6000/6000  High IRQ Int Handler
   4     566037   5548/6000  Console Uart
```

```
6           0  6000/6000  Parity interrupt
7   435491232  5612/6000  NMI Interrupt Handler
.
.
.
```

SHOW INTERFACES displays the status of all interfaces, the protocol addresses of each interface, signaling levels, and throughput statistics. Link states, errors, and connectivity are key components to look for in the SHOW INTERFACES output.

```
----------------- show interfaces -----------------


Ethernet1 is up, line protocol is up
  Hardware is Lance, address is 0060.471e.c71d (bia 0060.471e.c71d)
  Internet address is 10.4.1.5/24
  MTU 1500 bytes, BW 10000 Kbit, DLY 1000 usec, rely 255/255, load 1/255
  Encapsulation ARPA, loopback not set, keepalive set (10 sec)
  ARP type: ARPA, ARP Timeout 04:00:00
  Last input 00:00:00, output 00:00:00, output hang never
  Last clearing of "show interface" counters 5d06h
  Queueing strategy: fifo
  Output queue 0/40, 0 drops; input queue 0/75, 0 drops
  30 second input rate 3000 bits/sec, 4 packets/sec
  30 second output rate 9000 bits/sec, 4 packets/sec
     81273254 packets input, 2416126002 bytes, 0 no buffer
     Received 258670 broadcasts, 0 runts, 0 giants, 0 throttles
     0 input errors, 0 CRC, 0 frame, 0 overrun, 0 ignored, 0 abort
     0 input packets with dribble condition detected
     205598 packets output, 15925506 bytes, 0 underruns
     0 output errors, 477 collisions, 4 interface resets
     0 babbles, 0 late collision, 9411 deferred
     0 lost carrier, 0 no carrier
     0 output buffer failures, 0 output buffers swapped out
Loopback0 is up, line protocol is up
  Hardware is Loopback
  Internet address is 10.80.80.1/32
  MTU 1500 bytes, BW 8000000 Kbit, DLY 5000 usec, rely 255/255, load 1/255
  Encapsulation LOOPBACK, loopback not set, keepalive set (10 sec)
  Last input 00:00:00, output never, output hang never
  Last clearing of "show interface" counters 5d06h
  Queueing strategy: fifo
  Output queue 0/0, 0 drops; input queue 0/75, 0 drops
  5 minute input rate 0 bits/sec, 0 packets/sec
  5 minute output rate 0 bits/sec, 0 packets/sec
```

```
0 packets input, 0 bytes, 0 no buffer
Received 0 broadcasts, 0 runts, 0 giants, 0 throttles
0 input errors, 0 CRC, 0 frame, 0 overrun, 0 ignored, 0 abort
98395 packets output, 0 bytes, 0 underruns
0 output errors, 0 collisions, 0 interface resets
0 output buffer failures, 0 output buffers swapped out
```

SHOW PROCESS MEMORY displays all processes and the amount of memory each process is consuming. It is important to look for processes with memory leaks which are not freeing up available memory.

```
---------------- show process memory ------------------


Total: 20436512, Used: 1370904, Free: 19065608
 PID  TTY  Allocated     Freed     Holding    Getbufs     Retbufs Process
   0    0    206464      1236      841904          0           0 *Init*
   0    0       348    185656         348          0           0 *Sched*
   0    0   5425636   3474412      175952     807780           0 *Dead*
   1    0       256       256        3772          0           0 Load Meter
   2    2     23844     22292       14344          0           0 Virtual Exec
   3    0         0         0        6772          0           0 Check heaps
   4    0        92         0        6864          0           0 Pool Manager
   5    0       256       256        6772          0           0 Timers
   6    0      1096      2204        7080          0           0 ARP Input


                     1370436 Total
```

The CPU utilization displayed in SHOW PROCESS CPU indicates the level of CPU consumption by various processes. The header showing five-second and five-minute usage percentages gives a good snapshot as to the CPU state. In the event that the CPU is maxed, look deeper into the output and determine which process may be hung or overloaded.

```
---------------- show process cpu ------------------

CPU utilization for five seconds: 1%/0%; one minute: 1%; five minutes: 0%
 PID  Runtime(ms)  Invoked  uSecs    5Sec    1Min    5Min TTY Process
   1           0   348394      0    0.00%   0.00%   0.00%   0 Load Meter
   2        1160    25314     45    1.06%   0.81%   0.25%   2 Virtual Exec
   3      238224    32939   7232    0.00%   0.01%   0.00%   0 Check heaps
```

```
4          0          1          0   0.00%   0.00%   0.00%   0 Pool Manager
5          0          2          0   0.00%   0.00%   0.00%   0 Timers
6         20      29403         0   0.00%   0.00%   0.00%   0 ARP Input
.
.
.
```

The SHOW BUFFERS output lets you look at the allocation of buffer memory for various packet lengths. This is used to determine if excess packet-loss can be attributed to poorly allocated buffer sizes.

```
------------------ show buffers ------------------


Buffer elements:
     499 in free list (500 max allowed)
     7258135 hits, 0 misses, 0 created

Public buffer pools:
Small buffers, 104 bytes (total 50, permanent 50):
     50 in free list (20 min, 150 max allowed)
     1059407 hits, 0 misses, 0 trims, 0 created
     0 failures (0 no memory)
Middle buffers, 600 bytes (total 25, permanent 25):
     22 in free list (10 min, 150 max allowed)
     597811 hits, 2 misses, 6 trims, 6 created
     0 failures (0 no memory)
Big buffers, 1524 bytes (total 50, permanent 50):
     50 in free list (5 min, 150 max allowed)
     1665364 hits, 0 misses, 0 trims, 0 created
     0 failures (0 no memory)
VeryBig buffers, 4520 bytes (total 10, permanent 10):
     10 in free list (0 min, 100 max allowed)
     1091492 hits, 0 misses, 0 trims, 0 created
     0 failures (0 no memory)
Large buffers, 5024 bytes (total 0, permanent 0):
     0 in free list (0 min, 10 max allowed)
     0 hits, 0 misses, 0 trims, 0 created
     0 failures (0 no memory)
Huge buffers, 18024 bytes (total 0, permanent 0):
     0 in free list (0 min, 4 max allowed)
     597581 hits, 59 misses, 118 trims, 118 created
     0 failures (0 no memory)

Interface buffer pools:
Serial0 buffers, 1524 bytes (total 96, permanent 96):
     32 in free list (0 min, 96 max allowed)
```

```
     64 hits, 0 fallbacks
     32 max cache size, 32 in cache
Serial1 buffers, 1524 bytes (total 96, permanent 96):
     32 in free list (0 min, 96 max allowed)
     64 hits, 0 fallbacks
     32 max cache size, 32 in cache
Ethernet0 buffers, 1524 bytes (total 96, permanent 96):
     32 in free list (0 min, 96 max allowed)
     64 hits, 0 fallbacks
     32 max cache size, 32 in cache
Ethernet1 buffers, 1524 bytes (total 96, permanent 96):
     32 in free list (0 min, 96 max allowed)
     64 hits, 0 fallbacks
     32 max cache size, 31 in cache
```

CERTIFICATION SUMMARY

Advanced troubleshooting of Cisco routers and other devices requires a working knowledge of the devices and enabled software features. Whether you're looking at routing protocols, Frame Relay PVCs, or system hardware, an experienced troubleshooter needs to have a reference point for the router's expected behavior.

When using the DEBUG command, it may happen that an enormous amount of extremely technical information is presented to the troubleshooter and will overwhelm the user on the end of the display. Using DEBUG challenges the troubleshooter to gain a deeper understanding of the operations of certain hardware and software features, while also producing data that serves to resolve the problem.

In building a more scalable and manageable network environment, Cisco also provides a number of tools, including logging, SNMP polling for fault and performance information, sending alarms and traps to central servers, timestamping of messages, and using NTP for clock synchronization. Together, these tools provide robust management of large-scale networks.

Cisco also supports various out-of-band methods to access remote equipment, using terminal servers. Cisco IOS has built in various shortcuts and time-saving interconnectivity commands that will certainly be helpful during the CCIE lab. Over time, you will become more effective and intuitive with many commands during troubleshooting. In addition, Cisco continues to add more helpful "niche" commands with each IOS software release.

When working with TAC in identifying some of the lowest-level problems, you may be required to provide a CORE DUMP output, to be analyzed along with various other system-level and environmental information. It is important to provide Cisco with all relevant information and network documentation up front, so that network downtime can be minimized. Cisco provides a number of comprehensive commands that produce information necessary to the Cisco technician when resolving technical cases.

✓ TWO-MINUTE DRILL

- ❑ One of the more powerful tools in Cisco's command set is the DEBUG command for viewing ongoing protocol processes and state information.

- ❑ When using the debug command, be aware of the extra CPU and network overhead it imposes on the router and bandwidth.

- ❑ An extremely powerful feature of debugging is being able to use the router like a sniffer—you can debug certain packet-based information in a focused mode.

- ❑ In order to verify the level of debugging currently enabled on the Cisco router, use the SHOW DEBUG command.

- ❑ When you have to resolve WAN problems, Cisco provides a number of options designed for low-level debugging of Frame Relay, ATM, ISDN, and other WAN technologies.

- ❑ With the DEBUG FRAME-RELAY command, Cisco provides for extensive monitoring of Frame Relay connections within multiprotocol environments.

- ❑ The DEBUG ATM command provides robust ATM debugging information.

- ❑ If using a dial-up server or dial-on-demand routing (DDR), you will more than likely one day require the help of the DEBUG ISDN command for troubleshooting your ISDN connection.

- ❑ Typical misconfigurations of ISDN include errors in switch type and SPIDs. For instance, a mismatch of the ISDN switch type can be detected on an AS5300 when incoming calls keep failing and releasing.

❑ Failover occurs when an allocation request on a port fails and then attempts to allocate the next available port.

❑ The LOGGING command enables the logging of messages to a variety of sources.

❑ If the router is configured with the SERVICE TIMESTAMP command, you will see each event message in the log timestamped.

❑ You can use the TIMESTAMP command independently for debug or logging messages.

❑ Use of Network Time Protocol (NTP), RFC 1305, is suggested in order to keep the network timing synchronized.

❑ The "ntp clock-period" output displayed in the configuration should not be adjusted. The NTP clock-period is automatically stored in the NVRAM and is generated by the NTP process.

❑ Become intimately familiar with using a Cisco 2511 or 2611 as a multiconsole access device, and with switching between multiple reverse-Telnet sessions.

❑ When using the 2511, be sure that the line settings are correct on each of the async lines.

❑ When using a 2511 to access multiple routers, you will have to perform a *reverse Telnet* in order to gain access to the async lines.

❑ A *core dump* is a dump of the memory registers to a file. Cisco provides a tool for decoding a core dump, called Stack Decoder.

❑ Most newer IOS versions have bundled microcode within the software. Some older IOS versions require a separate microcode upload.

❑ The SHOW VERSION command is one of the most frequently used commands when you're looking at a Cisco device.

❑ The *configuration register* denotes how the router will boot. If the low-order hexadecimal digit is 0, then the router will boot into ROM monitor mode.

❑ Cisco IOS also provides a testing feature for examining various hardware and protocol criteria. The TEST commands will perform some hardware validation tests on various interfaces, protocols, and devices.

❑ Cisco also provides a means to gather valuable environmental status and measurements, using the SHOW ENV command.

SELF TEST

The following Self Test questions will help you measure your understanding of the material presented in this chapter. Read all the choices carefully, as there may be more than one correct answer. Choose all correct answers for each question.

1. You should enable DEBUG ALL when you log into a troubled router and don't know what the problem is.

   A. True

   B. False

2. If accessing the router via a VTY port and enabling debug, you should first enable what?

   A. Logging

   B. Terminal length

   C. Terminal monitor

   D. Virtual template

3. What should you do if the router appears to be hung up after you've enabled debug?

   A. Reboot the router

   B. Use the NO DEBUG ALL command

   C. Hit the break key

   D. Disconnect the WAN interface

4. Applying an access list to a DEBUG IP command is not a good idea because access lists require processing overhead.

   A. True

   B. False

5. In order to gain a comprehensive view of a LAN's operations, you may want to use a:

   A. Bridge

   B. Repeater

   C. Sniffer

   D. Router in DEBUG ALL mode

6. Frame Relay debugging allows for you to directly examine all except:

   A. IP

   B. IPX

   C. LMI

   D. DLSW

7. When trying to manage an ATM VC status from an ATM Service Provider, you may want to use:

   A. Individual VCCs

   B. A large VP

   C. SVCs

   D. OAM cells

8. Cisco supports the following remote authentication servers except:

   A. Radius

   B. TACACS

   C. TACACS+

   D. NIS+

9. If you're specifying an argument on the command line, Cisco will execute what command by default?

A. PING

B. TRACEROUTE

C. TELNET

D. HELP

10. The default setting for a console port on a router is:

A. 9600,N,1

B. 2400,N,1

C. 9600,E,2

D. 2400,N,1

11. From the console port of a 2511, to access an async line from the Octal interface into the console port of another router, what should you do?

A. Use the Kermit protocol.

B. Use L2F.

C. Use reverse Telnet.

D. Use LAT.

12. In order to switch to a different session of an async line to another async line, you first have to type which of the following key sequences:

A. ESC, BREAK

B. ESC-F4, !

C. CTRL-ALT-DEL

D. CTRL-SHIFT-6

13. In order to read a core dump, what utility do you use?

A. NROFF

B. Stack Decoder

C. vi

D. Microsoft Word

14. Core dumps can be written to a server using all the following methods except:

A. RCP

B. TFTP

C. SSH

D. FTP

15. New IOS microcode is available for free downloads from Cisco.

A. True

B. False

16. Which of the following commands is a good troubleshooting starting point when logging into a troubled router?

A. SHOW BUFFERS

B. DEBUG IP PACKET

C. TRACEROUTE WWW.CISCO.COM

D. SHOW VERSION

17. Which of the following commands helps you gain an overview of the router's operating environment?

A. SHOW ROUTER

B. SHOW ENV ALL

C. SHOW TEMP

D. SHOW HARDWARE

18. Cisco TAC will often request the output of which command when opening a case?

A. SHOW IP ROUTE

B. SHOW ARP

C. TRACE WWW.CISCO.COM

D. SHOW TECH

19. If you can't get a response from a reverse Telnet on a Cisco 2511 async line, what should you do?

    A. Reboot the router.

    B. Clear the line.

    C. Change the cable.

    D. Check the routing table.

20. By default, you can Telnet to any VTY interface.

    A. True

    B. False

11

Campus Switches and VLANs

Back when local-area networks (LANs) were cutting-edge technology, their multimillion-bps transmission speeds were considered more than adequate for even the largest networks. Likewise, 5MB hard drives were considered huge, and nobody needed more than 640KB of RAM. As the computers on the networks got faster and offered more storage, the networks became more heavily used. The two common methods for segmenting networks to improve performance were *bridging* and *subnetting*. These methods are still among the most preferred by network managers, and Cisco's Catalyst family of switches addresses both of them.

Note that we'll be using the term *station* to refer to a computer or device plugged into a LAN. This is consistent with the Cisco documentation and with discussions regarding Layer 2 networking. For *station,* you can freely substitute the words *client, server, host, network client, computer,* and so forth.

The Cisco Catalyst family includes a number of models, including the 2900, 5000, 5500, and 8500 families. This chapter concerns itself primarily with the 5000 and 5500 families, referred to as the 5000, or 5*xxx* family. Most of the features mentioned in this chapter are available on all the Catalyst families. If you're not sure if a command is available on your Catalyst, consult the documentation for your model, or see if a software upgrade is available that supports the feature you're looking for.

CERTIFICATION OBJECTIVE 11.01

Interface Configuration

When LAN switches were first created, they functioned like multiport intelligent bridges, usually with an internal backplane that ran at a significantly higher speed than the media connecting to it. In terms of features, the first generation of switches offered little beyond that. They also typically didn't address the subnetting issue, since the entire box was often one big broadcast domain. You could have logical subnetting for a protocol like IP or DECNet, but not AppleTalk or IPX, because they would automatically determine that they were on an existing network number. If you wanted a separate broadcast domain, you had to buy another switch and manually rewire.

To address network separation, switch manufacturers came up with the concept of *virtual LANs* or VLANs. Put simply, a VLAN is a logical broadcast domain that can span multiple switches. To get between broadcast domains, stations typically need to pass through some sort of Layer 3 (or higher) device, typically a router.

At their lowest level, Catalyst switches are VLAN-capable switches that work at the port level. They assign ports to VLANs and perform the intelligent bridging function within that VLAN as if there were a separate box per VLAN. This means you can have all the performance benefits of the bridging along with the ability to maintain separate networks. This can be done in one chassis (as long as you have enough ports), which typically saves money over multiple physical switches and adds the convenience of being able to move ports between VLANs remotely. The rest of our discussion will focus on the Catalyst family of switches.

Most of the commands we'll be using have to do with setting and viewing options on a port or group of ports. With a couple of exceptions (noted later), ports are organized in slots, and port numbers within that slot. For example, if there is a 48-port card in slot 3, the ports would be referred to as "slot 3, ports 1-48," and this is noted as "3/1-48." Many of the commands can take a range of ports, and that's how it would be typed, 3/1-48. If you're used to working with Cisco routers, then you're aware that slot numbers start at 0 on routers. On Cisco Catalysts, the slot numbers start at 1. The same goes for the port numbers; they start at 0 on the routers and at 1 on the Catalysts. So, the first port on a router is 0/0, but on a Catalyst it's 1/1.

For most network needs, the Catalyst comes with a very good set of defaults, and usually one doesn't have to change much more than the VLAN number on a set of ports, and set a VTP domain and version number (see the VTP section in this chapter.) The default VLAN is number 1, and if you're not mixing media and you don't need multiple VLANs, you can even leave the defaults as is and just connect your stations.

Here is the command to create additional VLANs:

SET VLAN <vlan_num> <mod/ports...>

Current versions of the software for the Catalysts permit VLAN numbers in the range of 1 through 1005, some of which are predefined. The range of valid modules and ports (<mod/ports...>) depends on what cards are installed. Generally, only ports that are already installed can be added to a VLAN.

We'll examine VLANs in more detail in a later section of this chapter. Let's examine some other common options we might need to set on ports.

Speed and Duplex Detection

On Fast Ethernet modules with a default configuration, when a station is plugged into the switch, the switch will attempt to automatically determine if the station is capable of 100MB operation and whether it can do full duplex.

Occasionally, a station will not be able to complete the negotiation process properly, and the port will have to be set manually. To set the port speed, use the following command:

SET PORT SPEED <mod_num/port_num> <4|10|16|100|auto>

This command, like many others, can set a range of ports at one time. For a Fast Ethernet module, setting the speed to auto will also set the half/full duplex to auto.

To set the duplex on a Fast Ethernet module, use the following command:

SET PORT DUPLEX <mod_num/port_num> <full||half>

You can't set the duplex manually if the speed is set to auto, and you can't set the duplex to auto if the speed has been set manually. To set the duplex to auto, you set the speed to auto.

Security

Security on a Catalyst switch has a very specific meaning. Implementing the security feature means that the Catalyst will only accept frames from a particular MAC address (this feature is for Ethernet modules only). The command is

SET PORT SECURITY *<mod_num/port_num>* *<enable|disable>* *[mac_addr]*

Specifying the MAC address is optional. If it's omitted, the first MAC address that transmits will be the one to which the port is secured. Because the security feature locks the port down to a single MAC address, only a single host can be plugged into that port. You cannot, for example, plug a hub into a port with security enabled, and plug multiple stations into the hub. Only one of them will work.

CERTIFICATION OBJECTIVE 11.02

Virtual LANs (VLANs)

As mentioned previously, a VLAN is most easily thought of as being equivalent to a *broadcast domain.* Put simply, a broadcast domain is the group of stations that gets a Layer 2 broadcast sent by one of the same group. An example would be an ARP request. When one station in a broadcast domain sends an ARP request, it is received by all the other stations in the broadcast domain.

Traditionally, separate broadcast domains were created by either separating network segments entirely, or by putting in a Layer 3 or higher gateway device, such as a router. Stations connected to a Catalyst switch will require a router (or similar device) in order to pass traffic between VLANs. This could be either a stand-alone external router, or an integrated router like the RSM card for the Catalyst 5*xxx* family.

Let's return to our ARP example. A question might have occurred to you: If an IP host didn't need to ARP another host (that is, it already knew the other host's MAC address), would it be able to communicate directly across VLANs? The answer is no. Even when two stations know all the information they would normally need to communicate at Layer 2, they won't be able to communicate if they're in different VLANs (and bridging hasn't been arranged between those VLANs). The two stations will need to go through an intermediate device, such as a router.

Let's examine some of the details for assigning and managing VLANs on a Catalyst switch.

VLAN Assignment

Assigning ports to a VLAN is simple. To do so, simply use the set vlan command:

> SET VLAN <vlan_num> <mod/ports...>

That's the simplified version of the command; we'll start with that.

Basically, to create a new VLAN, you pick a number between 2 and 1005, inclusive (1 is already there by default). You'll also want to assign some ports to the VLAN. Here's an example:

```
set vlan 10 5/1-24
```

You'll need to be in enable mode to do this. Also, if this is the first time the switch is being configured, you'll need to set a VTP name (see the section later in this chapter on "Virtual Trunking Protocol (VTP)"). The command just shown creates VLAN 10 (if it didn't already exist) and assigns ports 1 though 24 in slot 5 to that VLAN. That's it—VLAN 10 is up and functioning.

Let's examine some of the per-VLAN settings available.

VLAN Options

Table 11-1 defines the full set of options for set vlan, as follows:

> SET VLAN <vlan_num> [name <name>] [type <type>] [state <state>]
> [said <said>] [mtu <mtu>] [ring <hex_ring_number>]
> [decring <decimal_ring_number>]
> [bridge <bridge_number>] [parent <vlan_num>]
> [mode <bridge_mode>] [stp <stp_type>]
> [translation <vlan_num>] [backupcrf <off|on>]
> [aremaxhop <hopcount>] [stemaxhop <hopcount>]

TABLE 11-1	Options for **SET VLAN** Command	Description
Options for SET VLAN Command	SET VLAN <vlan_num> name <name>	Allows you to assign a descriptive name to the VLAN, up to 32 characters.
	SET VLAN <vlan_num> type <type>	Allows you to set the VLAN type. Valid types (at present) are ethernet, fddi, fddinet, trcrf, and trbrf. VLAN types are used when mapping between VLANs and with VTP (see the next section on VTP). If you're using only Ethernet in a single chassis, for example, you can leave the type at the default.
	SET VLAN <vlan_num> state <state>	Allows you to set the state (active or suspend) of the VLAN. Active is the default, which is what you will normally want. You may want to set the VLAN to suspend while testing.
	SET VLAN <vlan_num> said <said>	Allows you to set the security association identifier (SAID). The default SAID is 100000 plus the VLAN number (example: the default SAID for VLAN 10 is 100010). SAIDs are used as a VLAN identifier when trunking across 802.10 FDDI/CDDI networks. In general, you can leave SAID at the default unless you're already using conflicting SAIDs in an FDDI/CDDI network.
	SET VLAN <vlan_num> mtu <mtu>	Allows you to set the maximum transmission unit size. In general, you'll want to leave this at the default.
	SET VLAN <vlan_num> ring <hex_ring_number>	Allows you to set the ring number for FDDI or Token Ring VLANs. Use the default unless you're connecting to an existing ring with a different ring number. Valid values are 0x1 through 0xfff, hex.
	SET VLAN <vlan_num> decring <decimal_ring_number>	Same as just described, but in decimal. Valid range is 1-4095.

Most of the remaining vlan options have to do with other types of bridging, and some of them are only available in the newer versions of the Catalyst software. The type of bridging we've been discussing so far is called *transparent bridging*. It's called transparent because the end stations don't know the bridges are there and don't have to do anything special to use them. There are other types of bridging (for example, source route bridging) that require more work on the part of the end station, including providing a list of bridges to traverse in order to reach another station. This is done as part of the frame headers.

Nontransparent bridging is used mostly in conjunction with Token Ring or SNA networks and, even then, probably only when non-Catalyst bridges are also used. Much of the nontransparent bridging setup requires manual configuration of the Catalyst. In addition, significant features in this area have been added to the evolving Catalyst software, with additional capabilities likely to come.

If you plan to use the Catalyst equipment in nontrivial Token Ring networks or in conjunction with other brands of source route bridges, please consult the Cisco documentation as well as the documentation for the other equipment.

Virtual Trunking Protocol (VTP)

It's fairly easy to understand how to define and manage VLANs within a single switch. It's not so clear, however, whether manually defining VLANs is scalable, when there are dozens of interconnected switches running several trunking protocols. It could be difficult keeping the VLAN settings consistent across a group of Catalyst switches, especially if a number of the defaults have been changed. The problem gets worse when a mixture of trunking protocols have been used, such as ISL, 802.10, 802.1Q, and LANE.

Let's say you were manually configuring your VLANs in your switches, and you wanted to assign some ports on a switch to a VLAN that hadn't yet been defined there. You'd have to define the VLAN. Then you'd have to define the name. If you were using 802.10 anywhere with the VLAN, you'd have to make sure your SAID matched. Then you'd have to make sure your network type matched. You'd also have to assign an uplink of some sort to that VLAN to carry the traffic. Then, if anything ever changed, you'd have to manually find and update all the switches that had that VLAN on them.

Cisco has addressed this problem with the Virtual Trunking Protocol (VTP). With VTP, most of the changes and settings just discussed get propagated automatically. Add a set of trunk ports preconfigured to carry all your VLANs, and you've got a nearly automatic way to manage your VLAN settings.

Before we discuss what's needed to set up VTP, let's take a look at the VTP version. As of this writing, there are two versions of VTP, 1 and 2. VTP2 adds a number of features, including Token Ring features, a transparency option, and consistency checks. VTP2 was introduced in version 3.1(1) of the Catalyst software.

Note that mixing VTP versions does NOT work, and the default setting is for all Catalysts to do VTP1. Unless you change it, your Catalysts will be running VTP version 1. Cisco recommends that you use VTP2 if all of your switches are running a software version that is capable of VTP2. I recommend VTP2 as well, and the rest of this section will assume VTP2 will be used.

Here's the set vtp command syntax:

SET VTP [domain <*name*>] [mode <*mode*>] [passwd <*passwd*>] [pruning <enable|disable>] [V2 <enable|disable>

Pick a Catalyst to be a server. Type the following:

```
set vtp v2 enable
set vtp domain name
set vtp mode server
```

For *name,* pick a domain name between 1 and 32 characters long. Choose something simple and easy to remember. The domain name is unimportant except that it *must* match on all Catalysts that are connected (at least the ones you want to manage with VTP).

There—you've just configured a VTP server. Any VLAN changes you make (such as SAID, MTU size, or adding or removing a VLAN) will be propagated to VTP clients.

Now let's configure a VTP client:

```
set vtp v2 enable
set vtp domain name
set vtp mode client
```

Do this on each of the other switches, and you're basically done. Now any changes you make to a VLAN on a switch you've configured as a VTP server will be propagated. (VLAN changes cannot be made on Catalyst switches configured to be VTP clients.)

VTP2 also adds a transparent mode that allows passthrough of VTP information on a switch, without that switch having to participate in VTP itself. To enable that mode, use set vtp mode transparent instead of set vtp mode server.

A Closer Look at VTP

How does VTP work? Actually, if you're familiar with Layer 3 router advertisements, then VTP will look fairly familiar.

Catalyst switches use a Layer 2 multicast address to propagate VTP information. The Catalyst switches use this multicast address to send VTP information through trunk ports to neighboring Catalysts. Those Catalysts pick up the information, update their own tables, and then send their updated VTP information out of their trunk ports, thereby propagating the VTP information throughout the network.

VTP propagates a number of items, including:

- VLAN numbers
- ATM LANE names
- FDDI SAID numbers
- VTP domain name
- VTP version being used
- MTU for each VLAN

As you can see, VTP can be a great time-saver and can keep you from making a certain set of configuration errors. Is there any downside to VTP? What exactly have you accomplished by enabling VTP? Basically, what you've done is define every VLAN in your network on every switch. This creates a little extra traffic for passing the VTP information around, but that should be minimal.

Consider what happens, however, when an end-station broadcasts. Recall that every station has to get a copy of a broadcast. Traditional bridges will send a copy out of every port except the one it came in on. This behavior is known as *flooding*. VLAN-capable switches do much the same but within the VLAN, since a VLAN is defined as a broadcast domain. A Catalyst switch forwards broadcasts to all ports on itself in that VLAN, and forwards copies to any other switches that have that VLAN—but consider that we just defined *every* VLAN on *every* switch. Oops. When another Catalyst gets a copy of the broadcast frame, the Catalyst will drop the frame if it has no ports defined in that VLAN—but the Catalyst still has to use the CPU and bandwidth to get the frame there.

There's a solution, called *pruning*.

VTP Pruning

The obvious solution for this resource expenditure would be not forwarding the frames to a switch that doesn't need them. It's easy to set up, too. On one of your VTP servers, type the following:

```
set vtp pruning enable
```

This turns on pruning for the entire domain—every VLAN. This is probably exactly what you want, but if it's not, you can enable/disable pruning on a per-VLAN basis. Check your Catalyst documentation for other options.

Inter-Switch Link (ISL) Trunks

ISL (Inter-Switch Link) is Cisco's protocol for trunking VLANs over Fast Ethernet. By linking two Catalyst switches and running ISL over that link, you can pass Ethernet, FDDI, and Token Ring frames between them.

Here's the set trunk command syntax:

SET TRUNK <*mod_num/port_num*> [on|off|desirable|auto|nonnegotiate] [*vlans*]

And to configure a port to be a trunk port, use the SET TRUNK ON or SET TRUNK DESIRABLE command, like this:

```
set trunk 1/1 desirable
```

Use the DESIRABLE setting if you want the port to trunk when the other end is willing to do trunking. Use the ON setting if you want to force the port to be a trunk port regardless. By default, all-trunk capable ports are in AUTO mode, which means they will become a trunk port if the other end of a link is set to ON or DESIRABLE.

To set a port back to its default, use SET TRUNK AUTO. To disable trunking entirely on a port, use SET TRUNK OFF. The NONNEGOTIATE setting is similar to SET TRUNK ON, in that it forces the port to be a trunk port but does not send trunk negotiation frames. That is, it won't bring up a trunk with the other end set to AUTO; the other end would have to be set to ON or NONNEGOTIATE.

Optionally, a VLAN range ([*vlans*]) can be given, which will limit that trunk port to the VLANs given. By default, VLANs 1 through 1000 will be trunked.

As you can see from the SET TRUNK syntax, a port is designated as a trunk port, and VLANs to trunk over it are assigned to that port. Once that's done, those VLANs can pass across that trunk port, and the traffic can be kept separate while passing among switches.

ISL can also be used in Cisco routers. In newer router IOS versions, ISL can be configured on a physical Fast Ethernet port to provide virtual router ports—similar to Cisco Frame Relay subinterfaces. This allows you to route between multiple VLANs without having to buy physical interfaces for each. As long as there is enough bandwidth for all VLANs on that port, this solution works well. *Note:* Not all protocols are supported yet at the router with ISL. For example, AppleTalk is not supported over ISL as of IOS 11.3 on 75*xx* routers with VIP cards.

ISL is fundamentally a way to save physical ports and use logical ports instead. This can save a lot on extra interfaces—especially if they are high-speed ports, or router ports, which tend to be more expensive. Also, there may be a limited number of fiber or copper runs between two Catalyst switches, and using ISL solves that problem as well.

Let's look at an example:

```
set trunk 1/1 on
```

This will force port 1/1 to become a trunk port. If the switch on the other end is in auto mode, it will become a trunk port. Otherwise, the other switch will also have to be configured the same as port 1/1, to finish the trunk.

When you configure a trunk, all VLANs are allowed across it. Commands are available to remove certain VLANs from a trunk if desired; consult your documentation.

ISL in conjunction with VTP gives you a fairly easily managed VLAN environment.

Cisco's Web site provides a short document on configuring trunks, at

http://www.cisco.com/univercd/cc/td/doc/product/lan/cat5000/rel_4_2/config/e_trunk.htm

Also on their Web site, Cisco provides a short document that covers VTP and VLAN design issues and commands. This is recommended reading before planning your VLAN architecture:

http://www.cisco.com/univercd/cc/td/doc/product/lan/cat5000/rel_4_2/config/vlans.htm

CERTIFICATION OBJECTIVE 11.03

Spanning Tree Protocol

We've seen examples of how a switch learns which port a set of MAC addresses is attached to, so the switch can make intelligent forwarding decisions. Consider Figure 11-1.

Suppose Station A sends a unicast frame to Station B. That frame will go onto Segment A, and be seen by both Bridge 1 and Bridge 2. Both Bridge 1 and Bridge 2 have address tables that indicate Station B is on Segment B. Both bridges forward the frame onto Segment B, and Station B gets two

FIGURE 11-1   Multiple network paths

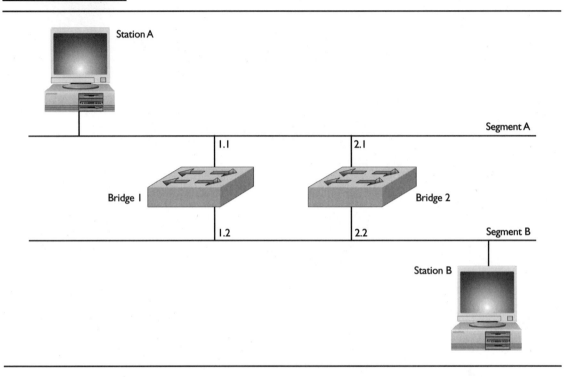

copies of the frame! Now, imagine that some station on either segment
sends a broadcast frame. The only rule for bridges to handle broadcast
frames is to not forward them to the segment they came from. Bridge 1 gets
a broadcast frame from Segment A and forwards it to Segment B. Bridge 2
gets a copy of the frame on Segment B and forwards it on to Segment A.
Bridge 1 picks it up again and forwards it to Segment B .... You get the
idea. The network would be instantly saturated on both segments.

Obviously bridges don't behave in this manner, or there would be a lot
of dead networks out there. One solution is for the network manager to
take care that multiple paths between any two network segments never
occur. This can be done, but what if the design in Figure 11-1 was done for
redundancy purposes? It's reasonable to design multiple paths so that one
can be used if the other fails.

The answer to this conflict is that bridges will arrange for their interfaces to be shut off automatically if there is a redundant path, or loop. In Figure 11-1, both interfaces on one of the bridges will be disabled, so there is only a single path between the two segments. If one of the links on the active bridge fails, the inactive bridge will take over.

The mechanism for bridges to coordinate all of this activity is the Spanning Tree protocol. A *spanning tree* is a way of representing a set of nodes and links (in our case, a network) such that there is only one path used between any two points. In a network of bridges with redundant links, this is accomplished by turning off certain ports, as in our example. Once the bridges have communicated and agreed upon a spanning-tree configuration, there are no active redundant paths in the network that would cause extra copies of frames to be forwarded. If there is a change in the topology due to the addition, removal, or failure of a bridge, the entire spanning tree is recalculated in every bridge.

As we've discussed, Catalyst switches are bridges. Therefore, every port on a Catalyst can participate in spanning-tree updates, unless the network manager turns off that feature. Caution should be used when considering which ports should and should not participate in the spanning-tree updates. If another path through the network is attached via a port on which spanning tree has been disabled, then loops can occur.

Let's examine how bridges communicate.

BPDU Hello Packets

Bridges communicate with other bridges via Bridge Protocol Data Units, or BPDUs. As bridges are Layer 2 devices, BPDU is a Layer 2 protocol. Bridges first discover each other by sending out frames with a Layer 2 multicast address as a destination. Here's a BPDU Hello packet captured with the Sniffer Pro software from Network Associates:

```
DLC:  ----- DLC Header -----
      DLC:
      DLC:  Frame 1 arrived at  18:46:35.5704; frame size is 60 (003C hex)
bytes.
      DLC:  Destination = Multicast 0180C2000000, Bridge_Group_Addr
      DLC:  Source      = Station 00605CC1BE25
```

```
         DLC:   802.3 length = 38
         DLC:
LLC:     ----- LLC Header ---
         LLC:
         LLC:   DSAP Address = 42, DSAP IG Bit = 00 (Individual Address)
         LLC:   SSAP Address = 42, SSAP CR Bit = 00 (Command)
         LLC:   Unnumbered frame: UI
         LLC:
BPDU:    ----- Bridge Protocol Data Unit Header -----
         BPDU:
         BPDU: Protocol Identifier = 0000
         BPDU: Protocol Version    = 00
         BPDU:
         BPDU: BPDU Type = 00 (Configuration)
         BPDU:
         BPDU: BPDU Flags = 00
         BPDU:  0... .... = Not Topology Change Acknowledgment
         BPDU:  .... ...0 = Not Topology Change
         BPDU:  .000 000. = Unused
         BPDU:
         BPDU: Root Identifier   = 8000.00102F174962
         BPDU:   Priority        = 8000
         BPDU:   MAC Address      = 00102F174962
         BPDU:
         BPDU: Root Path Cost    = 0
         BPDU:
         BPDU: Sending Bridge Id = 8000.00102F174962.8182
         BPDU:   Priority        = 8000
         BPDU:   MAC Address      = 00102F174962
         BPDU:   Port            = 8182
         BPDU:  Message Age         = 0.000 seconds
         BPDU:  Information Lifetime = 20.000 seconds
         BPDU:  Root Hello Time     = 2.000 seconds
         BPDU:  Forward Delay       = 15.000 seconds
         BPDU:
DLC:     Frame padding= 8 bytes
```

Without getting too deeply into the specifics of how BPDU works, let's just notice that the destination address is a multicast address, which the Sniffer Pro software has identified as being a bridge group address. This is just a Hello packet, so many of the fields aren't used here; but you can see some version information, flags for when a change is needed, some of the addressing schemes that are used, and timer information.

The bridging standards are maintained by the IEEE. You can find bridging standards documents at http://www.ieee.org, but you'll need membership to access them.

If you haven't disabled spanning tree, and you attach a sniffer of some sort, you'll see frames as shown in the previous sniffer capture, every two seconds by default. This interval can be modified; in the frame shown just above, it's identified as the Root Hello Time. In this context, the root is a particular bridge that is the root of the spanning tree.

PortFast

If you've ever tried moving a station between ports on a Catalyst with a default configuration, you may have noticed it takes a fair amount of time for the Catalyst to recognize that the station has moved, and to start passing traffic on the new port.

This delay is the result of the Catalyst going through several steps before it starts forwarding frames. Some of these steps may include speed and duplex detection, bridge table updates, and spanning-tree sensing, depending on how the switch is configured. This process can take around 30 to 60 seconds. Part of the delay is to avoid loops. If spanning tree is enabled on that port, it will try to ensure that there is no bridge reachable via that port before it starts forwarding packets. If such a bridge exists, a spanning-tree update will be required. The default configuration is for the Catalyst to err on the side of caution and check for bridges before forwarding any frames, to avoid even temporary loops.

If the network manager knows for sure that nothing but end-stations will ever be attached via those ports, the wait time can be reduced by enabling PortFast. Here's the syntax of the command:

SET SPANTREE PORTFAST <*mod_num/port_num*> <enable|disable>

Following is an example of enabling PortFast on ports 1 through 24 in slot 3:

```
Cat5500> (enable) set spantree portfast 3/1-24 enable

Warning: Spantree port fast start should only be enabled on ports connected
to a single host.  Connecting hubs, concentrators, switches, bridges, etc. to
a fast start port can cause temporary spanning tree loops.  Use with caution.

Spantree port 3/1-24 fast start enabled.
Cat5500> (enable)
```

UplinkFast

Because of the calculations and communication required when performing a spanning-tree update, substantial time may pass before the update completes—as much as 30 to 60 seconds. This is generally only disruptive when there is a failure situation, not when a bridge is added. Unfortunately, a failure event is when you're most interested in having the network reconfigure itself quickly. It doesn't sound like much, but 30 to 60 seconds is enough for some network applications to fail, and for users to pick up the phone and complain. The amount of time needed for the redundant links to become active is called the *convergence time*.

Cisco provides an enhancement to plain spanning tree, called UplinkFast. Basically, it takes a set of ports and constructs an uplink group. In this arrangement, one of the links is designated primary and the others are secondary. If the primary link goes down, the secondary can take over, but no spanning-tree convergence has to take place. When calculating spanning tree, the Catalyst treats the group as a single path; therefore, as long as part of the group is active, it doesn't have to perform a full spanning-tree convergence, which is much slower.

UplinkFast is generally useful only in networks where a deliberate switch hierarchy has been built. In this hierarchy, there's a set of switches at some central point, fed by access switches to which the stations are attached. In order to set up UplinkFast, you have to manually set a root for the spanning tree, and possibly a secondary. So if you've got such a physical layout already in place, designating the primary and secondary can be easy. When your network layout is fairly linear, however, this feature may not be appropriate for you.

Here is a highly abbreviated list of the steps required to set up UplinkFast:

1. **Designate a root switch.**

   SET SPANTREE ROOT *vlans* [DIA *network_diameter*] [HELLO *hello_time*]

   The *vlans* parameter is list of VLANs. The *diameter* is the maximum number of bridges between any two stations (from 1 to 7). The *hello_time* is the hello time you saw in the BPDU Hello packet earlier. This command is done on the root switch.

2. **Enable UplinkFast on each subordinate switch.**

   SET SPANTREE UPLINKFAST {enable|disable} [RATE *station_update_rate*]

   The enable|disable parameter is obvious. The *rate* is a Hello timer of sorts that allows the switches to verify that a link is alive. This number controls how many frames will be sent in a 100ms period of time.

These brief steps do not provide enough information to understand all that's required to start manually configuring spanning tree on the Catalysts, which is what these SET SPANTREE commands essentially do. Cisco's Web site provides an excellent document covering these topics in detail:

http://www.cisco.com/univercd/cc/td/doc/product/lan/cat5000/rel_4_2/config/spantree.htm

If you're considering reconfiguring your switch to allow for better convergence time, make sure to do your research and understand all the factors involved. It takes a fair amount of work to get to the point where you've manually configured the switches to do better than the defaults and automatic methods, and then you have to maintain it.

CERTIFICATION OBJECTIVE 11.04

Troubleshooting with the Span Port

One of the capabilities a network manager loses when a switch is used to replace a repeater is the ability to do packet capturing. On a repeated network segment, any of the stations on that segment, or any monitoring device attached to that segment, has the capability to get a copy of every frame or packet that goes by on the cable. This capability is commonly used by network managers to troubleshoot problems. Switches increase security on a network somewhat, by limiting network monitoring by unauthorized stations, but they also limit the legitimate network manager.

To retain this capability, Catalyst switches have the SPAN feature. SPAN is a slightly contrived acronym for Switch Port Analyzer—but good acronym or not, SPAN is a very useful feature. It allows a network manager, who has full rights on the switch, to designate a port to mirror frames that pass through the switch. There are a couple of ways to select the frames that will be copied to that port, and we'll go over those shortly.

Here are the SPAN commands:

```
SET SPAN ENABLE
SET SPAN DISABLE
SET SPAN src_mod/src_port dest_mod/dest_port [ rx | tx | both ]
SET SPAN src_vlan dest_mod/dest_port [ rx | tx | both ]
```

But before you enable SPAN, let's take a thorough look at the default settings.

By default, port 1/1 is the monitoring port, or the port to which the copies of the frames will be sent. The default monitoring source is all of VLAN 1, both transmit and receive. This means, if you were using 1/1 for anything important (like a critical station, a trunk port, an ISL link, etc.), and you type SET SPAN ENABLE without setting any ports, *you will have just killed it.*

Obviously, I emphasize this because I've made this mistake myself. SET SPAN ENABLE starts copying traffic immediately, whether you're ready or not. What you want to do *before* you issue SET SPAN ENABLE is to issue one of the last two SET SPAN commands just listed. The source can be either a single port or an entire VLAN (as it exists within that chassis). The settings RX, TX, and BOTH let you choose if you want to see traffic received, transmitted, or both by the port or VLAN being monitored. Most of the time, you'll want to do both.

Naturally, you'll need to attach your monitoring device (such as an RMON probe or Sniffer) to the port marked as the destination.

Spanning a Switch Port

Spanning a single port is fairly intuitive. When a port is spanned to another port for both transmit and receive, a copy of all the frames entering and leaving the monitored port are sent to the destination port. This allows you to attach your Sniffer or other packet analyzer, and troubleshoot conversations between that station and other stations. Some of what you *won't* see are problems in other parts of the network that are congested, or dropped packets. You'll simply see the symptom, which is dropped or retransmitted packets.

It should also be somewhat obvious that if you're monitoring from a low-speed port such as a 10MB link, and you're monitoring a higher-speed link such as a 100MB link, you may lose traffic at times. I've tried this configuration before, and on at least the older Catalyst software I got some unexpected behavior. Even though the amount of traffic on the 100MB link was much less than 10MB at any given time, I wasn't seeing all of the frames on my Sniffer. In fact, it seemed the Catalyst was "pulsing" packets at me. I'd get a few seconds of frames, followed by a few seconds of no traffic at all. I knew that the traffic was running continuously, so that wasn't the issue. This problem may have been fixed in newer versions of the Catalyst software, but try it ahead of time to make sure that a 100MB Sniffer isn't required— before you're stuck finding out during an emergency.

Spanning a VLAN

Many of the same caveats that apply for spanning a single port are also true for spanning a VLAN—more so, in fact. Obviously, for most VLANs, the aggregate traffic will be more than a single port normally generates, so using a high-speed port to attach your monitoring device is almost imperative. It's worth noting that this will only get you copies of traffic that cross the chassis you're attached to. The span feature will not collect copies of all traffic in that VLAN from other switches, despite the fact that they also contain that VLAN.

CERTIFICATION OBJECTIVE 11.05

Common Problems and Fixes

There's one basic problem to solve on the Catalyst switches: They don't pass frames the way you think they should, either at all or consistently. Reasons range from simple configuration errors to bugs in the Catalyst software. First we'll go over some specific things to examine when troubleshooting problems, and then we'll look at common problems and configuration errors.

The SHOW Commands (CAM DYNAMIC, VLAN, MODULE, and PORT)

Most of your initial troubleshooting will begin by using the SHOW commands. Let's look at each of the most common ones.

SHOW CAM DYNAMIC

All intelligent bridges have to keep tables of MAC addresses in order to make forwarding decisions. The bridges also have timers attached so that a bridge table entry doesn't stick around forever; if it did, and if a station were moved to a different switch, the station wouldn't be reachable from the first switch. Catalyst switches also can do VLANs, as we've discussed, so they keep per-VLAN bridge tables. Thus it's possible to have the same MAC address appear in two different VLANs, and the Catalyst will still be able to keep them separate.

Duplicate MAC addresses aren't supposed to happen, but Sun computers will typically have the same MAC address on all interfaces installed in one system. This can also occur with DECNet if duplicate DECNet addresses appear, because DECNet changes the MAC address to be a function of the DECNet address. This is not a problem for Catalyst switches, as long as the duplicate MAC addresses are in separate VLANs.

The SHOW CAM commands essentially show you the bridge tables of a Catalyst. This can be useful in verifying that a Catalyst has learned the location of a MAC address properly, or when for some reason you're trying to track down a station and all you have is the MAC address.

SHOW VLAN

The SHOW VLAN command tells you which ports are assigned to which VLAN, as well as the settings for each VLAN (the SAID and MTU, etc.).

You would normally use this command to sanity-check that you've got things configured the way you think you do—that is, to ensure the port you're trying to use is in the right VLAN.

SHOW MODULE

The SHOW MODULE command displays information about modules installed in the Catalyst chassis. You'd use this command to make sure that the supervisor recognizes that the card is installed, for example.

SHOW PORT

SHOW PORT is one of the commands you'll likely use often. It displays all the port-level configuration information and statistics. Here's a sample:

```
Cat5500> (enable) show port 1/1
Port  Name               Status      Vlan        Level  Duplex Speed Type
----  ------------------ ----------  ----------  ------ ------ ----- ---------
 1/1  uplink             connected   10          normal full    100 100BaseFX MM

Port   Security  Secure-Src-Addr    Last-Src-Addr      Shutdown  Trap
-----  --------  ----------------   ----------------   --------  --------
 1/1   disabled                                        No        disabled

Port      Broadcast-Limit Broadcast-Drop
--------  --------------- --------------
 1/1            -              -
Port   Status     Channel    Channel    Neighbor                  Neighbor
                  mode       status     device                    port
-----  ---------- ---------- ---------- ------------------------- ---------
 1/1   connected  auto       not channel

Port  Align-Err  FCS-Err    Xmit-Err   Rcv-Err    UnderSize
----- ---------- ---------- ---------- ---------- ----------
 1/1           0          0          0          0          0

Port  Single-Col Multi-Coll Late-Coll  Excess-Col Carri-Sen Runts      Giants
----- ---------- ---------- ---------- ---------- --------- ---------- ----------
 1/1           0          0          0          0         0          0          0
```

In this output you'll find all the information about what speed and duplex the port is running at, all your error statistics, and so on.

Disabled Ports

Use the show port command to see if all is well with the port in question. You can ensure that it's in the right VLAN, not shut down, doesn't have security enabled with the wrong MAC address, and so on. Some of these things are obvious, but network managers have to fix the obvious problems, too.

Missing VTP Domain

If you are having trouble with VLAN information being propagated, do a SHOW VTP and double-check your settings. Make sure your domain is set (not blank) and spelled exactly the same as on all the other Catalysts. Make sure the VTP versions match on all Catalyst switches. Make sure VTP is enabled. Make sure the VTP password matches if it's set on other Catalysts.

Deleted VLAN

What happens to ports in a particular VLAN if that VLAN is deleted? The ports become inactive, while retaining the old VLAN number. If you are troubleshooting and discover ports in an inactive state, make sure their VLAN is defined. The VLAN may have been deleted on this switch, or on a VTP server.

10/100 Autodetect Broken

Not all 10/100 NIC cards deal well with Autodetect. Problems range from less-than-optimal negotiated settings, to the cards' not being able to pass traffic at all, or only intermittently. The usual fix for difficulties of this nature is to hard-code the port to a particular speed and duplex. You'll probably find that older Sun hardware running SunOS 4.1.3 and earlier (unpatched) will have problems, as will various PC NICs. With the PC

NICs, a reboot will often take care of it, or sometimes an OS setting is needed.

Wrong Speed

If either the Catalyst or the NIC is running at the wrong speed, you won't be working very well. It's fairly easy to check the speed on the Catalyst, which gives you both a light and a software interface to investigate. Depending on the NIC type and OS running on the station, it might not be as easy at that end. One way to test would be to manually set a speed on the Catalyst.

Mismatched Duplex

Problems caused by duplex mismatches can be subtle and difficult to diagnose. In general, the communications will work...to a point. Duplex problems center around collisions: One side will think a collision occurred, but the other won't. This results in lost frames and transport retransmits, which tend to degrade performance significantly. The "half-collisions" go up as traffic increases.

Depending on which side thinks it's half duplex and which one thinks it's full duplex, you may or may not see errors on the Catalyst. (Most of the time you will.) Alignment errors are the most common result of this problem. The test and/or fix is to force the duplex by setting it to full or half on the Catalyst.

Code Rev Not Supporting New Module

Missing software support can range from obvious (module not recognized) to subtle. Subtle incompatibilities may look like card resets, partial functionality, and the like. In general, you'll want to be diligent about following the bug reports and keeping your Catalyst running with the newer code revs. Some of the bugs in even the most recent code are pretty serious.

QUESTIONS AND ANSWERS

What is the short list of steps to add a new Catalyst to an existing Catalyst network?	Install the hardware. Connect a terminal to the console. Assign a VTP domain and other VTP information to match the rest of the network. Assign an IP address to the switch. Assign a trunk port if needed. Assign ports to VLANs.
What do I do if the ports say they're inactive?	Check that the VLAN to which they're assigned is defined on that switch. If it's a new card, make sure your software version is new enough to support the card.
How do I track down a node on my switch network?	Get the MAC address, possibly via an ARP table. Do a SHOW CAM DYNAMIC on each switch that has the appropriate VLAN, and look for the MAC address.
I want to use a SPAN port to monitor traffic.	Set a destination port before you do a SET SPAN ENABLE. Also make sure that you're monitoring the right port or VLAN (default is all of VLAN 1 in that switch).
I plugged my running laptop into the switch, but I can't get a DHCP address.	With the default settings, it will take 30 to 60 seconds for a port on a switch to become "live." This is to avoid loops. If just waiting a minute is a problem in your situation, carefully read this chapter's section on PortFast.
Is there any way to reduce the amount of time it takes for the network to reroute to a redundant path when a link goes down?	With careful design, UplinkFast can be used in conjunction with normal spanning tree features to reduce convergence time for specific redundant links.
Some of my servers aren't running at 100MB, even though they have 100MB cards and I've got them patched into 100MB-capable switch ports. Why?	Various NIC cards don't always properly auto-sense 100MB and/or full duplex. Solutions may include forcing the switch to 100/full, rebooting the servers, or manually configuring the server software.

CERTIFICATION SUMMARY

VLANs provide the key features that network managers need in order to effectively manage their networks. These features include greater aggregate bandwidth, configuration flexibility, and easier management. To enable these features, Cisco Catalyst switches provide a number of features not found on standard bridges and less-capable switches.

Catalyst switches are port-assigned switches. A number of configuration options are available at the port level, including automatic speed and duplex detection for Fast Ethernet, and security options.

VLANs are a way of maintaining separate broadcast domains within the same physical chassis. Catalyst switches provide VLAN features for a number of LAN types, including Ethernet, FDDI, and Token Ring. Ports can be assigned to a VLAN individually or as a group. Some options can be set on a per-VLAN basis, including a descriptive name, MTU, SAID, and more. Cisco provides the VTP protocol to automatically distribute VLAN configuration information. This can be used to maintain consistency across multiple switches, and to ensure that changes are propagated to other switches. VTP pruning is provided to solve the problem of broadcasts being flooded to all switches.

ISL is a protocol that Cisco has developed to trunk multiple VLANs across a Fast Ethernet link while still keeping the VLANs distinct. By default, an ISL trunk when it is first assigned will carry all VLANs. When ISL is used in conjunction with VTP, it can provide a very effective and manageable VLAN solution.

Spanning tree is a Layer 2 protocol used by bridges to communicate with other bridges. This communication is needed to prevent loops in the network and to provide a degree of redundancy in case of a failed link. By default, all ports on a Catalyst participate in the spanning tree (unless they're disabled). This causes a delay when a station is first plugged into a Catalyst switch, before the station can communicate. One way to shorten that delay is to use the PortFast feature, if the network manager is sure there will be no loops created via that port. In order to improve the convergence time of the spanning tree, Cisco provides a feature called UplinkFast.

 # TWO-MINUTE DRILL

- ❑ The Cisco Catalyst family includes a number of models, including the 2900, 5000, 5500, and 8500 families.

- ❑ To address network separation, switch manufacturers came up with the concept of virtual LANs or VLANs. A VLAN is a logical broadcast domain that can span multiple switches.

- ❑ For most network needs, the Catalyst comes with a very good set of defaults, and usually one doesn't have to change much more than the VLAN number on a set of ports, and set a VTP domain and version number.

- ❑ On Fast Ethernet modules with a default configuration, when a station is plugged into the switch, the switch will attempt to automatically determine if the station is capable of 100MB operation and whether it can do full duplex.

- ❑ Implementing the security feature means that the Catalyst will only accept frames from a particular MAC address (this feature is for Ethernet modules only).

- ❑ Basically, to create a new VLAN, you pick a number between 2 and 1005, inclusive (1 is already there by default). You'll also want to assign some ports to the VLAN.

- ❑ With VTP, most of the changes and settings get propagated automatically.

- ❑ Note that mixing VTP versions does NOT work, and the default setting is for all Catalysts to do VTP1.

- ❑ Cisco recommends that you use VTP2 if all of your switches are running a software version that is capable of VTP2.

❑ ISL (Inter-Switch Link) is Cisco's protocol for trunking VLANs over Fast Ethernet.

❑ Bridges will arrange for their interfaces to be shut off automatically if there is a redundant path, or loop.

❑ A *spanning tree* is a way of representing a set of nodes and links (in our case, a network) such that there is only one path used between any two points.

❑ Bridges communicate with other bridges via Bridge Protocol Data Units, or BPDUs.

❑ Cisco provides an enhancement to plain spanning tree, called UplinkFast.

❑ SPAN allows a network manager, who has full rights on the switch, to designate a port to mirror frames that pass through the switch.

❑ When a port is spanned to another port for both transmit and receive, a copy of all the frames entering and leaving the monitored port are sent to the destination port.

❑ Many of the same caveats that apply for spanning a single port are also true for spanning a VLAN.

❑ There's one basic problem to solve on the Catalyst switches: They don't pass frames the way you think they should, either at all or consistently.

❑ Most of your initial troubleshooting will begin by using the SHOW commands.

❑ Use the show port command to see if all is well with the port in question.

❑ If you are having trouble with VLAN information being propagated, do a SHOW VTP and double-check your settings.

❑ If you are troubleshooting and discover ports in an inactive state, make sure their VLAN is defined.

❑ Not all 10/100 NIC cards deal well with Autodetect.

❑ It's fairly easy to check the speed on the Catalyst, which gives you both a light and a software interface to investigate.

❑ Duplex problems center around collisions: One side will think a collision occurred, but the other won't.

❑ In general, you'll want to be diligent about following the bug reports and keeping your Catalyst running with the newer code revs. Some of the bugs in even the most recent code are pretty serious.

SELF TEST

The following Self Test questions will help you measure your understanding of the material presented in this chapter. Read all the choices carefully, as there may be more than one correct answer. Choose all correct answers for each question.

1. A VLAN is equivalent to a:

   A. Trunk

   B. Broadcast domain

   C. Port

   D. Module

2. Switches are similar to what network device?

   A. Routers

   B. Repeaters

   C. Bridges

   D. Firewalls

3. Catalyst switches use what type of VLAN assignment, primarily?

   A. IP address

   B. MAC address

   C. SAID

   D. Port

4. Catalyst switches can auto-sense speed and duplex on which of the following LAN types?

   A. Token Ring

   B. Ethernet

   C. Fast Ethernet

   D. FDDI

5. Which protocol is used to distribute VLAN information between switches?

   A. Spanning Tree Protocol (STP)

   B. Virtual Trunking Protocol (VTP)

   C. Bridge Protocol Data Units (BPDU)

   D. 802.10

6. Of the following, which is the biggest disadvantage of VTP?

   A. Broadcasts flood to every switch by default

   B. Have to configure domain name on every switch

   C. Each switch has to have a different VTP password

   D. Slower than spanning tree

7. UplinkFast is recommended for what kind of network layout?

   A. Single switch

   B. Linear

   C. Hierarchical

   D. Full mesh

8. Which command is used to display the bridge tables in a Catalyst switch?

   A. SHOW MAC

   B. SHOW VLAN

C. SHOW PORT

D. SHOW CAM

9. Which command is used to set up a monitoring port to use with a Sniffer?

A. SET SPAN

B. SET CAM

C. SET VLAN

D. SET PORT

10. Which version of the Catalyst software introduced VTP version 2?

A. 2.3(4)

B. 3.1(1)

C. 4.1(1)

D. 5.1(2)

11. Disabling which of the following could lead to loops?

A. UplinkFast

B. PortFast

C. Spanning tree

D. VTP

12. What are the default SPAN settings?

A. Copy VLAN 1 to 1/1

B. Copy 1/1 to 1/2

C. Do ports defined

D. All VLANs to the fastest port

13. Which command is used to check for errors for a particular station?

A. SHOW MODULE

B. SHOW CAM

C. SHOW VLAN

D. SHOW PORT

14. The behavior of forwarding broadcasts to all ports in a bridge is called:

A. Spanning

B. Forwarding

C. Flooding

D. Pruning

15. In order for stations to communicate across VLANs without bridging them together, what is usually required?

A. A bridge

B. A hub

C. A router

D. A firewall

16. The default SAID is the VLAN number, plus

A. 1000

B. 10000

C. 100000

D. 1000000

17. Intelligent bridges keep tables of what kind of addresses?

A. IP

B. CAM

C. IPX

D. MAC

18. Configuring port security will accomplish what?

A. Keep hackers out

B. Turn off the port

C. Accept frames only from a particular MAC address

D. Turn off VLAN functions

19. BPDU Hello frames are addressed
    to what?

    A. MAC broadcast

    B. MAC multicast

    C. Catalyst switches

    D. IP broadcast

20. Cisco's enhancement to the Spanning
    Tree Protocol to reduce the amount of
    time it takes to bring up a redundant link
    is called:

    A. PortFast

    B. ISL

    C. UplinkFast

    D. VTP

CISCO CERTIFIED NETWORK PROFESSIONAL

12

Hands-on Troubleshooting

T

oday's networks come in a variety of topologies and are becoming increasingly more complex. The problems that can occur are equally varied and complex. In this chapter we will look at numerous technologies, from LANs to WANs. Topics include Ethernet, Token Ring, TCP/IP, IPX, and AppleTalk.

We will discuss common problems that occur on each network, and propose possible courses of action. These actions will aid in isolating the problem. This problem definition is a valuable step, since you must first isolate the problem before you can begin to solve it. Solutions can then be found by using the tools provided by Cisco, coupled with other helpful troubleshooting tools, such as the ping and trace commands and the protocol analyzers. The key is to follow a sound troubleshooting method.

Even if you are unable to solve a problem on your own, do not fear— Cisco has provided its customers with additional help. There are several places where you can get answers to your troubleshooting horrors. At the end of this chapter are lists of Cisco support functions that you can turn to for guidance.

CERTIFICATION OBJECTIVE 12.01

Troubleshooting LANs

In the category of LAN troubleshooting, we will cover three common LAN technologies: Ethernet, Token Ring, and FDDI. This section concentrates on Ethernet and Token Ring because they are the most widely used LAN technologies in the business world today. Troubleshooting FDDI networks will be covered briefly, as well. Before you can successfully troubleshoot any type of network, you must first have a good understanding of how the technology works.

Ethernet

Ethernet is the oldest and most prevalent LAN topology today. Ethernet stations operate on the principle of Carrier Sense Multiple Access with Collision Detection (CSMA/CD). CSMA/CD is an effective yet simple technology that forces stations to compete for access to the media. The contention-based nature of Ethernet prevents any one station from using all available 10 Mbps bandwidth. Hence the term *shared media,* which you will also see in connection with Ethernet.

Xerox Corporation's Palo Alto Research Center (PARC) initially developed Ethernet in the 1970s. Digital Equipment Corporation and Intel later joined Xerox in defining the "DIX" Ethernet specification, which was released in 1990. The IEEE 802.3 committee used Ethernet technology as its model for CSMA/CD LAN specification. Consequently, Ethernet and IEEE 802.3 are very similar. Today all CSMA/CD LANs are referred to as Ethernet.

Stations on a CSMA/CD LAN can gain access to the network at any point. To ensure the proper timing of transmission, before sending data the station listens to the network to see if it is currently being used. If so, then the station waits until the network is clear. If the network is not in use, the station begins to transmit. When the station transmits, collisions are possible. Collisions occur when two stations listen to the network, hear no ongoing transmission, and then send more or less simultaneously. When a collision happens, both stations must retransmit at a later time. Algorithms exist that determine when the stations can retransmit. Because Ethernet is a CSMA/CD-based technology, the stations detect collisions, thus knowing when retransmission is necessary.

To effectively troubleshoot an Ethernet LAN, you must first have an understanding of its physical wiring limitations and the frame format for Ethernet. Three defined wiring standards are 10BaseT, 10Base2, and 10Base5. Ethernet operates at a baseband signaling rate of 10 Mpbs, hence the "10Base" notation in the wiring standards.

10BaseT is the most popular cabling option. It uses unshielded twisted-pair cabling (UTP), uses a repeater to connect all stations together logically, and has a 100-meter distance limitation. 10Base2 uses RG58 AU cable, does not need a repeater, accommodates up to 30 stations, and has a total cable length limitation of 185 meters. 10Base5 uses coax cable, serves up to 100 stations, and allows total length not exceeding 500 meters.

An *Ethernet frame* consists of a preamble, destination address, source address, type field, data field, and the frame check sequence (FCS), as illustrated in Figure 12-1.

- The *preamble* announces to all receiving nodes that a frame is coming.

- The address fields are 6 bytes long. Addresses are found in the hardware interface cards in each station. The *destination address* field contains the address of the station receiving the data. The source address field contains the address of the station sending the data. The *source address* must be a single address, but the destination address can be multiple addresses, denoting a *multicast* (two or more stations) or *broadcast* (all stations).

- The *type field* identifies the protocol to use for receiving the data after processing is complete.

- The *data field* contains the actual data, which will eventually reach its destination and go to an upper-level protocol.

- The *FCS field* contains a cyclic redundancy check (CRC) value. This CRC value is used to ensure that the entire frame was delivered intact and correctly.

When troubleshooting Ethernet, the most useful Cisco IOS command is SHOW INTERFACES ETHERNET. We will now take a close look at the detailed information that can be extracted from this command. The syntax

---

FIGURE 12-1

Parts of an Ethernet frame

Preamble 8 bytes	Destination Address 6 bytes	Source Address 6 bytes	Type 2 bytes	Data	FCS 4 bytes

is shown in Table 12-1, and the command display is shown in Figure 12-2. Later, we will use this tool to solve several common Ethernet problems.

Note: To use the show interfaces command, you must be in privileged mode.

If you do not provide any additional options, the default command displays information on all network interfaces. The optional keywords let you show statistics on specific interfaces.

Common Ethernet Problems

■ Occurrence of collisions (jabbering—when an Ethernet NIC transmits data continuously)

Response: Check collision rate by using show interfaces ethernet command. The ratio of collisions to number of output packets should be 0.1. Check for unterminated Ethernet cables with a time-domain reflectometer (TDR). Check transceivers attached to stations; look for media problems.

TABLE 12-1	**Command**	**Options/Description**
Cisco IOS Ethernet Troubleshooting Commands	SHOW INTERFACES ETHERNET *unit* [accounting]	**unit** Must match a port number on the selected interface. **accounting** (Optional) Displays the number of packets of each protocol type that have been sent through the interface.
	SHOW INTERFACES ETHERNET [slot/port] [accounting] (for the Cisco 7200 series and Cisco 7500 series routers)	**slot** (Optional) Refer to the appropriate hardware manual for slot and port information. **port** (Optional) Refer to the appropriate hardware manual for slot and port information.
	SHOW INTERFACES ETHERNET [type slot/port-adapter/port] (for ports on VIPs in the Cisco 7500 series routers)	**type** (Optional) Type of interface. **port-adapter** (Optional) Refers to the appropriate hardware manual for information about port-adapter compatibility.

FIGURE 12-2   Command display for the SHOW INTERFACES ETHERNET command

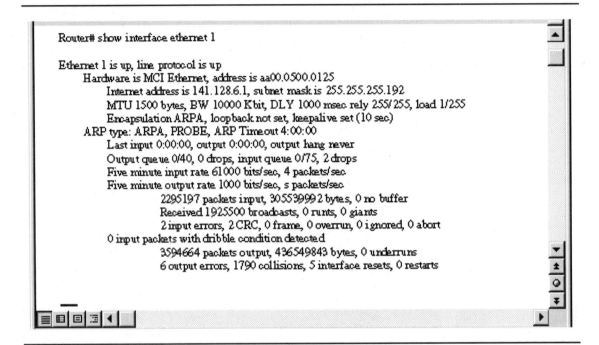

```
Router# show interface ethernet 1

Ethernet 1 is up, line protocol is up
     Hardware is MCI Ethernet, address is aa00.0500.0125
          Internet address is 141.128.6.1, subnet mask is 255.255.255.192
          MTU 1500 bytes, BW 10000 Kbit, DLY 1000 msec, rely 255/255, load 1/255
          Encapsulation ARPA, loopback not set, keepalive set (10 sec)
     ARP type: ARPA, PROBE, ARP Timeout 4:00:00
          Last input 0:00:00, output 0:00:00, output hang never
          Output queue 0/40, 0 drops, input queue 0/75, 2 drops
          Five minute input rate 61000 bits/sec, 4 packets/sec
          Five minute output rate 1000 bits/sec, s packets/sec
               2295197 packets input, 305539992 bytes, 0 no buffer
               Received 1925500 broadcasts, 0 runts, 0 giants
               2 input errors, 2 CRC, 0 frame, 0 overrun, 0 ignored, 0 abort
     0 input packets with dribble condition detected
               3594664 packets output, 436549843 bytes, 0 underruns
               6 output errors, 1790 collisions, 5 interface resets, 0 restarts
```

- **Occurrence of runt frames**

Response: There is a limit to the size of frames an Ethernet segment can transmit. The maximum is 1518 bytes and the minimum is 64 bytes. *Runt frames* are a violation of the minimum 64-byte frame size. Runt frames are a result of bad software on a network interface card (NIC), if the frame occurs with low collision rate or in a switched network. Find the source address of the bad frame with a protocol analyzer. Runt frames may also result from late collisions when shared media networks exceed maximum length specifications.

- **Occurrence of noise on wire**

Response: Check the CRC errors and collision rate by using show interfaces ethernet command. If numerous errors are occurring and there is a low collision rate, this usually indicates a high noise level. Check cabling for damage. Look for reflections being caused by bad taps spacing. Check to be sure that you are using the appropriate cabling (that is, Category 5 cabling is being used when necessary).

Token Ring

Token Ring networks operate by using a token-passing method. The second most popular LAN technology, Token Ring allows every station equal access to the media, thus solving Ethernet's problem with simultaneous transmissions causing collisions. With Token Ring, when a station wants to transmit, it waits until it has possession of a special frame called a *token*. Upon the arrival of the token, the station creates a data frame and transmits. All other stations on the ring relay the frame around until it reaches the designated station. Token Ring NICs are smarter than Ethernet NICs. Token Ring NICs manage the ring, in addition to sending and receiving data.

Token Ring was developed in the 1970s by IBM. IEEE 802.5 is very similar to Token Ring, and the term Token Ring often refers to both IEEE 802.5 networks and IBM's Token Ring networks.

Stations on a token-passing ring take turns using the media. A station can transmit only when it receives the token. This allows all stations equal access to the media, so no one station can dominate the cable. If the station has no data to send, it simply passes the token to the next station. However, when a station wants to transmit data, it receives the token by altering one bit of the token frame and then appends its information. The token and information are then forwarded to the next station on the ring. The token/information frame is forwarded around the ring until it reaches the destination station. The station copies the frame, then tags the frame as received. The frame continues around the ring until it reaches the source station, where it is removed from the ring. With token passing, only one frame can be on the ring at a time. All other stations must wait until they possess the token before they can transmit.

Traffic on a Token Ring consists of *data frames* and *token frames*. The data frame contains information similar to an Ethernet frame (destination address, source address, data field, and a frame check sequence (FCS). The token frame is simply 3 bytes long, consisting of a start delimiter, access control byte, and an end delimiter. Both frames are illustrated in Figure 12-3.

FIGURE 12-3

Parts of a token frame and
a data frame

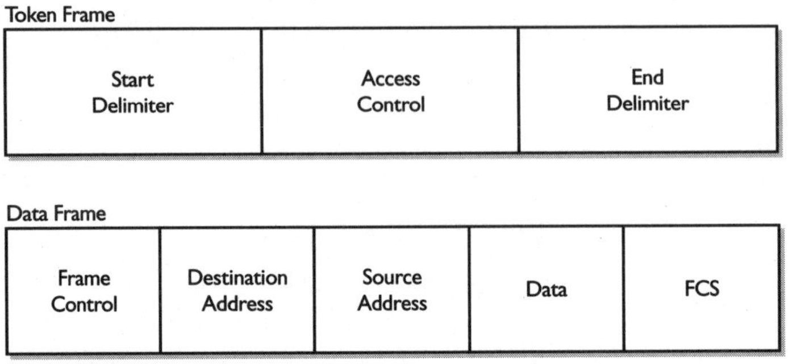

Token Frame

Start Delimiter	Access Control	End Delimiter

Data Frame

Frame Control	Destination Address	Source Address	Data	FCS

When troubleshooting a Token Ring network, use the SHOW INTERFACES TOKENRING command. We will now take a close look at the detailed information that can be extracted from this command. The syntax is shown in Table 12-2. Figure 12-4 shows the command display. Later, we will use this tool to solve several common token ring problems.

Note: To use the show interfaces command, you must be in privileged mode.

If you do not provide any additional options, the default command displays information on all network interfaces. The optional keywords let you show statistics on specific interfaces.

Common Token Ring Problems

■ **Ring is congested**

Response: Check to see if installation of ring is successful during low traffic periods. If so, then you may need to segment your network to distribute the traffic.

■ **Ring is not functioning**

Response: Check Token Ring statuses by using show interfaces tokenring command. If the status shows a line or protocol down, check physical cabling. If this is a new installation, verify that the multistation access unit (MSAU) is initialized.

Command	Options/Description
SHOW INTERFACES TOKENRING *unit* [accounting]	**unit** Must match a port number on the selected interface. **accounting** (Optional) Displays the number of packets of each protocol type that have been sent through the interface.
SHOW INTERFACES TOKENRING [slot/port] [accounting] (for the Cisco 7200 series and Cisco 7500 series routers)	**slot** (Optional) Refer to the appropriate hardware manual for slot and port information. **port** (Optional) Refer to the appropriate hardware manual for slot and port information.
SHOW INTERFACES TOKENRING [type slot/port-adapter/port] (for ports on VIPs in the Cisco 7500 series routers)	**type** (Optional) Type of interface. **port-adapter** (Optional) Refer to the appropriate hardware manual for information about port-adapter compatibility.

■ **"Open Lobe Fault" message at console**

Response: This message indicates a relay open in MAU. Check the cable to the MAU. Reset the interface by using the clear interface command. Verify the interface status by using show interfaces tokenring. The line protocol and interface should be in up/up status.

If the problem persists, disconnect devices from MAU and reset the MAU. Reconnect the router and verify interface status by using the show command. If the problem persists, connect the router to a MAU you know is working correctly, to help isolate the problem.

Check Token Ring cards and cable wiring. If the problem continues, replace cabling and check status of the interface to verify it is functional.

Fiber Distributed Data Interface (FDDI)

We will cover FDDI only briefly because it is not as prevalent as Ethernet or Token Ring. FDDI is a token-passing technology that uses a dual ring.

| FIGURE 12-4 | The command display for SHOW INTERFACES TOKENRING |

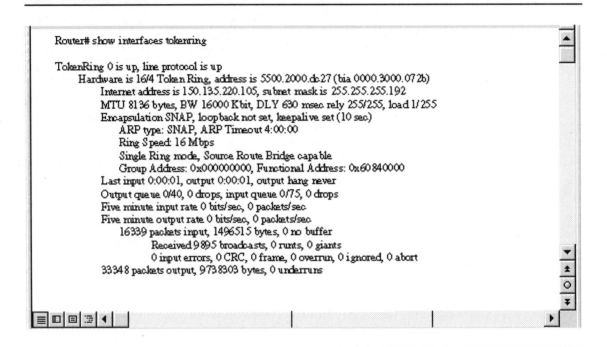

```
Router# show interfaces tokenring

TokenRing 0 is up, line protocol is up
    Hardware is 16/4 Token Ring, address is 5500.2000.dc27 (bia 0000.3000.072b)
        Internet address is 150.135.220.105, subnet mask is 255.255.255.192
        MTU 8136 bytes, BW 16000 Kbit, DLY 630 msec rely 255/255, load 1/255
        Encapsulation SNAP, loopback not set, keepalive set (10 sec)
            ARP type: SNAP, ARP Timeout 4:00:00
            Ring Speed: 16 Mbps
            Single Ring mode, Source Route Bridge capable
            Group Address: 0x00000000, Functional Address: 0x60840000
        Last input 0:00:01, output 0:00:01, output hang never
        Output queue 0/40, 0 drops, input queue 0/75, 0 drops
        Five minute input rate 0 bits/sec, 0 packets/sec
        Five minute output rate 0 bits/sec, 0 packets/sec
            16339 packets input, 1496515 bytes, 0 no buffer
                Received 9895 broadcasts, 0 runts, 0 giants
                0 input errors, 0 CRC, 0 frame, 0 overrun, 0 ignored, 0 abort
        33348 packets output, 9738303 bytes, 0 underruns
```

Networks with FDDI backbones do exist, but these network backbones are rapidly being replaced by newer technologies such as ATM and Gigabit Ethernet.

To troubleshoot an FDDI ring, you continue to use your basic troubleshooting techniques. The Cisco IOS command SHOW INTERFACES FDDI is helpful in solving FDDI problems. This command is used in a very similar manner to the show interfaces ethernet and show interfaces tokenring commands. Figure 12-5 shows the command display.

Note: Because an FDDI ring cannot have collisions, the collisions field is always zero.

FIGURE 12-5 The command display for SHOW INTERFACES FDDI

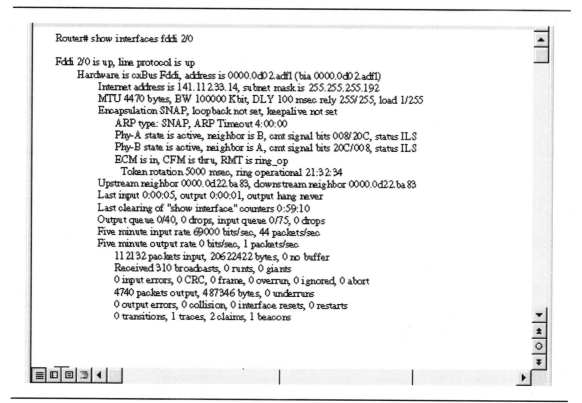

```
Router# show interfaces fddi 2/0

Fddi 2/0 is up, line protocol is up
    Hardware is cxBus Fddi, address is 0000.0d02.adf1 (bia 0000.0d02.adf1)
        Internet address is 141.11.2.33.14, subnet mask is 255.255.255.192
        MTU 4470 bytes, BW 100000 Kbit, DLY 100 msec, rely 255/255, load 1/255
        Encapsulation SNAP, loopback not set, keepalive not set
            ARP type: SNAP, ARP Timeout 4:00:00
            Phy-A state is active, neighbor is B, cmt signal bits 008/20C, status ILS
            Phy-B state is active, neighbor is A, cmt signal bits 20C/008, status ILS
            ECM is in, CFM is thru, RMT is ring_op
                Token rotation 5000 msec, ring operational 21:32:34
        Upstream neighbor 0000.0d22.ba83, downstream neighbor 0000.0d22.ba83
        Last input 0:00:05, output 0:00:01, output hang never
        Last clearing of "show interface" counters 0:59:10
        Output queue 0/40, 0 drops, input queue 0/75, 0 drops
        Five minute input rate 69000 bits/sec, 44 packets/sec
        Five minute output rate 0 bits/sec, 1 packets/sec
            112132 packets input, 20622422 bytes, 0 no buffer
            Received 310 broadcasts, 0 runts, 0 giants
            0 input errors, 0 CRC, 0 frame, 0 overrun, 0 ignored, 0 abort
            4740 packets output, 487346 bytes, 0 underruns
            0 output errors, 0 collision, 0 interface resets, 0 restarts
            0 transitions, 1 traces, 2 claims, 1 beacons
```

Common FDDI Problems

■ **FDDI ring is not functioning**

Response: Check status of FDDI interfaces by using show interfaces fddi command. Test connectivity between routers by pinging the gateway addresses. Verify that the MAC addresses of neighbors are correct. If you see all zeros in the address fields, then check physical connectivity.

exam
ⓦatch

In questions dealing with troubleshooting tools, be sure to look for the commands listed in this chapter's syntax tables. These are the most common commands used to troubleshoot each type of network.

CERTIFICATION OBJECTIVE 12.02

Troubleshooting WANs

Wide area networks (WANs) have the primary purpose of connecting LANs. There are several different methods of connecting local area networks into a wide area network. WAN types include dedicated point-to-point, X.25, Frame Relay, Switched 56, SMDS, and ATM. Although there are many different ways to interconnect LANs, we will focus on troubleshooting serial connections, Frame Relay networks, and Integrated Services Digital Network (ISDN) connections.

Serial Line Connections

This section discusses the use of show and debug commands to help troubleshoot serial line connections in a WAN environment.

Checking for errors in your serial line connections should be the first step in troubleshooting a WAN or serial line problem. To view the errors of your serial line, use the SHOW INTERFACES SERIAL command. Other useful show commands for troubleshooting a line problem are listed in Table 12-3.

TABLE 12-3	Command	Description
Cisco IOS Serial Line Troubleshooting Commands	SHOW INTERFACES SERIAL	Displays information about the serial interface. Usually a good indicator if the serial line is working correctly.
	SHOW LINE	Displays terminal line parameters. Useful when troubleshooting a modem problem.
	SHOW CONTROLLERS	Displays configuration and error information. Can be used with multiple parameters.
	SHOW BUFFERS	Displays buffer pools statistics.

exam
ⓌatcH

Be sure to familiarize yourself with the SHOW CONTROLLERS commands. Pay particular attention to the cable type (DCE or DTE). The syntax is **SHOW CONTROLLERS {bri|e1|ethernet|fddi|lex|mci|pcbus|serial|token}.**

The debug commands, as well, are helpful tools when troubleshooting a serial line.

- **DEBUG SERIAL INTERFACE** can be used to determine if HDLC keepalive packets are incrementing. There may be a timing problem on the interface card or on the network if the packets are not increasing.

- **DEBUG SERIAL PACKET** will print out error messages to indicate why a packet was not sent or why it was received incorrectly.

CSU/DSU (channel service unit/data service unit) loopback tests are extremely helpful in determining the source of WAN problems. Loopback tests do not apply to X.25 or Frame Relay networks. They work best in HDLC and PPP networks.

EXERCISE 12-1

Conducting a Loopback Test

1. Put the CSU/DSU in local loopback mode.

2. Check to see if the line status changes from "down" to "up" (looped) by using the show interfaces serial command. If the line remained "downed," the problem may be in the router, cabling, or CSU/DSU. Otherwise, the problem is likely on the other end of the serial connection.

3. If it is a local problem, turn on debug, with the debug serial interface command.

4. Take the CSU/DSU out of local loopback mode. View the output of the debug command and note that the keepalive counters are not incrementing.

5. Put the CSU/DSU back in local loopback mode. The keepalive packets should begin to increment. If they do not, then you probably have a router hardware problem. Replace the router interface.

6. Check the routers at both ends of the serial link. Use show interfaces serial on each router, and view the output for errors or abort messages.

7. Check the cabling, making sure it is within recommended lengths. Be sure all cabling is attached to the correct ports.

Common Serial Line Problems

Serial line problems can often be determined by viewing the status of the line interface.

■ **Serial connection is UP, but the line protocol is DOWN**

Response: This problem could be caused by router misconfiguration, a timing problem on the cable, router hardware failure, or keepalives not being sent by the remote router. Perform the CSU/DSU loopback test to isolate the problem. If the line protocol does come up during the loopback test, it is possible there is a telephone company problem.

■ **Serial connection is DOWN, and the line protocol is DOWN**

Response: This situation can be due to a telephone company problem, a cabling issue, or faulty hardware. Check to ensure you are using the correct cable and router interface. Make sure the CSU/DSU is working properly by checking the lights (LEDs) on the box. Contact your leased line carrier to determine if they are having difficulties.

ISDN

ISDN is a set of digital services available to end-users. It involves digitizing the telephone network so that data, graphics, text, video, and voice will flow over existing telephone wiring. The ISDN Basic Rate Interface (BRI) service offers two B channels and a D channel (2B+D). The B channel service operates at 64 Kbps and is used to carry data. The D channel operates at a slower 16 Kbps and is used for carrying signaling and control information.

The SHOW ISDN command displays information about calls, history, memory, status, and timers. This command is key when troubleshooting an

ISDN problem. Other helpful commands include SHOW ISDN SERVICE and SHOW ISDN NFAS GROUP.

Common ISDN Problems

■ **ISDN router does not dial**

Response: There are numerous possible causes for this problem. First, check your router configuration for ISDN to ensure it is correct. Possible router misconfigurations could be in your dialer-map command, or dialer-list, or even an access list could be the cause. Next, be sure to check the status of the interface, to be sure it is not in shutdown mode.

■ **Unable to communicate with remote ISDN router interface**

Response: Check to make sure there is a route to the remote network by using the show route command. Also check the configuration for dialer-map; it must point to the correct next-hop address. Dialer-group must be configured on both the local and remote routers.

This problem may also be caused by PPP (Point-to-Point Protocol) encapsulation or Challenge Handshake Authentication Protocol (CHAP) being misconfigured. Check your configurations and make sure they are correct.

■ **Slow performance across the ISDN link**

Response: Check for input or output errors by using the show interfaces commands. If you see errors, clear them and then see if the values are incrementing. If this happens, you should contact your carrier because this indicates poor line-quality.

Also check to see if a lot of packets are being dropped. You may need to adjust the hold queues, and this may solve your problem. To adjust hold queues, use the commands HOLD-QUEUE *<length>* OUT or HOLD-QUEUE *<length>* IN. Increase the queue that is dropping the packets.

■ **ISDN line disconnects when not being used**

Response: Check your configuration for the DIALER FAST-IDLE command. If the line disconnects too quickly when idle, this timer is too low and needs to be increased. Also be sure that the DIALER IDLE-TIMEOUT value is set. The default is 120 seconds. You may need to increase this timer, as well.

Frame Relay

Frame Relay was originally conceived as a protocol for use over ISDN interfaces. It provides a packet-switching data communications capability that is employed across the interface between user devices. These user devices are also referred to as data terminal equipment (DTE). The network equipment that interfaces with the DTE is called data circuit-terminating equipment (DCE). Useful commands when troubleshooting Frame Relay networks are listed in Table 12-4.

Useful debug tools for troubleshooting Frame Relay are

- **DEBUG FRAME-RELAY LMI**, which will help determine if a Frame Relay switch and router are sending and receiving LMI packets.

- **DEBUG FRAME-RELAY EVENTS** will help you see if any exchanges are taking place between a router and a Frame Relay switch.

TABLE 12-4	Command	Description
Cisco IOS Frame Relay Troubleshooting Commands	SHOW FRAME-RELAY PVC	Displays statistics on PVCs for Frame Relay interfaces
	SHOW FRAME-RELAY MAP	Displays current map entries and information about the connections
	SHOW FRAME-RELAY LMI	Displays statistics on Local Management Interface (LMI)
	SHOW FRAME-RELAY ROUTE	Displays all currently configured Frame Relay routes
	SHOW FRAME-RELAY TRAFFIC	Displays global statistics since reload

Common Frame Relay Problems

■ **Your Frame Relay link goes down**

Response: Use the show interfaces command to see the link status. Check for physical problems, such as cabling or hardware. Next check to see if keepalives are being sent. To do this, use the show interfaces command and set the keepalives if they're not yet configured. The default value for the KEEPALIVE *<seconds>* command is 10 seconds. If the keepalive command is already configured, check the encapsulation type. Encapsulation mismatch could also be the cause of the down link. Also, use the show frame-relay pvc command to check that the DLCIs are assigned to the correct subinterfaces.

■ **Unable to communicate with a remote router across Frame Relay link**

Response: Check for encapsulation mismatch and misconfigured access lists. Use the show frame-relay pvc command to check that the DLCIs are assigned to the correct subinterfaces. Also check to see if the frame-relay map command is missing from your configuration. To do this, use the show frame-relay map command. See if an address map has been entered for the DLCI, and if it's missing add a static address map (syntax for this command is listed in the next problem description).

■ **The permanent virtual circuit (PVC) in your Frame Relay network is UP, but you are unable to ping across to the other router**

Response: Check your frame-relay map statement. To do this, use the show frame-relay map command. Verify that the address is correct. If there is no map to the DLCI, add a static address map. The syntax is as follows:

FRAME-RELAY MAP
<protocol><protcol-address><dlci>[broadcast][ietf|cisco]

Verify that the DLCIs and next-hop addresses are correct. The *protocol-address* should be in the same network as your Frame Relay interface.

■ **Your site comes up automatically, but it fails after the frame mapping is done**

Response: Check your frame-relay map statement. Add the broadcast keyword. By default the broadcast keyword is added to dynamic maps learned through inverse ARP. Addition of the broadcast keyword identifies that all broadcasts should be forwarded to the specified address.

CERTIFICATION OBJECTIVE 12.03

Troubleshooting TCP/IP

Transmission Control Protocol/Internet Protocol (TCP/IP) is a well-known protocol that is often used to communicate across networks that are interconnected. TCP/IP can be used in a LAN environment, as well as a WAN environment. This section covers tools and commands useful when troubleshooting TCP/IP. It also presents common TCP/IP problems and techniques to solve these problems.

Since TCP/IP works at the Network layer, most tools you will use for troubleshooting will be with your router. These tools include the show and debug commands.

The show commands will display pertinent information about the status of the interface and protocol, as well as traffic and routes. Useful show commands are listed in Table 12-5.

Using debug commands will allow you to see messages that will help determine if your protocol is running correctly. Some valuable debugging commands are shown in Table 12-6.

Note: Be careful when using debug commands, because some of them will generate a lot of output for each processed packet. Try to use debug during off-peak hours.

The ping and trace commands are also very valuable when troubleshooting.

■ The ping command sends an Internet Control Message Protocol (ICMP) echo request to a group. If the request is received by a station, a reply is sent to the source host.

■ The trace command uses the error message generated by routers when a datagram exceeds its Time To Live (TTL). With trace, you can view the path taken to reach a specified destination.

Common TCP/IP Problems

■ **Users can access some hosts but not others on remote networks**

Response: This problem is often caused by misconfigured subnet masks or addresses on hosts. First check the subnet and IP information on host and router, to be sure it is configured correctly. Another possible cause is not having a default gateway specified on the local host. If a default gateway has not been configured, the host will be unable to reach any remote networks.

TABLE 12-5	Command	Description
Cisco IOS IP Troubleshooting Commands	SHOW IP ACCESS-LIST	Displays current IP access lists, similar to filtering
	SHOW IP ARP	Displays ARP (Address Resolution Protocol) cache
	SHOW IP INTERFACE	Displays usability status of interface
	SHOW IP MASKS	Displays masks applied to network addresses and number of subnets for each mask
	SHOW IP NAT STATISTICS	Displays NAT (Network Address Translation) statistics
	SHOW IP OSPF DATABASE	Displays database-related information; can be specified using parameters
	SHOW IP PROTOCOLS	Displays active routing protocol's status and parameters
	SHOW IP ROUTE	Displays entries in the routing table; very useful when troubleshooting
	SHOW IP TRAFFIC	Displays IP traffic statistics

Command	Description
DEBUG ARP	Displays information about ARP transactions. Shows whether router is sending and receiving ARP replies and requests.
DEBUG IP EIGRP	Lets you view Enhanced IGRP packets sent and received on an interface.
DEBUG IP ICMP	Helps determine whether router is sending or receiving ICMP messages. Useful when troubleshooting end-to-end connectivity.
DEBUG OSPF EVENTS	Displays information on OSPF events, such as flooding information, designated router, and shortest path first calculations.
DEBUG IP PACKET	Displays IP debugging information and security option transactions.
DEBUG IP RIP	Displays information on RIP routing table updates sent and received on an interface.

Also, be sure to check the router to see if restrictions are set using access lists. Access lists work as filters and will not allow access to a specified network or hosts.

■ **User tries to access hosts and receives "Host Not Found" replies; all hosts appear to be dead**

Response: First try reaching the host using the IP address. This will help you to determine if the problem is with the host or with your Domain Name System (DNS). If you are able to gain access using the IP address, try using the host name of other systems to see if you can reach them. If you are unable to reach any host using the name, DNS may no longer be up and running. Check your DNS software to resolve the issue. However, if the host name gets you access to some hosts, this may indicate that your DNS table is incomplete. DNS needs to be updated to include all IP address-to-host name mappings.

■ **User gets new machine and moves IP address; now no one is able to connect**

Response: Use the show ip arp command to view the ARP cache. The ARP table contains the MAC address-to-IP address mappings. The ARP cache may not have aged out. You will need to clear the cache by using clear arp-cache command. This should solve the problem because the new ARP table will reflect the new MAC address/IP address mapping.

■ **In a network running DHCP, a host is not receiving its address, default gateway, and other configuration information from the server**

Response: This problem occurs when the router is missing the necessary helper address for the DHCP server. The helper address should be set to the server address. To do this, use the command IP HELPER-ADDRESS *<ipaddress>*. This can be set per interface. If, on the other hand, you check the router and the helper address statements seem to be correct, the problem may be that all available addresses have been previously leased. To correct this problem, increase your address pool.

■ **Can ping some hosts but not others; there are no access control lists associated with the hosts**

Response: This problem is usually due to duplicate routes in the routing tables. Check the routing table, using the show commands, and adjust accordingly. This situation also may occur due to discontinuous subnets if you are using a distance vector protocol such as RIP.

exam

ⓦatch

Remember to review IP addressing and binary conversion before the exam. Oftentimes you will be asked to segment a network or apply a subnet mask. You need to be able to do the binary calculations by hand. Also, in troubleshooting, you sometimes will have to determine an incorrect mask to identify a problem.

QUESTIONS AND ANSWERS

My router is seeing duplicate routing updates.	A bridge is being used in conjunction with the router.
Some of my protocols are being routed, while others are not.	Incorrect access lists. Use your trace command to pinpoint the router that has the incorrect access list. This is usually the point where the tracert will stop. Telnet to the router and check the route table by using show ip route. To test the access list, try disabling them all, and then bring them back up one at a time while pinging the remote node. When the pings start to time out, you will know which access list had the undesirable effect. Correct the list and retest.
I lose my connection as the load of my serial link gets greater.	Overutilized serial line or dirty serial line.
My serial line goes down at a certain time every day.	Congested serial line, overused at a particular time of the day. Pay attention to the time of day your link is going down and try to determine what is causing the increase in traffic. It may be that backups being run at that time can be done during off-hours instead, thus solving your problem. Or the problem may be a symptom of a larger issue. Be sure to investigate to determine the root cause.
My Novell NetBIOS packets cannot get past the router.	Input the ipx type-20-propagation command into your router configuration. You must enter into configuration mode before you can add this command to your configuration.
I can't talk to my local IPX server.	Workstation is configured with wrong encapsulation frame type. Check the configuration files on the workstation to see if it is using the correct frame type.
I can't talk to my remote IPX server.	Workstation or router is configured with wrong encapsulation frame type. Check the configuration files on the workstation to see if it is using the correct frame type. Also, check the router by using the show run command; this will show you the current running router configuration. Check out what frame encapsulation is being used. Be careful not to use show config, because this will only show you the configuration that was last saved.

QUESTIONS AND ANSWERS

In my AppleTalk network, sometimes my services are dropped unexpectedly.	Check your routes, looking for an unstable route. Also check for a ZIP storm.
In my AppleTalk network, I can see the services but I can't connect to them.	Incorrect access list.

CERTIFICATION OBJECTIVE 12.04

Troubleshooting IPX

The Internetwork Packet Exchange (IPX) is a Network layer protocol whose purpose is to provide connectionless, best-effort transport service to upper-layer protocols such as SPX, NCP, and NetBIOS. IPX was created in the early 1980s by Novell, Inc. This section discusses useful tools and commands when troubleshooting an IPX network. We will also examine problems encountered while using IPX and techniques to solve these problems.

Under IPX, services are advertised using Service Advertising Protocol (SAP). One type of SAP advertisement is Get Nearest Server (GNS), which enables a client to locate the nearest login server. GNS runs when a client first powers up; it is a broadcast from the client. The nearest NetWare file server responds with a SAP. At that point, the client can log in to the server, make a connection, set the packet size, and use the server's resources.

Note: Cisco has modified the behavior of Get Nearest Server (GNS) responses. The router only responds if there are no servers on the local segment.

Because IPX also works at the Network layer, most tools you will use for troubleshooting include the show and debug commands.

The show commands will display pertinent information about the status of the interface and protocol, as well as traffic and routes. Useful show commands are listed in Table 12-7.

TABLE 12-7	Command	Description
Cisco IOS IPX Troubleshooting Commands	SHOW IPX ACCESS-LIST	Displays current IPX access lists, similar to filtering
	SHOW IPX CACHE	Displays IPX fast switching cache
	SHOW IPX INTERFACE	Displays status of IPX interface
	SHOW IPX SERVERS	Displays IPX servers found through SAP advertisements
	SHOW IPX NHRP	Displays Next Hop Resolution Protocol cache
	SHOW IPX NLSP DATABASE	Displays entries in link-state packet database; can be specified using parameters
	SHOW IPX EIGRP INTERFACES	Displays interfaces configured for Enhanced IGRP
	SHOW IPX ROUTE	Displays entries in the IPX routing table; very useful when troubleshooting
	SHOW IPX TRAFFIC	Displays IPX information about packets transmitted and received

Using debug commands allows you to see messages that will help you determine if the IPX protocol is running correctly. Some valuable IPX debugging commands are shown in Table 12-8.

Note: Be careful when using debug commands because some of them will generate a lot of output for each processed packet. Try to use debug during off-peak hours.

Common IPX Problems

■ **Server is not sending SAP updates**

Response: Use a protocol analyzer to check for SAP updates. Also, check the frame encapsulation for SAP updates.

If there is a mismatch between node and router, configure the proper encapsulation type by using the command ENCAPSULATION *<encapsulation type>*. Verify the new setting with the show interfaces command.

TABLE 12-8	Command	Description
Cisco IOS IPX Debug Troubleshooting Commands	DEBUG IPX PACKET	Displays information about packets received, forwarded, and sent.
	DEBUG IPX ROUTING	Displays information on IPX packets the router sends and receives.
	DEBUG IPX SAP	Displays information on SAP advertisements the router sends and receives. Additional parameters are available for this command to access more detailed information on SAP packets.

■ **While booting up, the host connects to a remote server instead of the local server**

Response: This problem is due to the gns-response-delay parameter that can be set in the router. In Cisco IOS software release 9.1(13), the default delay is set to zero milliseconds. If you are using earlier software versions, you may have to manually decrease the GNS response delay to improve response time. If you are using Cisco IOS 9.1(13) or later, you may have to manually increase the GNS response delay if a host has a slow processor or NIC. Otherwise, the host may miss the response from the router. The command to set GNS response delay is

IPX GNS-RESPONSE-DELAY *<#ofmilliseconds>*

■ **You created an access list that allows a SAP through, but you are still unable to see it at the next hop**

Response: Be careful when using access lists. In this case, check to see if the route to the next hop has been specified, as well.

■ **Host cannot connect to server on a remote LAN**

Response: A possible cause could be duplicate network numbers. Use the show ipx servers command to look for duplicates. Duplicate network numbers can prevent packets from being forwarded correctly. All network numbers must be unique throughout the entire internetwork.

If this is not the cause, check to ensure that the router interface is up; check encapsulation types; and check your hardware for problems such as a bad port.

■ **Client can see server but is unable to establish a connection**

Response: Check to see if any access lists have been applied that may prevent connectivity.

■ **Applications such as Windows 95 cannot connect to servers over the router**

Response: Using the debug ipx packet command, look for any Novell packets with a specification of type 20. Type 20 packets are NetBIOS service over IPX and can only be carried 7 hops from their origin in an IPX network. A file-server SAP can travel 15 hops, but the station attempting to connect to it from 8 hops away will fail. If you see these packets, be sure that you have executed the IPX TYPE-20-PROPAGATION command on each interface in the path from client to the server.

If there are packets other than type 20, check that your ipx helper-addresses are configured properly.

exam
ⓦatch

If you see the words "Novell" or "NetWare," in responses to debug commands, immediately look for answers regarding IPX or any components of IPX (such as SAP advertisements).

CERTIFICATION OBJECTIVE 12.05

Troubleshooting AppleTalk

AppleTalk is a proprietary network, developed in the early 1980s by Apple Computer, Inc. AppleTalk was designed as a client/server distributed network system to be used with Macintosh computers. Clients or nodes are assembled in logical groups called *zones*. Each node can be in only one zone.

When a client wants to access a service, a request is sent to the router for a list of zones. The Name Binding Protocol (NBP) looks for servers in the specified zone. The router forwards a request to each cable group in the specified zone. A multicast goes to all nodes that match the device type requested. Replies are sent by all available matching services. The reply is forwarded until it reaches the original router. The router sends the reply to the client, which then selects a service.

The show commands will display pertinent information about the status of the interface and protocol, as well as traffic and routes. Useful show commands are listed in Table 12-9.

With debug commands, you can see messages that will help determine if your protocol is running correctly. Some valuable debugging commands are shown in Table 12-10.

Note: Be careful when using debug commands, because some of them generate a lot of output for each processed AppleTalk packet. Try to use them during off-peak hours.

TABLE 12-9

Cisco IOS AppleTalk Troubleshooting Commands

Command	Description
SHOW APPLETALK ACCESS-LIST	Displays currently defined AppleTalk access lists
SHOW APPLETALK ARP	Displays Address Resolution Protocol (ARP) cache entries
SHOW APPLETALK INTERFACE	Displays usability status of interface
SHOW APPLETALK ZONE	Displays entries in zone information table
SHOW APPLETALK ROUTE	Displays entries in the AppleTalk routing table; very useful when troubleshooting
SHOW APPLETALK TRAFFIC	Displays AppleTalk traffic statistics
TEST APPLETALK	Can be used to perform informational lookups of NBP entities

	Command	Description
TABLE 12-10 Cisco IOS AppleTalk Debug Troubleshooting Commands	DEBUG APPLE ARP	Displays information about ARP transactions. Shows whether router is successfully sending and receiving AARP replies and requests. Note: ARPs in the Apple world are most commonly referred to by the acronym AARP.
	DEBUG APPLE NBP	Displays output from NBP routines.
	DEBUG APPLE ROUTING	Displays output from Routing Table Maintenance Protocol (RTMP) routines.
	DEBUG APPLE ZIP	Displays important Zone Information Protocol (ZIP) events.

Common AppleTalk Problems

■ Zones appear in the list, but no devices appear in the device list when a service is selected

Response: This problem is the result of a misconfigured access list. Use the show appletalk access-list command to view configuration of current access lists. Disable the access list, and then check to see if devices appear. If a device appears, that means that the access list needs to be reconfigured to filter appropriately.

■ User complains that network services are sometimes unavailable

Response: A possible cause is a duplicate network number or incorrect cable range. Check to be sure network numbers are unique and that cable ranges are not overlapping.

exam
ⓦatch

The two most common problems in an AppleTalk network are duplicate network numbers and unmatched configurations. So when you're presented with a problem, check to see if the routers all have the correct cable-range setting and list of zones. Then verify that the overlapping networks do not have the same cable ranges.

■ The router seems to be unable to discover routes; the port is trapped in acquiring mode

Response: Assign a network number or cable range to the router interface. This will put it in nondiscovery mode.

exam Watch

If you're given a problem with a Macintosh in your network, you must be running AppleTalk as a network protocol. This is usually in addition to running IP or IPX.

CERTIFICATION OBJECTIVE 12.06

Using Cisco Support Functions

If you have totally exhausted all possibilities and need some assistance in problem solving, Cisco provides support. You can get additional troubleshooting help online, by telephone, or in the form of a CD-ROM. Cisco has a broad range of services geared for helping Cisco customers.

Cisco Connection Online (CCO) help is available 24 hours a day, 7 days a week at http://www.cisco.com. CCO is a valuable self-help resource that provides Cisco customers with guided assistance. The CCO family includes CCO Documentation, CCO Open Forum, CCO CD-ROM, and the TAC (Technical Assistance Center).

exam Watch

Check out the Cisco Web site before taking any exam, because things are often changing. New developments may have occurred since the publishing of this book.

CCO Docs

The CCO Documentation area provides manuals and technical tips at Cisco's main Web site. Do a search to find specific product documentation.

CCO Open Forum

In the CCO Open Forum you can benefit from the wealth of knowledge of CCIEs and Cisco technical experts. This forum provides access to databases you can search for answers to your problems. For more difficult issues, you can consult technical experts willing to help.

CD-ROM

The Documentation CD-ROM is a library of product news, the newest bugs, end-user information, and other related topics. The latest and greatest versions of the documents can be found at

http://www.cisco.com/univercd/home/home.htm

Contact Cisco to order an annual subscription to the Documentation CD-ROM.

Cisco Technical Assistance Center (TAC)

For unsolved problems, you can open a ticket or case with the TAC, and qualified persons will help you. Your ticket will be tracked and followed through to a resolution. You can open a ticket online or by telephone.

CERTIFICATION SUMMARY

When faced with a network problem of any scope, your most powerful weapon will be knowledge. You must know about the network for which you're responsible, and understand how data flows throughout the network. This knowledge, coupled with a sound troubleshooting methodology and proper diagnostic tools, equip you with the necessary ammunition to effectively solve any network problem you may encounter. Be very familiar with the tools that are available to you; that will make it easier to determine the root of the problem and naturally lead you to possible solutions.

Remember: When troubleshooting, change only one variable at a time. A common mistake is to just jump into a problem and try to fix it. Don't assume anything, and keep an open mind. For example, a particular group of symptoms could falsely indicate a problem with a server, when in fact the server might be experiencing a problem due to another component's configuration issue.

Always be calm and don't panic. Take your time to analyze the symptoms, and determine a logical course of action. Of course, we hope the outcome of your actions will result in a solution. If your first action plan is unsuccessful, return the network to its original state and try action plan number two. Remember that Cisco does provide you with additional sources of help if needed.

Here are some additional troubleshooting tips:

- Never rule out physical hardware or cabling problems. Often, physical failure is the cause and is very easy to fix.

- Always verify encapsulation type with IPX.

- When working with IP, if you're unable to reach a node, check the subnet masking.

- When on any network with access lists configured and you're unable to reach a segment, always check the access list.

- Be familiar with all show protocol commands. They will be your windows into the network.

- Remember to use the many resources around you—your coworkers, online technical assistance, documentation, and your own common sense.

 TWO-MINUTE DRILL

- ❑ Ethernet stations operate on the principle of Carrier Sense Multiple Access with Collision Detection (CSMA/CD). CSMA/CD is an effective yet simple technology that forces stations to compete for access to the media.

- ❑ An Ethernet frame consists of a preamble, destination address, source address, type field, data field, and the frame check sequence (FCS).

- ❑ When troubleshooting Ethernet, the most useful Cisco IOS command is SHOW INTERFACES ETHERNET.

- ❑ There is a limit to the size of frames an Ethernet segment can transmit. The maximum is 1518 bytes and the minimum is 64 bytes. Runt frames are a violation of the minimum 64-byte frame size.

- ❑ The second most popular LAN technology, Token Ring allows every station equal access to the media, thus solving Ethernet's problem with simultaneous transmissions causing collisions.

❑ Traffic on a Token Ring consists of data frames and token frames.

❑ The data frame contains information similar to an Ethernet frame (destination address, source address, data field, and a frame check sequence (FCS).

❑ The token frame is simply 3 bytes long, consisting of a start delimiter, access control byte, and an end delimiter.

❑ When troubleshooting a Token Ring network, use the SHOW INTERFACES TOKENRING command.

❑ To use the show interfaces command, you must be in privileged mode.

❑ Because an FDDI ring cannot have collisions, the collisions field is always zero.

❑ Checking for errors in your serial line connections should be the first step in troubleshooting a WAN or serial line problem.

❑ DEBUG SERIAL INTERFACE can be used to determine if HDLC keepalive packets are incrementing.

❑ DEBUG SERIAL PACKET will print out error messages to indicate why a packet was not sent or why it was received incorrectly.

❑ The SHOW ISDN command displays information about calls, history, memory, status, and timers. This command is key when troubleshooting an ISDN problem.

❑ The ping command sends an Internet Control Message Protocol (ICMP) echo request to a group. If the request is received by a station, a reply is sent to the source host.

❑ The trace command uses the error message generated by routers when a datagram exceeds its Time To Live (TTL).

❑ Cisco has modified the behavior of Get Nearest Server (GNS) responses. The router only responds if there are no servers on the local segment.

❑ For unsolved problems, you can open a ticket or case with the TAC, and qualified persons will help you. Your ticket will be tracked and followed through to a resolution.

SELF TEST

This Self Test can be used as a tool to help measure your understanding of hands-on troubleshooting material covered in this chapter. Please read the questions carefully and choose the best answers.

1. To use the Cisco IOS show interfaces commands, you must be in which mode?

   A. Line

   B. Privileged

   C. User

   D. Config

2. What is the command to check collision rate?

   A. show interface rates

   B. show ethernet collisions

   C. show interface ethernet

   D. show collision rate

3. What is indicated by lots of errors with a low collision rate?

   A. Poor physical connection

   B. High noise-level

   C. Trouble with network monitoring software

   D. Runt frames

4. A Token Ring network works great during periods of low traffic, but sometimes gets congested. A possible solution is to:

   A. Segment the network.

   B. Switch to Ethernet.

   C. Reboot all routers.

   D. Add additional nodes to your network.

5. Which of the following is *not* a type of LAN technology?

   A. FDDI

   B. Ethernet

   C. TCP/IP

   D. Token Ring

6. What loopback tests are extremely helpful in determining the source of a WAN problem?

   A. CSU/DSU

   B. CDU/SCU

   C. Wide area network

   D. Local area network

7. Which of the following describes ISDN BRI service channeling?

   A. 2D+B

   B. B+D

   C. 2B+D

   D. 2C+D

8. If your Frame Relay link goes down, which of the following will you *not* check?

   A. Look for physical problems, such as cabling or hardware.

   B. Check to see if keepalives are being sent.

   C. Look for encapsulation mismatch.

   D. Check that token frames are not corrupt.

9. What difficulty may occur when you're using certain debug commands on your network?

   A. Runt frames

   B. Increase in traffic

   C. Serial line failure

   D. NIC interface problems

10. A user gets a new machine and moves the IP address. Suddenly no one is able to connect. What is the *most* likely cause?

   A. Router is misconfigured.

   B. ARP cache hasn't aged out.

   C. Token frame is corrupt.

   D. The new machine is not network compatible.

11. What command is used to set GNS response delay?

   A. ipx gns-response-delay <*#ofmilliseconds*>

   B. ipx gns-response-delay <*#ofseconds*>

   C. gns-response-delay <*#ofseconds*>

   D. gns-delay <*#ofseconds*>

12. You created an access list that allows a SAP through, but you are still unable to see it at the next hop. Which of the following are *not* likely causes? (Choose two.)

   A. Misconfigured access lists

   B. Unspecified route to next hop

   C. Incorrect IP address

   D. Incorrect subnet mask

13. What does the debug ipx sap command display?

   A. Information on SAP advertisements the router sends and receives

   B. Information on SAP advertisements the router sends

   C. Information on SAP advertisements the router receives

   D. IPX protocol status

14. What does the debug appletalk zip command display?

   A. Important Zone Information Protocol (ZIP) events

   B. Zone Information Protocol (ZIP) errors

   C. Zone Information Packet (ZIP) errors

   D. AppleTalk protocol status

15. The router seems to be unable to discover routes, and the port is trapped in acquiring mode. What is a possible solution?

   A. Replace cabling

   B. Assign a network number or cable range to the router interface

   C. Reboot the router

   D. Re-address workstations in your network

16. What does NBP stand for?

   A. Network Binding Protocol

   B. Name Bonding Protocol

   C. Name Binding Protocol

   D. Network Binding Packet

17. What is the Web site URL for Cisco Connection Online (CCO) help?

    A. http://www.cisco-help.com

    B. http://www.cisco.com

    C. http://www.cisco.help.com

    D. www.cisco.help.com

18. Where can you go to find Cisco software upgrades?

    A. CCO Software Center

    B. Cisco Technical Assistance Center

    C. CCO Documentation

    D. TAC

19. IPX works at what layer?

    A. Transport

    B. Internet

    C. Network

    D. Data link

13

Troubleshooting the ISDN Basic Rate Interface (BRI)

CERTIFICATION OBJECTIVES

I SDN, the Integrated Services Digital Network, enjoys continued growth in the networking world as service providers expand their ISDN offerings. Three markets in particular fuel the demand for ISDN services. First, ISDN is an excellent backup technology for primary WAN links, such as Frame Relay, in cases of failure and overload. ISDN also offers the appropriate price-to-performance ratio to the SOHO (Small Office Home Office) market, for intermittent connectivity to headquarters locations and the Internet. Finally, ISDN has been the method of choice for telecommuters whose bandwidth requirements often exceed the capabilities of the analog modem for dial-up access to corporate networks. The size of the ISDN installed base and its well-trained network professionals will ensure a place for ISDN in the network infrastructure of the future, even in the face of competing "last-mile" technologies.

We will examine a methodical, step-by-step approach to ISDN BRI (Basic Rate Interface) troubleshooting in this chapter. This approach empowers you with the ability to pinpoint and resolve ISDN issues in a matter of minutes (not days). We will begin at the Physical layer, using checkpoints along the way to verify our progress as we approach the upper layers of ISDN and PPP (Point-to-Point Protocol).

CERTIFICATION OBJECTIVE 13.01

The ISDN Physical Layer

ISDN Basic Rate Interface is a "last-mile" technology that allows digital connections over the same copper wires that deliver analog Plain Old Telephone Service (POTS). These digital connections allow data speeds that approach 128 Kbps. The ISDN BRI connection consists of three Time Division Multiplexed (TDM) channels—commonly referred to as 2B+D. The two Bearer (B) channels run at a 64 Kbps rate, while the D channel runs at a 16 Kbps rate. The D channel is responsible for call setup and control signaling for the two B channels. This method of signaling is what we refer to as "out-of-band" signaling, in which call setup and control information are carried in a logical channel separate from the data. The B channels carry actual user data, either together or separately.

ISDN is delivered from the telephone company central office (CO). The service utilizes the installed base of 2-wire local copper loops to the customer premise. ISDN's high data-rate over existing copper is achieved through the use of a Physical layer encoding called 2B1Q. This encoding scheme consists of four voltage levels between −3 volts and +3 volts, which each represent a 2-bit binary pattern. As a result, the actual bit rate is twice the signal baud (number of signal changes per second). They don't call it the International Signaling Device of Nerds (ISDN) for nothing, do they?

The ISDN CO Switch

The ISDN switch in the CO is loaded with special software that allows it to be an ISDN BRI switch. Unfortunately for us, the various ISDN switch vendors chose to implement the ISDN standard in various ways. The nice thing about standards is that we have so many to choose from! As a result, we have to configure the switch type in the Cisco router.

The IOS configuration commands to configure your switch type are as follows:

```
ATLANTA# CONFIGURE TERMINAL
ATLANTA(CONFIG)# ISDN SWITCH-TYPE {your switch-type}
```

Be aware that the *switch-type* entered in this command is a software load and not necessarily of the same type as the hardware or vendor of the actual switch. In North America the most common BRI switch types are the basic-5ess, the basic-dms100, and the basic-ni. The output shown in Figure 13-1 contains a list of switch types.

This *switch-type* parameter should be supplied by your ISDN service provider. If it is necessary to change your switch type after the initial configuration, be aware that a reload of the router will be necessary. In addition, keep in mind that the Cisco IOS can support multiple ISDN switch types on the same router if you are running IOS 11.3T or higher code. In this case, enter an isdn switch-type command in global configuration mode (as just shown), and also configure different switch types on a per-interface basis.

ISDN BRI switch-types
available on the
Cisco router

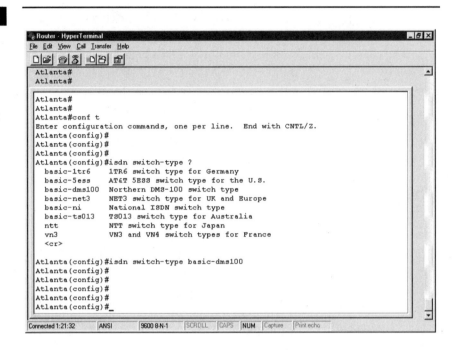

```
Router - HyperTerminal                                                    _ 8 X
File  Edit  View  Call  Transfer  Help

D |☞| ☺|☝| ☖☖| ☞|

Atlanta#                                                                    ▲
Atlanta#

Atlanta#
Atlanta#
Atlanta#conf t
Enter configuration commands, one per line.  End with CNTL/Z.
Atlanta(config)#
Atlanta(config)#
Atlanta(config)#
Atlanta(config)#isdn switch-type ?
  basic-1tr6    1TR6 switch type for Germany
  basic-5ess    AT&T 5ESS switch type for the U.S.
  basic-dms100  Northern DMS-100 switch type
  basic-net3    NET3 switch type for UK and Europe
  basic-ni      National ISDN switch type
  basic-ts013   TS013 switch type for Australia
  ntt           NTT switch type for Japan
  vn3           VN3 and VN4 switch types for France
  <cr>

Atlanta(config)#isdn switch-type basic-dms100
Atlanta(config)#
Atlanta(config)#
Atlanta(config)#
Atlanta(config)#
Atlanta(config)#_                                                          ▼
Connected 1:21:32    ANSI      9600 8-N-1   SCROLL  CAPS  NUM  Capture  Print echo
```

The NT1 Device

The NT1 device lies between the ISDN switch and the Cisco ISDN
interface or Terminal Adapter (both referenced as the *Terminal Endpoint* or
TE). The NT1 converts the 2-wire copper loop from the telephone
company (referred to as the U-loop), into a 4-wire ISDN interface (called
the S/T bus). To make it a bit clearer, the NT1 will be labeled with a U jack
and an S/T jack. The U jack plugs into the wall, and the S/T jack plugs into
your ISDN BRI interface on the Cisco router. Both are typically connected
with straight-through RJ-45 cables, even though some pins will go unused.

Be aware that many ISDN TE devices will have the NT1 built into the
BRI interface. In this case, the BRI interface will be labeled as a U interface
and cabled directly into the ISDN wall jack. Whether the NT1 is built into
the hardware or external to the ISDN device, look for an LED labeled
"NT1" or "Active." This LED is illuminated (usually green) when the
ISDN TE is activated by the ISDN NT1.

Verifying Layer 1 Activation

Layer 1 activation requires the following events: The TE begins the whole process by signaling "01111110" until the NT1 returns at least three 48-bit frames with the A (Active) bit set to 0. These frames consist of 16 bits for the B1 channel; 16 bits for the B2 channel; 4 bits for the D channel; the A bit; and 11 more bits for frame synch, DC balancing, and line management. The TE then begins sending its own 48-bit frames to the NT1. Upon receipt of these frames, the NT1 starts sending 48-bit frames with the A bit set to 1. At this point, Layer 1 is UP.

On the Cisco router, the command

SHOW ISDN STATUS

is the most heavily utilized command when troubleshooting ISDN BRI. A Layer 1 (the Physical layer) status of ACTIVE indicates proper cabling and Physical layer communication with the ISDN switch (see Figure 13-2). This

FIGURE 13-2

ISDN Physical Layer in ACTIVE state

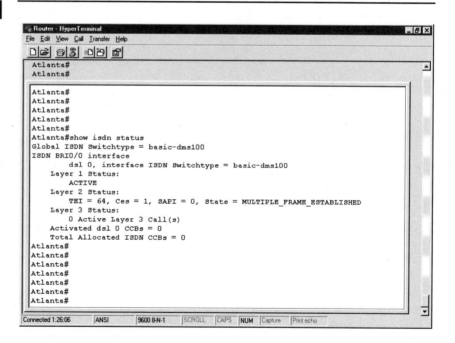

technique may be useful when you are not in the same physical location as the equipment you are configuring.

If you see a status of DEACTIVATED, the problem should have an easy solution. Confirm that the ISDN device and its NT1 are powered on and that the interface has not been shut down administratively. This can be verified with the following command:

```
Atlanta# show interface bri {interface-number}
```

Figure 13-3 shows you the output of this command.

If the interface is shut down, try the following series of commands:

```
Atlanta# configure terminal
Atlanta(config)# interface bri {interface-number}
Atlanta(config-if)# no shutdown
```

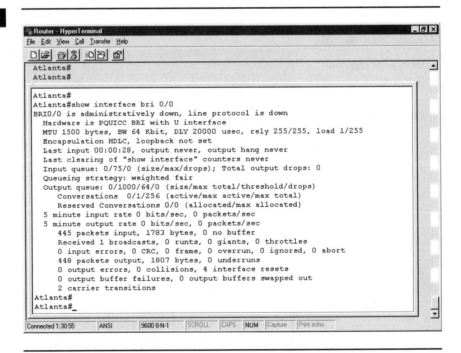

FIGURE 13-3

A BRI interface in an administratively shut down state

```
Atlanta#
Atlanta#

Atlanta#
Atlanta#show interface bri 0/0
BRI0/0 is administratively down, line protocol is down
  Hardware is PQUICC BRI with U interface
  MTU 1500 bytes, BW 64 Kbit, DLY 20000 usec, rely 255/255, load 1/255
  Encapsulation HDLC, loopback not set
  Last input 00:00:28, output never, output hang never
  Last clearing of "show interface" counters never
  Input queue: 0/75/0 (size/max/drops); Total output drops: 0
  Queueing strategy: weighted fair
  Output queue: 0/1000/64/0 (size/max total/threshold/drops)
     Conversations  0/1/256 (active/max active/max total)
     Reserved Conversations 0/0 (allocated/max allocated)
  5 minute input rate 0 bits/sec, 0 packets/sec
  5 minute output rate 0 bits/sec, 0 packets/sec
     445 packets input, 1783 bytes, 0 no buffer
     Received 1 broadcasts, 0 runts, 0 giants, 0 throttles
     0 input errors, 0 CRC, 0 frame, 0 overrun, 0 ignored, 0 abort
     448 packets output, 1807 bytes, 0 underruns
     0 output errors, 0 collisions, 4 interface resets
     0 output buffer failures, 0 output buffers swapped out
     2 carrier transitions
Atlanta#
Atlanta#_
```

Verify the RJ-45 cables and replace with known good cables, if necessary. As a final measure, contact your ISDN service provider and verify your switch type. Your service provider can also run tests on their local loop to verify ISDN service up to the customer side of the loop, if all else fails.

If the ISDN Layer 1 is ACTIVE, congratulations on a job well done! We will next test the ISDN Data Link layer.

CERTIFICATION OBJECTIVE 13.02

The ISDN Data Link Layer (Q.921)

The Data Link layer in ISDN has a dual personality. It goes by the name Q.921, which is the ITU (International Telecommunication Union) standard document for ISDN Layer 2; but it also goes by the name LAPD, which stands for "Link Access Procedure on the D channel." The latter name is a result of its close ties with LAPB, the Data Link layer for X.25, which is also standardized by the ITU. The Layer 2 frame structures are very similar and gave rise to the LAPF data-link standard for Frame Relay. You may be surprised to know that ISDN has been with us since the 1960s. It has formed the basis for the Frame Relay and ATM (a.k.a. B-ISDN) networks that are so prevalent today.

The ISDN Data Link layer has a simple but important job. Its mission is to deliver ISDN Layer 3 (ITU standard document Q.931) messages on the D channel, without error, from the TE BRI interface to the ISDN switch. To accomplish this, LAPD uses sequence numbers, error checking, and retransmissions at the Data Link layer. Since it is a Layer 2 technology, LAPD messages are only passed between the TE and ISDN switch, not end-to-end. Before LAPD can accomplish its mission, however, it must pass a few tests with the ISDN switch.

Q.921 Startup Procedures

The address field in an LAPD frame consists of a SAPI (Service Access Point Identifier) and a TEI (Terminal Endpoint Identifier). This combination is sometimes referred to as a DLCI (data-link connection identifier), out of which arises the equivalent term in Frame Relay. The SAPI is analogous to the SAP or Protocol fields in other Data Link layer technologies such as Ethernet and PPP. The SAPI's purpose is to tell the receiving station which application should process the Layer 3 "data" in this frame. It is simply a pointer to the appropriate Layer 3 service.

Initial Q.921 communication utilizes SAPI=63 during the TEI assignment phase, but later uses only SAPI=0 for Q.931 messages. It may also be useful to know that SAPI=16 can now be used to transfer X.25 data over the D channel at a maximum rate of 9.6 Kbps on the Cisco router, if your service provider offers an interconnection to an X.25 public data network.

TEI Assignment

When Layer 1 becomes ACTIVATED, the Cisco router or TA will begin asking the ISDN switch for an identity. We have been referring to these devices as Terminal Endpoints (TEs), so it is logical that their identifiers are called *Terminal Endpoint Identifiers* (TEIs). This identity request is sent on SAPI=63 with an initial TEI=127 (this is the all-1s TEI that indicates a broadcast); it is the IDREQ (ID Request) message. The ISDN switch should respond with an IDASSN (ID Assign) message indicating which TEI(s) to use for Q.921 communication. Though it's not required, TEI 64 only is commonly assigned, or TEIs 64 and 65, during normal BRI operation in North America.

The SABME and UA

Once an identity has been established and a TEI assigned, the TE will attempt to establish multiple-frame communication with the ISDN switch. This simply means that the TE will be able to send multiple frames before receiving an acknowledgment from the ISDN switch. The TE sends a SABME (Set Asynchronous Balanced Mode Extended) message in order move to the MULTIPLE FRAME ESTABLISHED state. The ISDN switch should respond with a UA (Unnumbered Acknowledgment). If the SABME and UA exchange succeeds, ISDN can move to the information transfer phase. At this point, Layer 2 is UP.

The switch and TE will continue to exchange keepalives every ten seconds (normally), in the form of RR (Receiver Ready) frames, in the absence of any Q.931 traffic. Figure 13-4 illustrates the IDREQ → IDASSN, SABME → UA , RR → RR sequence of events on a live ISDN switch.

Verifying LAPD Status

To check the status of ISDN Layer 2, use the SHOW ISDN STATUS IOS command. The Layer 2 status should indicate the assigned TEI(s), SAPI=0, and a state of MULTIPLE_FRAME_ESTABLISHED (see Figure 13-5). If you see that Layer 2 is NOT active, go back and verify the ISDN Physical layer as discussed earlier in this chapter. If you see a state of TEI_ASSIGNED for the ISDN Physical layer, it indicates that the ISDN switch is not responding to the SABMEs that the TE is sending. This

FIGURE 13-4

IDREQ/IDASSN and SABME/UA exchange between TE and ISDN switch, followed by 10-second RR keepalives

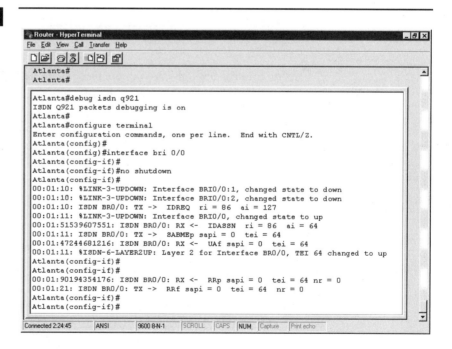

FIGURE 13-5

ISDN Layer 2 in the
MULTIPLE_FRAME_
ESTABLISHED state

```
Atlanta#
Atlanta#

Atlanta#
Atlanta#
Atlanta#
Atlanta#
Atlanta#
Atlanta#show isdn status
Global ISDN Switchtype = basic-dms100
ISDN BRI0/0 interface
        dsl 0, interface ISDN Switchtype = basic-dms100
    Layer 1 Status:
        ACTIVE
    Layer 2 Status:
        TEI = 64, Ces = 1, SAPI = 0, State = MULTIPLE_FRAME_ESTABLISHED
    Layer 3 Status:
        0 Active Layer 3 Call(s)
    Activated dsl 0 CCBs = 0
    Total Allocated ISDN CCBs = 0
Atlanta#
Atlanta#
Atlanta#
Atlanta#
Atlanta#
Atlanta#
Atlanta#
```

symptom has been observed in the field when the BRI cable has been
unplugged/re-inserted, or when the BRI interface has been through a
shutdown/no shutdown cycle (on *some* ISDN switch types). The
workaround is to reload the router so that the proper LAPD initialization
can take place.

Another helpful IOS tool is the command

```
debug isdn q921
```

used in the figures that accompany this chapter. All of the messages shown
here can be seen in real time with this debug command. To disable the
debug command, type

undebug all

If the ISDN Layer 2 is MULTIPLE_FRAME_ESTABLISHED,
congratulations! Let's move up the stack on the D channel to Q.931.

CERTIFICATION OBJECTIVE 13.03

ISDN Layer 3: SPIDs

One of the most common ISDN configuration errors is the lack of, or incorrect entry of, ISDN SPIDs (Service Profile Identifiers). ISDN's name, Integrated Services Digital Network, arose from its ability to support multiple types of services over one integrated infrastructure and one wire pair to the subscriber of those services. SPIDs are used predominantly in North America to indicate what service profile a subscriber is paying for. When the SPIDs are correctly configured, ISDN calls can then be placed.

Configuring SPIDs

exam
ⓦatch

One of the reasons for the widespread confusion over SPIDs is the fact that they are sometimes necessary and sometimes not. If the ISDN switch type is a Nortel dms100 or National ISDN (ni), SPIDs are required. If the switch is a 5ess, SPIDs may or may not be required.

So how do you decide? The answer should come from your service provider. The SPIDs given you (if any) should be documented in a safe place. A common—and wise—practice is to write your SPIDs above the wall jack for your BRI service. Many an ISDN cable has been unplugged, only to be plugged back into the wrong wall jack. This can be a disaster when router configurations of SPIDs do not match switch configurations of SPIDs. When SPIDs are required, you must configure them in your Cisco router exactly as given to you; otherwise, your ISDN service will not work.

A second reason for SPID confusion is the fact that there is no standard representation for SPIDs. SPIDs usually contain the 10-digit ISDN telephone number with an extra two to four digits at the beginning or end of the SPID, but your service provider will decide what format you will use.

SPID configuration involves setting up the correct SPIDs under the BRI interface and possibly an associated LDN, or Local Directory Number. The LDN is your seven-digit telephone number. Some switches require the LDN so that calls to the number assigned to the first B channel can roll over to the second B channel when the first B channel is in use. This operates similarly to a hunt group configuration. To configure SPIDs, use the following example (inserting your own numbers, of course):

```
Atlanta# configure terminal
Atlanta(config)# interface bri {interface-number}
Atlanta(config-if)# isdn spid1 21255512110101 5551211
Atlanta(config-if)# isdn spid2 21255512120101 5551212
```

It wouldn't hurt to do a shutdown/no shutdown on the BRI interface at this point in your configuration, although this step may not always be required in order for SPID verification to occur.

SPID Verification

SPID verification occurs after Q.921 is UP. SPIDs are sent to the switch for verification in Q.931 INFO messages. Figure 13-6 illustrates this process with the use of the DEBUG ISDN q931 command.

Since you will probably not see these real-time Q.931 messages, it is best to verify the SPID configuration—once again, with the SHOW ISDN STATUS command. Under the "SPID status:" heading, you would like to see that your SPIDs have been sent and are considered valid by the ISDN switch, as seen in Figure 13-7.

If your SPIDs are valid, congratulations! Your ISDN circuit is now ready to place calls (if it only knew whom to call!). Most ISDN texts would continue with a full discussion of Q.931 at this point, faithfully climbing the OSI stack. This text, however, is written to guide you through a working configuration from start to finish with logical checkpoints to confirm results along the way. Thus the next topic is DDR so that we can place calls. An illustrative discussion of Q.931 will follow.

FIGURE 13-6

ISDN switch verifying
SPIDs configured on the
Cisco router in
INFORMATION frames

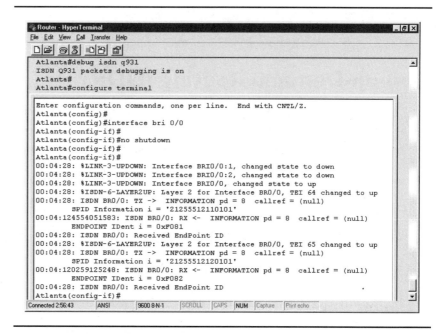

```
Atlanta#debug isdn q931
ISDN Q931 packets debugging is on
Atlanta#
Atlanta#configure terminal

Enter configuration commands, one per line.  End with CNTL/Z.
Atlanta(config)#
Atlanta(config)#interface bri 0/0
Atlanta(config-if)#
Atlanta(config-if)#no shutdown
Atlanta(config-if)#
Atlanta(config-if)#
00:04:28: %LINK-3-UPDOWN: Interface BRIO/0:1, changed state to down
00:04:28: %LINK-3-UPDOWN: Interface BRIO/0:2, changed state to down
00:04:28: %LINK-3-UPDOWN: Interface BRIO/0, changed state to up
00:04:28: %ISDN-6-LAYER2UP: Layer 2 for Interface BR0/0, TEI 64 changed to up
00:04:28: ISDN BRO/0: TX -> INFORMATION pd = 8  callref = (null)
           SPID Information i = '21255512110101'
00:04:28:124554051583: ISDN BRO/0: RX <- INFORMATION pd = 8  callref = (null)
           ENDPOINT IDent i = 0xF081
00:04:28: ISDN BRO/0: Received EndPoint ID
00:04:28: %ISDN-6-LAYER2UP: Layer 2 for Interface BR0/0, TEI 65 changed to up
00:04:28: ISDN BRO/0: TX -> INFORMATION pd = 8  callref = (null)
           SPID Information i = '21255512120101'
00:04:28:120259125248: ISDN BRO/0: RX <- INFORMATION pd = 8  callref = (null)
           ENDPOINT IDent i = 0xF082
00:04:28: ISDN BRO/0: Received EndPoint ID
Atlanta(config-if)#
```

FIGURE 13-7

SPID status verified with
the SHOW ISDN STATUS
command; both SPIDs are
"sent" and "valid"

```
Atlanta#
Atlanta#

Atlanta#
Atlanta#
Atlanta#show isdn status
Global ISDN Switchtype = basic-dms100
ISDN BRIO/0 interface
        dsl 0, interface ISDN Switchtype = basic-dms100
    Layer 1 Status:
        ACTIVE
    Layer 2 Status:
        TEI = 64, Ces = 1, SAPI = 0, State = MULTIPLE_FRAME_ESTABLISHED
        TEI = 65, Ces = 2, SAPI = 0, State = MULTIPLE_FRAME_ESTABLISHED
    Spid Status:
        TEI 64, ces = 1, state = 5(init)
            spid1 configured, spid1 sent, spid1 valid
            Endpoint ID Info: epsf = 0, usid = 70, tid = 1
        TEI 65, ces = 2, state = 5(init)
            spid2 configured, spid2 sent, spid2 valid
            Endpoint ID Info: epsf = 0, usid = 70, tid = 2
    Layer 3 Status:
        0 Active Layer 3 Call(s)
    Activated dsl 0 CCBs = 0
    Total Allocated ISDN CCBs = 0
Atlanta#
Atlanta#_
```

CERTIFICATION OBJECTIVE 13.04

Dial-on-Demand Routing (DDR)

Because BRI ISDN circuits need to connect only intermittently, they are, by nature, on-demand circuits. The Cisco router has to make decisions about what types of traffic are "interesting" enough to bring up (and pay for) the ISDN link, which is usually tariffed for businesses at a per-minute rate. After the "interesting" traffic decision is made, we must tell the router what telephone number to dial in order to reach a given destination. With the flexibility to call multiple destinations from one BRI interface, we may have many such telephone number/destination pairings. All of these issues are covered in this section.

Defining "Interesting" Traffic

The first question you must ask yourself when designing a DDR solution is, "What traffic am I willing to pay for?" Of course Telnet, SMTP, and FTP traffic are business applications and worthy of consideration, but what about that UDP port 666 application (the Doom game) that your boss is so fond of?

Filtering at this level is, of course, the job of access lists in the Cisco IOS. There are two ways to define "interesting" traffic. The simple method should be employed until the ISDN link is working to your satisfaction. The more advanced method should then be configured to reduce your monthly ISDN service charges.

Here's an example of the simple method:

```
Atlanta# configure terminal
Atlanta(config)# dialer-list 7 protocol ip permit
Atlanta(config)# interface bri {interface-number}
Atlanta(config-if)# dialer-group 7
```

This example allows all IP traffic to bring this ISDN link up. Use of this configuration reduces the number of things that can break in your ISDN call. A simple IP ping is now good enough to test this link. The dialer-list command selects the "interesting" traffic, and the dialer-group command ties the dialer-list to the BRI interface. Of course, we still need to configure a phone number to call, but we'll get to that shortly.

Once the link is tested and working, you can choose the advanced method for selecting "interesting" traffic to save money. Simply adjust the dialer-list command so that it references an IOS access list. Of course, you must also create the access list. Let's take a look:

```
Atlanta# dialer-list 8 protocol ip list 101

Atlanta(config)# access-list 101 permit tcp any any eq 23
Atlanta(config)# access-list 101 permit tcp any any eq 25
Atlanta(config)# access-list 101 permit tcp any any eq 21
Atlanta(config)# access-list 101 permit tcp any any eq 20

Atlanta(config)# interface bri {interface-number}
Atlanta(config-if)# dialer-group 8
```

This example allows our Telnet, SMTP, and FTP traffic to bring up the ISDN link. All other traffic is implicitly denied by the access list. We simply tie the new dialer-list to the interface with the dialer-group command as before.

Defining Whom to Call

The DIALER MAP command on the BRI interface is used to define whom to call. This command simply maps a telephone number to the next-hop Layer 3 protocol address. This next-hop address is normally the IP address of the BRI interface you are calling.

The whole process is very methodical. A packet enters the router, and a routing decision is made. When you look at a routing table, you can see that it simply maps destination networks to next-hop Layer 3 addresses. When the packet's destination is mapped to a next-hop address, the next step is to decide which interface is the best path to that next-hop address. The dialer map statement makes this decision. Once the route has been chosen and the outbound interface selected, we can decide whether the traffic is "interesting" enough to bring up the ISDN link via the dialer-list. Finally, if it passes the dialer-list, we use the telephone number in the dialer map statement to place the call. Got it? Let's look at an example:

```
Atlanta# configure terminal
Atlanta(config)# dialer-list 1 protocol ip permit

Atlanta(config)# interface bri {interface-number}
Atlanta(config-if)# dialer-group 1
Atlanta(config-if)# dialer map ip 10.1.1.1 14085551212

Atlanta(config-if)# ip address 10.1.1.2 255.255.255.0
```

The dialer map statement maps the IP address of the BRI interface in San Jose, CA, to a San Jose, CA telephone number. We configure an IP address on the same subnet for completeness. A simple ping to 10.1.1.1 should now attempt to bring up the ISDN link, assuming we have a like configuration on the San Jose router. I guess we now know the way to San Jose, right?

Troubleshooting DDR

Despite its technical accuracy, the call just described would quite likely fail, due to a speed mismatch. Most ISDN calls delivered across long distances (LATA boundaries) are only able to get 56 Kbps, whereas the default ISDN speed for calls from the Cisco router is 64 Kbps. A minor adjustment to the dialer map statement is required:

```
Atlanta(config-if)# dialer map ip 10.1.1.1 speed 56
14085551212
```

Now, if nothing seems to happen when you ping San Jose, try the DEBUG DIALER command. This will tell you if the traffic passed the dialer-list and also if a phone number is associated with that address. A normal DEBUG DIALER call is shown in Figure 13-8.

If you're lucky, ISDN will work for you on the first try. If you're like the rest of us, however, you may need to know a bit about Q.931 to make ISDN work its magic. We'll talk about Q.931 in the next section.

FIGURE 13-8

DEBUG DIALER output showing the dialing cause and dial string (5551211) for an ISDN call triggered by a ping to 10.1.1.2

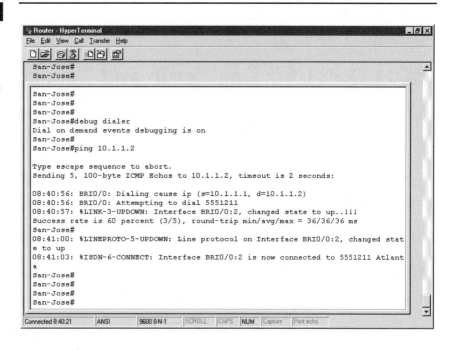

```
Router - HyperTerminal
File  Edit  View  Call  Transfer  Help

San-Jose#
San-Jose#

San-Jose#
San-Jose#
San-Jose#
San-Jose#debug dialer
Dial on demand events debugging is on
San-Jose#
San-Jose#ping 10.1.1.2

Type escape sequence to abort.
Sending 5, 100-byte ICMP Echos to 10.1.1.2, timeout is 2 seconds:

08:40:56: BRI0/0: Dialing cause ip (s=10.1.1.1, d=10.1.1.2)
08:40:56: BRI0/0: Attempting to dial 5551211
08:40:57: %LINK-3-UPDOWN: Interface BRI0/0:2, changed state to up..!!!
Success rate is 60 percent (3/5), round-trip min/avg/max = 36/36/36 ms
San-Jose#
08:41:00: %LINEPROTO-5-UPDOWN: Line protocol on Interface BRI0/0:2, changed stat
e to up
08:41:03: %ISDN-6-CONNECT: Interface BRI0/0:2 is now connected to 5551211 Atlant
a
San-Jose#
San-Jose#
San-Jose#
San-Jose#

Connected 8:40:21      ANSI      9600 8-N-1      SCROLL    CAPS    NUM    Capture    Print echo
```

QUESTIONS AND ANSWERS

Symptom from a Ping with DEBUG DIALER Enabled	Likely Cause
Unrecognized host, or protocol not running	No IP address configured on the BRI interface.
No output	"Interesting" packets are not being identified. Check your dialer-list and dialer-group for accuracy.
Dialing cause is identified, but you receive no dialer string and dialing cannot occur	The dialer map statement is not mapping the IP address you are pinging to a telephone number.
Wait for carrier timeout	ISDN Q.931 issues, such as "User Busy"

CERTIFICATION OBJECTIVE 13.05

ISDN Q.931 for Call Setup and Teardown

For all ISDN calls, the call setup, control, and teardown occur at Layer 3 on the D channel. Q.931 SETUP messages are created at the TE and carried reliably in Q.921 LAPD frames to the ISDN switch. The ISDN switch then routes calls over the PSTN (public switched telephone network) to their final destinations based on information in the Q.931 messages. At the receiving end of the ISDN call, new Q.931 messages with *most* of the originating Q.931 packet information are generated and sent to the receiving ISDN TE; thus Q.931 is technically not an end-to-end protocol.

The Q.931 architecture was created with a view for the future. Its flexibility allows it to be customized for use in environments other than ISDN in which call setup is necessary—such as Frame Relay SVCs, ATM SVCs, Voice-over IP, and digital cellular networks like PCS and GSM. Your Q.931 skills can be transferred to future technologies and environments.

Q.931 Call Establishment

ISDN calls progress through a series of Q.931 events from call establishment to call teardown. Each Q.931 event is given a name, called the *message type.*

Calls are initiated with the *Setup* message type. The next message may be any one of three message types:

- The most likely possibility is that the local ISDN switch will respond with a *Call Proceeding* message type, which indicates the successful initiation from the ISDN switch to the PSTN.

- After receiving the Call Proceeding message type, it is possible (but not required) that the remote ISDN switch will respond with an *Alerting* message type to indicate that the "phone is ringing," so to speak. This message type may not be seen when establishing a Data call, because the remote device normally responds instantly.

■ Finally, a *Connect* message type will be sent from the remote ISDN switch to the initiating party if the call is successful.

Q.931 Setup Messages

By far the most informative of the Q.931 messages, the Setup message is the first place to look once you've verified the Physical layer, the Data Link layer (Q.921), and DDR. All of the Q.931 message-type packets just mentioned contain fields called Information Elements (IEs). In the Setup message, these IEs contain information vital to the call establishment procedure. The most important IEs in the Setup packet are the Bearer Capability, Called Party Number, Calling Party Number, and the Call Reference Value.

The Bearer Capability IE is one of the best places to troubleshoot at the Q.931 layer. It defines which of the "integrated services," the IS part of ISDN, is being requested for this call. For ISDN BRI on Cisco routers, two values are commonly seen: 64-Kbps data calls and 56-Kbps data calls (other bearer capabilities are used in nondata environments). The assignment for 64-Kbps data is bearer capability 0x8890—the default for all Cisco routers not specifically configured otherwise. The 56-Kbps data call is assigned Bearer Capability 0x8890218F and is the most likely maximum achievable speed in nonlocal ISDN connections. Be aware that the latter value is *not* the default, yet is most likely a necessary configuration parameter in the dialer map statement.

The Called Party Number IE is simply the telephone number of the party to which the router is placing a call. Although a call may be placed to a Called Party Number of, for instance, 5551212, be aware that the Called Party Number delivered may or may not include the area code, such as 4085551212. This possibility exists because ISDN switch implementations differ slightly from vendor to vendor.

Why would this matter, you may ask? Let's see what happens when the area code is missing. First, a call will be placed on B channel 1 successfully. The receiving router, however, must return replies to the originating side of the call independently of the original packet sent (that is, at a different layer of router software code). The only way the receiving router can do so is to see if it is already connected to the originating router, as defined by its own dialer map statements (which map telephone numbers to next-hop IP addresses). When the dialer map contains a 7-digit number, but the delivered number is a 10-digit number, the receiving router thinks it is not already connected. The final result is that the receiving router will place a return call on B channel 2, thus effectively creating two half-duplex channels! This is obviously *not* cost effective. The solution to this problem, PPP authentication, will be presented later in this chapter.

The Calling Party Number IE is the originator of the ISDN call and can be used for Caller ID screening purposes. This feature is sometimes used by organizations as an additional security mechanism to ensure that only known callers may access a corporate ISDN dial-in service. The drawback to this method is that Calling Party Number information may or may not always be passed across the PSTN. When Caller ID screening is enabled, *only the configured numbers* will be able to access the ISDN service. If a user's Calling Party Number is not delivered by the PSTN, that user will be effectively locked out.

The last of the most important Setup message IEs is the Call Reference Value. It is simply a unique 8-bit random identifier used to distinguish one call from another between an ISDN switch and a TE. The Most Significant Bit (MSB) can be used to distinguish the originator of the Q.931 exchange from the receiver of the Q.931 exchange. The originator/receiver may be the local ISDN switch or the TE attached to that switch. The originator sets the MSB to 0 in the Setup message and in all subsequent Q.931 messages that refer to the same call, as seen in Figure 13-9. The remaining 7 bits are given a somewhat random value. The receiver will use the same remaining 7 bits, but will set the MSB to 1 in all subsequent messages that reference the same call. This process ensures that both sides (the TE and ISDN switch) will not establish different calls at the same time with the same Call Reference value.

In Figure 13-9 the callref parameter indicates the switch that originated the call; Bearer Capability is for 56 Kbps data; Calling Party Number is delivered with area code; Called Party Number has no area code. The callref

FIGURE 13-9

Q.931 Setup message at the
receiving end

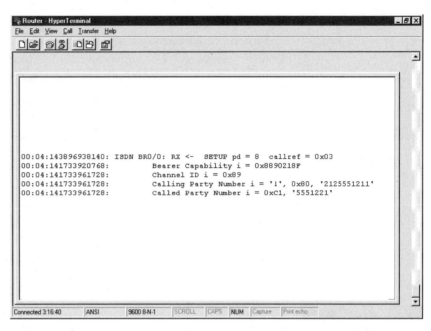

```
00:04:143896938140: ISDN BR0/0: RX <-  SETUP pd = 8  callref = 0x03
00:04:141733920768:       Bearer Capability i = 0x8890218F
00:04:141733961728:       Channel ID i = 0x89
00:04:141733961728:       Calling Party Number i = '1', 0x80, '2125551211'
00:04:141733961728:       Called Party Number i = 0xC1, '5551221'
```

on outbound messages for this call will be 0x83 because the inbound
callref is 0x03.

At this point, your Physical layer, your Q.921, and your Q.931 SPIDs
should be up and verified. If all DDR and Q.931 Setup parameters are
appropriate, you should be placing calls with no problems. Don't be afraid
to give yourself a pat on the back!

Now that your calls are up, how do you tear them down? Your service
provider would like it if you stopped reading here, of course. Your boss,
though, wants you to read on, so let's go.

Call Teardown

Q.931 call teardown involves three message types: Disconnect, Release, and
Release Complete. Either side can disconnect the call for one of several
reasons. The receiving side may be busy, may reject the call due to Caller
ID screening, or may not be able to provide the appropriate Bearer

Capability. Either side may disconnect the call after the line has been idle for a preconfigured amount of time.

By default, the Cisco router will disconnect all ISDN calls after 120 seconds (2 minutes). This timer can be tuned based on the average duration and frequency of your ISDN calls. To do so, try the following:

```
Atlanta# configure terminal
Atlanta(config)# interface bri 0/0
Atlanta(config-if)# dialer idle-timeout {number of seconds}
```

When calls have been established, the current idle time (and a bit of call history) can be observed with the SHOW DIALER command (see Figure 13-10). Be aware that this idle timer is reset every time "interesting" traffic (as defined by the dialer-list) passes through the interface.

For high-volume BRI lines, it may be helpful to know about one additional disconnect timer: the fast-idle timer. The fast-idle timer lowers

---

FIGURE 13-10

Output from the SHOW DIALER command: 6 call successes; idle timers set to 5 minutes; dial reason shown; and time until disconnect 296 secs

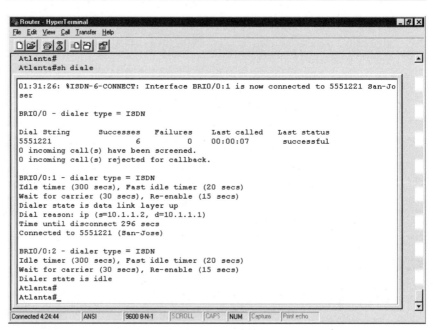

```
Atlanta#
Atlanta#sh diale

01:31:26: %ISDN-6-CONNECT: Interface BRI0/0:1 is now connected to 5551221 San-Jo
ser

BRI0/0 - dialer type = ISDN

Dial String      Successes   Failures    Last called   Last status
5551221                  6          0     00:00:07      successful
0 incoming call(s) have been screened.
0 incoming call(s) rejected for callback.

BRI0/0:1 - dialer type = ISDN
Idle timer (300 secs), Fast idle timer (20 secs)
Wait for carrier (30 secs), Re-enable (15 secs)
Dialer state is data link layer up
Dial reason: ip (s=10.1.1.2, d=10.1.1.1)
Time until disconnect 296 secs
Connected to 5551221 (San-Jose)

BRI0/0:2 - dialer type = ISDN
Idle timer (300 secs), Fast idle timer (20 secs)
Wait for carrier (30 secs), Re-enable (15 secs)
Dialer state is idle
Atlanta#
Atlanta#_
```

the time before disconnect if another call is contending with the current call for access to the link. The default value for this timer is 20 seconds, but it can be configured with the following:

```
Atlanta# configure terminal
Atlanta# interface bri 0/0
Atlanta# dialer fast-idle {number of seconds}
```

When a call is disconnected, either the Disconnect or Release Complete message will contain a cause code. This code is useful when troubleshooting ISDN call teardown. A good cause code is 0x8090 or 0x8290, both of which indicate a normal call-clearing. A cause code of 0x8291 indicates that the user is busy, and a code of 0x8095 indicates that the call was rejected.

Calls may be rejected based on configured Caller ID strings as shown in Figure 13-11. These strings can be configured via the following commands:

```
Atlanta# configure terminal
Atlanta(config)# interface bri 0/0
Atlanta(config-if)# isdn caller {Calling Party Number 1}
Atlanta(config-if)# isdn caller {Calling Party Number 2}
Atlanta(config-if)# isdn caller {Calling Party Number 3}
```

Another useful command when testing your initial ISDN Q.931 configuration is the

CLEAR INTERFACE BRI { *interface number* }

command. Instead of waiting for the dialer's idle-timeout to expire, you can clear the call instantly and begin testing new configurations.

If all layers up to and including Q.931 are now working, congratulations! You are well on your way to becoming an ISDN expert. The final layer to add to your ISDN configurations is PPP: the Point-to-Point Protocol.

CERTIFICATION OBJECTIVE 13.06

PPP: The Point-to-Point Protocol

Until now we have focused on Layers 1, 2, and 3 on the BRI D channel, which are predefined to use 2B1Q, Q.921, and Q.931, respectively. Layers

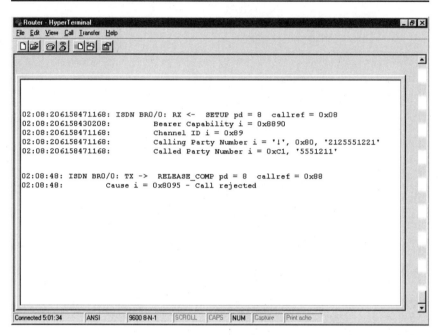

FIGURE 13-11

ISDN call teardown due to Caller ID rejection. When this occurs, the usual Disconnect and Release messages do not precede the RELEASE_COMP.

2 and 3 of the ISDN B channels, however, impose no such restrictions. You are free to run whatever protocols you like on the B channels. In our previous examples we used the default Layer 2 encapsulation of Cisco proprietary HDLC and IP as our Layer 3 protocol. PPP provides more flexibility and security than HDLC. It is the protocol of choice in ISDN environments.

PPP arose from the need for a more flexible Layer 2 protocol than had been used in the past. It is, however, based on the HDLC family of protocols, just like so many other networking Data Link layer protocols. PPP adds to HDLC capabilities for authentication, compression, IP address assignment, and bundling of multiple B channels into one logical pipe for data—in addition to many other standardized and proprietary features. This flexibility and these features are possible because the architects of PPP designed the LCP (Link Control Protocol) and NCP (Network Control Protocol) layers.

The Link Control Protocol

When the ISDN Q.931 CONNECT message has been sent, PPP can begin its negotiation at the LCP layer (see Figure 13-12). A few common options that Cisco routers negotiate are the AuthType, ACompression, PCompression, MagicNumber, and AsyncMap options, and we'll discuss these options in this section. Of these options, the AuthType *must* be agreed upon or the connection will drop.

So what is so special about the AuthType option? It defines which authentication protocol (if any) will be used to initiate this connection. The two authentication methods available on the Cisco router are PAP and CHAP.

PAP is the Password Authentication Protocol used in older PPP implementations and is the least preferred authentication type.

LCP negotiation of the AuthType and MagicNumber options. Both options are accepted on each side. LCP negotiation ends in an "open" state.

```
Router - HyperTerminal                                                    _ 8 X
File  Edit  View  Call  Transfer  Help
 D|e| e|3| D|e| e|
Atlanta#debug ppp negotiation                                                 ▲
PPP protocol negotiation debugging is on
Atlanta#
Atlanta#ping 10.1.1.1

Type escape sequence to abort.
Sending 5, 100-byte ICMP Echos to 10.1.1.1, timeout is 2 seconds:

00:15:50: %LINK-3-UPDOWN: Interface BRI0/0:2, changed state to up.
00:15:50: BR0/0:2 PPP: Treating connection as a callout
00:15:50: BR0/0:2 PPP: Phase is ESTABLISHING, Active Open
00:15:50: BR0/0:2 LCP: O CONFREQ [Closed] id 1 len 15
00:15:50: BR0/0:2 LCP:    AuthProto CHAP (0x0305C22305)
00:15:50: BR0/0:2 LCP:    MagicNumber 0x505E88E4 (0x0506505E88E4)
00:15:52: BR0/0:2 LCP: I CONFREQ [REQsent] id 1 len 15
00:15:52: BR0/0:2 LCP:    AuthProto CHAP (0x0305C22305)
00:15:52: BR0/0:2 LCP:    MagicNumber 0x505E8D8E (0x0506505E8D8E)
00:15:52: BR0/0:2 LCP: O CONFACK [REQsent] id 1 len 15
00:15:52: BR0/0:2 LCP:    AuthProto CHAP (0x0305C22305)
00:15:52: BR0/0:2 LCP:    MagicNumber 0x505E8D8E (0x0506505E8D8E)
00:15:52: BR0/0:2 LCP: TIMEout: State ACKsent
00:15:52: BR0/0:2 LCP: O CONFREQ [ACKsent] id 2 len 15
00:15:52: BR0/0:2 LCP:    AuthProto CHAP (0x0305C22305)
00:15.11:52: BR0/0:2 LCP:    MagicNumber 0x505E88E4 (0x0506505E88E4)
00:15:52: BR0/0:2 LCP: I CONFACK [ACKsent] id 2 len 15
00:15:52: BR0/0:2 LCP:    AuthProto CHAP (0x0305C22305)
00:15:52: BR0/0:2 LCP:    MagicNumber 0x505E88E4 (0x0506505E88E4)
00:15:52: BR0/0:2 LCP: State is Open                                          ▼
Connected 0:08:23    ANSI         9600 8-N-1   SCROLL  CAPS  NUM  Capture  Print echo
```

Its shortcoming is the fact that it sends the password over the link in cleartext format.

e x a m

ⓦa t c h

CHAP, the Challenge Handshake Authentication Protocol, is the successor to PAP. The CHAP password is never sent over the link in cleartext. Instead, the called party responds to the calling party by sending its host name and a random "challenge" string. The calling party encrypts the password (an identical password that was preconfigured on both sides) with this challenge string and then sends it back to the called party, along with the calling party's host name. The called party then encrypts its password configured for the calling party, with the same challenge. If the result is the same, the called party accepts the connection; otherwise, it rejects the connection. If a Cisco router calls another Cisco router, this CHAP process occurs in both directions (see Figure 13-13). If a PC PPP client (such as Windows Dial-Up Networking) dials into the router, only the PC is challenged.

FIGURE 13-13

PPP CHAP authentication occurring in both directions between two Cisco routers

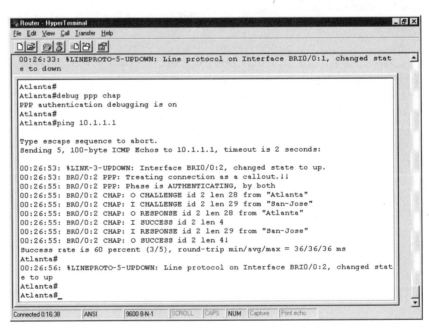

The following commands demonstrate an example of enabling CHAP authentication:

```
Atlanta# configure terminal
Atlanta(config)# username San-Jose password AuTuMn
Atlanta(config)# interface bri {interface number}
Atlanta(config-if)# encapsulation ppp
Atlanta(config-if)# ppp authentication chap
```

A few comments about this configuration are in order:

- The username chosen must be the host name of the *other* router (**San-Jose** in this case).

- The password chosen must be exactly the same on both routers and *is* case-sensitive (that's no typo; the password *is* case-sensitive!). The number-one ISDN configuration error is in the username statement, so be careful. This is usually evidenced by the occurrence of many 1- or 2-second calls. Q.931 accepts the call, but PPP CHAP quickly rejects the call.

- In addition, the interfaces must both be converted from the default encapsulation of HDLC to PPP with the ENCAPSULATION PPP command, and both sides must agree on CHAP as their authentication type.

By the way, using CHAP authentication also avoids that nasty situation of two half-duplex connections (one each way) created when the delivered Calling Party Number does not match what is in the dialer map statements (mentioned earlier in the Q.931 Setup Messages section). This doesn't occur because, with CHAP, the router now knows to whom it is connected. We are no longer depending on the PSTN to deliver Q.931 messages appropriately.

Using CHAP authentication does change our dialer map statement slightly. We must now add the NAME keyword to the dialer map statement using the host name of the router we are dialing. Lets take a look:

```
Atlanta# configure terminal
Atlanta(config)# interface bri {interface number}
Atlanta(config-if)# dialer map ip 10.1.1.1 name San-Jose speed 56 4085551212
```

The remaining LCP options can be briefly explained: The ACompression and PCompression options allow compression of the Address/Control and Protocol fields in the PPP header. The PPP Address and Control fields are always set to 255 and 3, respectively, and can be compressed. The Protocol field is a 16-bit field, which indicates which upper-layer protocol needs to receive the data in this PPP frame. A 16-bit field allows for over 65,000 Layer 3 protocols. In reality, only a few are used, and this field is easily compressed. The MagicNumber option is a random number that is used to detect links that have been placed in a "loopback" condition for testing purposes. Finally, the AsyncMap option defines a standard set of control and escape characters for the PPP session.

The Network Control Protocols

The Network Control Protocols (NCPs) have their turn when LCP negotiation is complete. An NCP is negotiated when a Layer 3 protocol has data to send over the PPP link. Common NCPs in use today with PPP are the IPCP (IP Control Protocol), the IPXCP (IPX Control Protocol), and the BRIDGECP (Bridging Control Protocol), just to name a few.

The IPCP allows the negotiation of IP parameters such as the IP address. This is no small matter—considering that the IP address space is being depleted even as you read this section. Dynamic IP address assignment by ISPs saves a large number of IP addresses over the alternative of assigning every subscriber a static IP address. Another popular IPCP option is the use of TCP/IP Header Compression. This option can be used to reduce the size of the TCP/IP header from 40 bytes down to 5 bytes in many cases. Those 35 bytes saved on every packet received can make a noticeable difference if your packets are typically small.

PPP options are negotiated with the following messages: CONFREQ (Configuration Request), CONFREJ (Configuration Reject), CONFACK (Configuration Acknowledge), and CONFNAK (Configuration Negative Acknowledge). The initial requests for support of LCP and NCP options are of course sent in the CONFREQ frames. If the other side of the PPP connection cannot or will not support an option, it simply returns a CONFREJ. If the receiving side can support the option, but not with the requested parameters for that option, that side will respond with a CONFNAK. In the CONFNAK frame, it is possible for the receiving side to "suggest" more appropriate or desired parameters for that option. If the option can be supported with the parameters indicated, then a CONFACK is sent. The PPP connection is UP when all LCPs and NCPs have been CONFACKed.

Multilink PPP

Multilink PPP allows multiple ISDN B channels to be logically combined into one virtual pipe for data to flow through. On a single ISDN line, this means we can have a dynamic jump from one B channel at a speed of 64 Kbps, to two B channels at a speed of 128 Kbps. This bandwidth on demand is enabled through the combination of two commands. Lets see:

```
Atlanta# configure terminal
Atlanta(config)# interface bri {interface number}
Atlanta(config-if)# ppp multilink
Atlanta(config-if)# dialer load-threshold {1-255}
```

The ppp multilink command simply allows both B channels to be used as one fast logical data pipe called a *multilink bundle*. Frames are fragmented at Layer 2 (PPP) and recombined at the other end of the link. This reduces overall latency for frame transmission. The DIALER LOAD-THRESHOLD {1-255} command specifies the load (expressed as a number out of 255) at which the next link in a multilink bundle will be added to increase data throughput. This allows true bandwidth on demand.

CERTIFICATION SUMMARY

ISDN installation and configuration may not be the most intuitive process in the world. This chapter's goal was to provide you with a step-by-step analysis of the tasks required to install and configure ISDN with verifiable checkpoints at each step along the way. We have seen that Cisco IOS SHOW and DEBUG commands provide very useful information to perform these checkpoint verifications.

The architects of ISDN intended to create an open architecture. Evidence of their success can be seen in ISDN's widespread use and adoption in other related industries. Now that you know and understand how ISDN operates in Cisco data networks, you will find it easy to apply this knowledge to other ISDN-related technologies. We hope your ISDN experiences will be enjoyable experiences now that you are empowered with the knowledge of its inner workings. Congratulations and happy networking!

 TWO-MINUTE DRILL

❑ ISDN Basic Rate Interface is a "last-mile" technology that allows digital connections over the same copper wires that deliver analog Plain Old Telephone Service (POTS).

❑ The ISDN BRI connection consists of three Time Division Multiplexed (TDM) channels—commonly referred to as 2B+D.

❑ The ISDN switch in the CO is loaded with special software that allows it to be an ISDN BRI switch.

❑ In North America the most common BRI switch types are the basic-5ess, the basic-dms100, and the basic-ni.

❑ The NT1 device lies between the ISDN switch and the Cisco ISDN interface or Terminal Adapter (both referenced as the *Terminal Endpoint* or TE).

❑ Be aware that many ISDN TE devices will have the NT1 built into the BRI interface.

❑ Layer 1 activation requires the following events: The TE begins the whole process by signaling "01111110" until the NT1 returns at least three 48-bit frames with the A (Active) bit set to 0.

❑ The Data Link layer in ISDN has a dual personality. It goes by the name Q.921, which is the ITU (International Telecommunication Union) standard document for ISDN Layer 2; but it also goes by the name LAPD, which stands for "Link Access Procedure on the D channel."

❑ The ISDN Data Link layer has a simple but important job. Its mission is to deliver ISDN Layer 3 (ITU standard document Q.931) messages on the D channel, without error, from the TE BRI interface to the ISDN switch.

❑ The address field in an LAPD frame consists of a SAPI (Service Access Point Identifier) and a TEI (Terminal Endpoint Identifier). This combination is sometimes referred to as a DLCI (data-link connection identifier), out of which arises the equivalent term in Frame Relay.

❑ To check the status of ISDN Layer 2, use the SHOW ISDN STATUS IOS command.

❑ One of the most common ISDN configuration errors is the lack of, or incorrect entry of, ISDN SPIDs (Service Profile Identifiers).

❑ One of the reasons for the widespread confusion over SPIDs is the fact that they are sometimes necessary and sometimes not. If the ISDN switch type is a Nortel dms100 or National ISDN (ni), SPIDs are required. If the switch is a 5ess, SPIDs may or may not be required.

❑ SPID verification occurs after Q.921 is UP. SPIDs are sent to the switch for verification in Q.931 INFO messages.

❑ Because BRI ISDN circuits need to connect only intermittently, they are, by nature, on-demand circuits.

❑ The dialer-list command selects the "interesting" traffic, and the dialer-group command ties the dialer-list to the BRI interface.

❑ The DIALER MAP command on the BRI interface is used to define whom to call.

❑ Most ISDN calls delivered across long distances (LATA boundaries) are only able to get 56 Kbps, whereas the default ISDN speed for calls from the Cisco router is 64 Kbps.

❑ For all ISDN calls, the call setup, control, and teardown occur at Layer 3 on the D channel.

❑ The Q.931 architecture was created with a view for the future. Its flexibility allows it to be customized for use in environments other than ISDN in which call setup is necessary—such as Frame Relay SVCs, ATM SVCs, Voice-over IP, and digital cellular networks like PCS and GSM.

❑ ISDN calls progress through a series of Q.931 events from call establishment to call teardown. Each Q.931 event is given a name, called the *message type*.

❑ By far the most informative of the Q.931 messages, the Setup message is the first place to look once you've verified the Physical layer, the Data-Link layer (Q.921), and DDR. All of the Q.931 message-type packets contain fields called *Information Elements* (IEs). In the Setup message, these IEs contain information vital to the call establishment procedure. The most important IEs in the Setup packet are the Bearer Capability, Called Party Number, Calling Party Number, and the Call Reference Value.

❑ Q.931 call teardown involves three message types: Disconnect, Release, and Release Complete.

❑ PPP adds to HDLC capabilities for authentication, compression, IP address assignment, and bundling of multiple B channels into one logical pipe for data—in addition to many other standardized and proprietary features.

❑ When the ISDN Q.931 CONNECT message has been sent, PPP can begin its negotiation at the LCP layer. A few common options that Cisco routers negotiate are the AuthType, ACompression, PCompression, MagicNumber, and AsyncMap options.

❑ CHAP, the Challenge Handshake Authentication Protocol, is the successor to PAP. The CHAP password is never sent over the link in cleartext. Instead, the called party responds to the calling party by sending its host name and a random "challenge" string. The calling party encrypts the password (an *identical* password that was preconfigured on both sides) with this challenge string and then sends it back to the called party, along with the calling party's host name. The called party then encrypts its password configured for the calling party, with the same challenge. If the result is the same, the called party accepts the connection; otherwise, it rejects the connection. If a Cisco router calls another Cisco router, this CHAP process occurs in both directions. If a PC PPP client (such as Windows Dial-Up Networking) dials into the router, only the PC is challenged.

❑ Multilink PPP allows multiple ISDN B channels to be logically combined into one virtual pipe for data to flow through.

SELF TEST

The following Self Test questions will help you measure your understanding of the material presented in this chapter. Read all the choices carefully, as there may be more than one correct answer. Choose all correct answers for each question.

1. ISDN is *not* used in which one of the following markets?

   A. Telecommuting

   B. ATM Permanent Virtual Circuits

   C. Frame Relay backup

   D. The SOHO market

2. ISDN is delivered from the CO to the customer via which of the following?

   A. 1 wire

   B. 2 wires

   C. 3 wires

   D. 4 wires

3. What does ISDN stand for?

   A. International Signaling Device of Nerds

   B. International Switched Data Network

   C. I Still Don't Know

   D. Integrated Services Digital Network

4. Individual ISDN B channels operate via which of the following?

   A. TDM at 48 Kbps

   B. FDM at 64 Kbps

   C. TDM at 64 Kbps

   D. QPSK at 56 Kbps

5. Which ISDN switch type is typically *not* used in the United States?

   A. NET3 switch type

   B. Nortel DMS-100

   C. NI switch type

   D. Lucent 5ESS

6. Which of the following completes Layer 1 activation?

   A. TE sends frames with the A bit = 0

   B. NT1 sends frames with the A bit = 0

   C. TE sends frames with the A bit = 1

   D. NT1 sends frames with the A bit = 1

7. The main job of Q.921 is to

   A. Send SETUP messages to the Called Party

   B. Verify SPIDs with the ISDN switch

   C. Deliver Q.931 messages safely to the ISDN switch

   D. Serve as a keepalive from the TE

8. A TEI is a:

   A. Transfer of Endpoint ISDN

   B. Terminal Endpoint Identifier

   C. Telephone Egress Indicator

   D. Terminal Exit Interface

9. Layer 2 status from the SHOW ISDN STATUS command should report

   A. MULTIPLE FRAME ESTABLISHED

   B. TEI ASSIGNED

   C. SABME

   D. LAPD

10. When are SPIDs required?

    A. SPIDs are always required

    B. When your service provider can lower costs with them

    C. When the switch is a DMS-100 or NI (National ISDN) switch

    D. When a Cisco router uses ISDN BRI

11. The best way to see if your configured SPIDs are valid is to

    A. Look for the Active light on the NT1

    B. Use the SHOW ISDN STATUS command

    C. Use the DEBUG ISDN Q921 command

    D. Use the SHOW DIALER command

12. Which command defines "interesting" traffic that will cause the ISDN link to dial?

    A. dialer-ping

    B. dialer map

    C. dialer-list

    D. dialer-match

13. Which command binds the dialer-list to the BRI interface?

    A. dialer map

    B. dialer-group

    C. dialer-bind

    D. dialer-link

14. The dialer map command links a _____ to a _____:

    A. dialer-list, interface

    B. Telephone number, IP address

15. Most long-distance ISDN BRI calls are placed at a maximum speed of

    A. 56 Kbps

    B. 64 Kbps

    C. 72 Kbps

    D. 164 Kbps

16. Which is *not* a part of the Q.931 SETUP message?

    A. Bearer Capability

    B. Called Party Number

    C. Calling Party Number

    D. Cause code

17. The Bearer Capability IE defines

    A. The reason for DISCONNECT

    B. The type of ISDN call requested

    C. The number of B channels used

    D. Who placed the ISDN call

18. The Most Significant Bit (MSB) of the Call Reference IE is set to

    A. 0 in messages from the TE to the switch

    B. 0 in messages from the originating side of the SETUP message

    C. 0 in messages to the originating side of the SETUP message

    D. 0 in messages from the switch to the TE

C. Calling Party Number, Called Party Number

D. Protocol, BRI interface

19. What is the default value of the dialer idle-timeout on Cisco routers?

    A. 60 seconds

    B. 180 seconds

    C. 300 seconds

    D. 120 seconds

20. Caller ID screening may be enabled on the Cisco router with the _____ command:

    A. ISDN CALLER {telephone number}

    B. ISDN FAST-IDLE {telephone number}

    C. ISDN CALLING-PARTY-NUMBER {telephone number}

    D. CALLING-PARTY-NUMBER {telephone number}

21. CHAP authentication does not send which of the following items over the link?

    A. The router host name

    B. The cleartext password

    C. A challenge string

    D. An encrypted password

22. The IPCP can negotiate which one of the following items?

    A. The compression type

    B. The IP routing protocol

    C. The IPX network number

    D. The IP address

A

Self Test
Answers

Answers to Chapter 1 Self Test

1. Which of the following agencies did early research in computer interconnectivity?

   A. Department of Defense

   B. Department of Technology

   C. Defense Advanced Research Projects Agency (DARPA)

   D. None of the above
   C. DARPA is the agency that conducted research for computer interconnectivity.

2. The Department of Defense presented what reference model for communication protocols?

   A. Ethernet

   B. Token Ring

   C. TCP

   D. TCP/IP
   D. Ethernet and Token Ring are communication protocols within the framework of the TCP/IP; however, TCP/IP is the actual model.

3. Which of the following are connection-oriented protocols?

   A. Token Ring

   B. Ethernet

   C. FDDI

   D. A and C

   E. A and B
   D. A and C. Token Ring and FDDI are connection-oriented protocols, requiring some type of

acknowledgment and using control mechanisms to ensure successful frame transmission. Ethernet frames may collide, so delivery is not guaranteed.

4. Which of the following are connectionless protocols?

   A. Ethernet

   B. IP

   C. ATM

   D. Frame Relay

   E. All of the above
   E. All of the above. These protocols are best-effort delivery protocols that require no acknowledgments or receipt of sent data. There are no control mechanisms in place to ensure data integrity.

5. Which of the following is the oldest LAN technology?

   A. ATM

   B. NetBIOS

   C. Ethernet

   D. Token Ring
   C. Ethernet has been around the longest—since early 1970s. ATM is not generally implemented in a LAN environment, although ATM LAN is a comparable solution implemented in a LAN environment. Token Ring is probably next oldest after Ethernet.

6. What layer or layers of the OSI reference model is/are equivalent to the Network Interface layer?

   A. Data Link

   B. Transport

C. Physical

D. A and C

D. A and C. The Data Link and Physical layers are equivalent to the Network Interface layer. Both Data Link and Physical layers correspond with the OSI model, and the Network Interface layer corresponds with the TCP/IP reference model. All the layers essentially are responsible for getting data across a physical network, delivering data between end-to-end stations.

7. The Application layer is responsible for which of the following tasks?

A. Managing sessions

B. Providing functionality to users

C. Providing functionality to programs

D. All of the above

D. All of the above. The Application layer does provide all these functions. Primarily, it manages interaction between applications, users, and services.

8. TCP and UDP are both what kind of protocol?

A. Connection-oriented

B. Connectionless

C. Transport

D. None of the above

C. Transport. TCP is connection-oriented, but UDP is connectionless. However, both protocols are Layer 4 protocols in the TCP/IP reference model.

9. What kind of protocol is UDP?

A. Unreliable

B. Reliable

C. Fast

D. IPX

A. UDP is a transport protocol that is unreliable.

10. An AppleTalk implementation consists of _____.

A. Zones

B. User segments

C. Network segments

D. All of the above

A. Zones. Network and user segments generally are parts of a particular LAN. AppleTalk uses zones to segment networks. Generally speaking, zones and network segments can be viewed as the same; however, in AppleTalk's implementation, zones are used to segment users and devices into logical groups.

11. Which of the following characterizes congestion on a network?

A. A statistical phenomenon

B. A normal state

C. Overloaded capacity

D. A and C

D. A and C are correct. Congestion is not normal. It is a deviation from the norm. Generally, traffic in a network environment should traverse the system without noticeable delays. Congestion is also a statistical phenomenon due to an overloaded capacity on a particular interface.

12. Which of the following applications sends packet information to the destination and then notifies the sender when a reply is received, indicating size of packets, packet loss, and time taken for a response?

A. Ping

B. Telnet

C. FTP

D. TFTP

E. None of the above
A. Ping. Although TFTP, FTP, and Telnet notify with a reply when a connection or session is established, these applications don't reply with packet information as it pertains to successfully reaching a device across the network.

13. What is the 80/20 rule?

A. Eighty percent of traffic should be local, and 20 percent requires internetworking.

B. Eighty percent of traffic requires internetworking, and 20 percent should be local.

C. All traffic (100 percent) requires internetworking.

D. None of the above.
A. The 80/20 rule implies that 80 percent of traffic is local, and the other 20 percent requires internetworking. The general rule is that most user resources are local or on the same LAN segment. This 80/20 rule is from the traditional approach to networking and communications.

14. What does the term *troubleshooting* mean?

A. Eliminating irrelevant information

B. Devising a corrective action plan to fix a problem

C. Isolating a problematic area

D. B and C

E. All of the above except D
E. All of the answers are troubleshooting procedures.

15. There are over 16,000,000 local addresses in which of the following address classes?

A. Class A

B. Class B

C. Class C

D. Class Z
A. Class A. Within their respective classes, Class B has 65,534 local addresses, and Class C has 254 local addresses. Class A has 16,777,214 local addresses.

16. Which of the following is a valid Class B address?

A. 129.23.2.264

B. 12.3.34.55

C. 128.233.23.260

D. 130.25.19.102
D. 130.25.19.102 is a valid Class B address. In a Class B addressing scheme, the valid host address range is from 128.1.0.0 to 191.255.0.0. Class

A ranges from 1.0.0.0 to 126.0.0.0 and Class C ranges from 192.0.1.0 to 233.255.254.0.

17. Which of the following layers is *not* included in the TCP/IP internetworking model?

A. Transport layer

B. Application layer

C. Data Link layer

D. Internet layer
    C. Data Link layer. In the OSI reference model, the Data Link layer resides on Layer 2. In the TCP/IP internetworking model, only the Network Interface, Internet, Transport, and Application layers are included.

18. IP addressing consists of what kind of address scheme?

A. 8-byte address scheme

B. 4-byte address scheme

C. 32-bit address scheme

D. B and C

E. A and C
    D. B and C. For every byte, 8 bits are reserved. Therefore, 4 bytes make up 32 bits, and 8 bytes make up 64 bits.

19. Which layer of the TCP/IP internetworking model is responsible for transmitting data across the physical network?

A. Data Link

B. Transport

C. Internet

D. Network Interface
   D. The Network Interface model is responsible for data transmission across the physical network. Transport primarily handles host-to-host interaction, data integrity, and control mechanisms to ensure data delivery. The Internet layer manages the entire TCP/IP model in a broad sense.

20. Which of these protocols transmits each data unit as an independent entity without establishing a logical connection between end-stations?

A. IP

B. IPX

C. SPX

D. A and B
   D. Both IP and IPX uses logical connection for data communications. SPX relies on peer-to-peer connections.

21. Which of the following is a valid IPX network address?

A. 141.10.10.4

B. 129.4.4.8

C. 4f.000.0c56.be45

D. A and C
   C. The correct answer is C. A and B are typically used in the IP world.

22. What is the native routing protocol for AppleTalk?

A. RIP

B. IPX

C. SNA

D. RTMP
D. RTMP is AppleTalk's native routing protocol. RIP is an IP routing protocol; IPX is for Novell implementation; and SNA is IBM's specific architecture primarily for mainframes.

Answers to Chapter 2 Self Test

1. What layer of the OSI model is responsible for providing signaling and mechanical functionality?

   A. Data Link
   B. Network
   C. Physical
   D. Transport
   C. The Physical layer provides the signaling and mechanical functionality in the protocol stack of the OSI model. The Data Link layer controls the flow of data across the network.

2. Name the layer of the OSI model that is divided into these two sublayers:

   A. Logical Link Control and Data Link
   B. Logical Link Control and Type 2 services
   C. Logical Link Control and Media Access Control (MAC)
   D. None of the above
   C. The LLC and MAC are the sublayer protocols for the Data Link layer.

3. Which of the following symptoms of trouble are found in Ethernet implementations?

   A. Runts
   B. Ring errors
   C. Beaconing
   D. Collisions
   E. A and D
   E. Ring errors and beaconing can be found in Token Ring implementations. Runts and collisions are indicative of Ethernet operation.

4. Xerox developed which LAN network technology?

   A. Frame Relay
   B. TCP/IP
   C. Ethernet
   D. Token Ring
   E. None of the above
   C. TCP/IP was developed by the Department of Defense. Token Ring is IBM's development. Xerox developed Ethernet.

5. Which of the following is a major difference between Ethernet and Token Ring?

   A. Access method
   B. Different vendors
   C. A and B
   D. None of the above
   C. One of the major differences between Ethernet and Token Ring is its access method, the way in which

data is transmitted. Ethernet developed by Xerox uses CSMA/CD algorithm and Token Ring developed by IBM is governed by token passing.

6. In order to transmit in the Token Ring network, you need to:

A. Possess token

B. Have a lot of bandwidth

C. Priority set

D. A and C

E. None of the above
A. In Token Ring implementation, the station that possesses the token is the transmitting station. All other stations must wait to seize the token for transmission.

7. What is the number of stations assigned to the active monitor role in Token Ring?

A. 4

B. 2

C. 3

D. 1
D. Only one station at a time can be designated as the active monitor in Token Ring operation.

8. The LAN Emulation (LANE) protocol uses which layer?

A. Data Link layer

B. Transport layer

C. Network layer

D. Physical layer
A. LAN Emulation uses the MAC network of Layer 2 to transmit packets.

9. LAN Emulation is an ATM Forum standard used to connect:

A. ATM switches to ATM desktop connections

B. Multiprotocol routers to an ATM network

C. WANs to an ATM network

D. Legacy LANs and ATM network
D. If a LAN Emulation service is provided for an ATM network, end-nodes such as servers and bridges can establish a connection to the ATM network while the back end, the software application, interacts as if it was attached to a traditional LAN.

10. In an LLC 802.2 layer, Type 2 is the _____.

A. More complicated

B. Least complicated

C. Most structured
A. Of the two services, LLC2 is the more complicated. This Type 2 service provides the functionality needed to provide reliable data transfer (quite similar to Layer 4 function). It also allows for error recovery, flow and congestion controls.

11. Token Ring uses what kind of process to help resolve the contention for the active monitoring role?

A. Ring

B. Token claiming

C. Priority

D. Access

B. If the active monitor leaves the ring or receives a lot of physical errors, existing stations must contend for the designated active monitor role by the process of token claiming.

12. Which of the following is a function of the MAC layer?

A. Transmitting data operations

B. Transmitting Media Access Management

C. Receiving Media Access Management

D. Receiving data operation

E. All of the above

E. The MAC provides transmitting and receiving data operations and transmitting and receiving Media Access Management. The MAC layer provides the interface between user data and the physical placement and retrieval of data on the network.

13. In an FDDI network, what provides for full redundancy?

A. Single Attached Station (SAS)

B. Dual Attached Station (DAS)

C. Node station

D. End-station

B. FDDI provides redundancy and failover capabilities by providing a secondary ring for operation. FDDI is able to loopback to the second ring in case of failures.

14. How do Token Ring frames traverse the network?

A. In two directions, downstream

B. In one direction, downstream

C. Vertically

D. Horizontally

B. Transmission in Token Ring implementation traverses the ring in one direction, downstream. The station possessing the token is transmitting. Once the destination is reached, the frame is copied and discarded when the originator receives.

15. MSAU can connect a maximum of how many Token Ring stations?

A. 16

B. 3

C. 4

D. 8

D. Typically a MSAU can connect up to eight Token Ring stations. If you connect two or more MSAUs, then the number of Token Ring stations will increase as well.

16. What is the minimum frame size for an Ethernet frame?

A. 56 bytes

B. 128 bytes

C. 64 bytes

C. The minimum frame size in Ethernet implementation is 64 bytes.

17. The active monitor role includes which of the following:

A. Detect lost tokens and data frames

B. Monitor the neighbor notification process

C. Purge ring

D. Ensure ring delay

E. All of the above
   E. The active monitor ensures ring delay, purges ring, monitors neighbor notification process, detects lost tokens and other important ring management functions.

18. ARP places hardware addresses in the data portion of which layer?

A. Physical layer

B. Data Link layer

C. Frame layer

D. None of the above
   B. When an ARP is sent, hardware addresses are mapped with an IP address.

19. LLC Type 1 Operation is used by all the following except:

A. IBM

B. Novell

C. Microsoft

D. Digital

E. Sun
   E. Sun.

20. What is the maximum frame size for an Ethernet frame?

A. 250 bytes

B. 320 bytes

C. 1518 bytes

D. 1616 bytes
   C. An Ethernet frame can be a maximum of 1518 bytes long. Anything exceeding this frame size is considered a jabber.

Answers to Chapter 3 Self Test

1. PPP was designed to do what?

A. Standardize IP encapsulation

B. Address error-detection issues

C. Improve WAN connectivity

D. All of the above
   D. All of the above. To accommodate communications needs, a standard Internet encapsulation protocol, the Point-to-Point Protocol (PPP), was designed. Not only did PPP standardize Internet encapsulation of IP over point-to-point links, it also addressed other issues such as encapsulation and error detection.

2. Which of the following fields are included in the PPP frame header?

A. Control

B. FCS

C. Data
   A. Control field. The PPP frame header is subdivided into an 8-bit address field, an 8-bit control field, and a 16-bit protocol field.

3. PPP operates on what layer of the OSI model?

A. Application

B. Session

C. Data Link

D. Transport
   C. PPP operates primarily on the second (Data Link) and third (Network) layers of the OSI model.

4. The NCP is utilized by PPP on which layer?

   A. Network

   B. Session

   C. Data Link

   D. Transport
      A. Network. The family of Network Control Protocols (NCPs) is used for establishing and configuring the various Network layer protocols.

5. The most intensive authentication standard for PPP is _____.

   A. PAP

   B. RADIUS

   C. CHAP

   D. TACACS
      C. CHAP. The Challenge Handshake Authentication Protocol is used to verify the credibility of a connection using a three-way handshake. After the initial link has been established, however, CHAP also periodically (and randomly) verifies the validity of the connection by sending a "challenge" message.

6. HDLC is considered a bit-stuffing _____.

   A. Protocol

   B. Algorithm

   C. Encryption

   D. Authentication
      B. Algorithm. Although HDLC is commonly referred to as a protocol, it isn't a protocol at all. HDLC (High Level Data Link Control) is actually a Data Link layer bit-stuffing algorithm that specifies a data encapsulation method for synchronous serial links.

7. CRC is primarily used for what?

   A. Error detection

   B. Framing

   C. Encoding

   D. Protocol identification
      A. Error detection. Each frame includes two CRC bytes for error checking.

8. SDLC is primarily used for what?

   A. Peer-to-peer communications

   B. Broadcasting

   C. Multiport networking
      C. Multiport networking. SDLC (Synchronous Data Link Control) differs from HDLC in that it is not used for peer-to-peer communications. It is used primarily for multipoint networking.

9. In Frame Relay headers, FECNs and BECNs (bits) are used for which of the following?

   A. Fragments

   B. Runts

   C. Congestion

   D. Lost frames
      C. Congestion. Along a PVC, the frame may experience latency due to congestion. This is where the FECNs and BECNs can be useful. These bits are meant to notify a subscriber's device of congestion on the network.

10. LMI recognizes only what type of IEs?

    A. Report-type

    B. Keepalive

    C. PVC status

    D. All of the above
       D. All of the above. The LMI protocol
       is designed so that the subscriber must
       initiate information exchange, so that
       the network is not taxed unnecessarily.
       The exchange consists of a requesting
       frame comprising a six-octet header
       and a list of IEs. These IEs are
       report-type, keepalive, and PVC
       status.

11. Which Cisco router command would you
    use to determine if LMI is up or down?

    A. SH INTB

    B. SH FR PVC

    C. SH FR LMI

    D. A and C
       D. Both the SH INTB and SH FR
       LMI commands identify the current
       status of the LMI.

12. SVCs identify that sending what signal has
    completed the signal transmission?

    A. An ACK

    B. A Clear Request

    C. A Termination Request

    D. A NACK
       B. Clear Request. To establish this
       connection, the DTE will send a
       Call Request with the necessary
       information (source/destination
       addresses) to establish a connection.
       If the receiving end sends an

acknowledgment back, then
transmissions begin and remain up
until the necessary information has
been passed. This is signaled with a
Clear Request packet.

13. SMDS supports which of the following?

    A. OC-3 speed

    B. Encryption

    C. End-to-end connectivity

    D. X.121 addressing
       C. One of SMDS's most appealing
       features is that it accommodates
       LAN-to-WAN connectivity.

14. How are ATM and SMDS similar?

    A. They use 53-byte uniform cells

    B. They use FCS for error detection

    C. They support VCIs

    D. They support SIP Relay
       A. ATM is similar to SMDS in that
       they share similar 53-byte cell-relay
       packets that have 48 bytes for data and
       a 5-byte address header.

15. What is the best ATM encapsulation
    method to use with SMDS?

    A. AAL5snap

    B. AAL34smds

    C. AAL5MUX

    D. QSAAL
       B. AAL34smds. This method supports
       both connectionless and connection-
       oriented protocols that utilize a
       variable bit rate such as SMDS. The
       actual encapsulation type is
       AAL34smds.

16. VCIs are segments of which of the following?

    A. LANs

    B. PVCs

    C. Virtual circuits

    C. A virtual channel is a segment of the virtual circuit. A virtual path consists of a set of these channels.

17. What type of ISDN standard supports two bearer channels and one signaling channel?

    A. ATM

    B. PRI

    C. X.25

    D. BRI

    D. ISDN BRI is often referred to as "2B+D" or "bonded ISDN" because it utilizes two Bearer channels with 64 Kbps for data, and one signaling channel with a 16 Kbps bandwidth.

18. Which of these WAN alarms is caused by a loss of synchronization?

    A. RA

    B. DF

    C. YA

    D. 1s

    A. Red alarms (RA) identify that the signal is out of frame or out of synchronization. RA generally indicates a break in the line before the device that detects or reports the alarm.

19. What type of signaling error is a result of pulses registered in consecutive polarity?

    A. BPVs

    B. Framing errors

    C. Bit errors

    D. WAN flaps

    A. A BPV occurs every time the number of times pulses of the same consecutive polarity are transmitted in violation of the bipolar signal format.

20. What T1 test stresses the circuit beyond the point where normal transmissions would be, in an attempt to replicate possible connectivity problems?

    A. 3/24

    B. All 1s

    C. QUASI

    D. All 0s

    C. QUASI testing randomly changes the bit pattern (using the pulses – ones) around in an attempt to create a signal that physically stresses the circuit past the level that normal data transmissions would cause.

Answers to Chapter 4 Self Test

1. Which of the following is a transport protocol?

    A. IP

    B. ICMP

    C. UDP

    D. ARP

C. UDP is the only true Layer 4 protocol in this list. They are all connectionless protocols.

2. What is the purpose of ARP?

   A. To map ports to IP addresses

   B. To connect TCP to IP

   C. To broadcast IP addresses

   D. To map Layer 2 addresses to Layer 3 addresses

   D. ARP is used to map IP addresses to Layer 2 addresses, so that IP packets can be sent to the right destination at Layer 2.

3. Which of the following programs can be used to connect to many TCP-based services?

   A. Ping

   B. FTP

   C. Telnet

   D. NETSTAT

   C. Telnet is a TCP client program, is available on almost all IP hosts, and can be used to manually issue commands to many servers, including SMTP, HTTP, and FTP servers.

4. Which range is known as the Well Known ports?

   A. 0 through 1023

   B. 0 through 1024

   C. 1024 through 49151

   D. 49152 through 65535

   A. 0 through 1023 is the Well Known ports range, and many popular services run from ports in this range.

In addition, on UNIX, the user must be root to start services listening on these ports.

5. To what IP address does a DHCP client send when requesting a new address?

   A. 0.0.0.0

   B. 10.0.0.1

   C. 127.0.0.1

   D. 255.255.255.255

   D. 255.255.255.255. Since a new DHCP client has no IP address, it must broadcast for one. Of the two broadcast addresses (0.0.0.0, 255.255.255.255) in the preceding list, the RFC for DHCP indicates to use 255.255.255.255.

6. IP multicast is associated with which IP class?

   A. Class A, 1–126

   B. Class B, 128–191

   C. Class C, 192–223

   D. Class D, 224–239

   D. Class D is the range of IP addresses that has been set aside for multicasts.

7. When an FTP client opens a port for the FTP server to connect to, this is called:

   A. Active mode

   B. Passive mode

   C. Control channel

   D. Data channel

   A. Active mode is the correct answer. Data channel could also be correct, except that it also refers to the mode where the *server* is listening (passive mode). The question is specific about the *client* listening, so active mode is a better answer.

8. Which is the correct sequence for a TCP three-way handshake?

    A. SYN, ACK, FIN

    B. SYN, SYN+ACK, FIN

    C. SYN, SYN+ACK, ACK

    D. SYN, SYN, ACK

    C. The client sends a SYN packet, the server responds with a SYN+ACK packet, and finally the client sends a SYN and the handshake is done. FIN is part of the teardown, not the initial handshake.

9. IP operates at which OSI layer?

    A. 2

    B. 3

    C. 4

    D. 7

    B. IP is a Layer 3 (network layer) protocol.

10. If a host can communicate with other hosts on its own subnet, but not with hosts on other subnets, what is a likely cause?

    A. Something is broken at Layer 1 or 2

    B. The router is malfunctioning

    C. The default gateway is not set

    D. DNS isn't working

    C. Given only the information here, most likely that one host has a bad or missing default gateway. If Layer 1 or 2 were broken, that host wouldn't be able to communicate on the same subnet. If DNS weren't working, the host also wouldn't likely be able to communicate properly on the local subnet. If the router were malfunctioning, you would have likely heard about other hosts on the same subnet having the same problem.

11. Which commands will display a route table on a host? (Select two.)

    A. NETSTAT -R

    B. ARP -A

    C. TRACEROUTE

    D. ROUTE PRINT

    A, D. On many operating systems, NETSTAT -R and ROUTE PRINT will display the local route table.

12. Which command displays the route table on a Cisco router?

    A. NETSTAT -R

    B. ROUTE PRINT

    C. SHOW IP ROUTE

    D. SHOW ROUTE

    C. SHOW IP ROUTE is the correct command. SHOW ROUTE isn't specific enough since Cisco routers are capable of maintaining route tables for many protocols. NETSTAT -R and ROUTE PRINT are for operating systems like UNIX and Windows.

13. Describe the function of the DEBUG IP ICMP command:

A. To send broadcast ICMP packets from the router to all hosts

B. To determine if the router is sending and receiving ICMP messages itself

C. To allow routing of ICMP debugging messages

D. To cause the router to send diagnostic information via ICMP

B. This command will display ICMP messages that the router itself is sending or receiving. These do not include messages that hosts are sending each other, even if they pass through the router.

14. If a host can communicate with some hosts and not others on its local and on remote subnets, a likely cause is:

A. Incorrect subnet mask

B. Misconfigured router

C. Partial network failure

D. Bad ARP table

A. Given the description, the most likely cause is a bad subnet mask. If the router were misconfigured or if a partial network failure had occurred, there would likely be complaints about other hosts. A bad ARP table would be a possible symptom of this problem rather than a root cause. An incorrect subnet mask will cause a host to determine that some hosts are directly reachable that aren't, or that it needs to use the default gateway when hosts are actually on the local subnet.

15. Which of the following is a characteristic of a connectionless protocol such as UDP?

A. Lost packets are retransmitted

B. There is less network traffic

C. Port numbers are used to differentiate communications

D. Packets are delivered in the correct order

B. When used for the appropriate application, connectionless protocols use fewer network resources because they don't have the overhead of connection-oriented protocols. Retransmitting and resequencing packets are characteristics of reliable protocols. Port numbers are used with both connection-oriented and connectionless protocols.

16. Which of the following is a routing protocol (used to exchange routes between routers)?

A. ARP

B. ICMP

C. IGMP

D. RIP

D. RIP (Routing Information Protocol) is one protocol that can be used for routers to exchange routes. ICMP can be used to fix bad route information, but it does not transfer route tables en masse.

17. Which command is used to display ARP information as the router processes it?

A. SHOW IP ARP

B. DEBUG ARP

C. SHOW ARP

D. DEBUG IP ARP

B. DEBUG ARP is the correct command. The DEBUG command will show ARP events as they happen. SHOW ARP and SHOW IP ARP actually display the same information, but they display the ARP table and don't provide any kind of real-time monitoring. DEBUG IP ARP isn't a valid command in Cisco IOS so far.

18. Which command is probably the best one to use when starting to debug a host-to-host IP networking problem?

   A. PING

   B. ARP

   C. TRACEROUTE

   D. NETSTAT

   A. PING encompasses many checks with one command, and is probably the best place to start narrowing things down. ARP and NETSTAT are more useful for checking specific things, and should be a later step. TRACEROUTE can give a lot of the same information, but takes longer typically.

19. What does the DEBUG IP PACKET command do?

   A. Causes a copy of each packet to be sent to another interface for monitoring by a protocol analyzer

   B. Causes the router to display information about each packet as it is routed

   C. Causes the router to send an ICMP message for each packet received

D. None of the above

   B. DEBUG IP PACKET will cause the router to display information about each packet as the router processes it. Again, be careful with this command as it may take your router down.

20. What is the command used to configure a Cisco router to forward DHCP broadcasts?

   A. DHCP FORWARD

   B. BOOTP FORWARD

   C. IP FORWARD

   D. IP HELPER

   D. IP HELPER is the correct command. This is an interface command, which means it must be applied to each interface on which you need this function.

Answers to Chapter 5 Self Test

1. What layer of the OSI model does IPX correspond to?

   A. Data Link

   B. Network

   C. Transport

   D. Session

   B. Network. IPX is a Layer 3 connectionless transport protocol that resides above the Data Link layer. This protocol receives data from the higher-layer protocols (such as SPX and NCP), encapsulates them in an

IPX datagram, and sends them to the Data Link layer for encapsulation in Ethernet frames.

2. What two Ethernet frame types support TCP/IP?

   A. Ethernet 802.3
   B. Ethernet 802.2
   C. Ethernet SNAP
   D. Ethernet II
   C, D. Ethernet SNAP and Ethernet II. Ethernet 802.3 supports IPX/SPX only. Ethernet 802.2 supports IPX/SPX and FTAM. Ethernet SNAP supports IPX/SPX, AppleTalk Phase II, and TCP/IP. Ethernet II supports IPX/SPX, AppleTalk Phase I, and TCP/IP.

3. Which one of the following three protocols uses a one-to-one acknowledgment for transmitted packets?

   A. IPX
   B. SPX
   C. SPX II
   B. SPX. The IPX protocol has no mechanism for guaranteed delivery, and requires no acknowledgment. SPX sends one packet and then waits for an acknowledgment before transmitting the next. SPX II improves the performance of SPX by allowing multiple packets to be sent before an acknowledgment is returned.

4. NetWare Core Protocols (NCP) uses SPX for guaranteed delivery.

   A. True
   B. False
   B. False. NCP uses its own built-in mechanism for guaranteed delivery and uses IPX as the transport protocol.

5. Packet Burst provides greater performance through what enhancement?

   A. Packet sizes are increased when connecting over a router.
   B. The burst mechanism greatly reduces network traffic.
   C. Multiple packets are transmitted in response to a single read or write request.
   C. Multiple packets are transmitted in response to a single read or write request. Packet Burst is built on top of NCP communications. Standard NCP communications require a one-to-one acknowledgment for each packet sent; each request is followed by a single packet, and then an acknowledgment must be received. Packet Burst allows multiple packets to be transmitted in response to a single request. A is incorrect—Large Internet Packet (LIP) is the technology that increases packet size between a client and a server.

6. What is the Cisco feature that allows an administrator to control the flow of IPX NetBIOS packets to a particular host?

   A. IPX helper addresses/IPX helper lists
   B. IPX NetBIOS flow control
   C. ipx netbios type-20-propagation

D. NetBIOS directional caching

A. IPX helper addresses/IPX helper lists. These addresses allow the administrator to specify a host to which broadcasts can be directed. IPX helper lists specify a list of attributes for the broadcast packets to meet. When used in conjunction with IPX helper lists, you have a mechanism to very tightly control the flow of broadcasts.

7. How often are RIP broadcasts sent by default by Novell servers?

A. Every 10 seconds

B. Every 30 seconds

C. Every 60 seconds

D. Every 5 minutes
C. Every 60 seconds. By default, Novell servers will broadcast their RIP tables every 60 seconds.

8. What is the command on Cisco routers to view the SAP entries?

A. SHOW IPX SAP-TABLE

B. DISPLAY SERVERS

C. SHOW IPX SERVERS

D. DISPLAY NETWORKS
C. SHOW IPX SERVERS. This will display the SAP entries the router has received. DISPLAY SERVERS and DISPLAY NETWORKS are commands used by Novell servers to view SAP tables and RIP tables.

9. What is the maximum number of hops that NLSP supports?

A. 15

B. 127

C. 45

D. 30
B. 127. Novell's older routing protocol, IPX RIP, only supports 15 hops. NLSP, however, supports a maximum of 127 hops.

10. What is the SAP type for a Novell File Server?

A. 0x0005

B. 0x0007

C. 0x0107

D. 0x0004
D. 0x0004 is the SAP type for a Novell file server. Another very common SAP type is 0x278, which is a Novell Directory Server.

11. When a workstation boots up and loads the drivers for a Bindery connection, what is it most likely trying to connect to?

A. An NDS tree

B. A Novell 4.*xx* server

C. A Novell 3.*xx* server

D. A Windows NT server
C. A Novell 3.*xx* server. The Bindery is the flat database that exists on a Novell 3.*xx* server and is used for user authentication. Novell 4.*xx* servers use an NDS database, which is a hierarchical database. The NDS database that clients log in to on a 4.*xx* network is called the tree.

12. When a workstation issues an SLIST command, it generates a SAP Get Nearest Server command and waits for responses from all network servers to build the list it displays.

A. True

B. False

B. False. When a workstation issues an SLIST command, it reads the Bindery of the server it is connected to, and pulls the entries from the server's SAP table.

13. A workstation printing on a Novell network does not directly send print jobs to the printer, but rather generates print jobs in a queue on the file server itself.

A. True

B. False

A. True. When a workstation prints, it uses NCP to generate a job in the NetWare queue. Once the job is in the queue, a print server pulls it from the queue and sends it to the printer.

14. How will a Cisco router handle workstations' Get Nearest Server requests by default if there are no servers on the same interface as the workstation?

A. The router will drop the request.

B. The router will forward the request onto all interfaces.

C. The router will proxy-answer for servers using servers listed in its SAP table.

D. The router will forward the request to the interface containing the first server in its SAP table.

C. The router will proxy-answer for servers using servers listed in its SAP table. By default, Cisco routers will issue Proxy GNS server requests using servers listed in their SAP table.

15. By default, what will servers do if they receive a SAP packet and there is no route for it in their routing table?

A. The server will send a RIP broadcast to find the route.

B. The server will drop the SAP packet.

C. The server will store the SAP information in its SAP tables.

D. The server will store the SAP until a route is discovered.

B. The server will drop the SAP packet. By default, if a server receives a SAP packet and there is no route in the routing tables, the SAP will be discarded.

Answers to Chapter 6 Self Test

1. Which of the following is a transport protocol?

A. ID

B. DDP

C. RTMP

D. AFP

C. RTMP is one of the transport protocols available in the AppleTalk protocol suite.

2. What is the purpose of AARP?

A. To map sockets to AppleTalk addresses

B. To get a list of zones

C. To transport packets

D. To map Layer 2 addresses to Layer 3 addresses

D. AARP is used to map AppleTalk addresses to Layer 2 addresses, so that DDP packets can be sent to the right destination at Layer 2.

3. What is the purpose of NBP?

A. To map a named service to its network number, node ID, and socket number

B. To retrieve the default zone for the local network segment

C. To access files on AppleShare servers

D. For printing

A. NBP is used to map a named service to a particular AppleTalk address and socket.

4. Which protocol is used for file transfers in AppleTalk?

A. FTP

B. AFP

C. PAP

D. DDP

B. AFP, the AppleTalk Filing Protocol, is the one used in AppleTalk networking to access files.

5. What is the range, in hex, designated as the startup network range?

A. FFF0-FFFF

B. FF00-FFFF

C. 65280-65534

D. FF00-FFFE

D. FF00-FFFE. Answer C is the correct answer in decimal, but D is the correct hex range.

6. What is AppleTalk's Layer 3 protocol?

A. ZIP

B. RTMP

C. AARP

D. DDP

D. DDP, the Datagram Delivery Protocol, is AppleTalk's Layer 3 protocol. AARP is a Layer 3-to-Layer 2 mapping protocol; ZIP and RTMP ride on top of DDP, making them Layer 4 or above protocols.

7. What is the maximum number of bytes in the DDP portion of an AppleTalk packet?

A. 65,535

B. 599

C. 1000

D. 1500

B. 599; 13 bytes of header and 586 bytes of data.

8. How does a node determine if its randomly picked address is already in use?

A. By sending an AARP request

B. By using ZIP to ask the router

C. By listening to RTMP broadcasts

D. By sending NBP requests

A. It sends an AARP request for the address it just picked. If the node gets a reply, the address is in use and unavailable. A valid address is needed to use all of the other protocols mentioned.

9. When will a Cisco router declare its own AppleTalk address invalid and refuse to function?

   A. When it's set to 128

   B. When another seed router tells the Cisco router that it's using an invalid configuration

   C. When it's in dynamic mode

   D. When it's in the Startup range
   B. Cisco routers will shut down AppleTalk if they determine they are in conflict with another seed router on the same network segment.

10. What's the most likely cause of one missing zone on a workstation?

   A. ZIP is running on the wrong socket

   B. The NBP broadcast didn't get a response

   C. The local router doesn't have that zone in its ZIT

   D. A name conflict
   C. If a workstation is missing only a single zone, it most likely didn't get the zone from the local router, because the local router itself didn't have the zone.

11. Which command is used to display AppleTalk routes on a Cisco router?

   A. SHOW APPLETALK ZONE

   B. SHOW APPLETALK ROUTE

   C. SHOW APPLETALK ARP

   D. TRACEROUTE APPLETALK ROUTE
   B. SHOW APPLETALK ROUTE. This will display the interface over which the router learned the route, and the AppleTalk address from which it learned the route.

12. How do you display the ZIT on a Cisco router?

   A. SHOW APPLETALK ZONE

   B. SHOW APPLETALK ROUTE

   C. SHOW APPLETALK ARP

   D. SHOW APPLETALK NBP
   A. SHOW APPLETALK ZONE will display the ZIT, or Zone Information Table.

13. In which zone will an AppleTalk device appear on a network segment that has more than one zone?

   A. The first alphabetically in the Chooser

   B. The default

   C. The longest

   D. The shortest
   B. The default. On Cisco routers, the default is the first one programmed in.

14. By default, RTMP sends updates how often?

   A. Every 10 seconds

   B. Every 20 seconds

   C. Every 30 seconds

   D. Every 60 seconds
   A. Every 10 seconds.

15. A zone is:

    A. A network number

    B. A cable range

    C. A device driver

    D. A group of AppleTalk devices

    D. A zone is a logical grouping of AppleTalk devices.

16. What is the broadcast host ID?

    A. 0

    B. 253

    C. 254

    D. 255

    D. 255 is the broadcast host ID.

17. What is the maximum number of hops in an AppleTalk network routed with RTMP?

    A. 8

    B. 15

    C. 16

    D. 255

    B. 15 hops is the maximum. At hop 15, the hop counter would be 16, since it starts at 1.

18. What type of packet does a workstation use to get a list of zone names?

    A. GetZoneList

    B. NBP

    C. ZIP

    D. GetNetInfo

    A. GetZoneList is a type of ZIP packet used by workstations to get a list of zone names only, without cable ranges.

19. What's the most likely cause of two zones with the same name in the Chooser?

    A. Duplicate ZIP packets

    B. Corrupted router memory

    C. One hasn't timed out yet

    D. An extra space

    D. The most likely cause is an extra space on the end of one of the names.

20. What's the best way to prepare for problems on an AppleTalk network?

    A. Use EIGRP

    B. Use Phase II

    C. Document the network

    D. Use a Sniffer

    C. Document your network. Right now.

Answers to Chapter 7 Self Test

1. Split-horizon is a feature intended to prevent which of the following?

    A. TTL Expiration

    B. Large Routing Loops

    C. Count-to-Infinity

    D. Two-node routing loops

    D. Two-node routing loops. Split-horizon updates ensure that routes are not advertised back to a source from which they came.

2. Which of the following metrics is *not* a basis for IGRP routing decisions?

A. Reliability

B. Bandwidth

C. Cost

D. Delay
   C. Cost. IGRP does not factor in a cost "biasing" value when selecting appropriate routes.

3. Which of the following IGRP timers is *not* used for routing updates?

   A. Update timers

   B. Flooding timers

   C. Holddown timers

   D. Flush timers
      B. Flooding timers. IGRP uses update, invalid, holddown, and flush timers.

4. EIGRP has advantages over IGRP based upon all the following criteria *except*

   A. Faster convergence

   B. Variable-length subnet masking

   C. Packet-loss metric

   D. Multiprotocol support
      C. Packet-loss metric. EIGRP supports the same metrics as IGRP.

5. Which EIGRP packet is *not* used within the EIGRP protocol suite?

   A. Hello

   B. Update

   C. Reply

   D. Close
      D. Close. EIGRP sends Hello, Update, Query, Reply, and Request packets. There is no Close packet.

6. An IPX Packet Address is a concatenation of

   A. 16-bit XNS address with a 32-bit network-assigned address

   B. 32-bit network-assigned address and a 48-bit MAC address

   C. 32-bit 802.2 address and a 32-bit MAC address

   D. 48-bit NetBIOS address and a 32-bit MAC address
      B. 32-bit network-assigned address and a 48-bit MAC address. An IPX address is formed by concatenating a 32-bit network-assigned network address with the device's 48-bit MAC address.

7. AppleTalk RTMP routing is a

   A. Distance vector, periodic broadcast routing protocol

   B. Link-state, event-driven routing protocol

   C. Distance vector, event-driven protocol

   D. Link-state periodic broadcast protocol
      A. Distance vector, periodic broadcast routing protocol. AppleTalk RTMP uses RIP, which is a distance vector periodic broadcast protocol.

8. OSPF is a routing protocol with all the following characteristics *except*

   A. It allows for hierarchical networks

   B. It's a link-state protocol

   C. It's a periodic broadcast protocol

   D. It's based on the Dijkstra algorithm
      C. It's a periodic broadcast protocol. Although OSPF does refresh link-state

advertisements periodically, OSPF is primarily an event-driven protocol.

9. Which of the following packet types is *not* included in OSPF?

A. Hello

B. Link State Reachability

C. Link State Request

D. Link State Update
B. Link State Reachability. OSPF includes Hello, Database Description, Link State Request, Link State Update, and Link State Acknowledgment packet types.

10. OSPF supports Type-of-Service-based routing.

A. True

B. False
A. True. OSPF can allow for delay, throughput, or reliability routing decisions based upon IP TOS bits.

11. BGP makes routing decisions based upon all the following criteria except

A. AS path length

B. Metric

C. Hop count

D. IP address
C. Hop count. BGP is used between autonomous systems and does not carry per-hop information.

12. BGP is a periodic broadcast protocol.

A. True

B. False
B. False. BGP synchronizes its tables once and then relies on event updates when certain network changes occur.

13. IPX can be routed via all the following routing protocols except

A. IPX RIP

B. RTMP

C. IPX EIGRP

D. NLSP
B. RTMP. RTMP is used for routing AppleTalk networks and does not support NetWare IPX.

14. IPX access lists can be applied to all of the following except

A. GNS requests

B. Service Advertising Protocol (SAP)

C. IPX addresses

D. NetBEUI addresses
D. NetBEUI addresses. Although NetBIOS is a supported IPX socket, NetBEUI is not.

15. BGP is completely independent of the IGP.

A. True

B. False
B. False. You must use the NO SYNCHRONIZATION configuration command to uncouple BGP and IGP.

16. AppleTalk addresses are dynamically assigned.

A. True

B. False
A. True. AppleTalk uses a media-dependent address selection protocol for dynamically attaining AppleTalk addresses.

17. Which of the following is *not* a limitation of RIP?

A. Subnetting

B. Maximum 15-router hop count

C. Classful routing

D. Not scalable
A. Subnetting. Although RIP does not allow for variable-length subnetting, subnetting is supported.

18. Nodes on extended AppleTalk networks can belong to multiple zones.

A. True

B. False
B. False. An AppleTalk node can only belong to one zone; however, an extended AppleTalk network can contain multiple zones.

19. OSPF has a higher administrative distance than IGRP.

A. True

B. False
A. True. An IGRP route is selected over an OSPF-based route.

20. IGRP is a

A. Distance vector, periodic broadcast routing protocol

B. Link-state, event-driven routing protocol

C. Distance vector, event-driven protocol

D. Link-state periodic broadcast protocol
A. Distance vector, periodic broadcast routing protocol. IGRP uses a distance vector algorithm and regularly updates routes whether they have changed or not.

Answers to Chapter 8 Self Test

1. SNMP can be used for which of the following tasks?

A. Configuring network equipment

B. Resetting router passwords

C. Collecting statistical information

D. All of the above
D. SNMP can be used for all of these.

2. The Telnet client built into IOS can be used to test connectivity to which of the following protocols?

A. SNMP

B. PING

C. SMTP

D. SNMP-TRAP
C. SMTP is the only TCP protocol in this list, and Telnet can only be used to test TCP services.

3. Which of the following is *not* a function of CiscoWorks?

A. Configuring a router for the first time

B. Discovering the logical network layout

C. Tracking a MAC address to a particular switch port

D. Keeping statistics about your network
   A. Configuring a router for the first time. A Cisco router needs to have some configuration done to it before it will respond to SNMP, so SNMP cannot be used for the initial configuration.

4. Which of these programs from the CMU SNMP package is used to dump the SNMP table from a network device?

   A. snmpget

   B. snmpgetnext

   C. snmpwalk

   D. snmpset
   C. The snmpwalk program will attempt to retrieve all of the SNMP values from a network device.

5. Traceroute is possible because IP hosts are required to send what?

   A. ICMP echo replies

   B. ICMP TTL-exceeded messages

   C. SNMP traps

   D. Traceroute response packets
   B. Traceroute works via a side-effect of hosts' sending ICMP TTL-exceeded messages.

6. With respect to wiring, what does "NEXT" mean?

   A. The next patch panel

   B. The next bridge hop

   C. The next router hop

D. Near-end crosstalk
   D. NEXT is the term used for near-end crosstalk, the tendency for signals to jump pairs at the ends of cables.

7. What's the best way to learn how to use a protocol analyzer?

   A. Read the documentation

   B. Monitor a working network

   C. Monitor a failing network

   D. Monitor for "top talkers"
   B. Monitor a working network. There's nothing wrong with reading the documentation, but you'll learn more by reading it *and* practicing with it. You'll be better off getting comfortable with it on a working network, so you can see what's normal.

8. Which router feature is used to track traffic between Layer 3 addresses?

   A. Accounting

   B. SNMP

   C. Debugging

   D. HTTP server
   A. The accounting feature will keep track of the number of packets and bytes transferred between pairs of Layer 3 addresses.

9. Which of the following CiscoWorks applications is used to maintain VLAN information in Catalyst switches?

   A. CWSI

   B. ATMDirector

   C. UserManager

D. VLANDirector
D. VLANDirector is used to maintain VLAN configuration on Catalysts.

10. Which protocol is used by Cisco devices to discover neighboring Cisco devices?

A. SNMP

B. CWSI

C. CDP

D. UDP
C. The Cisco Discovery Protocol (CDP) is a Layer 2 protocol used to discover neighboring Cisco equipment, allowing network-management systems to automatically build a logical view of a network.

11. What type of test is used to determine cable length, or distance to cable breaks?

A. PING

B. TDR

C. NEXT

D. Attenuation
B. Time-domain reflectometer (TDR) is the test related to cable length.

12. What is the name for the list of numbers used to refer to a particular SNMP value?

A. ICMP

B. CWSI

C. OID

D. CDP
C. Object identifier (OID) is the name for the string of numbers used to request or set a particular SNMP value.

13. If you want to configure your router to log messages outside itself, you will need what kind of server?

A. Windows NT

B. UNIX

C. CWSI

D. Syslog
D. A syslog server can run on just about any operating system. It can be on the same server as CiscoWorks, but CiscoWorks is not in any way required.

14. One of the more important tasks performed when using a packet analyzer is

A. Keeping copies of the packets

B. Narrowing down what's being monitored

C. Sending SNMP requests

D. Printing packets
B. To use a packet analyzer effectively, you need to be able to narrow down what you want to capture in order to get just what you want to see.

15. In what version of IOS was the HTTP server officially introduced?

A. 11.0(6)

B. 11.1

C. 11.2

D. 12.0
C. Version 11.2. The HTTP server existed in 11.0(6) but only for certain platforms, and it wasn't documented. It was officially supported on most platforms starting with 11.2.

16. What kind of IOS command is used to turn a router into a very rudimentary sniffer?

    A. Set sniffer
    B. Span port
    C. Debug
    D. PING
       C. A number of debug commands can be used to display portions of packets and frames as they pass through the router.

17. What command is used to configure a router to log into a remote host?

    A. logging *host*
    B. logging buffered
    C. logging syslog
    D. logging *remote*
       A. The logging *host* command, where *host* is the name or IP address of your syslog server. Answers C and D are incorrect, unless you've got syslog servers named syslog and remote.

18. What is used by network devices to notify a management station of some event occurring or threshold being reached?

    A. ICMP
    B. CDP
    C. SNMP
    D. SNMP trap
       D. SNMP trap.

19. Microsoft Windows uses what protocol in its tracert implementation?

    A. CDP
    B. TCP
    C. UDP
    D. ICMP
       D. Unlike the Traceroute implemented on UNIX and Cisco routers, Windows uses ICMP.

20. What is one important difference between most commercial SNMP packages and most free ones?

    A. The ability to do SNMP traps
    B. A GUI
    C. Working over IP
    D. Working with Cisco equipment
       B. In this list, the biggest difference is the GUI. Most commercial packages include a GUI, but most free SNMP tools are command-line based. (Price is another big difference.)

Answers to Chapter 9 Self Test

1. All the following IP IOS interface switching modes are supported, except:

   A. Flow
   B. Optimum
   C. Virtual
   D. Fast
      C. Virtual. IOS supports many types of switching modes, including Fast, Optimum, Flow, Autonomous, and

Process switching. The selected switching can have significant impact on the CPU processor and buffer usage.

2. A 10 Mbps Ethernet usually saturates at about:

   A. 1 Mbps

   B. 3 Mpbs

   C. 6 Mbps

   D. 10 Mbps

   B. 3 Mbps. A heavily used Ethernet network will generally not exceed more than 3 Mbps within a typical client/server environment. A single server on a LAN can sometimes peak at higher rates.

3. When using subinterfaces, split-horizon is disabled by default.

   A. True

   B. False

   B. False. Cisco *enables* split-horizon by default on Frame Relay subinterfaces. It is *disabled* by default on non-subinterfaces.

4. Cisco IOS supports all the following Novell IPX encapsulation methods except:

   A. MAC

   B. ARPA

   C. Novell-Ether

   D. SNAP

   A. MAC. IPX encapsulation methods include SAP, HDLC, ARPA, Novell-Ether, and SNAP. It is important to

make sure that the PCs on the LAN are using the appropriate encapsulation drivers.

5. The following indicators may represent interface or network problems, except:

   A. CRC

   B. Drops

   C. Load

   D. Aborts

   C. Load. The load on a circuit represents the utilization. CRC errors, drops, and aborts can be caused by line conditions, overutilized connections, or lack of resources on the routers.

6. Which of the following signaling states should *not* be up on an active circuit?

   A. CTS

   B. DCR

   C. DCD

   D. DTR

   B. DCR. A circuit will show active states for Ready-to-Send, Carrier-to-Send, Data Terminal Ready, Data Carrier Detect, and Data Send Ready. Generally, a circuit will not show up/up unless all these signals are active.

7. Which of the following Frame Relay LMI types is *not* supported?

   A. IETF

   B. ANSI

   C. Q.933a

D. Cisco

A. IETF. Cisco supports three LMI types: ANSI, Q.933a, and Cisco proprietary. A Frame Relay connection will not show up/up unless the LMI is properly defined.

8. ATM AAL5 "packet shredding" is indicated by:

A. Packet drops

B. Ignores

C. CRC errors

D. Overruns

C. CRC errors. A lost cell will cause the AAL5 CRC trailer to increment the CRC error counters. This problem is usually due to an ATM contract violation of either PCR, SCR, MBS, or CDVT.

9. Cisco ATM supports all the following AAL5 adaptations except:

A. AAL5MUX

B. AAL5snap

C. AAL5nlpid

D. AAL5head

D. AAL5head. Cisco supports the AAL5MUX, AAL5snap, and AAL5nlpid. Generally, AAL5snap is the default setting.

10. Packet loss is usually attributed to an oversubscribed connection.

A. True

B. False

A. True. Packet loss generally occurs when there are too many packets and too little bandwidth. The resolution of this problem is to either route traffic elsewhere or add more circuit capacity.

11. Which of the following is *not* a buffer size attributed to various packet sizes?

A. Little

B. Medium

C. VeryBig

D. Huge

A. Little. The buffer sizes include Small, Middle, Big, VeryBig, Large, and Huge. Designate these buffers to better allocate memory for packet size.

12. The default buffer size for Big is 1518 bytes.

A. True

B. False

B. False. An Ethernet packet is typically 1518 bytes, but the default buffer size for a Big buffer is 1524 bytes. Of course, this parameter is adjustable.

13. All of the following types of memory are within Cisco hardware, except:

A. NVRAM

B. Flash

C. Swap

D. ROM

C. Swap. Although Swap is often used for UNIX Virtual memory, Cisco does not have swap space. All of the other memory modules are used for specific functions.

14. All routing tables are stored in:

A. Flash

B. NVRAM

C. VRAM

D. ROM

C. VRAM. Routing tables use Volatile RAM and are subject to change or initialization at startup. Use the SHOW MEMORY SUMMARY to see available memory.

15. The startup configuration for booting the router is stored in the boot ROM.

A. True

B. False

B. False. The startup configuration is stored on NVRAM, which allows for retaining the configuration while rebooting the router.

16. Most newer releases of IOS make better use of memory.

A. True

B. False

B. False. It is not unusual to get a more recent Early Field Trial version of IOS with a memory leak that does not re-allocate freed memory. In addition, newer IOS versions have features that are often memory intensive.

17. Cisco logging supports all the following except:

A. Console

B. Print spooler

C. Syslog daemon

D. Local log

B. Print spooler. Cisco supports logging to the console port, terminal monitor, local logs, and syslog daemon. Logs are very important for tracking a network problem.

18. Ping is really an ICMP redirect.

A. True

B. False

B. False. A ping is an ICMP echo request/reply. The ICMP echo request is sent out, and the echo reply is returned.

19. Traceroute sends pings to each hop.

A. True

B. False

B. False. Traceroute sends a UDP packet with an incrementing TTL. Each hop then replies with an ICMP "Timeout Exceeded" reply when the TTL expires.

20. Extended pings allow for all the following features except:

A. Modifying packet size

B. Specifying the route

C. Replacing the source IP address with that of another router

D. Modifying the payload content

C. Replacing the source IP address with that of another router. You can modify the source IP address to be that of another interface on the originating router. If the source IP address of another router was specified, then the packet would return to the other router, bypassing the originating router, and could be used as a denial-of-service attack.

Answers to Chapter 10 Self Test

1. You should enable DEBUG ALL when you log into a troubled router and don't know what the problem is.

   A. True

   B. False
   B. False. Depending on the scope of the debug and the amount of data processing through the router, DEBUG ALL can lock up the CPU.

2. If accessing the router via a VTY port and enabling debug, you should first enable what?

   A. Logging

   B. Terminal length

   C. Terminal monitor

   D. Virtual template
   C. Terminal monitor. The terminal monitor will display all information normally sent to the console port, also to the VTY port.

3. What should you do if the router appears to be hung up after you've enabled debug?

   A. Reboot the router

   B. Use the NO DEBUG ALL command

   C. Hit the break key

   D. Disconnect the WAN interface
   B. Use the NO DEBUG ALL command. Although you may have to wait a little while for the debug buffer to empty, the NO DEBUG ALL command usually turns off debugging eventually.

4. Applying an access list to a DEBUG IP command is not a good idea because access lists require processing overhead.

   A. True

   B. False
   B. False. An access list is intended to reduce the debugging information and prevent the router from locking up.

5. In order to gain a comprehensive view of a LAN's operations, you may want to use a:

   A. Bridge

   B. Repeater

   C. Sniffer

   D. Router in DEBUG ALL mode
   C. Sniffer. Some intelligent sniffers require only that you plug them in, and they are able to provide extremely accurate feedback.

6. Frame Relay debugging allows for you to directly examine all except:

   A. IP

   B. IPX

   C. LMI

   D. DLSW
   B. IPX. Although you can look into the packet debugging, there is no IPX option for Frame Relay debugging.

7. When trying to manage an ATM VCC status from an ATM Service Provider, you may want to use:

    A. Individual VCCs

    B. A large VP

    C. SVCs

    D. OAM cells

    D. OAM cells. ATM OAM cells are specifically designed for ATM VCC management.

8. Cisco supports the following remote authentication servers except:

    A. Radius

    B. TACACS

    C. TACACS+

    D. NIS+

    D. NIS+. Radius, TACACS, and TACACS+ are all supported authentication methods.

9. If you're specifying an argument on the command line, Cisco will execute what command by default?

    A. PING

    B. TRACEROUTE

    C. TELNET

    D. HELP

    C. TELNET. If you're specifying an IP address, host name, DNS name, or nonreserved command, the IOS will attempt to execute a TELNET to whatever is specified on the command line.

10. The default setting for a console port on a router is:

    A. 9600,N,1

    B. 2400,N,1

    C. 9600,E,2

    D. 2400,N,1

    A. 9600,N,1. 9600 bps, no parity, 1 stop bit is the default console port setting.

11. From the console port of a 2511, to access an async line from the Octal interface into the console port of another router, what should you do?

    A. Use the Kermit protocol

    B. Use L2F

    C. Use reverse Telnet

    D. Use LAT

    C. Use reverse Telnet, which allows access to an async line from the 2511 itself.

12. In order to switch to a different session of an async line to another async line, you first have to type which of the following key sequences:

    A. ESC, BREAK

    B. ESC-F4, !

    C. CTRL-ALT-DEL

    D. CTRL-SHIFT-6

    D. CTRL-SHIFT-6. This sequence then allows you to select another async line.

13. In order to read a core dump, what utility do you use?

    A. NROFF

    B. Stack Decoder

    C. vi

D. Microsoft Word
   B. Stack Decoder. Core dumps are generally not readable. The Stack Decoder is a tool used by Cisco to view core dumps.

14. Core dumps can be written to a server using all the following methods except:

    A. RCP

    B. TFTP

    C. SSH

    D. FTP
       C. SSH. Core dumps can be written by FTP, RCP, or TFTP; but TFTP is limited to 16MB core files.

15. New IOS microcode is available for free downloads from Cisco.

    A. True

    B. False
       B. False. Contrary to popular practice, Cisco IOS is not free. In addition, the microcode is bundled in with the IOS.

16. Which of the following commands is a good troubleshooting starting point when logging into a troubled router?

    A. SHOW BUFFERS

    B. DEBUG IP PACKET

    C. TRACEROUTE WWW.CISCO.COM

    D. SHOW VERSION
       D. SHOW VERSION. The SHOW VERSION command is typically a good starting place to verify hardware and software configuration.

17. Which of the following commands helps you gain an overview of the router's operating environment?

    A. SHOW ROUTER

    B. SHOW ENV ALL

    C. SHOW TEMP

    D. SHOW HARDWARE
       B. SHOW ENV ALL, which displays the electrical, temperature, and controller information.

18. Cisco TAC will often request the output of which command when opening a case?

    A. SHOW IP ROUTE

    B. SHOW ARP

    C. TRACE WWW.CISCO.COM

    D. SHOW TECH
       D. SHOW TECH, which displays substantial essential configuration and operating information.

19. If you can't get a response from a reverse Telnet on a Cisco 2511 async line, what should you do?

    A. Reboot the router

    B. Clear the line

    C. Change the cable

    D. Check the routing table
       B. Clear the line. You may have to clear the line several times to get a response from the attached device.

20. By default, you can Telnet to any VTY interface.

    A. True

B. False

B. False. A VTY interface requires a user-supplied password before you can Telnet to it.

Answers to Chapter 11 Self Test

1. A VLAN is equivalent to a:

   A. Trunk

   B. Broadcast domain

   C. Port

   D. Module

   B. Broadcast domain. VLANs represent a group of stations that can broadcast to each other, hence they are equivalent to a broadcast domain.

2. Switches are similar to what network device?

   A. Routers

   B. Repeaters

   C. Bridges

   D. Firewalls

   C. Bridges. Switches are most similar to bridges in that they operate at Layer 2, and they forward based on learned Layer 2 information.

3. Catalyst switches use what type of VLAN assignment, primarily?

   A. IP address

   B. MAC address

   C. SAID

   D. Port

   D. Port. Catalyst switches are primarily port-assigned switches, because all the VLAN assignment is done per port or group of ports.

4. Catalyst switches can auto-sense speed and duplex on which of the following LAN types?

   A. Token Ring

   B. Ethernet

   C. Fast Ethernet

   D. FDDI

   C. Fast Ethernet. This is the only type that supports auto-sensing of both speed and duplex. FDDI is fixed for both, Token Ring is always full duplex, and Catalyst switches don't support full-duplex Ethernet (10MB).

5. Which protocol is used to distribute VLAN information between switches?

   A. Spanning Tree Protocol (STP)

   B. Virtual Trunking Protocol (VTP)

   C. Bridge Protocol Data Units (BPDU)

   D. 802.10

   B. Virtual Trunking Protocol (VTP). VTP is the protocol that Cisco created to distribute and maintain VLAN information automatically between switches.

6. Of the following, which is the biggest disadvantage of VTP?

   A. Broadcasts flood to every switch by default

B. Have to configure domain name on every switch

C. Each switch has to have a different VTP password

D. Slower than spanning tree
A. Broadcasts flood to every switch by default. This is the biggest potential problem with VTP, although it's easily configured away. Answers B, C, and D aren't true or don't apply.

7. UplinkFast is recommended for what kind of network layout?

A. Single switch

B. Linear

C. Hierarchical

D. Full mesh
C. Hierarchical. Due to the root switch requirements, the network has to be designed with this in mind. UplinkFast is useless on a single-switch or linear layout, and on a full-mesh network it would be difficult to decide how to assign the switches.

8. Which command is used to display the bridge tables in a Catalyst switch?

A. SHOW MAC

B. SHOW VLAN

C. SHOW PORT

D. SHOW CAM
D. SHOW CAM. This command shows the tracked information about MAC addresses in VLANs.

9. Which command is used to set up a monitoring port to use with a Sniffer?

A. SET SPAN

B. SET CAM

C. SET VLAN

D. SET PORT
A. The SET SPAN command is the one involved with monitoring traffic on a Catalyst switch.

10. Which version of the Catalyst software introduced VTP version 2?

A. 2.3(4)

B. 3.1(1)

C. 4.1(1)

D. 5.1(2)
B. Version 3.1(1). According to the Cisco documentation, VTP2 was introduced in Catalyst software version 3.1(1).

11. Disabling which of the following could lead to loops?

A. UplinkFast

B. PortFast

C. Spanning tree

D. VTP
C. Spanning tree is the protocol designed to detect Layer 2 loops.

12. What are the default SPAN settings?

A. Copy VLAN 1 to 1/1

B. Copy 1/1 to 1/2

C. Do ports defined

D. All VLANs to the fastest port
A. Copy VLAN 1 to 1/1. If you don't set a SPAN port before you turn it on, it will copy all of VLAN 1 to port 1/1 and disable port 1/1 for normal use.

13. Which command is used to check for errors for a particular station?

A. SHOW MODULE

B. SHOW CAM

C. SHOW VLAN

D. SHOW PORT
D. The SHOW PORT command is the one that displays error per port and, hence, per station.

14. The behavior of forwarding broadcasts to all ports in a bridge is called:

A. Spanning

B. Forwarding

C. Flooding

D. Pruning
C. Flooding. When a bridge forwards a broadcast frame to all ports (except the one it came in on), this is commonly called flooding.

15. In order for stations to communicate across VLANs without bridging them together, what is usually required?

A. A bridge

B. A hub

C. A router

D. A firewall
C. A router. Most commonly, a router is used to pass packets between VLANs at Layer 3.

16. The default SAID is the VLAN number, plus

A. 1000

B. 10000

C. 100000

D. 1000000
C. 100000. The default SAID is the VLAN plus 100,000 (one hundred thousand).

17. Intelligent bridges keep tables of what kind of addresses?

A. IP

B. CAM

C. IPX

D. MAC
D. MAC. Intelligent bridges keep tables of the Layer 2 (MAC) addresses. CAM does not refer to a network address type.

18. Configuring port security will accomplish what?

A. Keep hackers out

B. Turn off the port

C. Accept frames only from a particular MAC address

D. Turn off VLAN functions
C. Accept frames only from a particular MAC address. Security means that the port is "locked" to a particular MAC address.

19. BPDU Hello frames are addressed to what?

A. MAC broadcast

B. MAC multicast

C. Catalyst switches

D. IP broadcast
B. MAC multicast. BPDU Hello frames are sent to a Layer 2 multicast address.

20. Cisco's enhancement to Spanning Tree Protocol to reduce link failover time is called

A. PortFast

B. ISL

C. UplinkFast

D. VTP
C. UplinkFast is Cisco's solution to shortening the convergence time for redundant links.

Answers to Chapter 12 Self Test

1. To use the Cisco IOS show interfaces commands, you must be in which mode?

A. Line

B. Privileged

C. User

D. Config
B. Privileged mode.

2. What is the command to check collision rate?

A. show interface rates

B. show ethernet collisions

C. show interface ethernet

D. show collision rate
C. The show interface ethernet command displays the number of collisions and number of output packets.

3. What is indicated by lots of errors with a low collision rate?

A. Poor physical connection

B. High noise-level

C. Trouble with network monitoring software

D. Runt frames
B. High noise-level. Check the CRC errors and collision rate by using the show interface ethernet command.

4. A Token Ring network works great during periods of low traffic, but sometimes gets congested. A possible solution is to:

A. Segment the network

B. Switch to Ethernet

C. Reboot all routers

D. Add additional nodes to your network
A. Segmenting your network will distribute the traffic.

5. Which of the following is *not* a type of LAN technology?

A. FDDI

B. Ethernet

C. TCP/IP

D. Token Ring
C. TCP/IP is a network protocol, not a type of LAN technology.

6. What loopback tests are extremely helpful in determining the source of a WAN problem?

   A. CSU/DSU

   B. CDU/SCU

   C. Wide area network

   D. Local area network
   A. CSU/DSU (channel service unit/data service unit) is a hardware device about the size of an external modem that converts digital data frames from the communications technology used on a LAN into frames appropriate to a WAN.

7. Which of the following describes ISDN BRI service channeling?

   A. 2D+B

   B. B+D

   C. 2B+D

   D. 2C+D
   C. 2B+D. The B channel service operates at 64 Kbps and is used to carry data. The D channel operates at a slower 16 Kbps and is used for carrying signaling and control information.

8. If your Frame Relay link goes down, which of the following will you *not* check?

   A. Look for physical problems, such as cabling or hardware.

   B. Check to see if keepalives are being sent.

   C. Look for encapsulation mismatch.

   D. Check that token frames are not corrupt.
   D. Checking the token frame is something you would do if having problems with your LAN Token Ring network, not a Frame Relay network.

9. What difficulty may occur when you're using certain debug commands on your network?

   A. Runt frames

   B. Increase in traffic

   C. Serial line failure

   D. NIC interface problems
   B. Increase in traffic. Some debug commands will generate a lot of output for each processed packet. Try to use debug during off-peak hours.

10. A user gets a new machine and moves the IP address. Suddenly no one is able to connect. What is the *most* likely cause?

    A. Router is misconfigured

    B. ARP cache hasn't aged out

    C. Token frame is corrupt

    D. The new machine is not network compatible
    B. The ARP cache may not have aged out. The ARP table contains the MAC address to IP address mappings. You will need to clear the cache by using the clear arp-cache command. This should solve the problem because the new ARP table will reflect the new MAC address and IP address mapping.

11. What command is used to set GNS response delay?

    A. ipx gns-response-delay *<#ofmilliseconds>*

    B. ipx gns-response-delay *<#ofseconds>*

    C. gns-response-delay *<#ofseconds>*

    D. gns-delay *<#ofseconds>*
    A. ipx gns-response-delay *<#ofmilliseconds>*. You may have to manually decrease or increase the GNS response delay to improve response time.

12. You created an access list that allows a SAP through, but you are still unable to see it at the next hop. Which of the following are *not* likely causes? (Select two.)

    A. Misconfigured access lists

    B. Unspecified route to next hop

    C. Incorrect IP address

    D. Incorrect subnet mask
    C, D. Incorrect IP address and incorrect subnet mask. IP addresses and subnet masks are used with TCP/IP, not IPX.

13. What does the debug ipx sap command display?

    A. Information on SAP advertisements the router sends and receives

    B. Information on SAP advertisements the router sends

    C. Information on SAP advertisements the router receives

    D. IPX protocol status
    A. The debug ipx sap command is a useful IPX troubleshooting tool. It displays SAP advertisement information.

14. What does the debug appletalk zip command display?

    A. Important Zone Information Protocol (ZIP) events

    B. Zone Information Protocol (ZIP) errors

    C. Zone Information Packet (ZIP) errors

    D. AppleTalk protocol status
    B. The debug appletalk zip command displays important Zone Information Protocol (ZIP) events. This is a very useful tool when troubleshooting an AppleTalk network.

15. The router seems to be unable to discover routes, and the port is trapped in acquiring mode. What is a possible solution?

    A. Replace cabling

    B. Assign a network number or cable range to the router interface

    C. Reboot the router

    D. Re-address workstations in your network
    B. Assign a network number or cable range to the router interface. This will put it in nondiscovery mode.

16. What does NBP stand for?

    A. Network Binding Protocol

    B. Name Bonding Protocol

C. Name Binding Protocol

D. Network Binding Packet
C. Name Binding Protocol. In an AppleTalk network, when a client wants to access a service, a request is sent to the router for a list of zones. The Name Binding Protocol (NBP) looks for servers in the specified zone.

17. What is the Web site URL for Cisco Connection Online (CCO) help?

A. http://www.cisco-help.com

B. http://www.cisco.com

C. http://www.cisco.help.com

D. www.cisco.help.com
B. http://www.cisco.com. Cisco Connection Online (CCO) help is available 24 hours a day, 7 days a week.

18. Where can you go to find Cisco software upgrades?

A. CCO Software Center

B. Cisco Technical Assistance Center

C. CCO Documentation

D. TAC
A. CCO's Software Center makes it easier to find and download software updates and utilities for Cisco products.

19. IPX works at what layer?

A. Transport

B. Internet

C. Network

D. Data link
C. IPX is a Network layer protocol. IPX's purpose is to provide

connectionless, best-effort transport service to upper-layer protocols such as SPX, NCP, and NetBIOS.

Answers to Chapter 13 Self Test

1. ISDN is *not* used in which one of the following markets?

A. Telecommuting

B. ATM permanent virtual circuits

C. Frame Relay backup

D. The SOHO market
B. ATM permanent virtual circuits. ATM speeds of 1.5 Mbps to 155 Mbps are much higher than ISDN speeds of 64 to 128 Kbps.

2. ISDN is delivered from the CO to the customer via which of the following?

A. 1 wire

B. 2 wires

C. 3 wires

D. 4 wires
B. 2 wires are used from CO to NT1, but 4 wires from the NT1 to router.

3. What does ISDN stand for?

A. International Signaling Device of Nerds

B. International Switched Data Network

C. I Still Don't Know

D. Integrated Services Digital Network
D. Integrated Services Digital Network. ISDN allows multiple types

of services to be integrated onto one digital network.

4. Individual ISDN B channels operate via which of the following?

A. TDM at 48 Kbps

B. FDM at 64 Kbps

C. TDM at 64 Kbps

D. QPSK at 56 Kbps
   C. TDM at 64 Kbps. The two B channels are Time Division Multiplexed (TDM) and operate at a 64-Kbps rate.

5. Which ISDN switch type is typically *not* used in the United States?

A. NET3 switch type

B. Nortel DMS100

C. NI switch type

D. Lucent 5ESS
   A. NET3 switch type. The last three choices are the predominant switch types used in the U.S.

6. Which of the following completes Layer 1 activation?

A. TE sends frames with the A bit = 0

B. NT1 sends frames with the A bit = 0

C. TE sends frames with the A bit = 1

D. NT1 sends frames with the A bit = 1
   C. TE sends frames with the A bit = 1. Only frames originating at the TE have the A bit. This bit is set to 1 when activation is complete.

7. The main job of Q.921 is to

A. Send SETUP messages to the Called Party

B. Verify SPIDs with the ISDN switch

C. Deliver Q.931 messages safely to the ISDN switch

D. Serve as a keepalive from the TE
   C. Deliver Q.931 messages safely to the ISDN switch. Q.921 is a Layer 2 protocol that carries Layer 3 information (Q.931) safely to the other end of the data link.

8. A TEI is a:

A. Transfer of Endpoint ISDN

B. Terminal Endpoint Identifier

C. Telephone Egress Indicator

D. Terminal Exit Interface
   B. Terminal Endpoint Identifier. The Terminal Endpoint (TE) is identified by the TEI.

9. Layer 2 status from the SHOW ISDN STATUS command should report

A. MULTIPLE FRAME ESTABLISHED

B. TEI ASSIGNED

C. SABME

D. LAPD
   A. The MULTIPLE FRAME ESTABLISHED state is achieved after a successful SABME/UA exchange between the TE and ISDN switch.

10. When are SPIDs required?

A. SPIDs are always required

B. When your service provider can lower costs with them

C. When the switch is a DMS100 or NI (National ISDN) switch

D. When a Cisco router uses ISDN BRI
   C. When the switch is a DMS100 or
   NI (National ISDN) switch. DMS100
   and NI switches always want SPIDs.
   Other switches may or may not
   require SPIDs.

11. The best way to see if your configured
    SPIDs are valid is to

    A. Look for the Active light on the NT1

    B. Use the SHOW ISDN STATUS
       command

    C. Use the DEBUG ISDN Q.921
       command

    D. Use the SHOW DIALER command
       B. Use the SHOW ISDN STATUS
       command. Look for SPID status of
       "sent and valid" in the output
       of command.

12. Which command defines "interesting"
    traffic that will cause the ISDN link to dial?

    A. Dialer-ping

    B. Dialer-map

    C. Dialer-list

    D. Dialer-match
       C. The dialer-list command, which
       may point to an access list, defines
       which packets get through and which
       do not.

13. Which command binds the dialer-list to
    the BRI interface?

    A. Dialer-map

    B. Dialer-group

    C. Dialer-bind

    D. Dialer-link
       B. The dialer-group command binds
       the dialer-list to an interface, much as

the access-group command binds an
access list to an interface.

14. The dialer-map command links a
    _____ to a _____:

    A. Dialer-list, interface

    B. Telephone number, IP address

    C. Calling Party Number, Called Party
       Number

    D. Protocol, BRI interface
       B. Telephone number, IP address.
       The dialer-map links telephone
       numbers to next-hop IP addresses,
       which the routing table also utilizes.

15. Most long-distance ISDN BRI calls are
    placed at a maximum speed of

    A. 56 Kbps

    B. 64 Kbps

    C. 72 Kbps

    D. 164 Kbps
       A. 56 Kbps. Due to switch limitations,
       many ISDN connections can only
       achieve 56 Kbps and not the full 64
       Kbps.

16. Which is *not* a part of the Q.931
    SETUP message?

    A. Bearer Capability

    B. Called Party Number

    C. Calling Party Number

    D. Cause code
       D. Cause codes are necessary when
       calls are ended, not during call setup.

17. The Bearer Capability IE defines

    A. The reason for DISCONNECT

    B. The type of ISDN call requested

    C. The number of B channels used

D. Who placed the ISDN call
B. The type of ISDN call requested. The Bearer Capability IE dynamically requests call characteristics such as 56-Kbps versus 64-Kbps data on any given call.

18. The Most Significant Bit (MSB) of the Call Reference IE is set to

   A. 0 in messages from the TE to the switch

   B. 0 in messages from the originating side of the SETUP message

   C. 0 in messages to the originating side of the SETUP message

   D. 0 in messages from the switch to the TE
   B. 0 in messages from the originating side of the SETUP message. The originator (switch or TE) of the SETUP message sets the Call Reference Flag (MSB) to a 0. Replies from the receiver set this bit to a 1.

19. What is the default value of the dialer idle-timeout on Cisco routers?

   A. 60 seconds

   B. 180 seconds

   C. 300 seconds

   D. 120 seconds
   D. 120 seconds. Cisco defaults to tearing down ISDN calls two minutes after the last packet of "interesting" traffic has passed.

20. Caller ID screening may be enabled on the Cisco router with the _____ command:

   A. ISDN CALLER (telephone number)

   B. ISDN FAST-IDLE (telephone number)

   C. ISDN CALLING-PARTY-NUMBER (telephone number)

   D. CALLING-PARTY-NUMBER (telephone number)
   A. ISDN CALLER (telephone number). The ISDN CALLER command causes all incoming calls to be accepted only if the Calling Party Number is delivered in the SETUP message and configured on the Cisco router.

21. CHAP authentication does not send which of the following items over the link?

   A. The router host name

   B. The cleartext password

   C. A challenge string

   D. An encrypted password
   B. The cleartext password. CHAP never sends the cleartext password as a security mechanism.

22. The IPCP can negotiate which one of the following items?

   A. The compression type

   B. The IP routing protocol

   C. The IPX network number

   D. The IP address
   D. The IP address. IPCP is the IP Control Protocol and is responsible for dynamically negotiating an IP address.

CISCO CERTIFIED NETWORK PROFESSIONAL

B

About the CD

This CD-ROM contains a browser-based testing product, the *Personal Testing Center*. The *Personal Testing Center* is easy to install. Just click Setup and you will be walked through the installation. The Personal Testing Center program group will be created in the Start Programs folder.

The CD-ROM also contains a full HTML version of this book with a hyperlinked table of contents to help you find what you are looking for.

In addition, the CD contains a multimedia network training module from Global Knowledge Network. This module runs in your web browser. The module is taken from Global's "Essentials of Cisco Router Configuration" series, Volume 2, Router Configuration, and covers Interior Gateway Routing Protocol (IGRP).

The Essentials of Cisco Router Configuration product is a multi-volume series designed to instruct users on the installation, configuration, and management of Cisco routers. ECRC is a computer-based program designed for complete self-paced instruction, ensuring both short- and long-term understanding.

ECRC is authored by Cisco expert Neil Lovering, a CCIE who has taught thousands of students the workings of Cisco routers. Each of the ECRC training volumes, including the one on IGRP found here, is firmly rooted in the essentials of Cisco router configuration, meaning that you are taught exactly what you need to know to quickly set up your router. It uses graphics, animation, simulation, and audio for a full multimedia-training product. Each volume is web based, requiring only Internet Explorer or Netscape Navigator.

Personal Testing Center Test Type Choices

With the *Personal Testing Center*, you have three options in which to run the program: Live, Practice, and Review. Each test type will draw from a pool of over 250 potential questions. Your choice of test type will depend on whether you would like to simulate an actual Cisco exam, receive instant feedback on your answer choices, or review concepts using the testing simulator. Note that selecting the Full Screen icon on Internet Explorer's standard toolbar gives you the best display of the *Personal Testing Center*.

Live

The Live timed test type is meant to reflect the actual exam as closely as possible. You will have 90 minutes in which to complete the exam. You will have the option to skip questions and return to them later, move to the previous question, or end the exam. Once the timer has expired, you will automatically go to the scoring page to review your test results.

Managing Windows

The testing application runs inside an Internet Explorer 4.0 browser window. We recommend that you use the full-screen view to minimize the amount of text scrolling you need to do. However, the application will initiate a second iteration of the browser when you link to an Answer in Depth or a Review Graphic. If you are running in full-screen view, the second iteration of the browser will be covered by the first. You can toggle between the two windows with ALT-TAB, you can click your task bar to maximize the second window, or you can get out of full-screen mode and arrange the two windows so they are both visible on the screen at the same time. The application will not initiate more than two browser windows, so you aren't left with hundreds of open windows for each Answer in Depth or Review Graphic that you view.

Saving Scores as Cookies

Your exam score is stored as a browser cookie. If you've configured your browser to accept cookies, your score will be stored in a cookie named History. If you don't accept cookies, you cannot permanently save your scores. If you delete the History cookie, the scores will be deleted permanently.

Using the Browser Buttons

The test application runs inside the Internet Explorer 4.0 browser. You should navigate from screen to screen by using the application's buttons, not the browser's buttons.

JavaScript Errors

If you encounter a JavaScript error, you should be able to proceed within the application. If you cannot, shut down your Internet Explorer 4.0 browser session and re-launch the testing application.

Practice

When choosing the Practice exam type, you have the option of receiving instant feedback as to whether your selected answer is correct. The questions will be presented to you in numerical order, and you will see every question in the available question pool for each section you chose to be tested on.

As with the Live exam type, you have the option of continuing through the entire exam without seeing the correct answer for each question. The number of questions you answered correctly, along with the percentage of correct answers, will be displayed during the post-exam summary report. Once you have answered a question, click the Answer icon to display the correct answer.

You have the option of ending the Practice exam at any time, but your post-exam summary screen may reflect an incorrect percentage based on the number of questions you failed to answer. Questions that are skipped are counted as incorrect answers on the post-exam summary screen.

Review

During the Review exam type, you will be presented with questions similar to both the Live and Practice exam types. However, the Answer icon is not present, as every question will have the correct answer posted near the bottom of the screen. You have the option of answering the question without looking at the correct answer. In the Review exam type, you can also return to previous questions and skip to the next question, as well as end the exam by clicking the Stop icon.

The Review exam type is recommended when you have already completed the Live exam type once or twice, and would now like to determine which questions you answered correctly.

Questions with Answers

For the Practice and Review exam types, you will have the option of clicking a hyperlink titled Answers in Depth, which will present relevant study material aimed at exposing the logic behind the answer in a separate browser window. By having two browsers open (one for the test engine and one for the review information), you can quickly alternate between the two windows while keeping your place in the exam. You will find that additional windows are not generated as you follow hyperlinks throughout the test engine.

Scoring

The *Personal Testing Center* post-exam summary screen, called Benchmark Yourself, displays the results for each section you chose to be tested on, including a bar graph similar to the real exam, which displays the percentage of correct answers. You can compare your percentage to the actual passing percentage for each section. The percentage displayed on the post-exam summary screen is not the actual percentage required to pass the exam. You'll see the number of questions you answered correctly compared to the total number of questions you were tested on. If you choose to skip a question, it will be marked as incorrect. Ending the exam by clicking the End button with questions still unanswered lowers your percentage, as these questions will be marked as incorrect.

Clicking the End button and then the Home button allows you to choose another exam type, or test yourself on another section.

C

About the Web Site

Access Global Knowledge

As you know by now, Global Knowledge is the largest independent IT training company in the world. Just by purchasing this book, you have also secured a free subscription to the Global Knowledge Web site and its many resources. You can find it at: http://access.globalknowledge.com.

You can log in directly at the Global Knowledge site, and you will be e-mailed a new, secure password immediately upon registering.

What You'll Find There . . .

The wealth of useful information at the Global Knowledge site falls into three categories:

Skills Gap Analysis

Global Knowledge offers several ways for you to analyze your networking skills and discover where they may be lacking. Using Global Knowledge's trademarked Competence Key Tool, you can do a skills gap analysis and get recommendations for where you may need to do some more studying. (Sorry, it just might not end with this book!)

Networking

You'll also gain valuable access to another asset: people. At the Access Global site, you'll find threaded discussions, as well as live discussions. Talk to other CCIE candidates, get advice from folks who have already taken the exams, and get access to instructors and CCSIs.

Product Offerings

Of course, Global Knowledge also offers its products here, and you may find some valuable items for purchase—CBTs, books, or courses. Browse freely and see if there's something that could help you take that next step in career enhancement.

Glossary

10Base2   Ethernet specification using 50-ohm thin coaxial cable and a signaling rate of 10-Mbps baseband.

10Base5   Ethernet specification using standard (thick) 50-ohm baseband coaxial cable and a signaling rate of 10-Mbps baseband.

10BaseFL   Ethernet specification using fiber-optic cabling and a signaling rate of 10-Mbps baseband, and FOIRL.

10BaseT   Ethernet specification using two pairs of twisted-pair cabling (Category 3, 4, or 5): one pair for transmitting data and the other for receiving data, and a signaling rate of 10-Mbps baseband.

10Broad36   Ethernet specification using broadband coaxial cable and a signaling rate of 10 Mbps.

100BaseFX   Fast Ethernet specification using two strands of multimode fiber-optic cable per link and a signaling rate of 100-Mbps baseband. A 100BaseFX link cannot exceed 400 meters in length.

100BaseT   Fast Ethernet specification using UTP wiring and a signaling rate of 100-Mbps baseband. 100BaseT sends link pulses out on the wire when there is no data traffic present.

100BaseT4   Fast Ethernet specification using four pairs of Category 3, 4, or 5 UTP wiring and a signaling rate of 100-Mbps baseband. The maximum length of a 100BaseT4 segment is 100 meters.

100BaseTX   Fast Ethernet specification using two pairs of UTP or STP wiring and 100-Mbps baseband signaling. One pair of wires is used to receive data; the other is used to transmit. A 100BaseTX segment cannot exceed 100 meters in length.

100BaseX   100-Mbps baseband Fast Ethernet specification based on the IEEE 802.3 standard. 100BaseX refers to the whole 100Base family of standards for Fast Ethernet.

80/20 rule   General network standard that 80 percent of traffic on a given network is local (destined for targets in the same workgroup); and not more than 20 percent of traffic requires internetworking.

AAL (ATM adaptation layer)   Service-dependent sublayer of the Data Link layer. The function of the AAL is to accept data from different applications and present it to the ATM layer in 48-byte ATM segments.

AARP (AppleTalk Address Resolution Protocol)   The protocol that maps a data-link address to an AppleTalk network address.

ABR (area border router)   Router located on the border of an OSPF area, which connects that area to the backbone network. An ABR would be a member of both the OSPF backbone and the attached area. It maintains routing tables describing both the backbone topology and the topology of the other area.

access list   A sequential list of statements in a router configuration that identify network traffic for various purposes, including traffic and route filtering.

accounting   Cisco command option that, when applied to an interface, makes the router keep track of the number of bytes and packets sent between each pair of network addresses.

acknowledgment   Notification sent from one network device to another to acknowledge that a message or group of messages has been received. Sometimes abbreviated ACK. Opposite of **NACK**.

active hub   A multiport device that repeats and amplifies LAN signals at the Physical layer.

active monitor   A network device on a Token Ring that is responsible for managing ring operations. The active monitor ensures that tokens are not lost, or that frames do not circulate indefinitely on the ring.

address   A numbering convention used to identify a unique entity or location on a network.

address mapping   Technique that allows different protocols to operate together by associating addresses from one format with those of another.

address mask   A string of bits, which, when combined with an address, describes which portion of an address refers to the network or subnet and which part refers to the host. *See also* **subnet mask**.

address resolution   A technique for resolving differences between computer addressing schemes. Address resolution most often specifies a method for mapping network layer addresses to Data Link layer addresses. *See also* **address mapping**.

Address Resolution Protocol   *See* ARP.

administrative distance   A rating of the preferability of a routing information source. Administrative distance is expressed as a value between 0 and 255. The higher the value, the lower the preference.

advertising   A process in which a router sends routing or service updates at frequent intervals so that other routers on the network can maintain lists of usable routes or services.

algorithm   A specific process for arriving at a solution to a problem.

AMI (alternate mark inversion)   The line-code type that is used on T1 and E1 circuits. In this code, zeros are represented by 01 during each bit cell, and ones are represented by 11 or 00, alternately, during each bit cell.

ANSI (American National Standards Institute)   An organization of representatives of corporate, government, and other entities that coordinates standards-related activities, approves U.S. national standards, and develops positions for the United States in international standards organizations.

AppleTalk   A suite of communications protocols developed by Apple Computer for allowing communication among their devices over a network.

Application layer   Layer 7 of the OSI reference model. This layer provides services to end-user application processes such as electronic mail, file transfer, and terminal emulation.

ARP (Address Resolution Protocol)   Internet protocol used to map an IP address to a MAC address.

ASBR (autonomous system boundary router)   An ASBR is an ABR connecting an OSPF autonomous system to a non-OSPF network. ASBRs run two protocols: OSPF and another routing protocol. ASBRs must be located in a nonstub OSPF area.

asynchronous transmission   Describes digital signals that are transmitted without precise clocking or synchronization.

ATM (Asynchronous Transfer Mode)   An international standard for cell relay suitable for carrying multiple service types (such as voice, video, or data) in fixed-length (53-byte) cells. Fixed-length cells allow cell processing to occur in hardware, thereby reducing latency.

ATM adaptation layer   *See* AAL.

ATM Forum   International organization founded in 1991 by Cisco Systems, NET/ADAPTIVE, Northern Telecom, and Sprint to develop and promote standards-based implementation agreements for ATM technology.

AUI (attachment unit interface)   An interface between an MAU and a NIC (network interface card) described in the IEEE 802.3 specification. AUI often refers to the physical port to which an AUI cable attaches.

auto-discovery   A mechanism used by many network management products, including CiscoWorks, to build a map of a network.

autonomous system   A group of networks under a common administration that share in a common routing strategy. Sometimes abbreviated AS.

B channel (Bearer channel)   An ISDN term meaning a full-duplex, 64-Kbps channel used to send user data.

B8ZS (binary 8-zero substitution)   The line-code type that is used on T1 and E1 circuits. With B8ZS, a special code is substituted whenever eight consecutive zeros are sent over the link. This code is then interpreted at the remote end of the connection.

backoff   The retransmission delay used by contention-based MAC protocols such as Ethernet, after a network node determines that the physical medium is already in use.

bandwidth   The difference between the highest and lowest frequencies available for network signals. The term may also describe the throughput capacity of a network link or segment.

baseband   A network technology in which a single carrier frequency is used. Ethernet is a common example of a baseband network technology.

baud   Unit of signaling speed equal to the number of separate signal elements transmitted in one second. Baud is synonymous with bits per second (bps), as long as each signal element represents exactly one bit.

bearer channel   *See* B channel.

BECN (backward explicit congestion notification)   A Frame Relay network facility that allows switches in the network to advise DTE devices of congestion. The BECN bit is set in frames traveling in the opposite direction of frames encountering a congested path.

best-effort delivery   Describes a network system that does not use a system of acknowledgment to guarantee reliable delivery of information.

BGP (Border Gateway Protocol)   An interdomain path-vector routing protocol. BGP exchanges reachability information with other BGP systems. It is defined by RFC 1163.

binary   A numbering system in which there are only two digits, ones and zeros.

bit stuffing   A 0 insertion and deletion process defined by HDLC. This technique ensures that actual data never appears as flag characters.

BNC connector   Standard connector used to connect coaxial cable to an MAU or line card.

BOOTP (Bootstrap Protocol)   Part of the TCP/IP suite of protocols, used by a network node to determine the IP address of its network interfaces, in order to boot from a network server.

BPDU (Bridge Protocol Data Unit)   A Layer 2 protocol used for communication among bridges.

bps   Bits per second.

BRI (Basic Rate Interface)   ISDN interface consisting of two B channels and one D channel for circuit-switched communication. ISDN BRI can carry voice, video, and data.

bridge   Device that connects and forwards packets between two network segments that use the same data-link communications protocol. Bridges operate at the Data Link layer of the OSI reference model. A bridge will filter, forward, or flood an incoming frame based on the MAC address of the frame.

broadband   A data transmission system that multiplexes multiple independent signals onto one cable. Also, in telecommunications, any channel with a bandwidth greater than 4 KHz. In LAN terminology, a coaxial cable using analog signaling.

broadcast   Data packet addressed to all nodes on a network. Broadcasts are identified by a broadcast address that matches all addresses on the network.

broadcast address   Special address reserved for sending a message to all stations. At the Data Link layer, a broadcast address is a MAC destination address of all 1s.

broadcast domain   The group of all devices that will receive the same broadcast frame originating from any device within the group. Because routers do not forward broadcast frames, broadcast domains are typically bounded by routers.

buffer   A memory storage area used for handling data in transit. Buffers are used in internetworking to compensate for differences in processing speed between network devices or signaling rates of segments. Bursts of packets can be stored in buffers until they can be handled by slower devices.

bus   Common physical path composed of wires or other media, across which signals are sent from one part of a computer to another.

bus topology   A topology used in LANs. Transmissions from network stations propagate the length of the medium and are then received by all other stations.

byte   A series of consecutive binary digits that are operated upon as a unit, usually eight bits.

cable   Transmission medium of copper wire or optical fiber wrapped in a protective cover.

cable range   A range of network numbers on an extended AppleTalk network. The cable range value can be a single network number or a contiguous sequence of several network numbers. Nodes assign addresses within the cable range values provided.

CAM   Content-addressable memory.

carrier   Electromagnetic wave or alternating current of a single frequency, suitable for modulation by another, data-bearing signal.

Carrier Detect   *See* CD.

carrier sense multiple access with collision detection   *See* CSMA/CD.

Category 5 cabling   One of five grades of UTP cabling described in the EIA/TIA-586 standard. Category 5 cabling can transmit data at speeds up to 100 Mbps.

CCITT (Consultative Committee for International Telegraphy and Telephony)   International organization responsible for the development of communications standards. Now called the ITU-T. *See also* ITU-T.

CCO (Cisco Connection Online)   Self-help resource for Cisco customers. Available 24 hours a day, seven days a week at http://www.cisco.com. The CCO family includes CCO Documentation, CCO Open Forum, CCO CD-ROM, and the TAC (Technical Assistance Center).

CD (Carrier Detect)   Signal that indicates whether an interface is active.

CDDI (Copper Distributed Data Interface)   The implementation of FDDI protocols over STP and UTP cabling. CDDI transmits over distances of approximately 100 meters, providing data rates of 100 Mbps. CDDI uses a dual-ring architecture to provide redundancy.

CDP (Cisco Discovery Protocol)   Used to discover neighboring Cisco devices, and used by network management software. The CiscoWorks network management software takes advantage of CDP.

cell   The basic data unit for ATM switching and multiplexing. A cell consists of a five-byte header and 48 bytes of payload. Cells contain fields in their headers that identify the data stream to which they belong.

CHAP (Challenge Handshake Authentication Protocol)
Security feature used with PPP encapsulation, which prevents unauthorized access by identifying the remote end. The router or access server determines whether that user is allowed access.

checksum   Method for checking the integrity of transmitted data. A checksum is an integer value computed from a sequence of octets taken through a series of arithmetic operations. The value is recomputed at the receiving end and compared for verification.

CIDR (classless interdomain routing)   Technique supported by BGP4 and based on route aggregation. CIDR allows routers to group routes together in order to cut down on the quantity of routing information carried by the core routers. With CIDR, several IP networks appear to networks outside the group as a single, larger entity. With CIDR, IP addresses and their subnet masks are written as four octets, separated by periods, followed by a forward slash and a two-digit number that represents the subnet mask.

CIR (committed information rate)   The rate at which a Frame Relay network agrees to transfer information under normal conditions, averaged over a minimum increment of time. CIR, measured in bits per second, is one of the key negotiated tariff metrics.

circuit switching   A system in which a dedicated physical path must exist between sender and receiver for the entire duration of a call. Used heavily in telephone networks.

CiscoWorks   Network management package that provides a graphical view of a network, collects statistical information about a network, and offers various network management components.

client   Node or software program, or front-end device, that requests services from a server.

CLNS (Connectionless Network Service)   An OSI network layer service, for which no circuit need be established before data can be transmitted. Routing of messages to their destinations is independent of other messages.

CMU SNMP   A free command-line SNMP management package that comes in source code form. Originally developed at the Carnegie Mellon University, and available at http://www.net.cmu.edu/projects/snmp/.

collision   In Ethernet, the result of two nodes transmitting simultaneously. The frames from each device cause an increase in voltage when they meet on the physical media, and are damaged.

collision domain   A group of nodes such that any two or more of the nodes transmitting simultaneously will result in a collision.

congestion   Traffic in excess of network capacity.

connectionless   Term used to describe data transfer without the prior existence of a circuit.

console   A DTE device, usually consisting of a keyboard and display unit, through which users interact with a host.

contention   Access method in which network devices compete for permission to access the physical medium. Compare with **circuit switching** and **token passing**.

cost   A value, typically based on media bandwidth or other measures, that is assigned by a network administrator and used by routing protocols to compare various paths through an internetwork environment. Cost values are used to determine the most favorable path to a particular destination—the lower the cost, the better the path.

count to infinity   A condition in which routers continuously increment the hop count to particular networks. Often occurs in routing algorithms that are slow to converge. Usually, some arbitrary hop count ceiling is imposed to limit the extent of this problem.

CPE (customer premises equipment)   Terminating equipment, such as terminals, telephones, and modems, installed at customer sites and connected to the telephone company network.

CRC (cyclic redundancy check) An error-checking technique in which the receiving device performs a calculation on the frame contents and compares the calculated number to a value stored in the frame by the sending node.

CSMA/CD (carrier sense multiple access collision detect) Media-access mechanism used by Ethernet and IEEE 802.3. Devices use CSMA/CD to check the channel for a carrier before transmitting data. If no carrier is sensed, the device transmits. If two devices transmit at the same time, the collision is detected by all colliding devices. Collisions delay retransmissions from those devices for a randomly chosen length of time.

CSU (channel service unit) Digital interface device that connects end-user equipment to the local digital telephone loop. Often referred to together with DSU, as CSU/DSU.

D channel Data channel. Full-duplex, 16-kbps (BRI) or 64-kbps (PRI) ISDN channel.

datagram Logical unit of information sent as a network layer unit over a transmission medium without prior establishment of a circuit.

Data Link layer Layer 2 of the OSI reference model. This layer provides reliable transit of data across a physical link. The Data Link layer is concerned with physical addressing, network topology, access to the network medium, error detection, sequential delivery of frames, and flow control. The Data Link layer is divided into two sublayers: the MAC sublayer and the LLC sublayer.

DCE (data circuit-terminating equipment) The devices and connections of a communications network that represent the network end of the user-to-network interface. The DCE provides a physical connection to the network and provides a clocking signal used to synchronize transmission between DCE and DTE devices. Modems and interface cards are examples of DCE devices.

DDR (dial-on-demand routing)   Technique whereby a router can automatically initiate and close a circuit-switched session as transmitting stations demand. The router spoofs keepalives so that end-stations treat the session as active. DDR permits routing over ISDN or telephone lines using an external ISDN terminal adapter or modem.

de facto standard   A standard that exists because of its widespread use.

de jure standard   Standard that exists because of its development or approval by an official standards body.

DECNet   Group of communications products (including a protocol suite) developed and supported by Digital Equipment Corporation. DECNet/OSI (also called DECNet Phase V) is the most recent iteration and supports both OSI protocols and proprietary Digital protocols. Phase IV Prime supports inherent MAC addresses that allow DECNet nodes to coexist with systems running other protocols that have MAC address restrictions. *See also* **DNA.**

dedicated line   Communications line that is indefinitely reserved for transmissions, rather than switched as transmission is required. *See also* **leased line.**

default gateway   Another term for default router. The router that a host will use to reach another network when it has no specific information about how to reach that network.

default route   A routing table entry that is used to direct packets when there is no explicit route present in the routing table.

delay   The time between the initiation of a transaction by a sender and the first response received by the sender. Also, the time required to move a packet from source to destination over a network path.

demarc   The demarcation point between telephone carrier equipment and CPE.

demultiplexing   The separating of multiple streams of data that have been multiplexed into a common physical signal for transmission, back into multiple output streams. Opposite of **multiplexing**.

destination address   Address of a network device to receive data.

DHCP (Dynamic Host Configuration Protocol)   Provides a mechanism for allocating IP addresses dynamically so that addresses can be reassigned instead of belonging to only one host.

Dijkstra algorithm   Dijkstra's algorithm is a graph algorithm used to find the shortest path from one node on a graph to all others. Used in networking to determine the shortest path between routers.

discovery mode   Method by which an AppleTalk router acquires information about an attached network from an operational router and then uses this information to configure its own addressing information.

distance vector routing algorithm   Class of routing algorithms that use the number of hops in a route to find a shortest path to a destination network. Distance vector routing algorithms call for each router to send its entire routing table in each update to each of its neighbors. Also called Bellman-Ford routing algorithm.

DLCI (data-link connection identifier)   A value that specifies a virtual circuit in a Frame Relay network.

DNA (Digital Network Architecture)   Network architecture that was developed by Digital Equipment Corporation. DECNet is the collective term for the products that comprise DNA (including communications protocols).

DNIC (Data Network Identification Code)   Part of an X.121 address. DNICs are divided into two parts: the first specifying the country in which the addressed PSN is located and the second specifying the PSN itself. *See also* X.121.

DNS (Domain Name System)   System used in the Internet for translating names of network nodes into addresses.

DSP (domain specific part)   Part of an ATM address. A DSP is comprised of an area identifier, a station identifier, and a selector byte.

DTE (data terminal equipment)   Device at the user end of a user-network interface that serves as a data source, destination, or both. DTE connects to a data network through a DCE device (for example, a modem) and typically uses clocking signals generated by the DCE. DTE includes such devices as computers, routers and multiplexers.

DUAL (Diffusing Update Algorithm)   Convergence algorithm used in EIGRP. DUAL provides constant loop-free operation throughout a route computation by allowing routers involved in a topology change to synchronize at the same time, without involving routers that are unaffected by the change.

DVMRP (Distance Vector Multicast Routing Protocol)
DVMRP is an internetwork gateway protocol that implements a typical dense mode IP multicast scheme. Using IGMP, DVMRP exchanges routing datagrams with its neighbors.

dynamic routing   Routing that adjusts automatically to changes in network topology or traffic patterns.

E1   Wide-area digital transmission scheme used in Europe that carries data at a rate of 2.048 Mbps.

EIA/TIA-232   Common Physical layer interface standard, developed by EIA and TIA, that supports unbalanced circuits at signal speeds of up to 64 Kbps. Formerly known as RS-232.

EIGRP (Enhanced IGRP)   A multiservice routing protocol supporting IPX, AppleTalk, and IP. BGP is used for interconnecting networks and defining strict routing policies.

encapsulation   The process of attaching a particular protocol header to a unit of data prior to transmission on the network. For example, a frame of Ethernet data is given a specific Ethernet header before network transit.

endpoint   Device at which a virtual circuit or virtual path begins or ends.

enterprise network   A privately maintained network connecting most major points in a company or other organization. Usually spans a large geographic area and supports multiple protocols and services.

entity   Generally, an individual, manageable network device. Sometimes called an alias.

error control   Technique for detecting and correcting errors in data transmissions.

Ethernet   Baseband LAN specification invented by Xerox Corporation and developed jointly by Xerox, Intel, and Digital Equipment Corporation. Ethernet networks use the CSMA/CD method of media access control and run over a variety of cable types at 10 Mbps. Ethernet is similar to the IEEE 802.3 series of standards.

EtherTalk   Apple Computer's data-link product that allows an AppleTalk network to be connected by Ethernet cable.

EtherWave   A product from Netopia (formerly Farallon) used to connect AppleTalk devices with LocalTalk connectors to Ethernet networks. They are an alternative to LocalTalk-to-EtherTalk routers.

explorer packet   Generated by an end-station trying to find its way through a SRB network. Gathers a hop-by-hop description of a path through the network by being marked (updated) by each bridge that it traverses, thereby creating a complete topological map.

Fast Ethernet   Any of a number of 100-Mbps Ethernet specifications. Fast Ethernet offers a speed increase ten times that of the 10BaseT Ethernet specification, while preserving such qualities as frame format, MAC mechanisms, and MTU. Such similarities allow the use of existing 10BaseT applications and network management tools on Fast Ethernet networks. Based on an extension to the IEEE 802.3 specification. Compare with **Ethernet**. *See also* **100BaseFX; 100BaseT; 100BaseT4; 100BaseTX; 100BaseX; IEEE 802.3.**

FDDI (Fiber Distributed Data Interface)   LAN standard, defined by ANSI X3T9.5, specifying a 100-Mbps token-passing network using fiber-optic cable, with transmission distances of up to 2 km. FDDI uses a dual-ring architecture to provide redundancy. Compare with **CDDI**.

FECN (forward explicit congestion notification)   A facility in a Frame Relay network to inform DTE receiving the frame that congestion was experienced in the path from source to destination. DTE receiving frames with the FECN bit set can request that higher-level protocols take flow-control action as appropriate.

file transfer   Category of popular network applications that features movement of files from one network device to another.

filter   Generally, a process or device that screens network traffic for certain characteristics, such as source address, destination address, or protocol, and determines whether to forward or discard that traffic or routes based on the established criteria.

firewall   Router or other computer designated as a buffer between public networks and a private network. A firewall router uses access lists and other methods to ensure the security of the private network.

Flash memory   Nonvolatile storage that can be electrically erased and reprogrammed as necessary.

flash update   Routing update sent asynchronously when a change in the network topology occurs.

flat addressing   A system of addressing that does not incorporate a hierarchy to determine location.

flooding   Traffic-passing technique used by switches and bridges in which traffic received on an interface is sent out all of the interfaces of that device except the interface on which the information was originally received.

flow control   Technique for ensuring that a transmitting device, such as a modem, does not overwhelm a receiving device with data. When the buffers on the receiving device are full, a message is sent to the sending device to suspend transmission until it has processed the data in the buffers.

forwarding   The process of sending a frame or packet toward its destination.

fragment   Piece of a larger packet that has been broken down to smaller units.

fragmentation   Process of breaking a packet into smaller units when transmitting over a network medium that is unable to support a transmission unit the original size of the packet.

frame   Logical grouping of information sent as a Data Link layer unit over a transmission medium. Sometimes refers to the header and trailer, used for synchronization and error control, which surround the user data contained in the unit. The terms cell, datagram, message, packet, and segment are also used to describe logical information groupings at various layers of the OSI reference model and in various technology circles.

Frame Relay   Industry-standard, switched Data Link layer protocol that handles multiple virtual circuits over a single physical interface. Frame Relay is more efficient than X.25, for which it is generally considered a replacement.

Frame Relay Cloud   A generic term used to refer to a collective Frame Relay network. For Frame Relay carrier customers, it generally refers to the carrier's entire Frame Relay network. It's referred to as a "cloud" because the network layout is not visible to the customer.

frequency   Number of cycles, measured in hertz, of an alternating current signal per unit of time.

FTP (File Transfer Protocol)   An application protocol, part of the TCP/IP protocol stack, used for transferring files between hosts on a network.

full duplex   Capability for simultaneous data transmission and receipt of data between two devices.

full mesh   A network topology in which each network node has either a physical circuit or a virtual circuit connecting it to every other network node.

gateway   In the IP community, an older term referring to a routing device. Today, the term router is used to describe devices that perform this function, and gateway refers to a special-purpose device that performs an Application layer conversion of information from one protocol stack to another.

GB   Gigabyte. Approximately 1,000,000,000 bytes.

Gb   Gigabit. Approximately 1,000,000,000 bits.

GBps   Gigabytes per second.

Gbps Gigabits per second.

giants Ethernet frames over the maximum frame size.

GNS (Get Nearest Server) Request packet sent by a client on an IPX network to locate the nearest active server of a particular type. An IPX network client issues a GNS request to solicit either a direct response from a connected server or a response from a router that tells it where on the internetwork the service can be located. GNS is part of the IPX SAP.

half-duplex Capability for data transmission in only one direction at a time between a sending station and a receiving station.

handshake Sequence of messages exchanged between two or more network devices to ensure transmission synchronization.

hardware address *See* MAC address.

HDLC (High-level Data Link Control) Bit-oriented synchronous Data Link layer protocol developed by ISO and derived from SDLC. HDLC specifies a data encapsulation method for synchronous serial links and includes frame characters and checksums in its headers.

header Control information placed before data when encapsulating that data for network transmission.

Hello packet Multicast packet that is used by routers for neighbor discovery and recovery. Hello packets also indicate that a client is still operating on the network.

Hello protocol Protocol used by OSPF and other routing protocols for establishing and maintaining neighbor relationships.

hierarchical addressing   A scheme of addressing that uses a logical hierarchy to determine location. For example, IP addresses consist of network numbers, subnet numbers, and host numbers, which IP routing algorithms use to route the packet to the appropriate location.

holddown   State of a routing table entry in which routers will neither advertise the route nor accept advertisements about the route for a specific length of time (known as the holddown period).

hop   Term describing the passage of a data packet between two network nodes (for example, between two routers). *See also* **hop count**.

hop count   Routing metric used to measure the distance between a source and a destination. RIP uses hop count as its metric.

host   A computer system on a network. Similar to the term node except that host usually implies a computer system, whereas node can refer to any networked system, including routers.

host number   Part of an IP address that designates which node is being addressed. Also called a host address.

hub   A term used to describe a device that serves as the center of a star topology network; or, an Ethernet multiport repeater, sometimes referred to as a concentrator.

ICMP (Internet Control Message Protocol)   A network layer Internet protocol that provides reports of errors and other information about IP packet processing. ICMP is documented in RFC 792.

IEEE (Institute of Electrical and Electronics Engineers)   A professional organization among whose activities are the development of communications and networking standards. IEEE LAN standards are the most common LAN standards today.

IEEE 802.3   IEEE LAN protocol for the implementation of the Physical layer and the MAC sublayer of the Data Link layer. IEEE 802.3 uses CSMA/CD access at various speeds over various physical media.

IEEE 802.5   IEEE LAN protocol for the implementation of the Physical layer and MAC sublayer of the Data Link layer. Similar to Token Ring, IEEE 802.5 uses token-passing access over STP cabling.

IGP (Interior Gateway Protocol)   A generic term for an Internet routing protocol used to exchange routing information within an autonomous system. Examples of common Internet IGPs include IGRP, OSPF, and RIP.

InARP (Inverse Address Resolution Protocol)   A basic Frame Relay protocol that allows routers on the Frame network to learn the protocol addresses of other routers.

interface   A connection between two systems or devices; or in routing terminology, a network connection.

Internet   Term used to refer to the global internetwork that evolved from the ARPANET, that now connects tens of thousands of networks worldwide.

Internet protocol   Any protocol that is part of the TCP/IP protocol stack. *See* **TCP/IP**.

internetwork   Collection of networks interconnected by routers and other devices that functions (generally) as a single network.

internetworking   General term used to refer to the industry that has arisen around the problem of connecting networks together. The term may be used to refer to products, procedures, and technologies.

Inverse ARP (Inverse Address Resolution Protocol)   Method of building dynamic address mappings in a Frame Relay network. Allows a device to discover the network address of a device associated with a virtual circuit.

IP (Internet Protocol)   Network layer protocol in the TCP/IP stack offering a connectionless datagram service. IP provides features for addressing, type-of-service specification, fragmentation and reassembly, and security. Documented in RFC 791.

IP address   A 32-bit address assigned to hosts using the TCP/IP suite of protocols. An IP address is written as four octets separated by dots (dotted decimal format). Each address consists of a network number, an optional subnetwork number, and a host number. The network and subnetwork numbers together are used for routing, while the host number is used to address an individual host within the network or subnetwork. A subnet mask is often used with the address to extract network and subnetwork information from the IP address.

IPX (Internetwork Packet Exchange)   NetWare network layer (Layer 3) protocol used for transferring data from servers to workstations. IPX is similar to IP in that it is a connectionless datagram service.

IPXCP (IPX Control Protocol)   The protocol that establishes and configures IPX over PPP.

IPXWAN   A protocol that negotiates end-to-end options for new links on startup. When a link comes up, the first IPX packets sent across are IPXWAN packets negotiating the options for the link. When the IPXWAN options have been successfully determined, normal IPX transmission begins, and no more IPXWAN packets are sent. Defined by RFC 1362.

ISDN (Integrated Services Digital Network)   Communication protocol, offered by telephone companies, that permits telephone networks to carry data, voice, and other source traffic.

ISL (Inter-Switch Link)   Cisco's protocol for trunking VLANs over Fast Ethernet.

ITU-T (International Telecommunication Union Telecommunication Standardization Sector)   International body dedicated to the development of worldwide standards for telecommunications technologies. ITU-T is the successor to CCITT.

jabbers   Long, continuous frames exceeding 1518 bytes that prevent all stations on the Ethernet network from transmitting data. Jabbering violates CSMA/CD implementation by prohibiting stations from transmitting data.

jam pattern   Initiated by Ethernet transmitting station when a collision is detected during transmission.

KB   Kilobyte. Approximately 1,000 bytes.

Kb   Kilobit. Approximately 1,000 bits.

KBps   Kilobytes per second.

Kbps   Kilobits per second.

keepalive interval   Period of time between keepalive messages sent by a network device.

keepalive message   Message sent by one network device to inform another network device that it is still active.

LAN (local area network) High-speed, low-error data network covering a relatively small geographic area. LANs connect workstations, peripherals, terminals, and other devices in a single building or other geographically limited area. LAN standards specify cabling and signaling at the physical and Data Link layers of the OSI model. Ethernet, FDDI, and Token Ring are the most widely used LAN technologies.

LANE (LAN Emulation) Technology that allows an ATM network to function as a LAN backbone. In this situation LANE provides multicast and broadcast support, address mapping (MAC-to-ATM), and virtual circuit management.

LAPB (Link Access Procedure, Balanced) The Data Link layer protocol in the X.25 protocol stack. LAPB is a bit-oriented protocol derived from HDLC.

LAPD (Link Access Procedure on the D channel) ISDN Data Link layer protocol for the D channel. LAPD was derived from the LAPB protocol and is designed to satisfy the signaling requirements of ISDN basic access. Defined by ITU-T Recommendations Q.920 and Q.921.

LAPF Data link standard for Frame Relay.

late collision Collision that is detected only after a station places a complete frame of the network.

latency The amount of time elapsed between the time a device requests access to a network and the time it is allowed to transmit; or, amount of time between the point at which a device receives a frame and the time that frame is forwarded out the destination port.

LCP (Link Control Protocol) A protocol used with PPP, which establishes, configures, and tests data-link connections.

leased line Transmission line reserved by a communications carrier for the private use of a customer. A leased line is a type of dedicated line.

link   Network communications channel consisting of a circuit or transmission path and all related equipment between a sender and a receiver. Most often used to refer to a WAN connection. Sometimes called a line or a transmission link.

link-state routing algorithm   Routing algorithm in which each router broadcasts or multicasts information regarding the cost of reaching each of its neighbors to all nodes in the internetwork. Link state algorithms require that routers maintain a consistent view of the network and are therefore not prone to routing loops.

LLC (Logical Link Control)   Higher of two Data Link layer sublayers defined by the IEEE. The LLC sublayer handles error control, flow control, framing, and MAC-sublayer addressing. The most common LLC protocol is IEEE 802.2, which includes both connectionless and connection-oriented types.

LMI (Local Management Interface)   A set of enhancements to the basic Frame Relay specification. LMI includes support for keepalives, a multicast mechanism; global addressing, and a status mechanism.

load balancing   In routing, the ability of a router to distribute traffic over all its network ports that are the same distance from the destination address. Load balancing increases the utilization of network segments, thus increasing total effective network bandwidth.

local loop   A line from the premises of a telephone subscriber to the telephone company central office.

LocalTalk   Apple Computer's proprietary baseband protocol that operates at the Dat Link and Physical layers of the OSI reference model. LocalTalk uses CSMA/CA and supports transmissions at speeds of 230.4 Kbps.

loop   A situation in which packets never reach their destination, but are forwarded in a cycle repeatedly through a group of network nodes.

MAC (Media Access Control)   Lower of the two sublayers of the Data Link layer defined by the IEEE. The MAC sublayer handles access to shared media.

MAC address   Standardized Data Link layer address that is required for every port or device that connects to a LAN. Other devices in the network use these addresses to locate specific ports in the network and to create and update routing tables and data structures. MAC addresses are 48 bits long and are controlled by the IEEE. Also known as a hardware address, a MAC-layer address, or a physical address.

MAN (metropolitan-area network)   A network that spans a metropolitan area. Generally, a MAN spans a larger geographic area than a LAN, but a smaller geographic area than a WAN.

Mb   Megabit. Approximately 1,000,000 bits.

Mbps   Megabits per second.

media   The various physical environments through which transmission signals pass. Common network media include cable (twisted-pair, coaxial, and fiber optic) and the atmosphere (through which microwave, laser, and infrared transmission occurs). Sometimes referred to as physical media.

Media Access Control   *See* MAC.

mesh   Network topology in which devices are organized in a segmented manner with redundant interconnections strategically placed between network nodes.

message   Application layer logical grouping of information, often composed of a number of lower-layer logical groupings such as packets.

MSAU (multistation access unit)   A wiring concentrator to which all end stations in a Token Ring network connect. Sometimes abbreviated MAU.

multiaccess network   A network that allows multiple devices to connect and communicate by sharing the same medium, such as a LAN.

multicast   A single packet copied by the network and sent to a specific subset of network addresses. These addresses are specified in the Destination Address field.

multicast address   A single address that refers to multiple network devices. Sometimes called a group address.

multiplexing   A technique that allows multiple logical signals to be transmitted simultaneously across a single physical channel.

mux   A multiplexing device. A mux combines multiple input signals for transmission over a single line. The signals are demultiplexed, or separated, before they are used at the receiving end.

NACK (negative acknowledgment)   A response sent from a receiving device to a sending device indicating that the information received contained errors.

name resolution   The process of associating a symbolic name with a network location or address.

NAT (Network Address Translation)   A technique for reducing the need for globally unique IP addresses. NAT allows an organization with addresses that may conflict with others in the IP address space, to connect to the Internet by translating those addresses into unique ones within the globally routable address space.

NBMA (nonbroadcast multiaccess)   Term describing a multiaccess network that either does not support broadcasting (such as X.25) or in which broadcasting is not feasible.

NBP (Name Binding Protocol)   AppleTalk transport level protocol that translates a character string name into the DDP address of the corresponding socket client.

NCP (Network Control Protocol)   Protocols that establish and configure various network layer protocols. Used for AppleTalk over PPP.

NDS (NetWare Directory Services)   A feature added in NetWare 4.0 as a replacement for individual bindaries. NDS allows NetWare and related resources to be grouped in a tree hierarchy to better provide central administration.

NetBIOS (Network Basic Input/Output System)   An application programming interface used by applications on an IBM LAN to request services from lower-level network processes such as session establishment and termination, and information transfer.

netmask   A number, usually used as a bit-mask, to separate an address into its network portion and host portion.

NetWare   A network operating system developed by Novell, Inc. Provides remote file access, print services, and numerous other distributed network services.

network   Collection of computers, printers, routers, switches, and other devices that are able to communicate with each other over some transmission medium.

network interface   Border between a carrier network and a privately owned installation.

Network layer   Layer 3 of the OSI reference model. This layer provides connectivity and path selection between two end systems. The Network layer is the layer at which routing takes place.

NLSP (NetWare Link Services Protocol)   Link-state routing protocol for IPX based on IS-IS.

node   Endpoint of a network connection or a junction common to two or more lines in a network. Nodes can be processors, controllers, or workstations. Nodes, which vary in their functional capabilities, can be interconnected by links, and serve as control points in the network.

NVRAM (nonvolatile RAM)   RAM that retains its contents when a device is powered off.

ODI   Novell's Open Data-link Interface.

OSI reference model (Open System Interconnection reference model)   A network architectural framework developed by ISO and ITU-T. The model describes seven layers, each of which specifies a particular network. The lowest layer, called the Physical layer, is closest to the media technology. The highest layer, the Application layer, is closest to the user. The OSI reference model is widely used as a way of understanding network functionality.

OSPF (Open Shortest Path First)   A link-state, hierarchical IGP routing algorithm, which includes features such as least-cost routing, multipath routing, and load balancing. OSPF was based on an early version of the IS-IS protocol.

out-of-band signaling   Transmission using frequencies or channels outside the frequencies or channels used for transfer of normal data. Out-of-band signaling is often used for error reporting when normal channels are unusable for communicating with network devices.

packet   Logical grouping of information that includes a header containing control information and (usually) user data. Packets are most often used to refer to network layer units of data. The terms datagram, frame, message, and segment are also used to describe logical information groupings at various layers of the OSI reference model, and in various technology circles. *See also* **PDU.**

packet analyzer   A software package (also sometimes including specialized hardware) used to monitor network traffic. Most packet analyzer packages will also do packet decoding, making the packets easier for humans to read.

packet burst   Allows multiple packets to be transmitted between Novell clients and servers in response to a single read or write request. It also allows NCP connections to greatly improve throughput by reducing the number of acknowledgments.

packet starvation effect   On Ethernet, when packets experience latencies up to 100 times the average, or completely starve out due to 16 collisions. Occurs as a result of the CSMA/CD implementation.

PAP (Password Authentication Protocol)   Authentication protocol that allows PPP peers to authenticate one another. The remote router attempting to connect to the local router is required to send an authentication request. Unlike CHAP, PAP passes the password and host name or username in the clear (unencrypted). PAP does not itself prevent unauthorized access, but merely identifies the remote end. The router or access server then determines if that user is allowed access. PAP is supported only on PPP lines.

partial mesh   Term describing a network in which devices are organized in a mesh topology, with some network nodes organized in a full mesh, but with others that are only connected to one or two other nodes in the network. A partial mesh does not provide the level of redundancy of a full mesh topology, but is less expensive to implement. Partial mesh topologies are generally used in the peripheral networks that connect to a fully meshed backbone. *See also* **full mesh; mesh.**

PDU (protocol data unit)   The OSI term for a packet.

Physical layer   Layer 1 of the OSI reference model; it corresponds with the Physical control layer in the SNA model. The Physical layer defines the specifications for activating, maintaining, and deactivating the physical link between end systems.

ping (packet internet groper)   ICMP echo message and its reply. Often used in IP networks to test the reachability of a network device.

poison reverse updates   Routing updates that explicitly indicate that a network or subnet is unreachable, rather than implying that a network is unreachable by not including it in updates. Poison reverse updates are sent to defeat large routing loops.

port   1. Interface on an internetworking device (such as a router). 2. In IP terminology, an upper-layer process that receives information from lower layers. Ports are numbered, and each numbered port is associated with a specific process. For example, SMTP is associated with port 25. A port number is also known as a well-known address. 3. To rewrite software or microcode so that it will run on a different hardware platform or in a different software environment than that for which it was originally designed.

PPP (Point-to-Point Protocol)   A successor to SLIP that provides router-to-router and host-to-network connections over synchronous and asynchronous circuits. Whereas SLIP was designed to work with IP, PPP was designed to work with several network layer protocols, such as IP, IPX, and ARA. PPP also has built-in security mechanisms, such as CHAP and PAP. PPP relies on two protocols: LCP and NCP. *See also* **CHAP; LCP; NCP; PAP; SLIP.**

Presentation layer   Layer 6 of the OSI reference model. This layer ensures that information sent by the Application layer of one system will be readable by the Application layer of another. The Presentation layer is also concerned with the data structures used by programs and therefore negotiates data transfer syntax for the Application layer.

PRI (Primary Rate Interface)   ISDN interface to primary rate access. Primary rate access consists of a single 64-Kbps D channel plus 23 (T1) or 30 (E1) B channels for voice or data. Compare to **BRI**.

protocol   Formal description of a set of rules and conventions that govern how devices on a network exchange information.

protocol stack   Set of related communications protocols that operate together and, as a group, address communication at some or all of the seven layers of the OSI reference model. Not every protocol stack covers each layer of the model, and often a single protocol in the stack will address a number of layers at once. TCP/IP is a typical protocol stack.

proxy ARP (proxy Address Resolution Protocol)   Variation of the ARP protocol in which an intermediate device (for example, a router) sends an ARP response on behalf of an end node to the requesting host. Proxy ARP can lessen bandwidth use on slow-speed WAN links. *See also* **ARP**.

PVC (permanent virtual circuit)   Permanently established virtual circuits save bandwidth in situations where certain virtual circuits must exist all the time, such as during circuit establishment and tear down.

Q.921   ITU (International Telecommunication Union) standard document for ISDN Layer 2 (Data Link layer).

Q.931   ITU (International Telecommunication Union) standard document for ISDN Layer 3.

query   Message used to inquire about the value of some variable or set of variables.

queue   A backlog of packets stored in buffers and waiting to be forwarded over a router interface.

RAM (random-access memory)   Volatile memory that can be read and written by a computer.

reassembly   The putting back together of an IP datagram at the destination after it has been fragmented either at the source or at an intermediate node. *See also* **fragmentation**.

reload   The event of a Cisco router rebooting, or the command that causes the router to reboot.

reverse path forwarding   If a packet server receives a packet through different interfaces from the same source, the server drops all packets after the first.

reverse Telnet   Using a router to connect to a serial device, frequently a modem, in order to connect out. For example, telnetting to a special port on an access router in order to access a modem to dial out. Called "reverse" because it's the opposite of the router's usual function, to accept calls into the modem.

RFC (Request For Comments)   Document series used as the primary means for communicating information about the Internet. Some RFCs are designated by the IAB as Internet standards.

ring   Connection of two or more stations in a logically circular topology. Information is passed sequentially between active stations. Token Ring, FDDI, and CDDI are based on this topology.

ring topology   Network topology that consists of a series of repeaters connected to one another by unidirectional transmission links to form a single closed loop. Each station on the network connects to the network at a repeater.

RIP (Routing Information Protocol)   A routing protocol for TCP/IP networks. The most common routing protocol in the Internet. RIP uses hop count as a routing metric.

RMON (Remote monitor)   A set of SNMP standards used to collect statistical network information. RMON is divided into groups, with each additional group providing more statistical information.

ROM (read-only memory)   Nonvolatile memory that can be read, but not written, by the computer.

routed protocol   Protocol that carries user data so it can be routed by a router. A router must be able to interpret the logical internetwork as specified by that routed protocol. Examples of routed protocols include AppleTalk, DECNet, and IP.

router   Network layer device that uses one or more metrics to determine the optimal path along which network traffic should be forwarded. Routers forward packets from one network to another based on network layer information.

routing   Process of finding a path to a destination host.

routing metric   Method by which a routing algorithm determines preferability of one route over another. This information is stored in routing tables. Metrics include bandwidth, communication cost, delay, hop count, load, MTU, path cost, and reliability. Sometimes referred to simply as a metric.

routing protocol   Protocol that accomplishes routing through the implementation of a specific routing algorithm. Examples of routing protocols include IGRP, OSPF, and RIP.

routing table   Table stored in a router or some other internetworking device that keeps track of routes to particular network destinations and, in some cases, metrics associated with those routes.

routing update   Message sent from a router to indicate network reachability and associated cost information. Routing updates are typically sent at regular intervals and after a change in network topology. Compare with **flash update**.

RSRB (remote source-route bridging)   Equivalent to an SRB over WAN links.

RTMP (Routing Table Maintenance Protocol)   The protocol used by AppleTalk devices to communicate routing information. Structurally similar to RIP.

runts   Ethernet frames that are smaller than 64 bytes.

SAP (service access point)   1. Field defined by the IEEE 802.2 specification that is part of an address specification. Thus, the destination plus the DSAP define the recipient of a packet. The same applies to the SSAP. 2. Service Advertising Protocol. IPX protocol that provides a means of informing network routers and servers of the location of available network resources and services.

segment   1. Section of a network that is bounded by bridges, routers, or switches. 2. In a LAN using a bus topology, a segment is a continuous electrical circuit that is often connected to other such segments with repeaters. 3. Term used in the TCP specification to describe a single Transport layer unit of information.

serial transmission   Method of data transmission in which the bits of a data character are transmitted sequentially over a single channel.

session   1. Related set of communications transactions between two or more network devices. 2. In SNA, a logical connection that enables two NAUs to communicate.

Session layer   Layer 5 of the OSI reference model. This layer establishes, manages, and terminates sessions between applications and manages data exchange between Presentation layer entities. Corresponds to the data flow control layer of the SNA model. *See also* **Application layer; Data Link layer; Network layer; Physical layer; Presentation layer; Transport layer.**

sliding window flow control   Method of flow control in which a receiver gives a transmitter permission to transmit data until a window is full. When the window is full, the transmitter must stop transmitting until the receiver acknowledges some of the data, or advertises a larger window. TCP, other transport protocols, and several Data Link layer protocols use this method of flow control.

SLIP (Serial Line Internet Protocol)   Uses a variation of TCP/IP to make point-to-point serial connections. Succeeded by PPP.

SNAP (Subnetwork Access Protocol)   Internet protocol that operates between a network entity in the subnetwork and a network entity in the end system. SNAP specifies a standard method of encapsulating IP datagrams and ARP messages on IEEE networks.

SNMP (Simple Network Management Protocol)   Network management protocol used almost exclusively in TCP/IP networks. SNMP provides a means to monitor and control network devices, and to manage configurations, statistics collection, performance, and security.

SNMP Manager   Software used to manage network devices via SNMP. Often includes graphical representation of the network and individual devices, and the ability to set and respond to SNMP traps.

SNMP Trap   A threshold of some sort which, when reached, causes the SNMP managed device to notify the SNMP Manager. This allows for immediate notification, instead of having to wait for the SNMP Manager to poll again.

socket   Software structure operating as a communications endpoint within a network device.

SONET (Synchronous Optical Network)   High-speed synchronous network specification developed by Bellcore and designed to run on optical fiber.

source address   Address of a network device that is sending data.

spanning tree   Loop-free subset of a network topology. *See also* Spanning Tree Protocol.

Spanning Tree Protocol   Developed to eliminate loops in the network. The Spanning Tree Protocol ensures a loop-free path by placing one of the bridge ports in "blocking mode," preventing the forwarding of packets.

SPF (shortest path first algorithm)   Routing algorithm that sorts routes by length of path to determine a shortest-path spanning tree. Commonly used in link-state routing algorithms. Sometimes called Dijkstra's algorithm.

SPIDs (Service Profile Identifiers)   These function as addresses for B channels on ISDN BRI circuits. When call information is passed over the D channel, the SPIDs are used to identify which channel is being referred to. SPIDs are usually some variant of the phone number for the channel.

split-horizon updates   Routing technique in which information about routes is prevented from being advertised out the router interface through which that information was received. Split-horizon updates are used to prevent routing loops.

SPX (Sequenced Packet Exchange)   Reliable, connection-oriented protocol at the Transport layer that supplements the datagram service provided by IPX.

SR/TLB (source-route translational bridging)   Method of bridging that allows source-route stations to communicate with transparent bridge stations, using an intermediate bridge that translates between the two bridge protocols.

SRB (source-route bridging)   Method of bridging in Token Ring networks. In an SRB network, before data is sent to a destination, the entire route to that destination is predetermined in real time.

SRT (source-route transparent bridging)   IBM's merging of SRB and transparent bridging into one bridging scheme, which requires no translation between bridging protocols.

standard   Set of rules or procedures that are either widely used or officially specified.

star topology   LAN topology in which endpoints on a network are connected to a common central switch by point-to-point links. A ring topology that is organized as a star implements a unidirectional closed-loop star, instead of point-to-point links. Compare with **bus topology**, **ring topology**, and **tree topology**.

static route   Route that is explicitly configured and entered into the routing table. Static routes take precedence over routes chosen by dynamic routing protocols.

subinterface   A virtual interface defined as a logical subdivision of a physical interface.

subnet address   Portion of an IP address that is specified as the subnetwork by the subnet mask. *See also* **IP address**; **subnet mask**; **subnetwork.**

subnet mask   32-bit address mask used in IP to indicate the bits of an IP address that are being used for the subnet address. Sometimes referred to simply as mask. *See also* **address mask**; **IP address.**

subnetwork   1. In IP networks, a network sharing a particular subnet address. 2. Subnetworks are networks arbitrarily segmented by a network administrator in order to provide a multilevel, hierarchical routing structure while shielding the subnetwork from the addressing complexity of attached networks. Sometimes called a subnet.

SVC (switched virtual circuit)   Virtual circuit that can be established dynamically on demand, and which is torn down after a transmission is complete. SVCs are used when data transmission is sporadic.

switch   1. Network device that filters, forwards, and floods frames based on the destination address of each frame. The switch operates at the Data Link layer of the OSI model. 2. General term applied to an electronic or mechanical device that allows a connection to be established as necessary and terminated when there is no longer a session to support.

T1   Digital WAN carrier facility. T1 transmits DS-1-formatted data at 1.544 Mbps through the telephone-switching network, using AMI or B8ZS coding. Compare with **E1**. *See also* **AMI**; **B8ZS.**

TCP (Transmission Control Protocol)   Connection-oriented Transport layer protocol that provides reliable full-duplex data transmission. TCP is part of the TCP/IP protocol stack.

TCP/IP (Transmission Control Protocol/Internet Protocol)
Common name for the suite of protocols developed by the U.S. DoD in the 1970s to support the construction of worldwide internetworks. TCP and IP are the two best-known protocols in the suite.

TDR (time-domain reflectometer)   A TDR test is used to measure the length of a cable, or the distance to a break. This is accomplished by sending a signal down a wire, and measuring how long it takes for an echo of the signal to bounce back.

TEI (Terminal Endpoint Identifier)   Field in the LAPD address that identifies a device on an ISDN interface.

TFTP (Trivial File Transfer Protocol)   Simplified version of FTP that allows files to be transferred from one computer to another over a network.

three-way handshake   The three required packets to set up a TCP connection. It consists of a SYN packet, acknowledged by a SYN+ACK packet, which is finally acknowledged by an ACK packet. During this handshake, sequence numbers are exchanged.

throughput   Rate of information arriving at, and possibly passing through, a particular point in a network system.

timeout   Event that occurs when one network device expects to hear from another network device within a specified period of time, but does not. A timeout usually results in a retransmission of information or the termination of the session between the two devices.

token   Frame that contains only control information. Possession of the token allows a network device to transmit data onto the network. *See also* **token passing**.

token passing   Method by which network devices access the physical medium based on possession of a small frame called a token. Compare this method to **circuit switching** and **contention**.

Token Ring   Token-passing LAN developed and supported by IBM. Token Ring runs at 4 or 16 Mbps over a ring topology. Similar to IEEE 802.5. *See also* **IEEE 802.5; ring topology; token passing.**

TokenTalk   Apple Computer's data-link product that allows an AppleTalk network to be connected by Token Ring cables.

transparent bridging   Bridging scheme used in Ethernet and IEEE 802.3 networks. Allows bridges to pass frames along one hop at a time, based on tables that associate end nodes with bridge ports. Bridges are transparent to network end nodes.

Transport layer   Layer 4 of the OSI reference model. This layer is responsible for reliable network communication between end nodes. The Transport layer provides mechanisms for the establishment, maintenance, and termination of virtual circuits, transport fault detection and recovery, and information flow control.

tree topology   A LAN topology that resembles a bus topology. Tree networks can contain branches with multiple nodes. In a tree topology, transmissions from a station propagate the length of the physical medium, and are received by all other stations.

twisted-pair   Relatively low-speed transmission medium consisting of two insulated wires arranged in a regular spiral pattern. The wires can be shielded or unshielded. Twisted-pair is common in telephony applications and is increasingly common in data networks.

UDP (User Datagram Protocol) Connectionless Transport layer protocol in the TCP/IP protocol stack. UDP is a simple protocol that exchanges datagrams without acknowledgments or guaranteed delivery, requiring that error processing and retransmission be handled by other protocols. UDP is defined in RFC 768.

unicast Regular IP packet sent from a single host to a single host.

UTP (unshielded twisted-pair) Four-pair wire medium used in a variety of networks. UTP does not require the fixed spacing between connections that is necessary with coaxial-type connections.

virtual circuit Logical circuit created to ensure reliable communication between two network devices. A virtual circuit is defined by a VPI/VCI pair, and can be either permanent or switched. Virtual circuits are used in Frame Relay and X.25. In ATM, a virtual circuit is called a virtual channel. Sometimes abbreviated VC.

VLAN (virtual LAN) Group of devices on one or more LANs that are configured (using management software) so that they can communicate as if they were attached to the same wire, when in fact they are located on a number of different LAN segments. Because VLANs are based on logical instead of physical connections, they are extremely flexible.

VLSM (Variable-length Subnet Masking) Ability to specify a different length subnet mask for the same network number at different locations in the network. VLSM can help optimize available address space.

VTY (Virtual Terminal) VTYs work like physical terminal ports on routers so they can be managed across a network, usually via Telnet.

WAN (wide area network) Data communications network that serves users across a broad geographic area and often uses transmission devices provided by common carriers. Frame Relay, SMDS, and X.25 are examples of WANs. Compare with **LAN** and **MAN**.

wildcard mask   32-bit quantity used in conjunction with an IP address to determine which bits in an IP address should be matched and ignored when comparing that address with another IP address. A wildcard mask is specified when defining access list statements.

X.121   ITU-T standard describing an addressing scheme used in X.25 networks. X.121 addresses are sometimes called IDNs (International Data Numbers).

X.21   ITU-T standard for serial communications over synchronous digital lines. The X.21 protocol is used primarily in Europe and Japan.

X.25   ITU-T standard that defines how connections between DTE and DCE are maintained for remote terminal access and computer communications in public data networks. X.25 specifies LAPB, a Data Link layer protocol, and PLP, a network layer protocol. Frame Relay has to some degree superseded X.25.

ZIP broadcast storm   Occurs when a route advertisement without a corresponding zone triggers the network with a flood of Zone Information Protocol requests.

zone   In AppleTalk, a logical group of network devices.

Zone Information Protocol (ZIP)   A protocol used in AppleTalk to communicate information about AppleTalk zone names and cable ranges.

Zone Information Table (ZIT)   A table of zone name to cable range mappings in AppleTalk. These tables are maintained in each AppleTalk router.

INDEX

M

N

Custom Corporate Network Training

Train on Cutting Edge Technology   We can bring the best in skill-based training to your facility to create a real-world hands-on training experience. Global Knowledge has invested millions of dollars in network hardware and software to train our students on the same equipment they will work with on the job. Our relationships with vendors allow us to incorporate the latest equipment and platforms into your on-site labs.

Maximize Your Training Budget   Global Knowledge provides experienced instructors, comprehensive course materials, and all the networking equipment needed to deliver high quality training. You provide the students; we provide the knowledge.

Avoid Travel Expenses   On-site courses allow you to schedule technical training at your convenience, saving time, expense, and the opportunity cost of travel away from the workplace.

Discuss Confidential Topics   Private on-site training permits the open discussion of sensitive issues such as security, access, and network design. We can work with your existing network's proprietary files while demonstrating the latest technologies.

Customize Course Content   Global Knowledge can tailor your courses to include the technologies and the topics which have the greatest impact on your business. We can complement your internal training efforts or provide a total solution to your training needs.

Corporate Pass   The Corporate Pass Discount Program rewards our best network training customers with preferred pricing on public courses, discounts on multimedia training packages, and an array of career planning services.

Global Knowledge Training Lifecycle   Supporting the Dynamic and Specialized Training Requirements of Information Technology Professionals

- Define Profile
- Assess Skills
- Design Training
- Deliver Training
- Test Knowledge
- Update Profile
- Use New Skills

College Credit Recommendation Program   The American Council on Education's CREDIT program recommends 53 Global Knowledge courses for college credit. Now our network training can help you earn your college degree while you learn the technical skills needed for your job. When you attend an ACE-certified Global Knowledge course and pass the associated exam, you earn college credit recommendations for that course. Global Knowledge can establish a transcript record for you with ACE, which you can use to gain credit at a college or as a written record of your professional training that you can attach to your resume.

Registration Information

COURSE FEE: The fee covers course tuition, refreshments, and all course materials. Any parking expenses that may be incurred are not included. Payment or government training form must be received six business days prior to the course date. We will also accept Visa/ MasterCard and American Express. For non-U.S. credit card users, charges will be in U.S. funds and will be converted by your credit card company. Checks drawn on Canadian banks in Canadian funds are acceptable.

COURSE SCHEDULE: Registration is at 8:00 a.m. on the first day. The program begins at 8:30 a.m. and concludes at 4:30 p.m. each day.

CANCELLATION POLICY: Cancellation and full refund will be allowed if written cancellation is received in our office at least six business days prior to the course start date. Registrants who do not attend the course or do not cancel more than six business days in advance are responsible for the full registration fee; you may transfer to a later date provided the course fee has been paid in full. Substitutions may be made at any time. If Global Knowledge must cancel a course for any reason, liability is limited to the registration fee only.

GLOBAL KNOWLEDGE: Global Knowledge programs are developed and presented by industry professionals with "real-world" experience. Designed to help professionals meet today's interconnectivity and interoperability challenges, most of our programs feature hands-on labs that incorporate state-of-the-art communication components and equipment.

ON-SITE TEAM TRAINING: Bring Global Knowledge's powerful training programs to your company. At Global Knowledge, we will custom design courses to meet your specific network requirements. Call 1 (919) 461-8686 for more information.

YOUR GUARANTEE: Global Knowledge believes its courses offer the best possible training in this field. If during the first day you are not satisfied and wish to withdraw from the course, simply notify the instructor, return all course materials, and receive a 100% refund.

In the US:

CALL: 1 (888) 762-4442

FAX: 1 (919) 469-7070

VISIT OUR WEBSITE:

www.globalknowledge.com

MAIL CHECK AND THIS FORM TO:

Global Knowledge

Suite 200

114 Edinburgh South

P.O. Box 1187

Cary, NC 27512

In Canada:

CALL: 1 (800) 465-2226

FAX: 1 (613) 567-3899

VISIT OUR WEBSITE:

www.globalknowledge.com.ca

MAIL CHECK AND THIS FORM TO:

Global Knowledge

Suite 1601

393 University Ave.

Toronto, ON M5G 1E6

REGISTRATION INFORMATION:

Course title _____

Course location _____ Course date _____

Name/title _____ Company _____

Name/title _____ Company _____

Name/title _____ Company _____

Address _____ Telephone _____ Fax _____

City _____ State/Province _____ Zip/Postal Code _____

Credit card _____ Card # _____ Expiration date _____

Signature _____

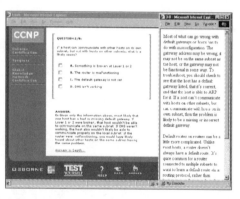

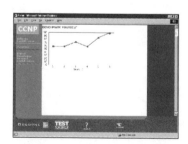